WALL·TO·WALL
BABY BLUES®

Other *Baby Blues*® Books from Andrews McMeel Publishing

Guess Who Didn't Take a Nap?
I Thought Labor Ended When the Baby Was Born
We Are Experiencing Parental Difficulties . . . Please Stand By
Night of the Living Dad
I Saw Elvis in My Ultrasound
One More and We're Outnumbered!
Check, Please . . .
threats, bribes & videotape
If I'm a Stay-At-Home Mom, Why Am I Always in the Car?
Lift and Separate
I Shouldn't Have to Scream More Than Once!
Motherhood Is Not for Wimps
Baby Blues®: Unplugged
Dad to the Bone
Never a Dry Moment

Treasuries

The Super-Absorbent Biodegradable Family-Size Baby Blues®
Baby Blues®: Ten Years and Still in Diapers
Butt-Naked Baby Blues®

WALL·TO·WALL
BABY BLUES®

BY RICK KIRKMAN & JERRY SCOTT

**Andrews McMeel
Publishing**

Kansas City

Baby Blues® is syndicated internationally by King Features Syndicate, Inc. For information, write King Features Syndicate, Inc., 888 Seventh Avenue, New York, New York 10019.

03 04 05 06 07 BAM 10 9 8 7 6 5 4 3 2 1

ISBN: 0-7407-3811-9

Library of Congress Control Number: 2003106113

Find **Baby Blues**® on the Web at
www.babyblues.com.

──── **ATTENTION: SCHOOLS AND BUSINESSES** ────

Andrews McMeel books are available at quantity discounts with bulk purchase for educational, business, or sales promotional use. For information, please write to: Special Sales Department, Andrews McMeel Publishing, 4520 Main Street, Kansas City, Missouri 64111.

"To Corey and Niki, lawyers in love."

—J.S.

**"To my part-time mentor, Mell, and Sally—
with love and friendship."**

—R.K.

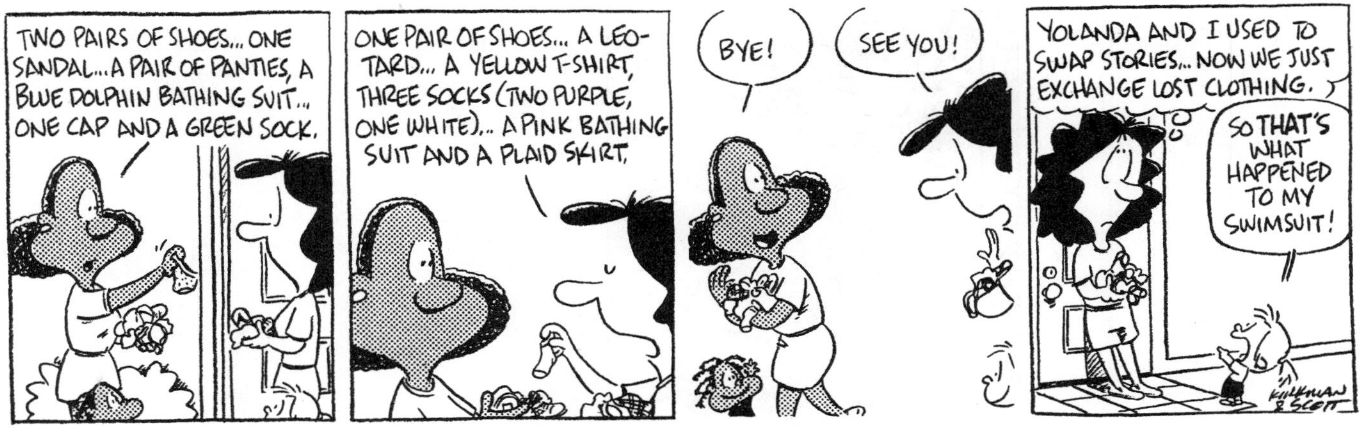
TWO PAIRS OF SHOES... ONE SANDAL... A PAIR OF PANTIES, A BLUE DOLPHIN BATHING SUIT... ONE CAP AND A GREEN SOCK.
ONE PAIR OF SHOES... A LEOTARD... A YELLOW T-SHIRT, THREE SOCKS (TWO PURPLE, ONE WHITE)... A PINK BATHING SUIT AND A PLAID SKIRT.
BYE!
SEE YOU!
YOLANDA AND I USED TO SWAP STORIES... NOW WE JUST EXCHANGE LOST CLOTHING.
SO THAT'S WHAT HAPPENED TO MY SWIMSUIT!
KIRKMAN & SCOTT

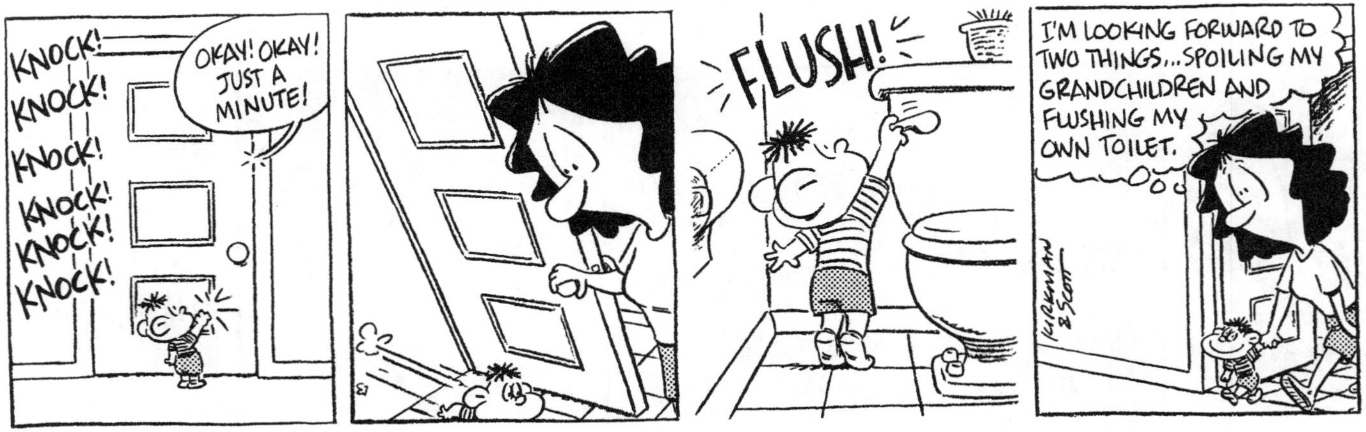
KNOCK! KNOCK! KNOCK! KNOCK! KNOCK! KNOCK!
OKAY! OKAY! JUST A MINUTE!
FLUSH!
I'M LOOKING FORWARD TO TWO THINGS... SPOILING MY GRANDCHILDREN AND FLUSHING MY OWN TOILET.
KIRKMAN & SCOTT

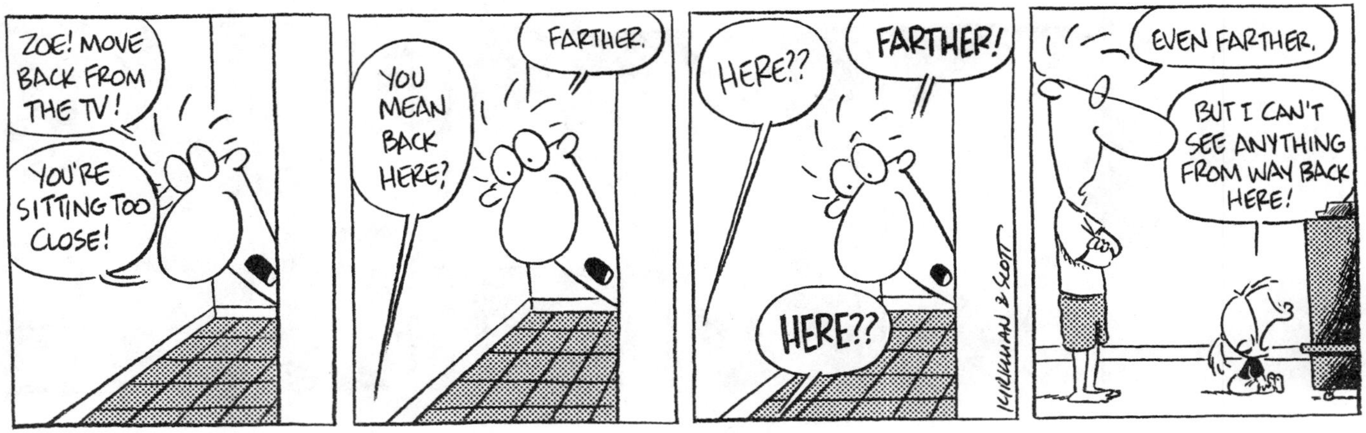
ZOE! MOVE BACK FROM THE TV!
YOU'RE SITTING TOO CLOSE!
YOU MEAN BACK HERE?
FARTHER.
HERE??
FARTHER!
HERE??
KIRKMAN & SCOTT
EVEN FARTHER.
BUT I CAN'T SEE ANYTHING FROM WAY BACK HERE!

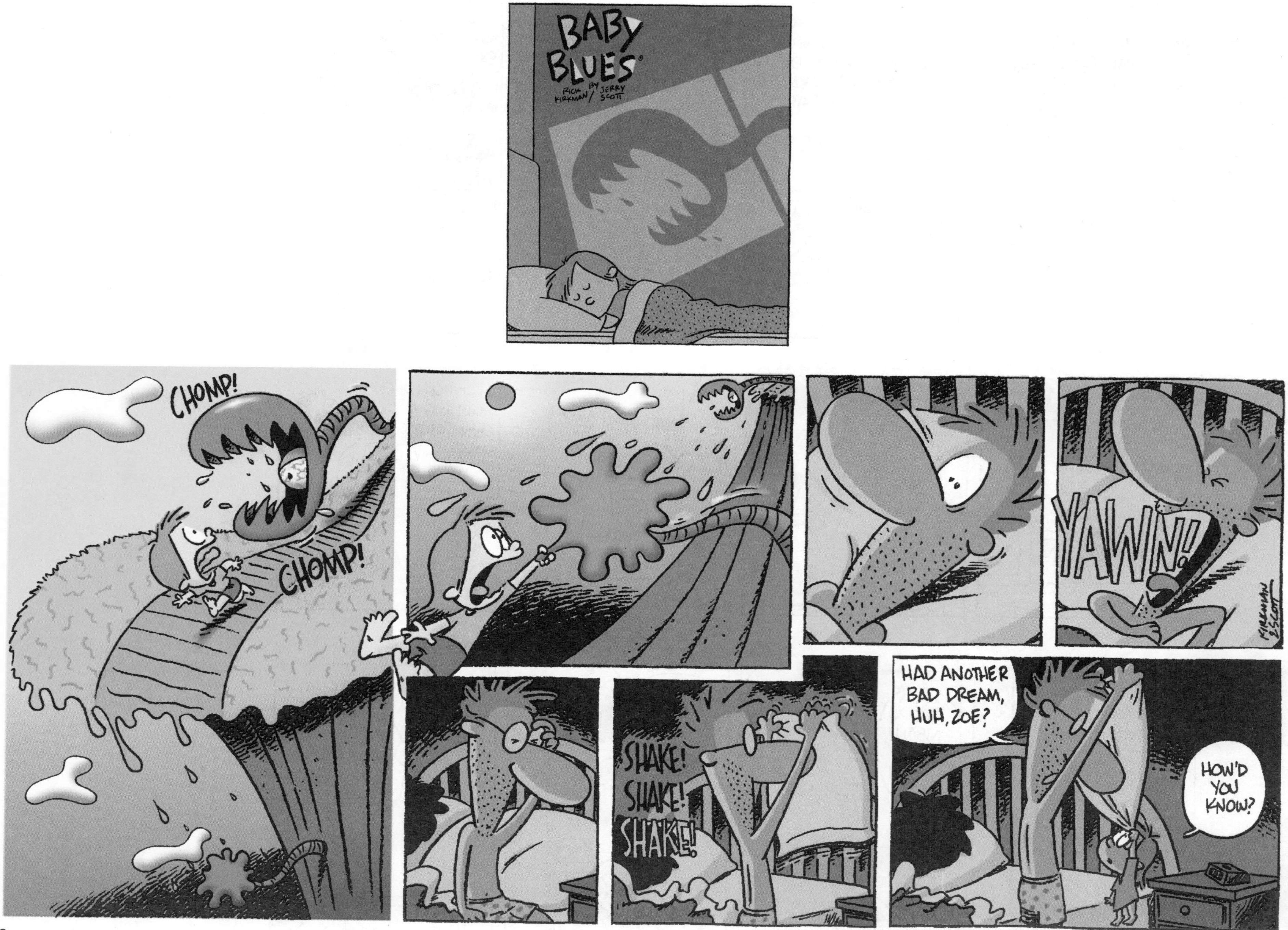
BABY BLUES®
BY RICK KIRKMAN / JERRY SCOTT
CHOMP!
CHOMP!
YAWN!
SHAKE!
SHAKE!
SHAKE!
HAD ANOTHER BAD DREAM, HUH, ZOE?
HOW'D YOU KNOW?

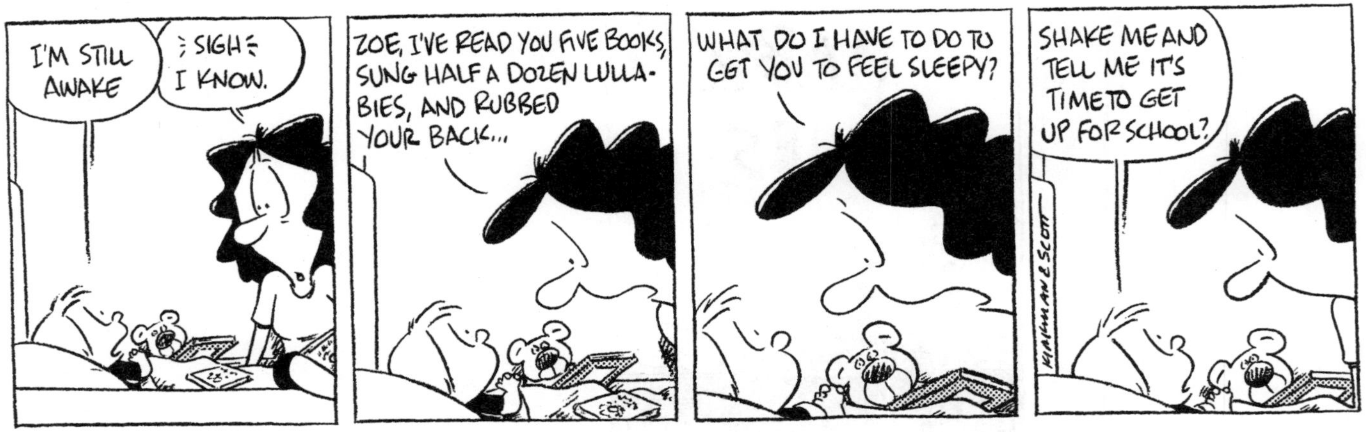
I'M STILL AWAKE
SIGH
I KNOW.
ZOE, I'VE READ YOU FIVE BOOKS, SUNG HALF A DOZEN LULLABIES, AND RUBBED YOUR BACK...
WHAT DO I HAVE TO DO TO GET YOU TO FEEL SLEEPY?
SHAKE ME AND TELL ME IT'S TIME TO GET UP FOR SCHOOL?
KIRKMAN & SCOTT

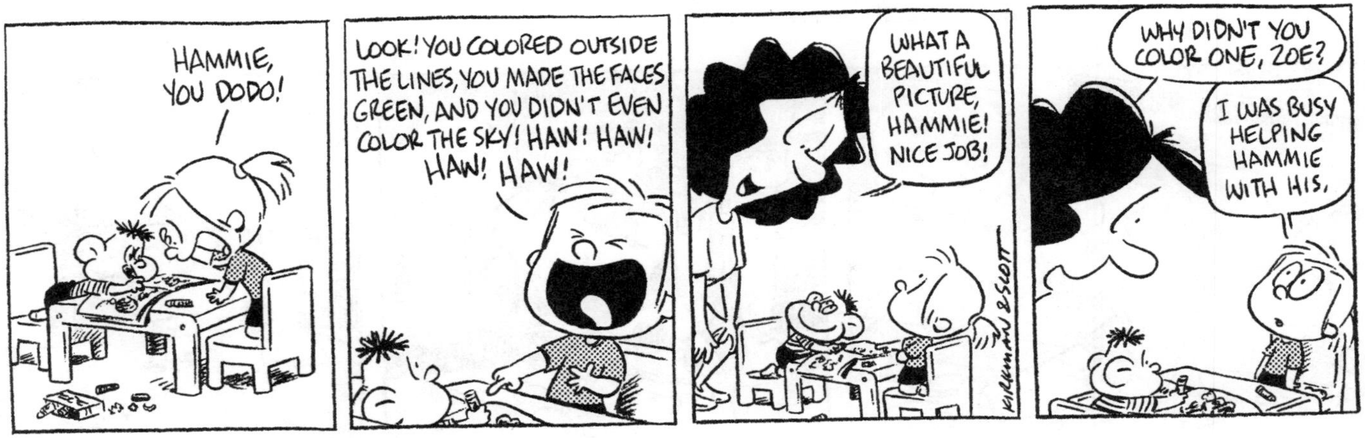
HAMMIE, YOU DODO!
LOOK! YOU COLORED OUTSIDE THE LINES, YOU MADE THE FACES GREEN, AND YOU DIDN'T EVEN COLOR THE SKY! HAW! HAW! HAW! HAW!
WHAT A BEAUTIFUL PICTURE, HAMMIE! NICE JOB!
KIRKMAN & SCOTT
WHY DIDN'T YOU COLOR ONE, ZOE?
I WAS BUSY HELPING HAMMIE WITH HIS.

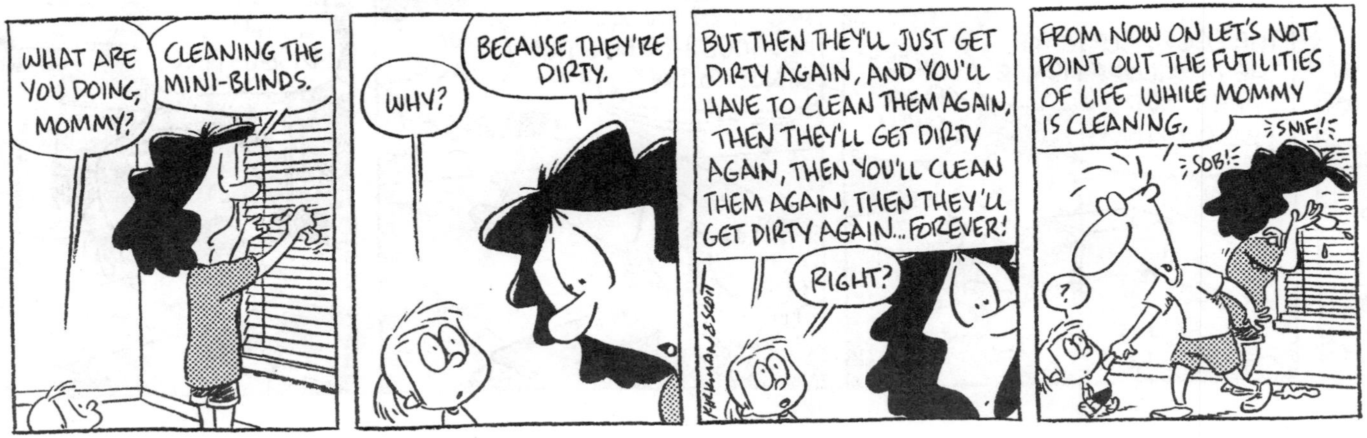
WHAT ARE YOU DOING, MOMMY?
CLEANING THE MINI-BLINDS.
WHY?
BECAUSE THEY'RE DIRTY.
BUT THEN THEY'LL JUST GET DIRTY AGAIN, AND YOU'LL HAVE TO CLEAN THEM AGAIN, THEN THEY'LL GET DIRTY AGAIN, THEN YOU'LL CLEAN THEM AGAIN, THEN THEY'LL GET DIRTY AGAIN... FOREVER!
RIGHT?
KIRKMAN & SCOTT
FROM NOW ON LET'S NOT POINT OUT THE FUTILITIES OF LIFE WHILE MOMMY IS CLEANING.
SNIF!
SOB!
?

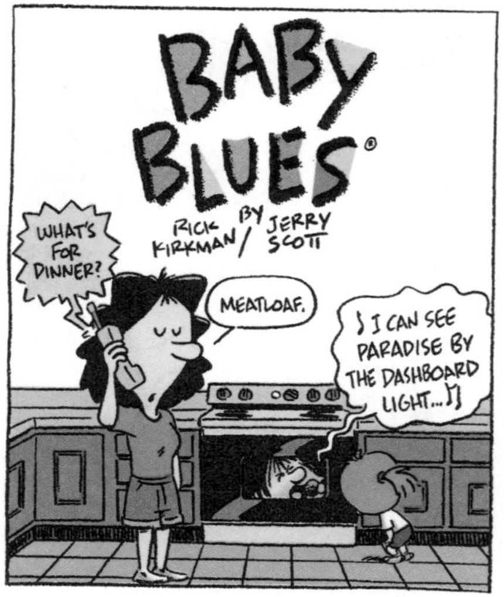
BABY BLUES®
BY RICK KIRKMAN / JERRY SCOTT
WHAT'S FOR DINNER?
MEATLOAF.
♪ I CAN SEE PARADISE BY THE DASHBOARD LIGHT... ♪

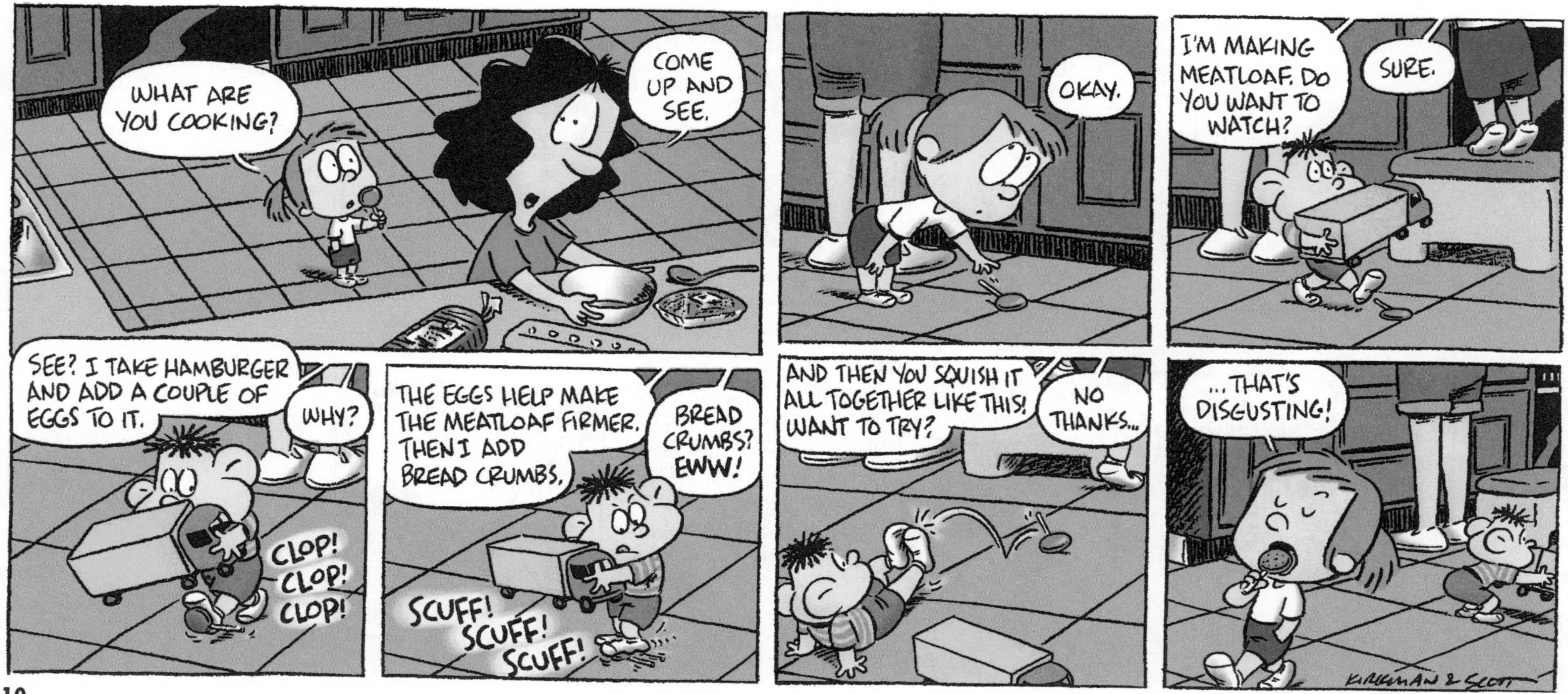
WHAT ARE YOU COOKING?
COME UP AND SEE.
OKAY.
I'M MAKING MEATLOAF. DO YOU WANT TO WATCH?
SURE.
SEE? I TAKE HAMBURGER AND ADD A COUPLE OF EGGS TO IT.
WHY?
CLOP! CLOP! CLOP!
THE EGGS HELP MAKE THE MEATLOAF FIRMER. THEN I ADD BREAD CRUMBS.
BREAD CRUMBS? EWW!
SCUFF! SCUFF! SCUFF!
AND THEN YOU SQUISH IT ALL TOGETHER LIKE THIS! WANT TO TRY?
NO THANKS...
...THAT'S DISGUSTING!
KIRKMAN & SCOTT

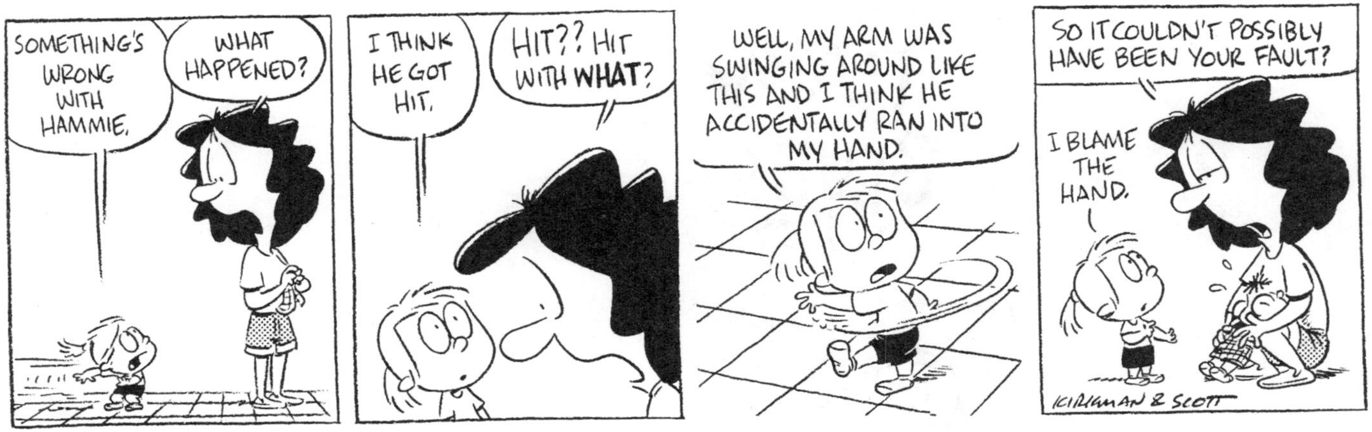
SOMETHING'S WRONG WITH HAMMIE.
WHAT HAPPENED?
I THINK HE GOT HIT.
HIT?? HIT WITH **WHAT**?
WELL, MY ARM WAS SWINGING AROUND LIKE THIS AND I THINK HE ACCIDENTALLY RAN INTO MY HAND.
SO IT COULDN'T POSSIBLY HAVE BEEN YOUR FAULT?
I BLAME THE HAND.
KIRKMAN & SCOTT

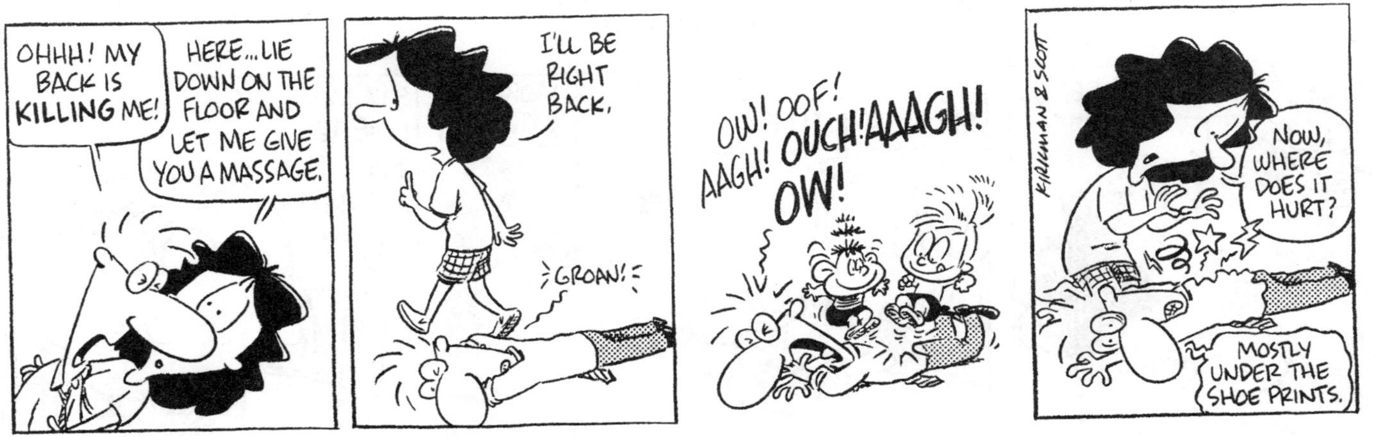
OHHH! MY BACK IS **KILLING** ME!
HERE...LIE DOWN ON THE FLOOR AND LET ME GIVE YOU A MASSAGE.
I'LL BE RIGHT BACK.
GROAN!
OW! OOF! AAGH! OUCH! AAAGH! OW!
KIRKMAN & SCOTT
NOW, WHERE DOES IT HURT?
MOSTLY UNDER THE SHOE PRINTS.

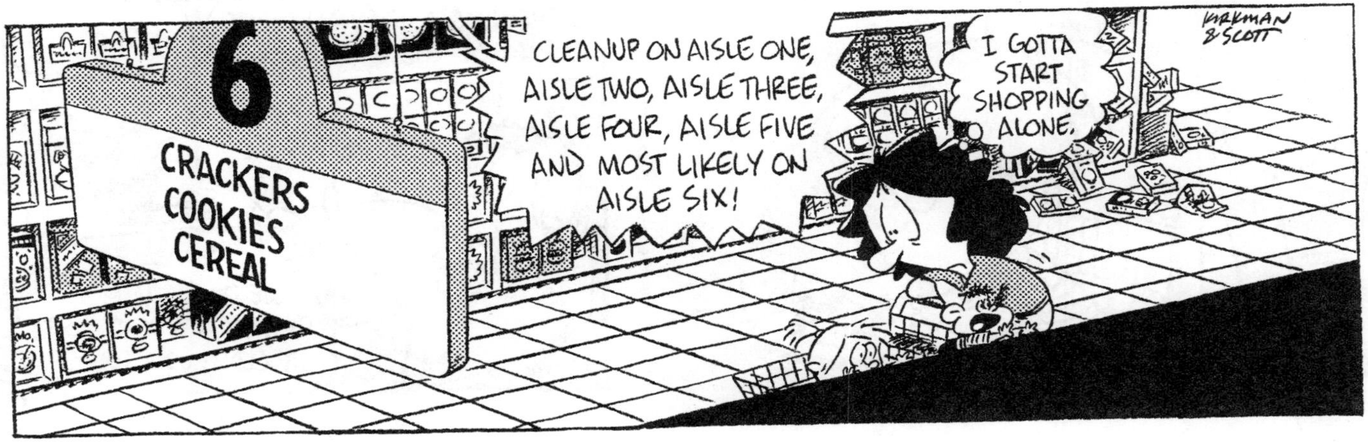
6
CRACKERS
COOKIES
CEREAL
CLEANUP ON AISLE ONE, AISLE TWO, AISLE THREE, AISLE FOUR, AISLE FIVE AND MOST LIKELY ON AISLE SIX!
I GOTTA START SHOPPING ALONE.
KIRKMAN & SCOTT

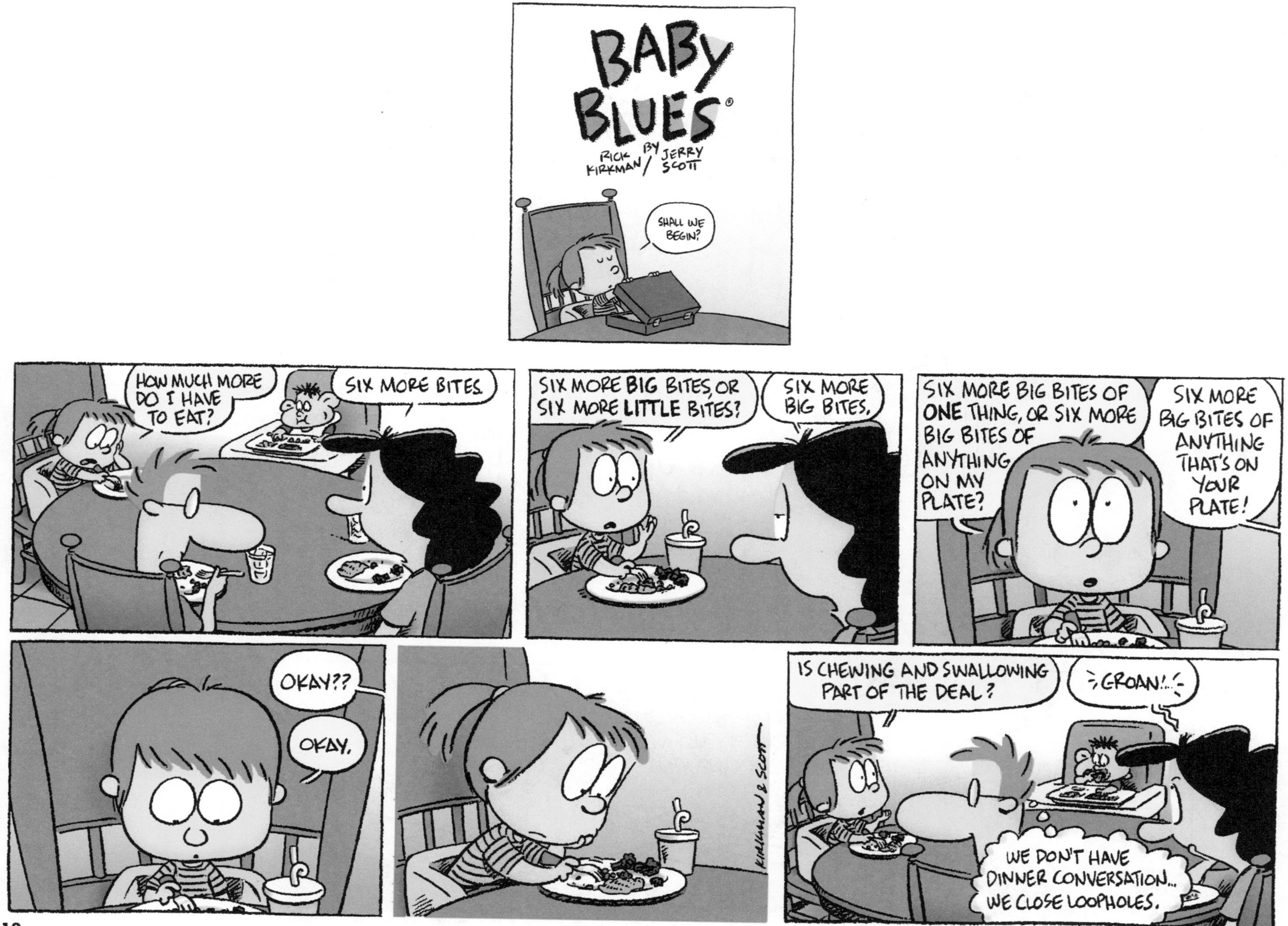
BABY BLUES®
BY RICK KIRKMAN / JERRY SCOTT
SHALL WE BEGIN?
HOW MUCH MORE DO I HAVE TO EAT?
SIX MORE BITES.
SIX MORE BIG BITES, OR SIX MORE LITTLE BITES?
SIX MORE BIG BITES.
SIX MORE BIG BITES OF ONE THING, OR SIX MORE BIG BITES OF ANYTHING ON MY PLATE?
SIX MORE BIG BITES OF ANYTHING THAT'S ON YOUR PLATE!
OKAY??
OKAY.
KIRKMAN & SCOTT
IS CHEWING AND SWALLOWING PART OF THE DEAL?
GROAN!...
WE DON'T HAVE DINNER CONVERSATION... WE CLOSE LOOPHOLES.

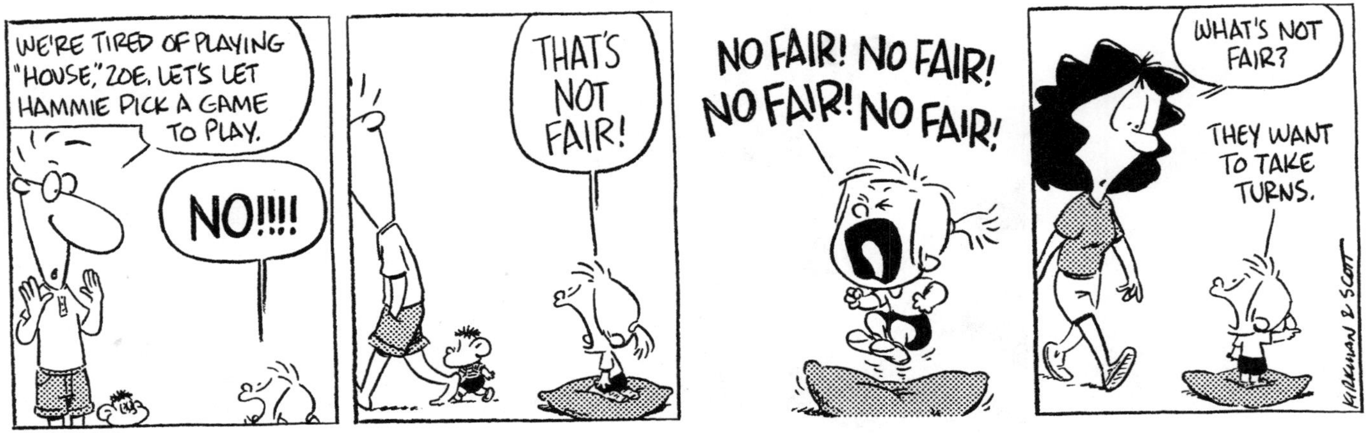
WE'RE TIRED OF PLAYING "HOUSE," ZOE. LET'S LET HAMMIE PICK A GAME TO PLAY.
NO!!!!
THAT'S NOT FAIR!
NO FAIR! NO FAIR! NO FAIR! NO FAIR!
WHAT'S NOT FAIR?
THEY WANT TO TAKE TURNS.
KIRKMAN & SCOTT

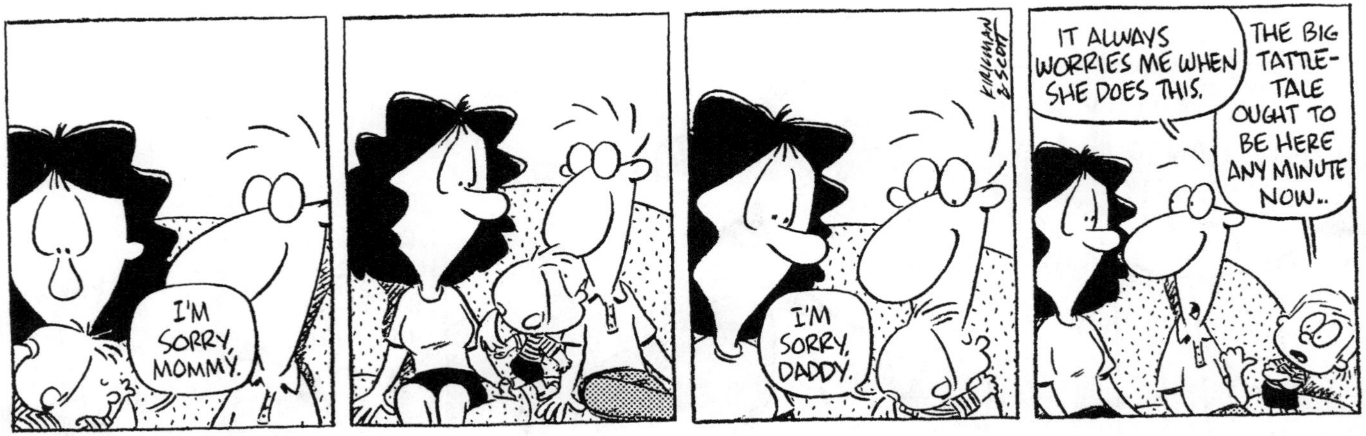
I'M SORRY, MOMMY.
KIRKMAN & SCOTT
I'M SORRY, DADDY.
IT ALWAYS WORRIES ME WHEN SHE DOES THIS.
THE BIG TATTLE-TALE OUGHT TO BE HERE ANY MINUTE NOW..

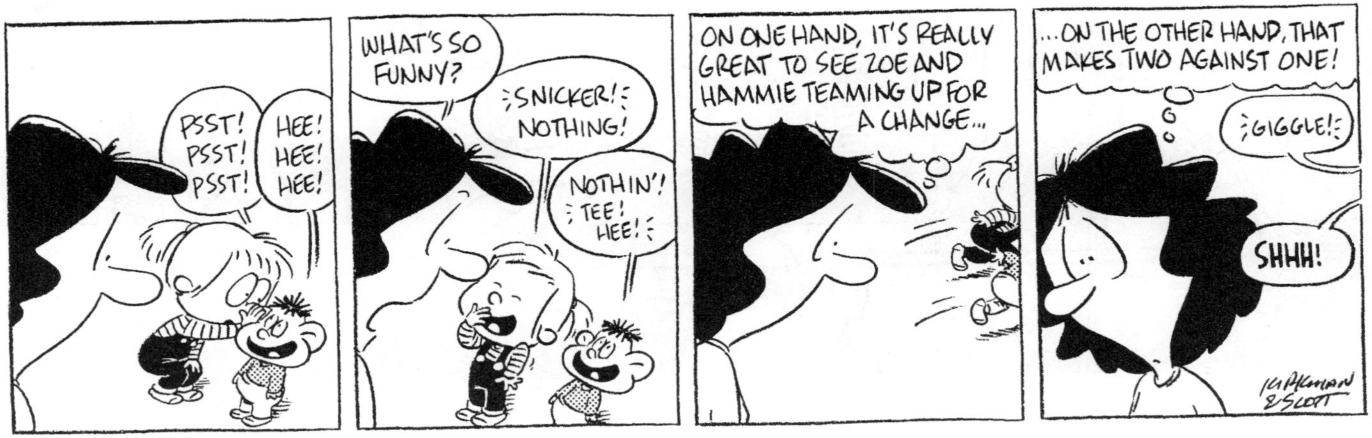
PSST! PSST! PSST!
HEE! HEE! HEE!
WHAT'S SO FUNNY?
SNICKER! NOTHING!
NOTHIN'! TEE! HEE!
ON ONE HAND, IT'S REALLY GREAT TO SEE ZOE AND HAMMIE TEAMING UP FOR A CHANGE...
...ON THE OTHER HAND, THAT MAKES TWO AGAINST ONE!
GIGGLE!
SHHH!
KIRKMAN & SCOTT

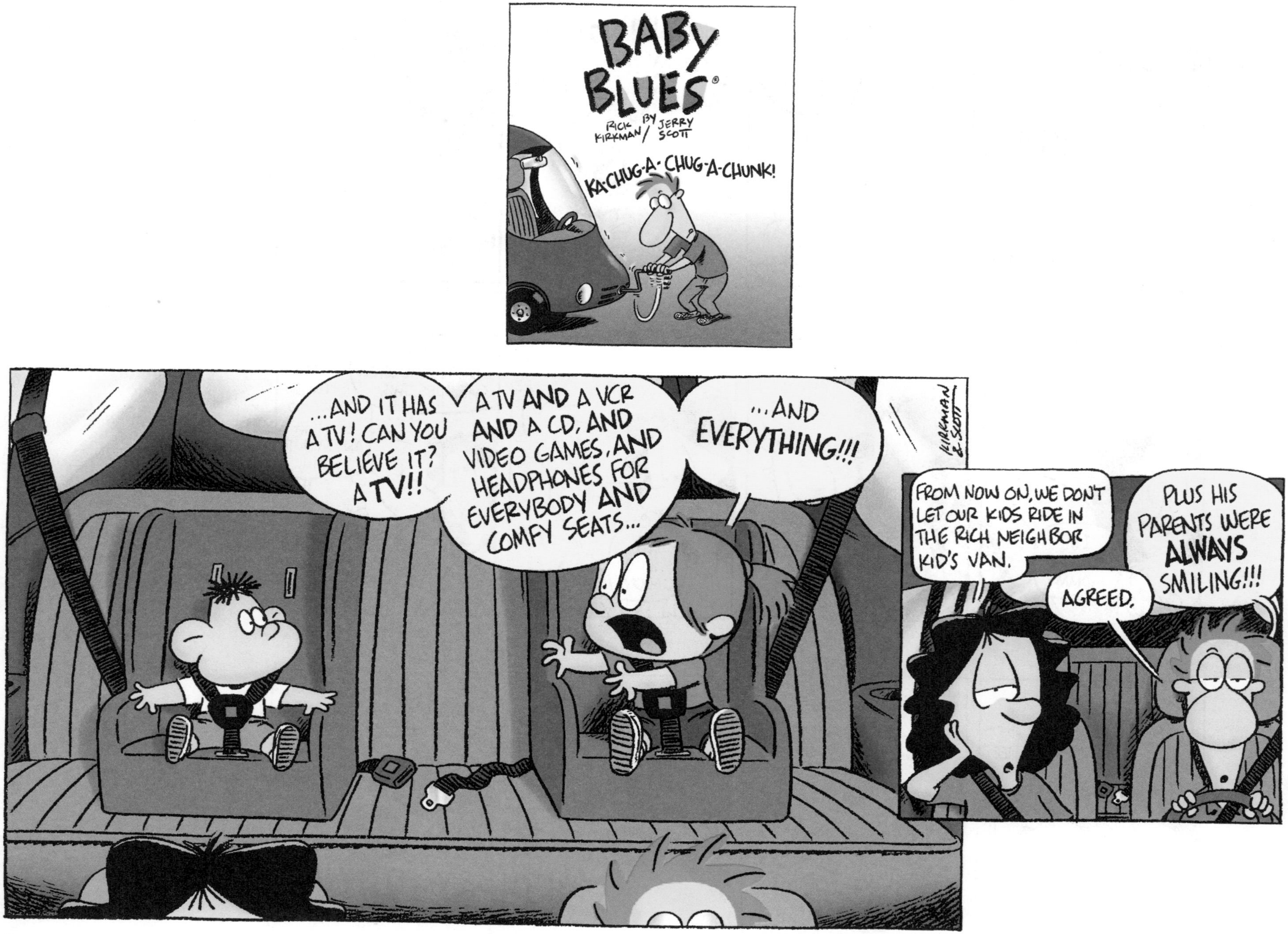
BABY BLUES®
RICK KIRKMAN / BY JERRY SCOTT
KA-CHUG-A-CHUG-A-CHUNK!
...AND IT HAS A TV! CAN YOU BELIEVE IT? A TV!!
A TV AND A VCR AND A CD, AND VIDEO GAMES, AND HEADPHONES FOR EVERYBODY AND COMFY SEATS...
...AND EVERYTHING!!!
KIRKMAN & SCOTT
FROM NOW ON, WE DON'T LET OUR KIDS RIDE IN THE RICH NEIGHBOR KID'S VAN.
AGREED.
PLUS HIS PARENTS WERE ALWAYS SMILING!!!

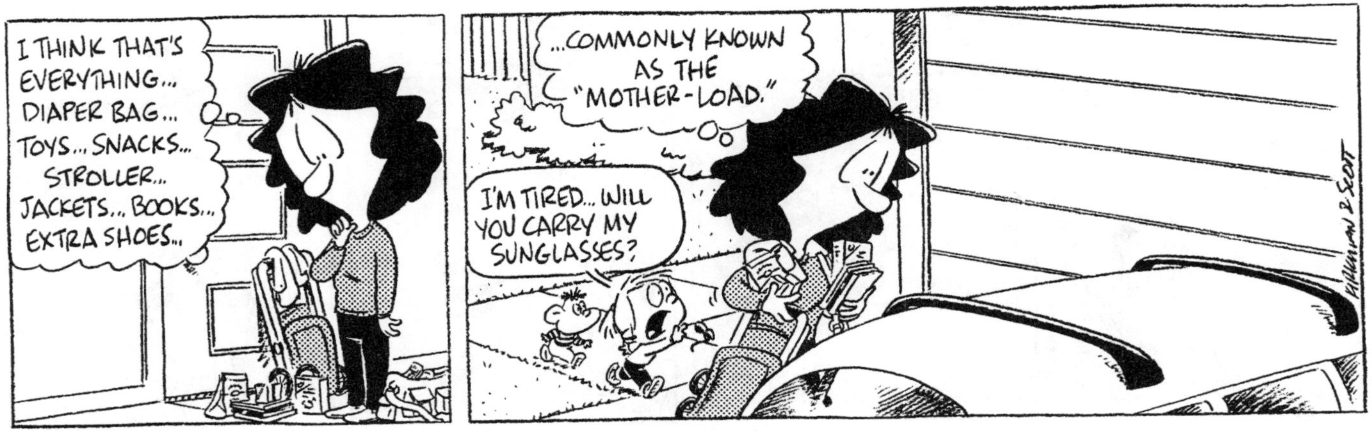
I THINK THAT'S EVERYTHING... DIAPER BAG... TOYS... SNACKS... STROLLER... JACKETS... BOOKS... EXTRA SHOES...
...COMMONLY KNOWN AS THE "MOTHER-LOAD."
I'M TIRED... WILL YOU CARRY MY SUNGLASSES?
KIRKMAN & SCOTT

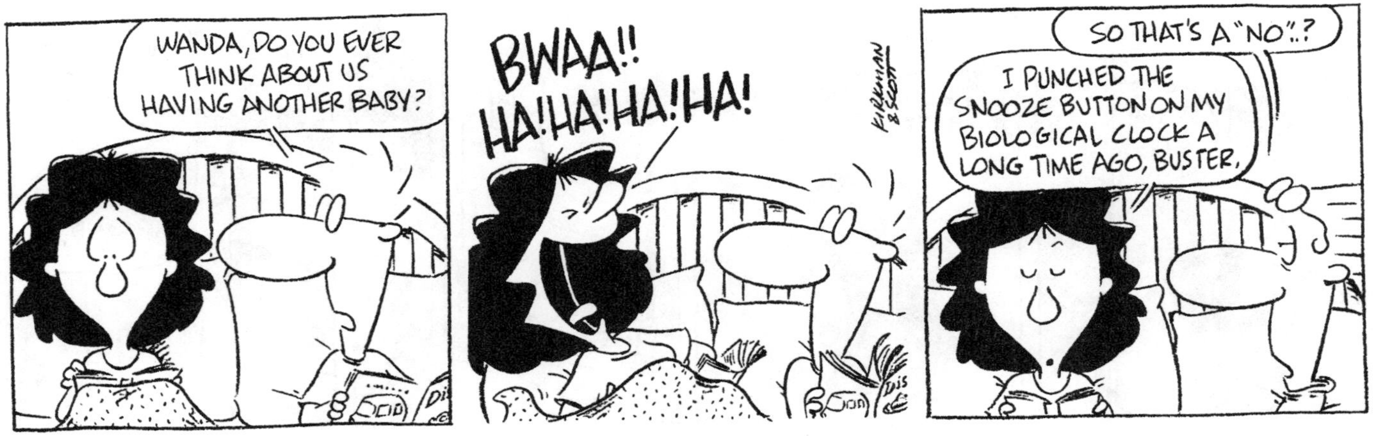
WANDA, DO YOU EVER THINK ABOUT US HAVING ANOTHER BABY?
BWAA!! HA!HA!HA!HA!
KIRKMAN & SCOTT
I PUNCHED THE SNOOZE BUTTON ON MY BIOLOGICAL CLOCK A LONG TIME AGO, BUSTER.
SO THAT'S A "NO"..?

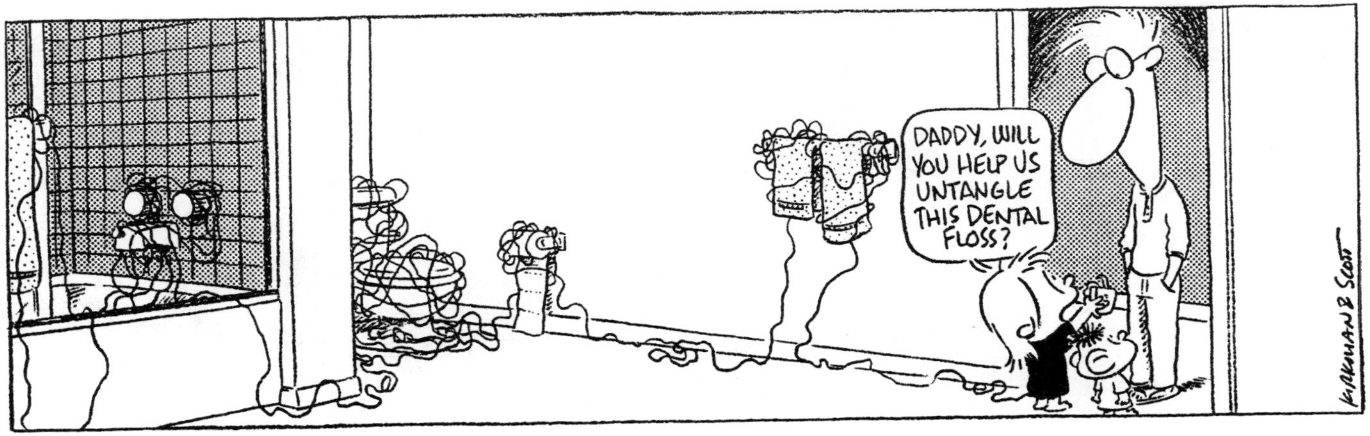
DADDY, WILL YOU HELP US UNTANGLE THIS DENTAL FLOSS?
KIRKMAN & SCOTT

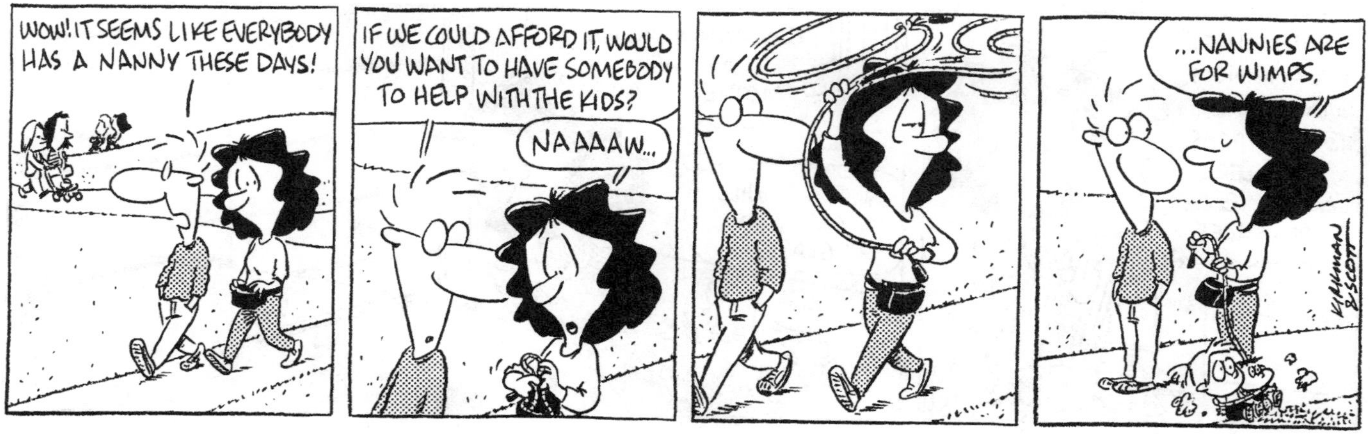
WOW! IT SEEMS LIKE EVERYBODY HAS A NANNY THESE DAYS!
IF WE COULD AFFORD IT, WOULD YOU WANT TO HAVE SOMEBODY TO HELP WITH THE KIDS?
NAAAAW...
...NANNIES ARE FOR WIMPS.

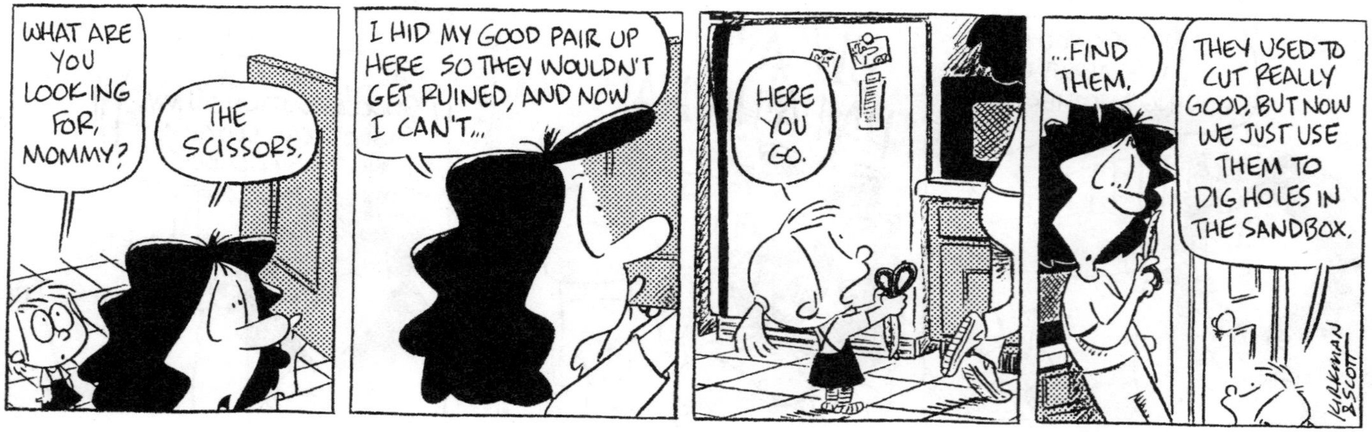
WHAT ARE YOU LOOKING FOR, MOMMY?
THE SCISSORS.
I HID MY GOOD PAIR UP HERE SO THEY WOULDN'T GET RUINED, AND NOW I CAN'T...
HERE YOU GO.
...FIND THEM.
THEY USED TO CUT REALLY GOOD, BUT NOW WE JUST USE THEM TO DIG HOLES IN THE SANDBOX.

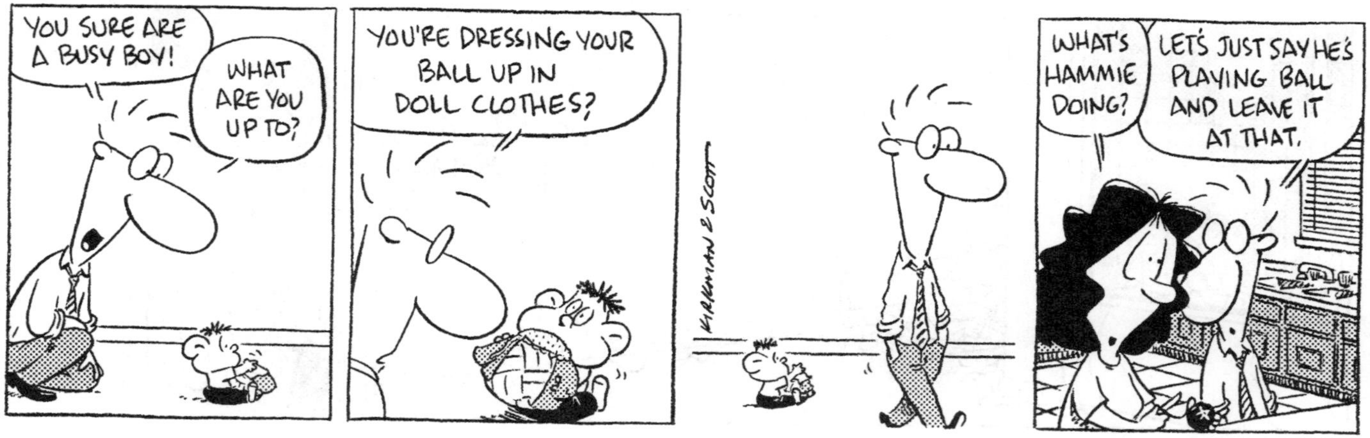
YOU SURE ARE A BUSY BOY!
WHAT ARE YOU UP TO?
YOU'RE DRESSING YOUR BALL UP IN DOLL CLOTHES?
WHAT'S HAMMIE DOING?
LET'S JUST SAY HE'S PLAYING BALL AND LEAVE IT AT THAT.

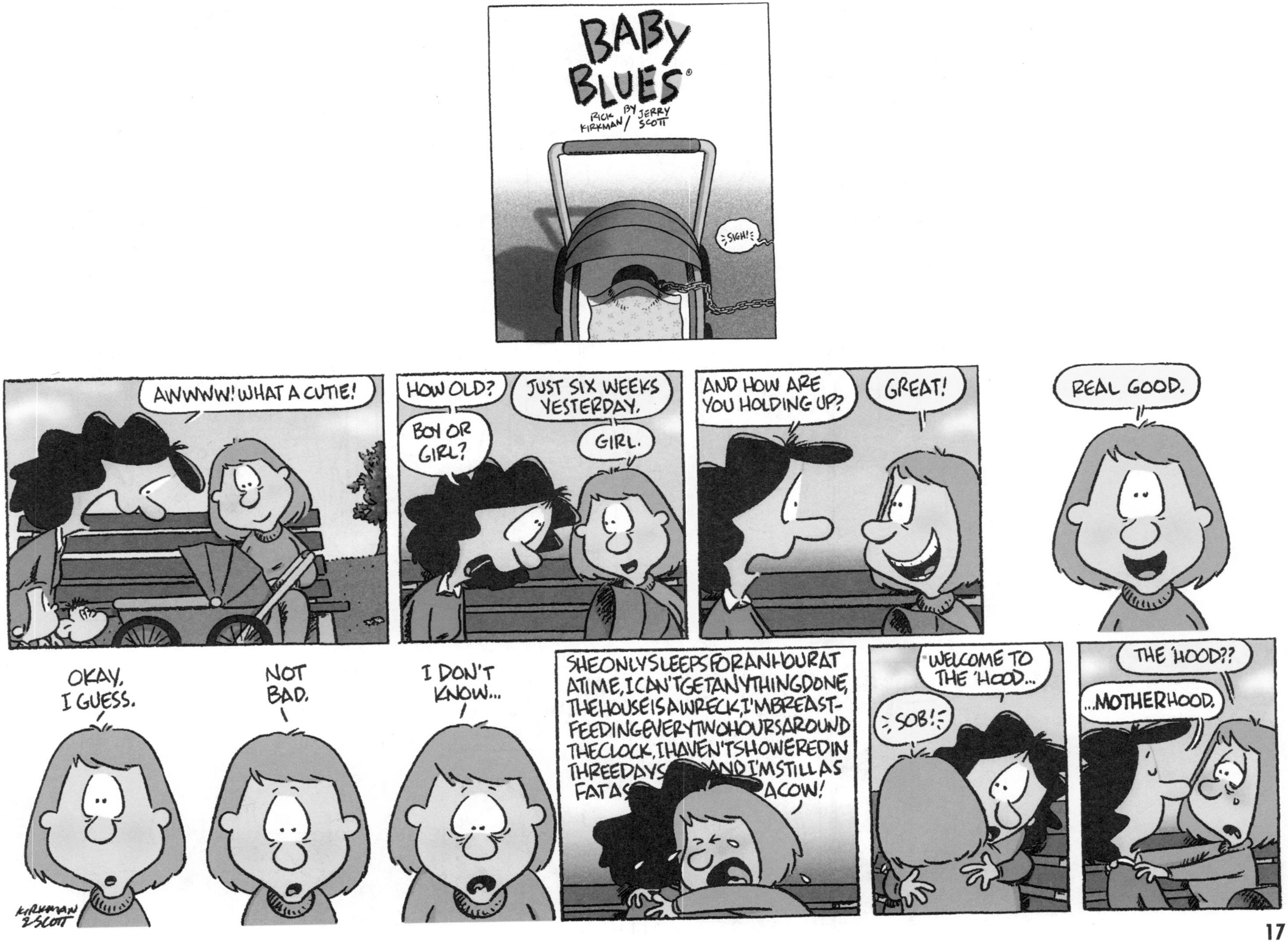
BABY BLUES®
BY RICK KIRKMAN / JERRY SCOTT
SIGH!
AWWWW! WHAT A CUTIE!
HOW OLD?
BOY OR GIRL?
JUST SIX WEEKS YESTERDAY.
GIRL.
AND HOW ARE YOU HOLDING UP?
GREAT!
REAL GOOD.
OKAY, I GUESS.
NOT BAD.
I DON'T KNOW...
SHEONLYSLEEPSFORANHOURAT ATIME, ICAN'TGETANYTHINGDONE, THEHOUSEISAWRECK, I'MBREAST-FEEDINGEVERYTWOHOURSAROUND THECLOCK, IHAVEN'TSHOWEREDIN THREEDAYS ANDI'MSTILLAS FATAS ACOW!
SOB!
WELCOME TO THE 'HOOD...
THE 'HOOD??
...MOTHERHOOD.
KIRKMAN & SCOTT

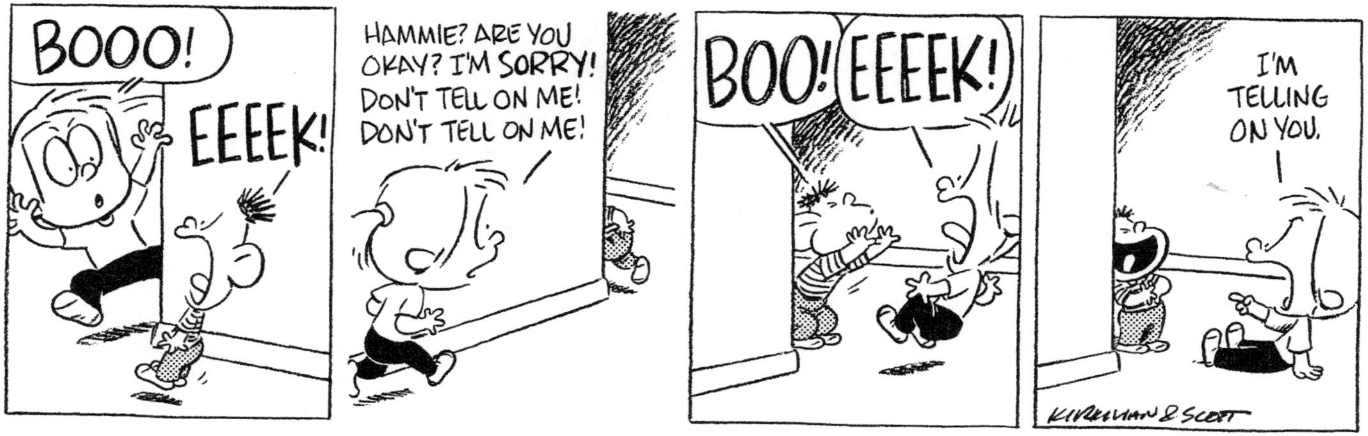
BOOO!
EEEEK!
HAMMIE? ARE YOU OKAY? I'M SORRY! DON'T TELL ON ME! DON'T TELL ON ME!
BOO!
EEEEK!
I'M TELLING ON YOU.
KIRKMAN & SCOTT

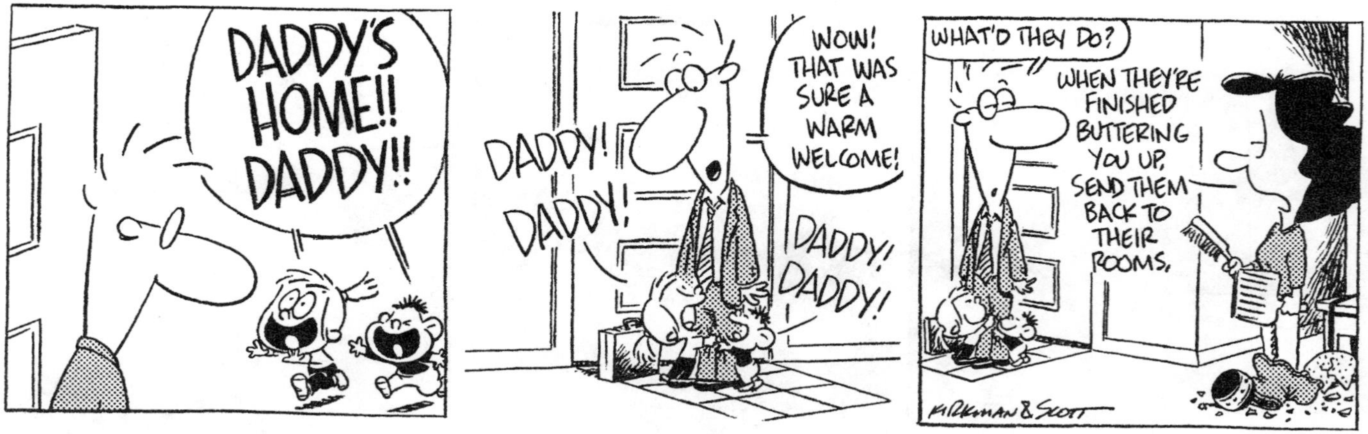
DADDY'S HOME!! DADDY!!
DADDY! DADDY!
WOW! THAT WAS SURE A WARM WELCOME!
DADDY! DADDY!
WHAT'D THEY DO?
WHEN THEY'RE FINISHED BUTTERING YOU UP, SEND THEM BACK TO THEIR ROOMS.
KIRKMAN & SCOTT

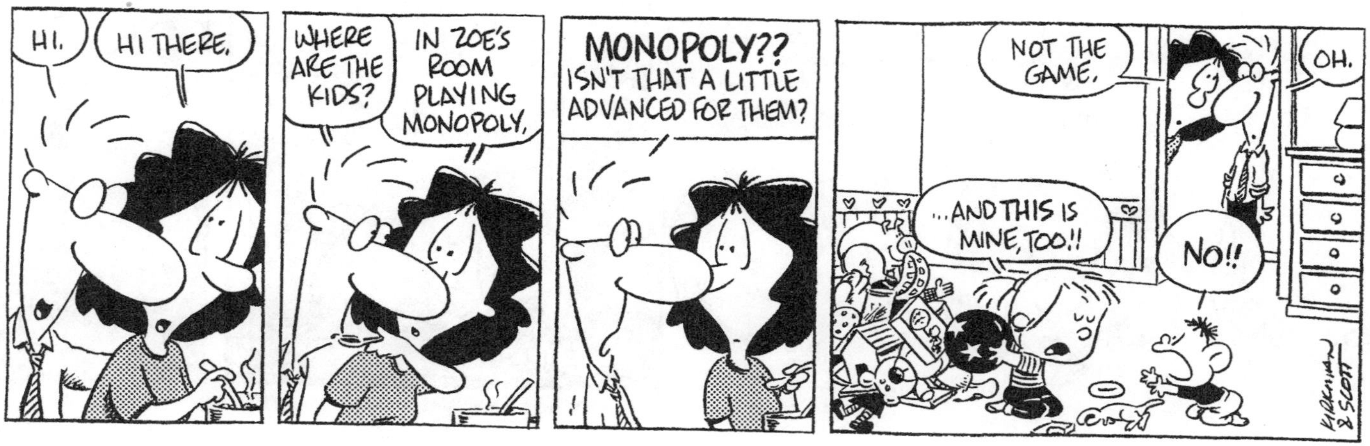
HI.
HI THERE.
WHERE ARE THE KIDS?
IN ZOE'S ROOM PLAYING MONOPOLY.
MONOPOLY?? ISN'T THAT A LITTLE ADVANCED FOR THEM?
NOT THE GAME.
OH.
...AND THIS IS MINE, TOO!!
NO!!
KIRKMAN & SCOTT

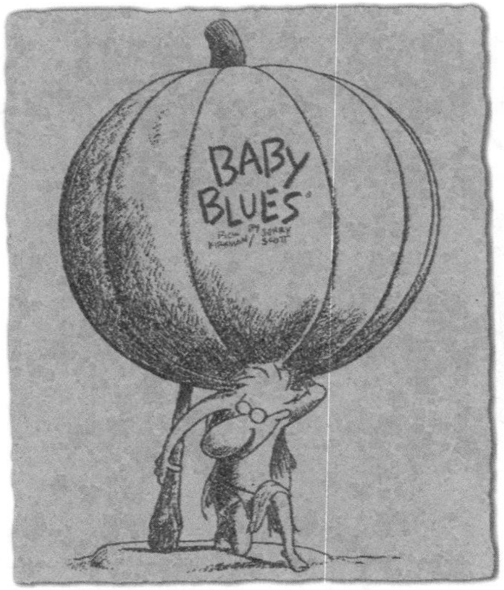
BABY BLUES

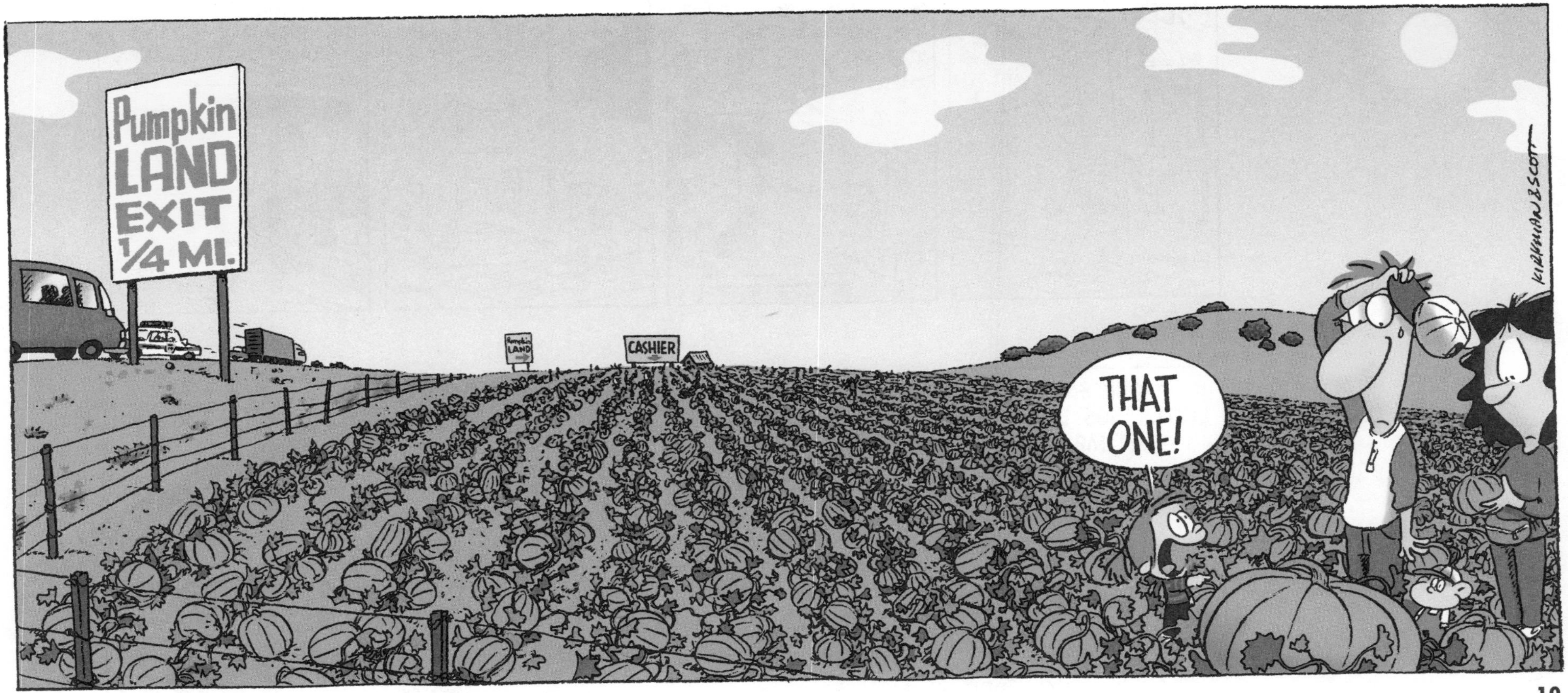
Pumpkin
LAND
EXIT
1/4 MI.
Pumpkin LAND
CASHIER
THAT ONE!
KIRKMAN & SCOTT

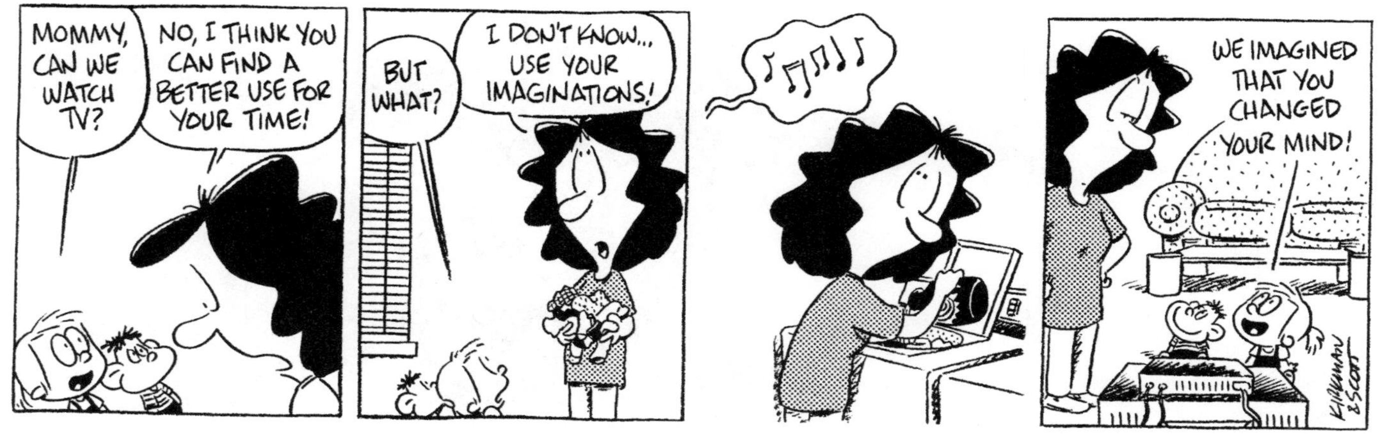
MOMMY, CAN WE WATCH TV?
NO, I THINK YOU CAN FIND A BETTER USE FOR YOUR TIME!
BUT WHAT?
I DON'T KNOW... USE YOUR IMAGINATIONS!
WE IMAGINED THAT YOU CHANGED YOUR MIND!
KIRKMAN & SCOTT

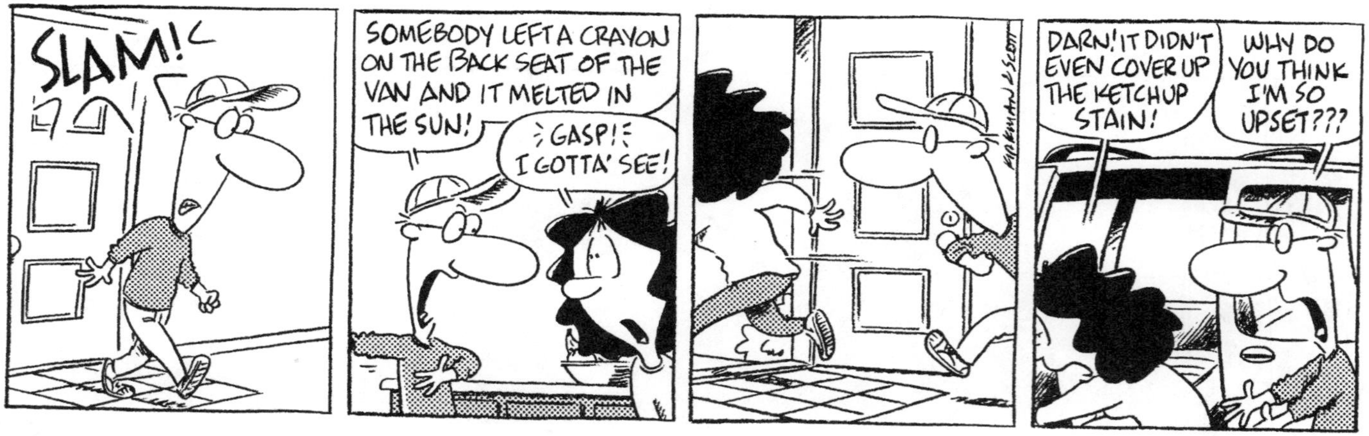
SLAM!
SOMEBODY LEFT A CRAYON ON THE BACK SEAT OF THE VAN AND IT MELTED IN THE SUN!
GASP! I GOTTA' SEE!
KIRKMAN & SCOTT
DARN! IT DIDN'T EVEN COVER UP THE KETCHUP STAIN!
WHY DO YOU THINK I'M SO UPSET???

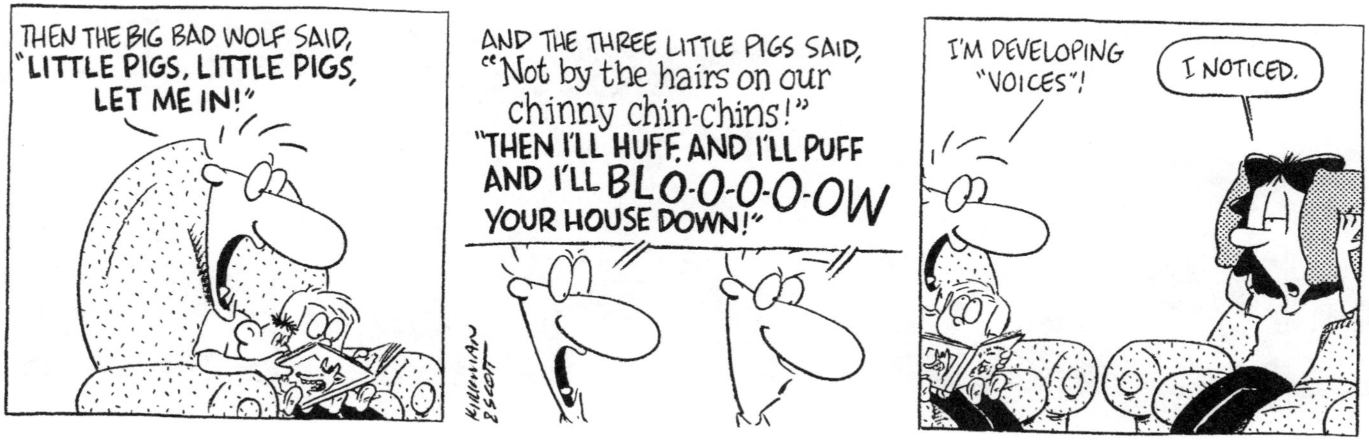
THEN THE BIG BAD WOLF SAID, "LITTLE PIGS, LITTLE PIGS, LET ME IN!"
KIRKMAN & SCOTT
AND THE THREE LITTLE PIGS SAID, "Not by the hairs on our chinny chin-chins!"
"THEN I'LL HUFF, AND I'LL PUFF AND I'LL BLO-O-O-O-O-OW YOUR HOUSE DOWN!"
I'M DEVELOPING "VOICES"!
I NOTICED.

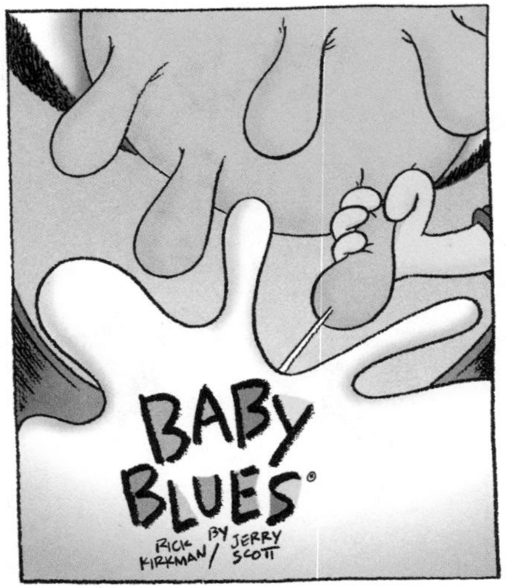
BABY BLUES®
BY RICK KIRKMAN / JERRY SCOTT

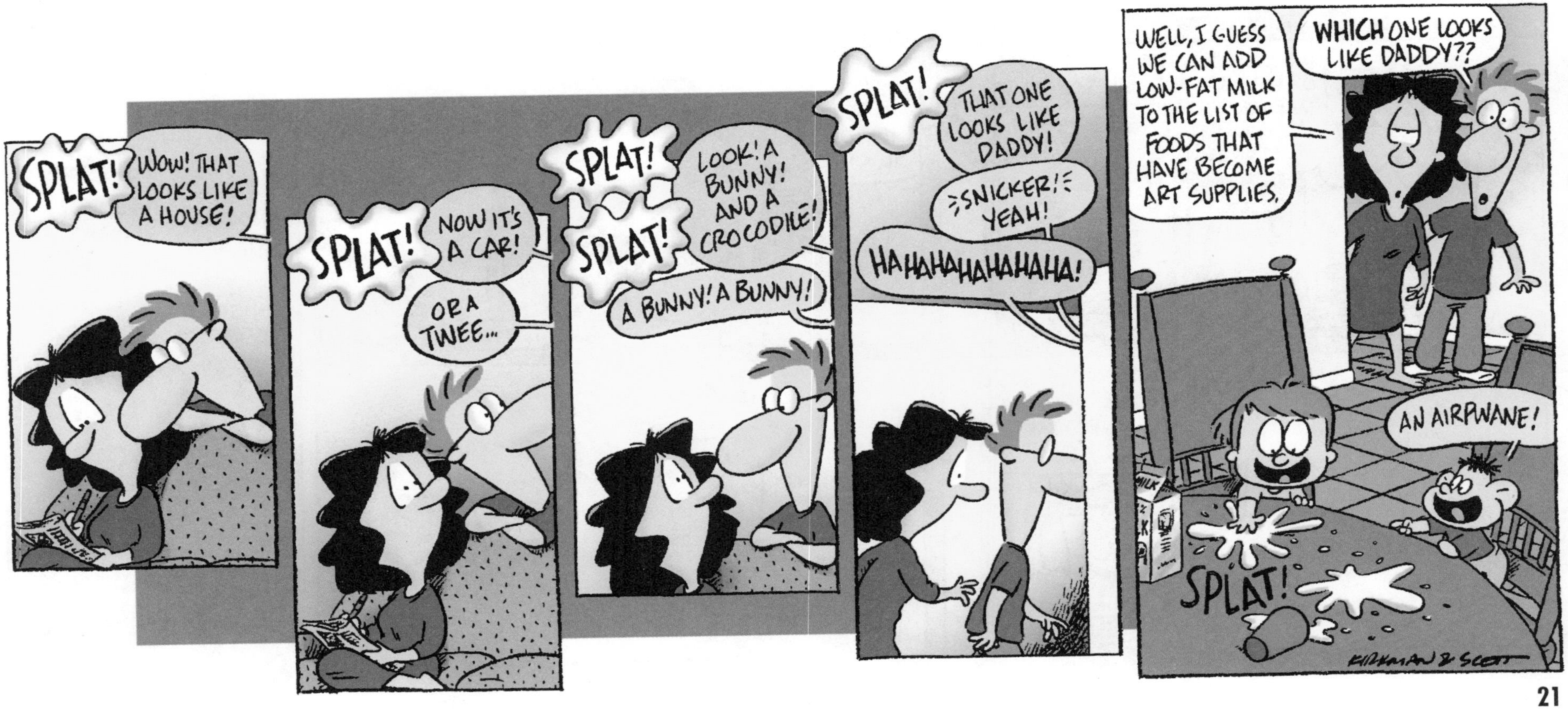
SPLAT!
WOW! THAT LOOKS LIKE A HOUSE!
SPLAT!
NOW IT'S A CAR!
OR A TWEE...
SPLAT!
SPLAT!
LOOK! A BUNNY! AND A CROCODILE!
A BUNNY! A BUNNY!
SPLAT!
THAT ONE LOOKS LIKE DADDY!
SNICKER! YEAH!
HAHAHAHAHAHAHA!
WELL, I GUESS WE CAN ADD LOW-FAT MILK TO THE LIST OF FOODS THAT HAVE BECOME ART SUPPLIES.
WHICH ONE LOOKS LIKE DADDY??
AN AIRPWANE!
SPLAT!
MILK
KIRKMAN & SCOTT

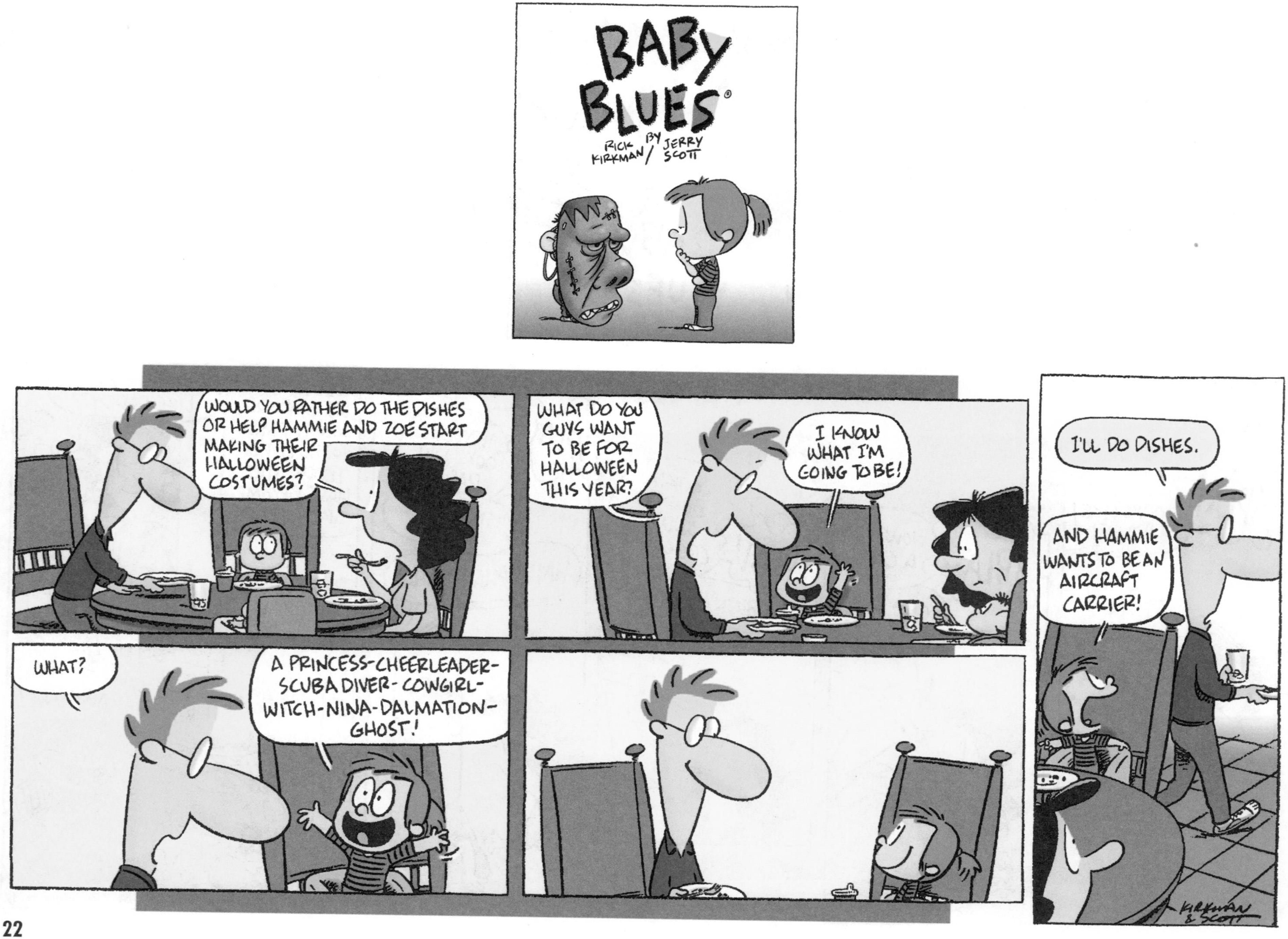
BABY BLUES®
BY RICK KIRKMAN / JERRY SCOTT
WOULD YOU RATHER DO THE DISHES OR HELP HAMMIE AND ZOE START MAKING THEIR HALLOWEEN COSTUMES?
WHAT DO YOU GUYS WANT TO BE FOR HALLOWEEN THIS YEAR?
I KNOW WHAT I'M GOING TO BE!
WHAT?
A PRINCESS-CHEERLEADER-SCUBA DIVER-COWGIRL-WITCH-NINA-DALMATION-GHOST!
I'LL DO DISHES.
AND HAMMIE WANTS TO BE AN AIRCRAFT CARRIER!
KIRKMAN & SCOTT

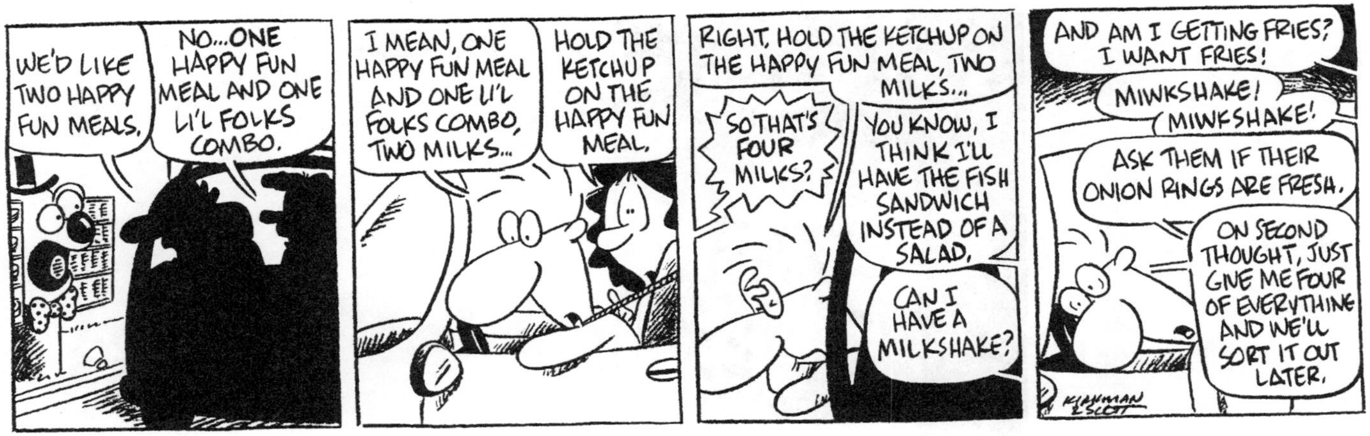
WE'D LIKE TWO HAPPY FUN MEALS.
NO...ONE HAPPY FUN MEAL AND ONE LI'L FOLKS COMBO.
I MEAN, ONE HAPPY FUN MEAL AND ONE LI'L FOLKS COMBO, TWO MILKS...
HOLD THE KETCHUP ON THE HAPPY FUN MEAL.
RIGHT, HOLD THE KETCHUP ON THE HAPPY FUN MEAL, TWO MILKS...
SO THAT'S FOUR MILKS?
YOU KNOW, I THINK I'LL HAVE THE FISH SANDWICH INSTEAD OF A SALAD.
CAN I HAVE A MILKSHAKE?
AND AM I GETTING FRIES? I WANT FRIES!
MIWKSHAKE!
MIWKSHAKE!
ASK THEM IF THEIR ONION RINGS ARE FRESH.
ON SECOND THOUGHT, JUST GIVE ME FOUR OF EVERYTHING AND WE'LL SORT IT OUT LATER.
KIRKMAN & SCOTT

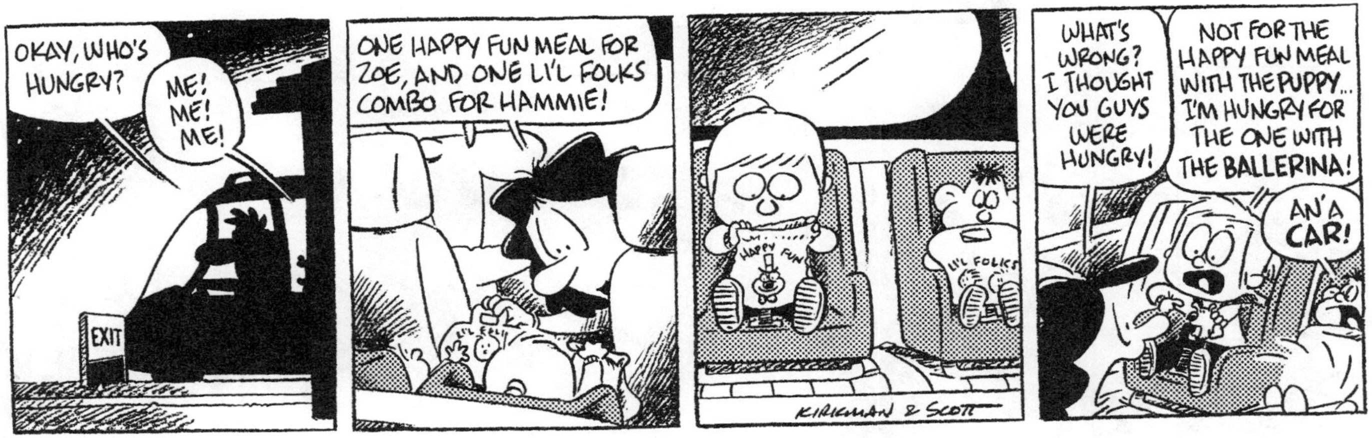
OKAY, WHO'S HUNGRY?
ME! ME! ME!
EXIT
ONE HAPPY FUN MEAL FOR ZOE, AND ONE LI'L FOLKS COMBO FOR HAMMIE!
HAPPY FUN
LI'L FOLKS
KIRKMAN & SCOTT
WHAT'S WRONG? I THOUGHT YOU GUYS WERE HUNGRY!
NOT FOR THE HAPPY FUN MEAL WITH THE PUPPY... I'M HUNGRY FOR THE ONE WITH THE BALLERINA!
AN'A CAR!

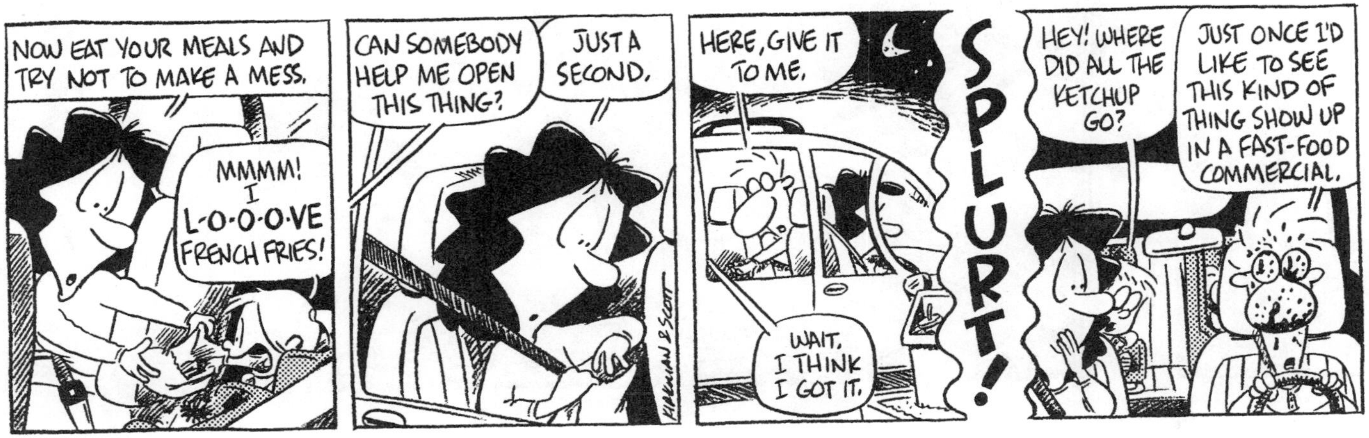
NOW EAT YOUR MEALS AND TRY NOT TO MAKE A MESS.
MMMM! I L-O-O-O-VE FRENCH FRIES!
CAN SOMEBODY HELP ME OPEN THIS THING?
JUST A SECOND.
KIRKMAN & SCOTT
HERE, GIVE IT TO ME.
WAIT. I THINK I GOT IT.
SPLURT!
HEY! WHERE DID ALL THE KETCHUP GO?
JUST ONCE I'D LIKE TO SEE THIS KIND OF THING SHOW UP IN A FAST-FOOD COMMERCIAL.

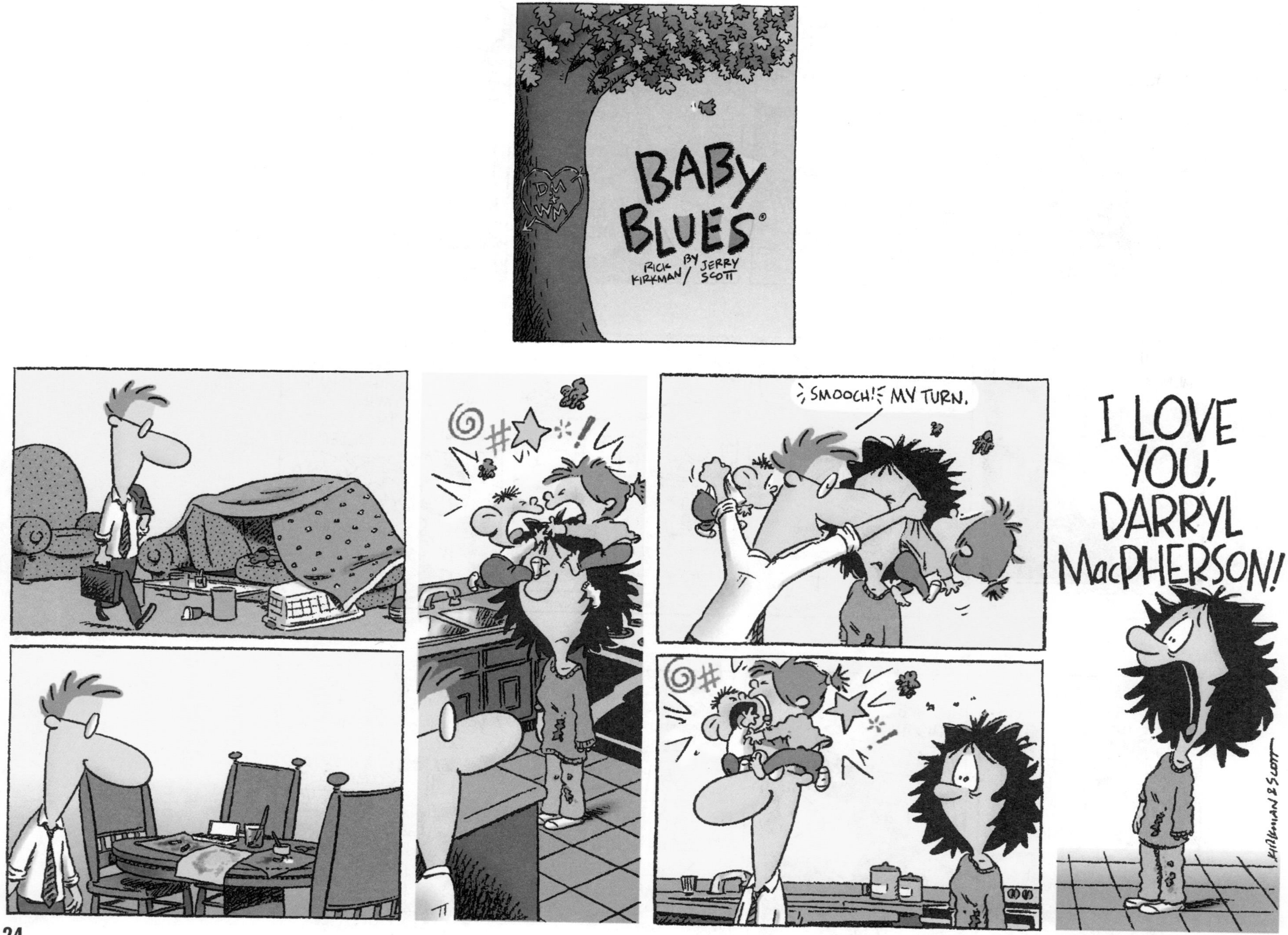
BABY BLUES®
BY RICK KIRKMAN / JERRY SCOTT
D.M. + W.M.
SMOOCH!
MY TURN.
I LOVE YOU, DARRYL MacPHERSON!
KIRKMAN & SCOTT

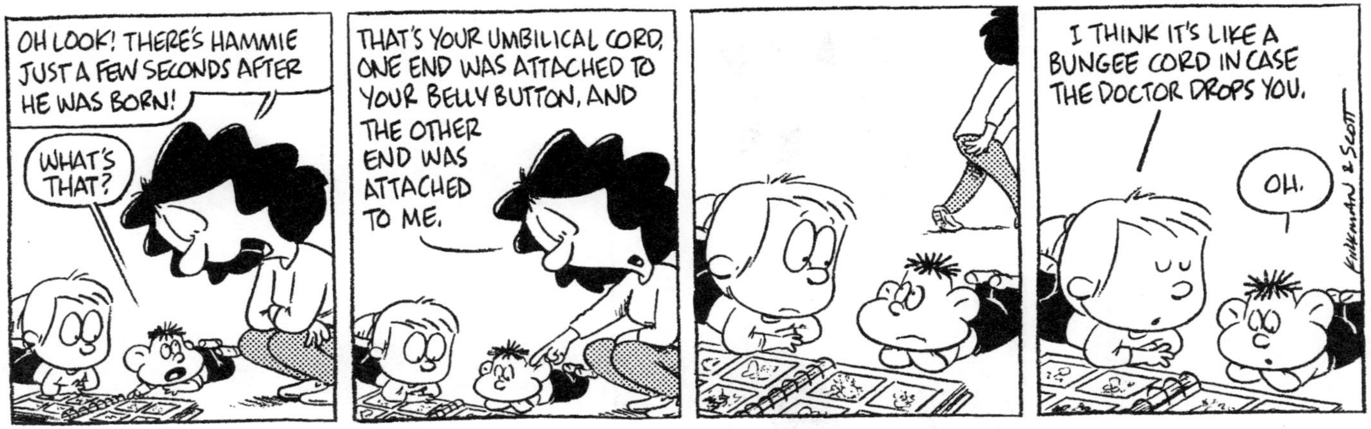
OH LOOK! THERE'S HAMMIE JUST A FEW SECONDS AFTER HE WAS BORN!
WHAT'S THAT?
THAT'S YOUR UMBILICAL CORD, ONE END WAS ATTACHED TO YOUR BELLY BUTTON, AND THE OTHER END WAS ATTACHED TO ME.
I THINK IT'S LIKE A BUNGEE CORD IN CASE THE DOCTOR DROPS YOU.
OH.
KIRKMAN & SCOTT

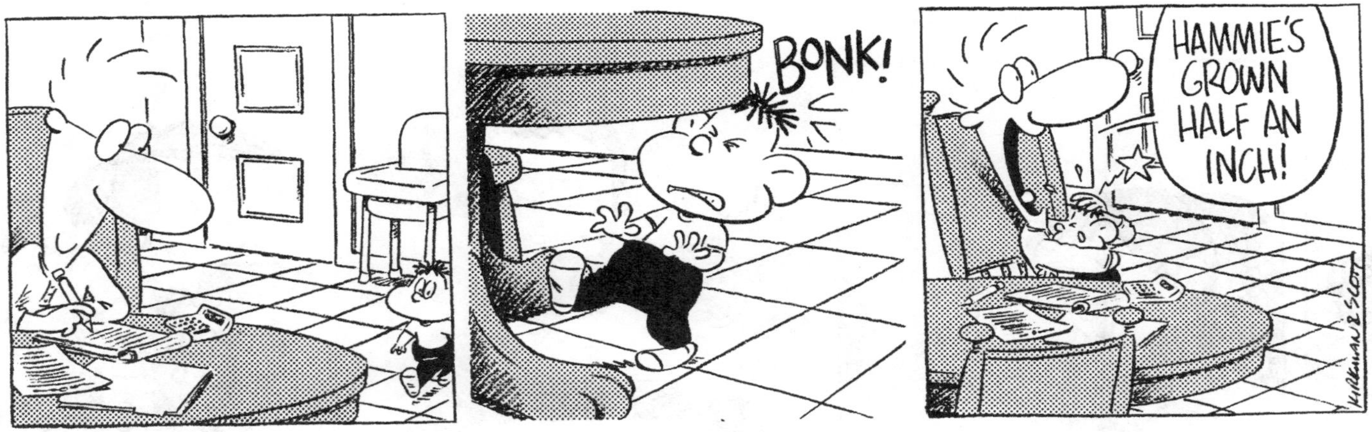
BONK!
HAMMIE'S GROWN HALF AN INCH!
KIRKMAN & SCOTT

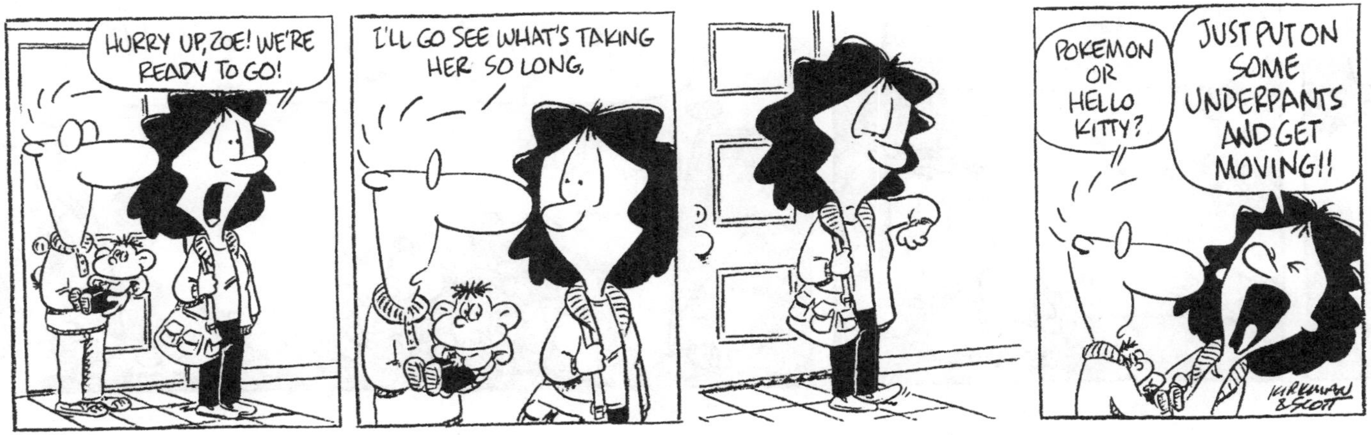
HURRY UP, ZOE! WE'RE READY TO GO!
I'LL GO SEE WHAT'S TAKING HER SO LONG.
POKEMON OR HELLO KITTY?
JUST PUT ON SOME UNDERPANTS AND GET MOVING!!
KIRKMAN & SCOTT

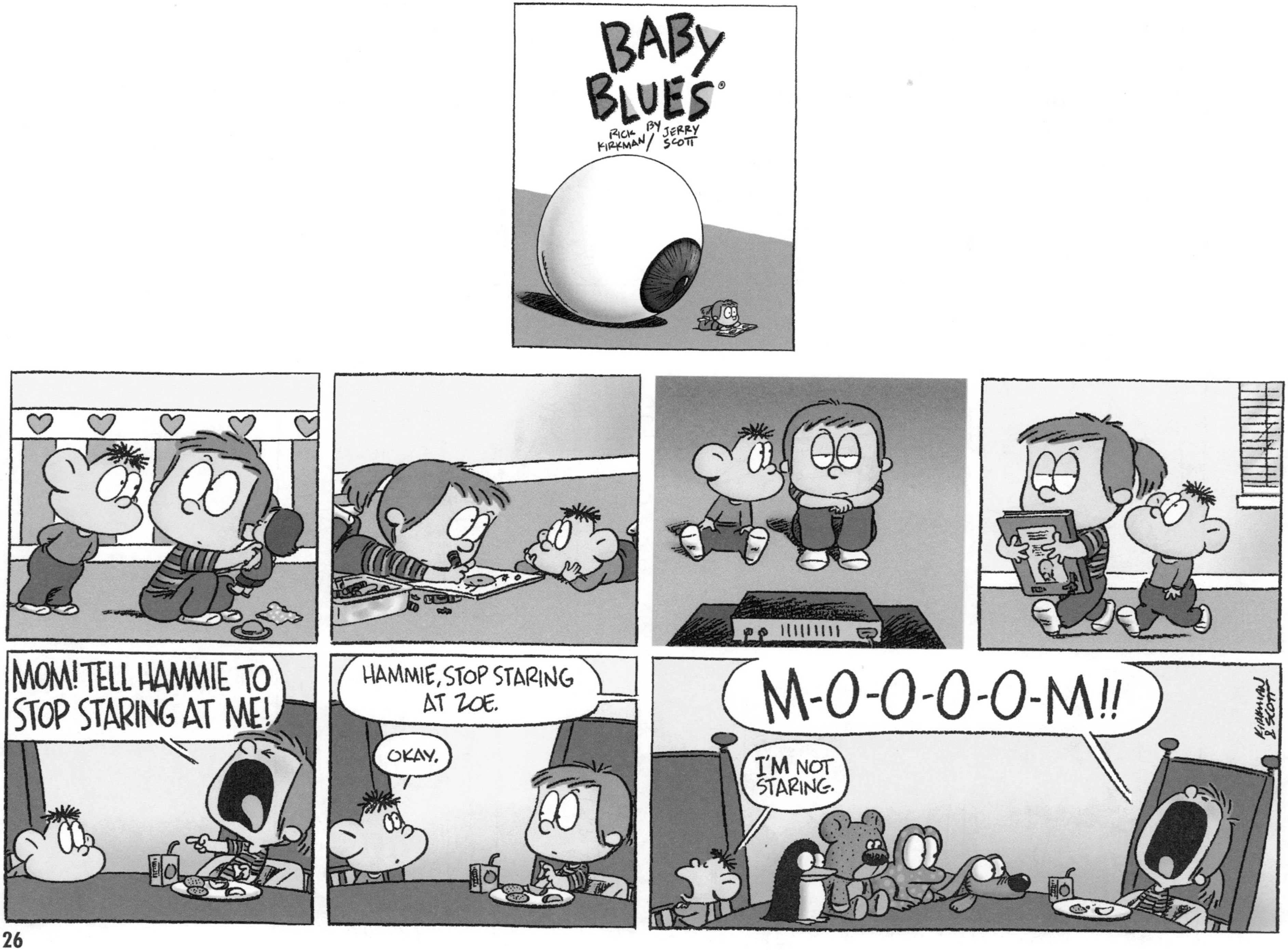
BABY BLUES®
BY RICK KIRKMAN / JERRY SCOTT
MOM! TELL HAMMIE TO STOP STARING AT ME!
HAMMIE, STOP STARING AT ZOE.
OKAY.
M-O-O-O-O-M!!
I'M NOT STARING.
KIRKMAN & SCOTT

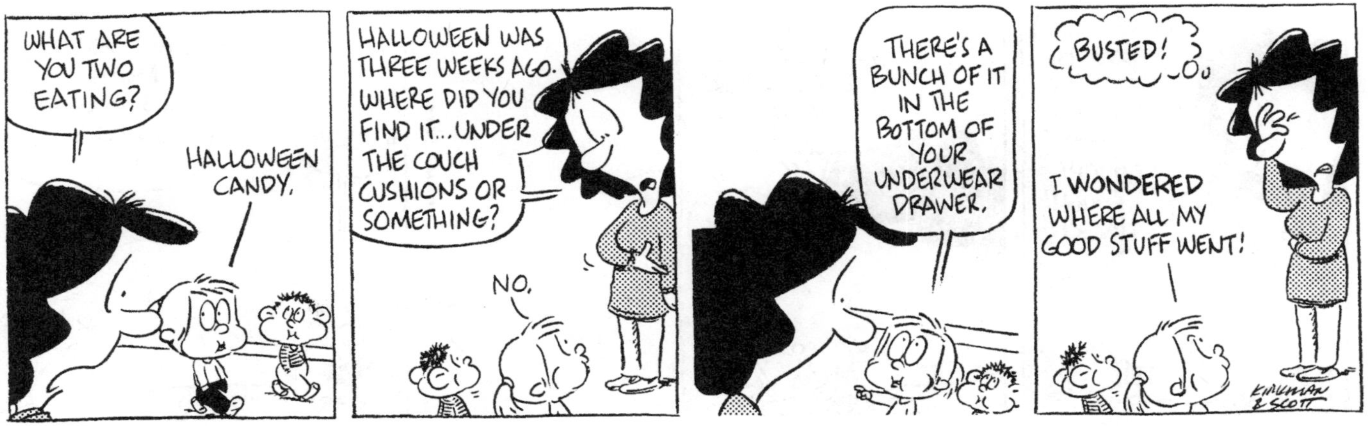
WHAT ARE YOU TWO EATING?
HALLOWEEN CANDY.
HALLOWEEN WAS THREE WEEKS AGO. WHERE DID YOU FIND IT... UNDER THE COUCH CUSHIONS OR SOMETHING?
NO.
THERE'S A BUNCH OF IT IN THE BOTTOM OF YOUR UNDERWEAR DRAWER.
BUSTED!
I WONDERED WHERE ALL MY GOOD STUFF WENT!
KIRKMAN & SCOTT

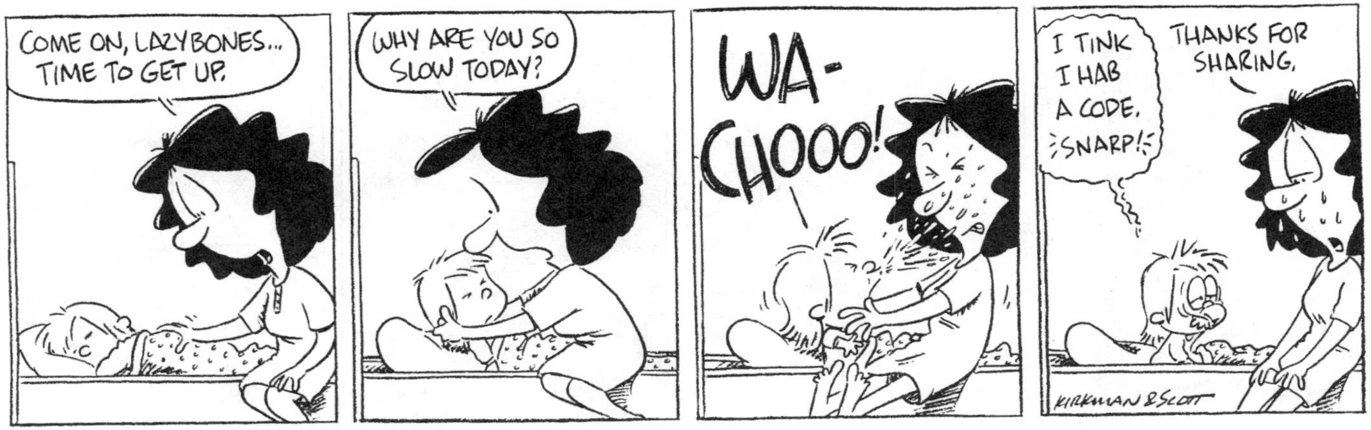
COME ON, LAZYBONES... TIME TO GET UP.
WHY ARE YOU SO SLOW TODAY?
WA-CHOOO!
I TINK I HAB A CODE. SNARP!
THANKS FOR SHARING.
KIRKMAN & SCOTT

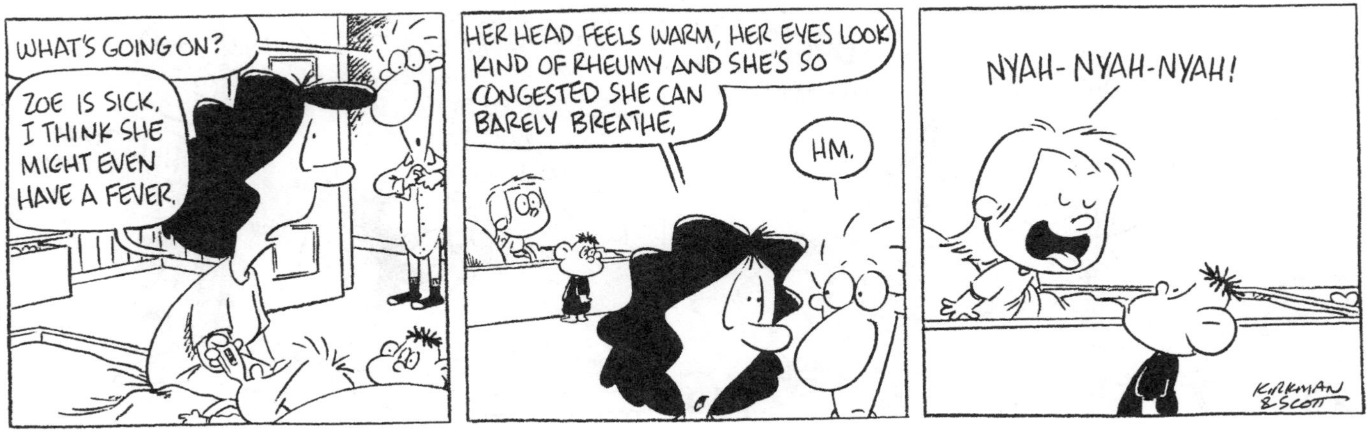
WHAT'S GOING ON?
ZOE IS SICK. I THINK SHE MIGHT EVEN HAVE A FEVER.
HER HEAD FEELS WARM, HER EYES LOOK KIND OF RHEUMY AND SHE'S SO CONGESTED SHE CAN BARELY BREATHE.
HM.
NYAH-NYAH-NYAH!
KIRKMAN & SCOTT

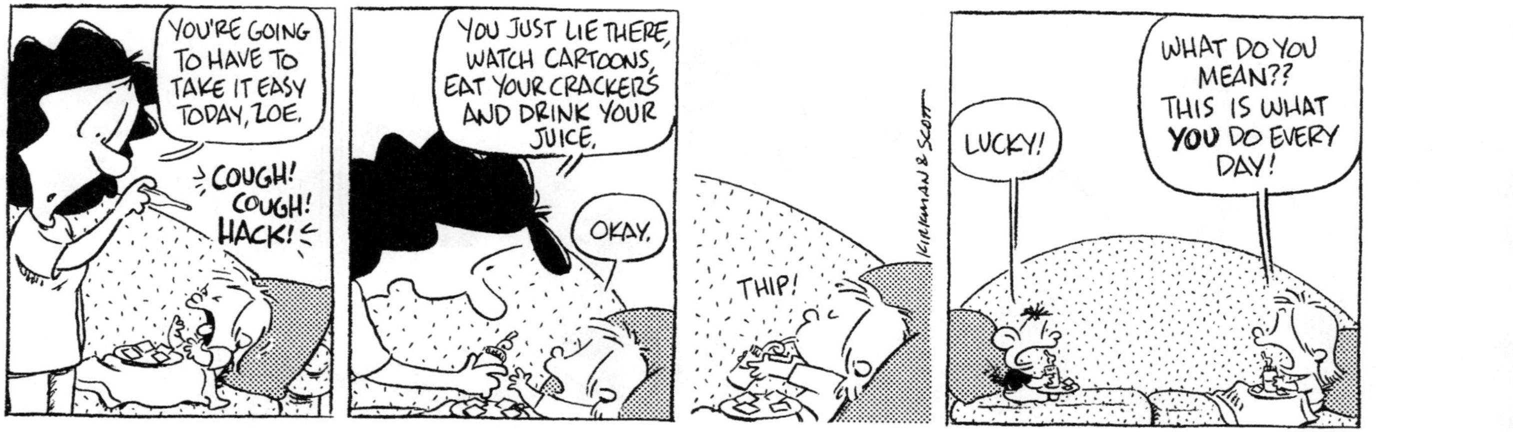
YOU'RE GOING TO HAVE TO TAKE IT EASY TODAY, ZOE.
COUGH! COUGH! HACK!
YOU JUST LIE THERE, WATCH CARTOONS, EAT YOUR CRACKERS AND DRINK YOUR JUICE.
OKAY.
THIP!
KIRKMAN & SCOTT
LUCKY!
WHAT DO YOU MEAN?? THIS IS WHAT YOU DO EVERY DAY!

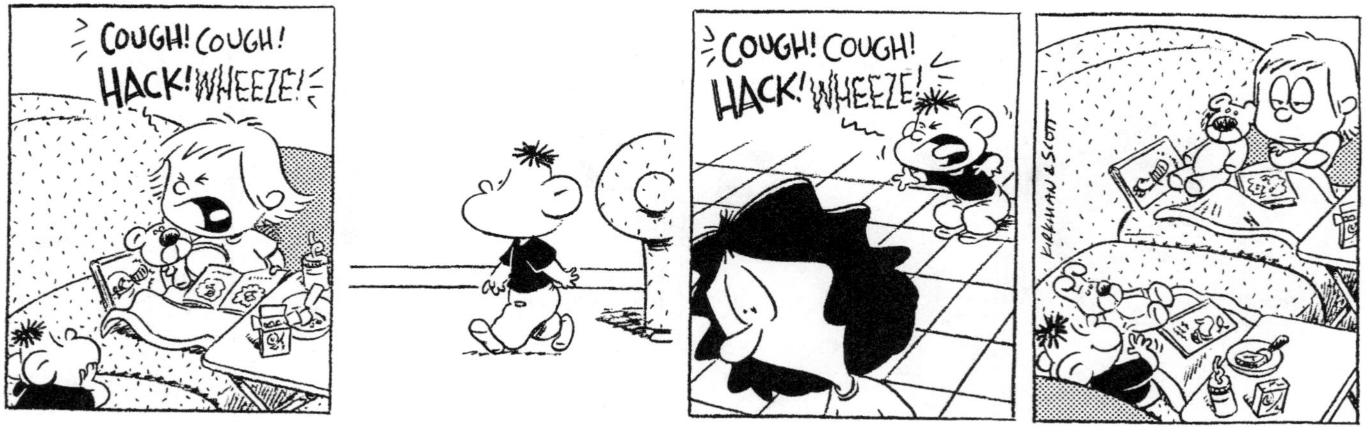
COUGH! COUGH! HACK! WHEEZE!
COUGH! COUGH! HACK! WHEEZE!
KIRKMAN & SCOTT

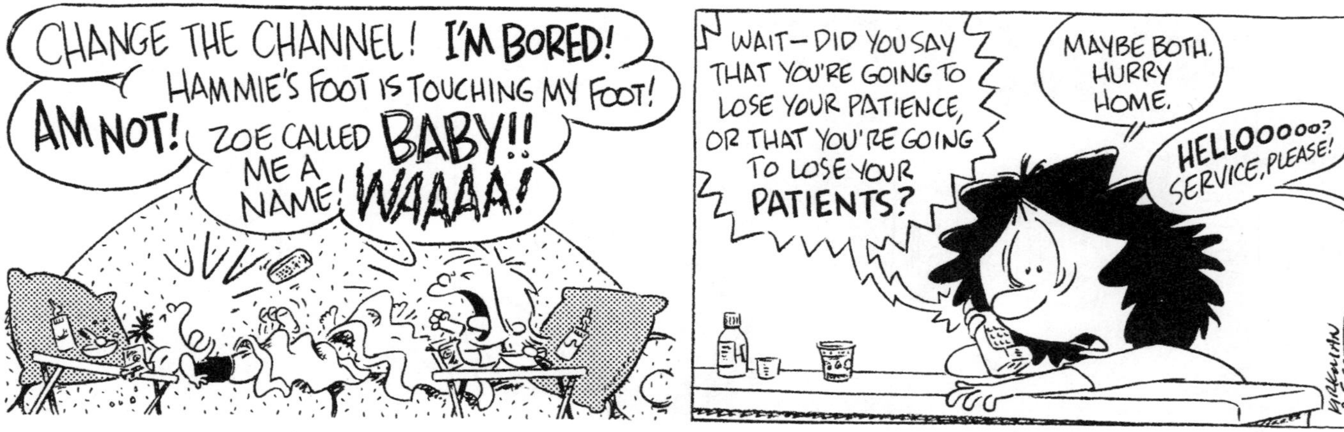
CHANGE THE CHANNEL! I'M BORED!
HAMMIE'S FOOT IS TOUCHING MY FOOT!
AM NOT!
ZOE CALLED ME A NAME!
BABY!! WAAAA!
WAIT— DID YOU SAY THAT YOU'RE GOING TO LOSE YOUR PATIENCE, OR THAT YOU'RE GOING TO LOSE YOUR PATIENTS?
MAYBE BOTH. HURRY HOME.
HELLOOOoo? SERVICE, PLEASE!
KIRKMAN & SCOTT

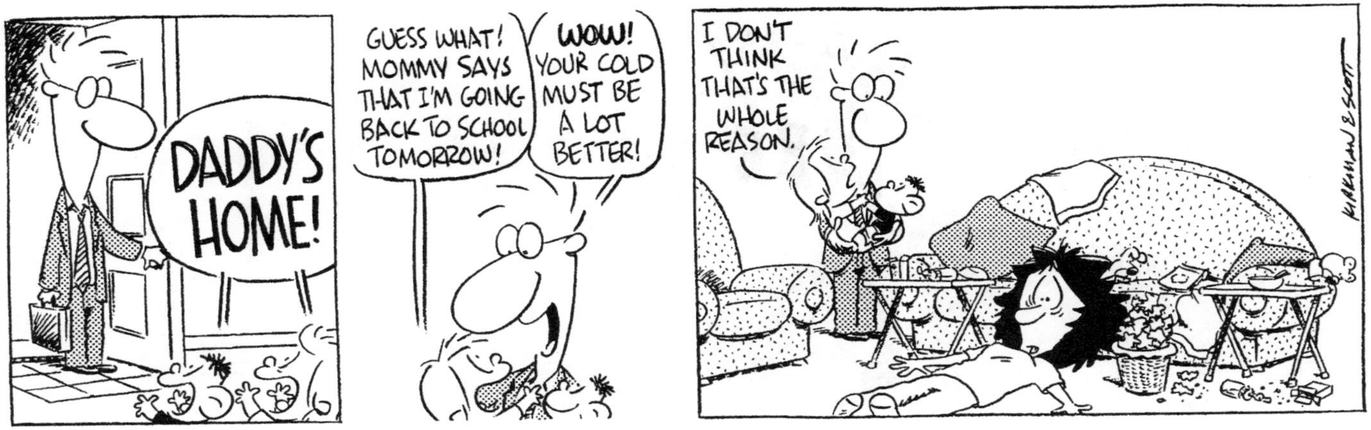
DADDY'S HOME!
GUESS WHAT! MOMMY SAYS THAT I'M GOING BACK TO SCHOOL TOMORROW!
WOW! YOUR COLD MUST BE A LOT BETTER!
I DON'T THINK THAT'S THE WHOLE REASON.
KIRKMAN & SCOTT

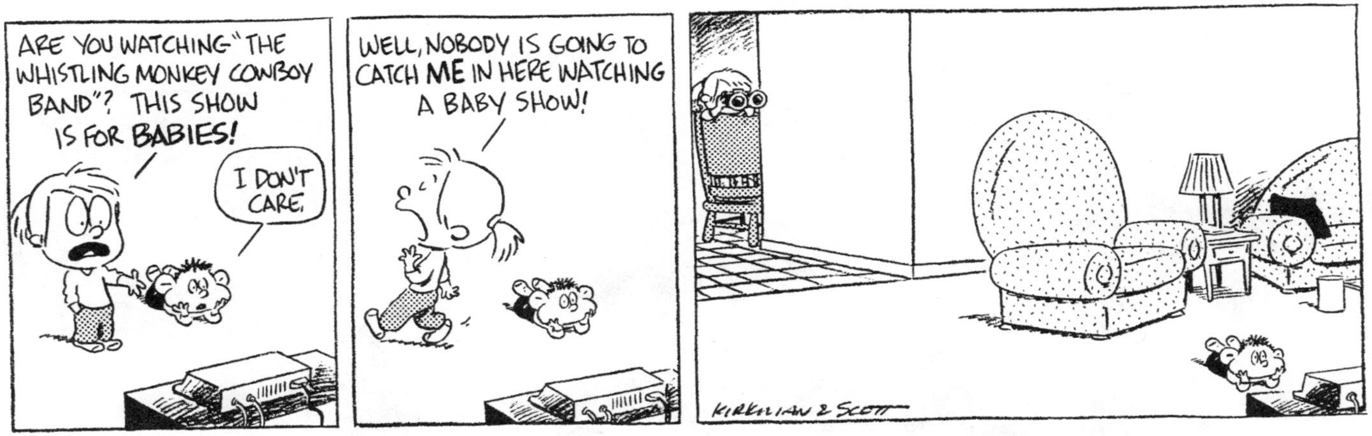
ARE YOU WATCHING "THE WHISTLING MONKEY COWBOY BAND"? THIS SHOW IS FOR BABIES!
I DON'T CARE.
WELL, NOBODY IS GOING TO CATCH ME IN HERE WATCHING A BABY SHOW!
KIRKMAN & SCOTT

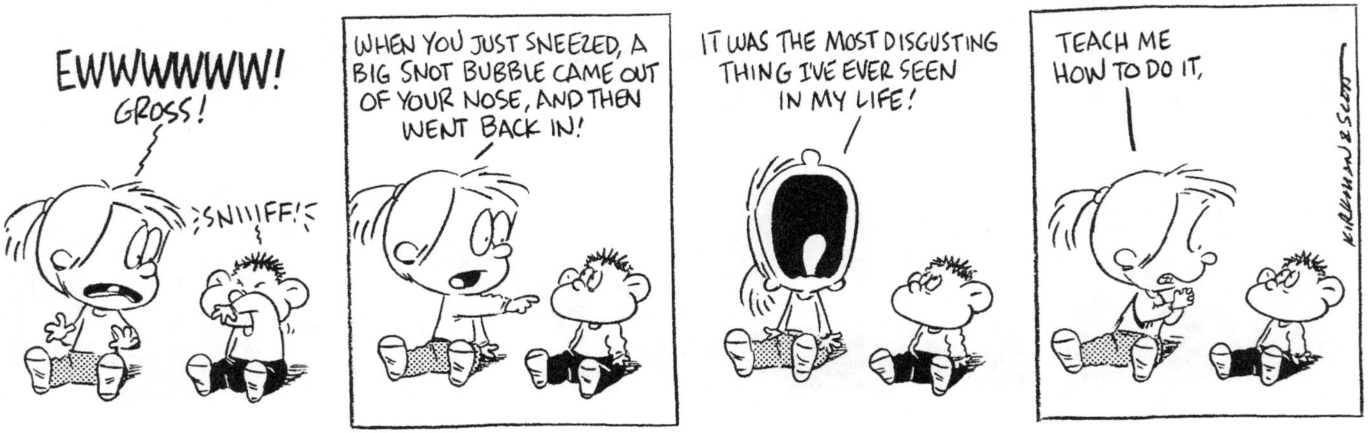
EWWWWWW! GROSS!
SNIIIFF!
WHEN YOU JUST SNEEZED, A BIG SNOT BUBBLE CAME OUT OF YOUR NOSE, AND THEN WENT BACK IN!
IT WAS THE MOST DISGUSTING THING I'VE EVER SEEN IN MY LIFE!
TEACH ME HOW TO DO IT.
KIRKMAN & SCOTT

BABY BLUES®

by Rick Kirkman / Jerry Scott

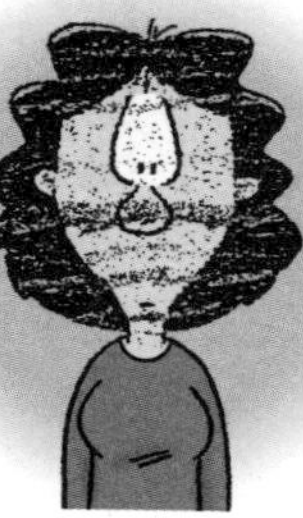

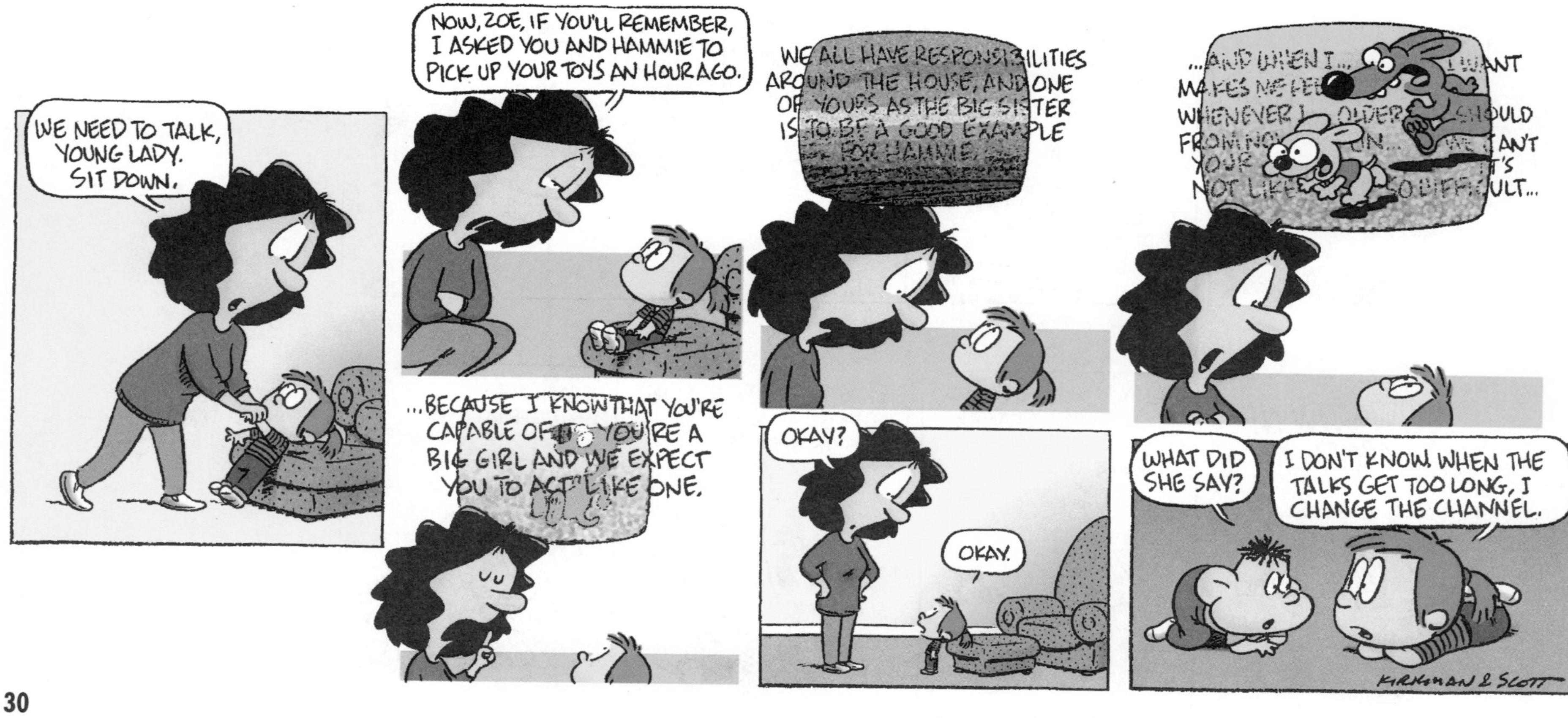

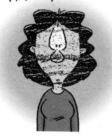

WE NEED TO TALK, YOUNG LADY. SIT DOWN.
NOW, ZOE, IF YOU'LL REMEMBER, I ASKED YOU AND HAMMIE TO PICK UP YOUR TOYS AN HOUR AGO.
WE ALL HAVE RESPONSIBILITIES AROUND THE HOUSE, AND ONE OF YOURS AS THE BIG SISTER IS TO BE A GOOD EXAMPLE FOR HAMMIE.
...BECAUSE I KNOW THAT YOU'RE CAPABLE OF IT. YOU'RE A BIG GIRL AND WE EXPECT YOU TO ACT LIKE ONE.
OKAY?
OKAY.
WHAT DID SHE SAY?
I DON'T KNOW. WHEN THE TALKS GET TOO LONG, I CHANGE THE CHANNEL.
KIRKMAN & SCOTT

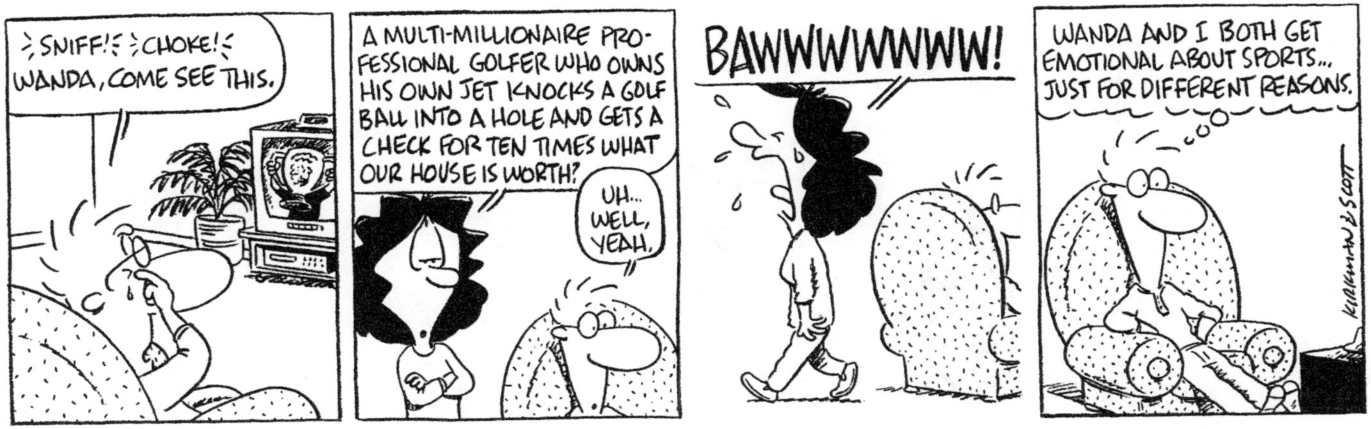
SNIFF! CHOKE! WANDA, COME SEE THIS.
A MULTI-MILLIONAIRE PROFESSIONAL GOLFER WHO OWNS HIS OWN JET KNOCKS A GOLF BALL INTO A HOLE AND GETS A CHECK FOR TEN TIMES WHAT OUR HOUSE IS WORTH?
UH... WELL, YEAH.
BAWWWWWWW!
WANDA AND I BOTH GET EMOTIONAL ABOUT SPORTS... JUST FOR DIFFERENT REASONS.
KIRKMAN & SCOTT

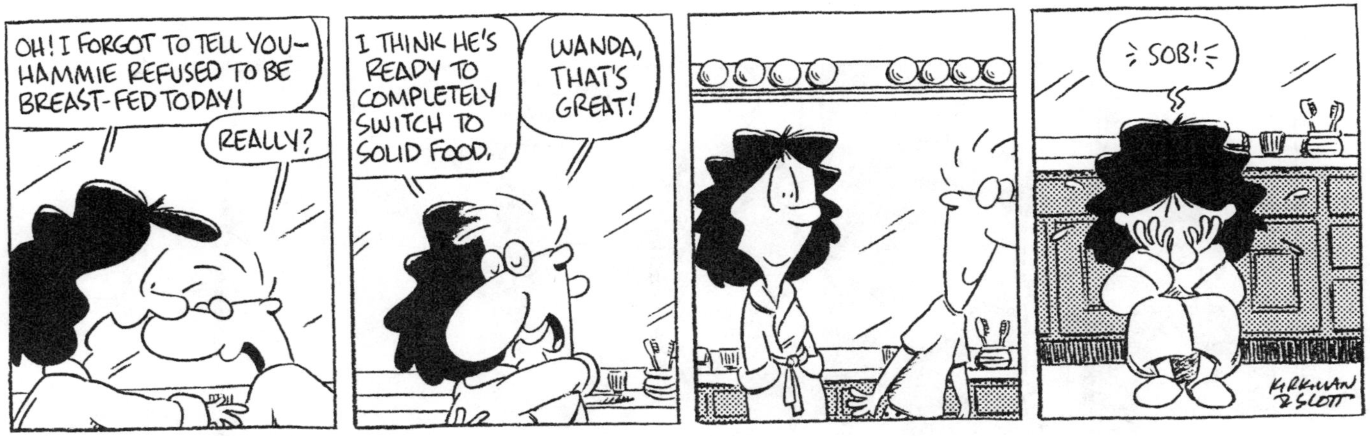
OH! I FORGOT TO TELL YOU-HAMMIE REFUSED TO BE BREAST-FED TODAY!
REALLY?
I THINK HE'S READY TO COMPLETELY SWITCH TO SOLID FOOD.
WANDA, THAT'S GREAT!
SOB!
KIRKMAN & SCOTT

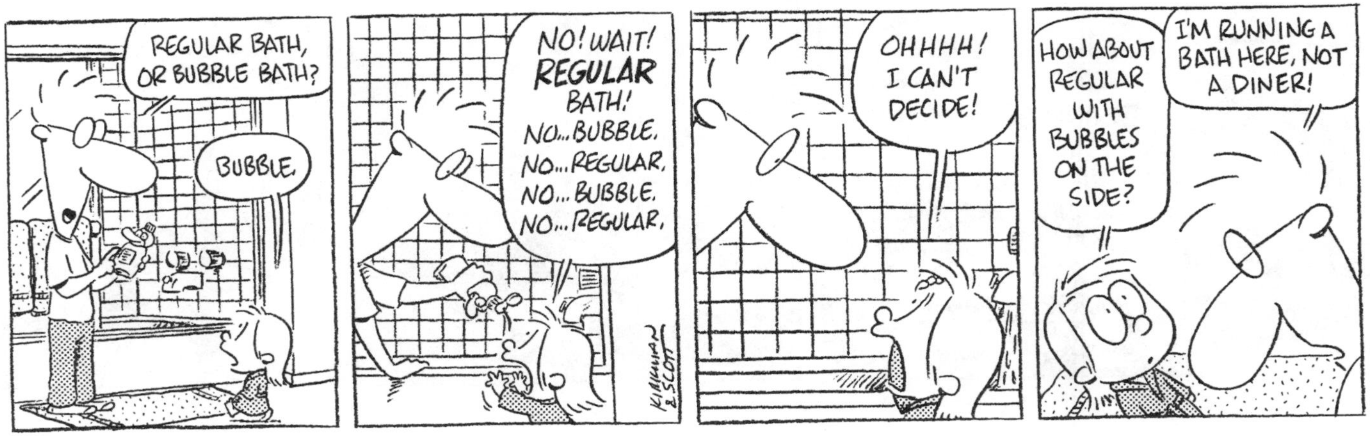
REGULAR BATH, OR BUBBLE BATH?
BUBBLE.
NO! WAIT! REGULAR BATH! NO... BUBBLE. NO... REGULAR. NO... BUBBLE. NO... REGULAR.
KIRKMAN & SCOTT
OHHHH! I CAN'T DECIDE!
HOW ABOUT REGULAR WITH BUBBLES ON THE SIDE?
I'M RUNNING A BATH HERE, NOT A DINER!

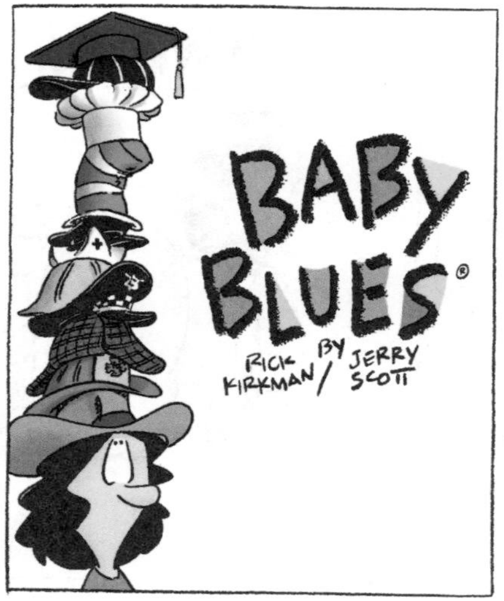
BABY BLUES®
BY RICK KIRKMAN / JERRY SCOTT

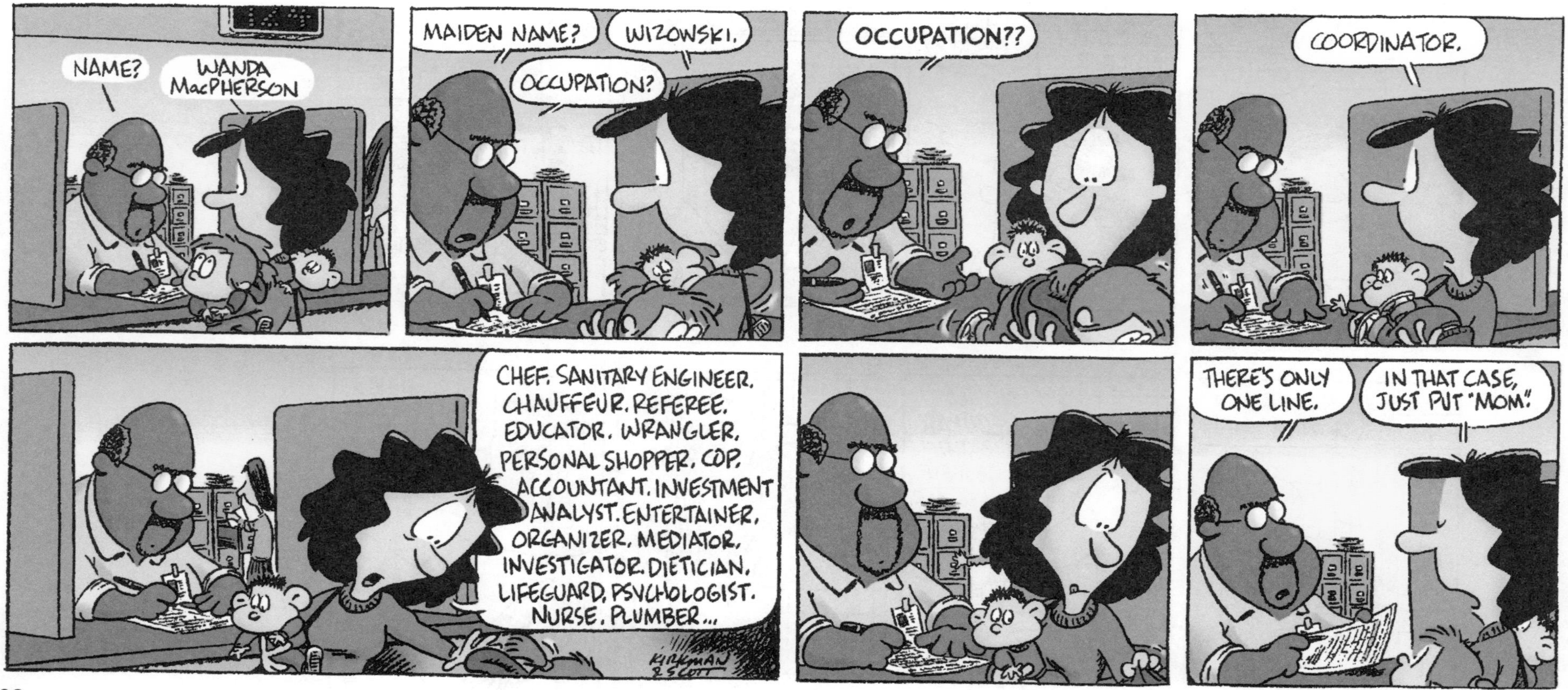
NAME?
WANDA MacPHERSON
MAIDEN NAME?
WIZOWSKI.
OCCUPATION?
OCCUPATION??
COORDINATOR.
CHEF. SANITARY ENGINEER. CHAUFFEUR. REFEREE. EDUCATOR. WRANGLER. PERSONAL SHOPPER. COP. ACCOUNTANT. INVESTMENT ANALYST. ENTERTAINER. ORGANIZER. MEDIATOR. INVESTIGATOR. DIETICIAN. LIFEGUARD. PSYCHOLOGIST. NURSE. PLUMBER...
KIRKMAN & SCOTT
THERE'S ONLY ONE LINE.
IN THAT CASE, JUST PUT "MOM."

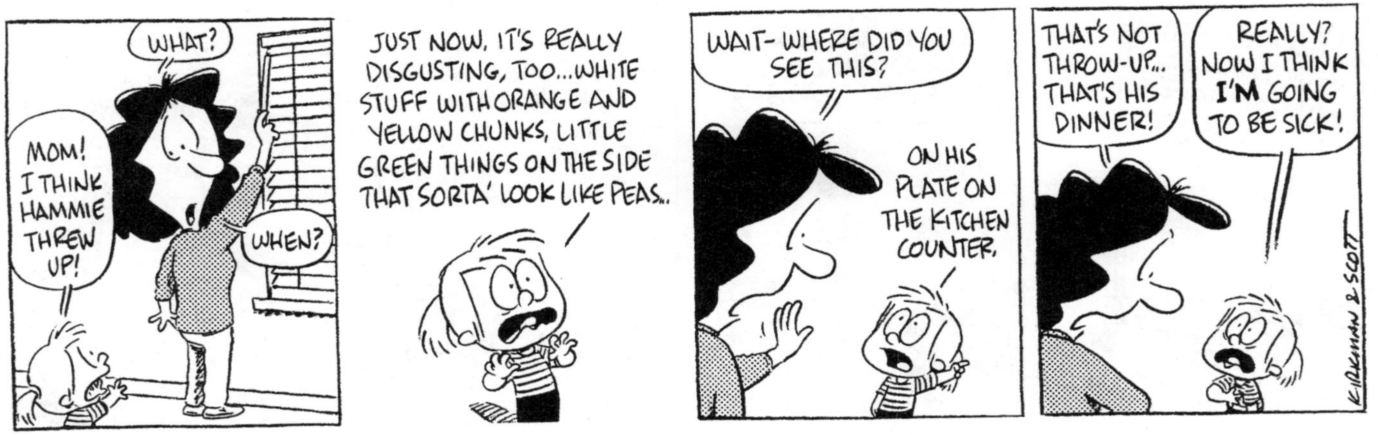
MOM! I THINK HAMMIE THREW UP!
WHAT?
WHEN?
JUST NOW. IT'S REALLY DISGUSTING, TOO...WHITE STUFF WITH ORANGE AND YELLOW CHUNKS, LITTLE GREEN THINGS ON THE SIDE THAT SORTA' LOOK LIKE PEAS...
WAIT- WHERE DID YOU SEE THIS?
ON HIS PLATE ON THE KITCHEN COUNTER.
THAT'S NOT THROW-UP... THAT'S HIS DINNER!
REALLY? NOW I THINK **I'M** GOING TO BE SICK!
KIRKMAN & SCOTT

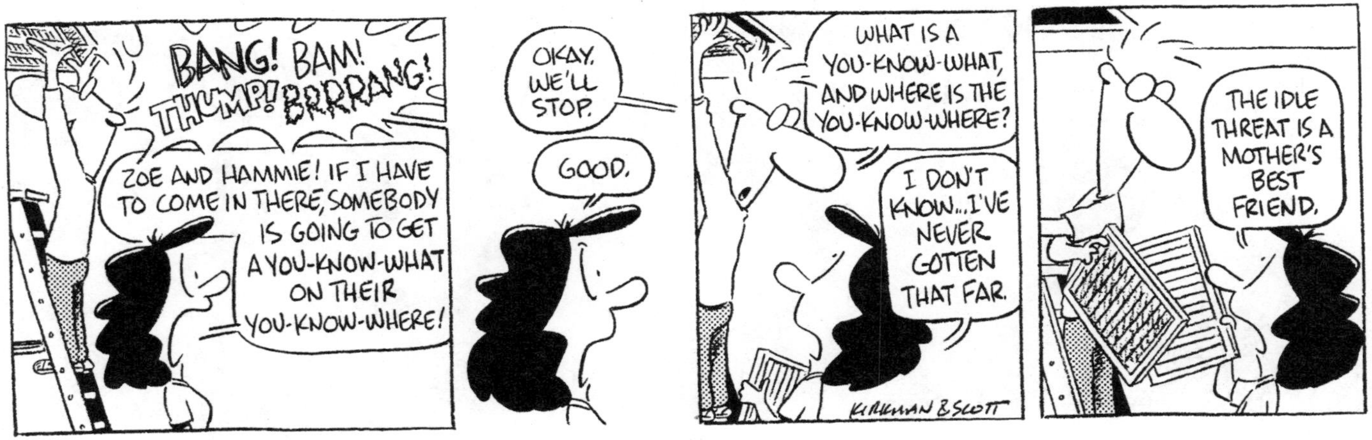
BANG! BAM! THUMP! BRRRANG!
ZOE AND HAMMIE! IF I HAVE TO COME IN THERE, SOMEBODY IS GOING TO GET A YOU-KNOW-WHAT ON THEIR YOU-KNOW-WHERE!
OKAY. WE'LL STOP.
GOOD.
WHAT IS A YOU-KNOW-WHAT, AND WHERE IS THE YOU-KNOW-WHERE?
I DON'T KNOW...I'VE NEVER GOTTEN THAT FAR.
KIRKMAN & SCOTT
THE IDLE THREAT IS A MOTHER'S BEST FRIEND.

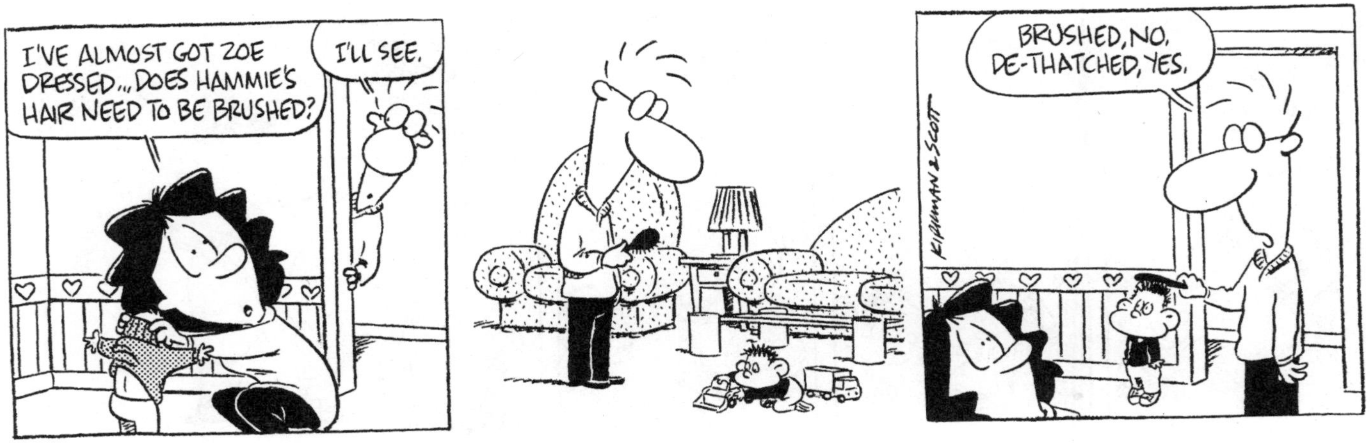
I'VE ALMOST GOT ZOE DRESSED... DOES HAMMIE'S HAIR NEED TO BE BRUSHED?
I'LL SEE.
KIRKMAN & SCOTT
BRUSHED, NO. DE-THATCHED, YES.

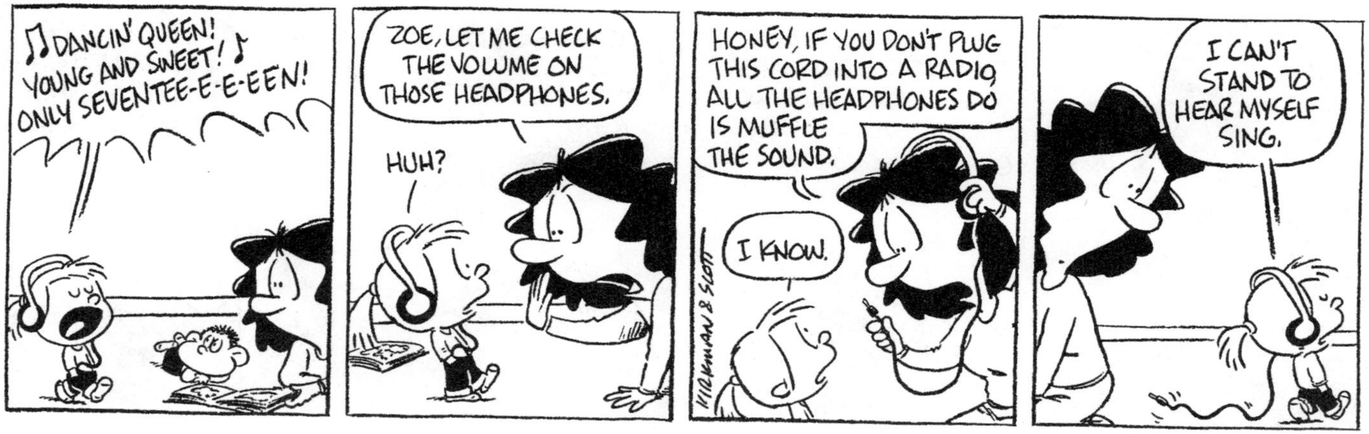
DANCIN' QUEEN! YOUNG AND SWEET! ONLY SEVENTEE-E-E-EEN!
ZOE, LET ME CHECK THE VOLUME ON THOSE HEADPHONES.
HUH?
HONEY, IF YOU DON'T PLUG THIS CORD INTO A RADIO, ALL THE HEADPHONES DO IS MUFFLE THE SOUND.
I KNOW.
KIRKMAN & SCOTT
I CAN'T STAND TO HEAR MYSELF SING.

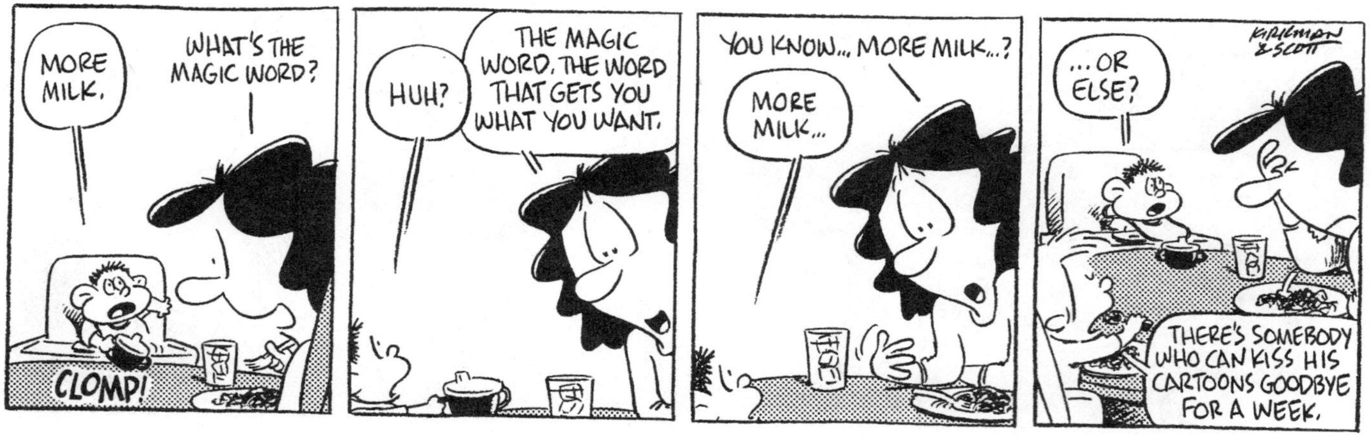
MORE MILK.
WHAT'S THE MAGIC WORD?
CLOMP!
HUH?
THE MAGIC WORD. THE WORD THAT GETS YOU WHAT YOU WANT.
YOU KNOW... MORE MILK...?
MORE MILK...
KIRKMAN & SCOTT
...OR ELSE?
THERE'S SOMEBODY WHO CAN KISS HIS CARTOONS GOODBYE FOR A WEEK.

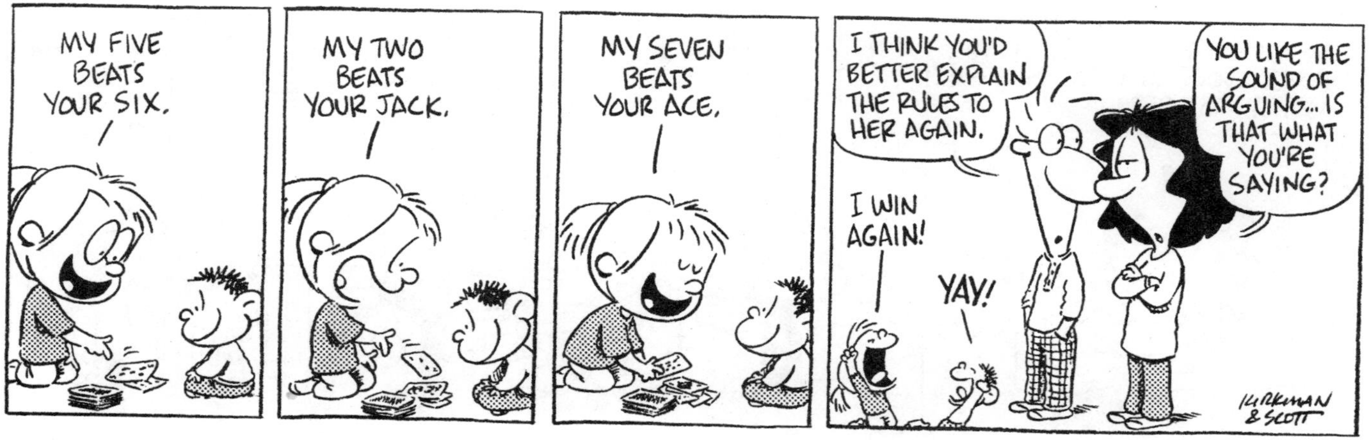
MY FIVE BEATS YOUR SIX.
MY TWO BEATS YOUR JACK.
MY SEVEN BEATS YOUR ACE.
I THINK YOU'D BETTER EXPLAIN THE RULES TO HER AGAIN.
YOU LIKE THE SOUND OF ARGUING... IS THAT WHAT YOU'RE SAYING?
I WIN AGAIN!
YAY!
KIRKMAN & SCOTT

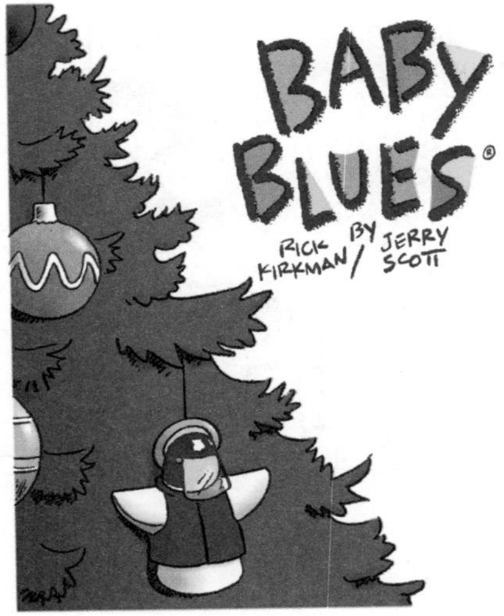
BABY BLUES®
BY RICK KIRKMAN / JERRY SCOTT

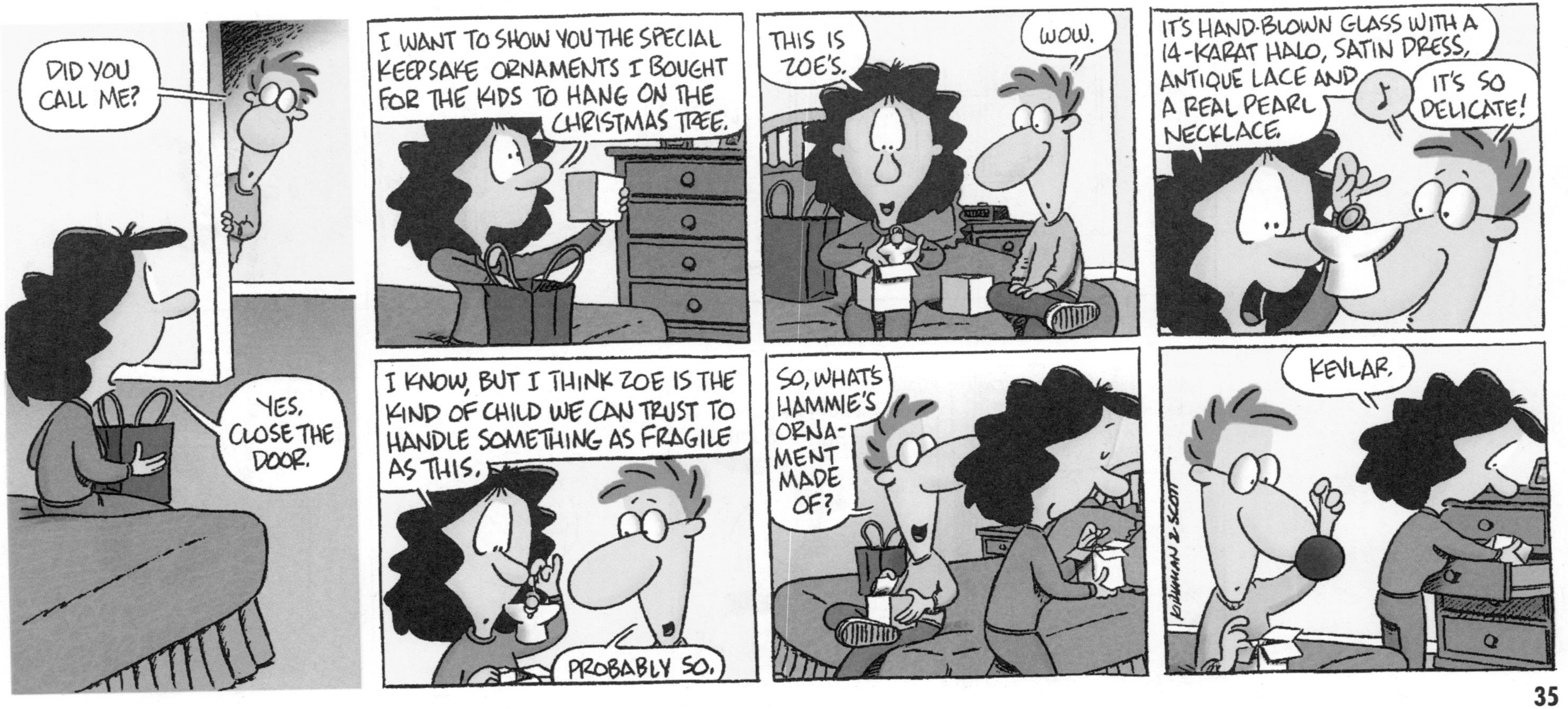
DID YOU CALL ME?
YES. CLOSE THE DOOR.
I WANT TO SHOW YOU THE SPECIAL KEEPSAKE ORNAMENTS I BOUGHT FOR THE KIDS TO HANG ON THE CHRISTMAS TREE.
THIS IS ZOE'S.
WOW.
IT'S HAND-BLOWN GLASS WITH A 14-KARAT HALO, SATIN DRESS, ANTIQUE LACE AND A REAL PEARL NECKLACE.
IT'S SO DELICATE!
I KNOW, BUT I THINK ZOE IS THE KIND OF CHILD WE CAN TRUST TO HANDLE SOMETHING AS FRAGILE AS THIS.
PROBABLY SO.
SO, WHAT'S HAMMIE'S ORNAMENT MADE OF?
KEVLAR.
KIRKMAN & SCOTT

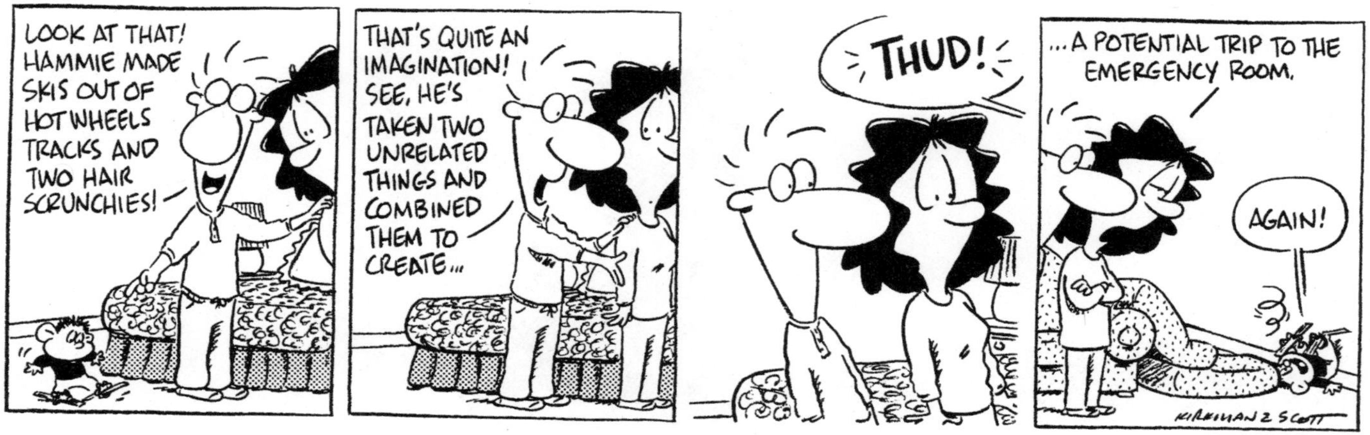
LOOK AT THAT! HAMMIE MADE SKIS OUT OF HOT WHEELS TRACKS AND TWO HAIR SCRUNCHIES!
THAT'S QUITE AN IMAGINATION! SEE, HE'S TAKEN TWO UNRELATED THINGS AND COMBINED THEM TO CREATE...
THUD!
...A POTENTIAL TRIP TO THE EMERGENCY ROOM.
AGAIN!
KIRKMAN & SCOTT

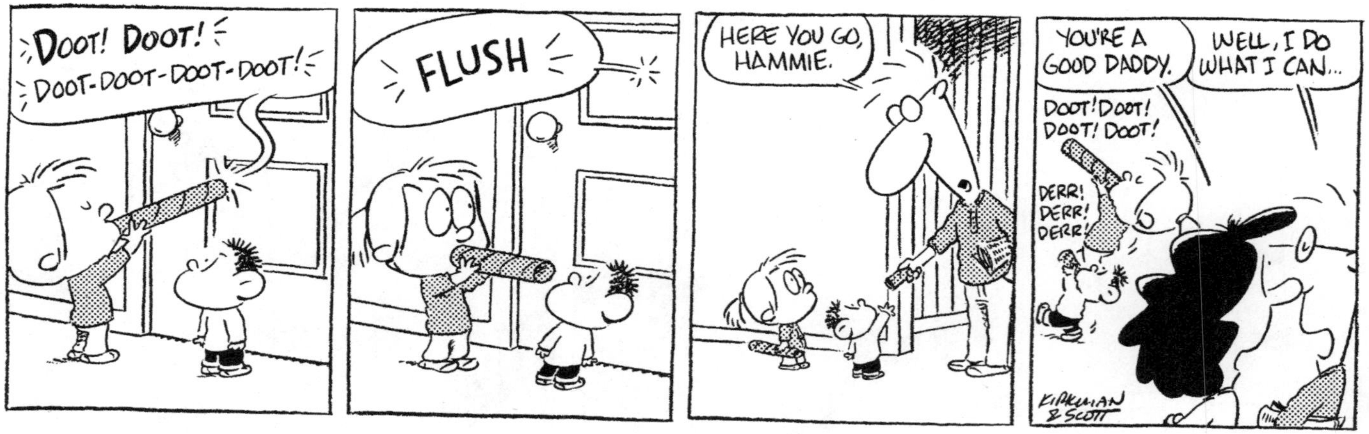
DOOT! DOOT! DOOT-DOOT-DOOT-DOOT!
FLUSH
HERE YOU GO, HAMMIE.
YOU'RE A GOOD DADDY.
WELL, I DO WHAT I CAN...
DOOT! DOOT! DOOT! DOOT!
DERR! DERR! DERR!
KIRKMAN & SCOTT

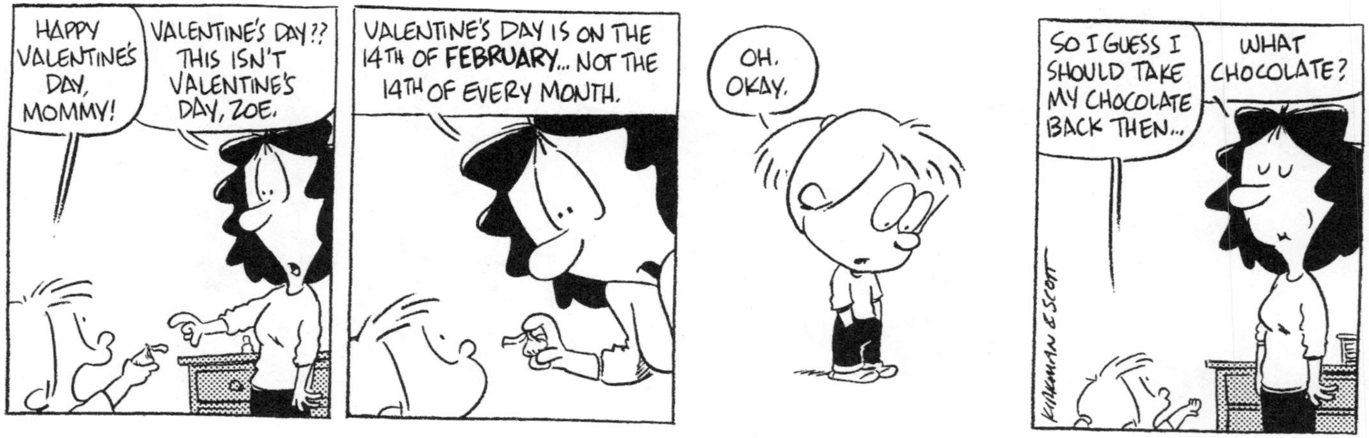
HAPPY VALENTINE'S DAY, MOMMY!
VALENTINE'S DAY?? THIS ISN'T VALENTINE'S DAY, ZOE.
VALENTINE'S DAY IS ON THE 14TH OF FEBRUARY... NOT THE 14TH OF EVERY MONTH.
OH. OKAY.
SO I GUESS I SHOULD TAKE MY CHOCOLATE BACK THEN...
WHAT CHOCOLATE?
KIRKMAN & SCOTT

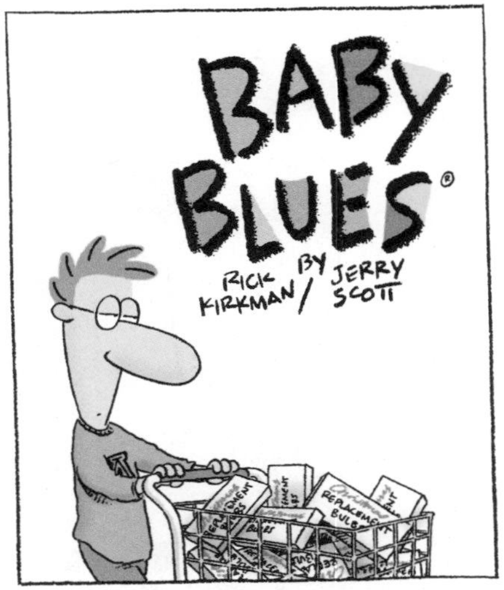
BABY BLUES®
BY RICK KIRKMAN / JERRY SCOTT

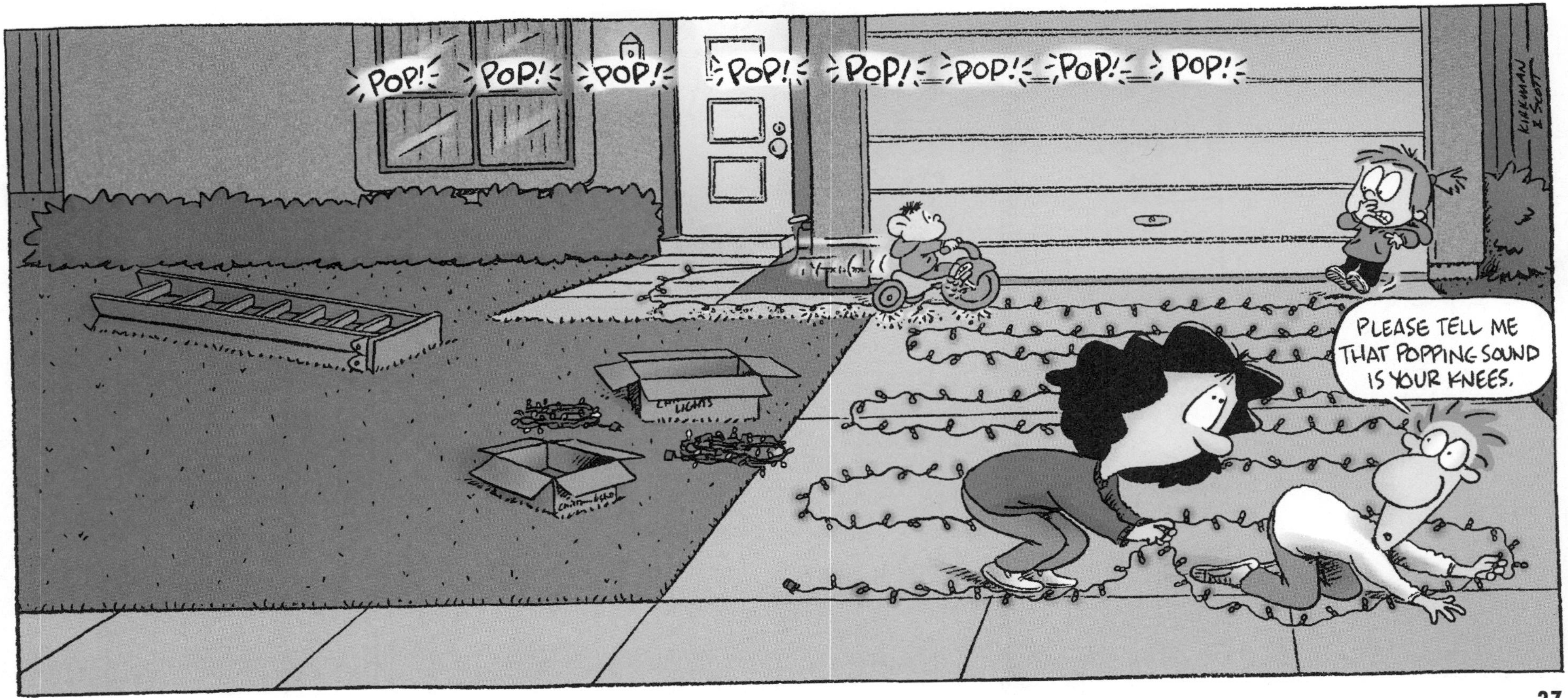
POP! POP! POP! POP! POP! POP! POP! POP!
PLEASE TELL ME THAT POPPING SOUND IS YOUR KNEES.
KIRKMAN & SCOTT

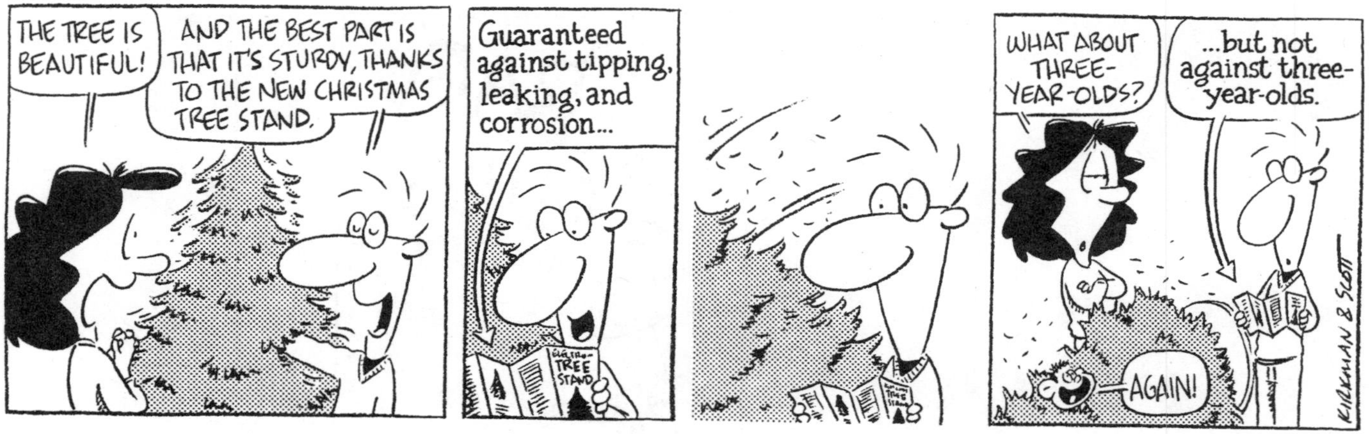
THE TREE IS BEAUTIFUL!
AND THE BEST PART IS THAT IT'S STURDY, THANKS TO THE NEW CHRISTMAS TREE STAND.
Guaranteed against tipping, leaking, and corrosion...
WHAT ABOUT THREE-YEAR-OLDS?
...but not against three-year-olds.
AGAIN!
KIRKMAN & SCOTT

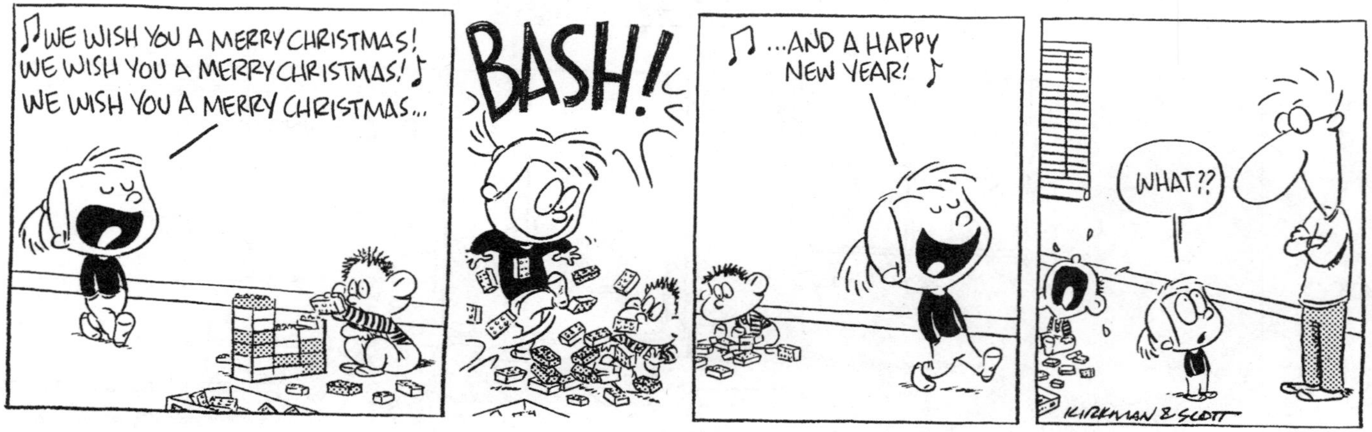
♪ WE WISH YOU A MERRY CHRISTMAS! WE WISH YOU A MERRY CHRISTMAS! ♪ WE WISH YOU A MERRY CHRISTMAS...
BASH!
♫ ...AND A HAPPY NEW YEAR! ♪
WHAT??
KIRKMAN & SCOTT

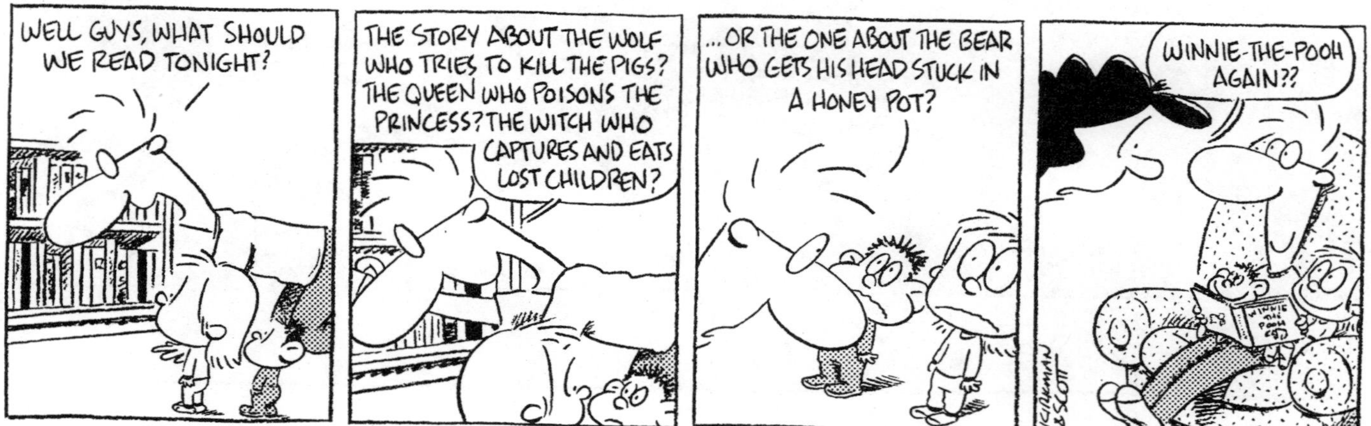
WELL GUYS, WHAT SHOULD WE READ TONIGHT?
THE STORY ABOUT THE WOLF WHO TRIES TO KILL THE PIGS? THE QUEEN WHO POISONS THE PRINCESS? THE WITCH WHO CAPTURES AND EATS LOST CHILDREN?
...OR THE ONE ABOUT THE BEAR WHO GETS HIS HEAD STUCK IN A HONEY POT?
KIRKMAN & SCOTT
WINNIE-THE-POOH AGAIN??

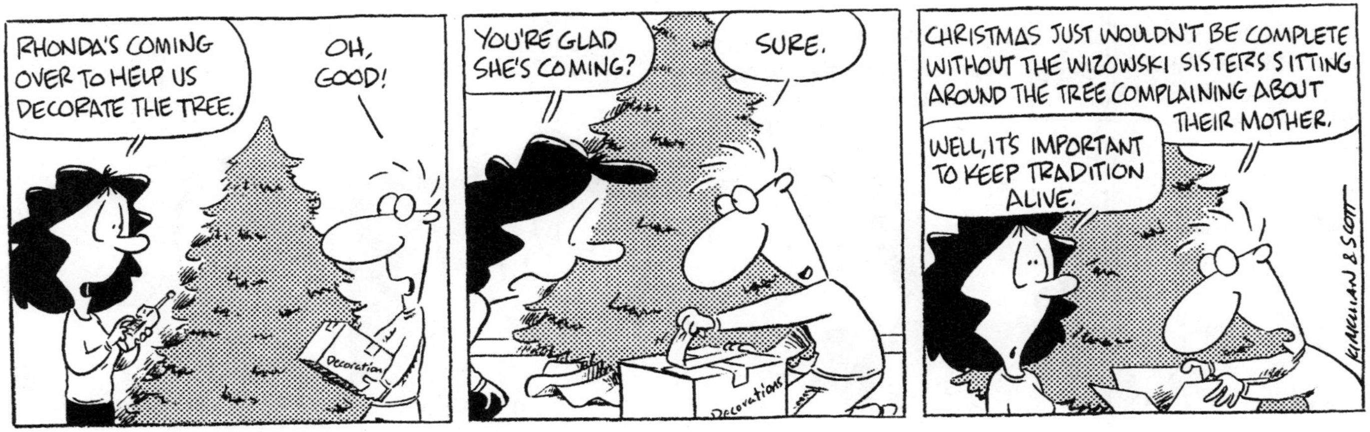
RHONDA'S COMING OVER TO HELP US DECORATE THE TREE.
OH, GOOD!
YOU'RE GLAD SHE'S COMING?
SURE.
CHRISTMAS JUST WOULDN'T BE COMPLETE WITHOUT THE WIZOWSKI SISTERS SITTING AROUND THE TREE COMPLAINING ABOUT THEIR MOTHER.
WELL, IT'S IMPORTANT TO KEEP TRADITION ALIVE.
KIRKMAN & SCOTT

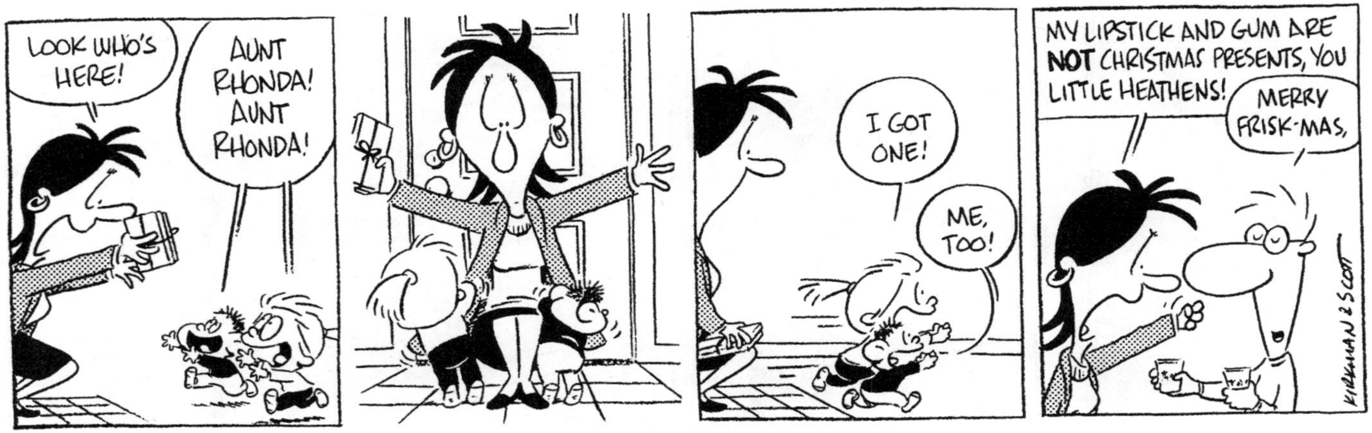
LOOK WHO'S HERE!
AUNT RHONDA! AUNT RHONDA!
I GOT ONE!
ME, TOO!
MY LIPSTICK AND GUM ARE **NOT** CHRISTMAS PRESENTS, YOU LITTLE HEATHENS!
MERRY FRISK-MAS,
KIRKMAN & SCOTT

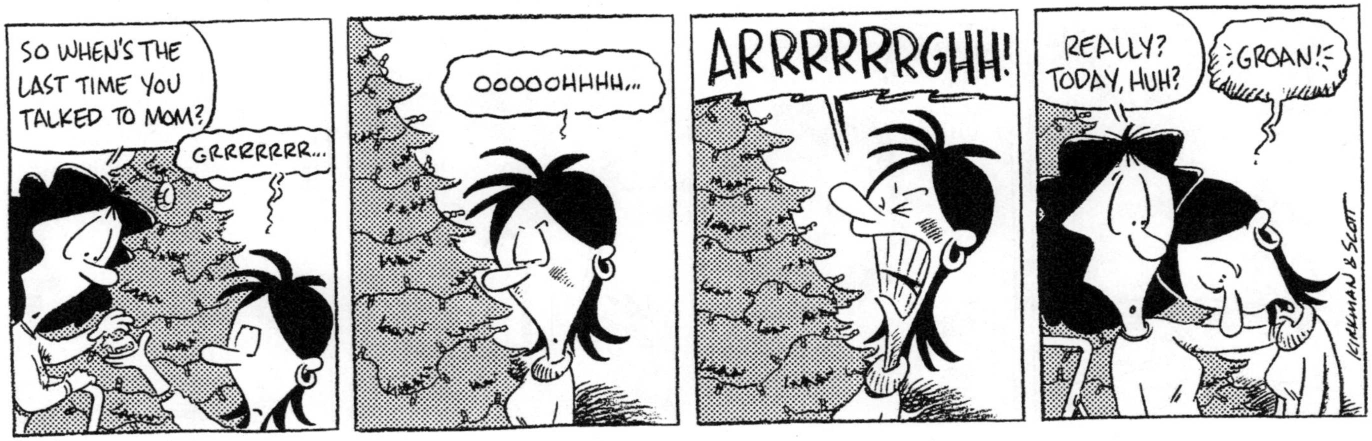
SO WHEN'S THE LAST TIME YOU TALKED TO MOM?
GRRRRRRR...
OOOOOHHHH...
ARRRRRRGHH!
REALLY? TODAY, HUH?
GROAN!
KIRKMAN & SCOTT

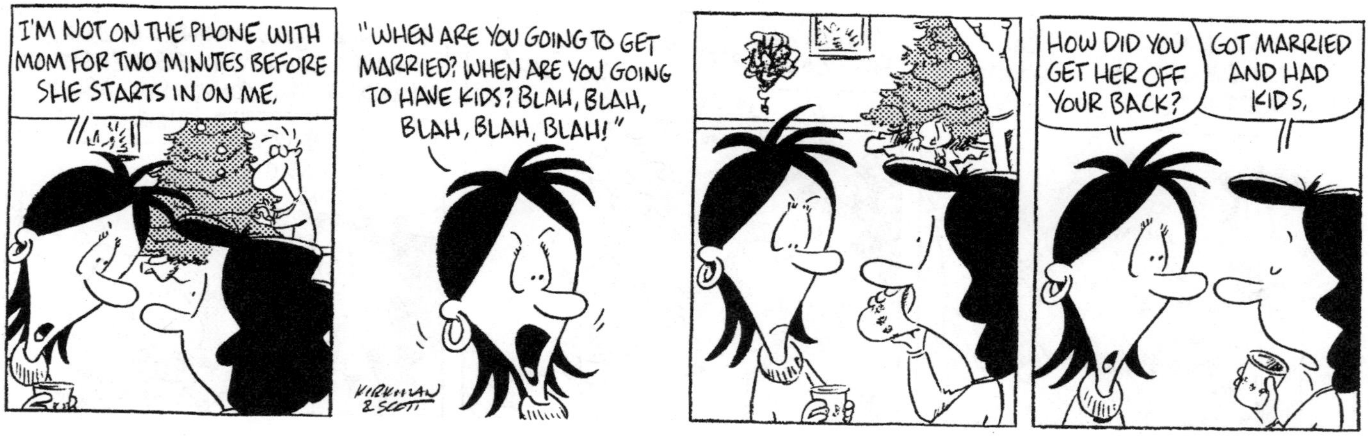
I'M NOT ON THE PHONE WITH MOM FOR TWO MINUTES BEFORE SHE STARTS IN ON ME.
"WHEN ARE YOU GOING TO GET MARRIED? WHEN ARE YOU GOING TO HAVE KIDS? BLAH, BLAH, BLAH, BLAH, BLAH!"
KIRKMAN & SCOTT
HOW DID YOU GET HER OFF YOUR BACK?
GOT MARRIED AND HAD KIDS.

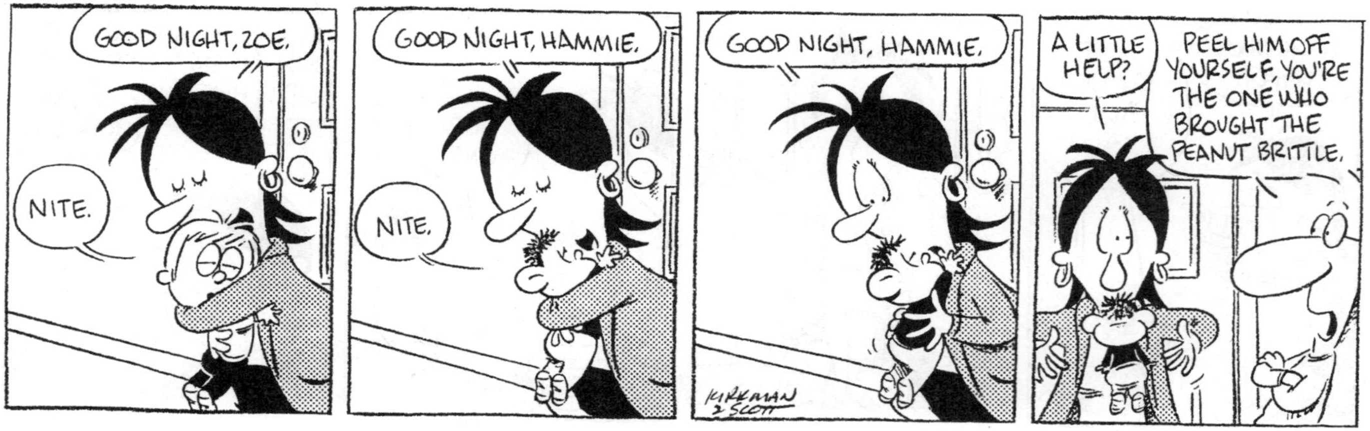
GOOD NIGHT, ZOE.
NITE.
GOOD NIGHT, HAMMIE.
NITE.
GOOD NIGHT, HAMMIE.
KIRKMAN & SCOTT
A LITTLE HELP?
PEEL HIM OFF YOURSELF. YOU'RE THE ONE WHO BROUGHT THE PEANUT BRITTLE.

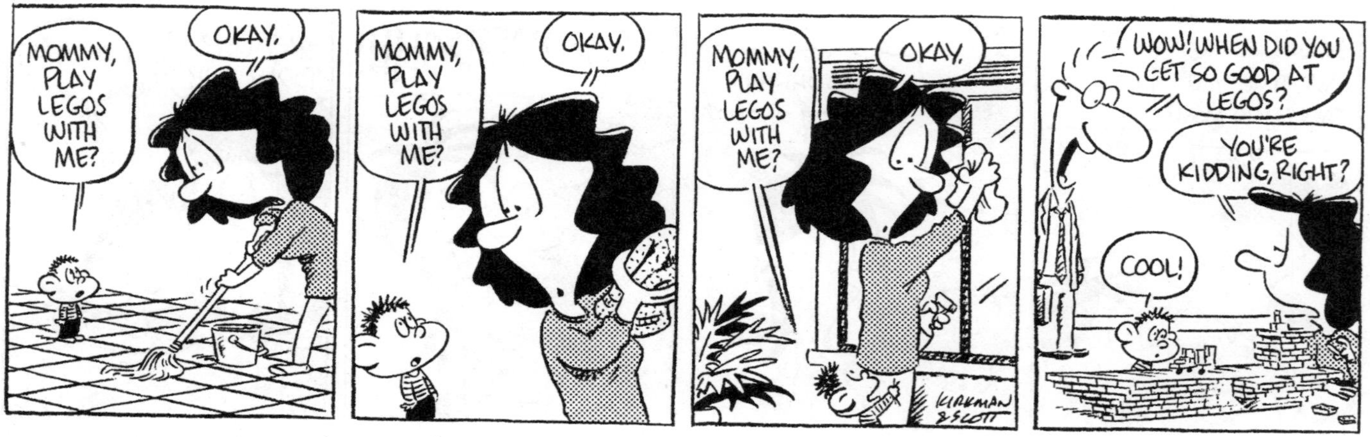
MOMMY, PLAY LEGOS WITH ME?
OKAY.
MOMMY, PLAY LEGOS WITH ME?
OKAY.
MOMMY, PLAY LEGOS WITH ME?
OKAY.
KIRKMAN & SCOTT
WOW! WHEN DID YOU GET SO GOOD AT LEGOS?
YOU'RE KIDDING, RIGHT?
COOL!

BABY BLUES®

BY RICK KIRKMAN / JERRY SCOTT

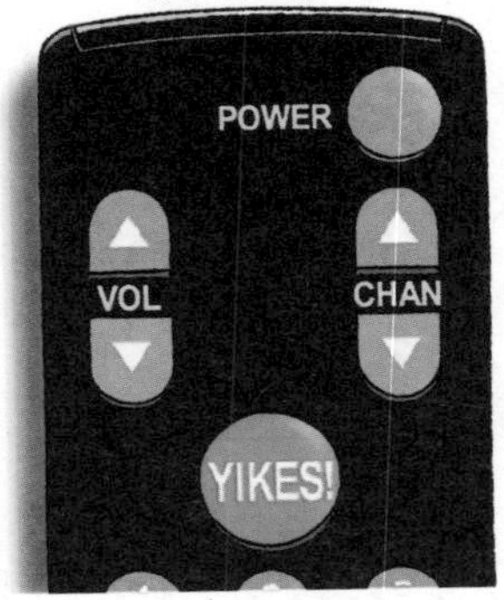
POWER
VOL
CHAN
YIKES!

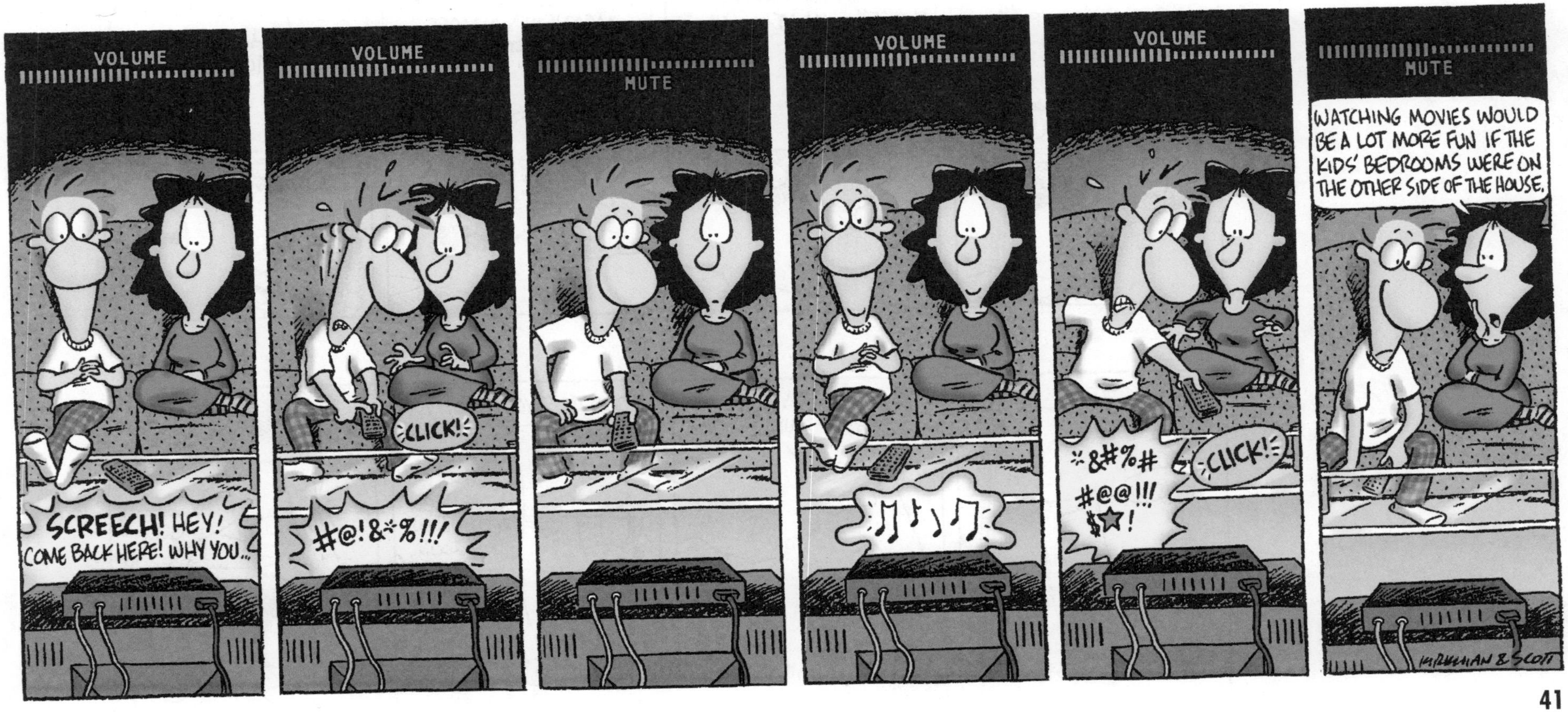
VOLUME
SCREECH! HEY! COME BACK HERE! WHY YOU...
VOLUME
CLICK!
#@!&*%!!!
MUTE
VOLUME
♫♪♪♫
VOLUME
*&#%# #@@!!! $☆!
CLICK!
MUTE
WATCHING MOVIES WOULD BE A LOT MORE FUN IF THE KIDS' BEDROOMS WERE ON THE OTHER SIDE OF THE HOUSE.
KIRKMAN & SCOTT

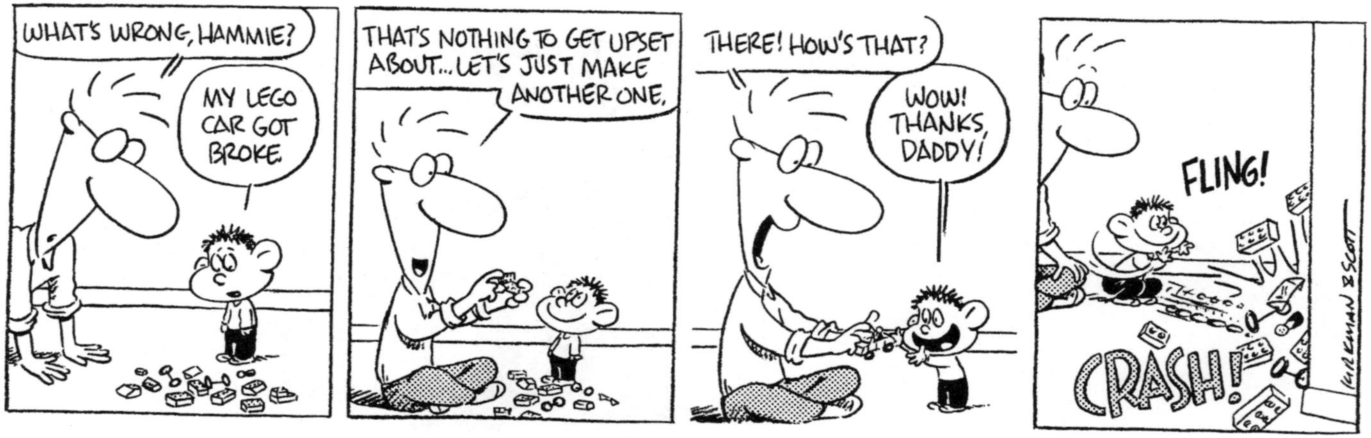
WHAT'S WRONG, HAMMIE?
MY LEGO CAR GOT BROKE.
THAT'S NOTHING TO GET UPSET ABOUT... LET'S JUST MAKE ANOTHER ONE.
THERE! HOW'S THAT?
WOW! THANKS, DADDY!
FLING!
CRASH!
KIRKMAN & SCOTT

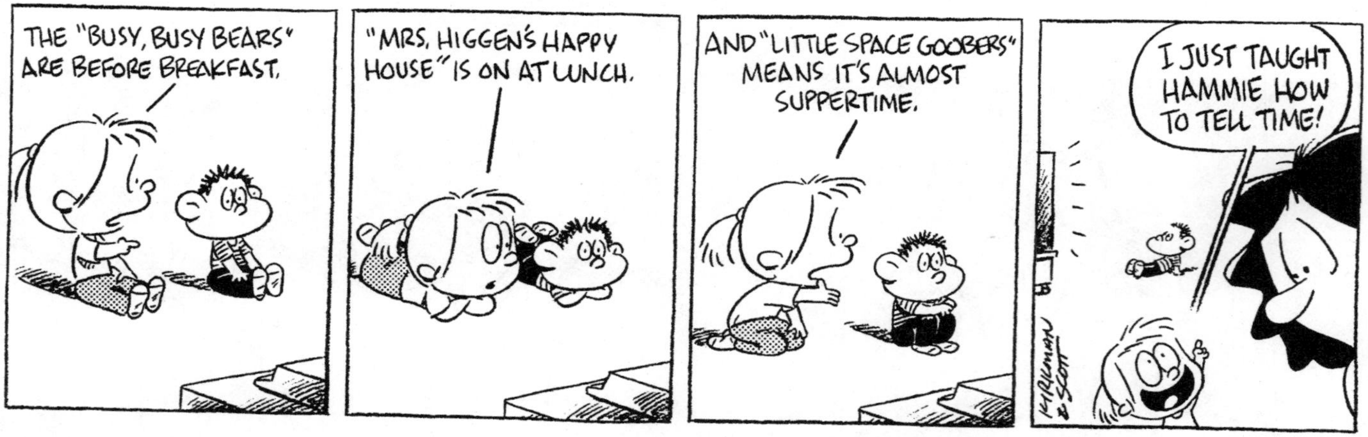
THE "BUSY, BUSY BEARS" ARE BEFORE BREAKFAST.
"MRS. HIGGEN'S HAPPY HOUSE" IS ON AT LUNCH.
AND "LITTLE SPACE GOOBERS" MEANS IT'S ALMOST SUPPERTIME.
KIRKMAN & SCOTT
I JUST TAUGHT HAMMIE HOW TO TELL TIME!

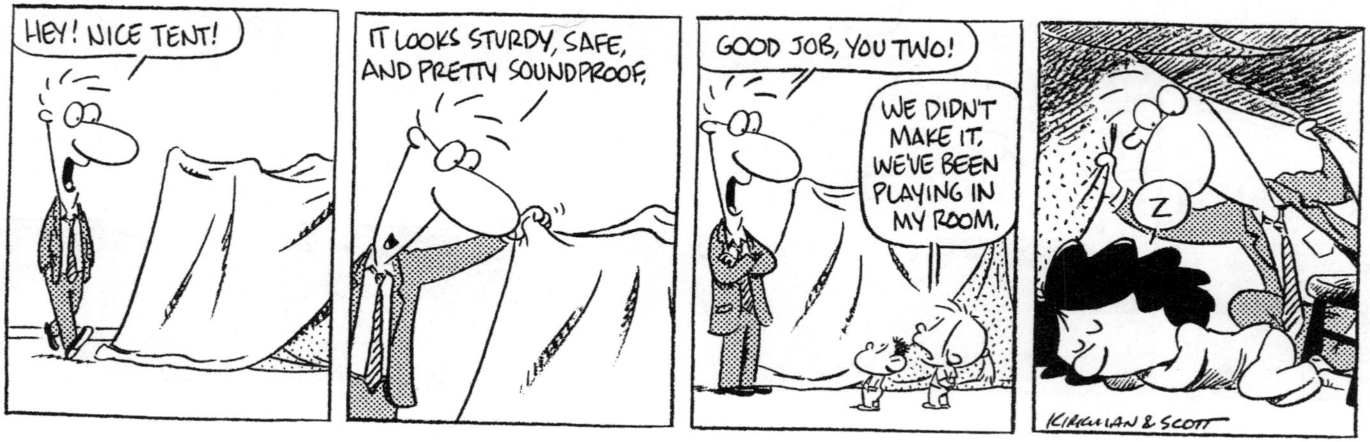
HEY! NICE TENT!
IT LOOKS STURDY, SAFE, AND PRETTY SOUNDPROOF.
GOOD JOB, YOU TWO!
WE DIDN'T MAKE IT. WE'VE BEEN PLAYING IN MY ROOM.
Z
KIRKMAN & SCOTT

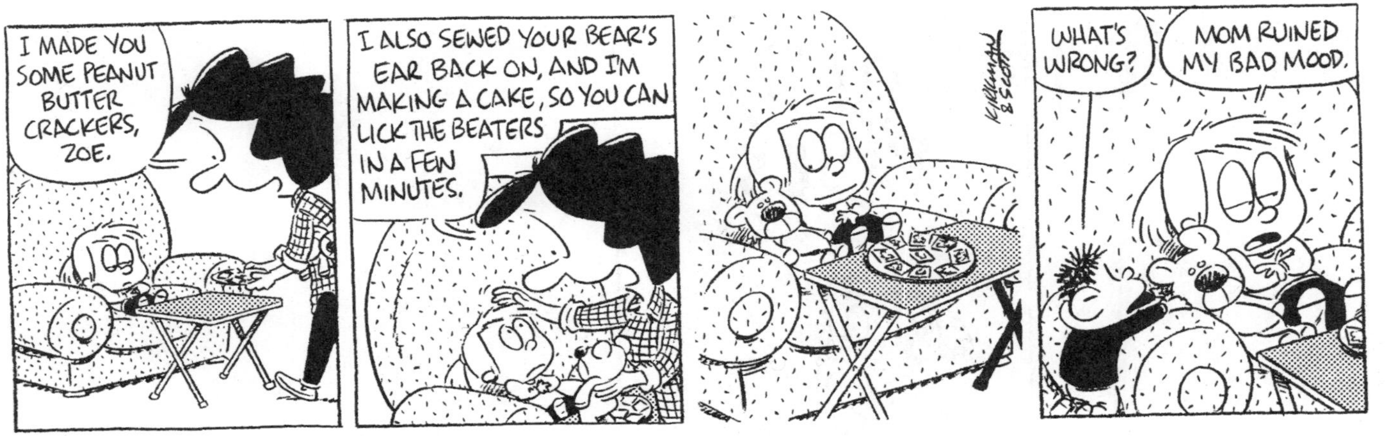
I MADE YOU SOME PEANUT BUTTER CRACKERS, ZOE.
I ALSO SEWED YOUR BEAR'S EAR BACK ON, AND I'M MAKING A CAKE, SO YOU CAN LICK THE BEATERS IN A FEW MINUTES.
KIRKMAN & SCOTT
WHAT'S WRONG?
MOM RUINED MY BAD MOOD.

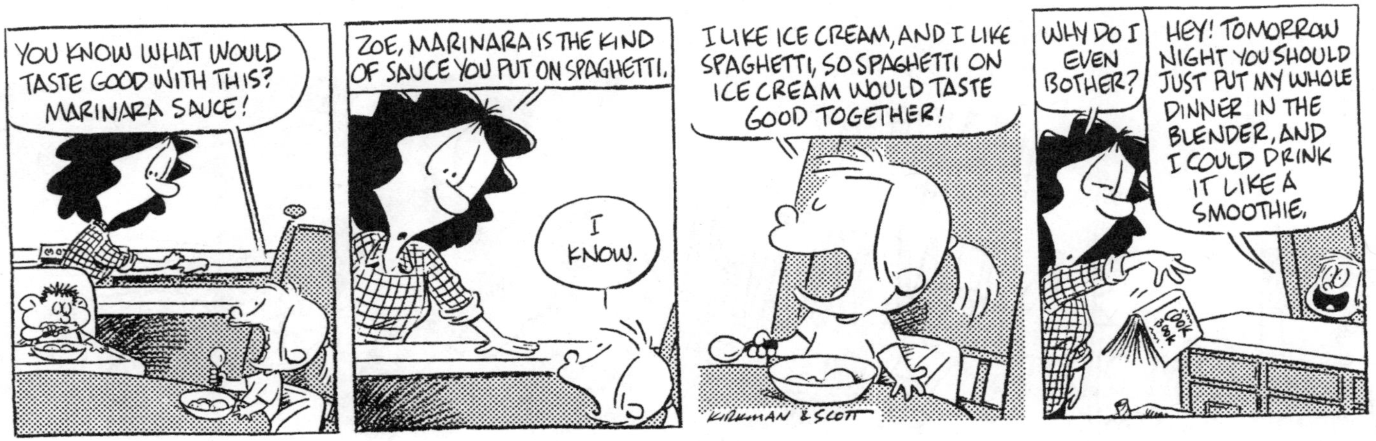
YOU KNOW WHAT WOULD TASTE GOOD WITH THIS? MARINARA SAUCE!
ZOE, MARINARA IS THE KIND OF SAUCE YOU PUT ON SPAGHETTI.
I KNOW.
I LIKE ICE CREAM, AND I LIKE SPAGHETTI, SO SPAGHETTI ON ICE CREAM WOULD TASTE GOOD TOGETHER!
KIRKMAN & SCOTT
WHY DO I EVEN BOTHER?
HEY! TOMORROW NIGHT YOU SHOULD JUST PUT MY WHOLE DINNER IN THE BLENDER, AND I COULD DRINK IT LIKE A SMOOTHIE.

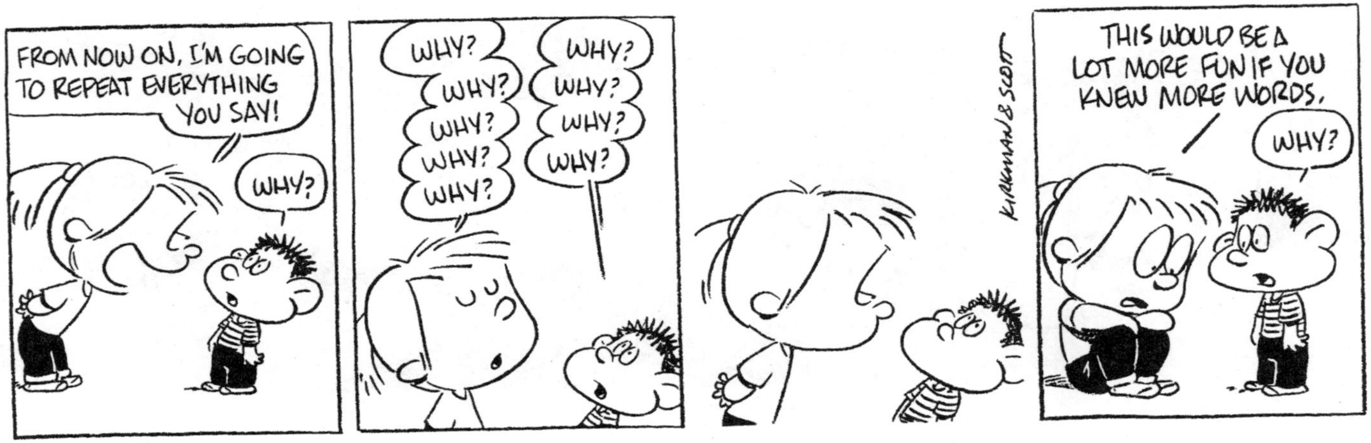
FROM NOW ON, I'M GOING TO REPEAT EVERYTHING YOU SAY!
WHY?
WHY?
WHY?
WHY?
WHY?
WHY?
WHY?
WHY?
WHY?
WHY?
KIRKMAN & SCOTT
THIS WOULD BE A LOT MORE FUN IF YOU KNEW MORE WORDS.
WHY?

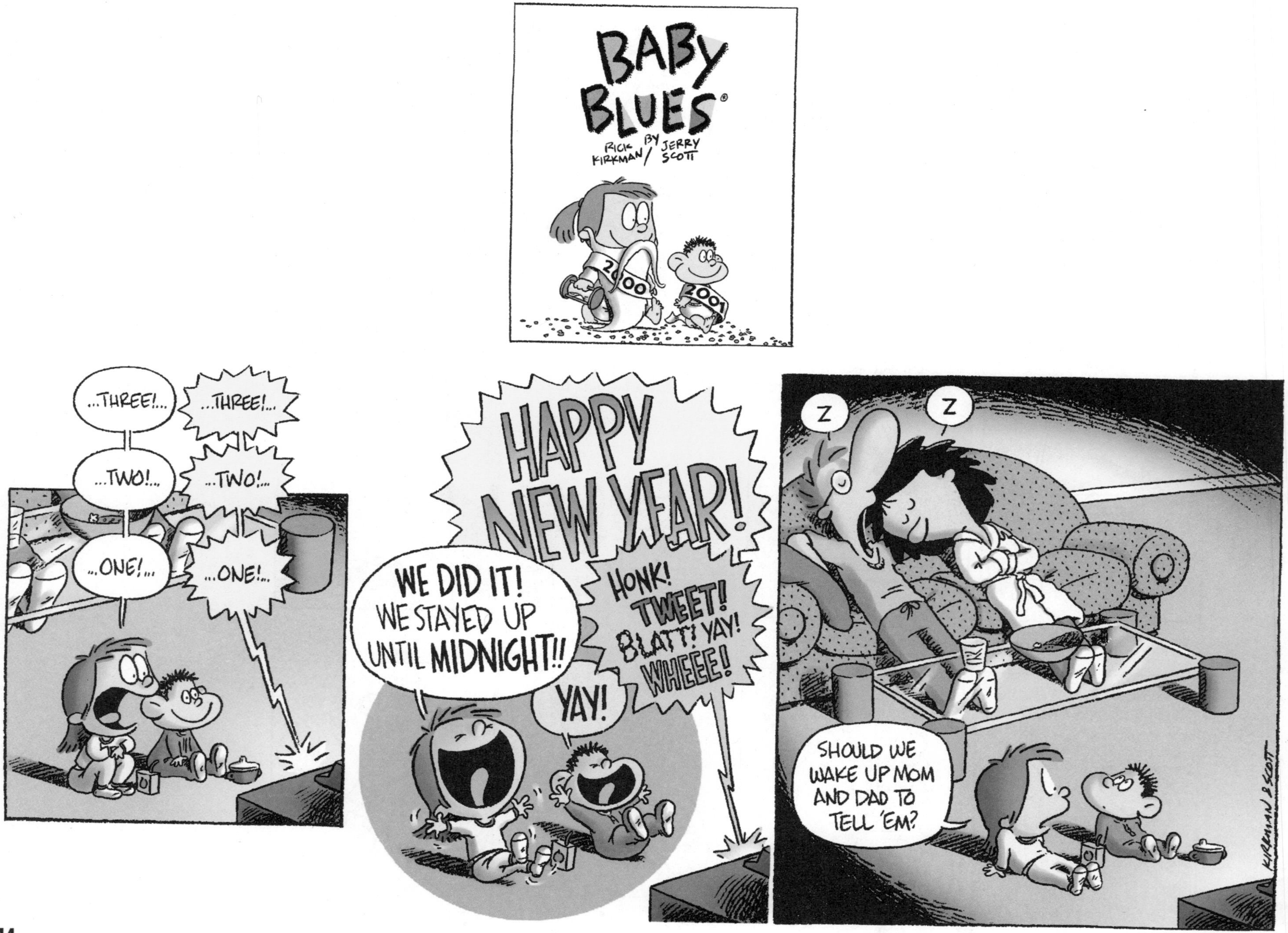
BABY BLUES®
BY RICK KIRKMAN / JERRY SCOTT
2000
2001
...THREE!...
...THREE!...
...TWO!...
...TWO!...
...ONE!...
...ONE!...
HAPPY NEW YEAR!
WE DID IT! WE STAYED UP UNTIL MIDNIGHT!!
YAY!
HONK! TWEET! BLATT! YAY! WHEEE!
Z
Z
SHOULD WE WAKE UP MOM AND DAD TO TELL 'EM?
KIRKMAN & SCOTT

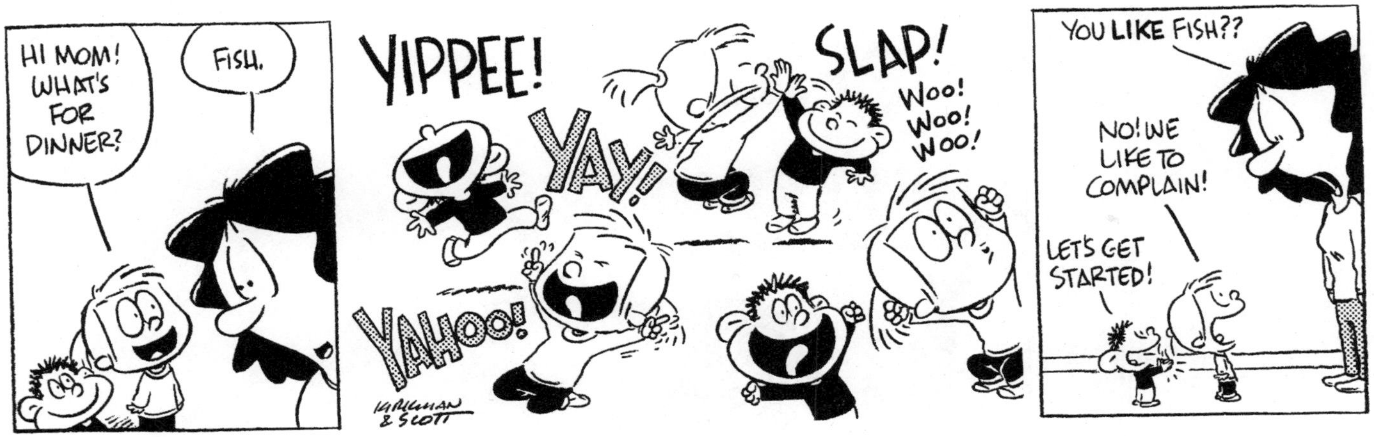
HI MOM! WHAT'S FOR DINNER?
FISH.
YIPPEE!
YAY!
SLAP!
WOO! WOO! WOO!
YAHOO!
KIRKMAN & SCOTT
YOU LIKE FISH??
NO! WE LIKE TO COMPLAIN!
LET'S GET STARTED!

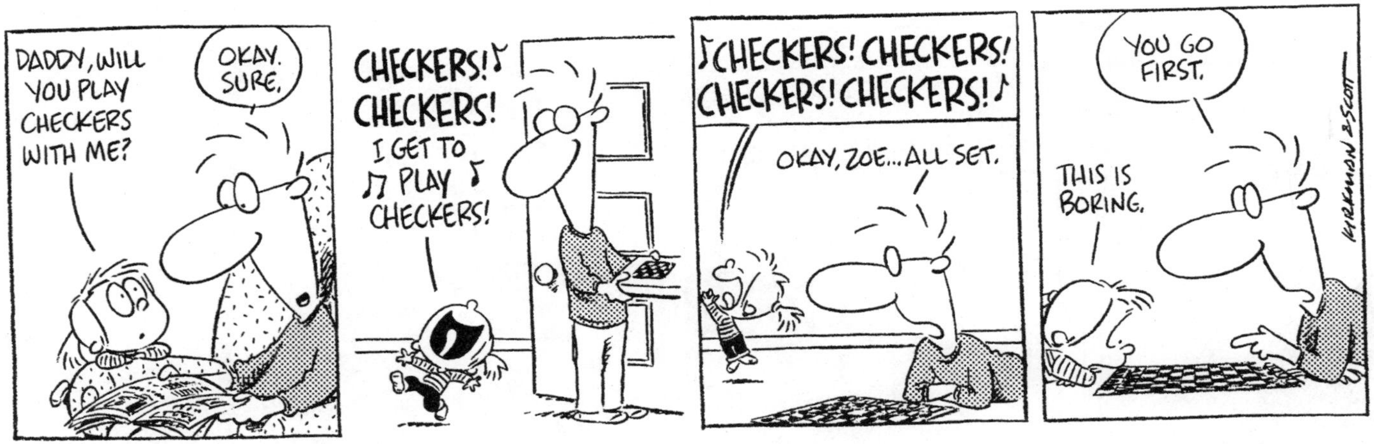
DADDY, WILL YOU PLAY CHECKERS WITH ME?
OKAY. SURE.
CHECKERS! CHECKERS! I GET TO PLAY CHECKERS!
CHECKERS! CHECKERS! CHECKERS! CHECKERS!
OKAY, ZOE... ALL SET.
YOU GO FIRST.
THIS IS BORING.
KIRKMAN & SCOTT

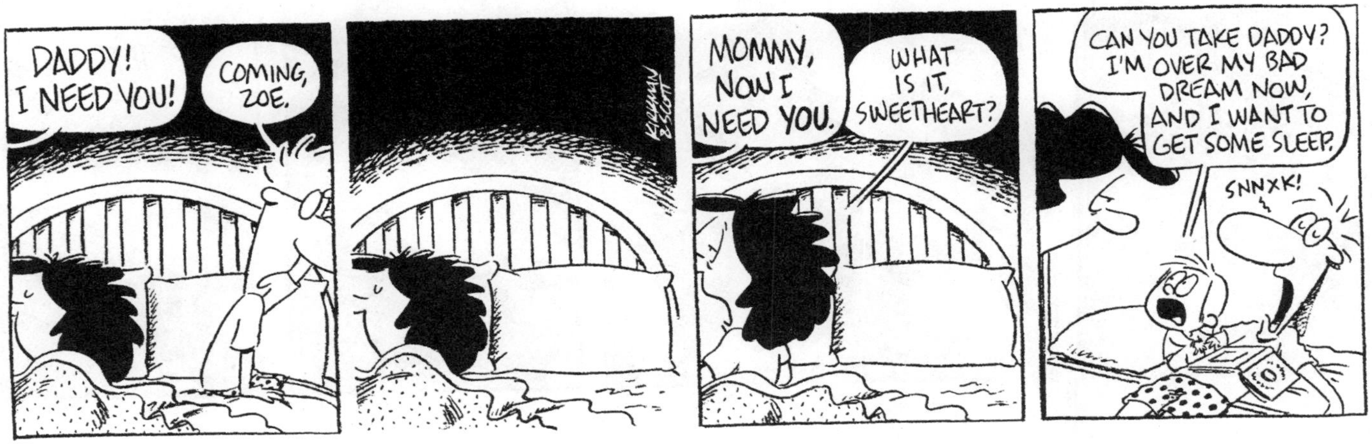
DADDY! I NEED YOU!
COMING, ZOE.
KIRKMAN & SCOTT
MOMMY, NOW I NEED YOU.
WHAT IS IT, SWEETHEART?
CAN YOU TAKE DADDY? I'M OVER MY BAD DREAM NOW, AND I WANT TO GET SOME SLEEP.
SNNXK!

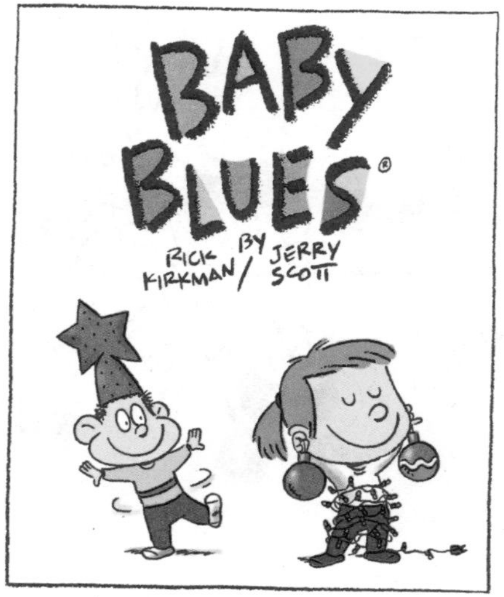
BABY BLUES®
BY RICK KIRKMAN / JERRY SCOTT

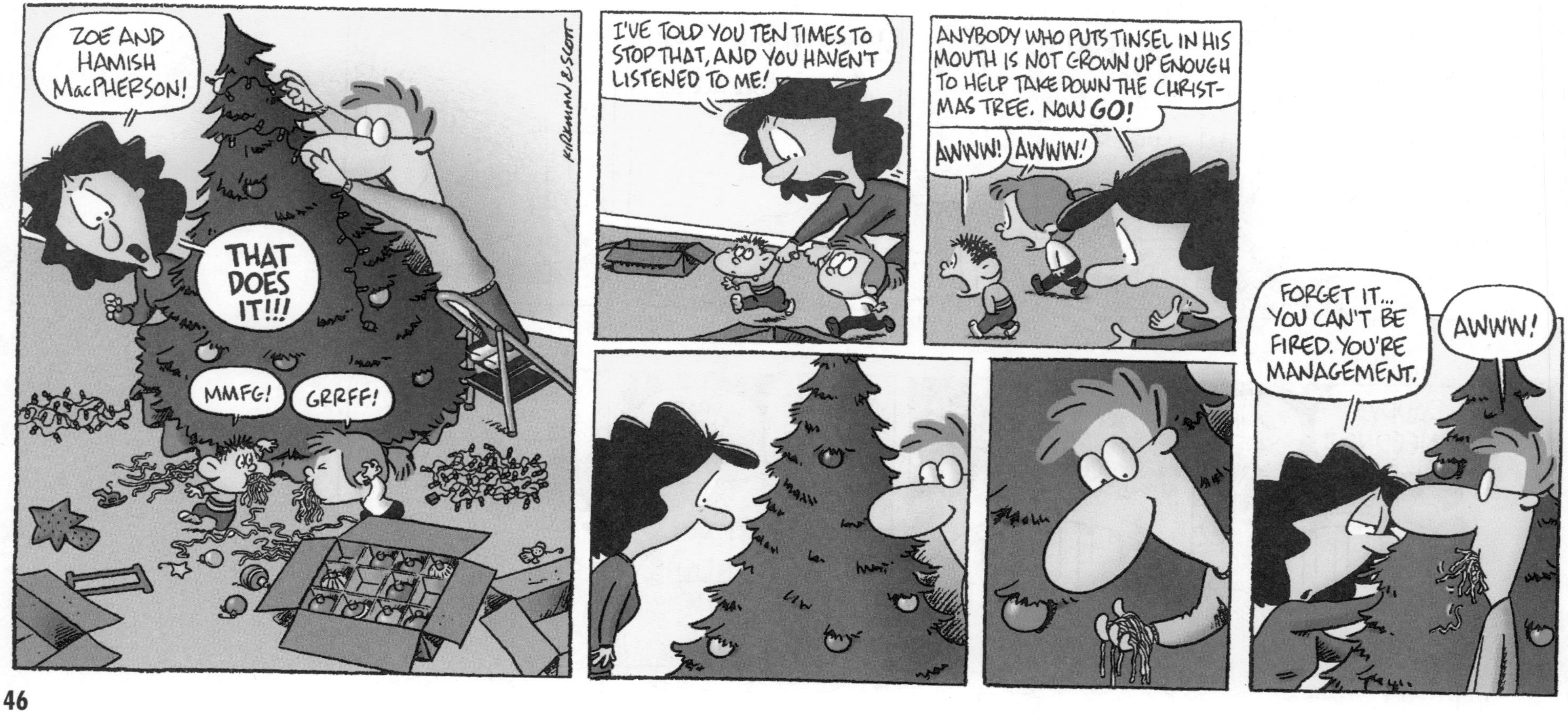
ZOE AND HAMISH MacPHERSON!
THAT DOES IT!!!
MMFG!
GRRFF!
KIRKMAN & SCOTT
I'VE TOLD YOU TEN TIMES TO STOP THAT, AND YOU HAVEN'T LISTENED TO ME!
ANYBODY WHO PUTS TINSEL IN HIS MOUTH IS NOT GROWN UP ENOUGH TO HELP TAKE DOWN THE CHRISTMAS TREE. NOW GO!
AWWW!
AWWW!
FORGET IT... YOU CAN'T BE FIRED. YOU'RE MANAGEMENT.
AWWW!

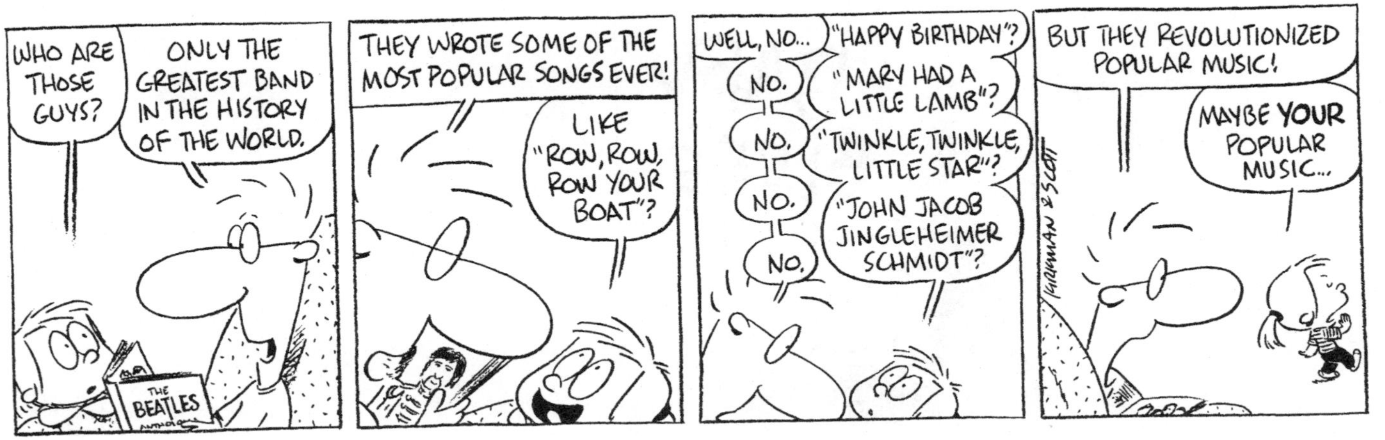
WHO ARE THOSE GUYS?
ONLY THE GREATEST BAND IN THE HISTORY OF THE WORLD.
THE BEATLES
THEY WROTE SOME OF THE MOST POPULAR SONGS EVER!
LIKE "ROW, ROW, ROW YOUR BOAT"?
WELL, NO...
"HAPPY BIRTHDAY"?
NO.
"MARY HAD A LITTLE LAMB"?
NO.
"TWINKLE, TWINKLE, LITTLE STAR"?
NO.
"JOHN JACOB JINGLEHEIMER SCHMIDT"?
NO.
KIRKMAN & SCOTT
BUT THEY REVOLUTIONIZED POPULAR MUSIC!
MAYBE **YOUR** POPULAR MUSIC...

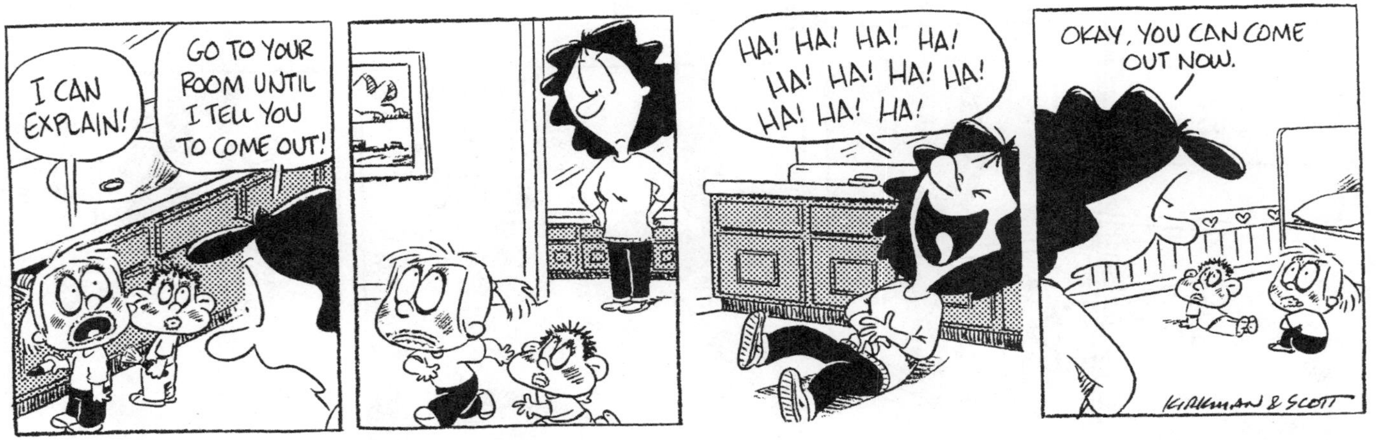
I CAN EXPLAIN!
GO TO YOUR ROOM UNTIL I TELL YOU TO COME OUT!
HA! HA! HA! HA! HA! HA! HA! HA! HA! HA! HA!
OKAY, YOU CAN COME OUT NOW.
KIRKMAN & SCOTT

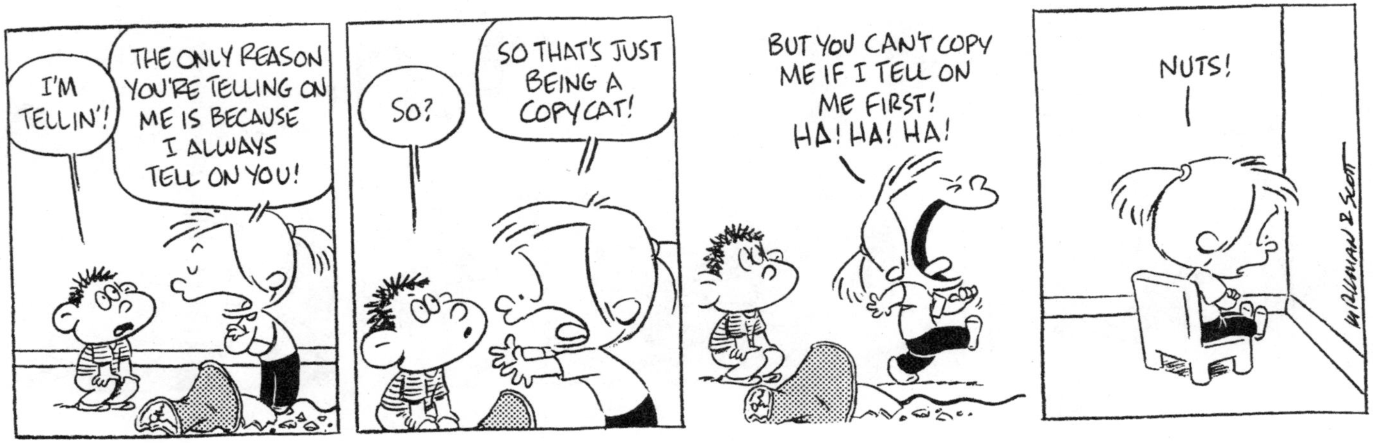
I'M TELLIN'!
THE ONLY REASON YOU'RE TELLING ON ME IS BECAUSE I ALWAYS TELL ON YOU!
SO?
SO THAT'S JUST BEING A COPYCAT!
BUT YOU CAN'T COPY ME IF I TELL ON ME FIRST! HA! HA! HA!
NUTS!
KIRKMAN & SCOTT

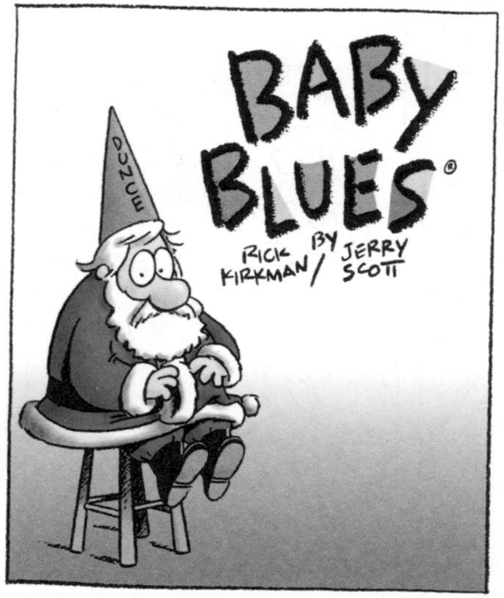
BABY BLUES®
DUNCE
BY RICK KIRKMAN / JERRY SCOTT

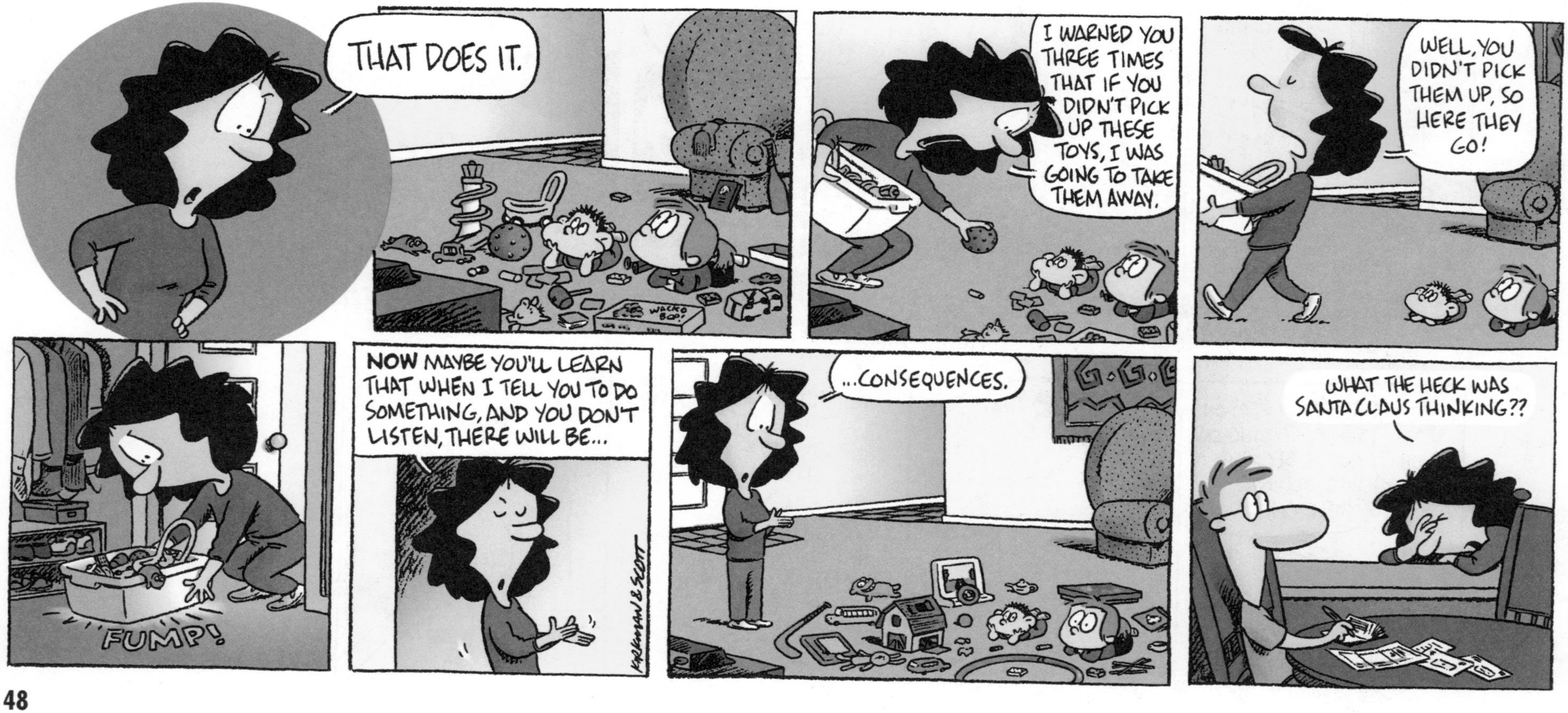
THAT DOES IT.
WACKO BOP!
I WARNED YOU THREE TIMES THAT IF YOU DIDN'T PICK UP THESE TOYS, I WAS GOING TO TAKE THEM AWAY.
WELL, YOU DIDN'T PICK THEM UP, SO HERE THEY GO!
FUMP!
NOW MAYBE YOU'LL LEARN THAT WHEN I TELL YOU TO DO SOMETHING, AND YOU DON'T LISTEN, THERE WILL BE...
KIRKMAN & SCOTT
...CONSEQUENCES.
WHAT THE HECK WAS SANTA CLAUS THINKING??

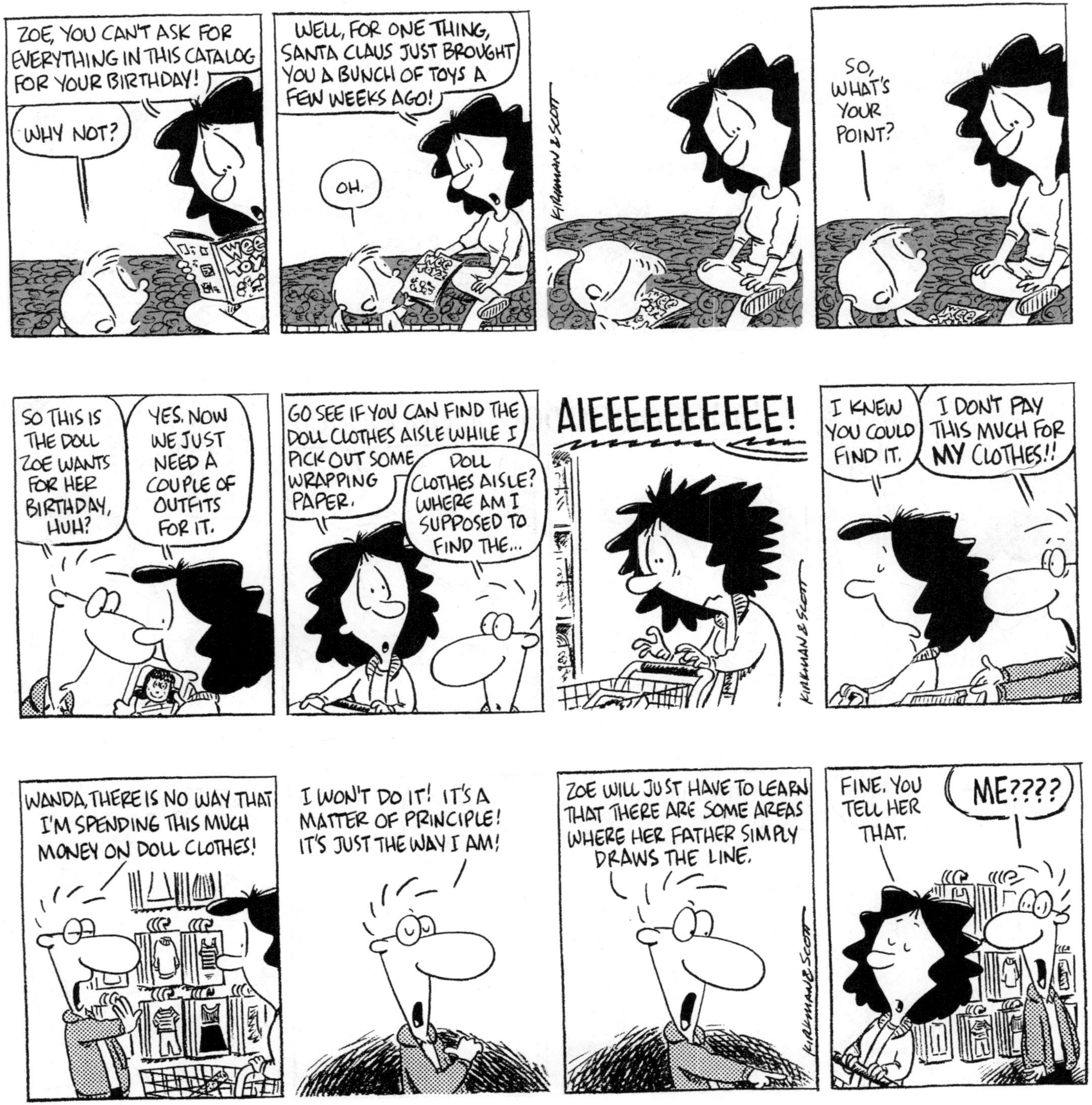
ZOE, YOU CAN'T ASK FOR EVERYTHING IN THIS CATALOG FOR YOUR BIRTHDAY!
WHY NOT?
WEE TOYS
WELL, FOR ONE THING, SANTA CLAUS JUST BROUGHT YOU A BUNCH OF TOYS A FEW WEEKS AGO!
OH.
KIRKMAN & SCOTT
SO, WHAT'S YOUR POINT?
SO THIS IS THE DOLL ZOE WANTS FOR HER BIRTHDAY, HUH?
YES. NOW WE JUST NEED A COUPLE OF OUTFITS FOR IT.
GO SEE IF YOU CAN FIND THE DOLL CLOTHES AISLE WHILE I PICK OUT SOME WRAPPING PAPER.
DOLL CLOTHES AISLE? WHERE AM I SUPPOSED TO FIND THE...
AIEEEEEEEEEE!
KIRKMAN & SCOTT
I KNEW YOU COULD FIND IT.
I DON'T PAY THIS MUCH FOR MY CLOTHES!!
WANDA, THERE IS NO WAY THAT I'M SPENDING THIS MUCH MONEY ON DOLL CLOTHES!
I WON'T DO IT! IT'S A MATTER OF PRINCIPLE! IT'S JUST THE WAY I AM!
ZOE WILL JUST HAVE TO LEARN THAT THERE ARE SOME AREAS WHERE HER FATHER SIMPLY DRAWS THE LINE.
KIRKMAN & SCOTT
FINE. YOU TELL HER THAT.
ME????

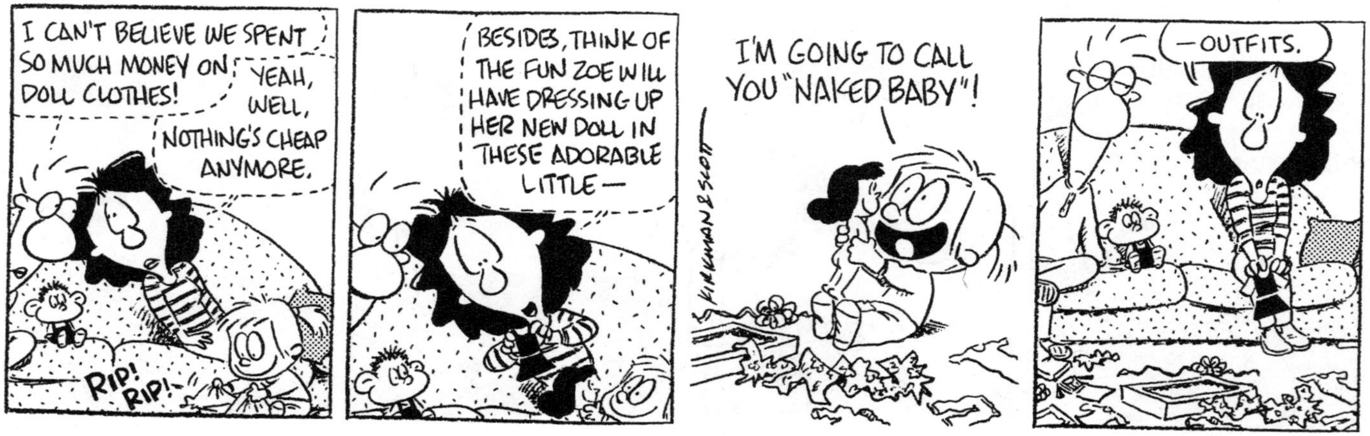
I CAN'T BELIEVE WE SPENT SO MUCH MONEY ON DOLL CLOTHES!
YEAH, WELL, NOTHING'S CHEAP ANYMORE.
RIP! RIP!
BESIDES, THINK OF THE FUN ZOE WILL HAVE DRESSING UP HER NEW DOLL IN THESE ADORABLE LITTLE —
I'M GOING TO CALL YOU "NAKED BABY"!
— OUTFITS.
KIRKMAN & SCOTT

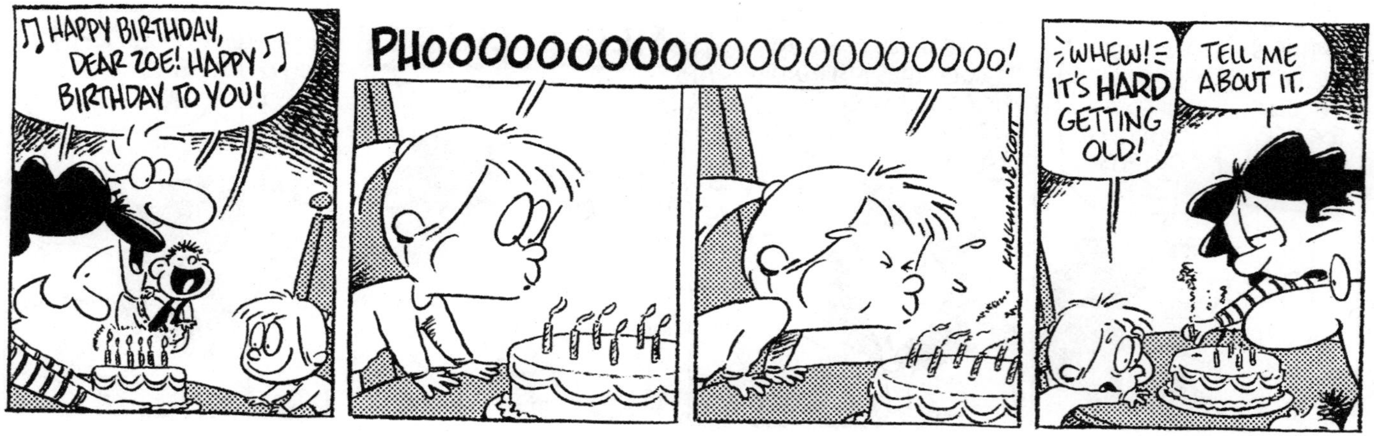
HAPPY BIRTHDAY, DEAR ZOE! HAPPY BIRTHDAY TO YOU!
PHOOOOOOOOOOOOOOOOOOOOOOo!
WHEW! IT'S HARD GETTING OLD!
TELL ME ABOUT IT.
KIRKMAN & SCOTT

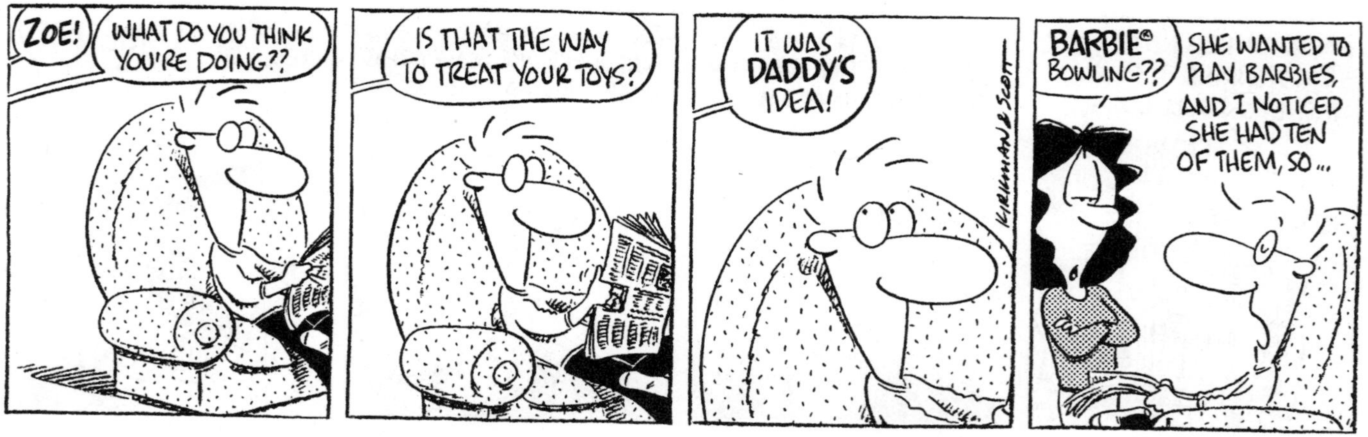
ZOE!
WHAT DO YOU THINK YOU'RE DOING??
IS THAT THE WAY TO TREAT YOUR TOYS?
IT WAS DADDY'S IDEA!
BARBIE® BOWLING??
SHE WANTED TO PLAY BARBIES, AND I NOTICED SHE HAD TEN OF THEM, SO...
KIRKMAN & SCOTT

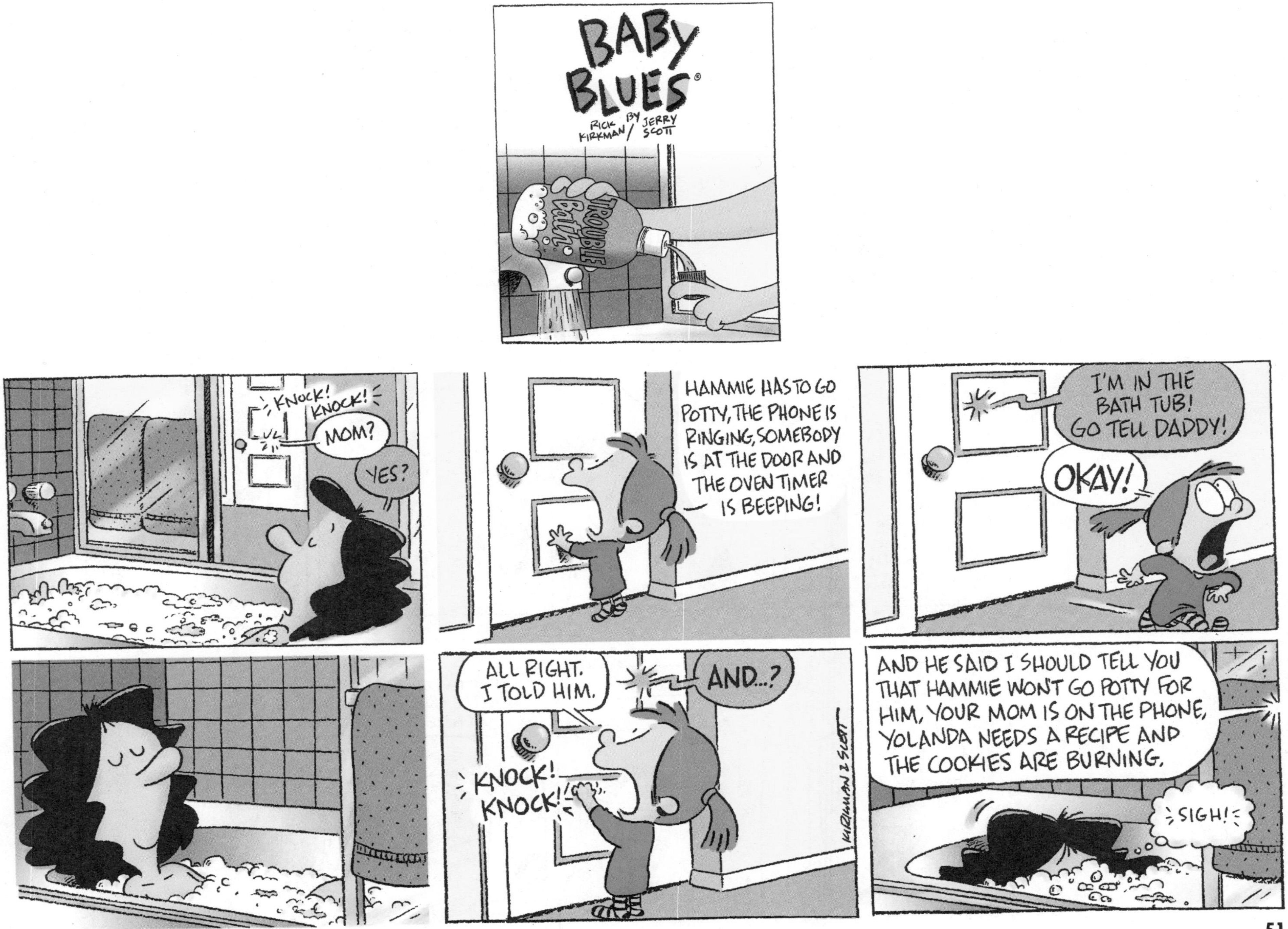
BABY BLUES®
RICK KIRKMAN / BY JERRY SCOTT
TROUBLE Bath
KNOCK! KNOCK!
MOM?
YES?
HAMMIE HAS TO GO POTTY, THE PHONE IS RINGING, SOMEBODY IS AT THE DOOR AND THE OVEN TIMER IS BEEPING!
I'M IN THE BATH TUB! GO TELL DADDY!
OKAY!
ALL RIGHT. I TOLD HIM.
AND...?
KNOCK! KNOCK!
KIRKMAN & SCOTT
AND HE SAID I SHOULD TELL YOU THAT HAMMIE WON'T GO POTTY FOR HIM, YOUR MOM IS ON THE PHONE, YOLANDA NEEDS A RECIPE AND THE COOKIES ARE BURNING.
SIGH!

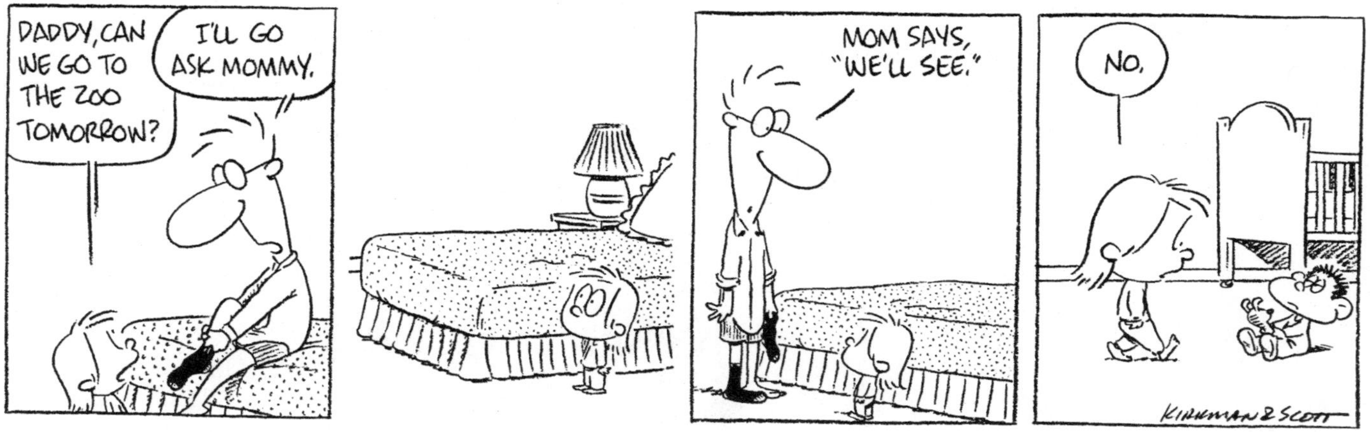
DADDY, CAN WE GO TO THE ZOO TOMORROW?
I'LL GO ASK MOMMY.
MOM SAYS, "WE'LL SEE."
NO.
KIRKMAN & SCOTT

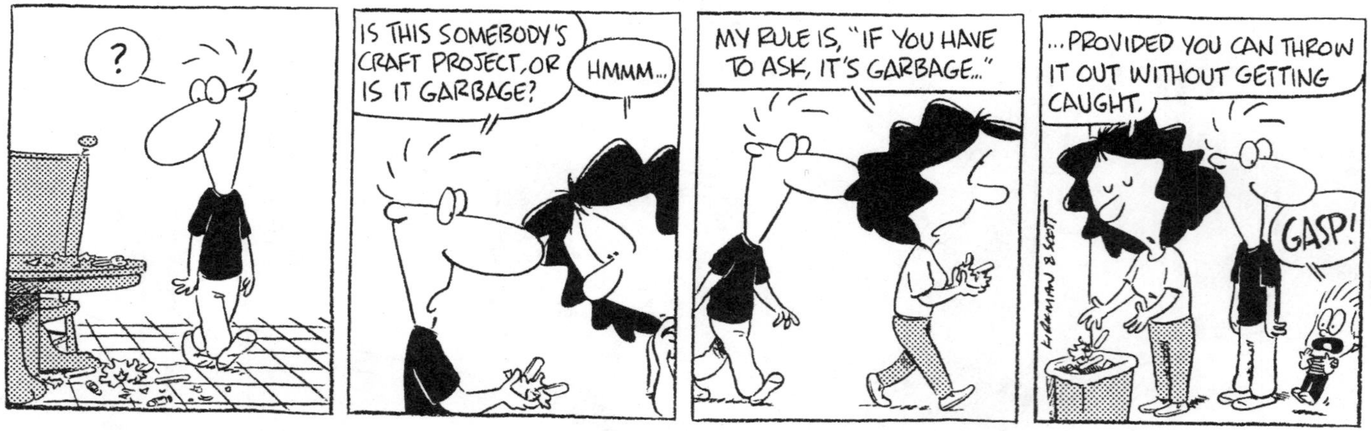
?
IS THIS SOMEBODY'S CRAFT PROJECT, OR IS IT GARBAGE?
HMMM...
MY RULE IS, "IF YOU HAVE TO ASK, IT'S GARBAGE..."
...PROVIDED YOU CAN THROW IT OUT WITHOUT GETTING CAUGHT.
GASP!
KIRKMAN & SCOTT

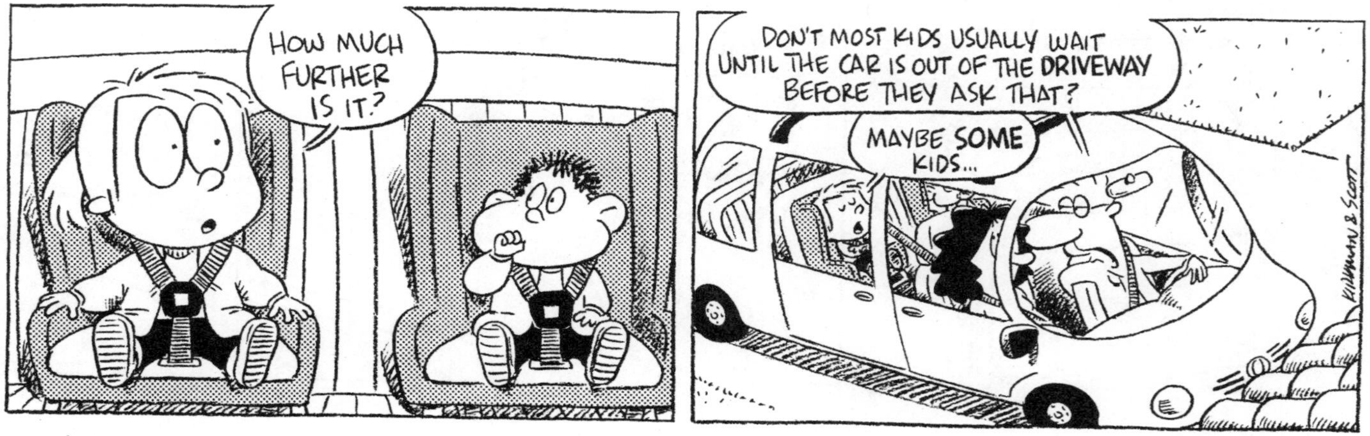
HOW MUCH FURTHER IS IT?
DON'T MOST KIDS USUALLY WAIT UNTIL THE CAR IS OUT OF THE DRIVEWAY BEFORE THEY ASK THAT?
MAYBE SOME KIDS...
KIRKMAN & SCOTT

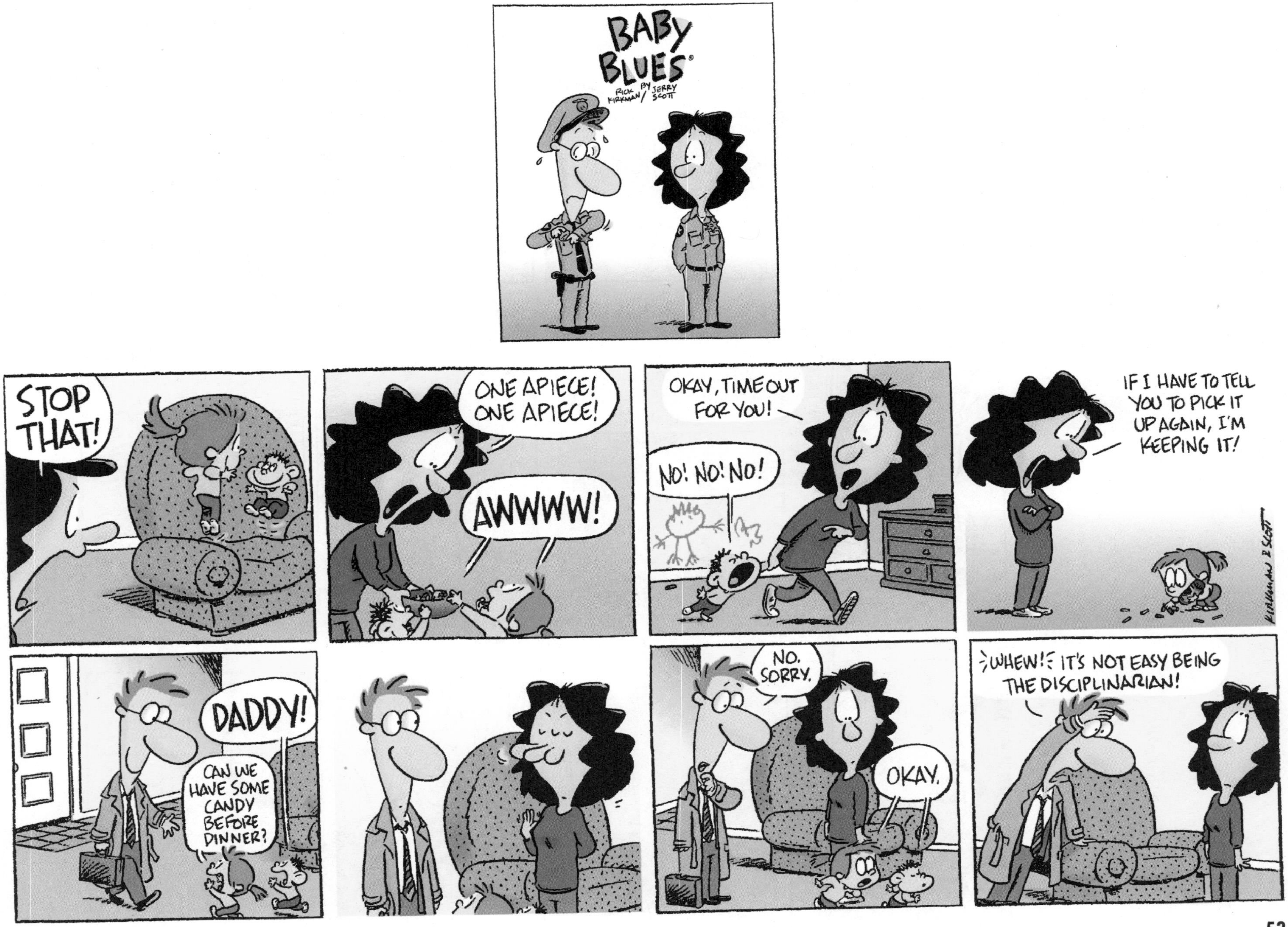
BABY BLUES®
BY RICK KIRKMAN / JERRY SCOTT
STOP THAT!
ONE APIECE! ONE APIECE!
AWWWW!
OKAY, TIME OUT FOR YOU!
NO! NO! NO!
IF I HAVE TO TELL YOU TO PICK IT UP AGAIN, I'M KEEPING IT!
KIRKMAN & SCOTT
DADDY!
CAN WE HAVE SOME CANDY BEFORE DINNER?
NO. SORRY.
OKAY.
WHEW! IT'S NOT EASY BEING THE DISCIPLINARIAN!

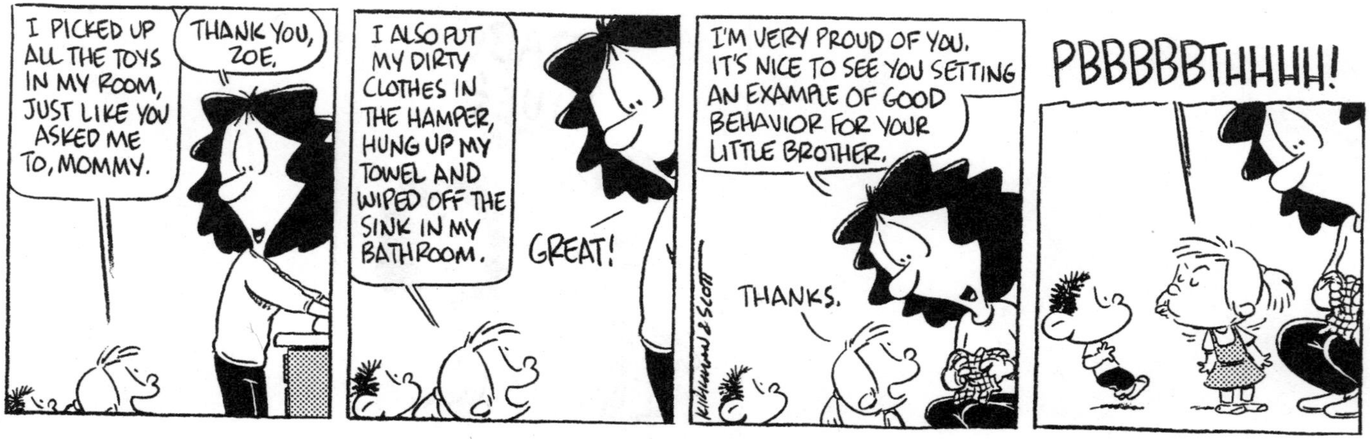
I PICKED UP ALL THE TOYS IN MY ROOM, JUST LIKE YOU ASKED ME TO, MOMMY.
THANK YOU, ZOE.
I ALSO PUT MY DIRTY CLOTHES IN THE HAMPER, HUNG UP MY TOWEL AND WIPED OFF THE SINK IN MY BATHROOM.
GREAT!
I'M VERY PROUD OF YOU. IT'S NICE TO SEE YOU SETTING AN EXAMPLE OF GOOD BEHAVIOR FOR YOUR LITTLE BROTHER.
THANKS.
KIRKMAN & SCOTT
PBBBBBTHHHH!

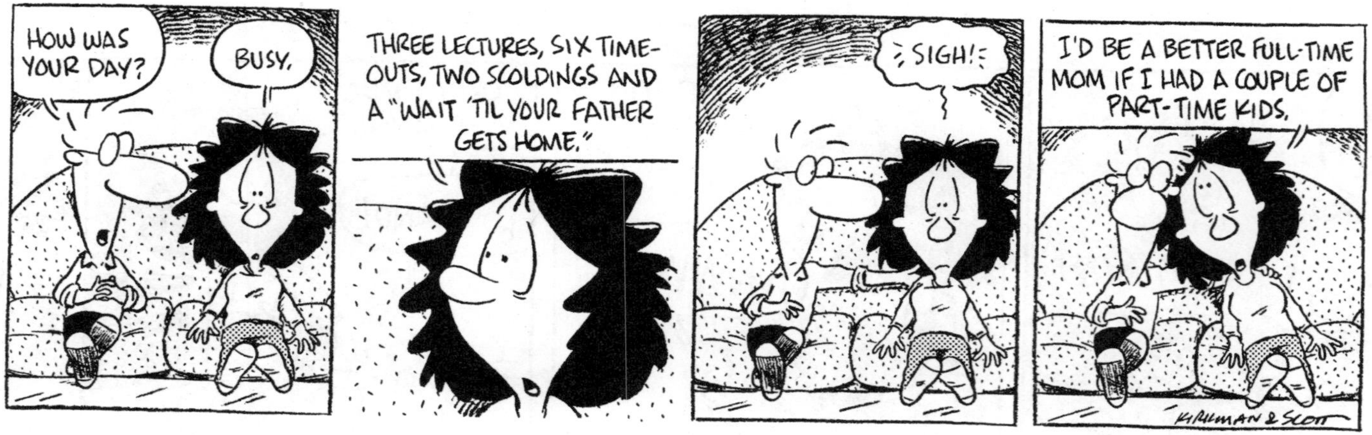
HOW WAS YOUR DAY?
BUSY.
THREE LECTURES, SIX TIME-OUTS, TWO SCOLDINGS AND A "WAIT 'TIL YOUR FATHER GETS HOME."
SIGH!
I'D BE A BETTER FULL-TIME MOM IF I HAD A COUPLE OF PART-TIME KIDS.
KIRKMAN & SCOTT

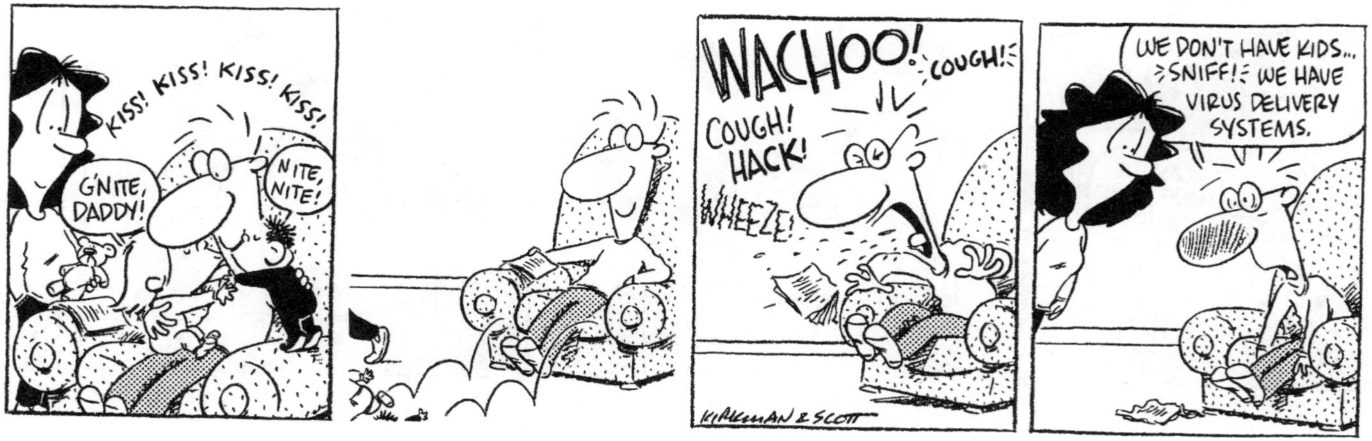
KISS! KISS! KISS! KISS!
G'NITE, DADDY!
NITE, NITE!
WACHOO!
COUGH!
COUGH! HACK!
WHEEZE!
KIRKMAN & SCOTT
WE DON'T HAVE KIDS... SNIFF! WE HAVE VIRUS DELIVERY SYSTEMS.

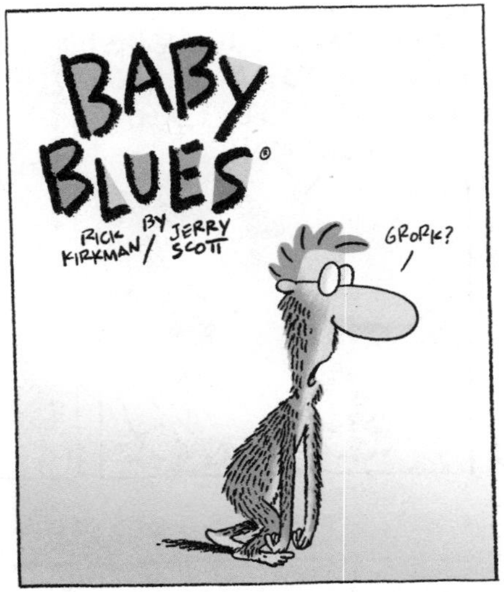
BABY BLUES®
RICK KIRKMAN / BY JERRY SCOTT
GRORK?

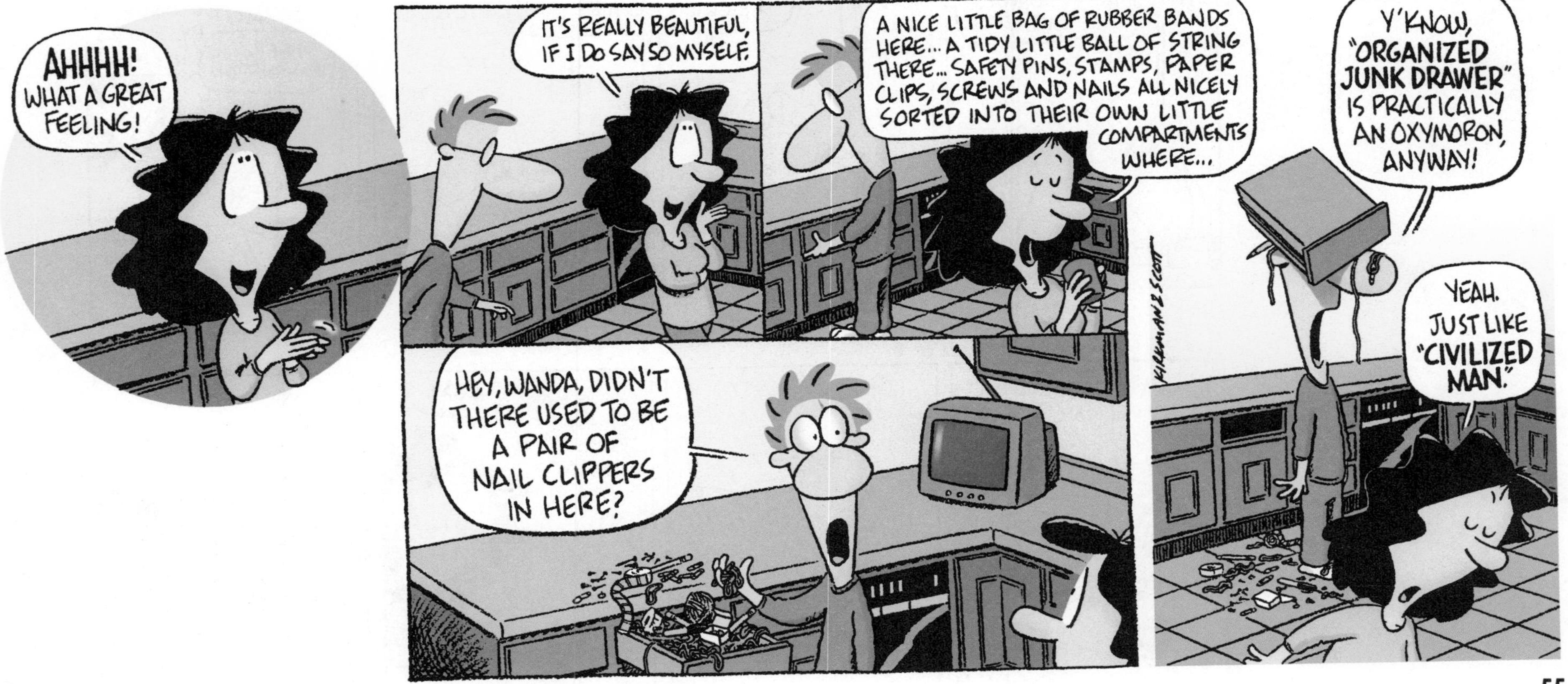
AHHHH! WHAT A GREAT FEELING!
IT'S REALLY BEAUTIFUL, IF I DO SAY SO MYSELF.
A NICE LITTLE BAG OF RUBBER BANDS HERE... A TIDY LITTLE BALL OF STRING THERE... SAFETY PINS, STAMPS, PAPER CLIPS, SCREWS AND NAILS ALL NICELY SORTED INTO THEIR OWN LITTLE COMPARTMENTS WHERE...
HEY, WANDA, DIDN'T THERE USED TO BE A PAIR OF NAIL CLIPPERS IN HERE?
Y'KNOW, "ORGANIZED JUNK DRAWER" IS PRACTICALLY AN OXYMORON, ANYWAY!
YEAH. JUST LIKE "CIVILIZED MAN."
KIRKMAN & SCOTT

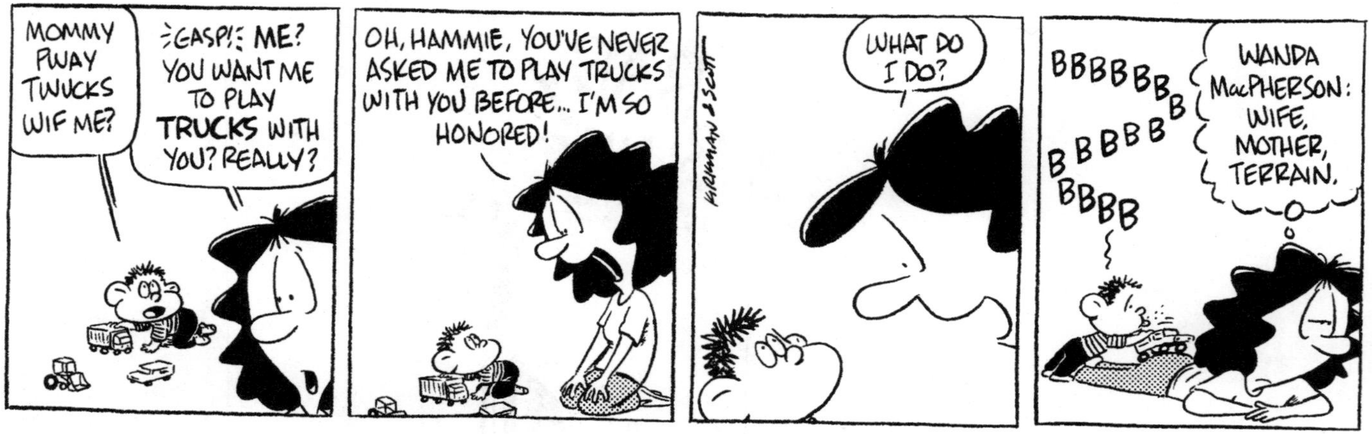
MOMMY PWAY TWUCKS WIF ME?
GASP! ME? YOU WANT ME TO PLAY TRUCKS WITH YOU? REALLY?
OH, HAMMIE, YOU'VE NEVER ASKED ME TO PLAY TRUCKS WITH YOU BEFORE... I'M SO HONORED!
KIRKMAN & SCOTT
WHAT DO I DO?
BBBBBBBB BBBBBB BBBB
WANDA MacPHERSON: WIFE, MOTHER, TERRAIN.

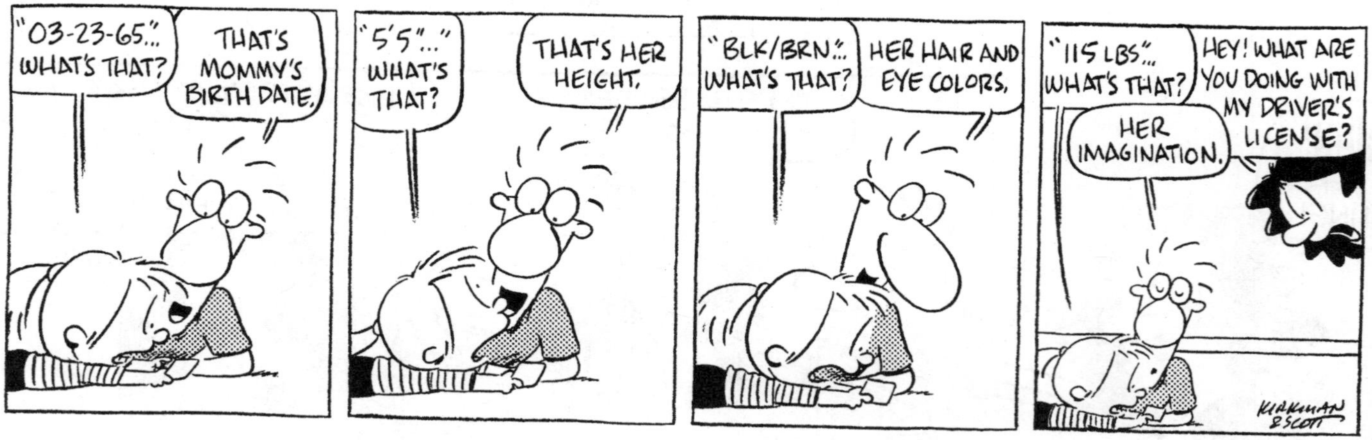
"03-23-65"... WHAT'S THAT?
THAT'S MOMMY'S BIRTH DATE.
"5'5"..." WHAT'S THAT?
THAT'S HER HEIGHT.
"BLK/BRN"... WHAT'S THAT?
HER HAIR AND EYE COLORS.
"115 LBS"... WHAT'S THAT?
HER IMAGINATION.
HEY! WHAT ARE YOU DOING WITH MY DRIVER'S LICENSE?
KIRKMAN & SCOTT

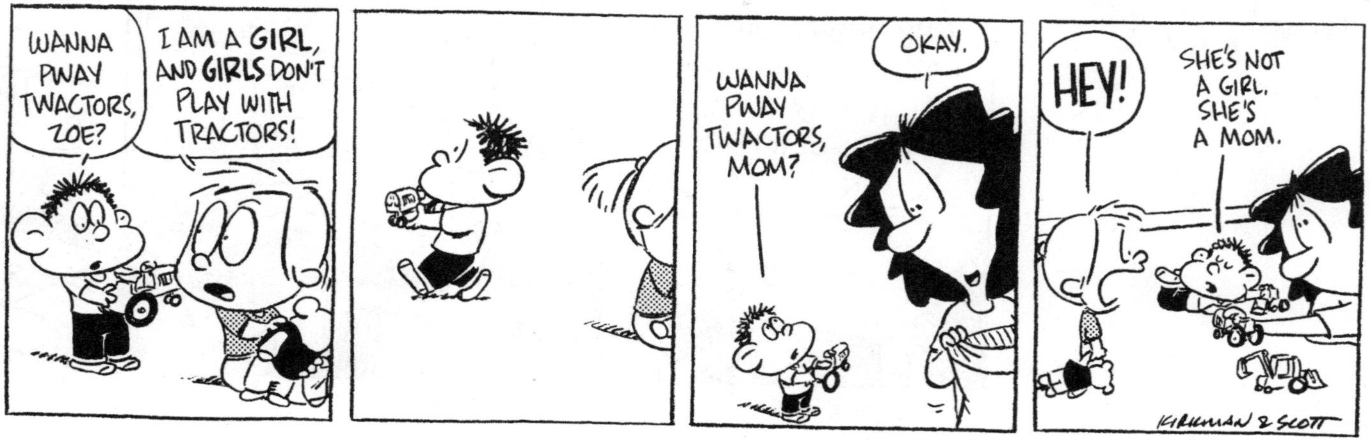
WANNA PWAY TWACTORS, ZOE?
I AM A GIRL, AND GIRLS DON'T PLAY WITH TRACTORS!
WANNA PWAY TWACTORS, MOM?
OKAY.
HEY!
SHE'S NOT A GIRL. SHE'S A MOM.
KIRKMAN & SCOTT

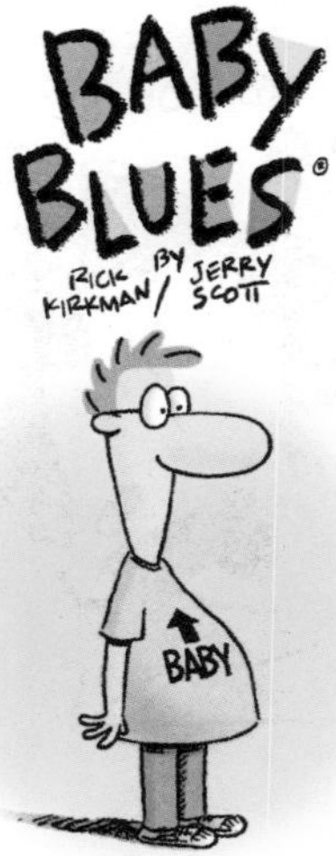
BABY BLUES®
BY RICK KIRKMAN / JERRY SCOTT
BABY

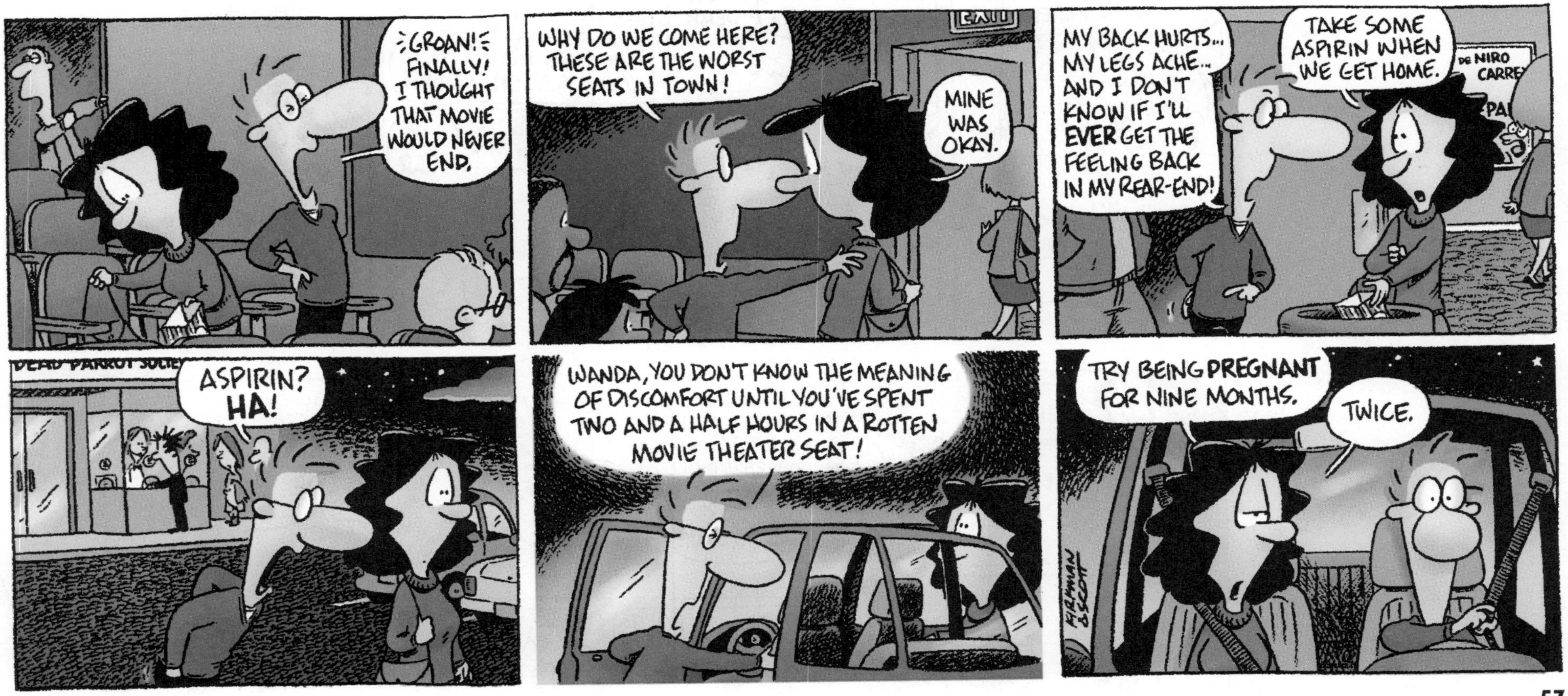
GROAN! FINALLY! I THOUGHT THAT MOVIE WOULD NEVER END.
WHY DO WE COME HERE? THESE ARE THE WORST SEATS IN TOWN!
MINE WAS OKAY.
MY BACK HURTS... MY LEGS ACHE... AND I DON'T KNOW IF I'LL **EVER** GET THE FEELING BACK IN MY REAR-END!
TAKE SOME ASPIRIN WHEN WE GET HOME.
ASPIRIN? **HA!**
WANDA, YOU DON'T KNOW THE MEANING OF DISCOMFORT UNTIL YOU'VE SPENT TWO AND A HALF HOURS IN A ROTTEN MOVIE THEATER SEAT!
TRY BEING **PREGNANT** FOR NINE MONTHS.
TWICE.
KIRKMAN & SCOTT

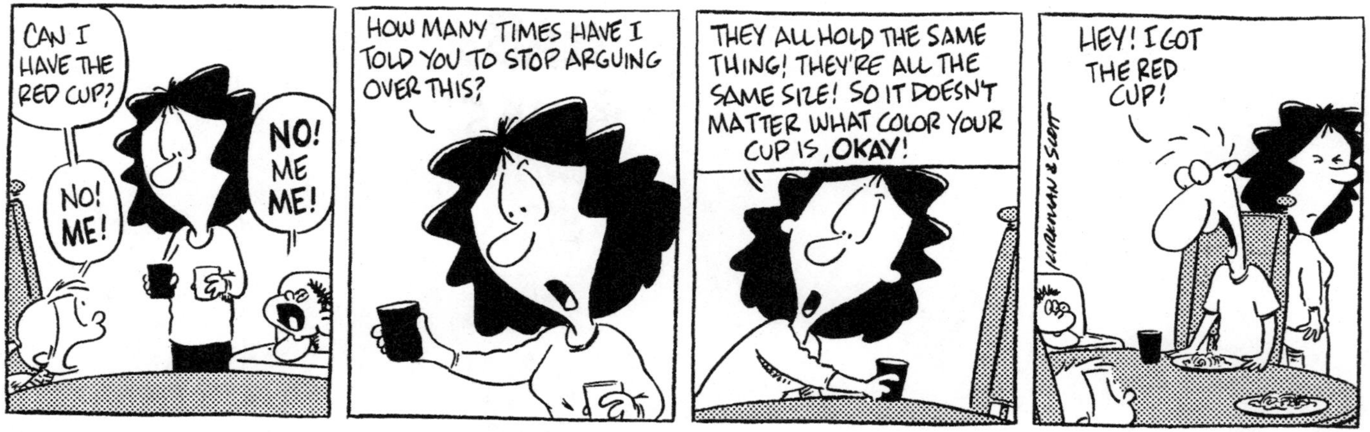
CAN I HAVE THE RED CUP?
NO! ME!
NO! ME ME!
HOW MANY TIMES HAVE I TOLD YOU TO STOP ARGUING OVER THIS?
THEY ALL HOLD THE SAME THING! THEY'RE ALL THE SAME SIZE! SO IT DOESN'T MATTER WHAT COLOR YOUR CUP IS, OKAY!
KIRKMAN & SCOTT
HEY! I GOT THE RED CUP!

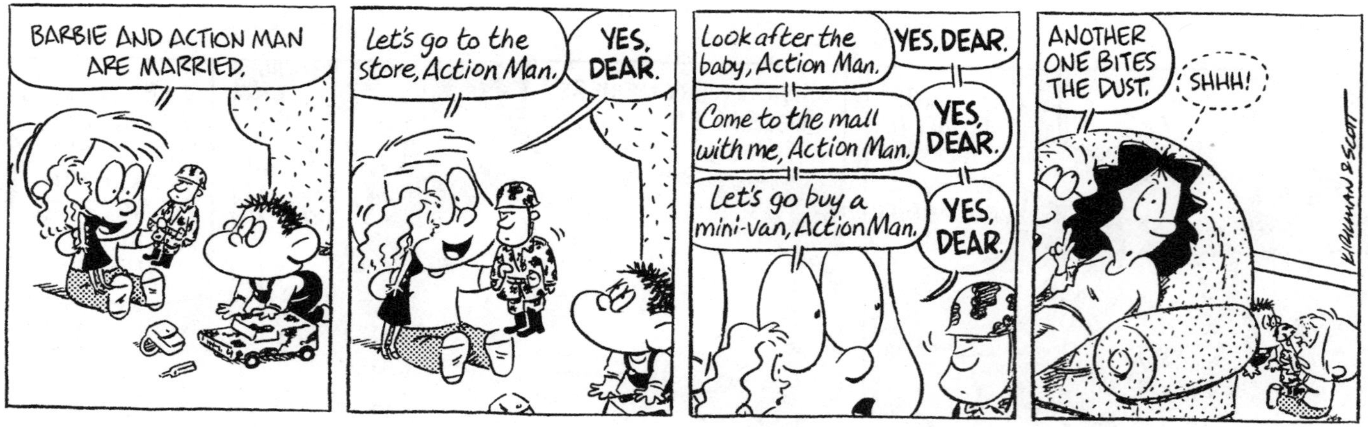
BARBIE AND ACTION MAN ARE MARRIED.
Let's go to the store, Action Man.
YES, DEAR.
Look after the baby, Action Man.
YES, DEAR.
Come to the mall with me, Action Man.
YES, DEAR.
Let's go buy a mini-van, Action Man.
YES, DEAR.
ANOTHER ONE BITES THE DUST.
SHHH!
KIRKMAN & SCOTT

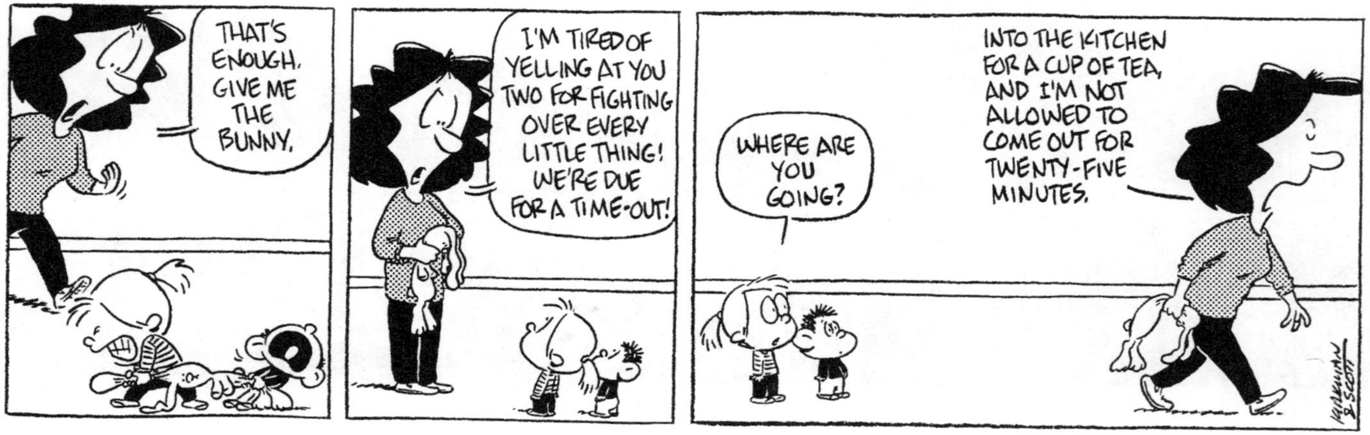
THAT'S ENOUGH. GIVE ME THE BUNNY.
I'M TIRED OF YELLING AT YOU TWO FOR FIGHTING OVER EVERY LITTLE THING! WE'RE DUE FOR A TIME-OUT!
WHERE ARE YOU GOING?
INTO THE KITCHEN FOR A CUP OF TEA, AND I'M NOT ALLOWED TO COME OUT FOR TWENTY-FIVE MINUTES.
KIRKMAN & SCOTT

Baby Blues®

BY RICK KIRKMAN / JERRY SCOTT

Hammie and Me

WHEREVER I AM,
THERE'S ALWAYS HAM,
BUT WE ALL JUST CALL
HIM "HAMMIE."
WHATEVER I DO,
HE WANTS TO, TOO,
EVEN WHEN I TELL
HIM TO "SCRAMMIE!"

"WHERE ARE YOU GOING?
WHAT SHOULD WE DO?"
HE WANTS TO KNOW
ONE OR THE OTHER.
"LEAVE ME ALONE,"
I WEARILY GROAN,
IT AIN'T EASY
HAVING A BROTHER.

HE WANTS TO PLAY
TRUCKS OR CARS OR TRAINS
(IT IS CONSTANTLY
SOMETHING WITH WHEELS).
HE WON'T DRESS-UP
WITH ME ANYMORE
EVEN THOUGH HE LOOKS
GREAT IN HIGH HEELS.

ONE TIME GRAPE JUICE
GOT SPILLED ON THE COUCH,
WHEN MOM SAW IT
I KNEW SHE WOULD SNAP.
I HAD NO DOUBT
I'D GET A TIME-OUT,
BUT HEROICALLY,
HAM TOOK THE RAP.

SO WHEREVER I AM,
THERE'S ALWAYS HAM,
AND SOMETIMES I THINK
I MIGHT SMOTHER.
BUT ORNERY, STINKY
AND CLINGY ASIDE,
THER'RE WORSE THINGS
THAN HAVING A BROTHER.

With apologies to A. A. Milne

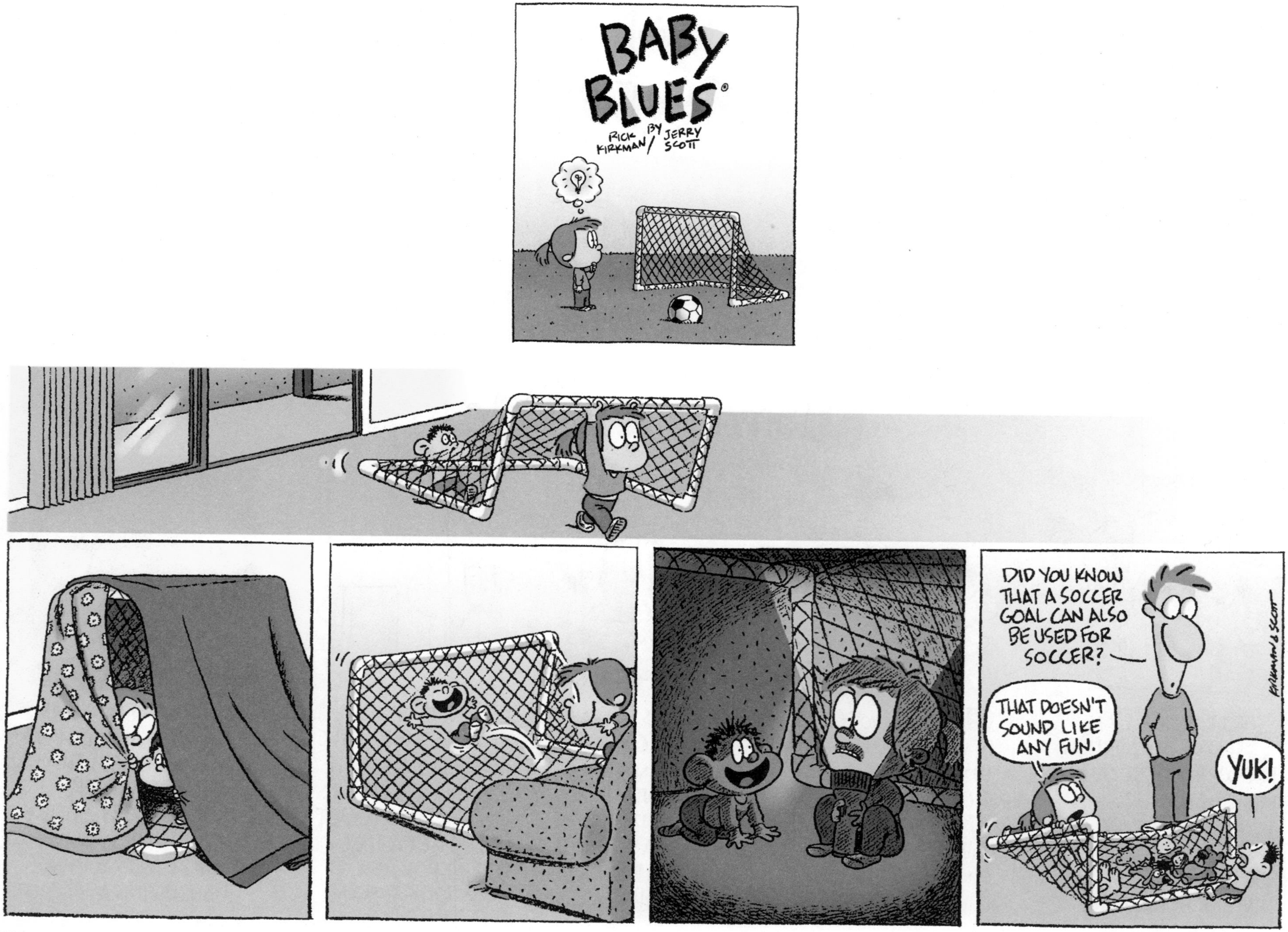
BABY BLUES®
RICK KIRKMAN / BY JERRY SCOTT
DID YOU KNOW THAT A SOCCER GOAL CAN ALSO BE USED FOR SOCCER?
THAT DOESN'T SOUND LIKE ANY FUN.
YUK!
KIRKMAN & SCOTT

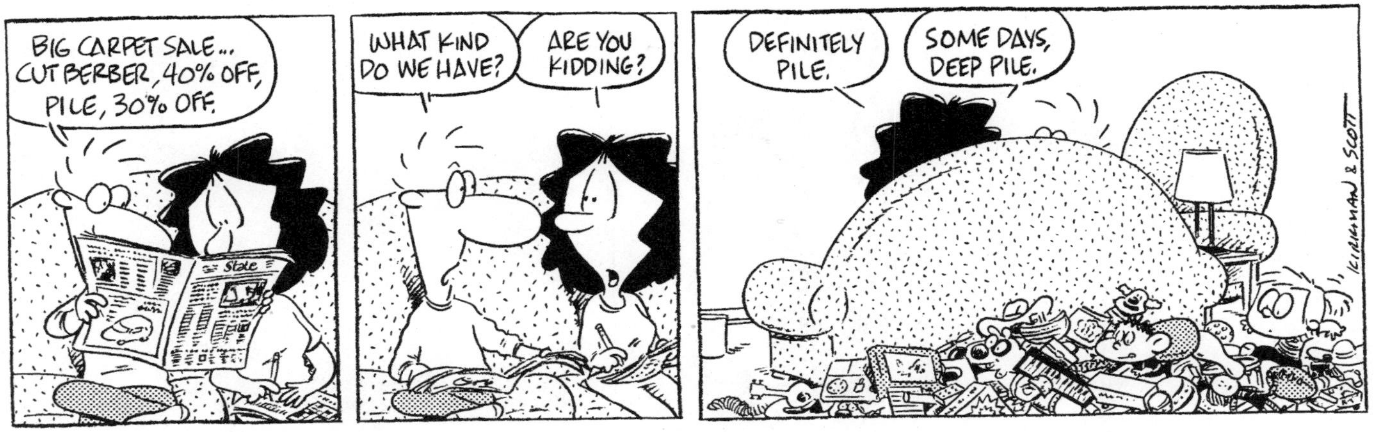
BIG CARPET SALE... CUT BERBER, 40% OFF, PILE, 30% OFF.
WHAT KIND DO WE HAVE?
ARE YOU KIDDING?
DEFINITELY PILE.
SOME DAYS, DEEP PILE.
KIRKMAN & SCOTT

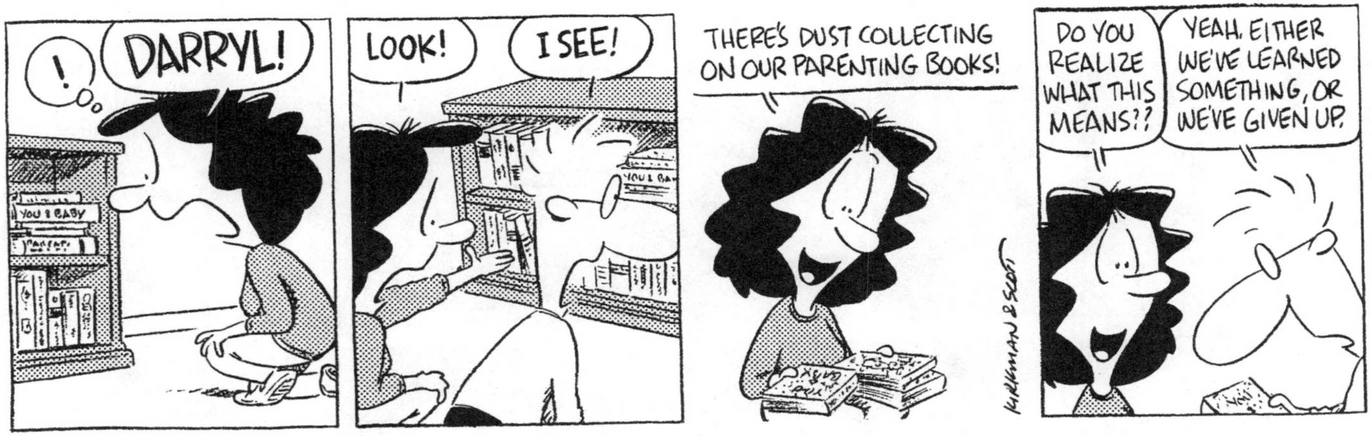
!
DARRYL!
YOU & BABY
LOOK!
I SEE!
THERE'S DUST COLLECTING ON OUR PARENTING BOOKS!
KIRKMAN & SCOTT
DO YOU REALIZE WHAT THIS MEANS??
YEAH. EITHER WE'VE LEARNED SOMETHING, OR WE'VE GIVEN UP.

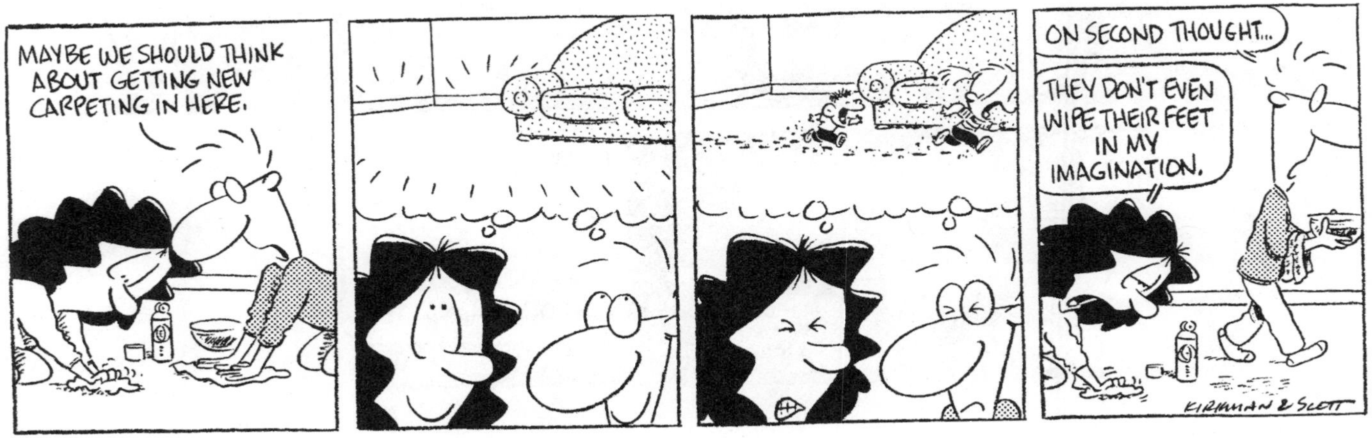
MAYBE WE SHOULD THINK ABOUT GETTING NEW CARPETING IN HERE.
ON SECOND THOUGHT...
THEY DON'T EVEN WIPE THEIR FEET IN MY IMAGINATION.
KIRKMAN & SCOTT

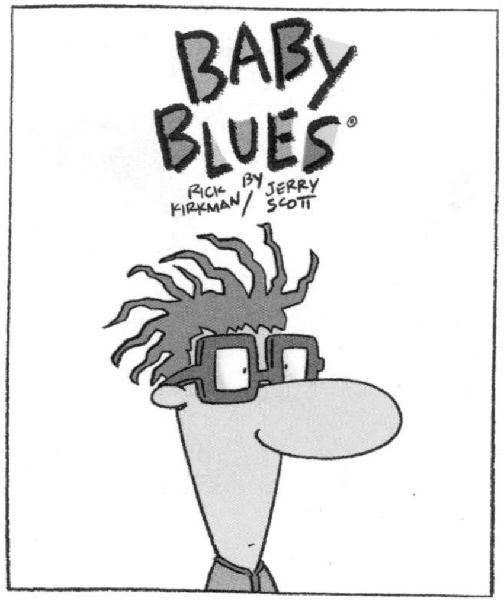
BABY BLUES®
RICK KIRKMAN / BY JERRY SCOTT

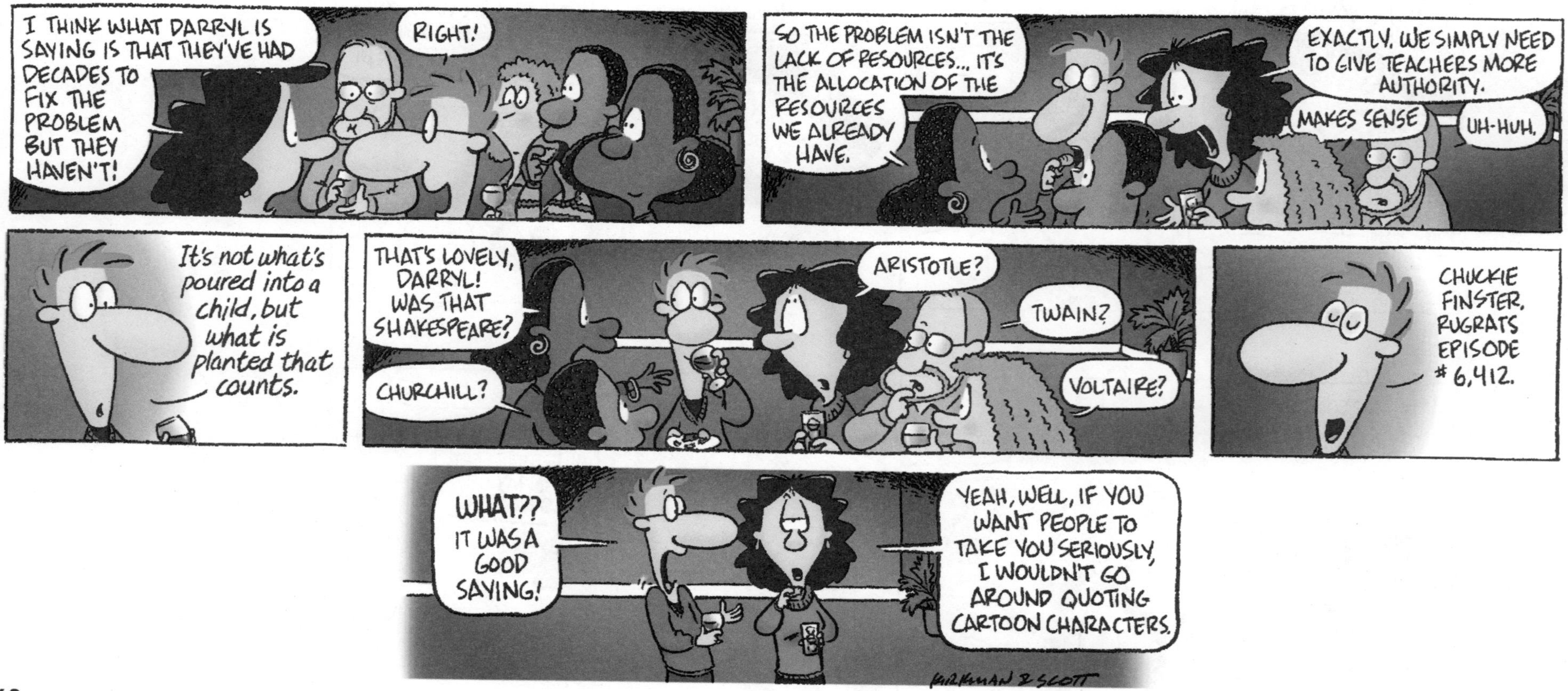
I THINK WHAT DARRYL IS SAYING IS THAT THEY'VE HAD DECADES TO FIX THE PROBLEM BUT THEY HAVEN'T!
RIGHT!
SO THE PROBLEM ISN'T THE LACK OF RESOURCES... IT'S THE ALLOCATION OF THE RESOURCES WE ALREADY HAVE.
EXACTLY. WE SIMPLY NEED TO GIVE TEACHERS MORE AUTHORITY.
MAKES SENSE
UH-HUH.
It's not what's poured into a child, but what is planted that counts.
THAT'S LOVELY, DARRYL! WAS THAT SHAKESPEARE?
ARISTOTLE?
TWAIN?
CHURCHILL?
VOLTAIRE?
CHUCKIE FINSTER, RUGRATS EPISODE # 6,412.
WHAT?? IT WAS A GOOD SAYING!
YEAH, WELL, IF YOU WANT PEOPLE TO TAKE YOU SERIOUSLY, I WOULDN'T GO AROUND QUOTING CARTOON CHARACTERS.
KIRKMAN & SCOTT

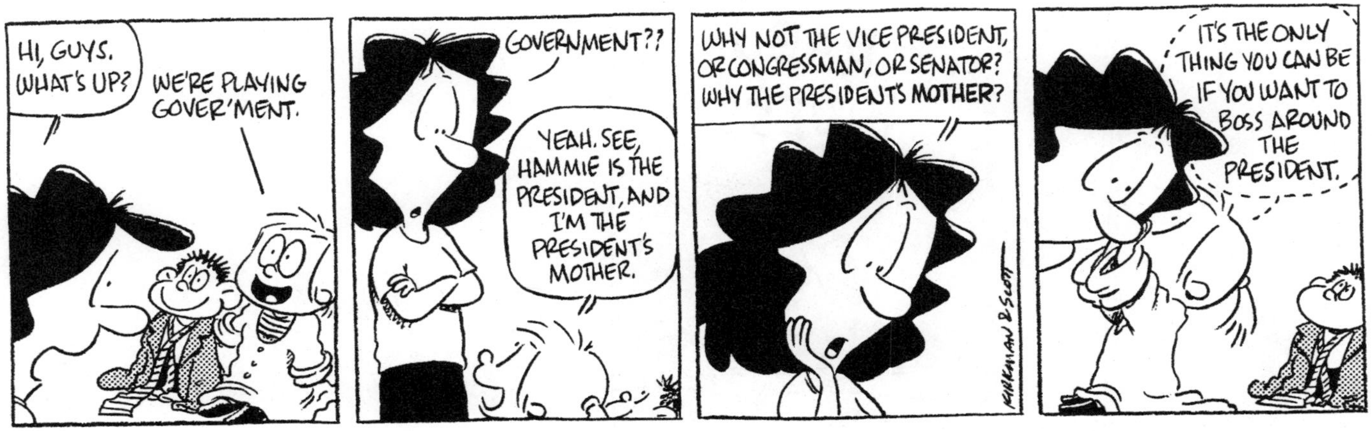
HI, GUYS. WHAT'S UP?
WE'RE PLAYING GOVER'MENT.
GOVERNMENT??
YEAH. SEE, HAMMIE IS THE PRESIDENT, AND I'M THE PRESIDENT'S MOTHER.
WHY NOT THE VICE PRESIDENT, OR CONGRESSMAN, OR SENATOR? WHY THE PRESIDENT'S **MOTHER**?
KIRKMAN & SCOTT
IT'S THE ONLY THING YOU CAN BE IF YOU WANT TO BOSS AROUND THE PRESIDENT.

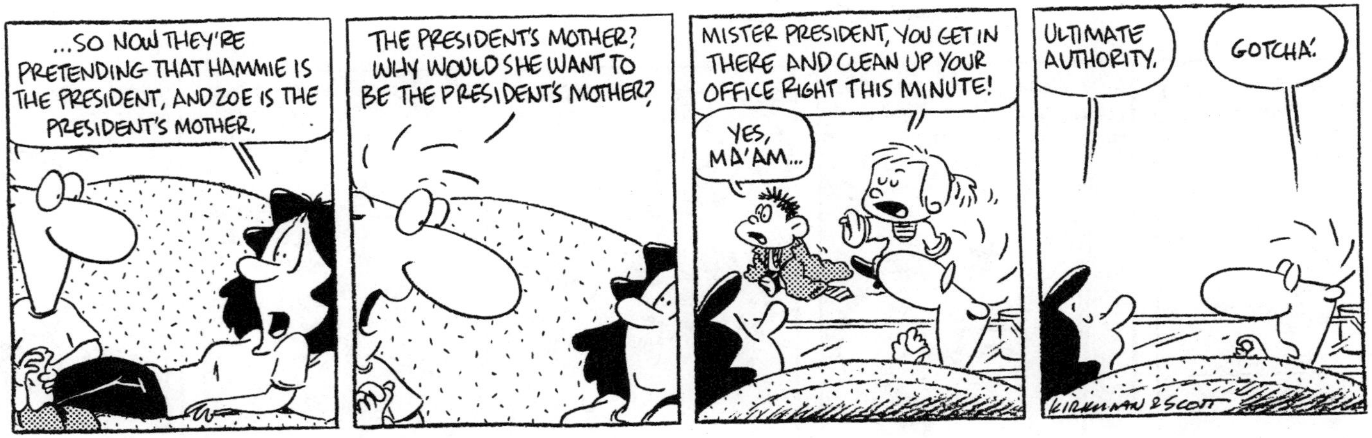
...SO NOW THEY'RE PRETENDING THAT HAMMIE IS THE PRESIDENT, AND ZOE IS THE PRESIDENT'S MOTHER.
THE PRESIDENT'S MOTHER? WHY WOULD SHE WANT TO BE THE PRESIDENT'S MOTHER?
MISTER PRESIDENT, YOU GET IN THERE AND CLEAN UP YOUR OFFICE RIGHT THIS MINUTE!
YES, MA'AM...
ULTIMATE AUTHORITY.
GOTCHA.
KIRKMAN & SCOTT

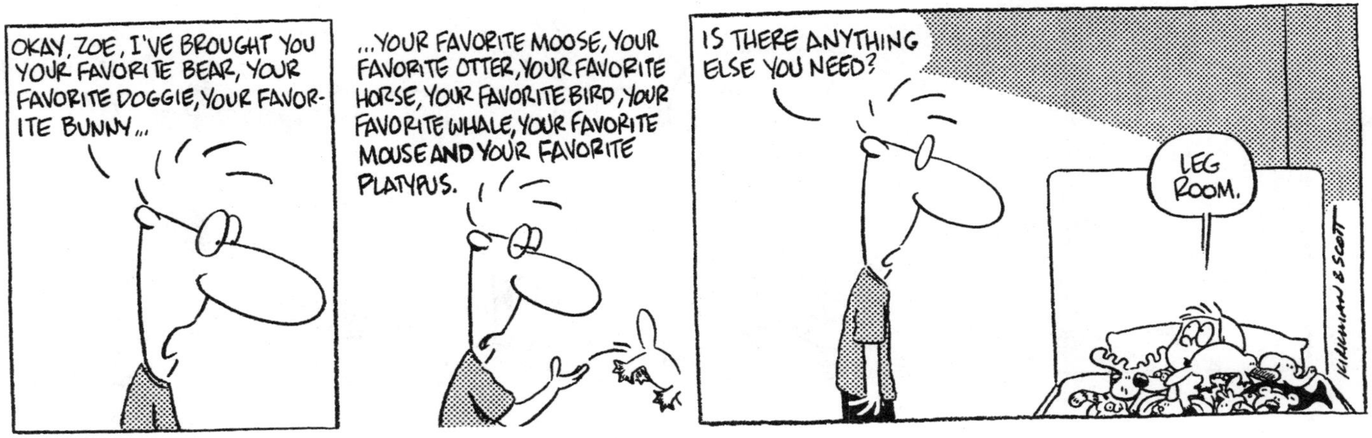
OKAY, ZOE, I'VE BROUGHT YOU YOUR FAVORITE BEAR, YOUR FAVORITE DOGGIE, YOUR FAVORITE BUNNY...
...YOUR FAVORITE MOOSE, YOUR FAVORITE OTTER, YOUR FAVORITE HORSE, YOUR FAVORITE BIRD, YOUR FAVORITE WHALE, YOUR FAVORITE MOUSE AND YOUR FAVORITE PLATYPUS.
IS THERE ANYTHING ELSE YOU NEED?
LEG ROOM.
KIRKMAN & SCOTT

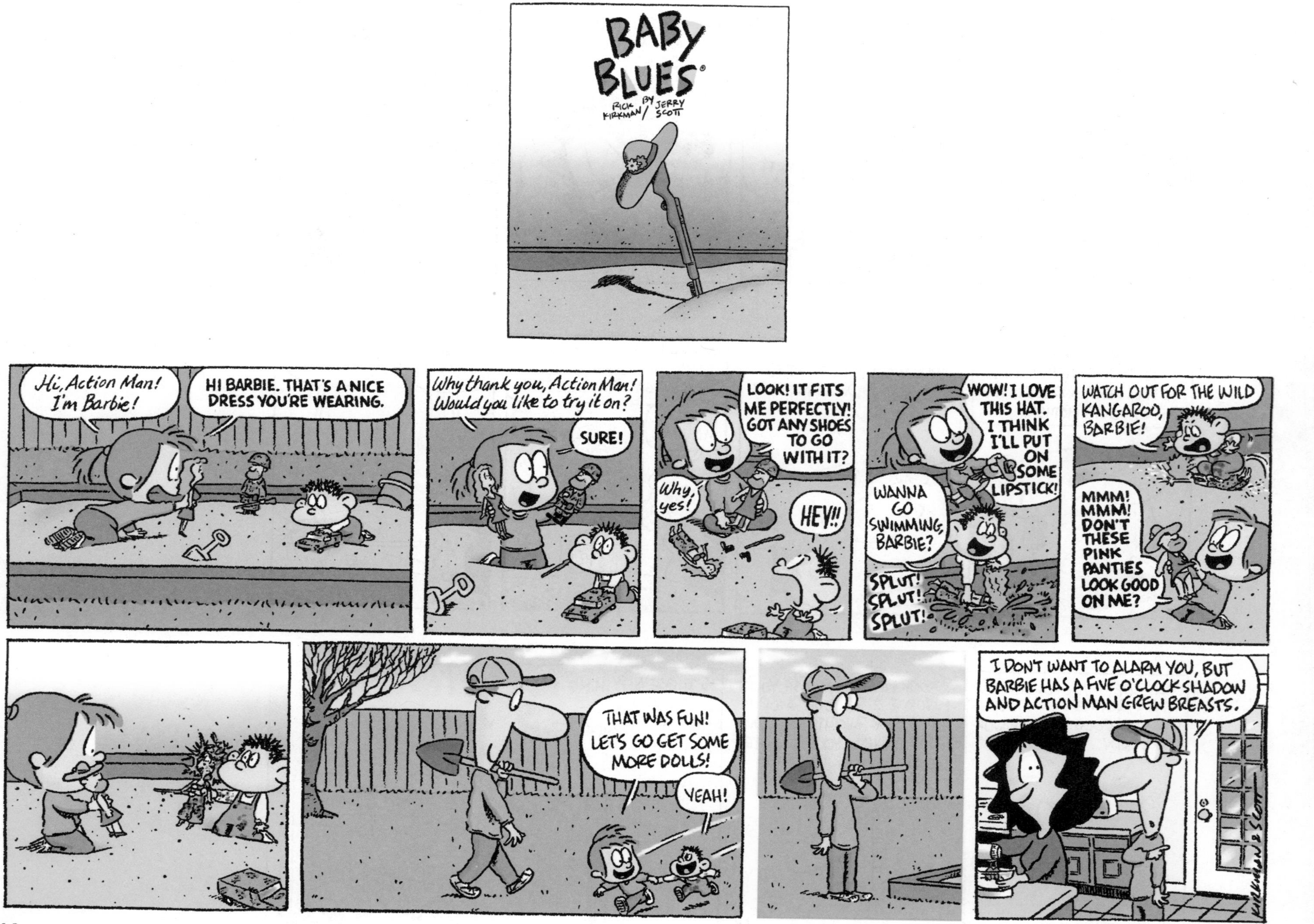
BABY BLUES®
BY RICK KIRKMAN / JERRY SCOTT
Hi, Action Man! I'm Barbie!
HI BARBIE. THAT'S A NICE DRESS YOU'RE WEARING.
Why thank you, Action Man! Would you like to try it on?
SURE!
LOOK! IT FITS ME PERFECTLY! GOT ANY SHOES TO GO WITH IT?
Why, yes!
HEY!!
WOW! I LOVE THIS HAT. I THINK I'LL PUT ON SOME LIPSTICK!
WANNA GO SWIMMING, BARBIE?
SPLUT! SPLUT! SPLUT!
WATCH OUT FOR THE WILD KANGAROO, BARBIE!
MMM! MMM! DON'T THESE PINK PANTIES LOOK GOOD ON ME?
THAT WAS FUN! LET'S GO GET SOME MORE DOLLS!
YEAH!
I DON'T WANT TO ALARM YOU, BUT BARBIE HAS A FIVE O'CLOCK SHADOW AND ACTION MAN GREW BREASTS.
KIRKMAN & SCOTT

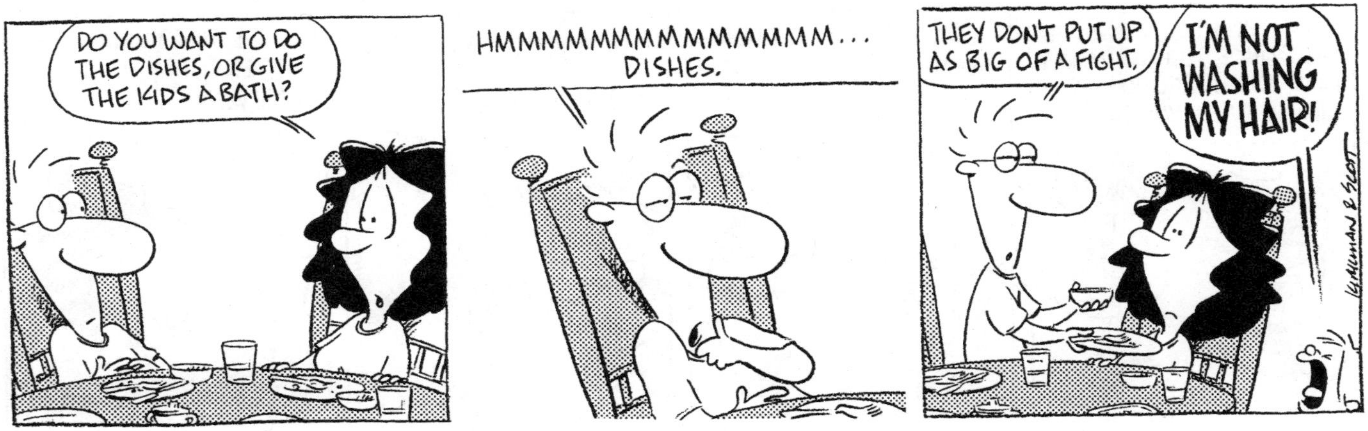
DO YOU WANT TO DO THE DISHES, OR GIVE THE KIDS A BATH?
HMMMMMMMMMMMMMM... DISHES.
THEY DON'T PUT UP AS BIG OF A FIGHT.
I'M NOT WASHING MY HAIR!
KIRKMAN & SCOTT

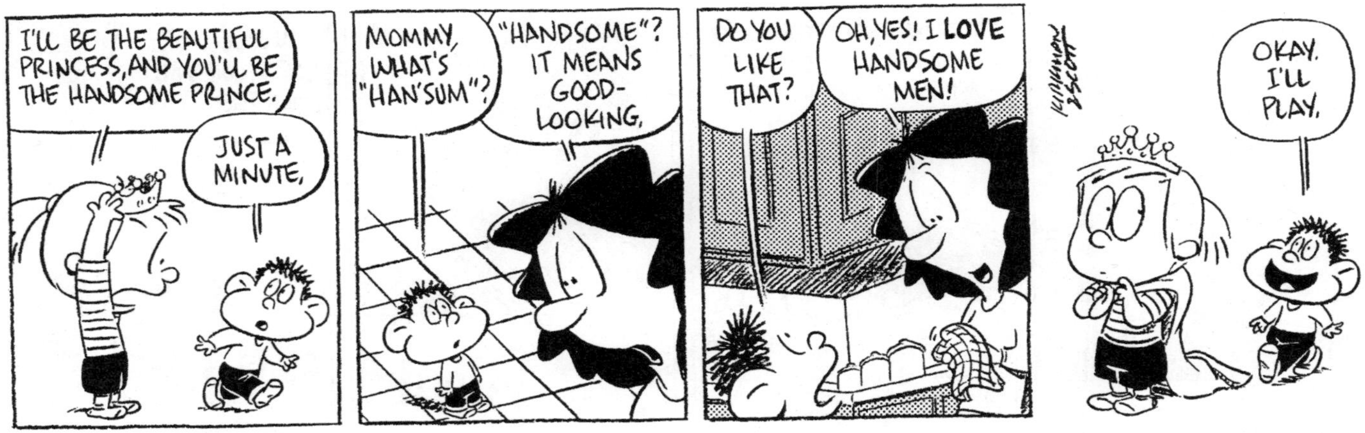
I'LL BE THE BEAUTIFUL PRINCESS, AND YOU'LL BE THE HANDSOME PRINCE.
JUST A MINUTE.
MOMMY, WHAT'S "HAN'SUM"?
"HANDSOME"? IT MEANS GOOD-LOOKING.
DO YOU LIKE THAT?
OH, YES! I LOVE HANDSOME MEN!
KIRKMAN & SCOTT
OKAY. I'LL PLAY.

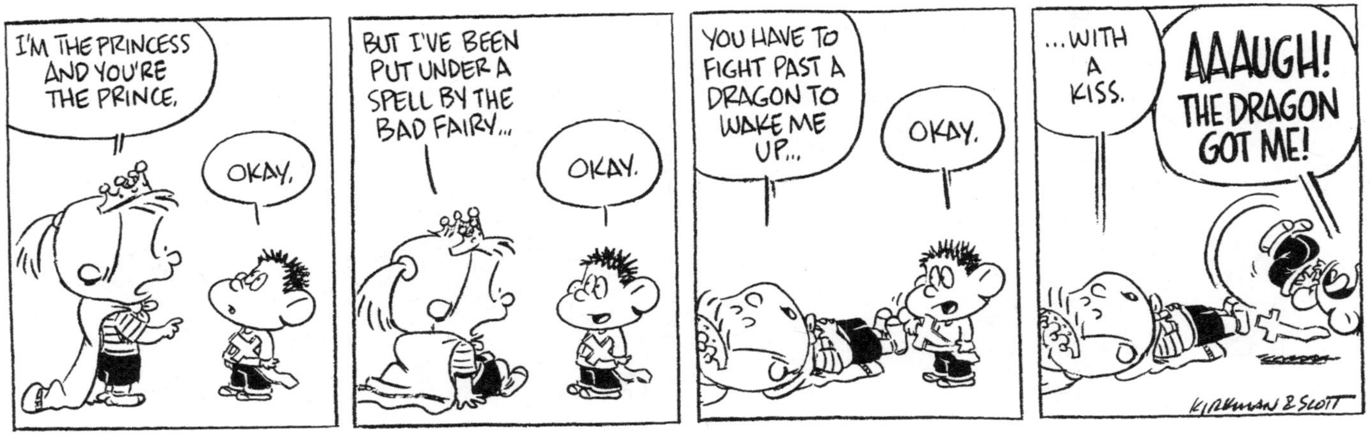
I'M THE PRINCESS AND YOU'RE THE PRINCE.
OKAY.
BUT I'VE BEEN PUT UNDER A SPELL BY THE BAD FAIRY...
OKAY.
YOU HAVE TO FIGHT PAST A DRAGON TO WAKE ME UP...
OKAY.
...WITH A KISS.
AAAUGH! THE DRAGON GOT ME!
KIRKMAN & SCOTT

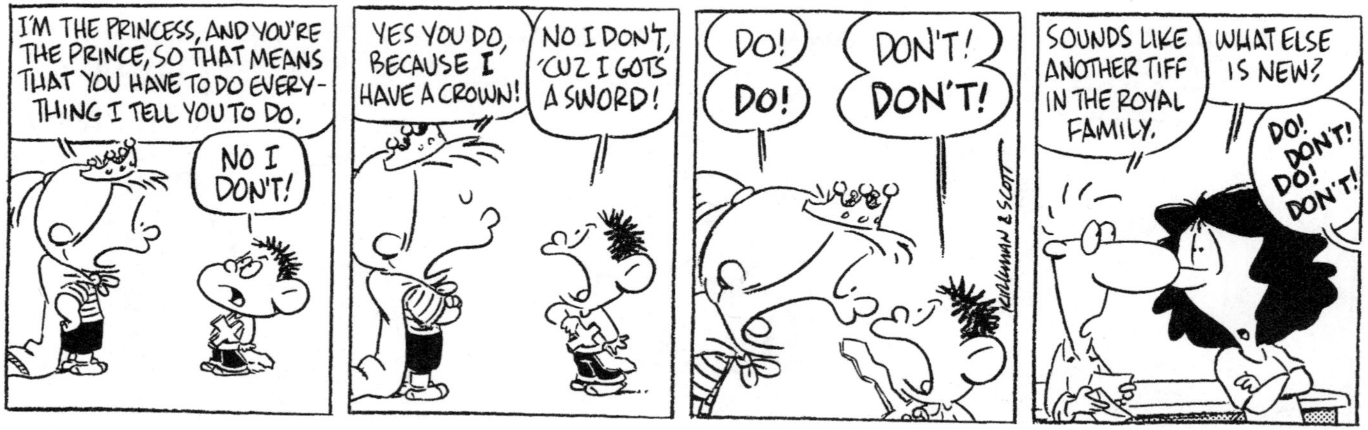
I'M THE PRINCESS, AND YOU'RE THE PRINCE, SO THAT MEANS THAT YOU HAVE TO DO EVERYTHING I TELL YOU TO DO.
NO I DON'T!
YES YOU DO, BECAUSE I HAVE A CROWN!
NO I DON'T, 'CUZ I GOTS A SWORD!
DO! DO!
DON'T! DON'T!
KIRKMAN & SCOTT
SOUNDS LIKE ANOTHER TIFF IN THE ROYAL FAMILY.
WHAT ELSE IS NEW?
DO! DON'T! DO! DON'T!

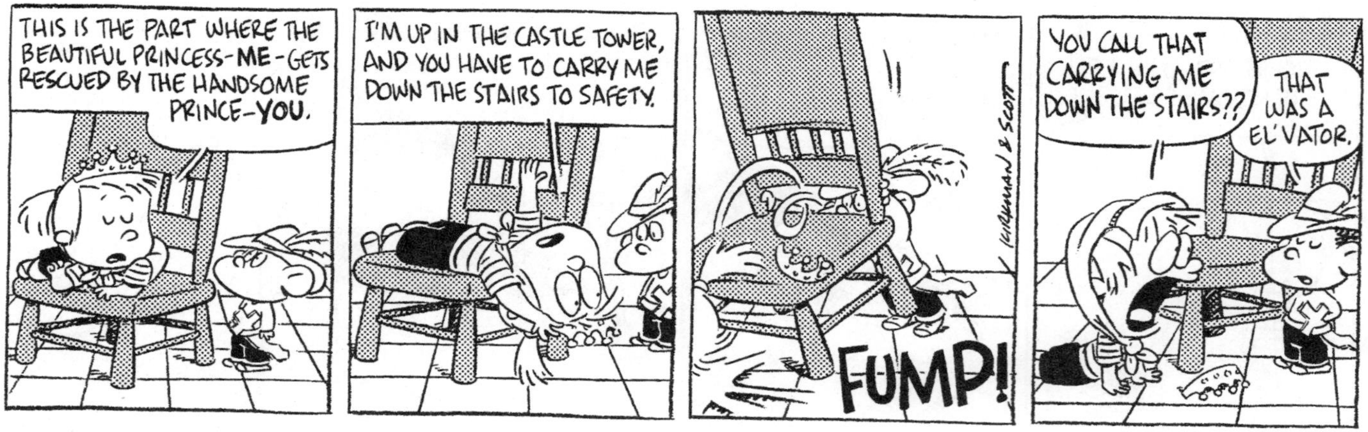
THIS IS THE PART WHERE THE BEAUTIFUL PRINCESS-ME-GETS RESCUED BY THE HANDSOME PRINCE-YOU.
I'M UP IN THE CASTLE TOWER, AND YOU HAVE TO CARRY ME DOWN THE STAIRS TO SAFETY.
KIRKMAN & SCOTT
FUMP!
YOU CALL THAT CARRYING ME DOWN THE STAIRS??
THAT WAS A EL'VATOR.

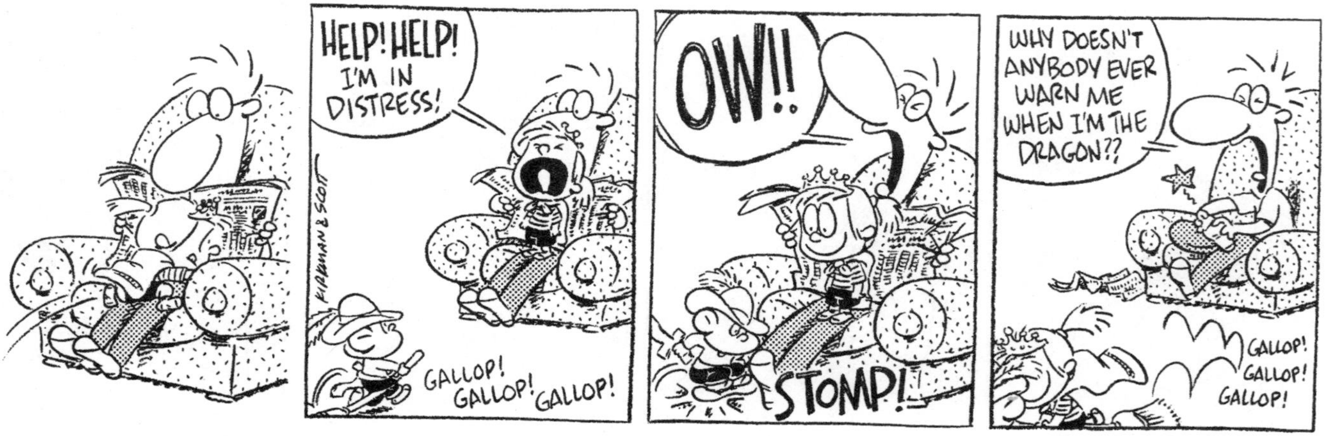
KIRKMAN & SCOTT
HELP! HELP! I'M IN DISTRESS!
GALLOP! GALLOP! GALLOP!
OW!!
STOMP!
WHY DOESN'T ANYBODY EVER WARN ME WHEN I'M THE DRAGON??
GALLOP! GALLOP! GALLOP!

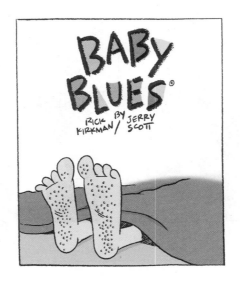

BABY BLUES®

By Rick Kirkman / Jerry Scott

DARRYL?

MFGLBM?

WOULD YOU GET ME A DRINK OF WATER?

UH, YEAH. SURE... OKAY.

OW!

OUCH! OOCH!

YEOW!

OW! OW! OW! OW!

OUCH!

OW! OOH!

AAGHK!

NFVH!

MAYBE NEXT TIME I'LL TELL YOU TO GET YOUR OWN WATER.

AND MAYBE NEXT TIME YOU PROMISE TO PICK UP THE KIDS' LEGOS, YOU'LL DO IT.

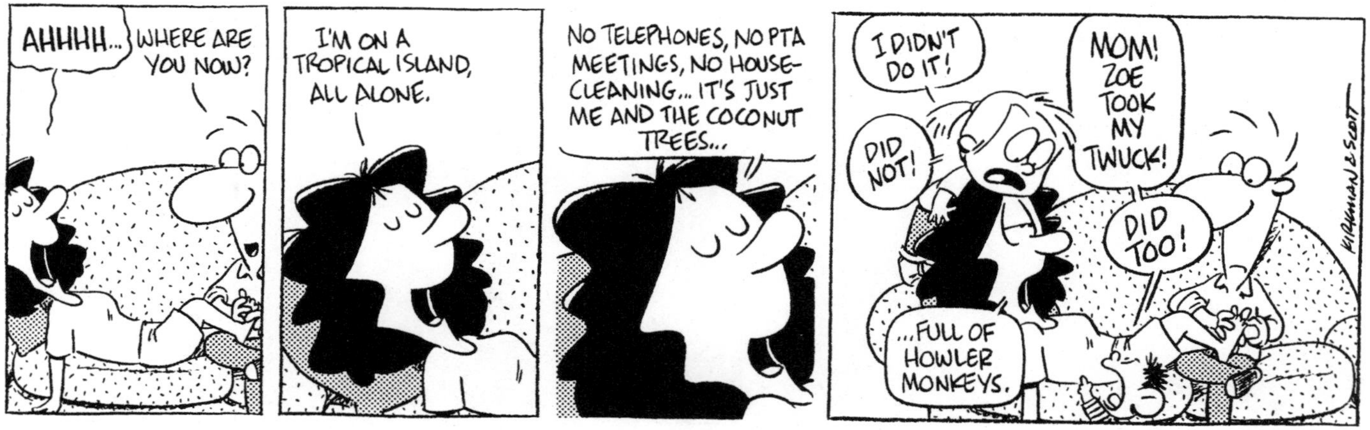
AHHHH...
WHERE ARE YOU NOW?
I'M ON A TROPICAL ISLAND, ALL ALONE.
NO TELEPHONES, NO PTA MEETINGS, NO HOUSE-CLEANING... IT'S JUST ME AND THE COCONUT TREES...
I DIDN'T DO IT!
MOM! ZOE TOOK MY TWUCK!
DID NOT!
DID TOO!
...FULL OF HOWLER MONKEYS.
KIRKMAN & SCOTT

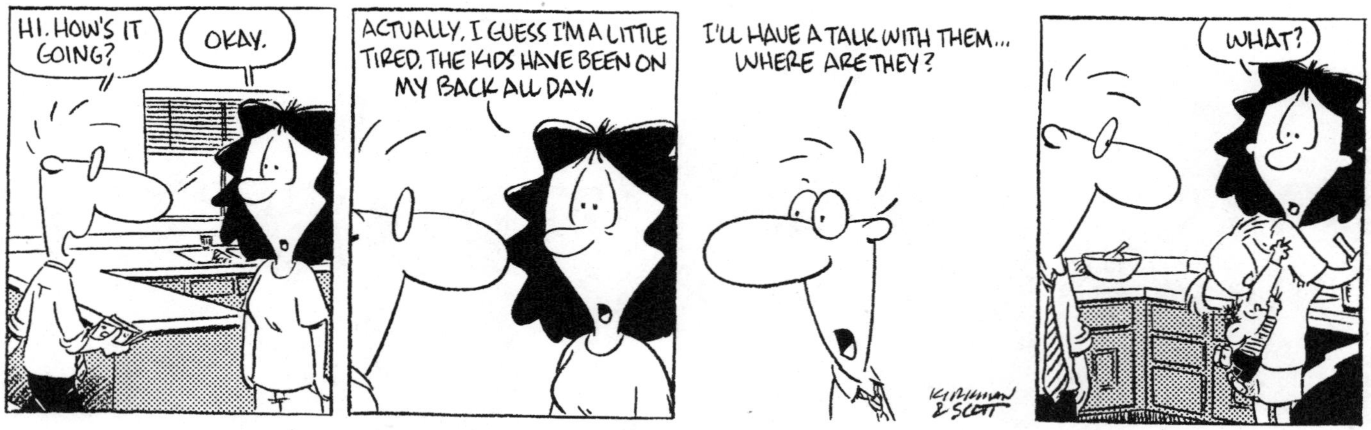
HI. HOW'S IT GOING?
OKAY.
ACTUALLY, I GUESS I'M A LITTLE TIRED. THE KIDS HAVE BEEN ON MY BACK ALL DAY.
I'LL HAVE A TALK WITH THEM... WHERE ARE THEY?
KIRKMAN & SCOTT
WHAT?

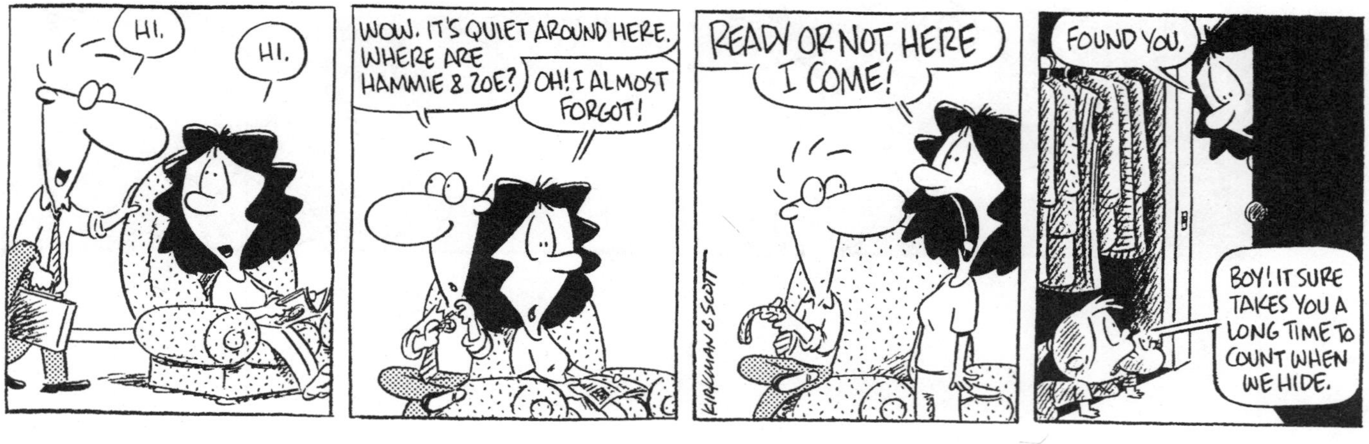
HI.
HI.
WOW. IT'S QUIET AROUND HERE. WHERE ARE HAMMIE & ZOE?
OH! I ALMOST FORGOT!
KIRKMAN & SCOTT
READY OR NOT, HERE I COME!
FOUND YOU.
BOY! IT SURE TAKES YOU A LONG TIME TO COUNT WHEN WE HIDE.

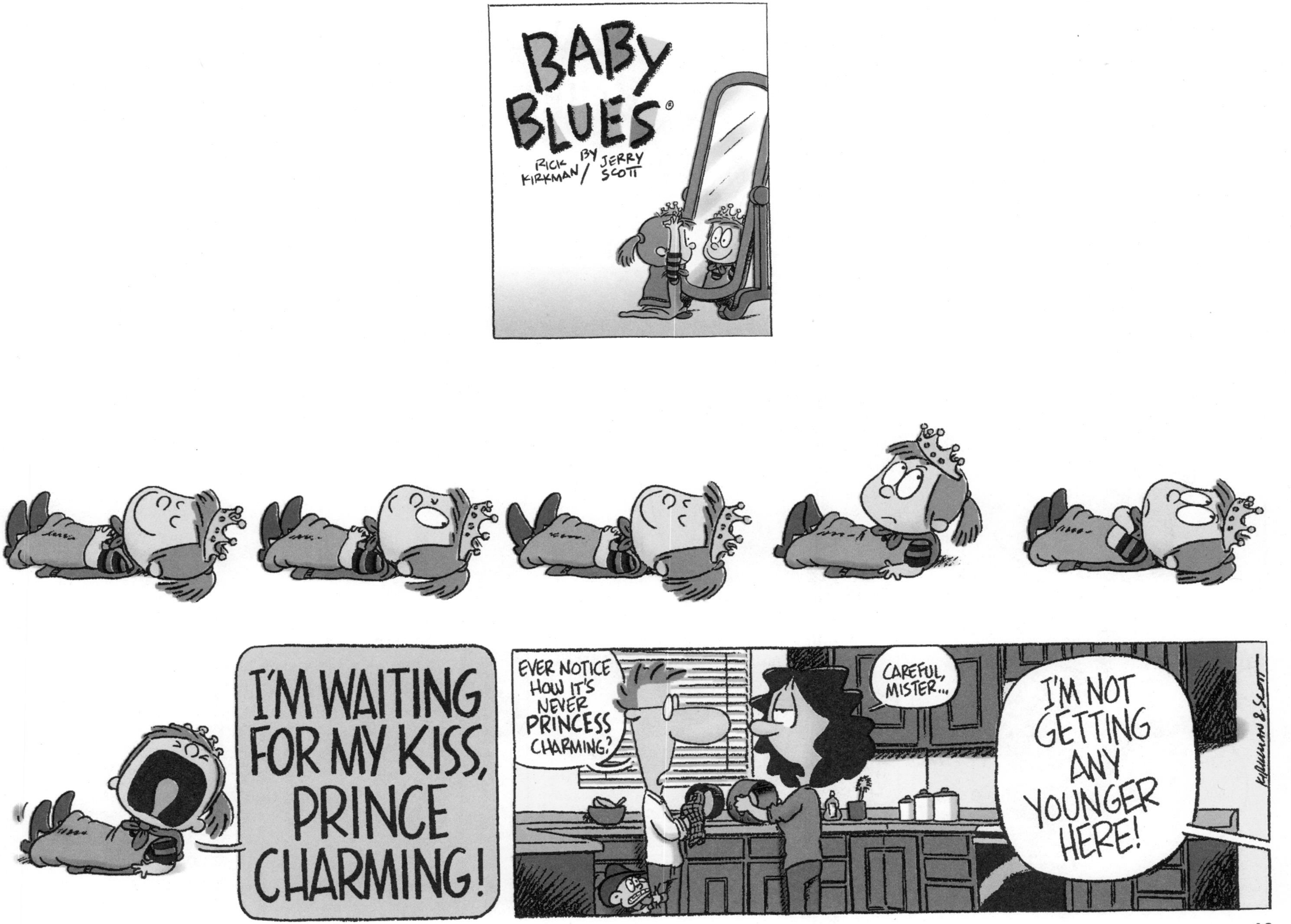
BABY BLUES®
BY RICK KIRKMAN / JERRY SCOTT
I'M WAITING FOR MY KISS, PRINCE CHARMING!
EVER NOTICE HOW IT'S NEVER PRINCESS CHARMING?
CAREFUL, MISTER...
I'M NOT GETTING ANY YOUNGER HERE!
KIRKMAN & SCOTT

BABY BLUES®
BY RICK KIRKMAN / JERRY SCOTT

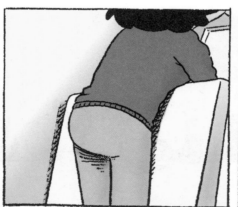

ZOE? WHAT ARE Y—?

DADDY SHOWED ME HOW TO USE THE VIDEO CAMERA!

DID DADDY ALSO WARN YOU ABOUT THE DANGERS OF FILMING MOMMY FROM BEHIND?

NEXT LESSON: TEMPERAMENTAL STARS.

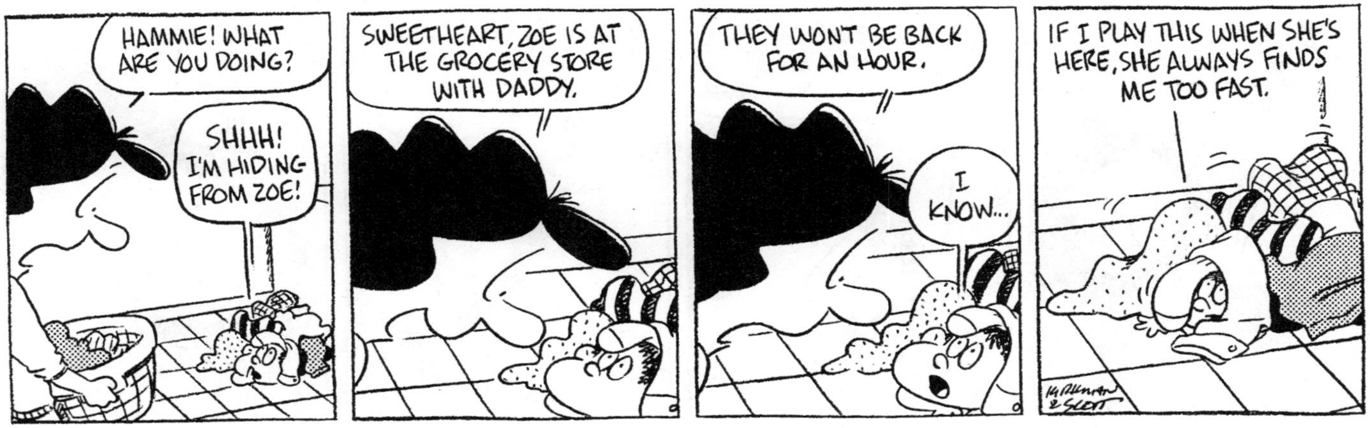
HAMMIE! WHAT ARE YOU DOING?
SHHH! I'M HIDING FROM ZOE!
SWEETHEART, ZOE IS AT THE GROCERY STORE WITH DADDY.
THEY WON'T BE BACK FOR AN HOUR.
I KNOW...
IF I PLAY THIS WHEN SHE'S HERE, SHE ALWAYS FINDS ME TOO FAST.
KIRKMAN & SCOTT

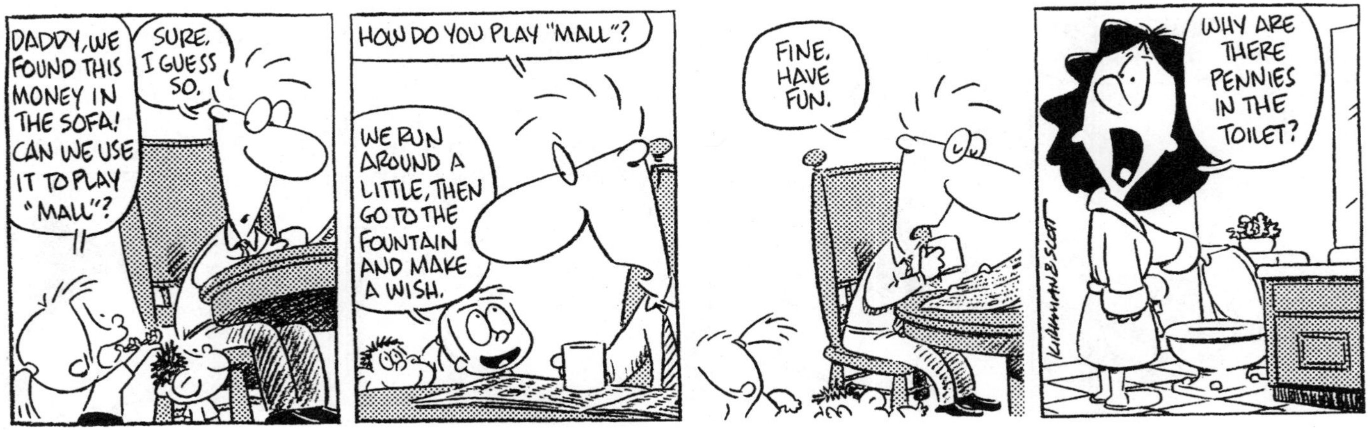
DADDY, WE FOUND THIS MONEY IN THE SOFA! CAN WE USE IT TO PLAY "MALL"?
SURE. I GUESS SO.
HOW DO YOU PLAY "MALL"?
WE RUN AROUND A LITTLE, THEN GO TO THE FOUNTAIN AND MAKE A WISH.
FINE. HAVE FUN.
WHY ARE THERE PENNIES IN THE TOILET?
KIRKMAN & SCOTT

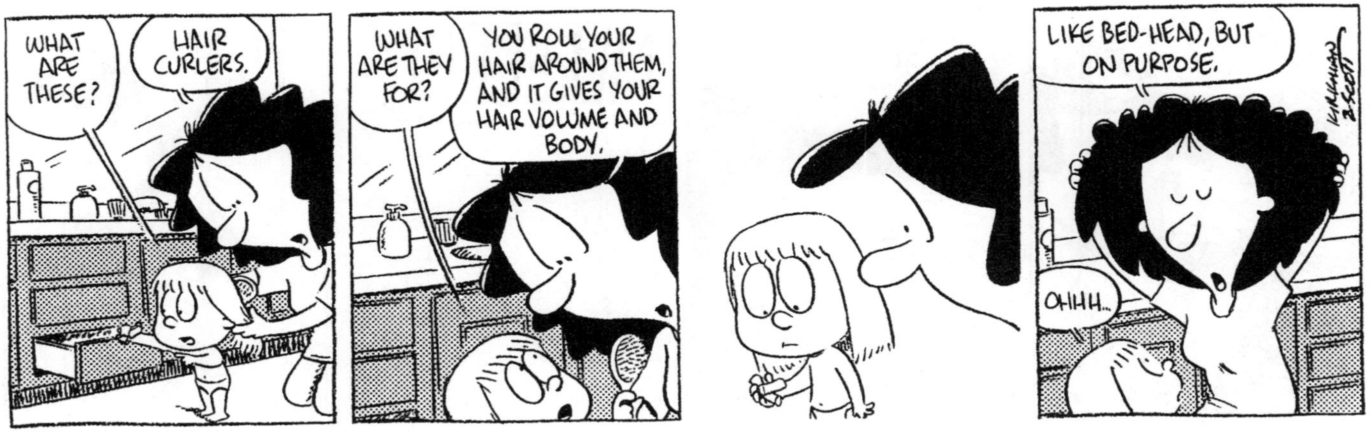
WHAT ARE THESE?
HAIR CURLERS.
WHAT ARE THEY FOR?
YOU ROLL YOUR HAIR AROUND THEM, AND IT GIVES YOUR HAIR VOLUME AND BODY.
LIKE BED-HEAD, BUT ON PURPOSE.
OHHH...
KIRKMAN & SCOTT

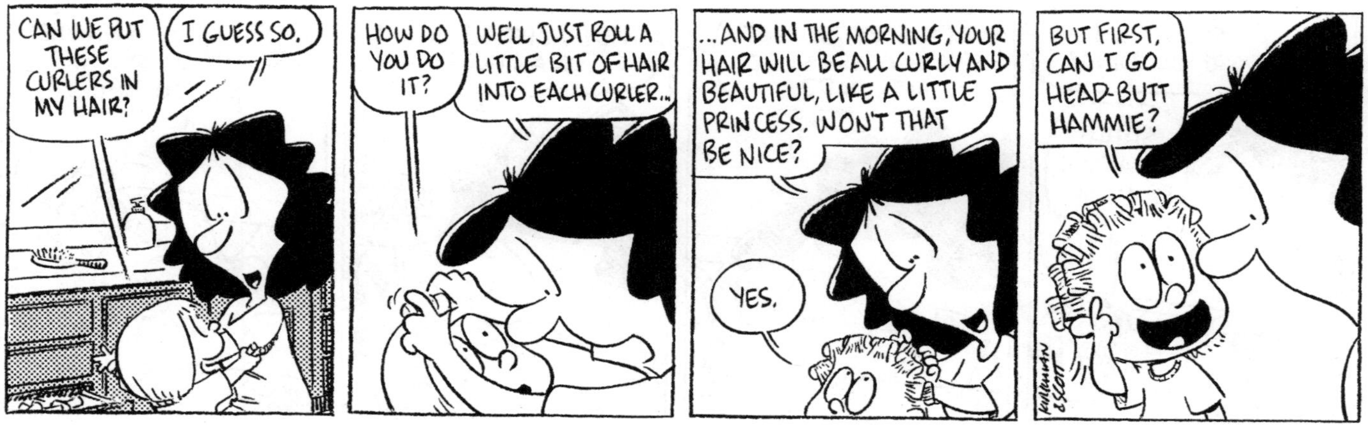
CAN WE PUT THESE CURLERS IN MY HAIR?
I GUESS SO.
HOW DO YOU DO IT?
WE'LL JUST ROLL A LITTLE BIT OF HAIR INTO EACH CURLER...
...AND IN THE MORNING, YOUR HAIR WILL BE ALL CURLY AND BEAUTIFUL, LIKE A LITTLE PRINCESS. WON'T THAT BE NICE?
YES.
BUT FIRST, CAN I GO HEAD-BUTT HAMMIE?

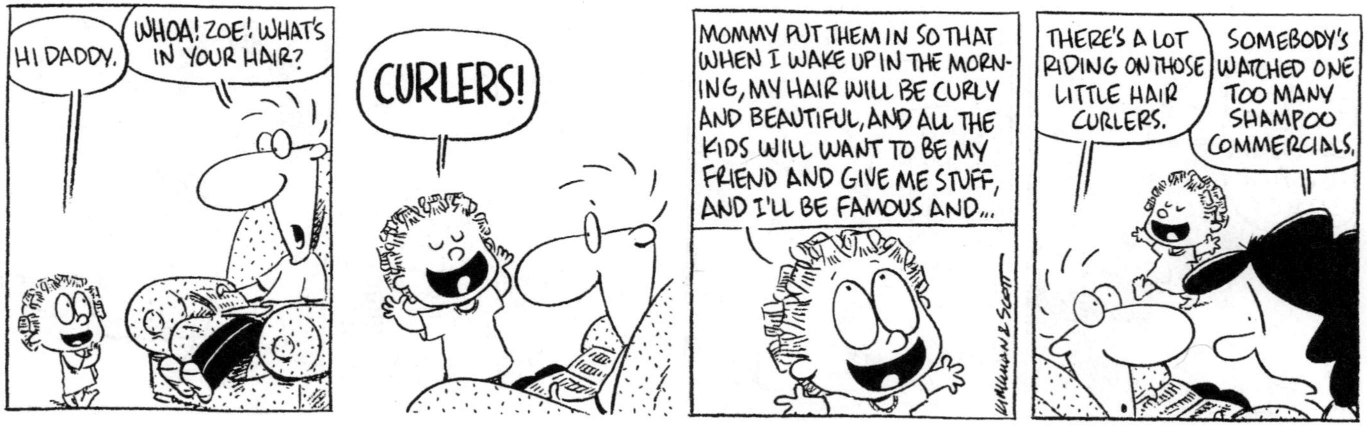
HI DADDY.
WHOA! ZOE! WHAT'S IN YOUR HAIR?
CURLERS!
MOMMY PUT THEM IN SO THAT WHEN I WAKE UP IN THE MORNING, MY HAIR WILL BE CURLY AND BEAUTIFUL, AND ALL THE KIDS WILL WANT TO BE MY FRIEND AND GIVE ME STUFF, AND I'LL BE FAMOUS AND...
THERE'S A LOT RIDING ON THOSE LITTLE HAIR CURLERS.
SOMEBODY'S WATCHED ONE TOO MANY SHAMPOO COMMERCIALS.

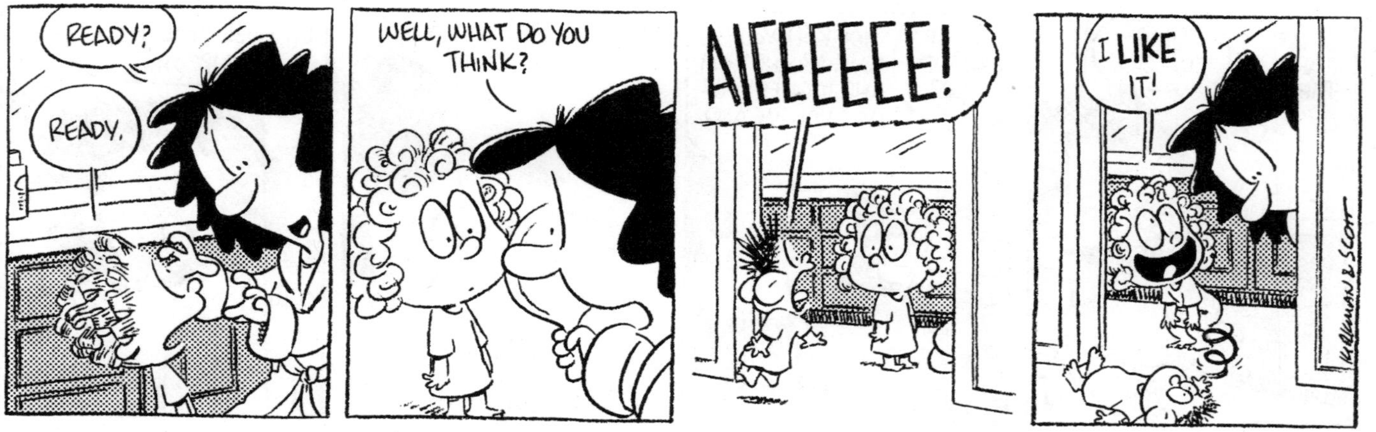
READY?
READY.
WELL, WHAT DO YOU THINK?
AIEEEEEE!
I LIKE IT!

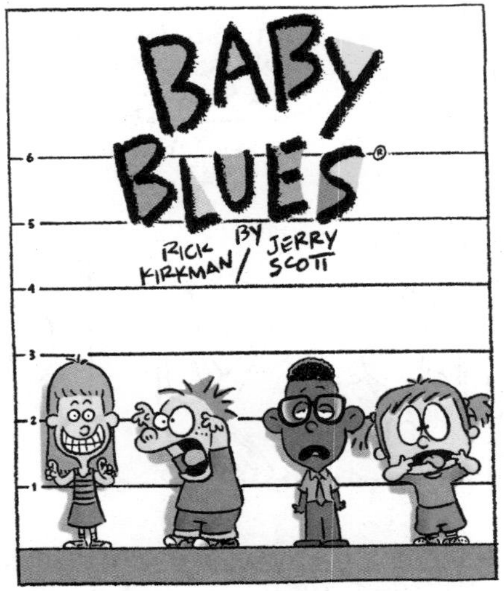
BABY BLUES®
RICK KIRKMAN / BY JERRY SCOTT

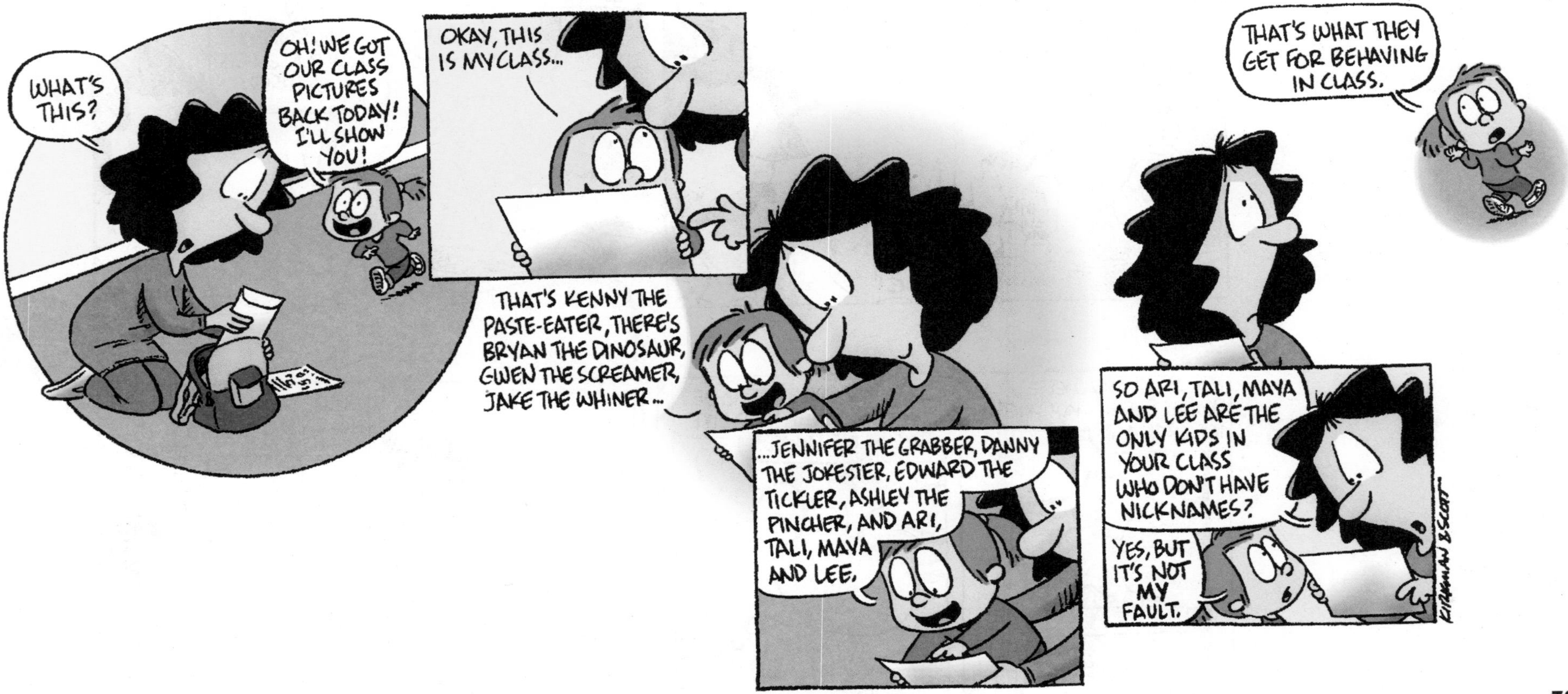
WHAT'S THIS?
OH! WE GOT OUR CLASS PICTURES BACK TODAY! I'LL SHOW YOU!
OKAY, THIS IS MY CLASS...
THAT'S KENNY THE PASTE-EATER, THERE'S BRYAN THE DINOSAUR, GWEN THE SCREAMER, JAKE THE WHINER...
...JENNIFER THE GRABBER, DANNY THE JOKESTER, EDWARD THE TICKLER, ASHLEY THE PINCHER, AND ARI, TALI, MAYA AND LEE.
SO ARI, TALI, MAYA AND LEE ARE THE ONLY KIDS IN YOUR CLASS WHO DON'T HAVE NICKNAMES?
YES, BUT IT'S NOT MY FAULT.
THAT'S WHAT THEY GET FOR BEHAVING IN CLASS.

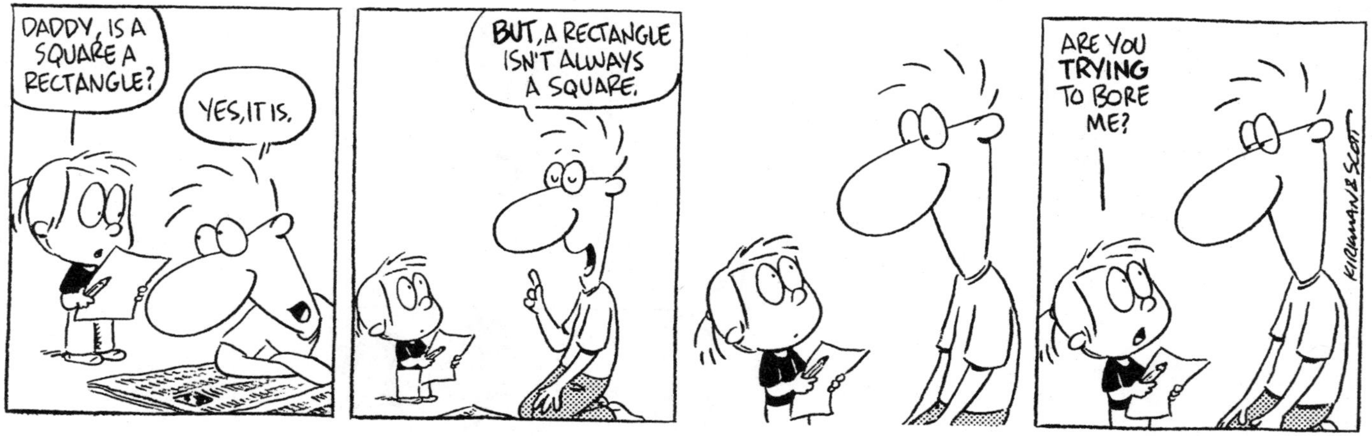
DADDY, IS A SQUARE A RECTANGLE?
YES, IT IS.
BUT, A RECTANGLE ISN'T ALWAYS A SQUARE.
ARE YOU TRYING TO BORE ME?
KIRKMAN & SCOTT

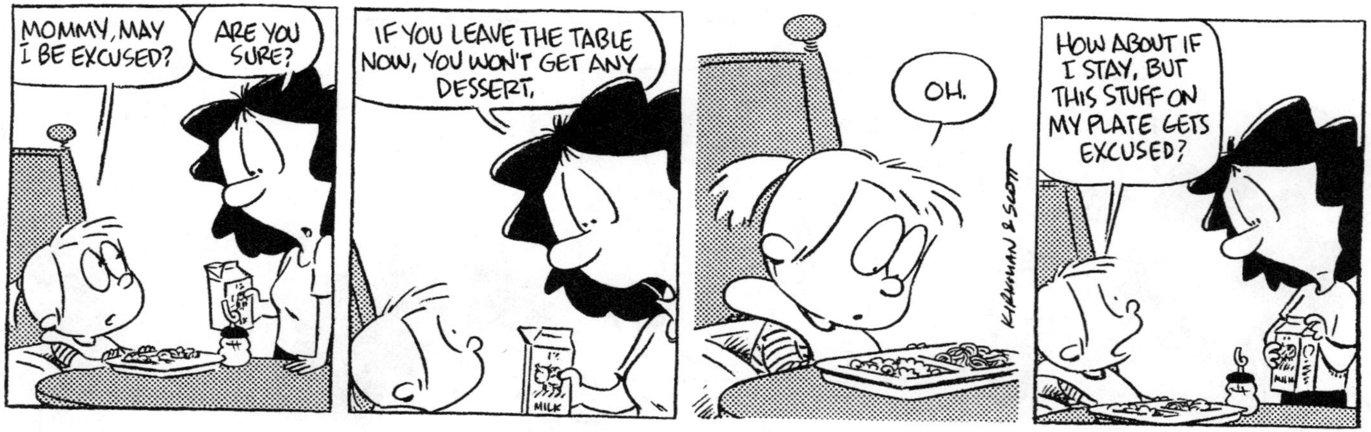
MOMMY, MAY I BE EXCUSED?
ARE YOU SURE?
IF YOU LEAVE THE TABLE NOW, YOU WON'T GET ANY DESSERT.
OH.
KIRKMAN & SCOTT
HOW ABOUT IF I STAY, BUT THIS STUFF ON MY PLATE GETS EXCUSED?

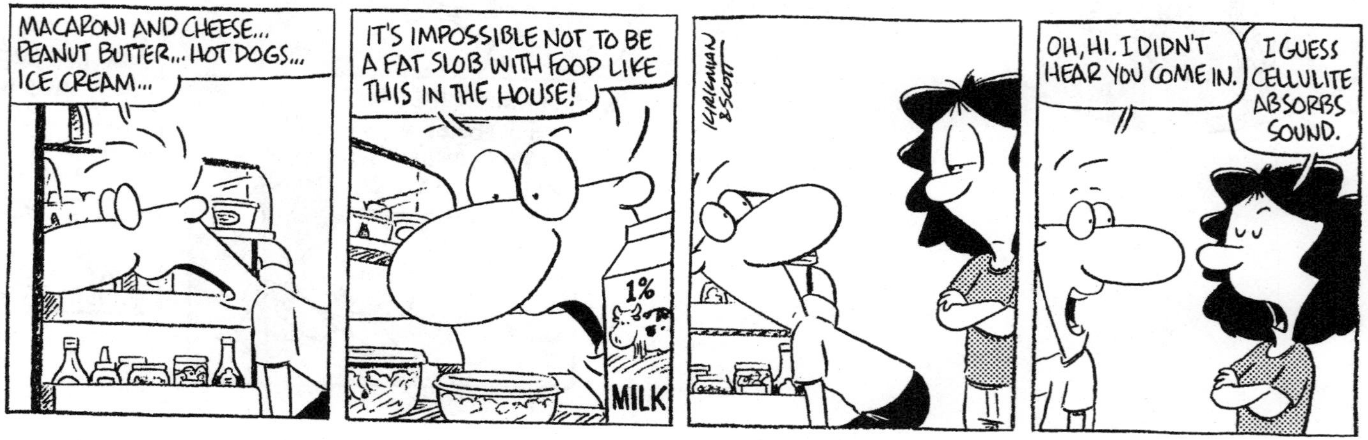
MACARONI AND CHEESE... PEANUT BUTTER... HOT DOGS... ICE CREAM...
IT'S IMPOSSIBLE NOT TO BE A FAT SLOB WITH FOOD LIKE THIS IN THE HOUSE!
1%
MILK
KIRKMAN & SCOTT
OH, HI. I DIDN'T HEAR YOU COME IN.
I GUESS CELLULITE ABSORBS SOUND.

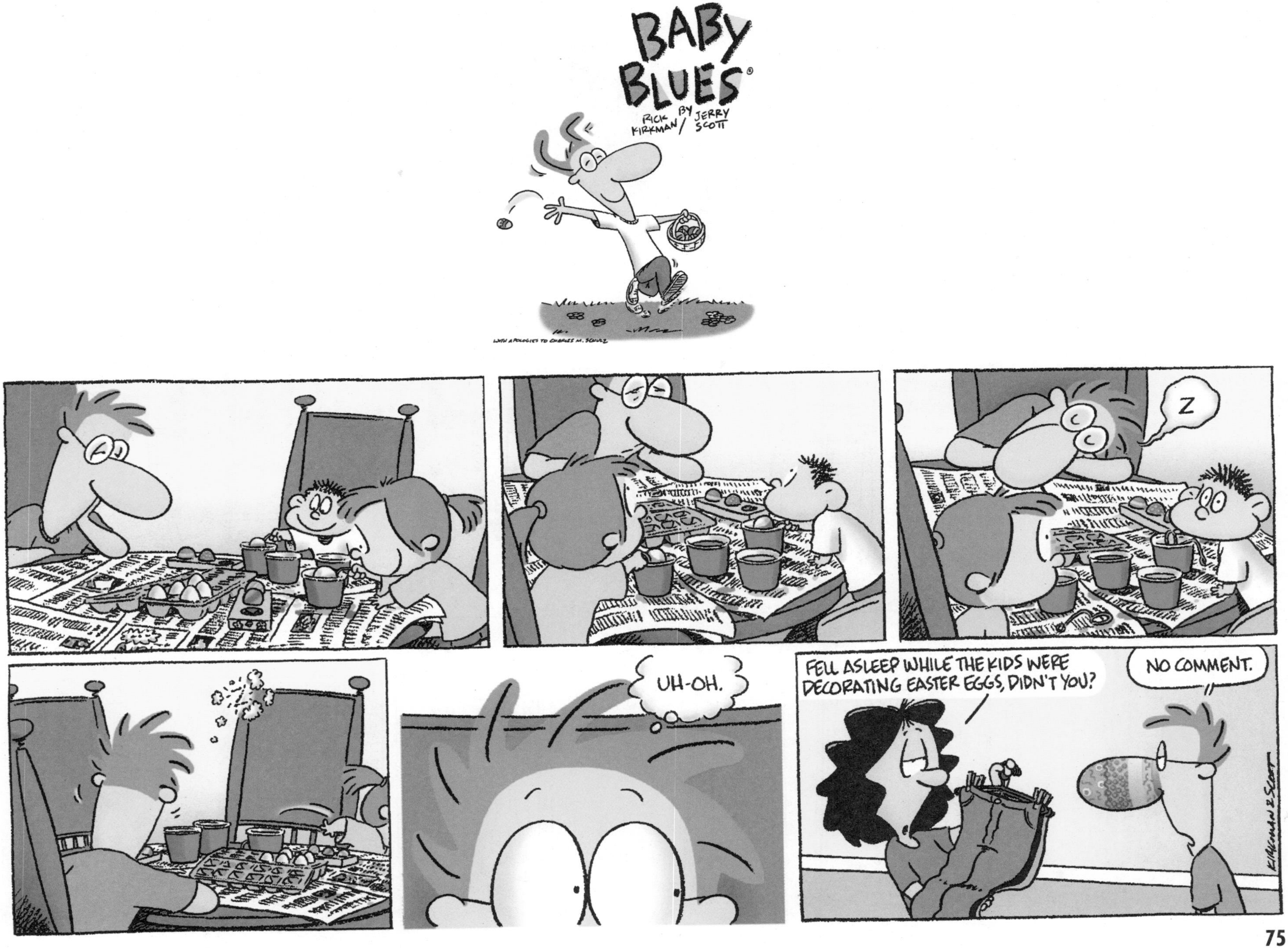
BABY BLUES®
BY RICK KIRKMAN / JERRY SCOTT
WITH APOLOGIES TO CHARLES M. SCHULZ
Z
UH-OH.
FELL ASLEEP WHILE THE KIDS WERE DECORATING EASTER EGGS, DIDN'T YOU?
NO COMMENT.
KIRKMAN & SCOTT

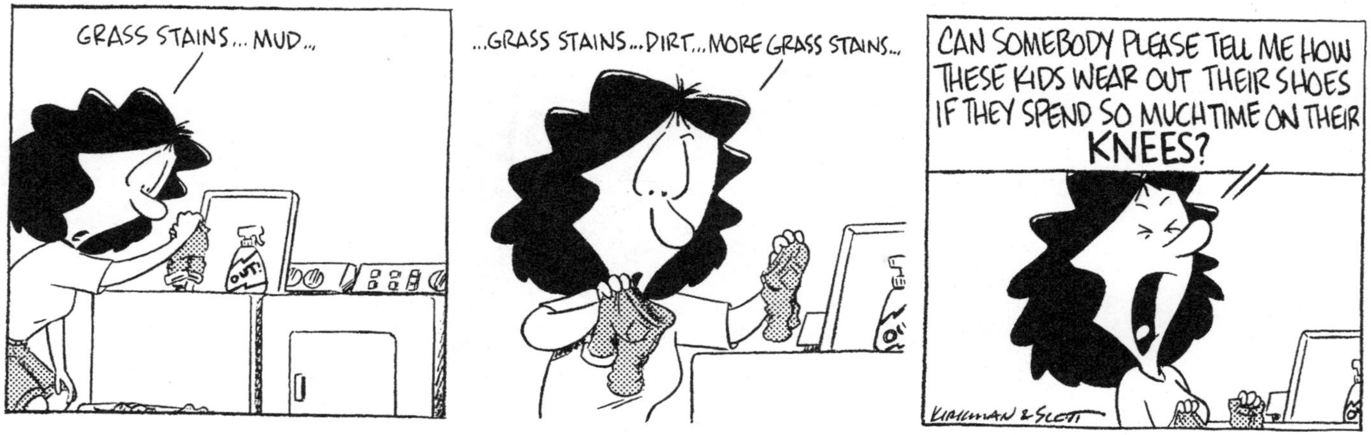
GRASS STAINS... MUD...
...GRASS STAINS... DIRT... MORE GRASS STAINS...
CAN SOMEBODY PLEASE TELL ME HOW THESE KIDS WEAR OUT THEIR SHOES IF THEY SPEND SO MUCH TIME ON THEIR KNEES?
OUT!
KIRKMAN & SCOTT

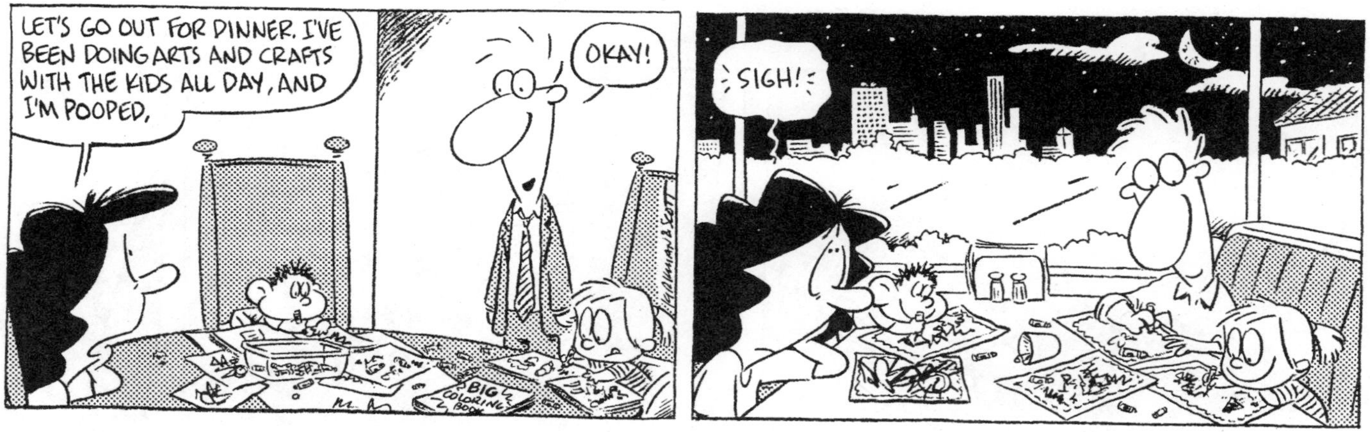
LET'S GO OUT FOR DINNER. I'VE BEEN DOING ARTS AND CRAFTS WITH THE KIDS ALL DAY, AND I'M POOPED.
OKAY!
BIG COLORING BOOK
KIRKMAN & SCOTT
SIGH!

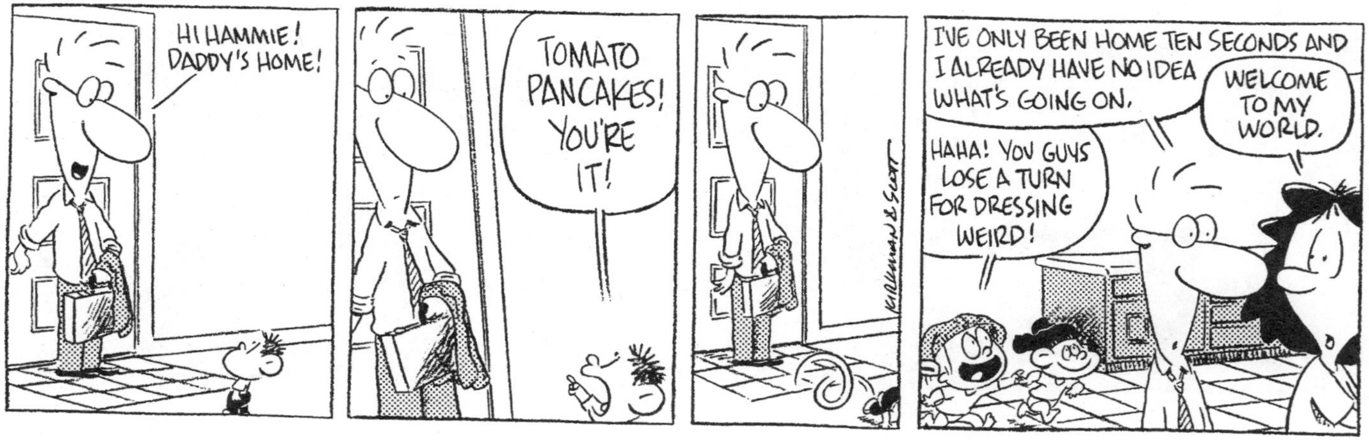
HI HAMMIE! DADDY'S HOME!
TOMATO PANCAKES! YOU'RE IT!
KIRKMAN & SCOTT
I'VE ONLY BEEN HOME TEN SECONDS AND I ALREADY HAVE NO IDEA WHAT'S GOING ON.
WELCOME TO MY WORLD.
HAHA! YOU GUYS LOSE A TURN FOR DRESSING WEIRD!

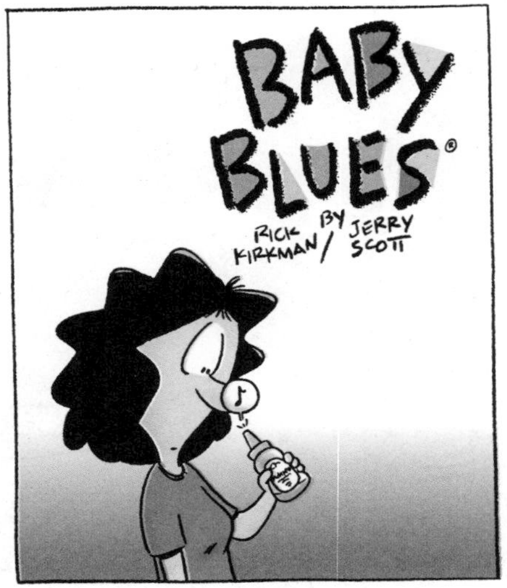
BABY BLUES®
BY RICK KIRKMAN / JERRY SCOTT

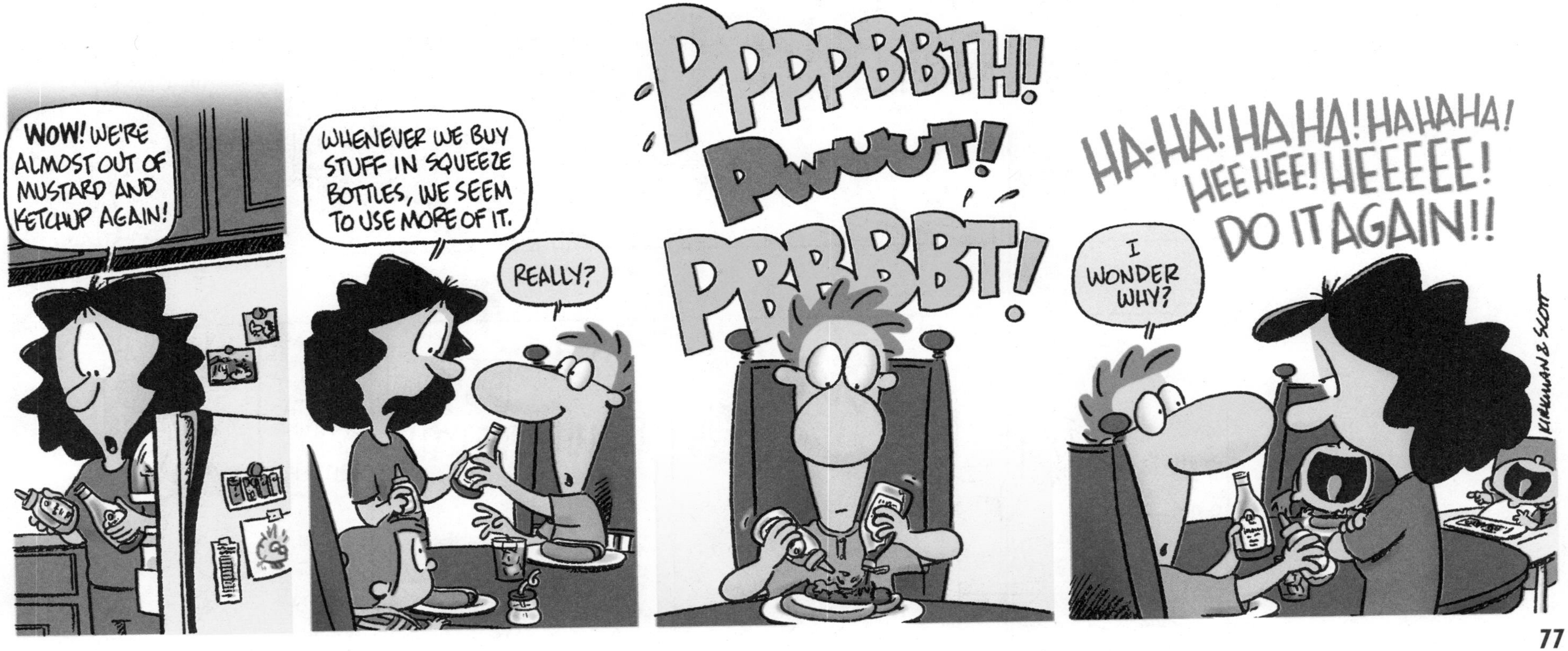
WOW! WE'RE ALMOST OUT OF MUSTARD AND KETCHUP AGAIN!
WHENEVER WE BUY STUFF IN SQUEEZE BOTTLES, WE SEEM TO USE MORE OF IT.
REALLY?
PPPPBBTH!
PWUUT!
PBBBBT!
I WONDER WHY?
HA-HA! HA HA! HA HA HA! HEE HEE! HEEEEE! DO IT AGAIN!!
KIRKMAN & SCOTT

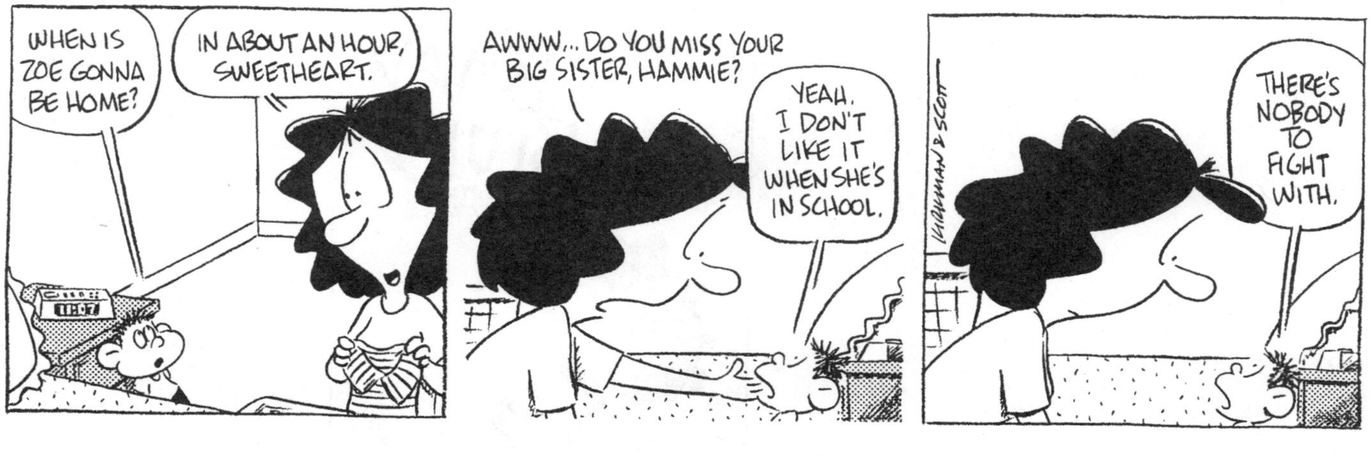
WHEN IS ZOE GONNA BE HOME?
IN ABOUT AN HOUR, SWEETHEART.
AWWW... DO YOU MISS YOUR BIG SISTER, HAMMIE?
YEAH. I DON'T LIKE IT WHEN SHE'S IN SCHOOL.
THERE'S NOBODY TO FIGHT WITH.
KIRKMAN & SCOTT

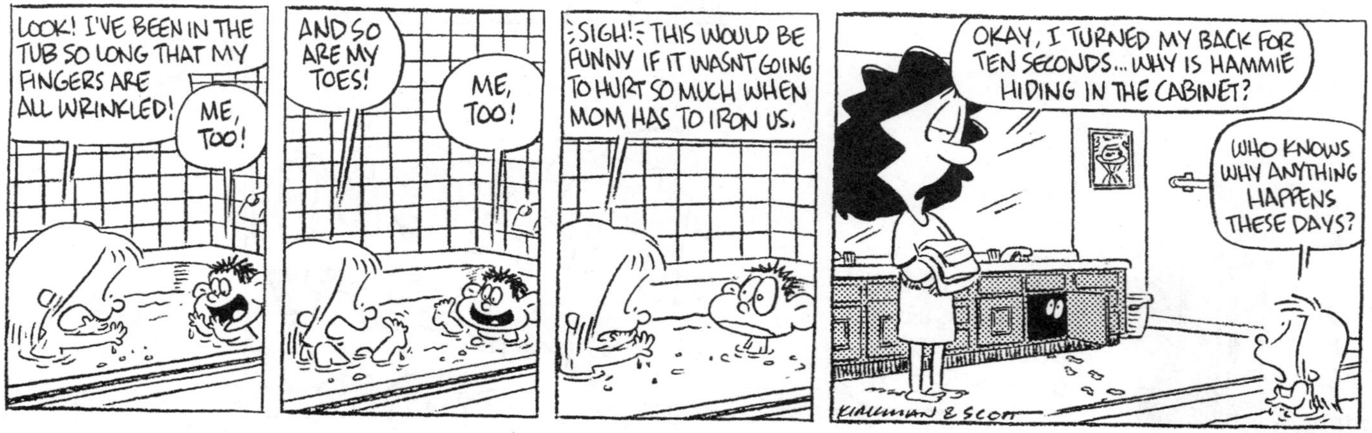
LOOK! I'VE BEEN IN THE TUB SO LONG THAT MY FINGERS ARE ALL WRINKLED!
ME, TOO!
AND SO ARE MY TOES!
ME, TOO!
SIGH! THIS WOULD BE FUNNY IF IT WASN'T GOING TO HURT SO MUCH WHEN MOM HAS TO IRON US.
OKAY, I TURNED MY BACK FOR TEN SECONDS... WHY IS HAMMIE HIDING IN THE CABINET?
WHO KNOWS WHY ANYTHING HAPPENS THESE DAYS?
KIRKMAN & SCOTT

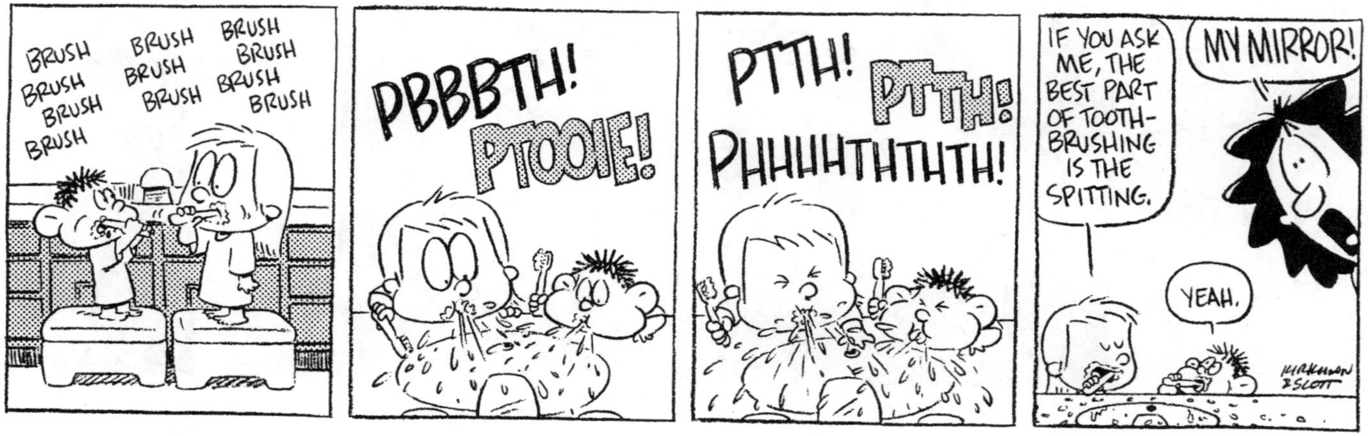
BRUSH BRUSH BRUSH BRUSH
BRUSH BRUSH BRUSH
BRUSH BRUSH BRUSH BRUSH
PBBBTH! PTOOIE!
PTTH! PTTH! PHHHHTHTHTH!
IF YOU ASK ME, THE BEST PART OF TOOTH-BRUSHING IS THE SPITTING.
MY MIRROR!
YEAH.
KIRKMAN & SCOTT

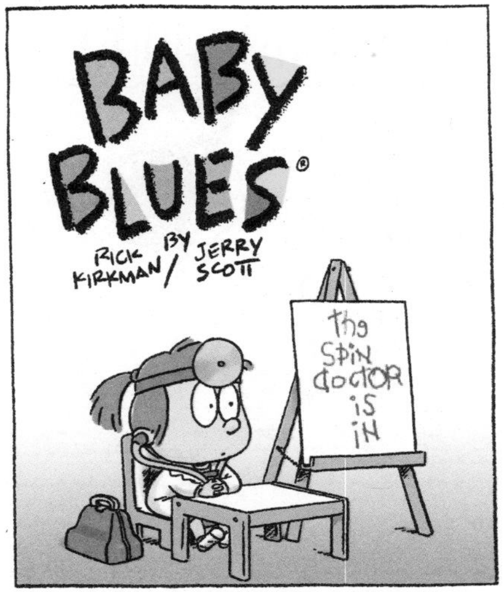
BABY BLUES®
BY RICK KIRKMAN / JERRY SCOTT
the SPIN doctor is iN

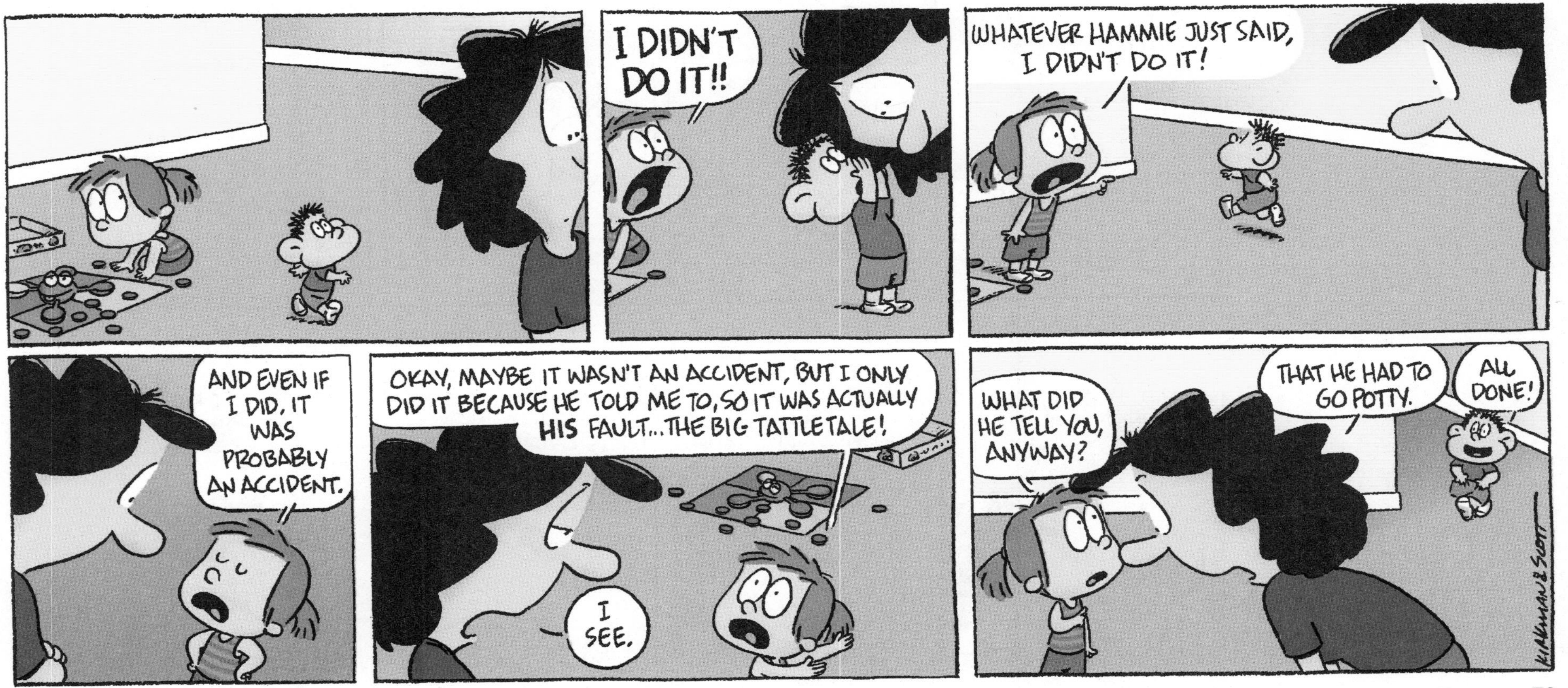
I DIDN'T DO IT!!
WHATEVER HAMMIE JUST SAID, I DIDN'T DO IT!
AND EVEN IF I DID, IT WAS PROBABLY AN ACCIDENT.
OKAY, MAYBE IT WASN'T AN ACCIDENT, BUT I ONLY DID IT BECAUSE HE TOLD ME TO, SO IT WAS ACTUALLY **HIS** FAULT... THE BIG TATTLETALE!
I SEE.
WHAT DID HE TELL YOU, ANYWAY?
THAT HE HAD TO GO POTTY.
ALL DONE!
KIRKMAN & SCOTT

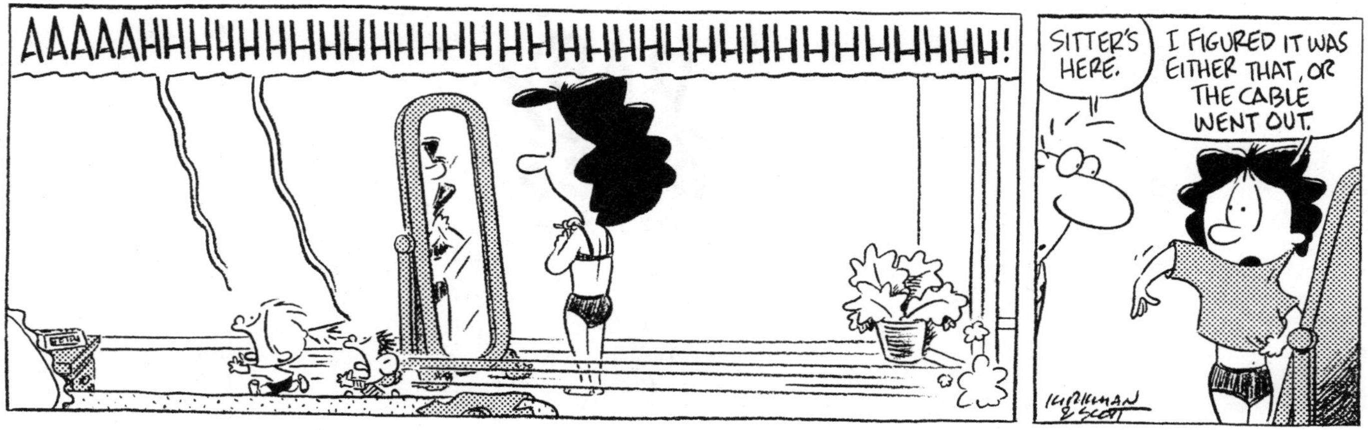
AAAAAHHHHHHHHHHHHHHHHHHHHHHHHHHHHHHHHHHHHH!
SITTER'S HERE.
I FIGURED IT WAS EITHER THAT, OR THE CABLE WENT OUT.

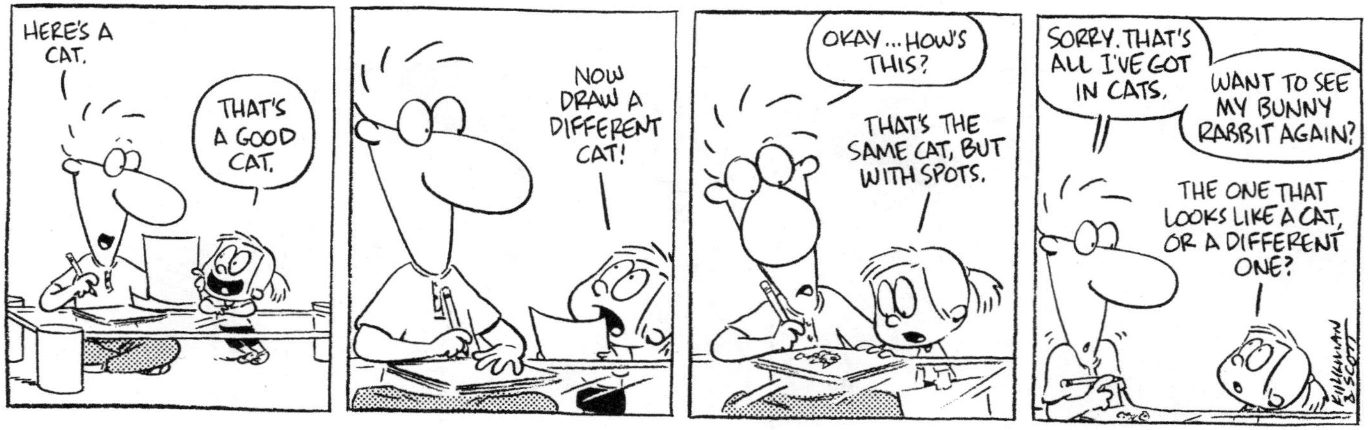
HERE'S A CAT.
THAT'S A GOOD CAT.
NOW DRAW A DIFFERENT CAT!
OKAY... HOW'S THIS?
THAT'S THE SAME CAT, BUT WITH SPOTS.
SORRY. THAT'S ALL I'VE GOT IN CATS.
WANT TO SEE MY BUNNY RABBIT AGAIN?
THE ONE THAT LOOKS LIKE A CAT, OR A DIFFERENT ONE?

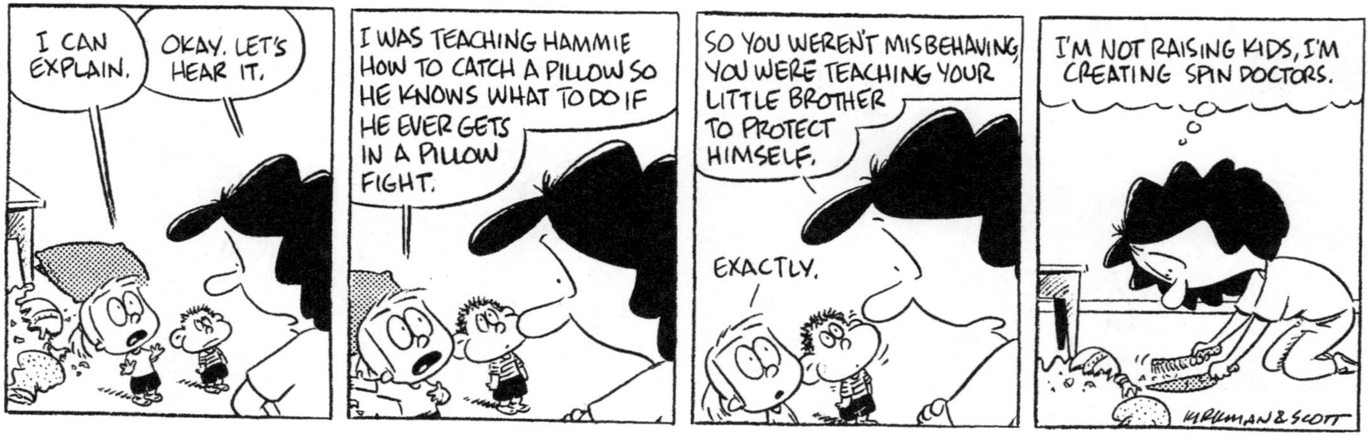
I CAN EXPLAIN.
OKAY. LET'S HEAR IT.
I WAS TEACHING HAMMIE HOW TO CATCH A PILLOW SO HE KNOWS WHAT TO DO IF HE EVER GETS IN A PILLOW FIGHT.
SO YOU WEREN'T MISBEHAVING, YOU WERE TEACHING YOUR LITTLE BROTHER TO PROTECT HIMSELF.
EXACTLY.
I'M NOT RAISING KIDS, I'M CREATING SPIN DOCTORS.

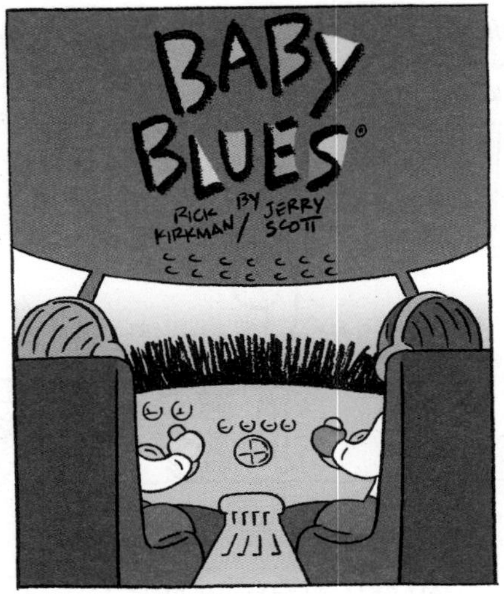
BABY BLUES®
RICK KIRKMAN / BY JERRY SCOTT

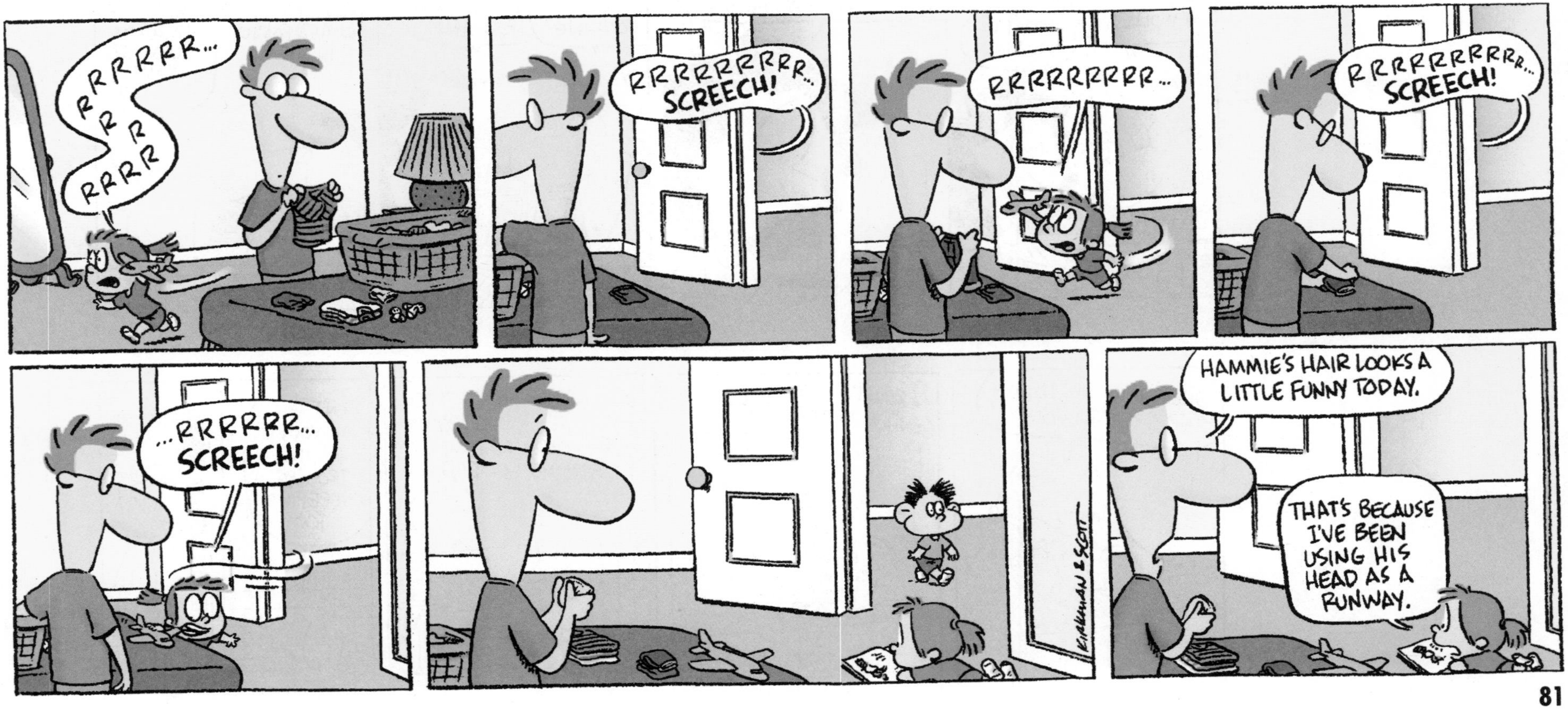
RRRRRR... R R R RRRR
RRRRRRRRRR... SCREECH!
RRRRRRRRR...
RRRRRRRRRR... SCREECH!
...RRRRRR... SCREECH!
KIRKMAN & SCOTT
HAMMIE'S HAIR LOOKS A LITTLE FUNNY TODAY.
THAT'S BECAUSE I'VE BEEN USING HIS HEAD AS A RUNWAY.

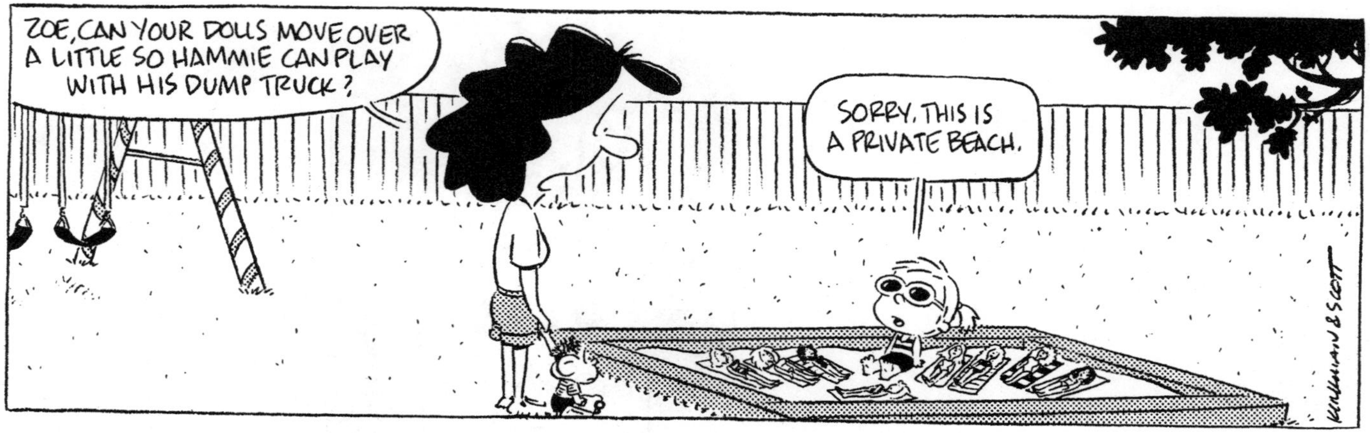
ZOE, CAN YOUR DOLLS MOVE OVER A LITTLE SO HAMMIE CAN PLAY WITH HIS DUMP TRUCK?
SORRY. THIS IS A PRIVATE BEACH.
KIRKMAN & SCOTT

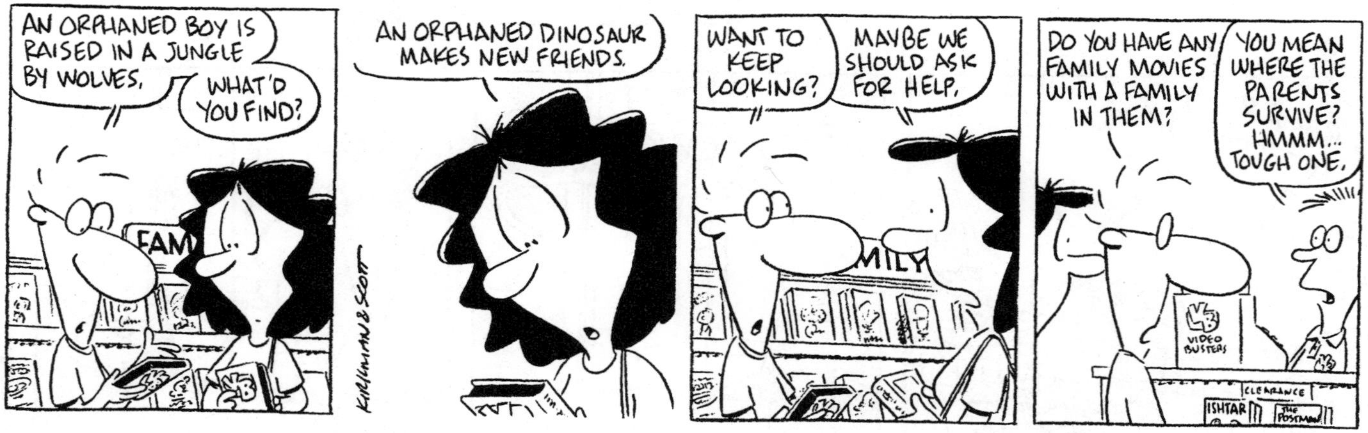
AN ORPHANED BOY IS RAISED IN A JUNGLE BY WOLVES.
WHAT'D YOU FIND?
FAM
KIRKMAN & SCOTT
AN ORPHANED DINOSAUR MAKES NEW FRIENDS.
WANT TO KEEP LOOKING?
MAYBE WE SHOULD ASK FOR HELP.
MILY
DO YOU HAVE ANY FAMILY MOVIES WITH A FAMILY IN THEM?
YOU MEAN WHERE THE PARENTS SURVIVE? HMMM... TOUGH ONE.
VIDEO BUSTERS
CLEARANCE
ISHTAR
THE POSTMAN

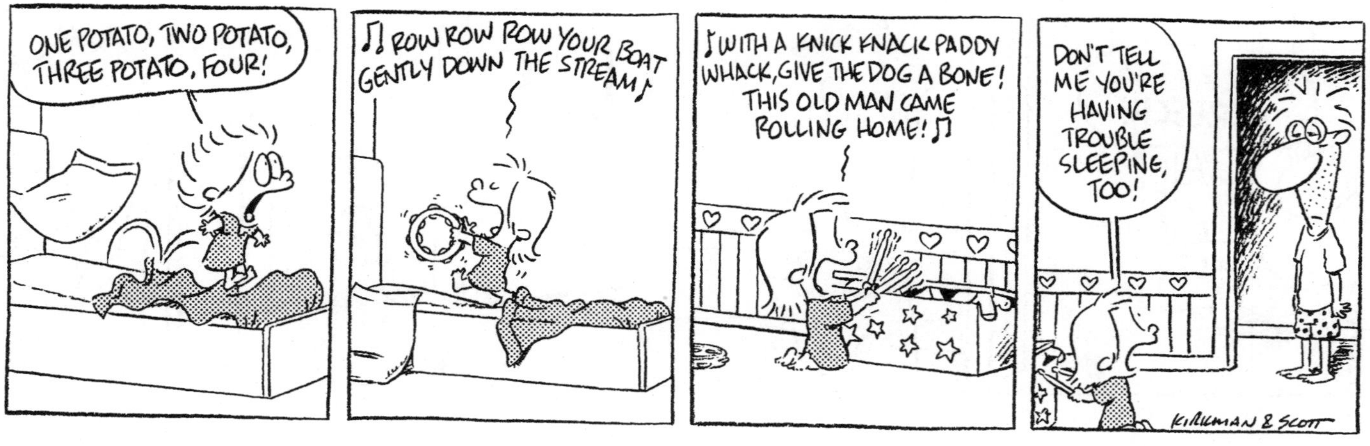
ONE POTATO, TWO POTATO, THREE POTATO, FOUR!
♫ ROW ROW ROW YOUR BOAT GENTLY DOWN THE STREAM ♪
♪ WITH A KNICK KNACK PADDY WHACK, GIVE THE DOG A BONE! THIS OLD MAN CAME ROLLING HOME! ♫
DON'T TELL ME YOU'RE HAVING TROUBLE SLEEPING, TOO!
KIRKMAN & SCOTT

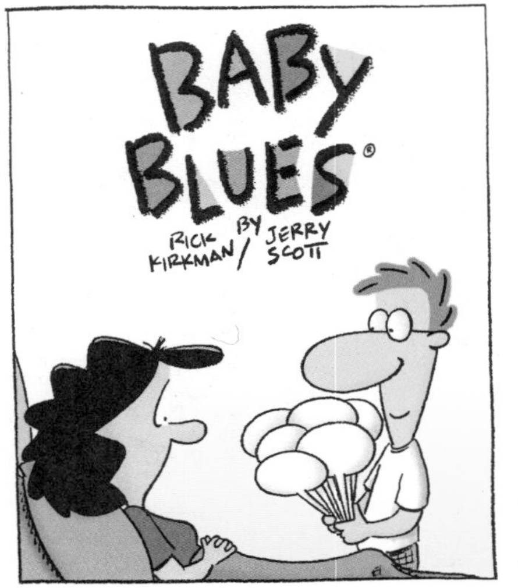
BABY BLUES®
BY RICK KIRKMAN / JERRY SCOTT

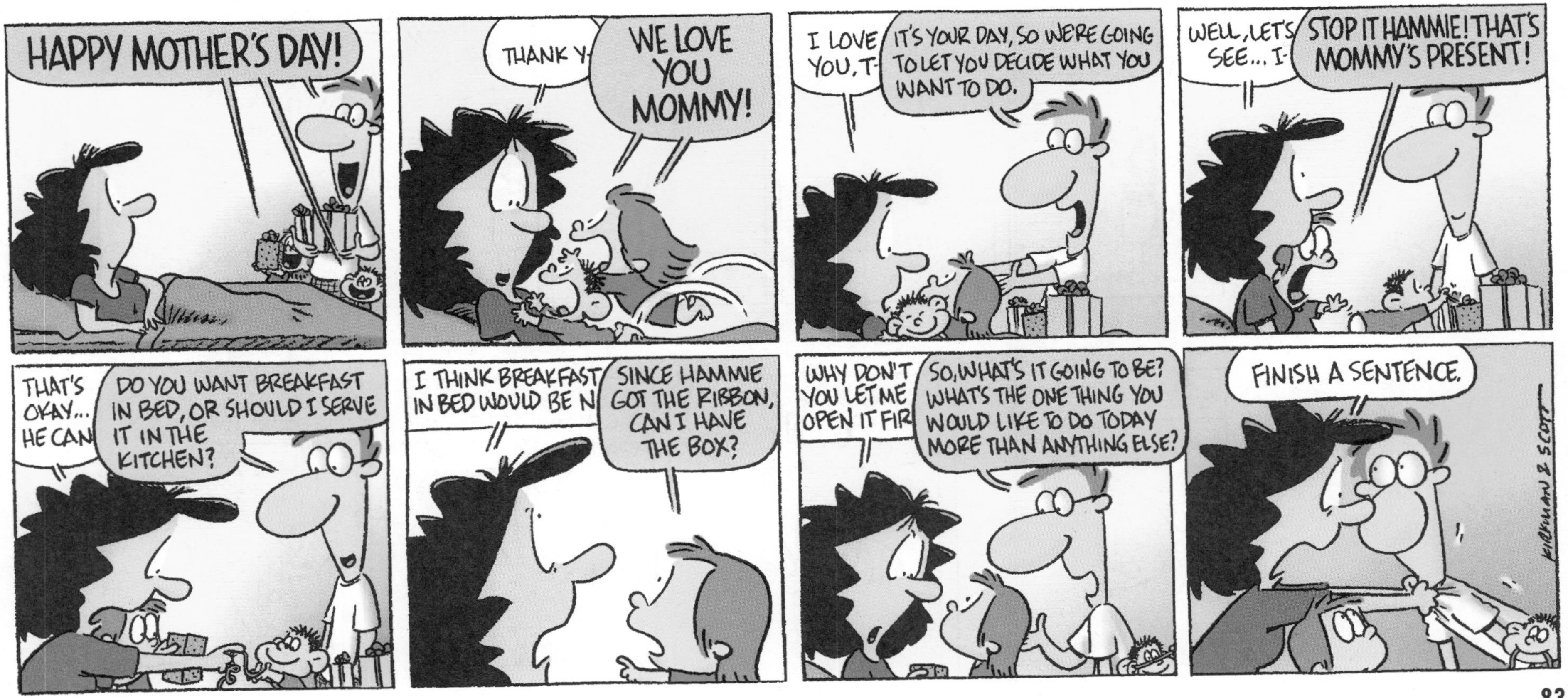
HAPPY MOTHER'S DAY!
THANK Y-
WE LOVE YOU MOMMY!
I LOVE YOU, T-
IT'S YOUR DAY, SO WE'RE GOING TO LET YOU DECIDE WHAT YOU WANT TO DO.
WELL, LET'S SEE... I-
STOP IT HAMMIE! THAT'S MOMMY'S PRESENT!
THAT'S OKAY... HE CAN
DO YOU WANT BREAKFAST IN BED, OR SHOULD I SERVE IT IN THE KITCHEN?
I THINK BREAKFAST IN BED WOULD BE N
SINCE HAMMIE GOT THE RIBBON, CAN I HAVE THE BOX?
WHY DON'T YOU LET ME OPEN IT FIR
SO, WHAT'S IT GOING TO BE? WHAT'S THE ONE THING YOU WOULD LIKE TO DO TODAY MORE THAN ANYTHING ELSE?
FINISH A SENTENCE.
KIRKMAN & SCOTT

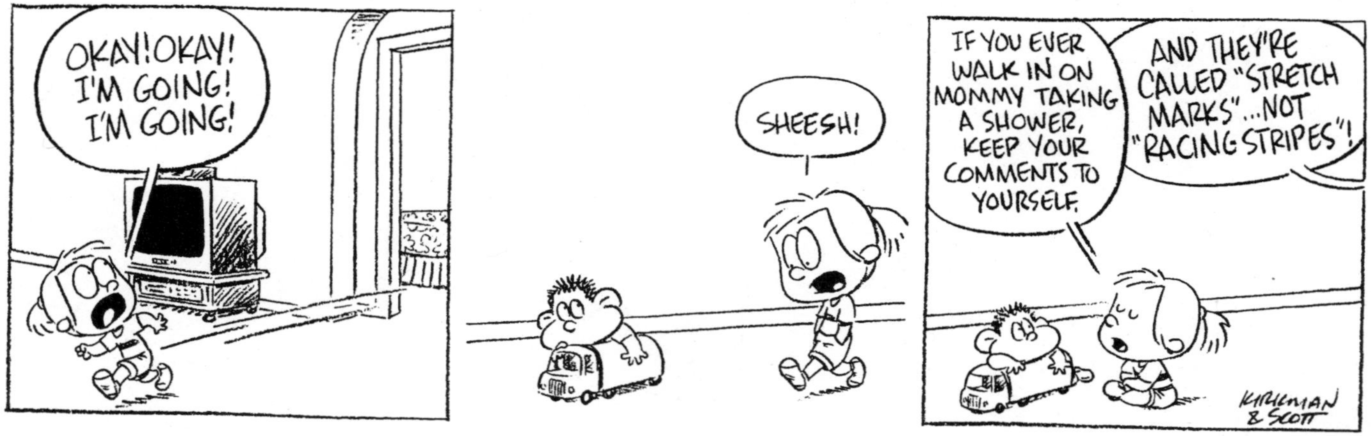
OKAY! OKAY! I'M GOING! I'M GOING!
SHEESH!
IF YOU EVER WALK IN ON MOMMY TAKING A SHOWER, KEEP YOUR COMMENTS TO YOURSELF.
AND THEY'RE CALLED "STRETCH MARKS"... NOT "RACING STRIPES"!
KIRKMAN & SCOTT

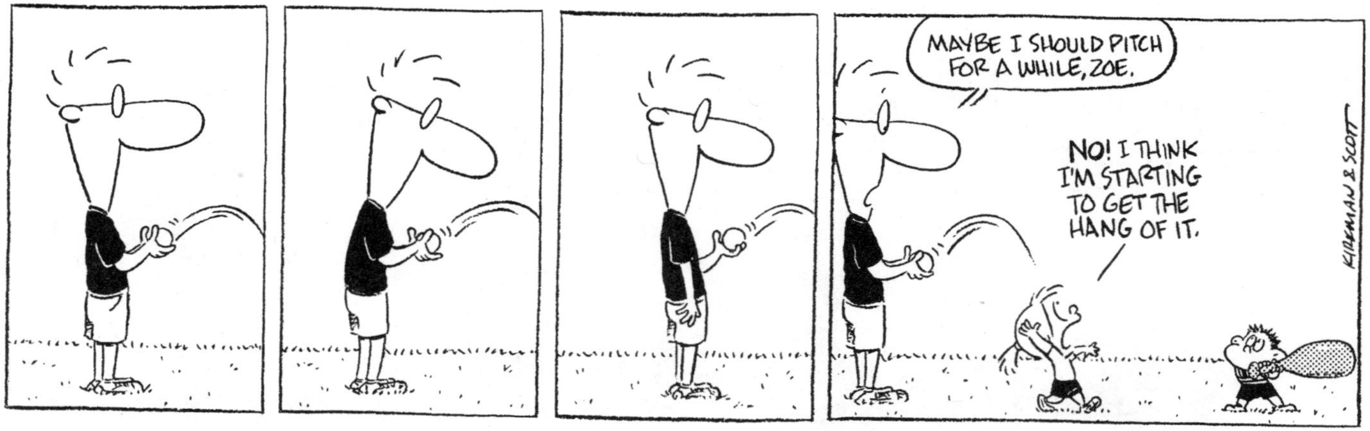
MAYBE I SHOULD PITCH FOR A WHILE, ZOE.
NO! I THINK I'M STARTING TO GET THE HANG OF IT.
KIRKMAN & SCOTT

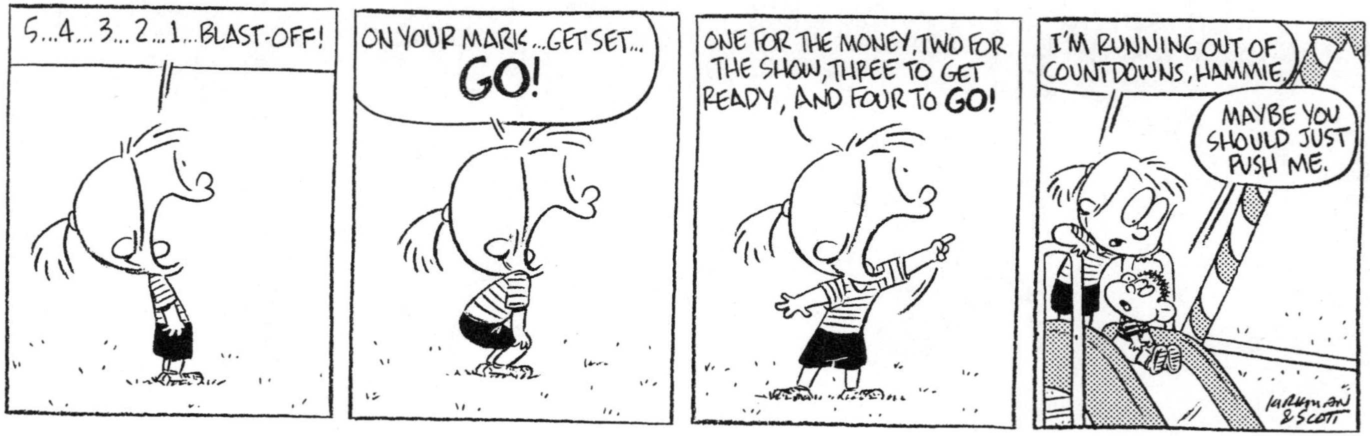
5... 4... 3... 2... 1... BLAST-OFF!
ON YOUR MARK... GET SET... GO!
ONE FOR THE MONEY, TWO FOR THE SHOW, THREE TO GET READY, AND FOUR TO GO!
I'M RUNNING OUT OF COUNTDOWNS, HAMMIE.
MAYBE YOU SHOULD JUST PUSH ME.
KIRKMAN & SCOTT

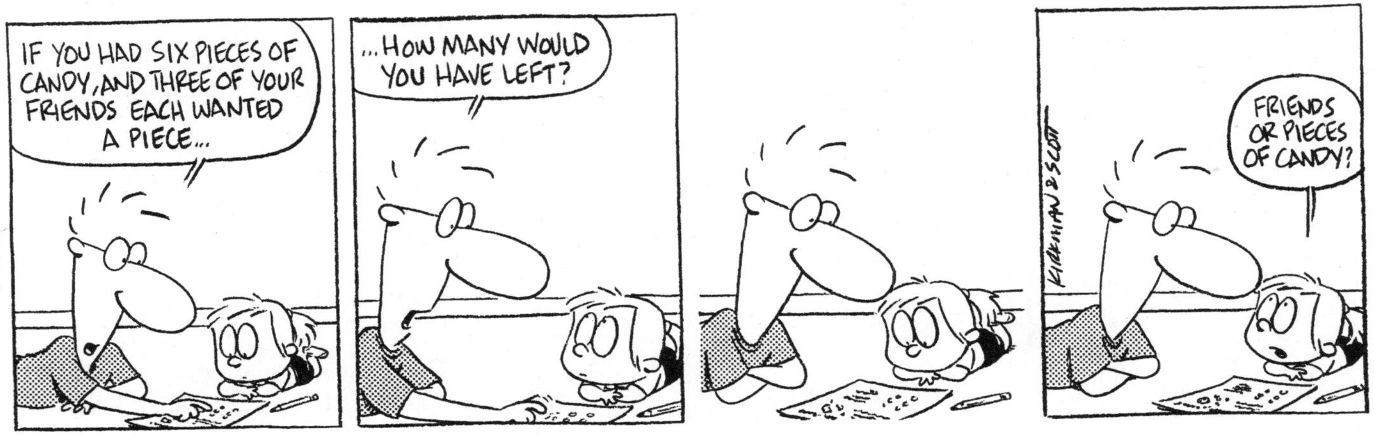
IF YOU HAD SIX PIECES OF CANDY, AND THREE OF YOUR FRIENDS EACH WANTED A PIECE...
...HOW MANY WOULD YOU HAVE LEFT?
KIRKMAN & SCOTT
FRIENDS OR PIECES OF CANDY?

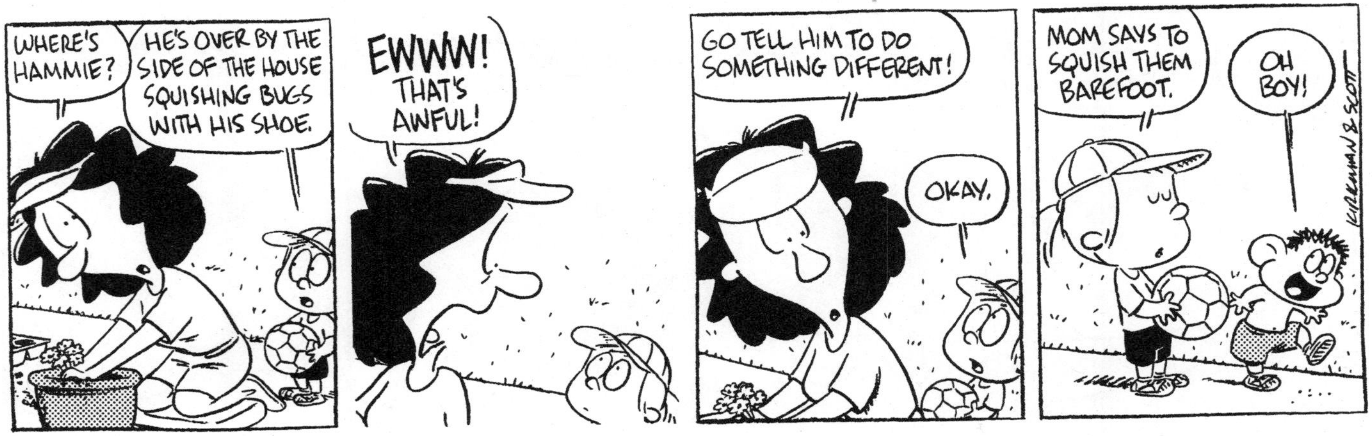
WHERE'S HAMMIE?
HE'S OVER BY THE SIDE OF THE HOUSE SQUISHING BUGS WITH HIS SHOE.
EWWW! THAT'S AWFUL!
GO TELL HIM TO DO SOMETHING DIFFERENT!
OKAY.
MOM SAYS TO SQUISH THEM BAREFOOT.
OH BOY!
KIRKMAN & SCOTT

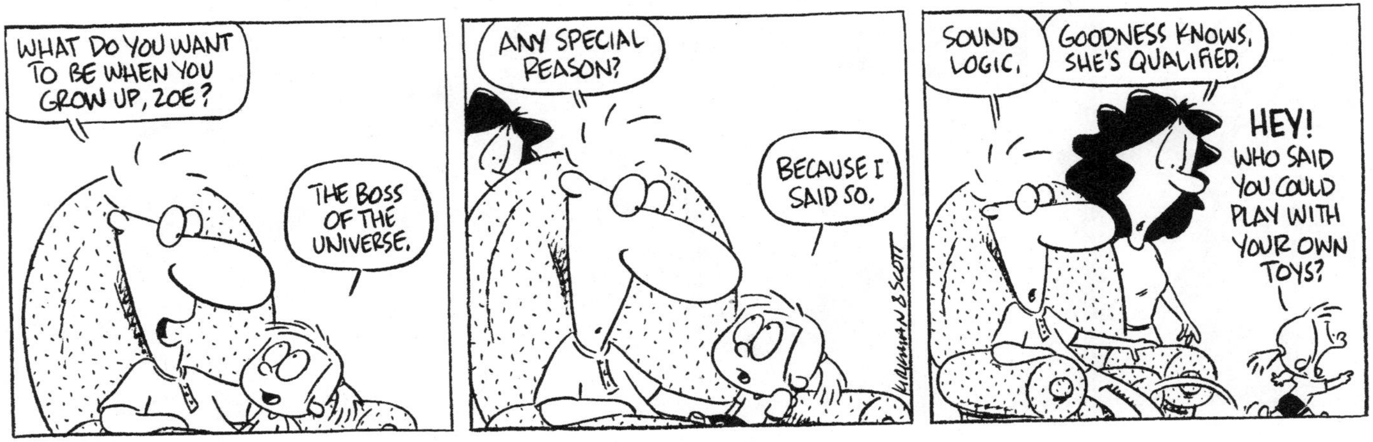
WHAT DO YOU WANT TO BE WHEN YOU GROW UP, ZOE?
THE BOSS OF THE UNIVERSE.
ANY SPECIAL REASON?
BECAUSE I SAID SO.
KIRKMAN & SCOTT
SOUND LOGIC.
GOODNESS KNOWS, SHE'S QUALIFIED.
HEY! WHO SAID YOU COULD PLAY WITH YOUR OWN TOYS?

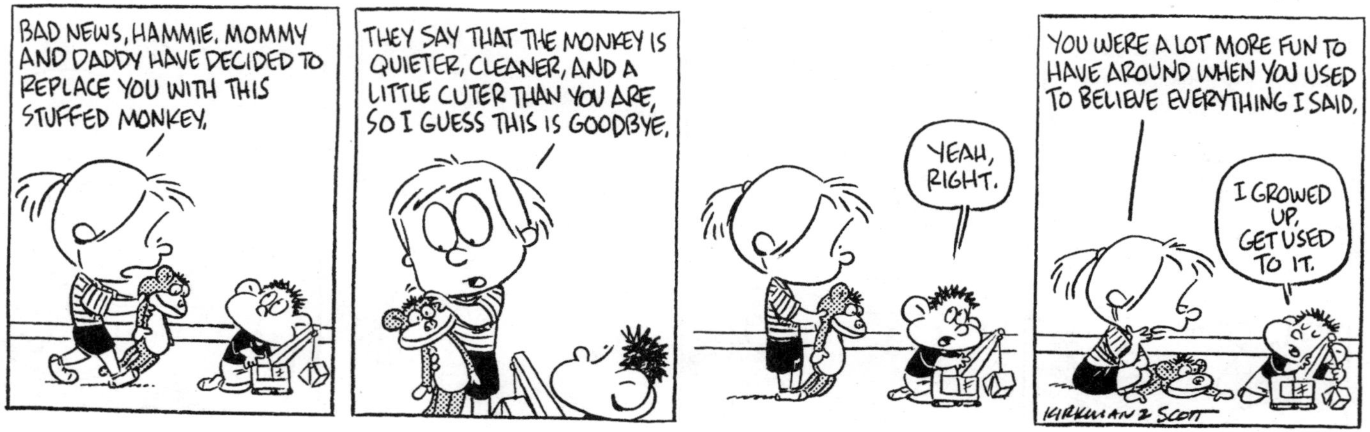
BAD NEWS, HAMMIE. MOMMY AND DADDY HAVE DECIDED TO REPLACE YOU WITH THIS STUFFED MONKEY.
THEY SAY THAT THE MONKEY IS QUIETER, CLEANER, AND A LITTLE CUTER THAN YOU ARE, SO I GUESS THIS IS GOODBYE.
YEAH, RIGHT.
YOU WERE A LOT MORE FUN TO HAVE AROUND WHEN YOU USED TO BELIEVE EVERYTHING I SAID.
I GROWED UP. GET USED TO IT.
KIRKMAN & SCOTT

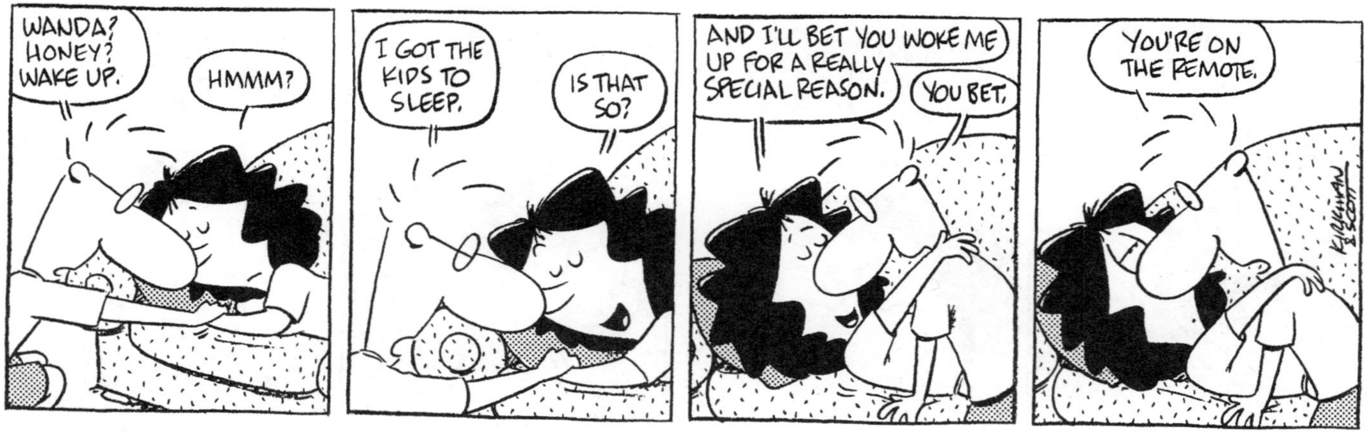
WANDA? HONEY? WAKE UP.
HMMM?
I GOT THE KIDS TO SLEEP.
IS THAT SO?
AND I'LL BET YOU WOKE ME UP FOR A REALLY SPECIAL REASON.
YOU BET.
YOU'RE ON THE REMOTE.
KIRKMAN & SCOTT

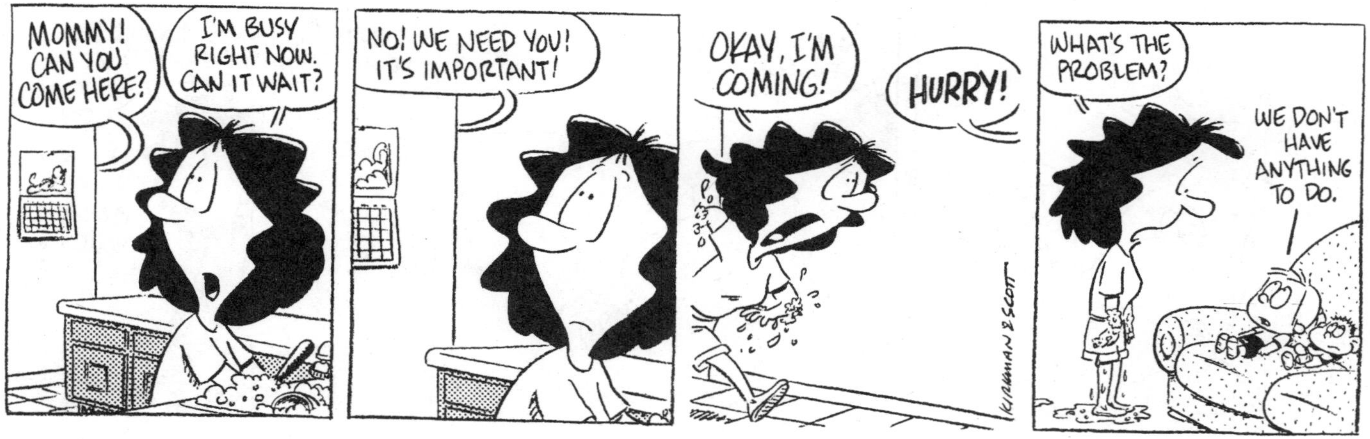
MOMMY! CAN YOU COME HERE?
I'M BUSY RIGHT NOW. CAN IT WAIT?
NO! WE NEED YOU! IT'S IMPORTANT!
OKAY, I'M COMING!
HURRY!
WHAT'S THE PROBLEM?
WE DON'T HAVE ANYTHING TO DO.
KIRKMAN & SCOTT

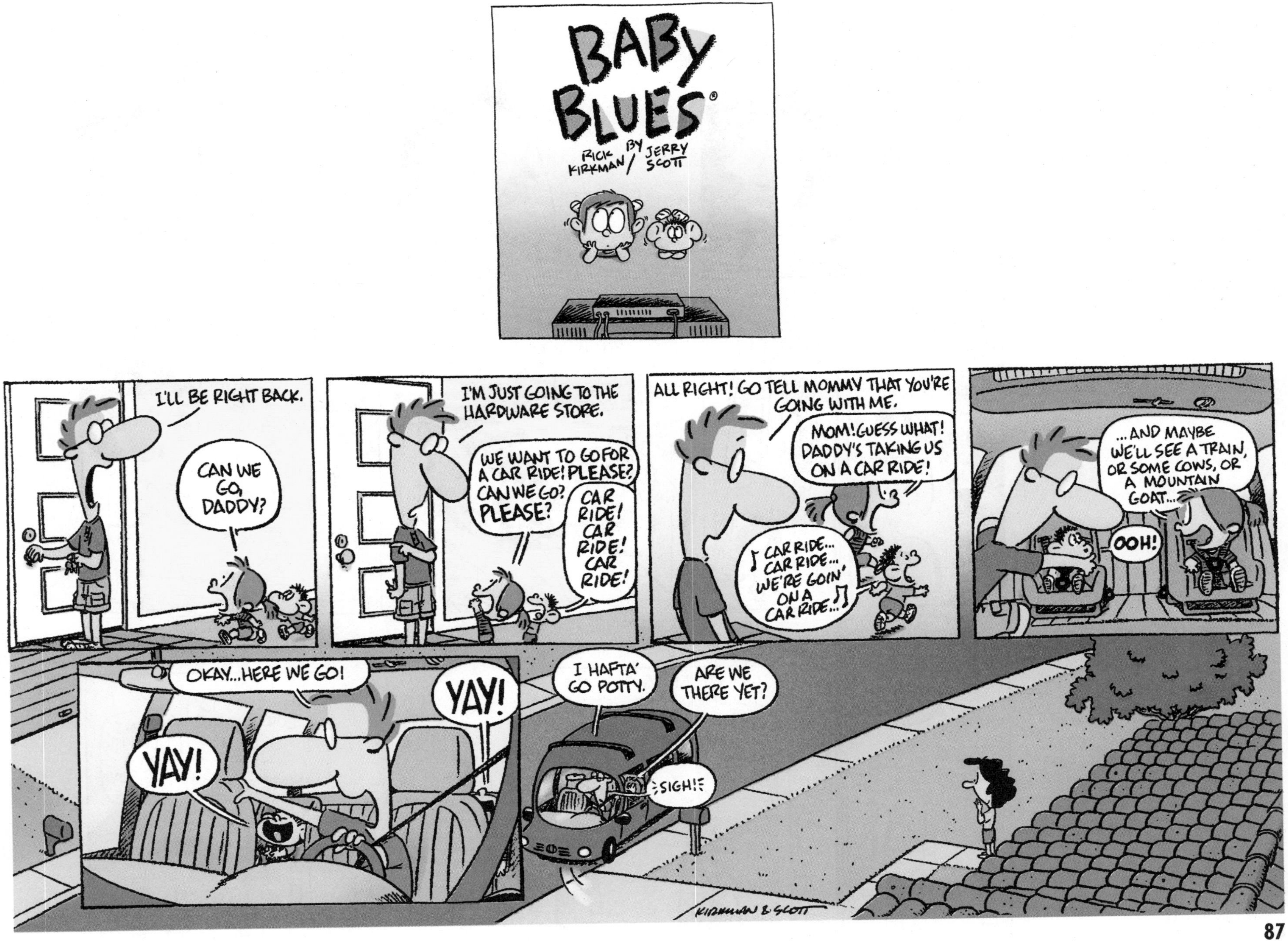
BABY BLUES®
BY RICK KIRKMAN / JERRY SCOTT
I'LL BE RIGHT BACK.
CAN WE GO, DADDY?
I'M JUST GOING TO THE HARDWARE STORE.
WE WANT TO GO FOR A CAR RIDE! PLEASE? CAN WE GO? PLEASE?
CAR RIDE! CAR RIDE! CAR RIDE!
ALL RIGHT! GO TELL MOMMY THAT YOU'RE GOING WITH ME.
MOM! GUESS WHAT! DADDY'S TAKING US ON A CAR RIDE!
♪ CAR RIDE... CAR RIDE... WE'RE GOIN' ON A CAR RIDE... ♫
...AND MAYBE WE'LL SEE A TRAIN, OR SOME COWS, OR A MOUNTAIN GOAT...
OOH!
OKAY...HERE WE GO!
YAY!
YAY!
I HAFTA' GO POTTY.
ARE WE THERE YET?
SIGH!
KIRKMAN & SCOTT

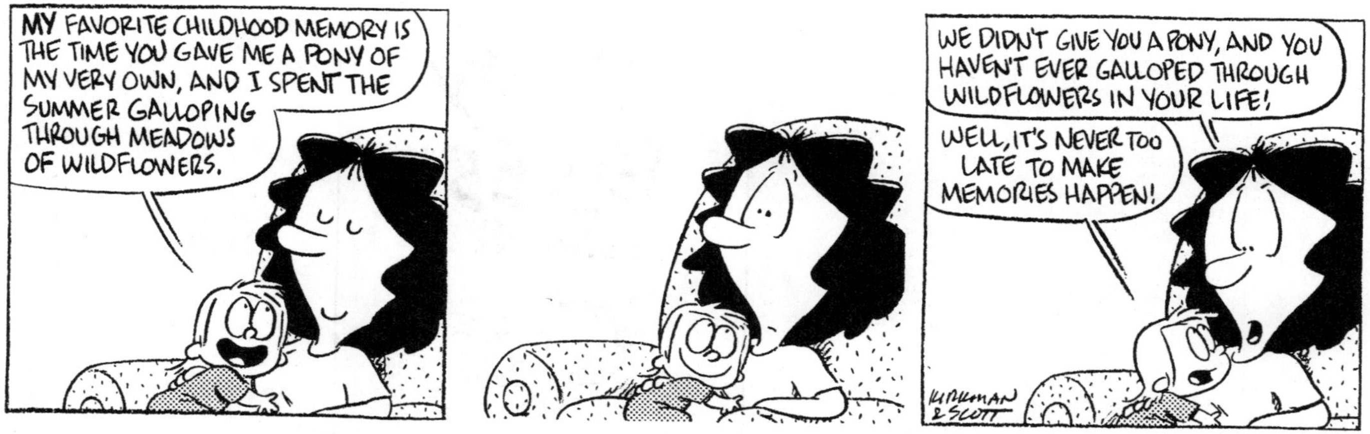
MY FAVORITE CHILDHOOD MEMORY IS THE TIME YOU GAVE ME A PONY OF MY VERY OWN, AND I SPENT THE SUMMER GALLOPING THROUGH MEADOWS OF WILDFLOWERS.
WE DIDN'T GIVE YOU A PONY, AND YOU HAVEN'T EVER GALLOPED THROUGH WILDFLOWERS IN YOUR LIFE!
WELL, IT'S NEVER TOO LATE TO MAKE MEMORIES HAPPEN!
KIRKMAN & SCOTT

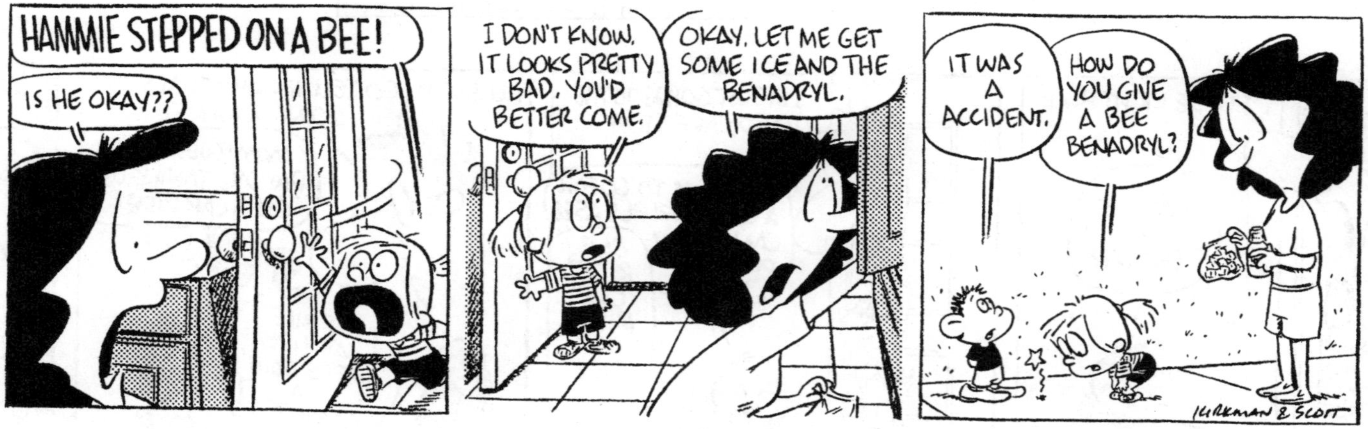
HAMMIE STEPPED ON A BEE!
IS HE OKAY??
I DON'T KNOW. IT LOOKS PRETTY BAD. YOU'D BETTER COME.
OKAY. LET ME GET SOME ICE AND THE BENADRYL.
IT WAS A ACCIDENT.
HOW DO YOU GIVE A BEE BENADRYL?
KIRKMAN & SCOTT

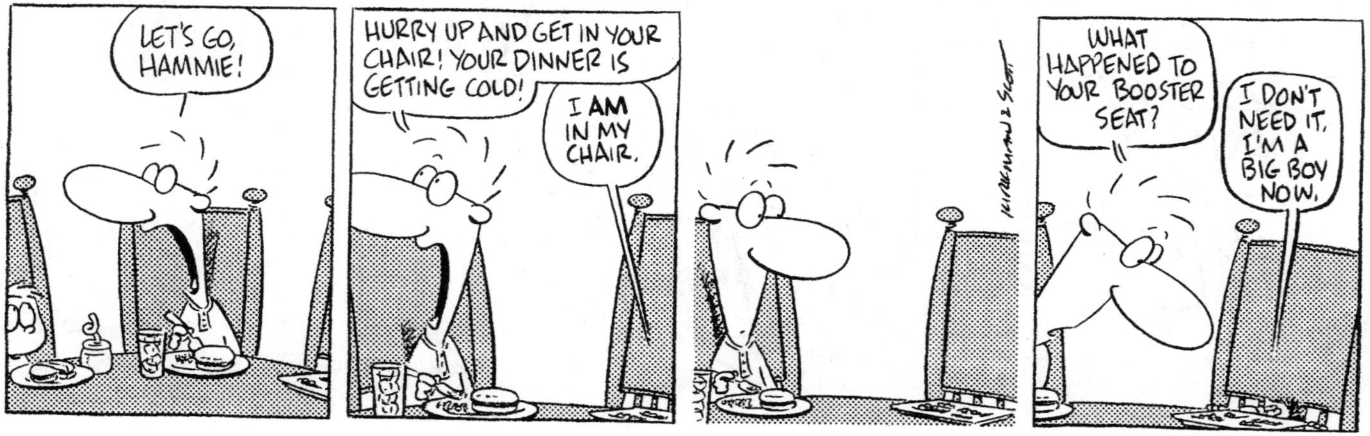
LET'S GO, HAMMIE!
HURRY UP AND GET IN YOUR CHAIR! YOUR DINNER IS GETTING COLD!
I AM IN MY CHAIR.
WHAT HAPPENED TO YOUR BOOSTER SEAT?
I DON'T NEED IT. I'M A BIG BOY NOW.

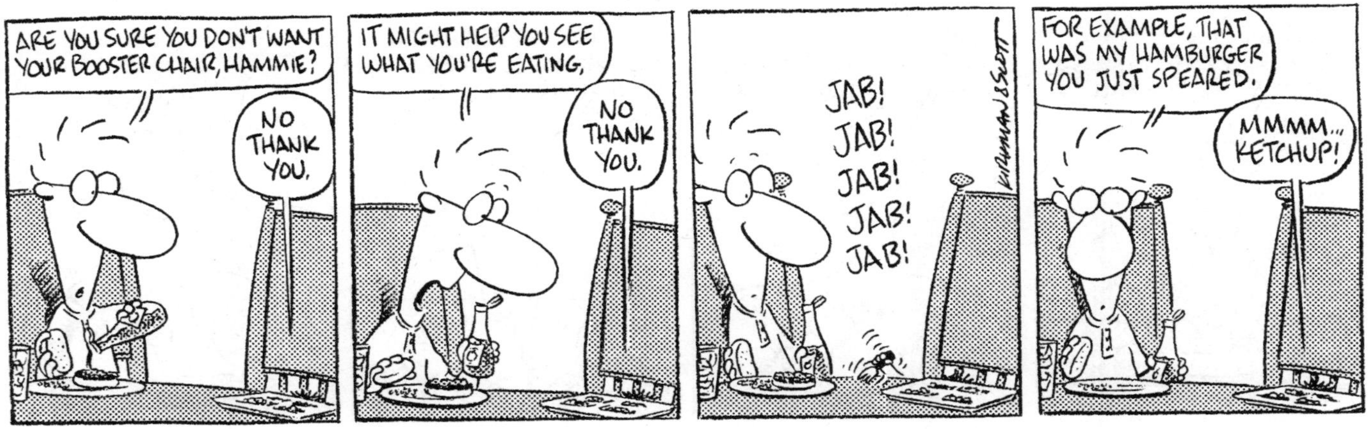
ARE YOU SURE YOU DON'T WANT YOUR BOOSTER CHAIR, HAMMIE?
NO THANK YOU.
IT MIGHT HELP YOU SEE WHAT YOU'RE EATING.
NO THANK YOU.
JAB! JAB! JAB! JAB! JAB!
FOR EXAMPLE, THAT WAS MY HAMBURGER YOU JUST SPEARED.
MMMM... KETCHUP!

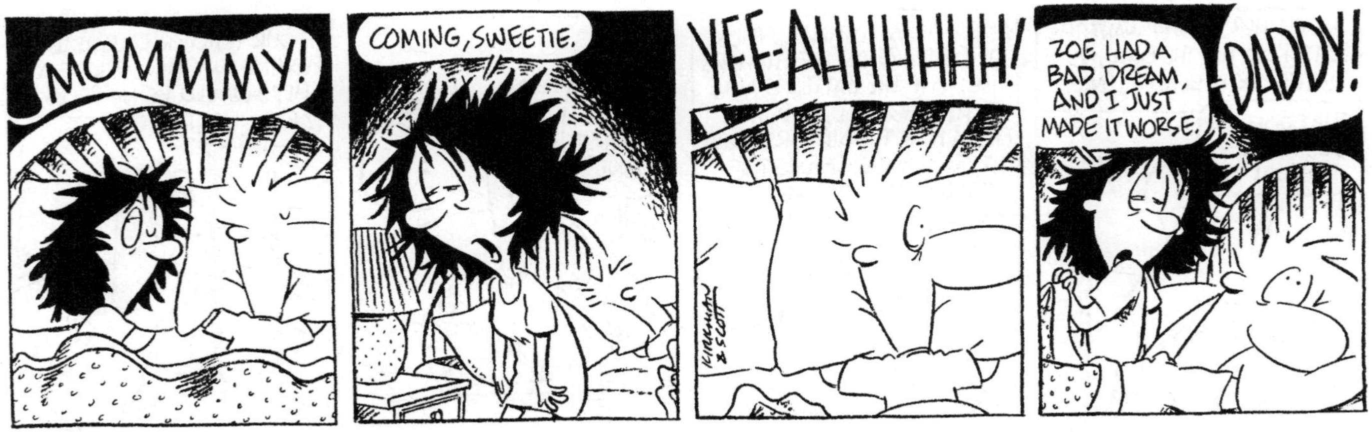
MOMMMY!
COMING, SWEETIE.
YEE-AHHHHHH!
ZOE HAD A BAD DREAM, AND I JUST MADE IT WORSE.
DADDY!

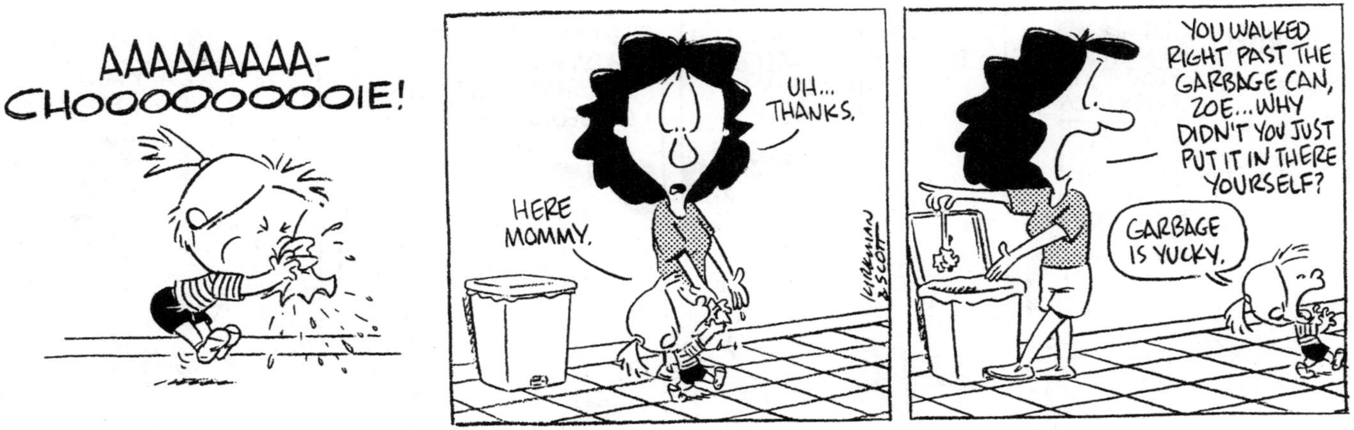
AAAAAAAAA-CHOOOOOOOOIE!
HERE MOMMY.
UH... THANKS.
YOU WALKED RIGHT PAST THE GARBAGE CAN, ZOE... WHY DIDN'T YOU JUST PUT IT IN THERE YOURSELF?
GARBAGE IS YUCKY.

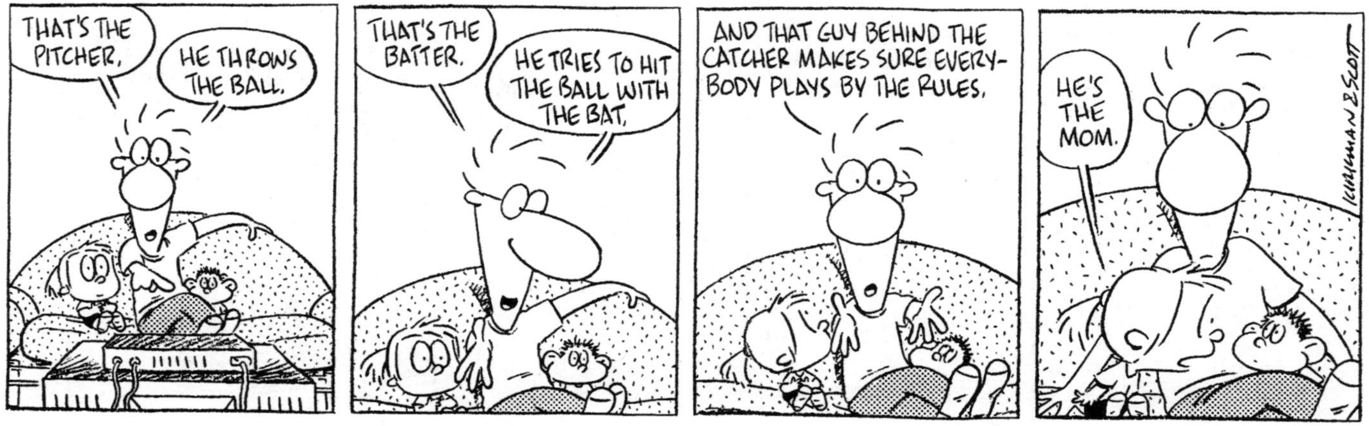
THAT'S THE PITCHER,
HE THROWS THE BALL.
THAT'S THE BATTER.
HE TRIES TO HIT THE BALL WITH THE BAT.
AND THAT GUY BEHIND THE CATCHER MAKES SURE EVERYBODY PLAYS BY THE RULES.
HE'S THE MOM.
KIRKMAN & SCOTT

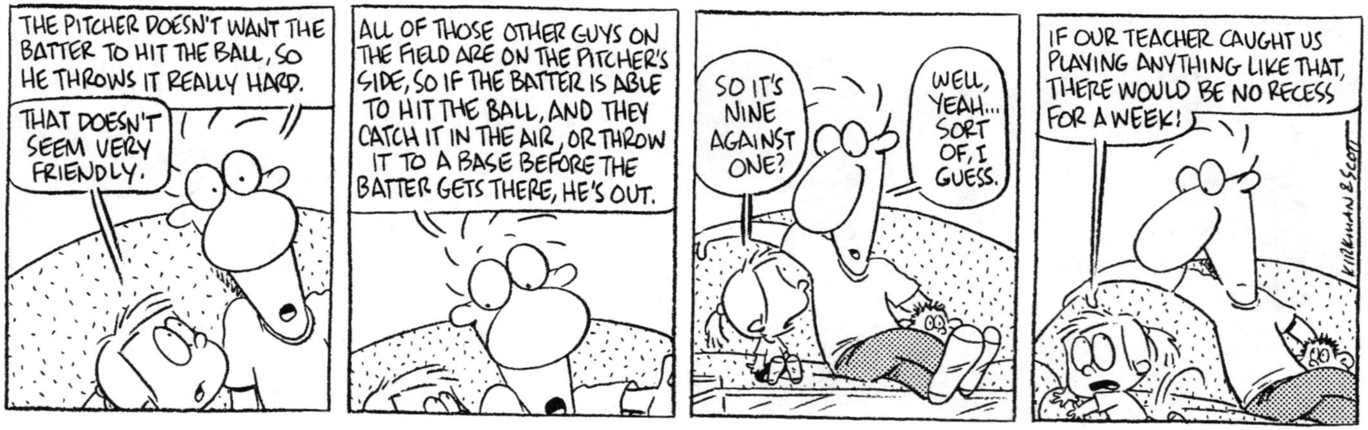
THE PITCHER DOESN'T WANT THE BATTER TO HIT THE BALL, SO HE THROWS IT REALLY HARD.
THAT DOESN'T SEEM VERY FRIENDLY.
ALL OF THOSE OTHER GUYS ON THE FIELD ARE ON THE PITCHER'S SIDE, SO IF THE BATTER IS ABLE TO HIT THE BALL, AND THEY CATCH IT IN THE AIR, OR THROW IT TO A BASE BEFORE THE BATTER GETS THERE, HE'S OUT.
SO IT'S NINE AGAINST ONE?
WELL, YEAH... SORT OF, I GUESS.
IF OUR TEACHER CAUGHT US PLAYING ANYTHING LIKE THAT, THERE WOULD BE NO RECESS FOR A WEEK!
KIRKMAN & SCOTT

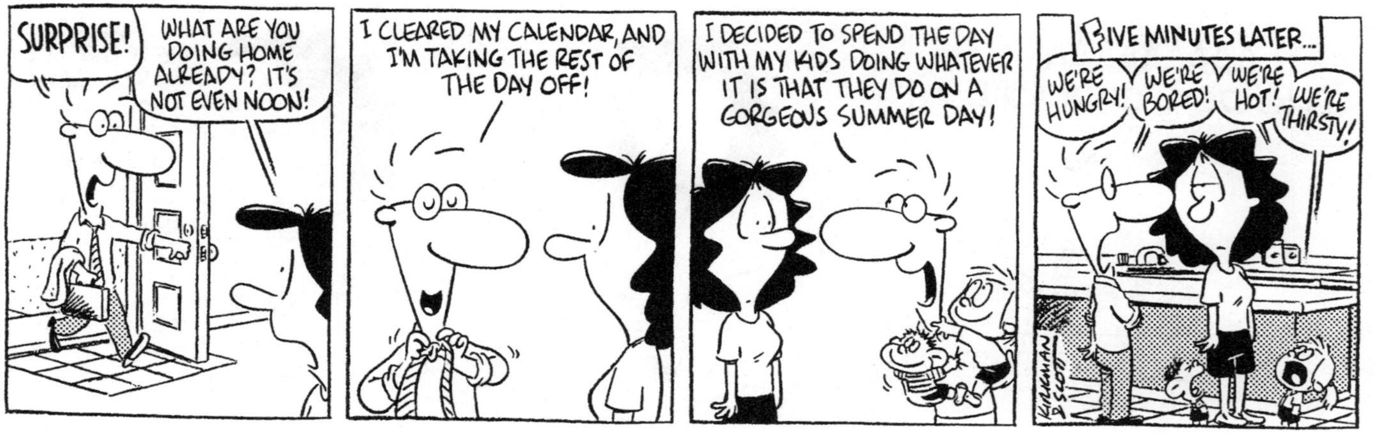
SURPRISE!
WHAT ARE YOU DOING HOME ALREADY? IT'S NOT EVEN NOON!
I CLEARED MY CALENDAR, AND I'M TAKING THE REST OF THE DAY OFF!
I DECIDED TO SPEND THE DAY WITH MY KIDS DOING WHATEVER IT IS THAT THEY DO ON A GORGEOUS SUMMER DAY!
FIVE MINUTES LATER...
WE'RE HUNGRY!
WE'RE BORED!
WE'RE HOT!
WE'RE THIRSTY!
KIRKMAN & SCOTT

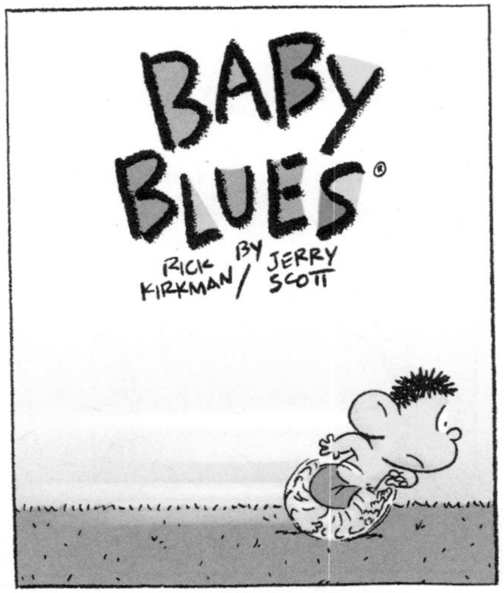
BABY BLUES®
BY RICK KIRKMAN / JERRY SCOTT

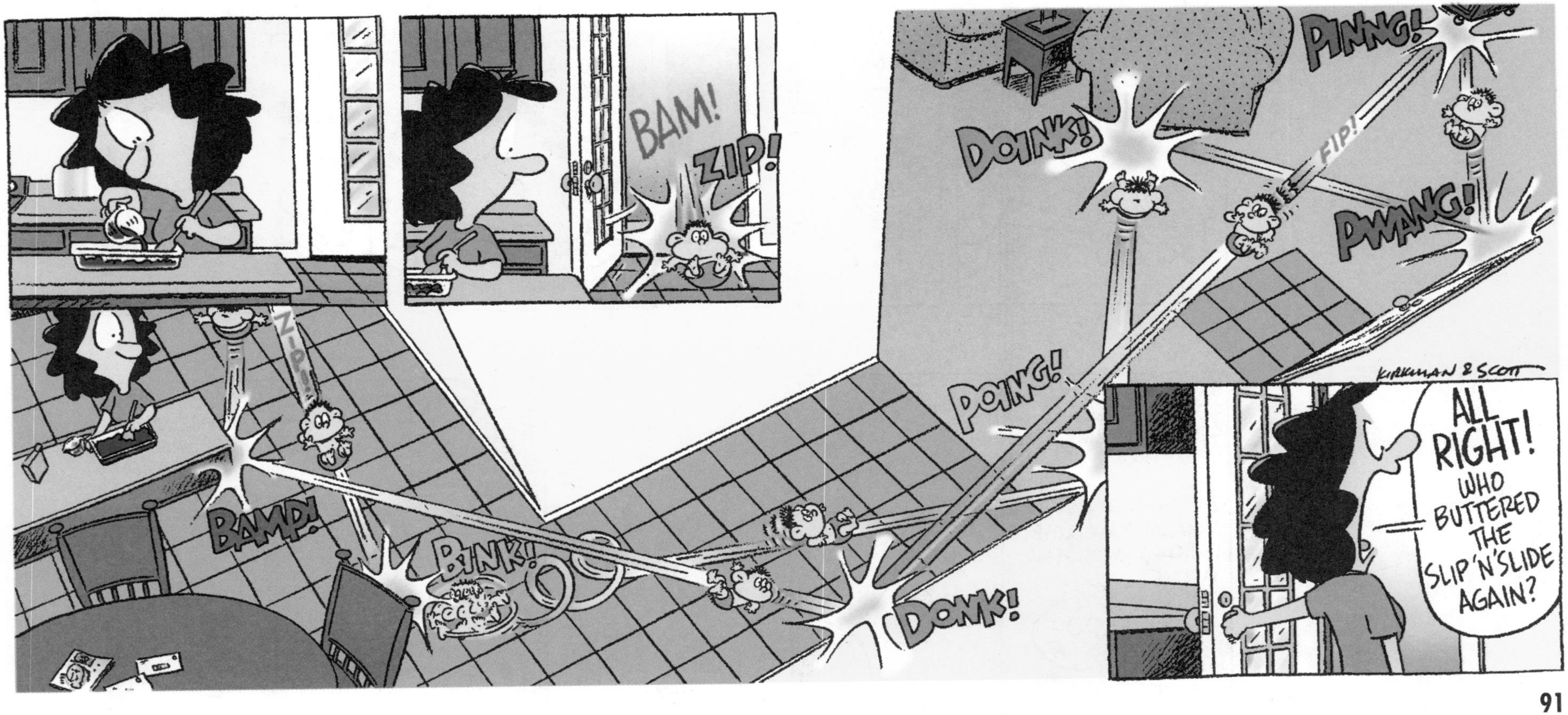
BAM!
ZIP!
ZIP!
BAMP!
BINK!
DONK!
POING!
DOINK!
FIP!
PWANG!
PINNG!
KIRKMAN & SCOTT
ALL RIGHT! WHO BUTTERED THE SLIP'N'SLIDE AGAIN?

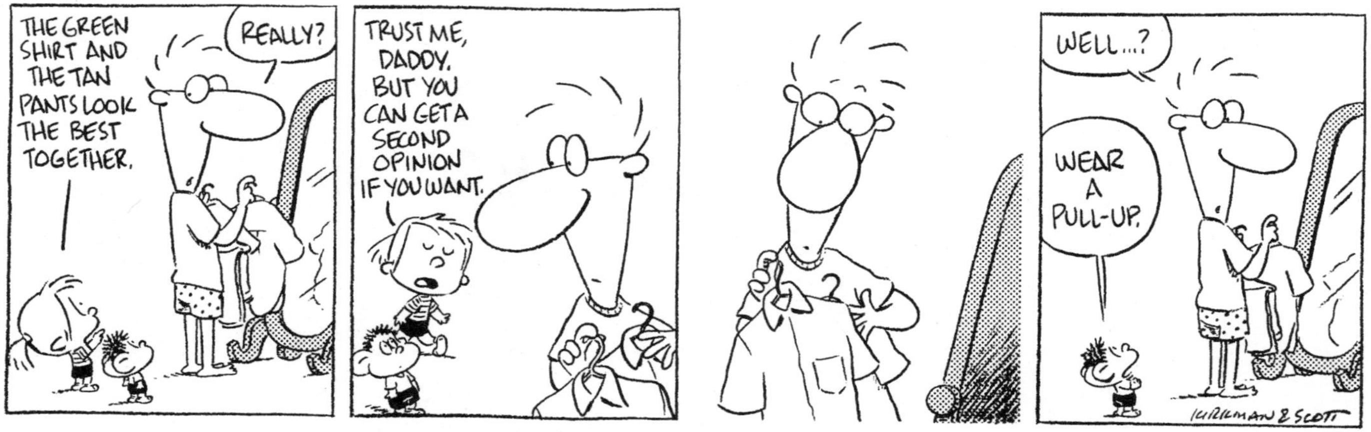
THE GREEN SHIRT AND THE TAN PANTS LOOK THE BEST TOGETHER.
REALLY?
TRUST ME, DADDY. BUT YOU CAN GET A SECOND OPINION IF YOU WANT.
WELL...?
WEAR A PULL-UP.
KIRKMAN & SCOTT

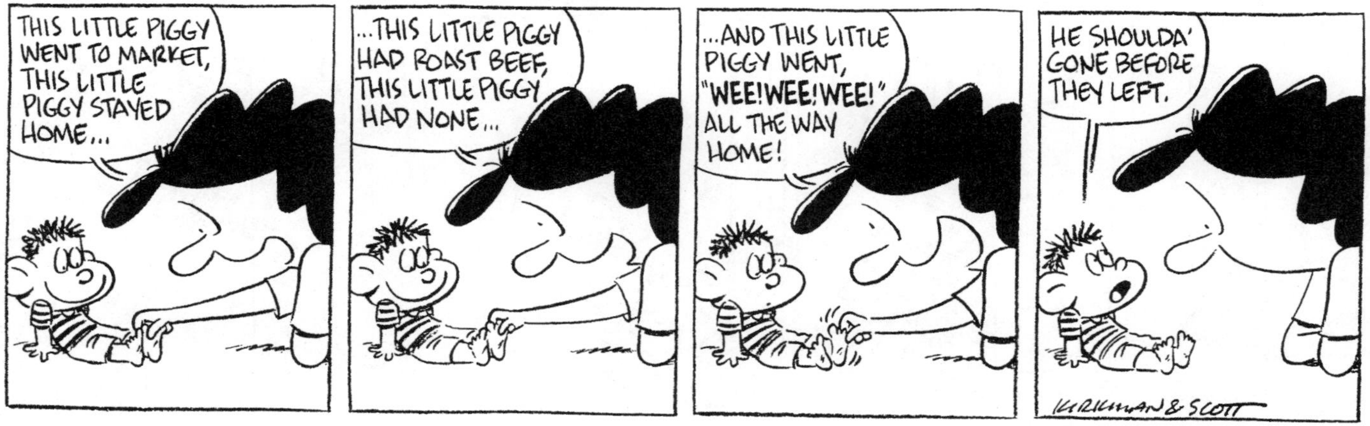
THIS LITTLE PIGGY WENT TO MARKET, THIS LITTLE PIGGY STAYED HOME...
...THIS LITTLE PIGGY HAD ROAST BEEF, THIS LITTLE PIGGY HAD NONE...
...AND THIS LITTLE PIGGY WENT, "WEE! WEE! WEE!" ALL THE WAY HOME!
HE SHOULDA' GONE BEFORE THEY LEFT.
KIRKMAN & SCOTT

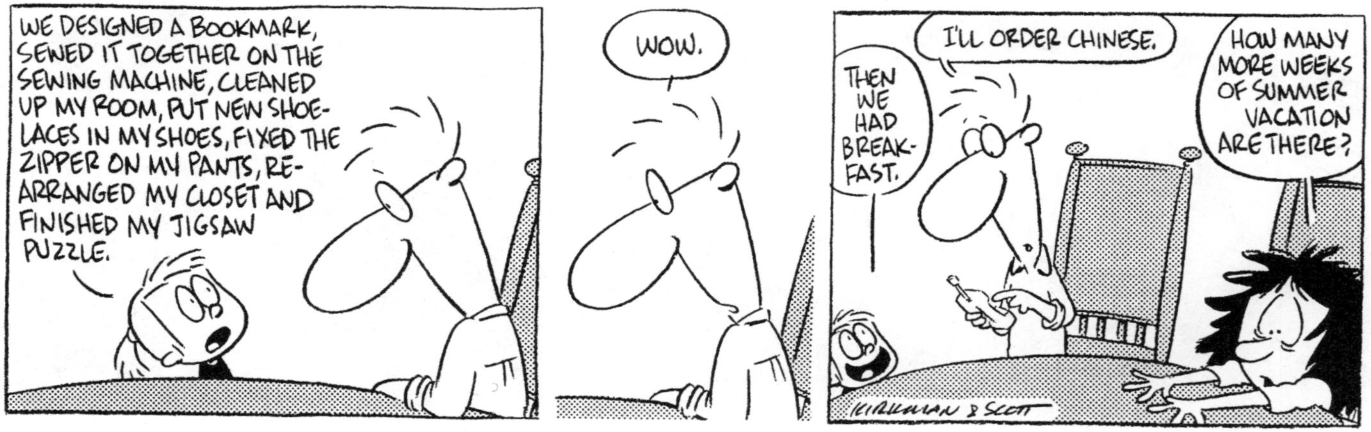
WE DESIGNED A BOOKMARK, SEWED IT TOGETHER ON THE SEWING MACHINE, CLEANED UP MY ROOM, PUT NEW SHOE-LACES IN MY SHOES, FIXED THE ZIPPER ON MY PANTS, RE-ARRANGED MY CLOSET AND FINISHED MY JIGSAW PUZZLE.
WOW.
THEN WE HAD BREAK-FAST.
I'LL ORDER CHINESE.
HOW MANY MORE WEEKS OF SUMMER VACATION ARE THERE?
KIRKMAN & SCOTT

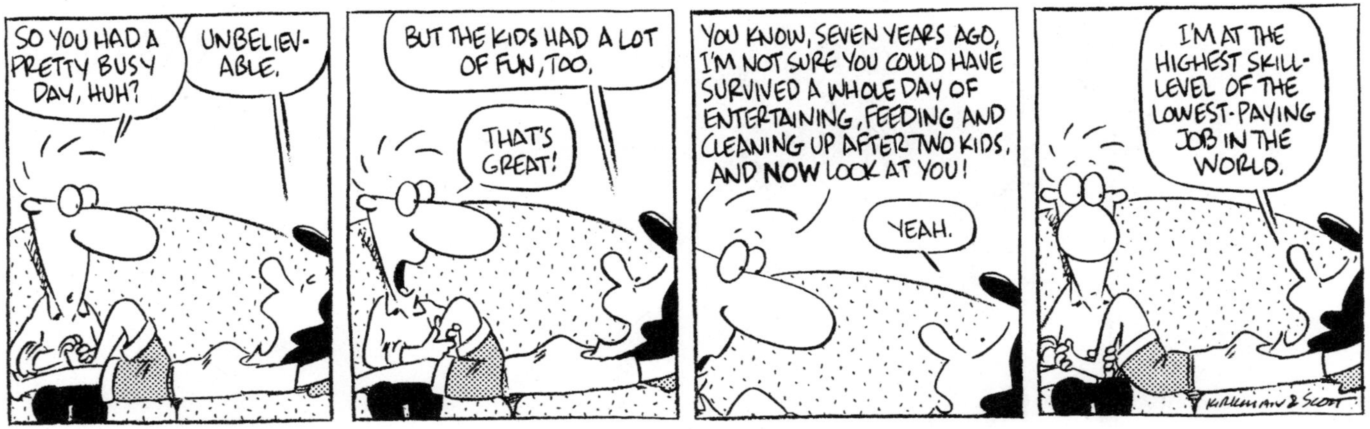
SO YOU HAD A PRETTY BUSY DAY, HUH?
UNBELIEV-ABLE.
BUT THE KIDS HAD A LOT OF FUN, TOO.
THAT'S GREAT!
YOU KNOW, SEVEN YEARS AGO, I'M NOT SURE YOU COULD HAVE SURVIVED A WHOLE DAY OF ENTERTAINING, FEEDING AND CLEANING UP AFTER TWO KIDS, AND NOW LOOK AT YOU!
YEAH.
I'M AT THE HIGHEST SKILL-LEVEL OF THE LOWEST-PAYING JOB IN THE WORLD.
KIRKMAN & SCOTT

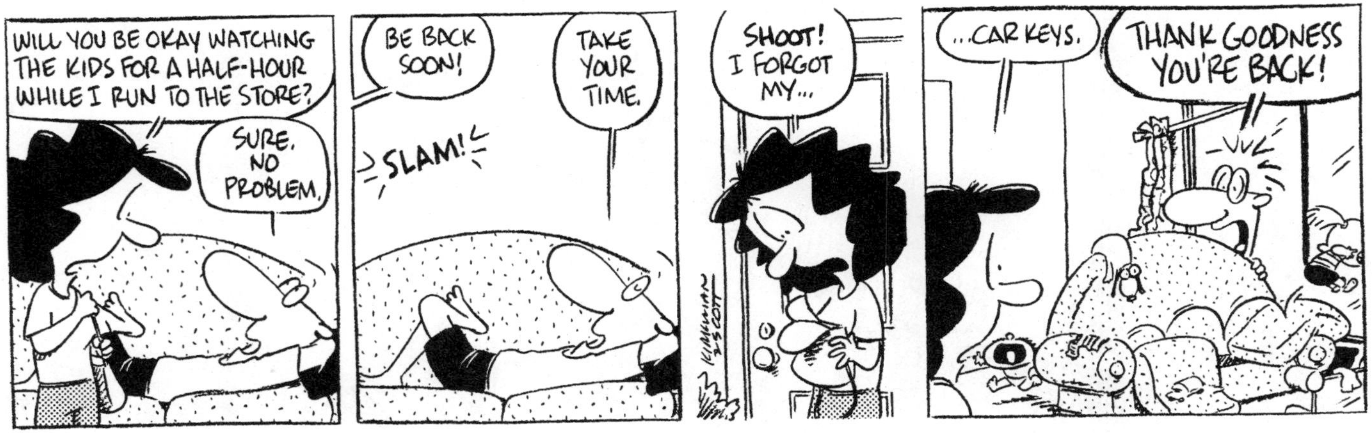
WILL YOU BE OKAY WATCHING THE KIDS FOR A HALF-HOUR WHILE I RUN TO THE STORE?
SURE. NO PROBLEM.
BE BACK SOON!
TAKE YOUR TIME.
SLAM!
SHOOT! I FORGOT MY...
...CAR KEYS.
THANK GOODNESS YOU'RE BACK!

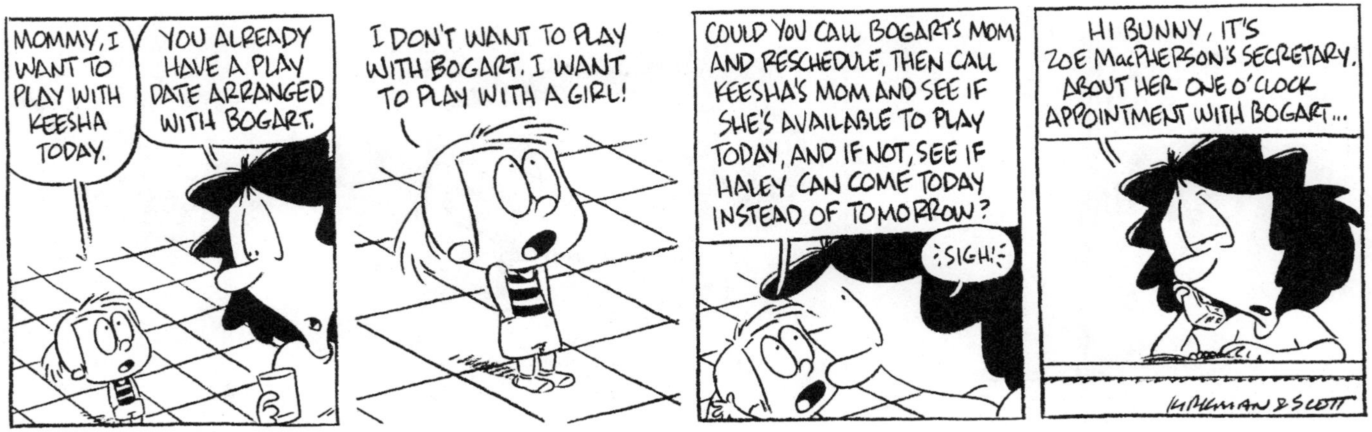
MOMMY, I WANT TO PLAY WITH KEESHA TODAY.
YOU ALREADY HAVE A PLAY DATE ARRANGED WITH BOGART.
I DON'T WANT TO PLAY WITH BOGART. I WANT TO PLAY WITH A GIRL!
COULD YOU CALL BOGART'S MOM AND RESCHEDULE, THEN CALL KEESHA'S MOM AND SEE IF SHE'S AVAILABLE TO PLAY TODAY, AND IF NOT, SEE IF HALEY CAN COME TODAY INSTEAD OF TOMORROW?
SIGH!
HI BUNNY, IT'S ZOE MacPHERSON'S SECRETARY. ABOUT HER ONE O'CLOCK APPOINTMENT WITH BOGART...
KIRKMAN & SCOTT

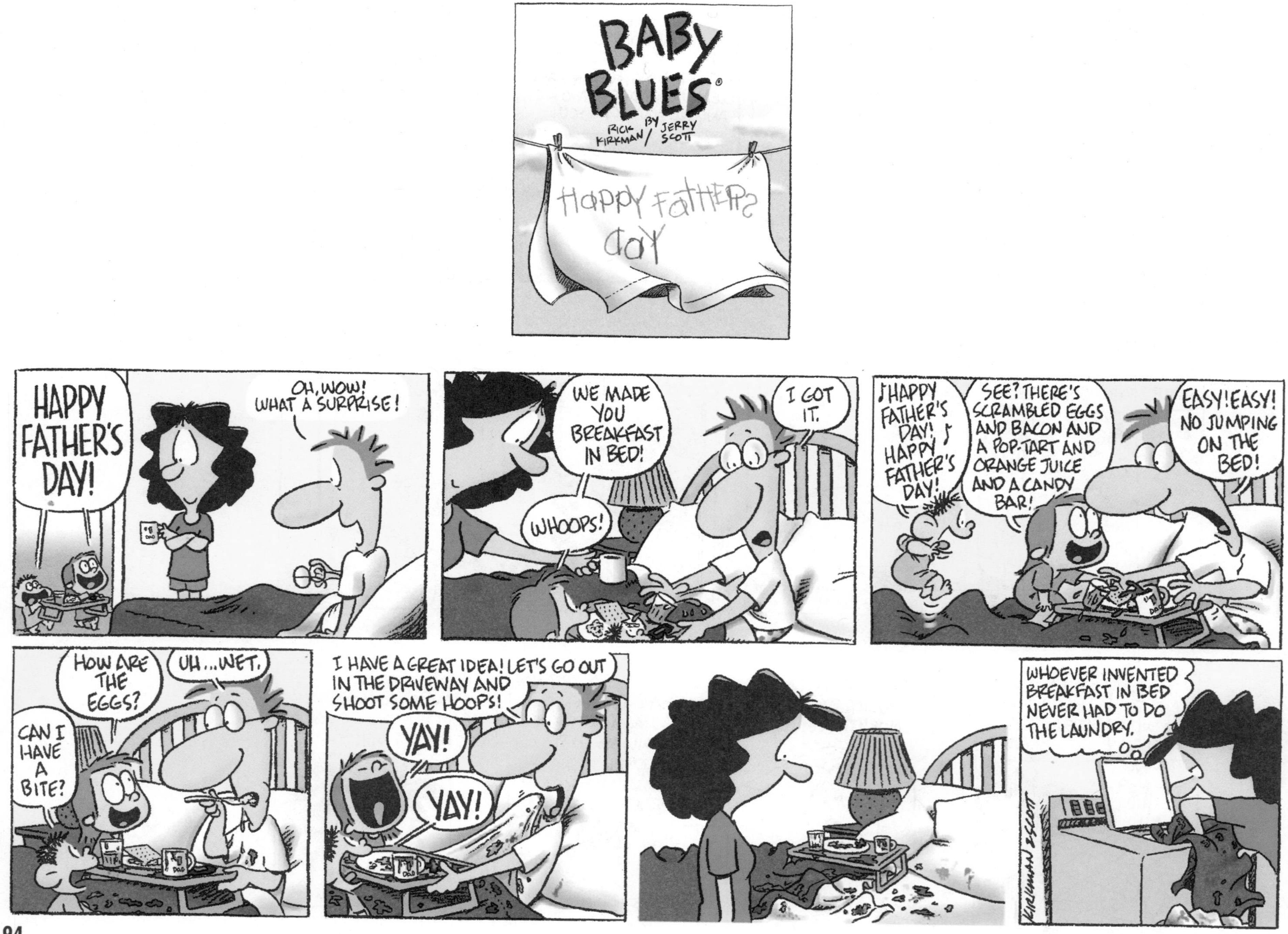
BABY BLUES®
BY RICK KIRKMAN / JERRY SCOTT
HAPPY FATHERS DAY
HAPPY FATHER'S DAY!
OH, WOW! WHAT A SURPRISE!
WE MADE YOU BREAKFAST IN BED!
WHOOPS!
I GOT IT.
♪HAPPY FATHER'S DAY! HAPPY FATHER'S DAY!♪
SEE? THERE'S SCRAMBLED EGGS AND BACON AND A POP-TART AND ORANGE JUICE AND A CANDY BAR!
EASY! EASY! NO JUMPING ON THE BED!
HOW ARE THE EGGS?
UH...WET.
CAN I HAVE A BITE?
I HAVE A GREAT IDEA! LET'S GO OUT IN THE DRIVEWAY AND SHOOT SOME HOOPS!
YAY!
YAY!
WHOEVER INVENTED BREAKFAST IN BED NEVER HAD TO DO THE LAUNDRY.
KIRKMAN & SCOTT

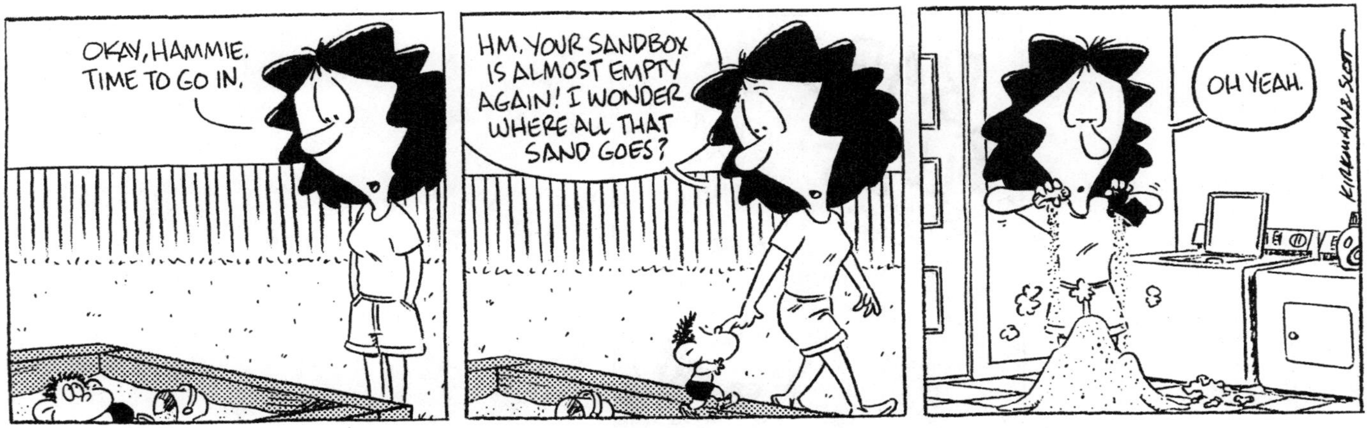
OKAY, HAMMIE. TIME TO GO IN.
HM. YOUR SANDBOX IS ALMOST EMPTY AGAIN! I WONDER WHERE ALL THAT SAND GOES?
OH YEAH.
KIRKMAN & SCOTT

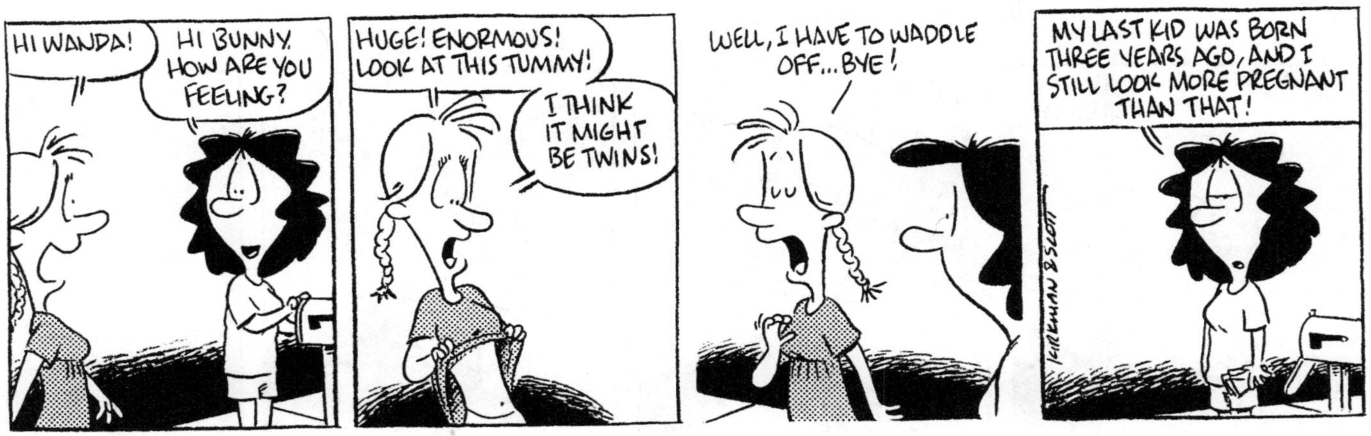
HI WANDA!
HI BUNNY. HOW ARE YOU FEELING?
HUGE! ENORMOUS! LOOK AT THIS TUMMY!
I THINK IT MIGHT BE TWINS!
WELL, I HAVE TO WADDLE OFF... BYE!
KIRKMAN & SCOTT
MY LAST KID WAS BORN THREE YEARS AGO, AND I STILL LOOK MORE PREGNANT THAN THAT!

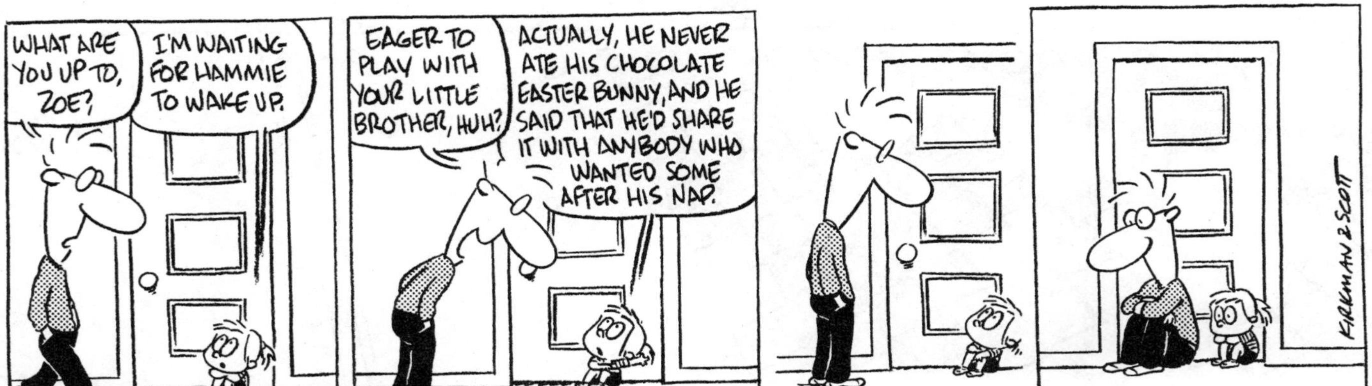
WHAT ARE YOU UP TO, ZOE?
I'M WAITING FOR HAMMIE TO WAKE UP.
EAGER TO PLAY WITH YOUR LITTLE BROTHER, HUH?
ACTUALLY, HE NEVER ATE HIS CHOCOLATE EASTER BUNNY, AND HE SAID THAT HE'D SHARE IT WITH ANYBODY WHO WANTED SOME AFTER HIS NAP.
KIRKMAN & SCOTT

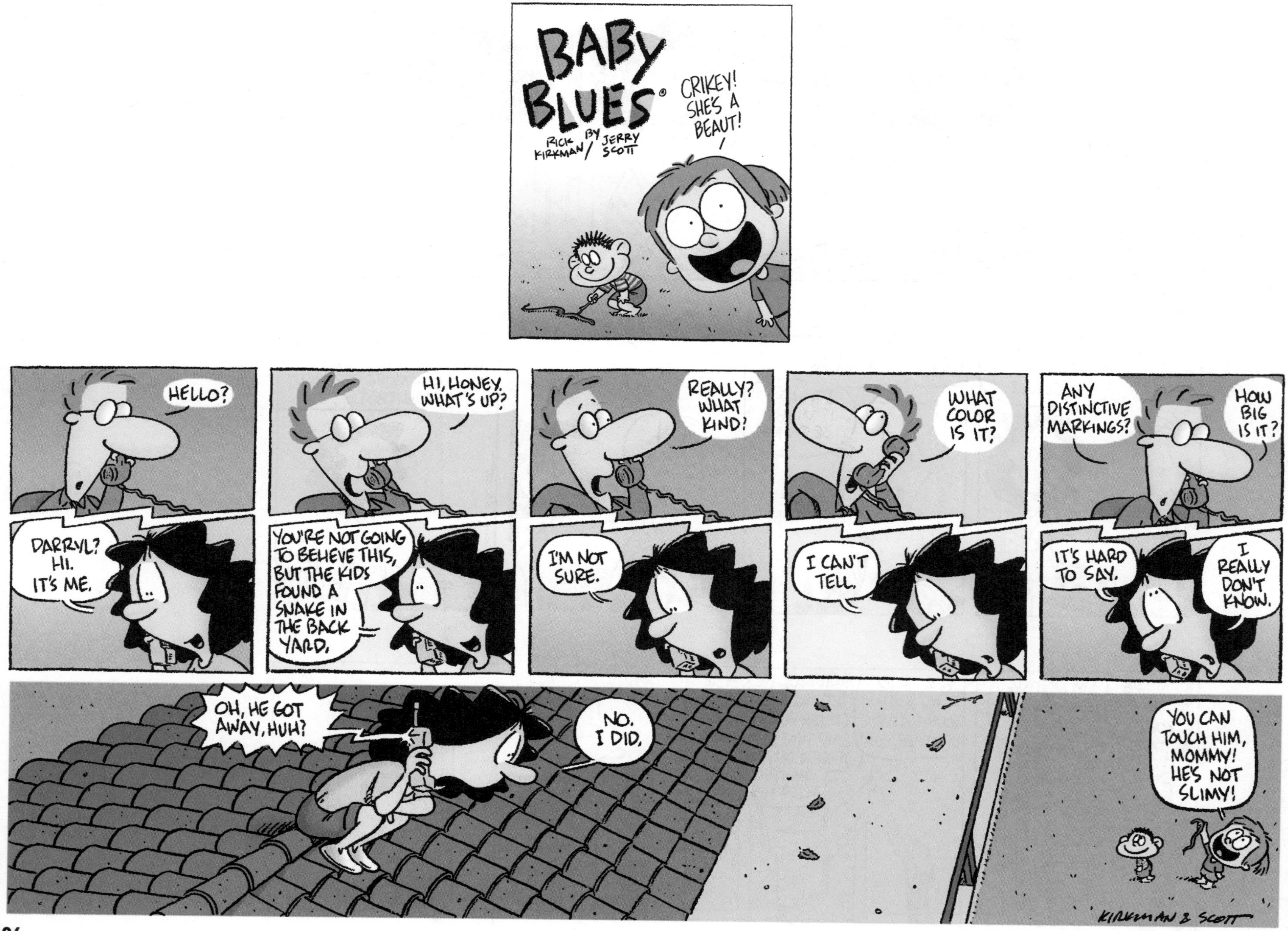
BABY BLUES®
BY RICK KIRKMAN / JERRY SCOTT
CRIKEY! SHE'S A BEAUT!
HELLO?
DARRYL? HI. IT'S ME.
HI, HONEY. WHAT'S UP?
YOU'RE NOT GOING TO BELIEVE THIS, BUT THE KIDS FOUND A SNAKE IN THE BACK YARD.
REALLY? WHAT KIND?
I'M NOT SURE.
WHAT COLOR IS IT?
I CAN'T TELL.
ANY DISTINCTIVE MARKINGS?
IT'S HARD TO SAY.
HOW BIG IS IT?
I REALLY DON'T KNOW.
OH, HE GOT AWAY, HUH?
NO. I DID.
YOU CAN TOUCH HIM, MOMMY! HE'S NOT SLIMY!
KIRKMAN & SCOTT

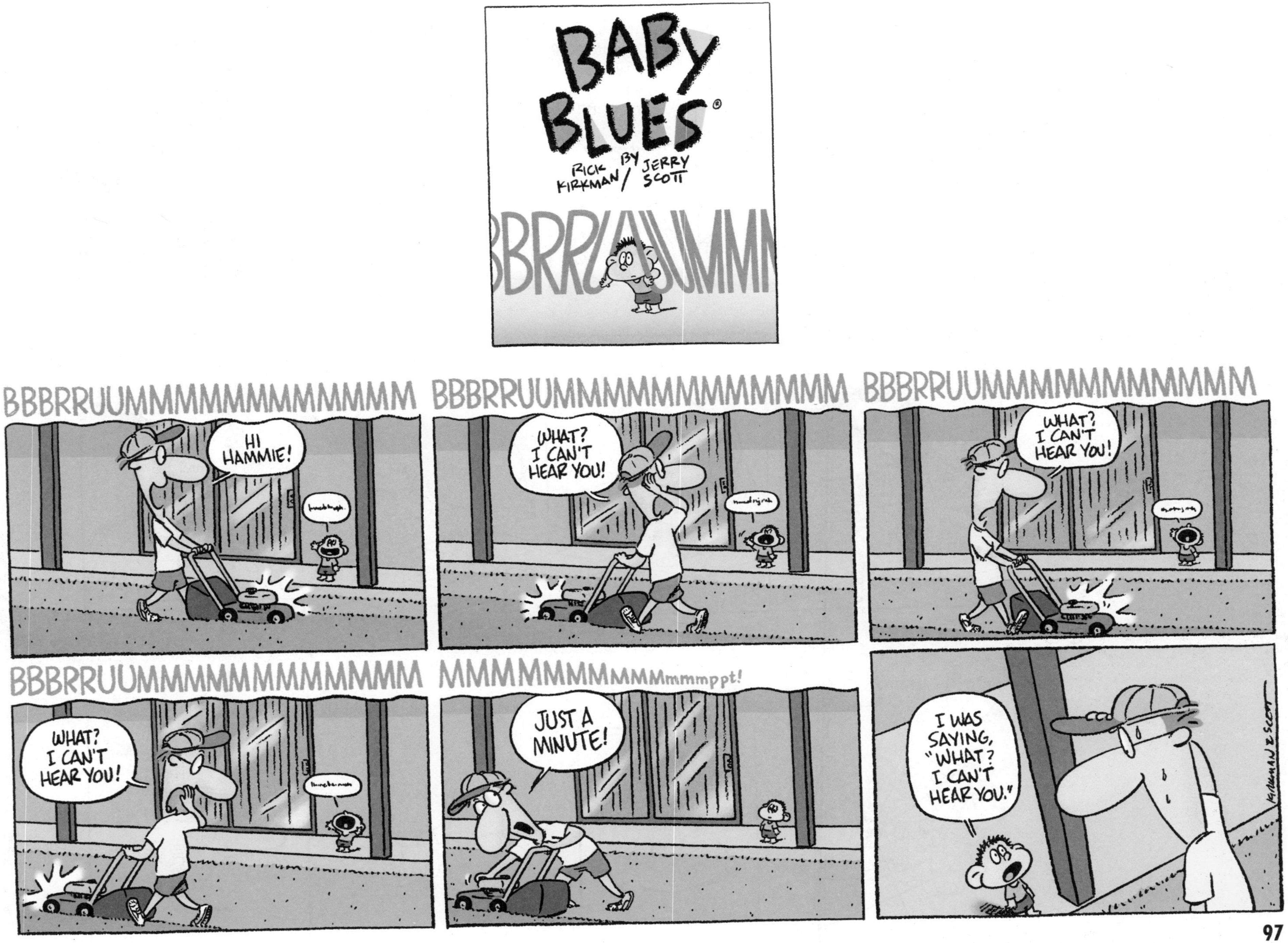
BABY BLUES®
BY RICK KIRKMAN / JERRY SCOTT
BBRRUUMMM
BBBRRUUMMMMMMMMMMMM
HI HAMMIE!
BBBRRUUMMMMMMMMMMMMMM
WHAT? I CAN'T HEAR YOU!
BBBRRUUMMMMMMMMMMMMM
WHAT? I CAN'T HEAR YOU!
BBBRRUUMMMMMMMMMMMMM
WHAT? I CAN'T HEAR YOU!
MMMMMMMMMMmmmppt!
JUST A MINUTE!
I WAS SAYING, "WHAT? I CAN'T HEAR YOU."
KIRKMAN & SCOTT

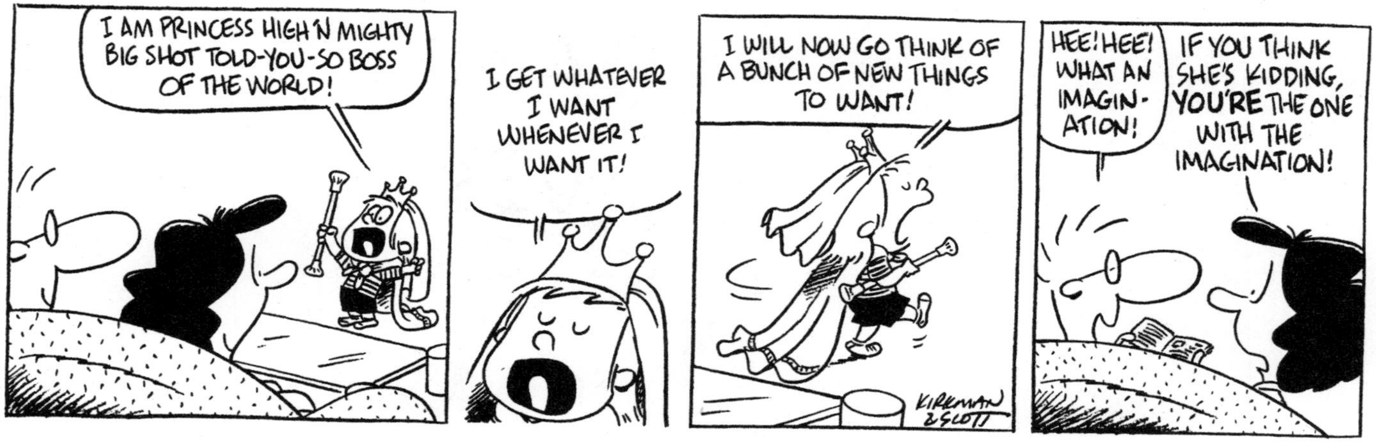
I AM PRINCESS HIGH 'N MIGHTY BIG SHOT TOLD-YOU-SO BOSS OF THE WORLD!
I GET WHATEVER I WANT WHENEVER I WANT IT!
I WILL NOW GO THINK OF A BUNCH OF NEW THINGS TO WANT!
KIRKMAN & SCOTT
HEE! HEE! WHAT AN IMAGIN-ATION!
IF YOU THINK SHE'S KIDDING, **YOU'RE** THE ONE WITH THE IMAGINATION!

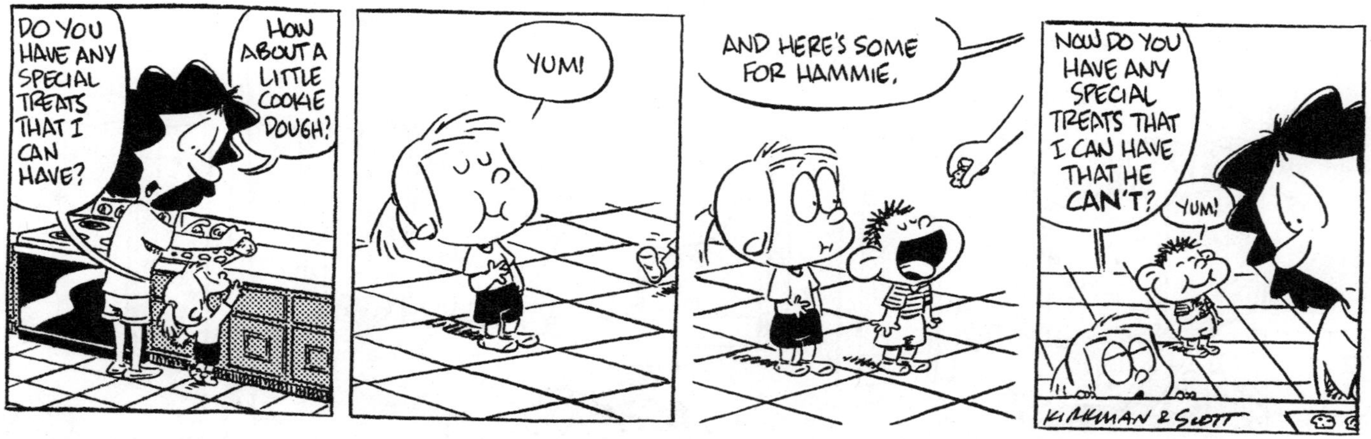
DO YOU HAVE ANY SPECIAL TREATS THAT I CAN HAVE?
HOW ABOUT A LITTLE COOKIE DOUGH?
YUM!
AND HERE'S SOME FOR HAMMIE.
NOW DO YOU HAVE ANY SPECIAL TREATS THAT I CAN HAVE THAT HE **CAN'T**?
YUM!
KIRKMAN & SCOTT

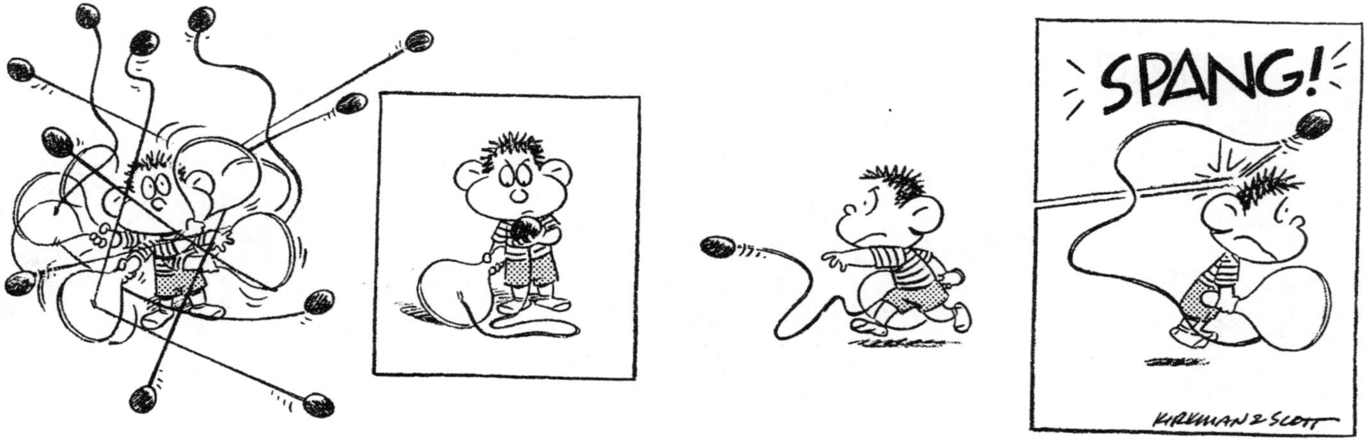
SPANG!
KIRKMAN & SCOTT

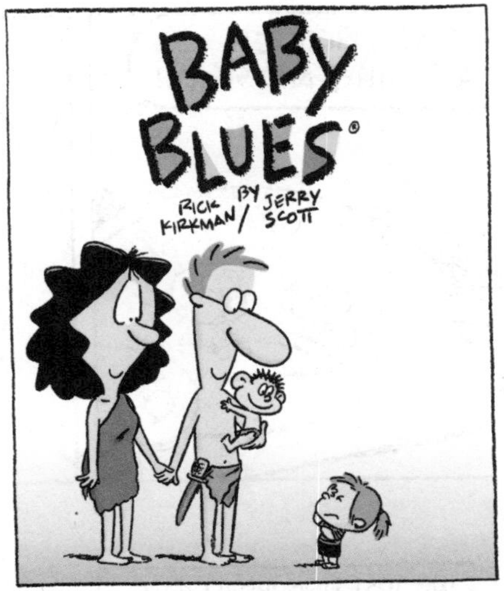
BABY BLUES®
BY RICK KIRKMAN/ JERRY SCOTT

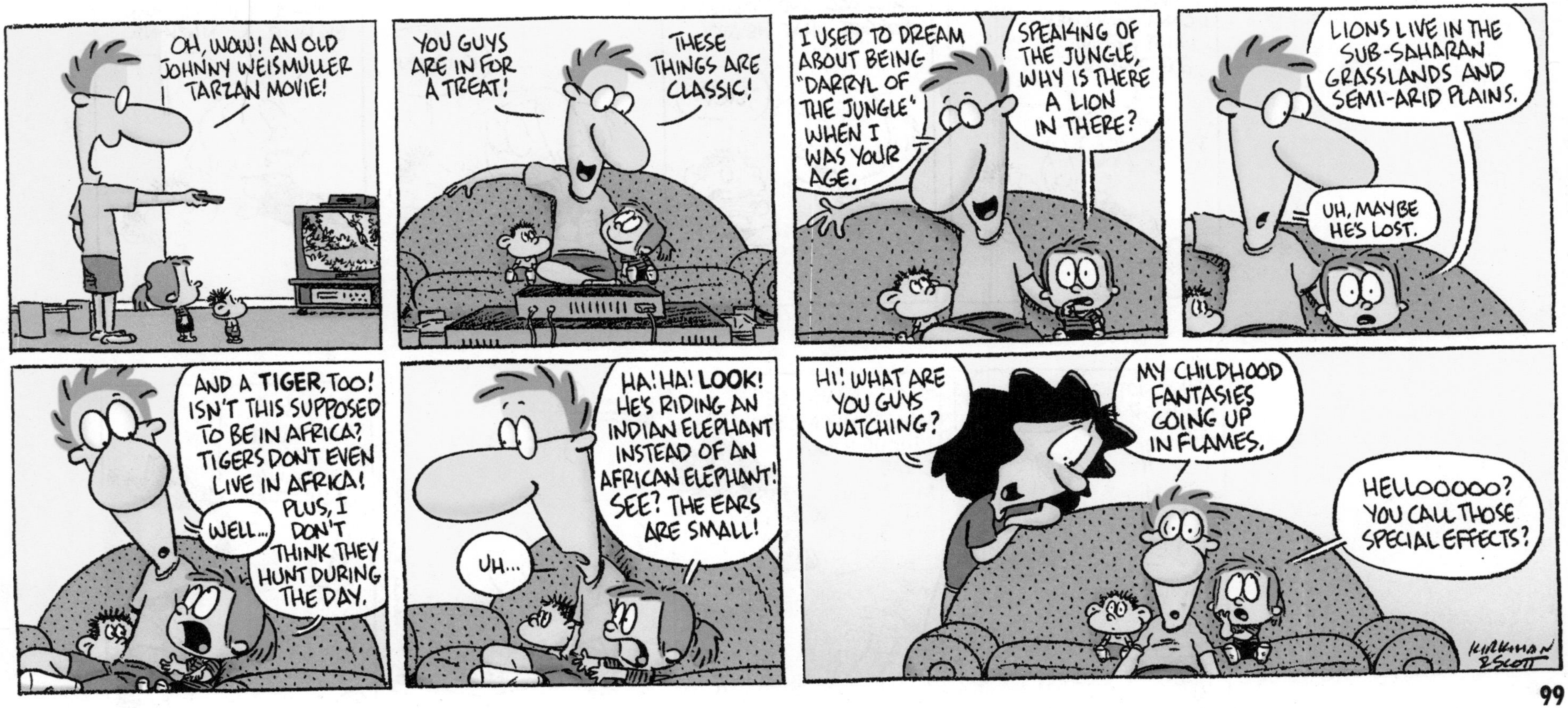
OH, WOW! AN OLD JOHNNY WEISMULLER TARZAN MOVIE!
YOU GUYS ARE IN FOR A TREAT!
THESE THINGS ARE CLASSIC!
I USED TO DREAM ABOUT BEING "DARRYL OF THE JUNGLE" WHEN I WAS YOUR AGE.
SPEAKING OF THE JUNGLE, WHY IS THERE A LION IN THERE?
LIONS LIVE IN THE SUB-SAHARAN GRASSLANDS AND SEMI-ARID PLAINS.
UH, MAYBE HE'S LOST.
AND A **TIGER**, TOO! ISN'T THIS SUPPOSED TO BE IN AFRICA? TIGERS DON'T EVEN LIVE IN AFRICA! PLUS, I DON'T THINK THEY HUNT DURING THE DAY.
WELL...
HA! HA! **LOOK!** HE'S RIDING AN INDIAN ELEPHANT INSTEAD OF AN AFRICAN ELEPHANT! SEE? THE EARS ARE SMALL!
UH...
HI! WHAT ARE YOU GUYS WATCHING?
MY CHILDHOOD FANTASIES GOING UP IN FLAMES.
HELLOOOOO? YOU CALL THOSE SPECIAL EFFECTS?
KIRKMAN & SCOTT

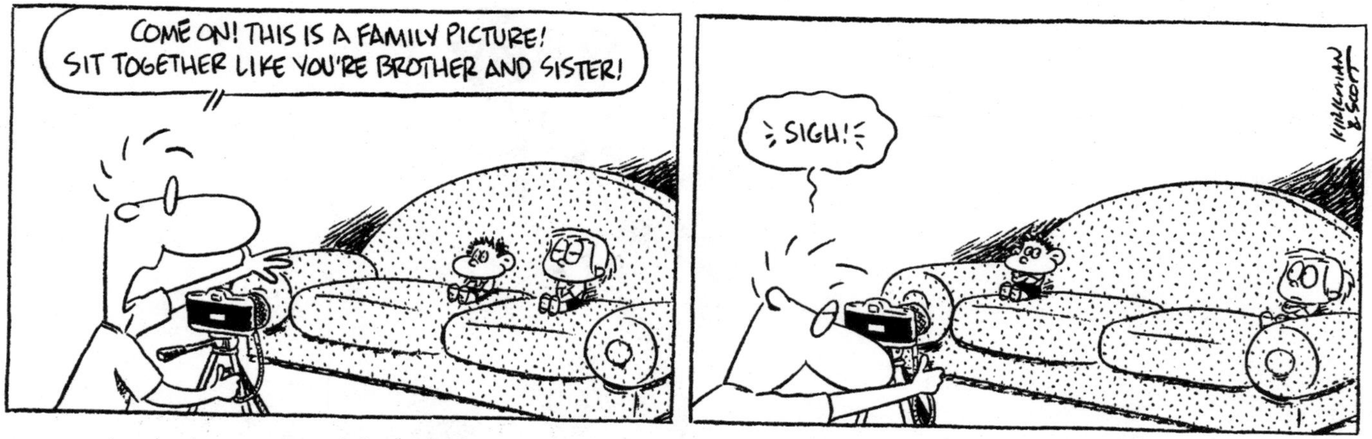
COME ON! THIS IS A FAMILY PICTURE! SIT TOGETHER LIKE YOU'RE BROTHER AND SISTER!
SIGH!
KIRKMAN & SCOTT

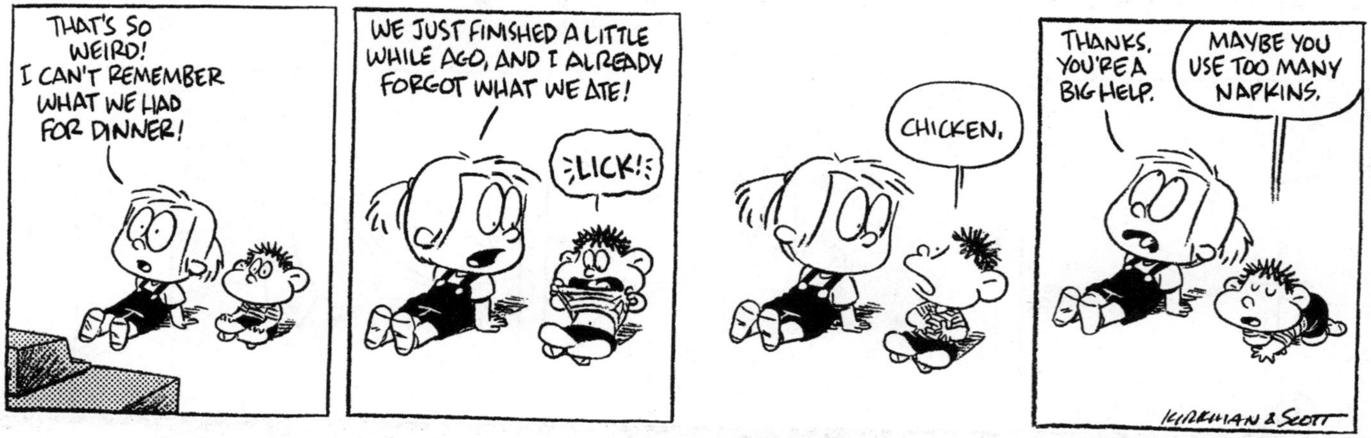
THAT'S SO WEIRD! I CAN'T REMEMBER WHAT WE HAD FOR DINNER!
WE JUST FINISHED A LITTLE WHILE AGO, AND I ALREADY FORGOT WHAT WE ATE!
LICK!
CHICKEN.
THANKS. YOU'RE A BIG HELP.
MAYBE YOU USE TOO MANY NAPKINS.
KIRKMAN & SCOTT

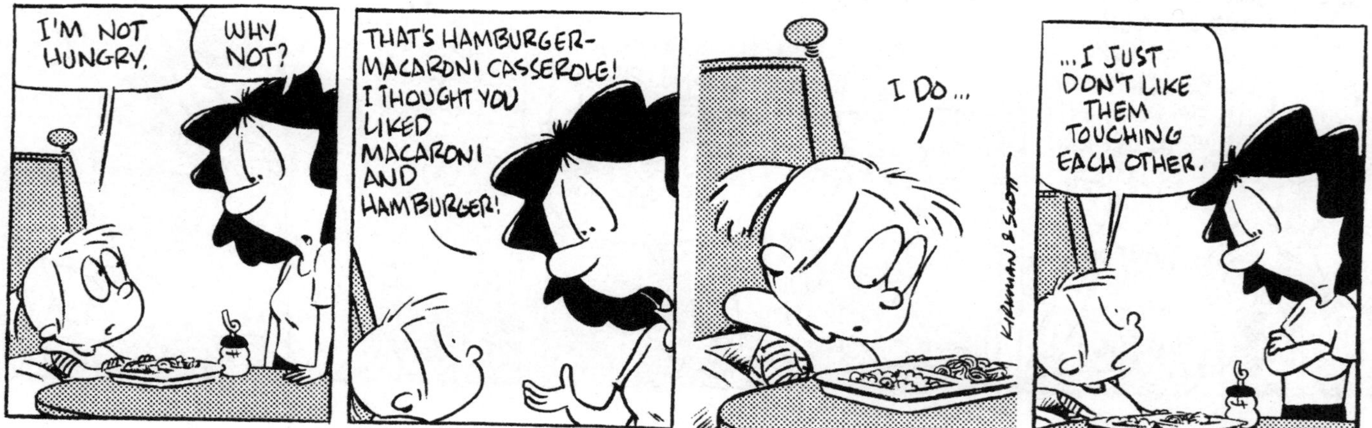
I'M NOT HUNGRY.
WHY NOT?
THAT'S HAMBURGER-MACARONI CASSEROLE! I THOUGHT YOU LIKED MACARONI AND HAMBURGER!
I DO...
KIRKMAN & SCOTT
...I JUST DON'T LIKE THEM TOUCHING EACH OTHER.

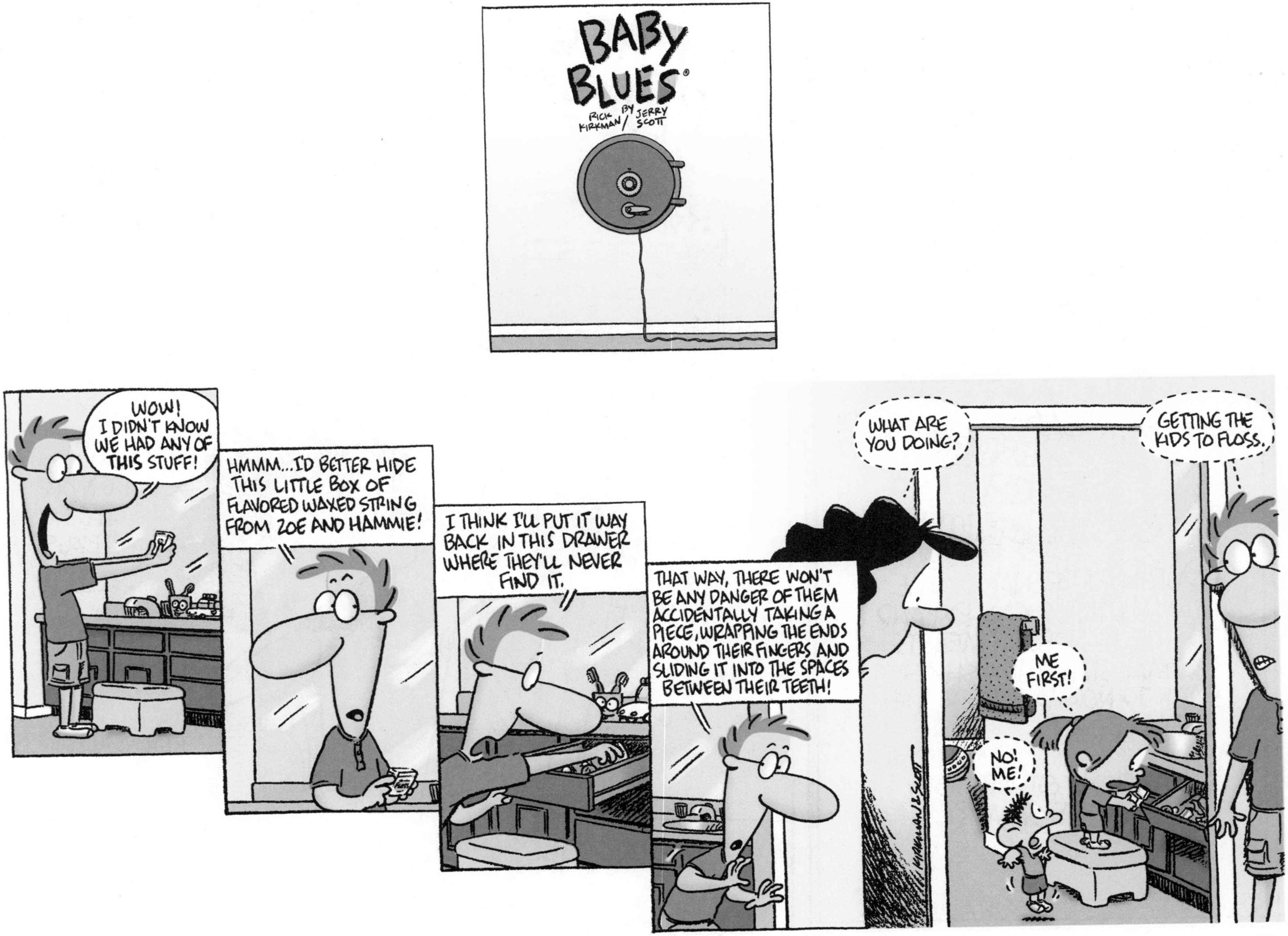
BABY BLUES®
BY RICK KIRKMAN / JERRY SCOTT
WOW! I DIDN'T KNOW WE HAD ANY OF THIS STUFF!
HMMM...I'D BETTER HIDE THIS LITTLE BOX OF FLAVORED WAXED STRING FROM ZOE AND HAMMIE!
I THINK I'LL PUT IT WAY BACK IN THIS DRAWER WHERE THEY'LL NEVER FIND IT.
THAT WAY, THERE WON'T BE ANY DANGER OF THEM ACCIDENTALLY TAKING A PIECE, WRAPPING THE ENDS AROUND THEIR FINGERS AND SLIDING IT INTO THE SPACES BETWEEN THEIR TEETH!
WHAT ARE YOU DOING?
GETTING THE KIDS TO FLOSS.
ME FIRST!
NO! ME!

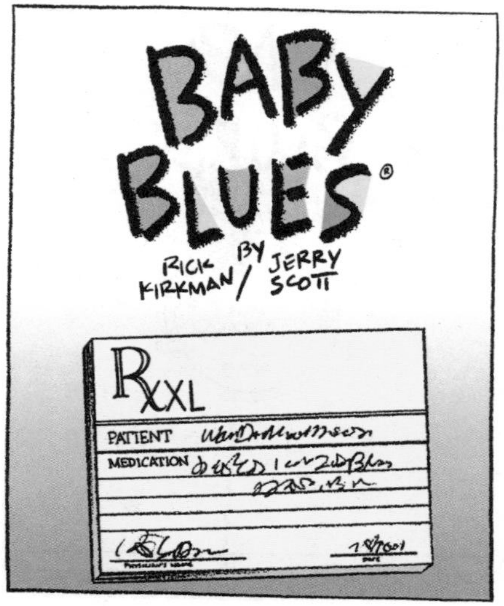
BABY BLUES®
BY RICK KIRKMAN / JERRY SCOTT
RXXL
PATIENT
MEDICATION

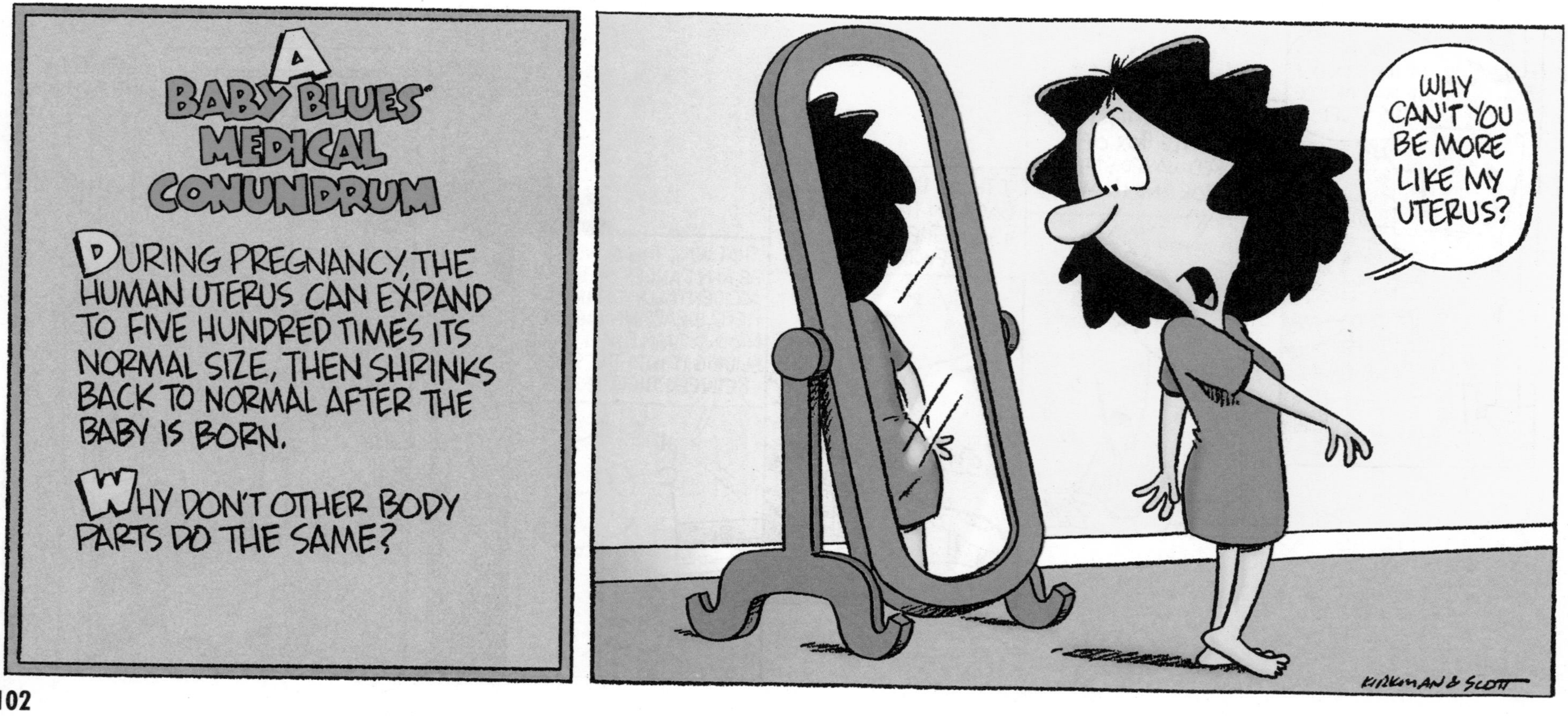
A BABY BLUES® MEDICAL CONUNDRUM
DURING PREGNANCY, THE HUMAN UTERUS CAN EXPAND TO FIVE HUNDRED TIMES ITS NORMAL SIZE, THEN SHRINKS BACK TO NORMAL AFTER THE BABY IS BORN.
WHY DON'T OTHER BODY PARTS DO THE SAME?
WHY CAN'T YOU BE MORE LIKE MY UTERUS?
KIRKMAN & SCOTT

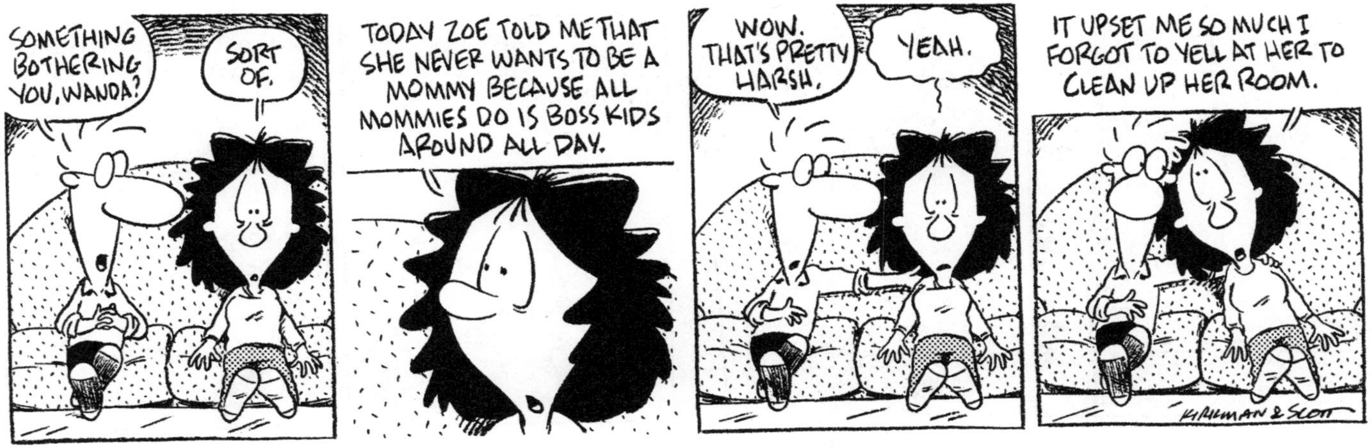
SOMETHING BOTHERING YOU, WANDA?
SORT OF.
TODAY ZOE TOLD ME THAT SHE NEVER WANTS TO BE A MOMMY BECAUSE ALL MOMMIES DO IS BOSS KIDS AROUND ALL DAY.
WOW. THAT'S PRETTY HARSH.
YEAH.
IT UPSET ME SO MUCH I FORGOT TO YELL AT HER TO CLEAN UP HER ROOM.
KIRKMAN & SCOTT

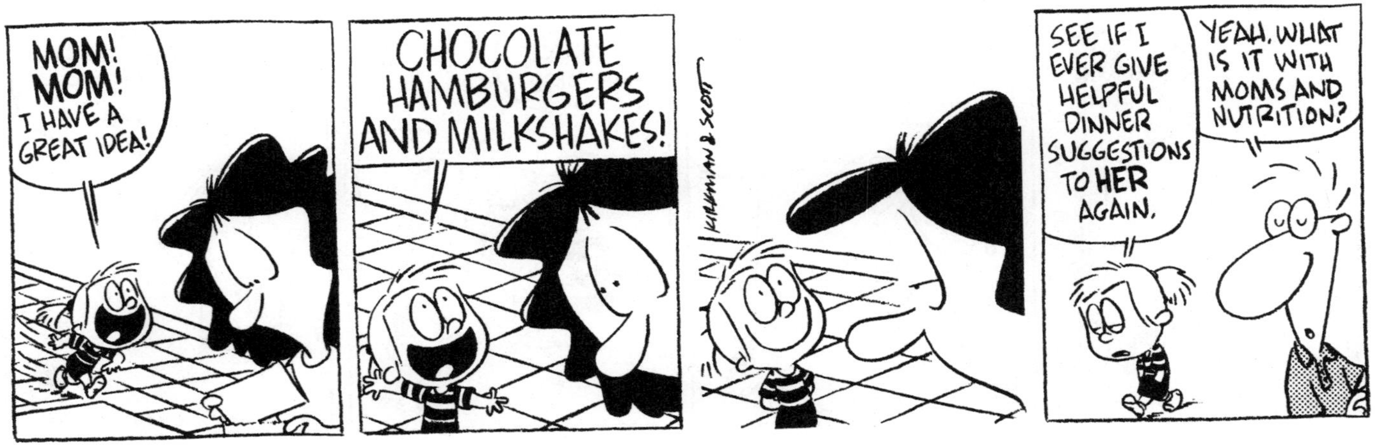
MOM! **MOM!** I HAVE A GREAT IDEA!
CHOCOLATE HAMBURGERS AND MILKSHAKES!
KIRKMAN & SCOTT
SEE IF I EVER GIVE HELPFUL DINNER SUGGESTIONS TO **HER** AGAIN.
YEAH. WHAT IS IT WITH MOMS AND NUTRITION?

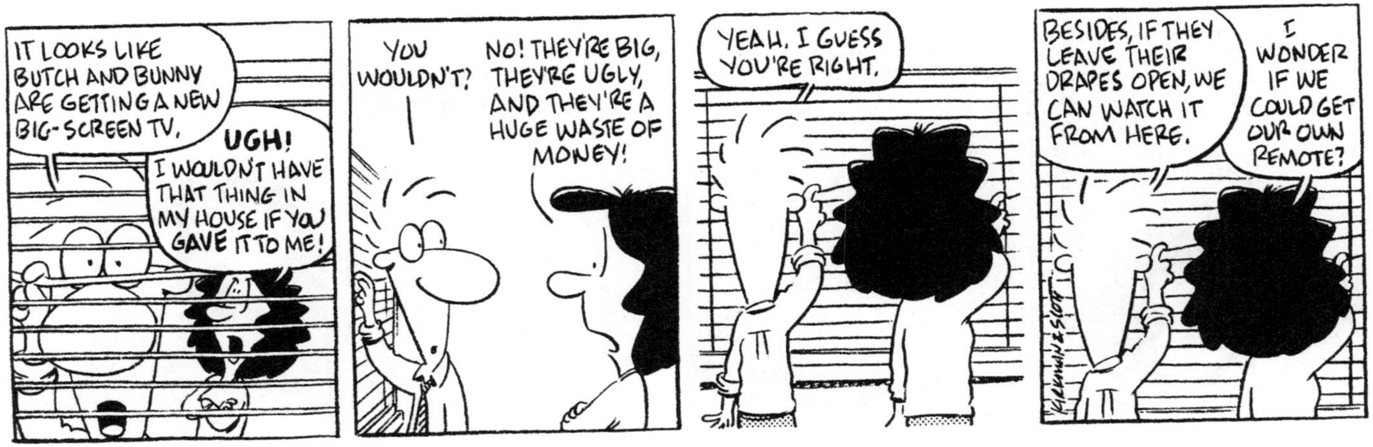
IT LOOKS LIKE BUTCH AND BUNNY ARE GETTING A NEW BIG-SCREEN TV.
UGH! I WOULDN'T HAVE THAT THING IN MY HOUSE IF YOU **GAVE** IT TO ME!
YOU WOULDN'T?
NO! THEY'RE BIG, THEY'RE UGLY, AND THEY'RE A HUGE WASTE OF MONEY!
YEAH. I GUESS YOU'RE RIGHT.
BESIDES, IF THEY LEAVE THEIR DRAPES OPEN, WE CAN WATCH IT FROM HERE.
I WONDER IF WE COULD GET OUR OWN REMOTE?
KIRKMAN & SCOTT

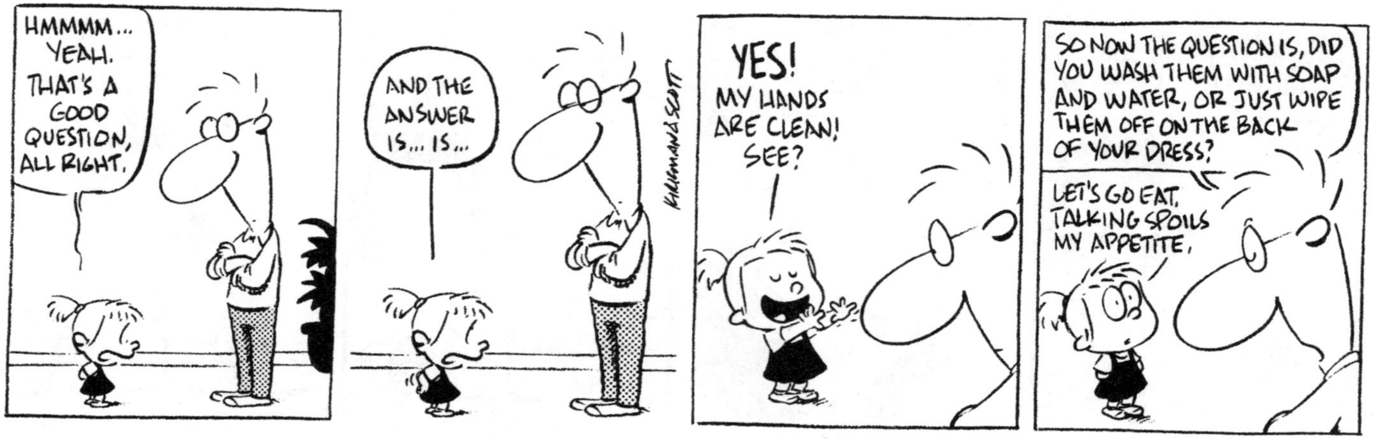
HMMMM... YEAH. THAT'S A GOOD QUESTION, ALL RIGHT.
AND THE ANSWER IS... IS...
KIRKMAN & SCOTT
YES! MY HANDS ARE CLEAN! SEE?
SO NOW THE QUESTION IS, DID YOU WASH THEM WITH SOAP AND WATER, OR JUST WIPE THEM OFF ON THE BACK OF YOUR DRESS?
LET'S GO EAT. TALKING SPOILS MY APPETITE.

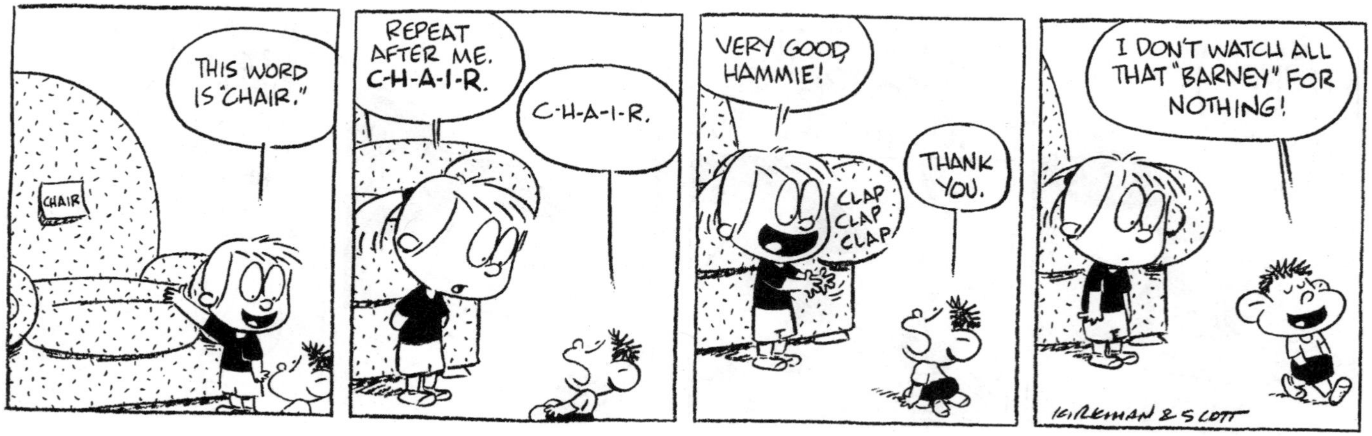
CHAIR
THIS WORD IS "CHAIR."
REPEAT AFTER ME. C-H-A-I-R.
C-H-A-I-R.
VERY GOOD, HAMMIE!
CLAP CLAP CLAP
THANK YOU.
I DON'T WATCH ALL THAT "BARNEY" FOR NOTHING!
KIRKMAN & SCOTT

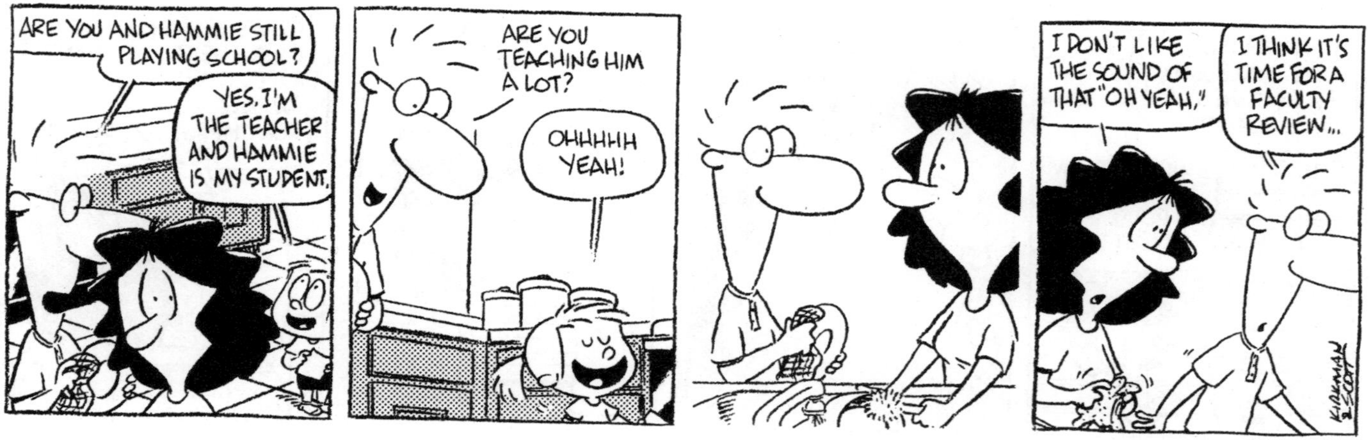
ARE YOU AND HAMMIE STILL PLAYING SCHOOL?
YES. I'M THE TEACHER AND HAMMIE IS MY STUDENT.
ARE YOU TEACHING HIM A LOT?
OHHHHH YEAH!
I DON'T LIKE THE SOUND OF THAT "OH YEAH."
I THINK IT'S TIME FOR A FACULTY REVIEW...
KIRKMAN & SCOTT

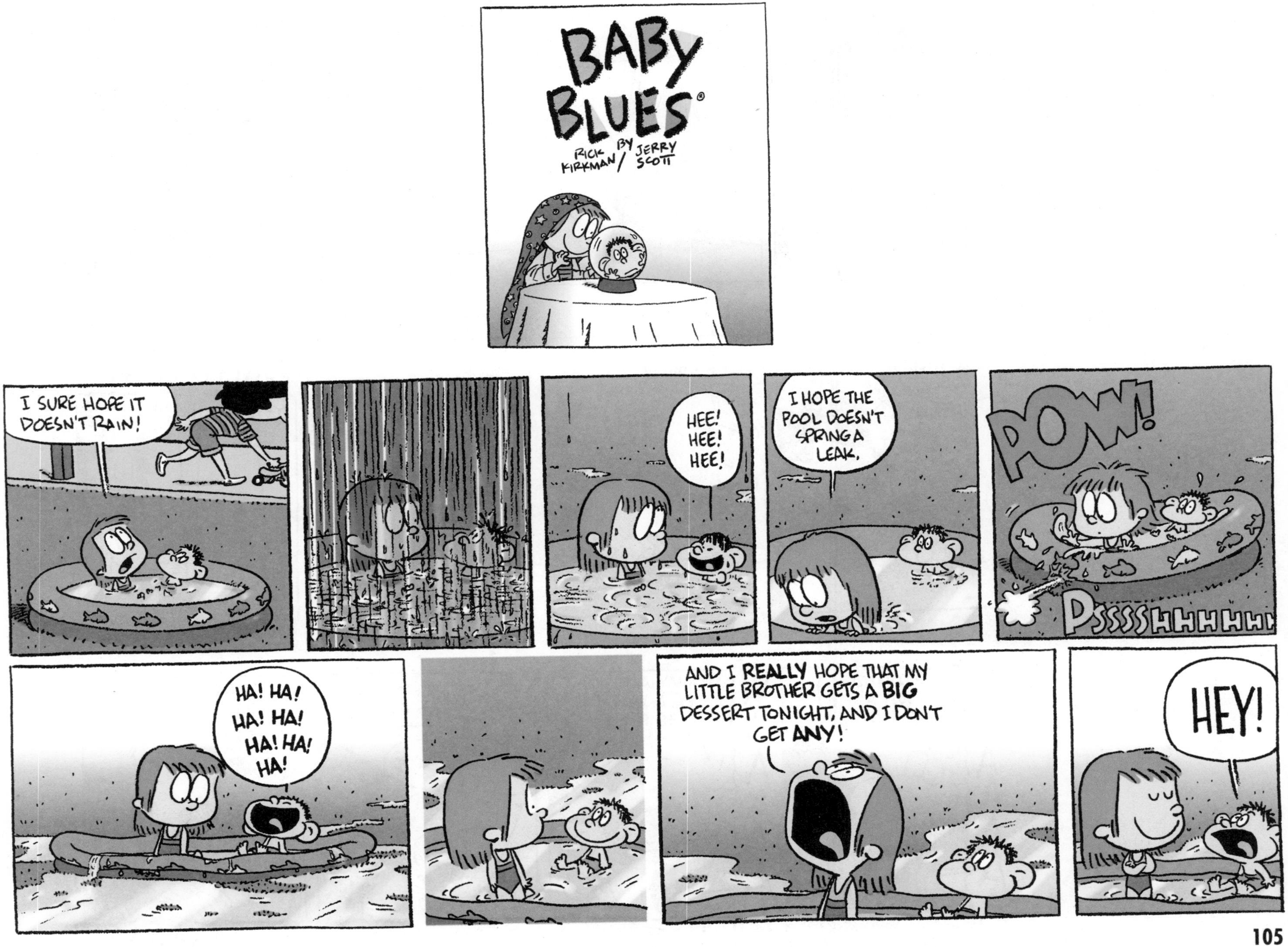
BABY BLUES®
BY RICK KIRKMAN / JERRY SCOTT
I SURE HOPE IT DOESN'T RAIN!
HEE! HEE! HEE!
I HOPE THE POOL DOESN'T SPRING A LEAK.
POW!
PSSSSHHHHHH
HA! HA! HA! HA! HA! HA! HA!
AND I REALLY HOPE THAT MY LITTLE BROTHER GETS A BIG DESSERT TONIGHT, AND I DON'T GET ANY!
HEY!

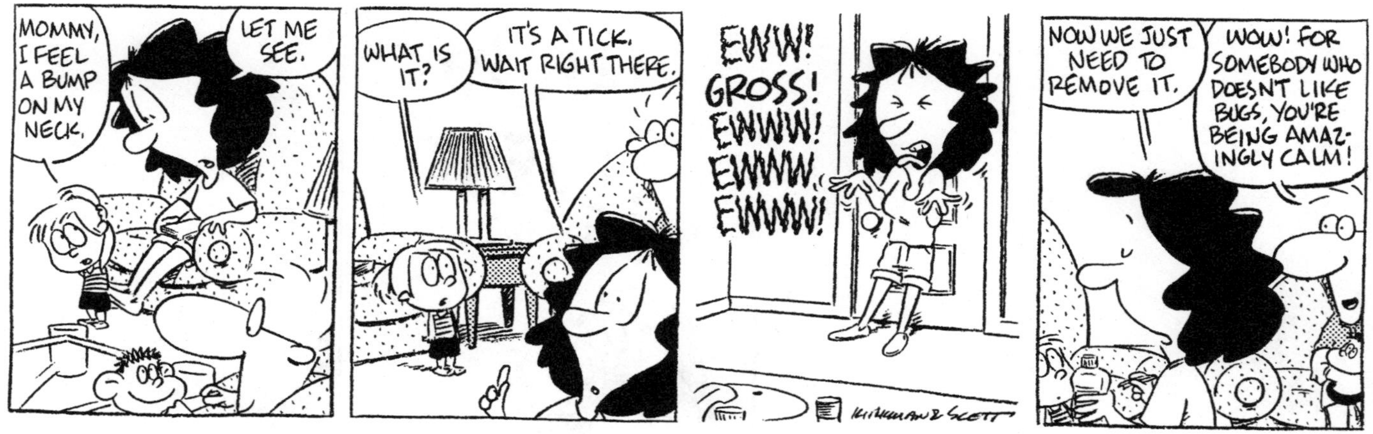
MOMMY, I FEEL A BUMP ON MY NECK.
LET ME SEE.
WHAT IS IT?
IT'S A TICK. WAIT RIGHT THERE.
EWW! GROSS! EWWW! EWWW. EWWW!
KIRKMAN & SCOTT
NOW WE JUST NEED TO REMOVE IT.
WOW! FOR SOMEBODY WHO DOESN'T LIKE BUGS, YOU'RE BEING AMAZINGLY CALM!

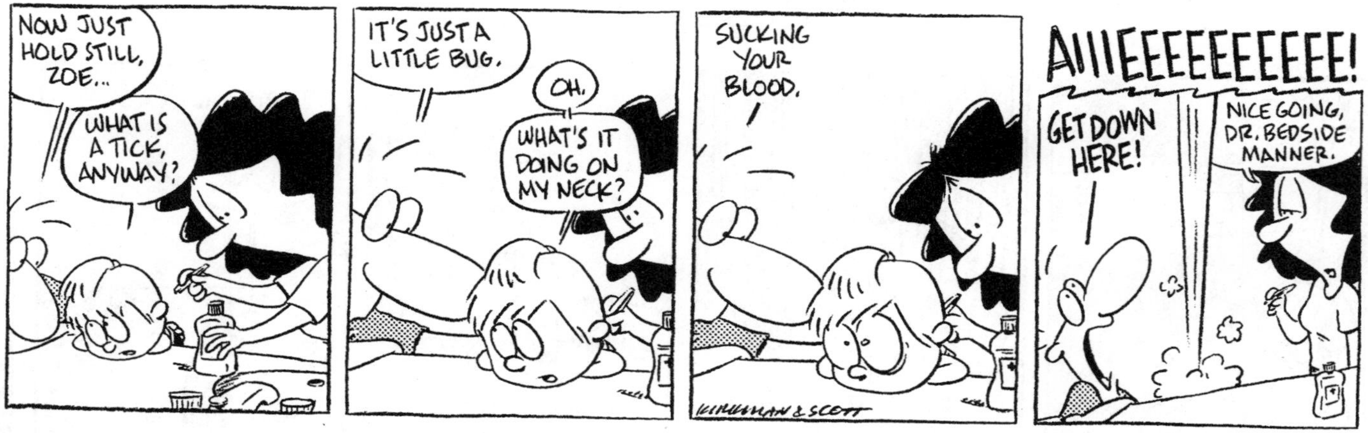
NOW JUST HOLD STILL, ZOE...
WHAT IS A TICK, ANYWAY?
IT'S JUST A LITTLE BUG.
OH.
WHAT'S IT DOING ON MY NECK?
SUCKING YOUR BLOOD.
KIRKMAN & SCOTT
AIIIEEEEEEEEEE!
GET DOWN HERE!
NICE GOING, DR. BEDSIDE MANNER.

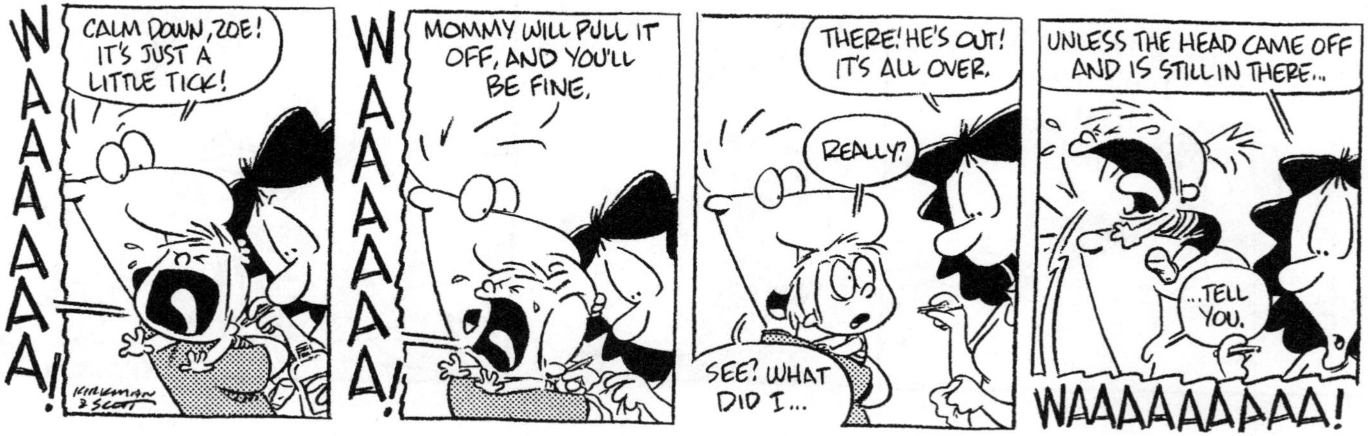
WAAAAAA!
CALM DOWN, ZOE! IT'S JUST A LITTLE TICK!
KIRKMAN & SCOTT
WAAAAAA!
MOMMY WILL PULL IT OFF, AND YOU'LL BE FINE.
THERE! HE'S OUT! IT'S ALL OVER.
REALLY?
SEE? WHAT DID I...
UNLESS THE HEAD CAME OFF AND IS STILL IN THERE...
...TELL YOU.
WAAAAAAAAA!

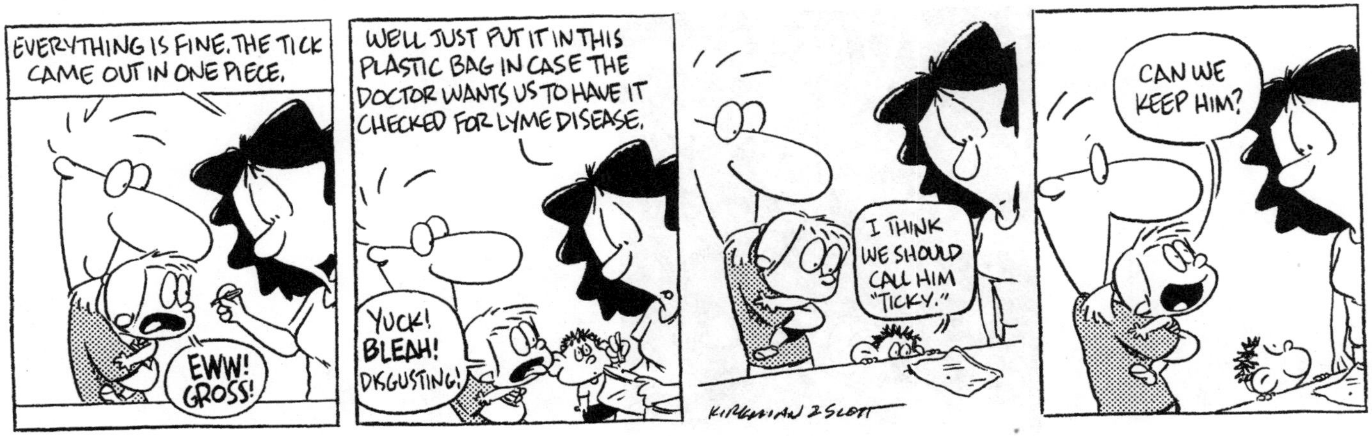
EVERYTHING IS FINE. THE TICK CAME OUT IN ONE PIECE.
EWW! GROSS!
WE'LL JUST PUT IT IN THIS PLASTIC BAG IN CASE THE DOCTOR WANTS US TO HAVE IT CHECKED FOR LYME DISEASE.
YUCK! BLEAH! DISGUSTING!
I THINK WE SHOULD CALL HIM "TICKY."
KIRKMAN & SCOTT
CAN WE KEEP HIM?

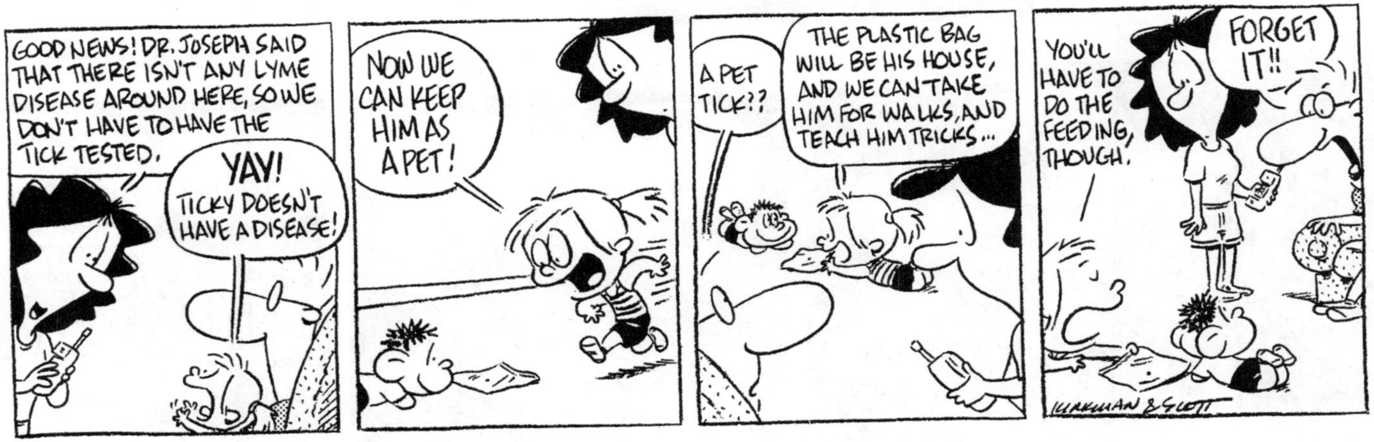
GOOD NEWS! DR. JOSEPH SAID THAT THERE ISN'T ANY LYME DISEASE AROUND HERE, SO WE DON'T HAVE TO HAVE THE TICK TESTED.
YAY! TICKY DOESN'T HAVE A DISEASE!
NOW WE CAN KEEP HIM AS A PET!
A PET TICK??
THE PLASTIC BAG WILL BE HIS HOUSE, AND WE CAN TAKE HIM FOR WALKS, AND TEACH HIM TRICKS...
YOU'LL HAVE TO DO THE FEEDING, THOUGH.
FORGET IT!!
KIRKMAN & SCOTT

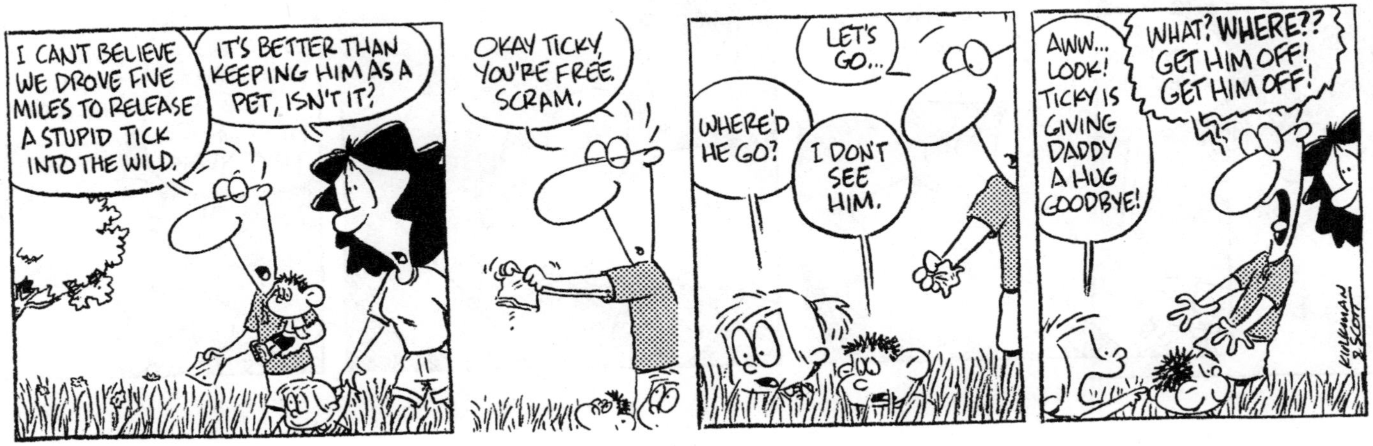
I CAN'T BELIEVE WE DROVE FIVE MILES TO RELEASE A STUPID TICK INTO THE WILD.
IT'S BETTER THAN KEEPING HIM AS A PET, ISN'T IT?
OKAY TICKY, YOU'RE FREE. SCRAM.
LET'S GO...
WHERE'D HE GO?
I DON'T SEE HIM.
AWW... LOOK! TICKY IS GIVING DADDY A HUG GOODBYE!
WHAT? WHERE?? GET HIM OFF! GET HIM OFF!
KIRKMAN & SCOTT

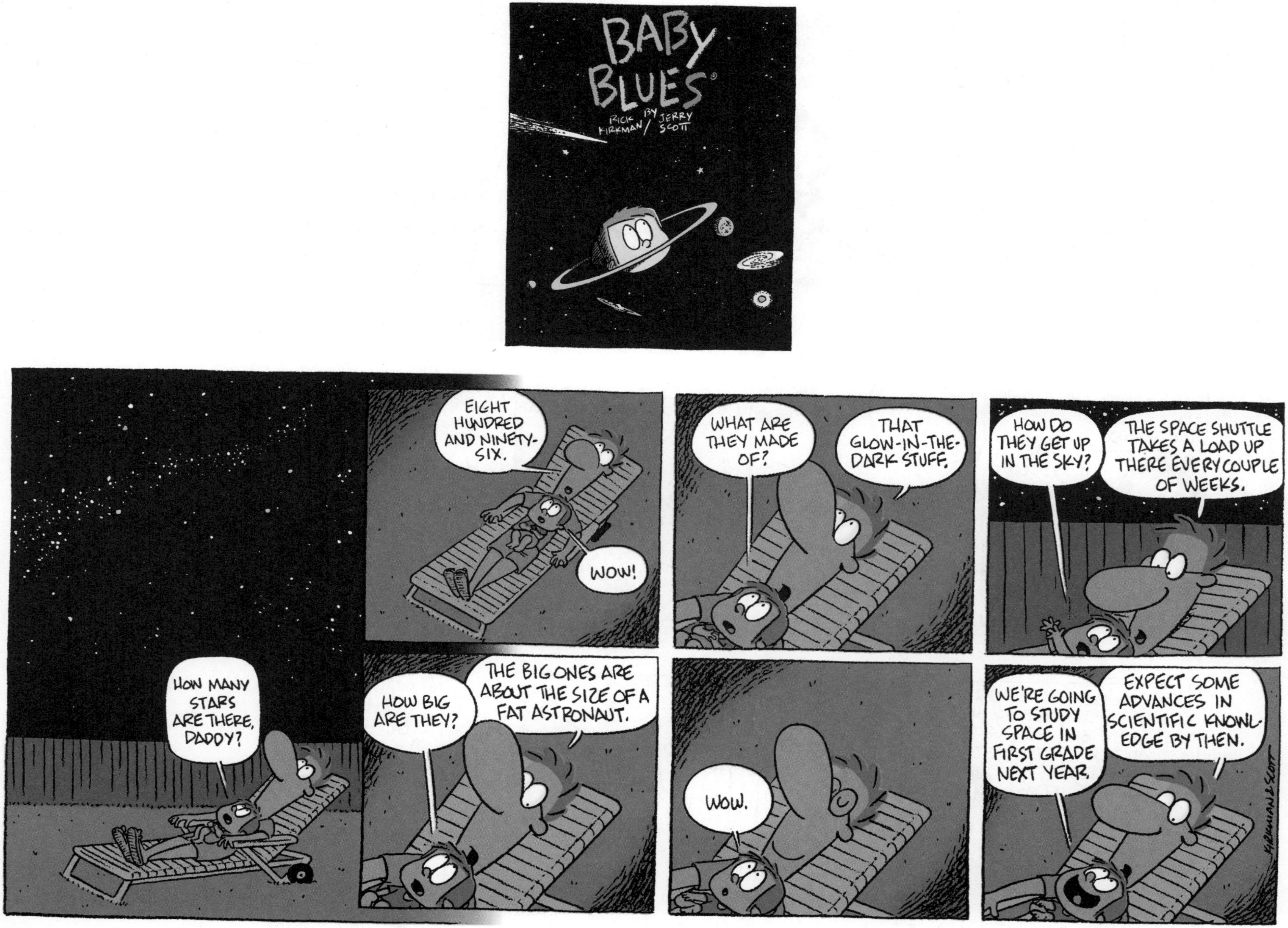
BABY BLUES
RICK KIRKMAN / BY JERRY SCOTT
HOW MANY STARS ARE THERE, DADDY?
EIGHT HUNDRED AND NINETY-SIX.
WOW!
WHAT ARE THEY MADE OF?
THAT GLOW-IN-THE-DARK STUFF.
HOW DO THEY GET UP IN THE SKY?
THE SPACE SHUTTLE TAKES A LOAD UP THERE EVERY COUPLE OF WEEKS.
HOW BIG ARE THEY?
THE BIG ONES ARE ABOUT THE SIZE OF A FAT ASTRONAUT.
WOW.
WE'RE GOING TO STUDY SPACE IN FIRST GRADE NEXT YEAR.
EXPECT SOME ADVANCES IN SCIENTIFIC KNOWLEDGE BY THEN.
KIRKMAN & SCOTT

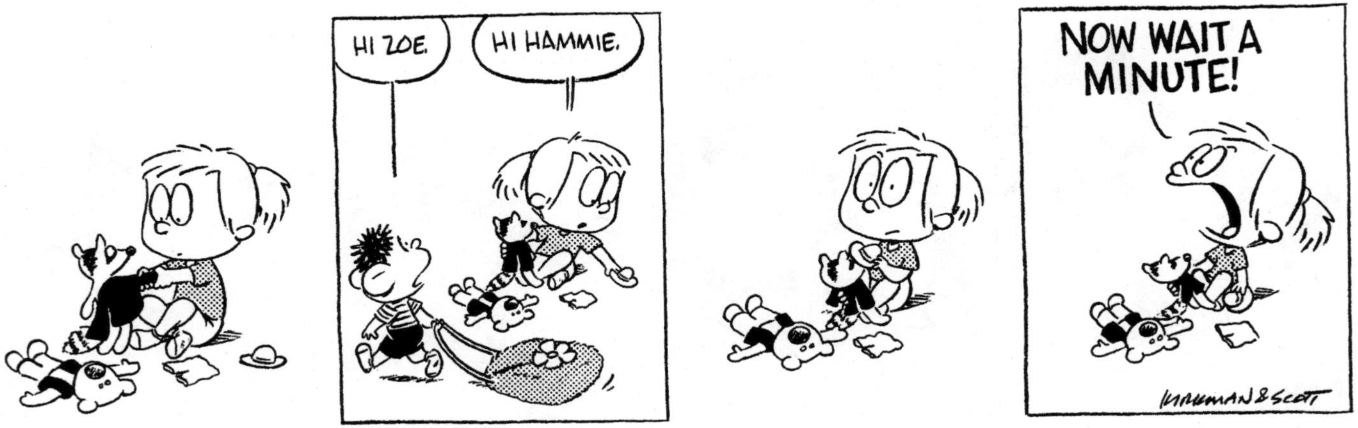
HI ZOE.
HI HAMMIE.
NOW WAIT A MINUTE!
KIRKMAN & SCOTT

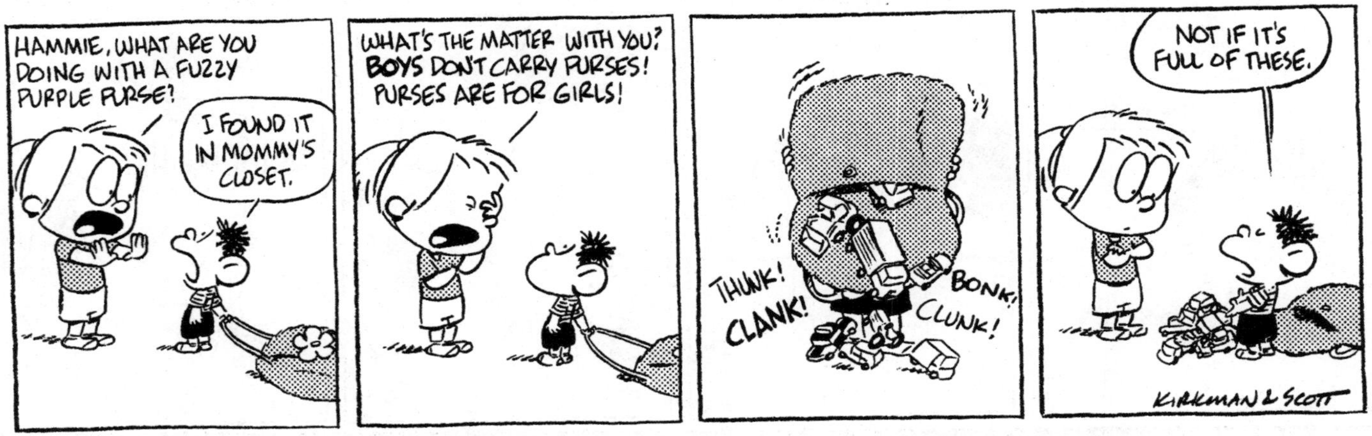
HAMMIE, WHAT ARE YOU DOING WITH A FUZZY PURPLE PURSE?
I FOUND IT IN MOMMY'S CLOSET.
WHAT'S THE MATTER WITH YOU? BOYS DON'T CARRY PURSES! PURSES ARE FOR GIRLS!
THUNK!
CLANK!
BONK!
CLUNK!
NOT IF IT'S FULL OF THESE.
KIRKMAN & SCOTT

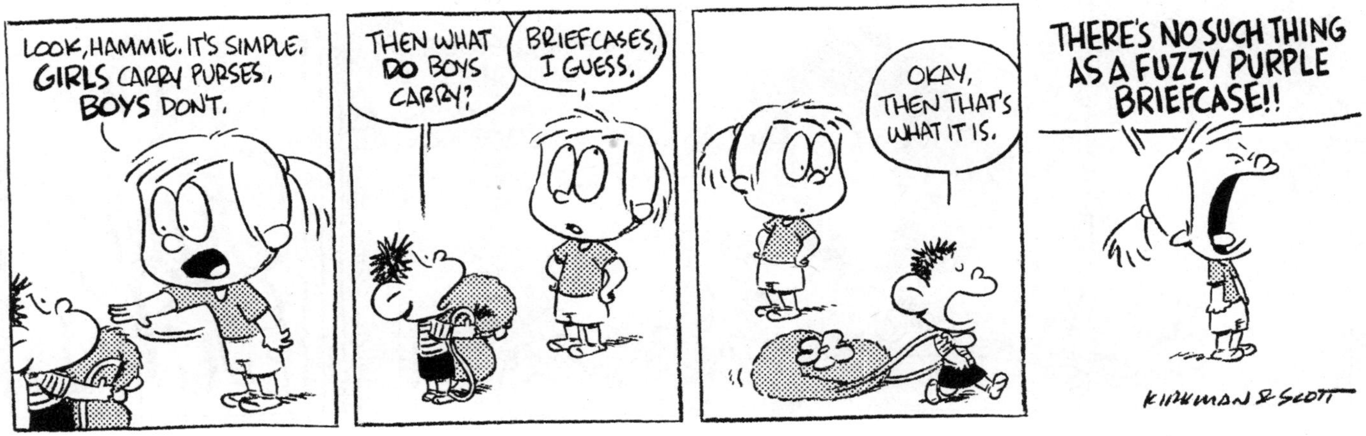
LOOK, HAMMIE. IT'S SIMPLE. GIRLS CARRY PURSES. BOYS DON'T.
THEN WHAT DO BOYS CARRY?
BRIEFCASES, I GUESS.
OKAY, THEN THAT'S WHAT IT IS.
THERE'S NO SUCH THING AS A FUZZY PURPLE BRIEFCASE!!
KIRKMAN & SCOTT

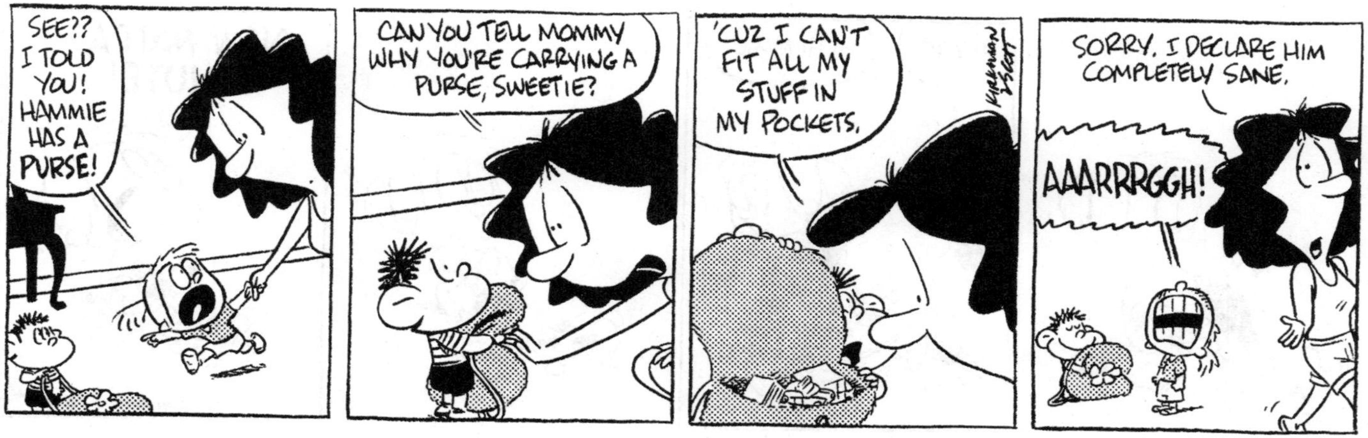
SEE?? I TOLD YOU! HAMMIE HAS A PURSE!
CAN YOU TELL MOMMY WHY YOU'RE CARRYING A PURSE, SWEETIE?
'CUZ I CAN'T FIT ALL MY STUFF IN MY POCKETS.
KIRKMAN & SCOTT
SORRY. I DECLARE HIM COMPLETELY SANE.
AAARRRGGH!

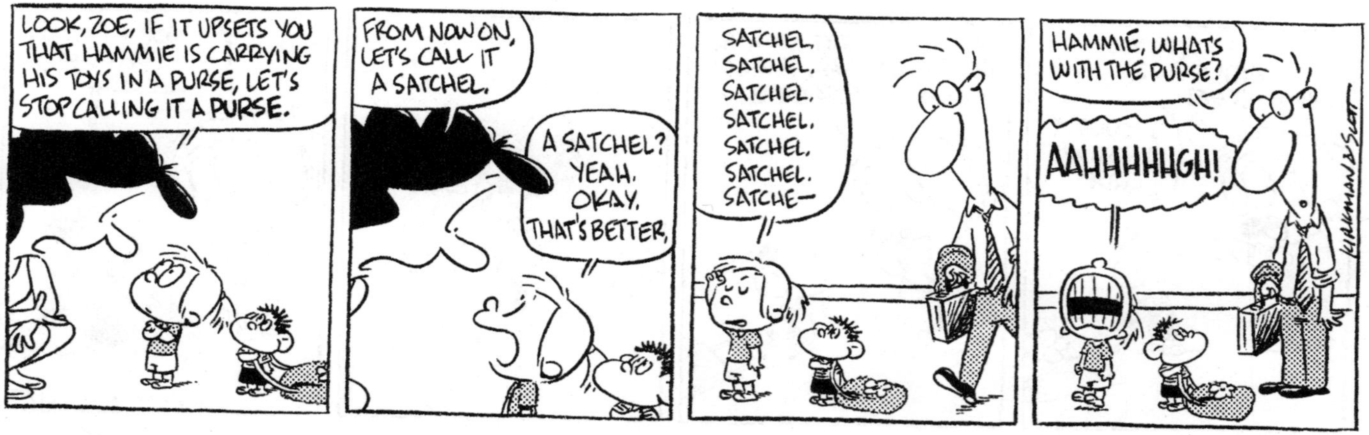
LOOK, ZOE, IF IT UPSETS YOU THAT HAMMIE IS CARRYING HIS TOYS IN A PURSE, LET'S STOP CALLING IT A PURSE.
FROM NOW ON, LET'S CALL IT A SATCHEL.
A SATCHEL? YEAH. OKAY. THAT'S BETTER.
SATCHEL. SATCHEL. SATCHEL. SATCHEL. SATCHEL. SATCHEL. SATCHE—
HAMMIE, WHAT'S WITH THE PURSE?
AAHHHHHGH!
KIRKMAN & SCOTT

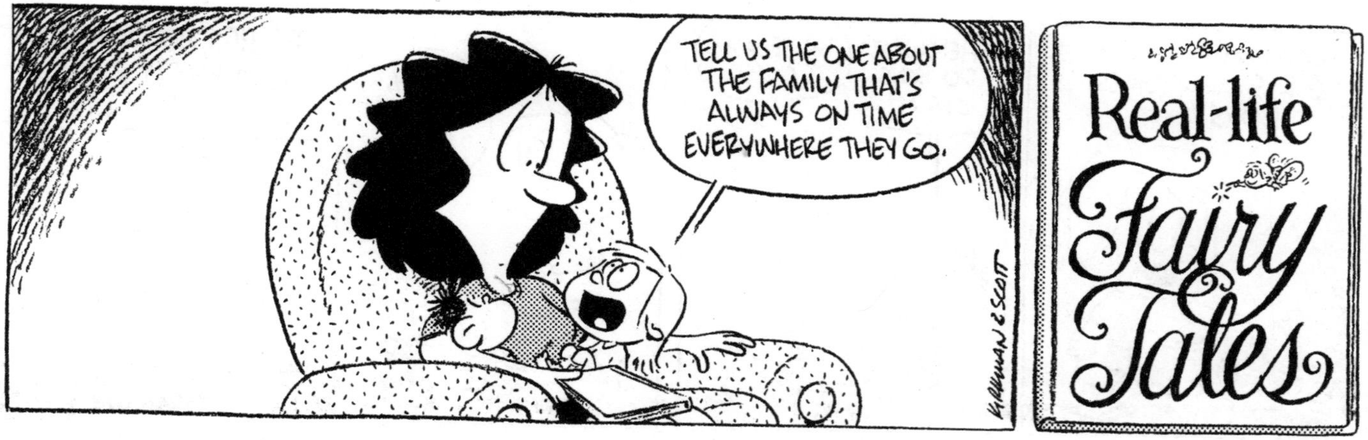
TELL US THE ONE ABOUT THE FAMILY THAT'S ALWAYS ON TIME EVERYWHERE THEY GO.
KIRKMAN & SCOTT
Real-life Fairy Tales

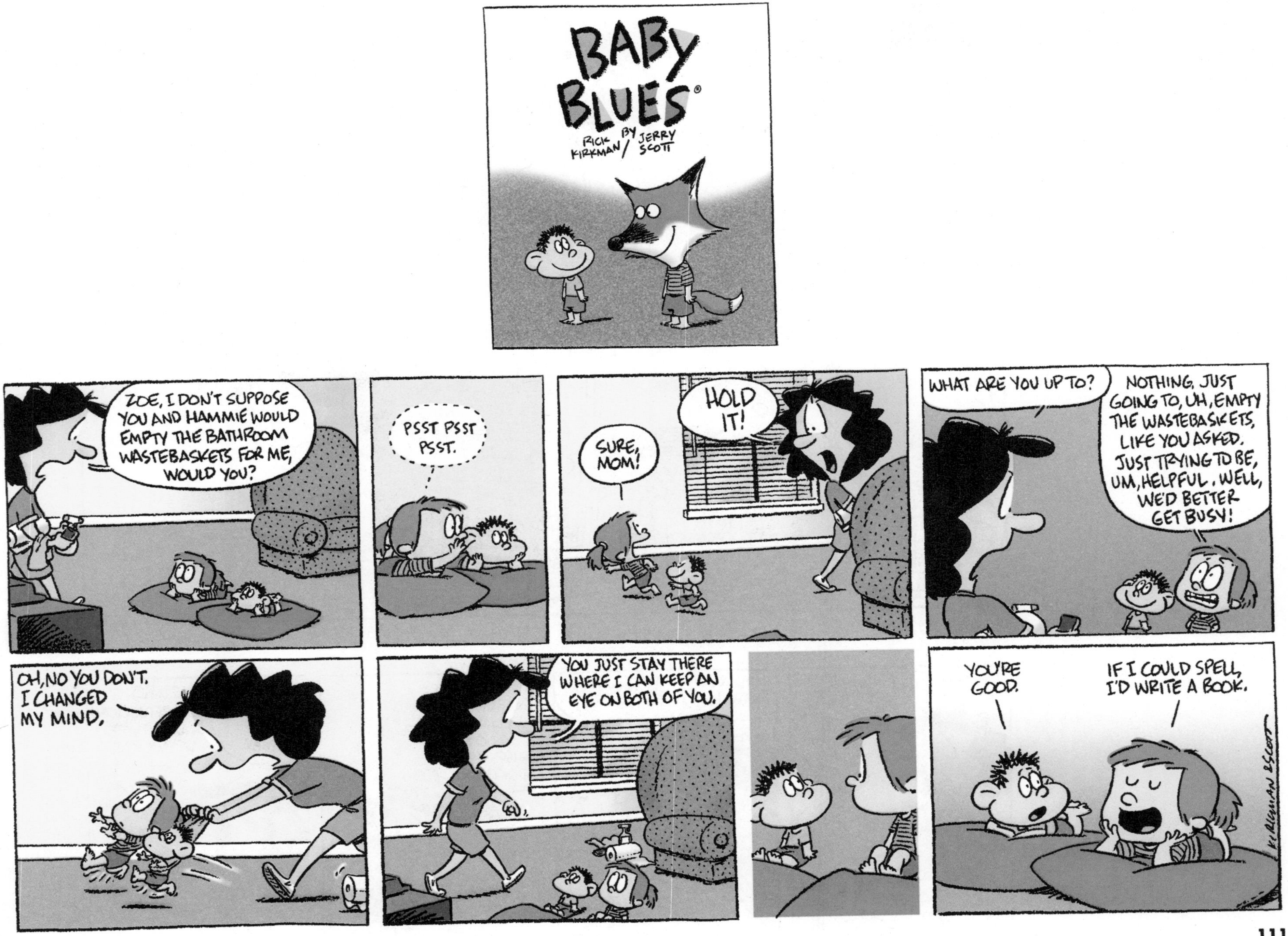
BABY BLUES®
RICK KIRKMAN / BY JERRY SCOTT
ZOE, I DON'T SUPPOSE YOU AND HAMMIE WOULD EMPTY THE BATHROOM WASTEBASKETS FOR ME, WOULD YOU?
PSST PSST PSST.
SURE, MOM!
HOLD IT!
WHAT ARE YOU UP TO?
NOTHING. JUST GOING TO, UH, EMPTY THE WASTEBASKETS, LIKE YOU ASKED. JUST TRYING TO BE, UM, HELPFUL. WELL, WE'D BETTER GET BUSY!
OH, NO YOU DON'T. I CHANGED MY MIND.
YOU JUST STAY THERE WHERE I CAN KEEP AN EYE ON BOTH OF YOU.
YOU'RE GOOD.
IF I COULD SPELL, I'D WRITE A BOOK.
KIRKMAN & SCOTT

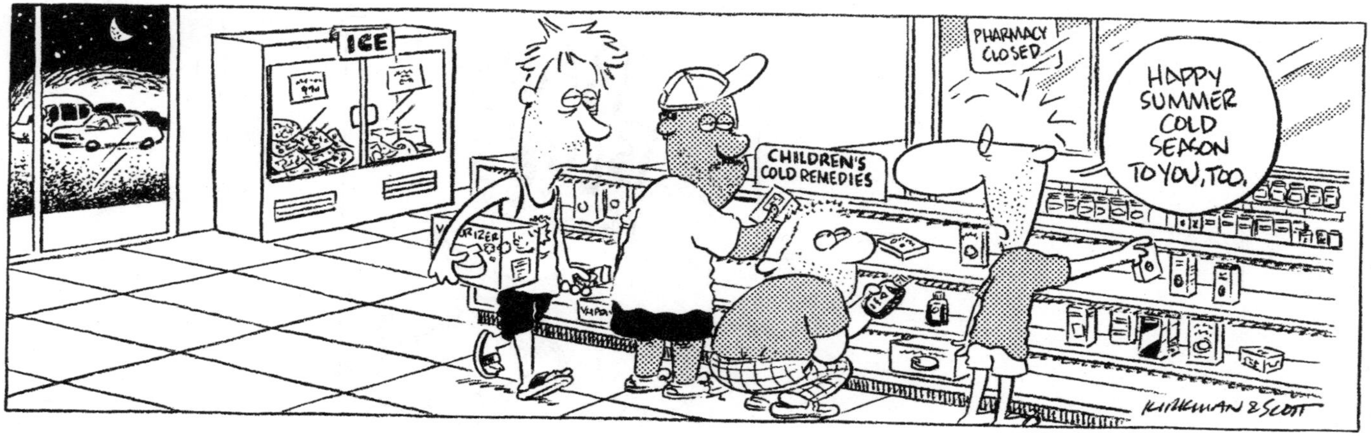
ICE
PHARMACY CLOSED
CHILDREN'S COLD REMEDIES
HAPPY SUMMER COLD SEASON TO YOU, TOO.
KIRKMAN & SCOTT

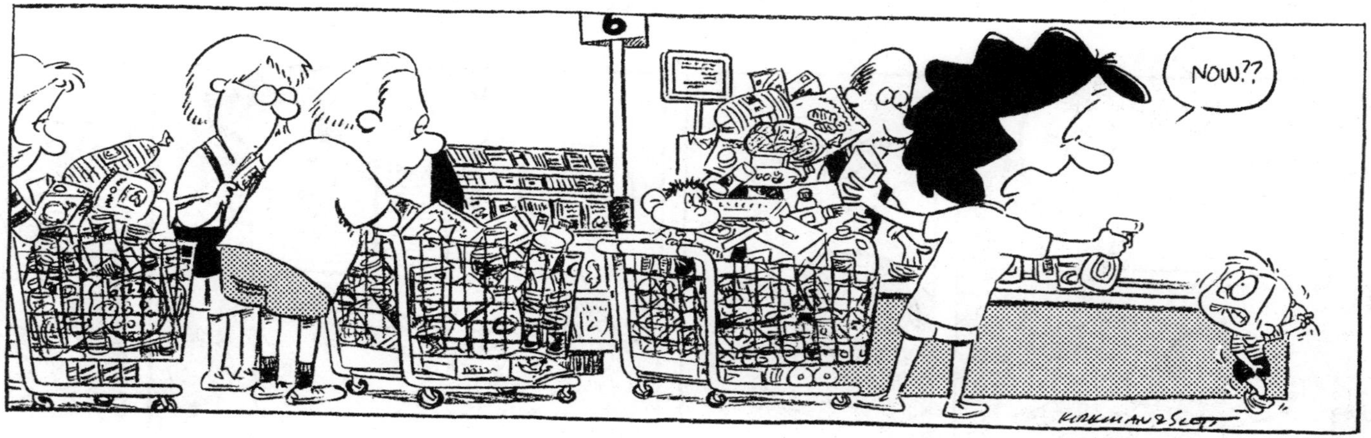
6
NOW??
KIRKMAN & SCOTT

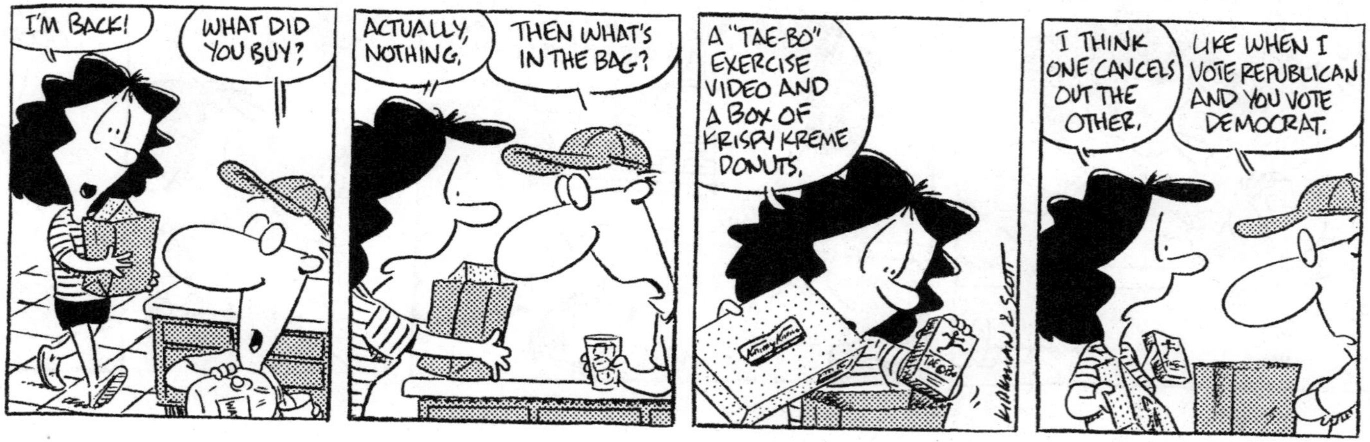
I'M BACK!
WHAT DID YOU BUY?
ACTUALLY, NOTHING.
THEN WHAT'S IN THE BAG?
A "TAE-BO" EXERCISE VIDEO AND A BOX OF KRISPY KREME DONUTS.
KIRKMAN & SCOTT
I THINK ONE CANCELS OUT THE OTHER.
LIKE WHEN I VOTE REPUBLICAN AND YOU VOTE DEMOCRAT.

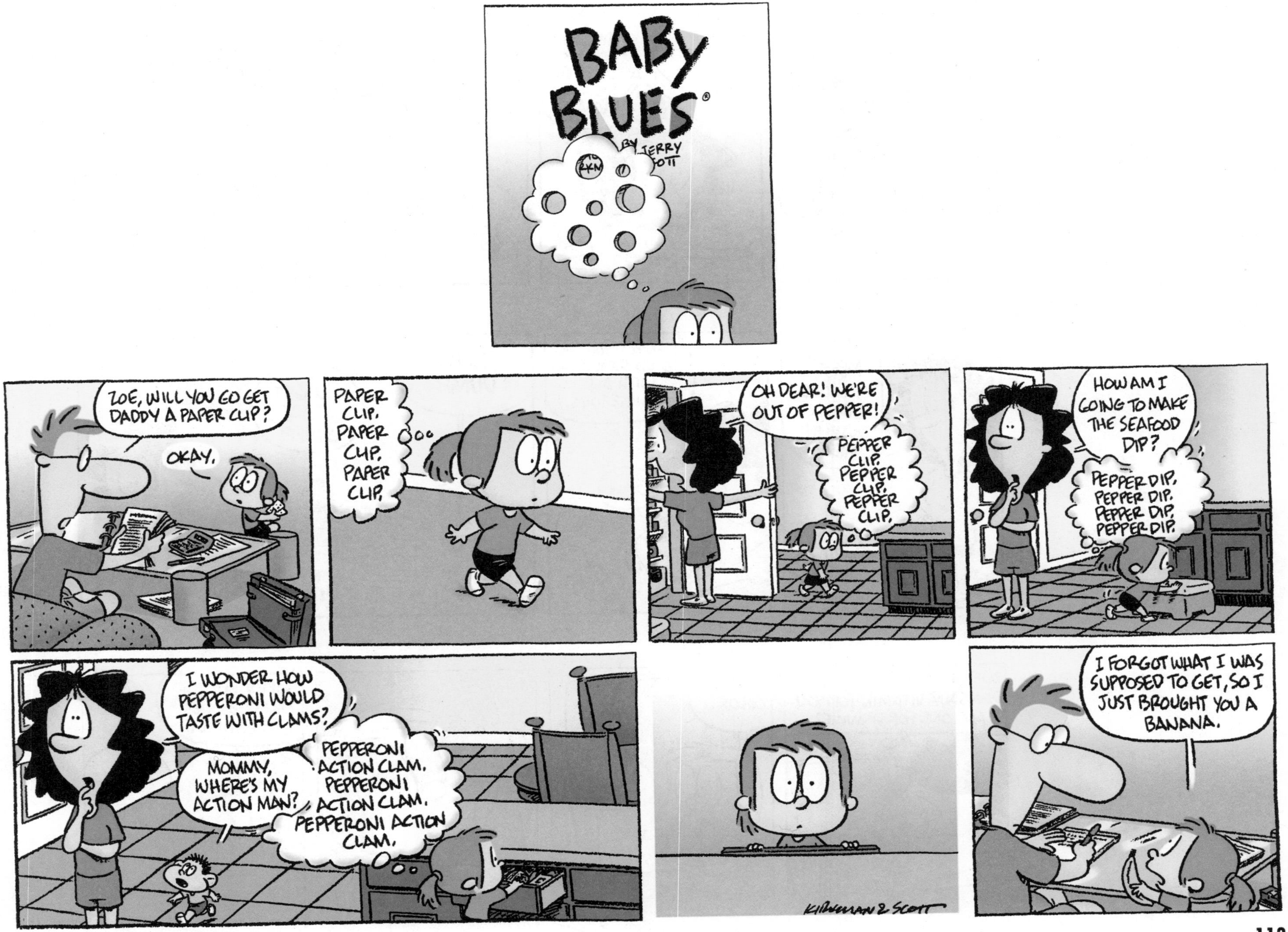
BABY BLUES®
ZOE, WILL YOU GO GET DADDY A PAPER CLIP?
OKAY.
PAPER CLIP, PAPER CLIP, PAPER CLIP.
OH DEAR! WE'RE OUT OF PEPPER!
PEPPER CLIP, PEPPER CLIP, PEPPER CLIP.
HOW AM I GOING TO MAKE THE SEAFOOD DIP?
PEPPER DIP, PEPPER DIP, PEPPER DIP, PEPPER DIP.
I WONDER HOW PEPPERONI WOULD TASTE WITH CLAMS?
MOMMY, WHERE'S MY ACTION MAN?
PEPPERONI ACTION CLAM, PEPPERONI ACTION CLAM, PEPPERONI ACTION CLAM.
KIRKMAN & SCOTT
I FORGOT WHAT I WAS SUPPOSED TO GET, SO I JUST BROUGHT YOU A BANANA.

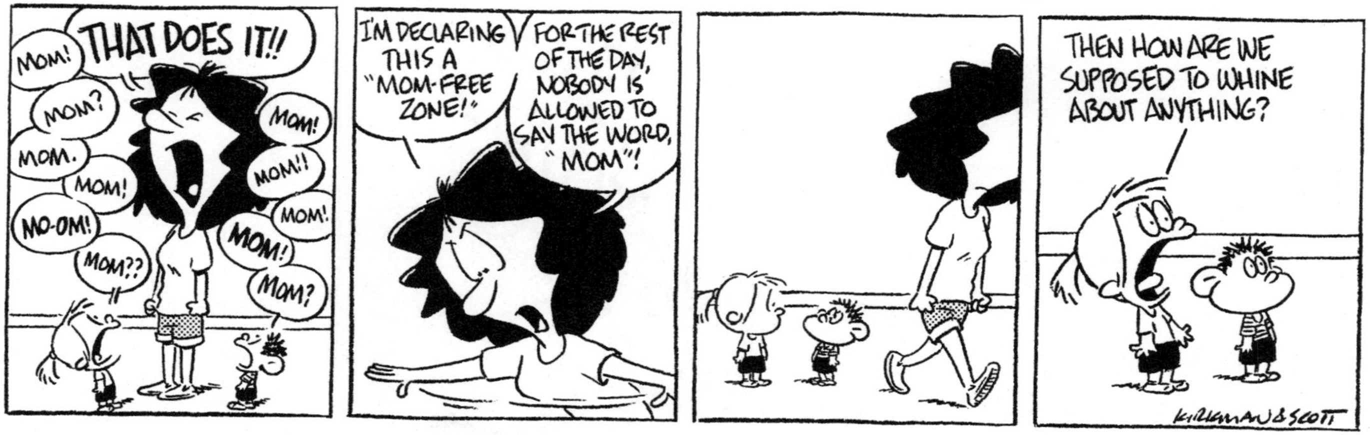
MOM!
THAT DOES IT!!
MOM?
MOM.
MOM!
MO-OM!
MOM??
MOM!
MOM!!
MOM!
MOM!
MOM?
I'M DECLARING THIS A "MOM-FREE ZONE!"
FOR THE REST OF THE DAY, NOBODY IS ALLOWED TO SAY THE WORD, "MOM"!
THEN HOW ARE WE SUPPOSED TO WHINE ABOUT ANYTHING?
KIRKMAN & SCOTT

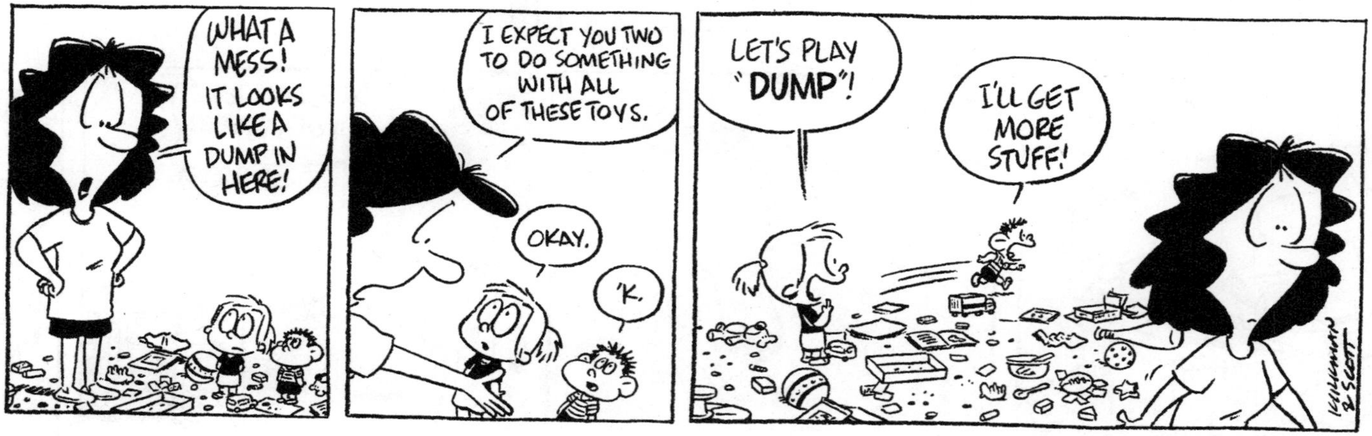
WHAT A MESS! IT LOOKS LIKE A DUMP IN HERE!
I EXPECT YOU TWO TO DO SOMETHING WITH ALL OF THESE TOYS.
OKAY.
'K.
LET'S PLAY "DUMP"!
I'LL GET MORE STUFF!
KIRKMAN & SCOTT

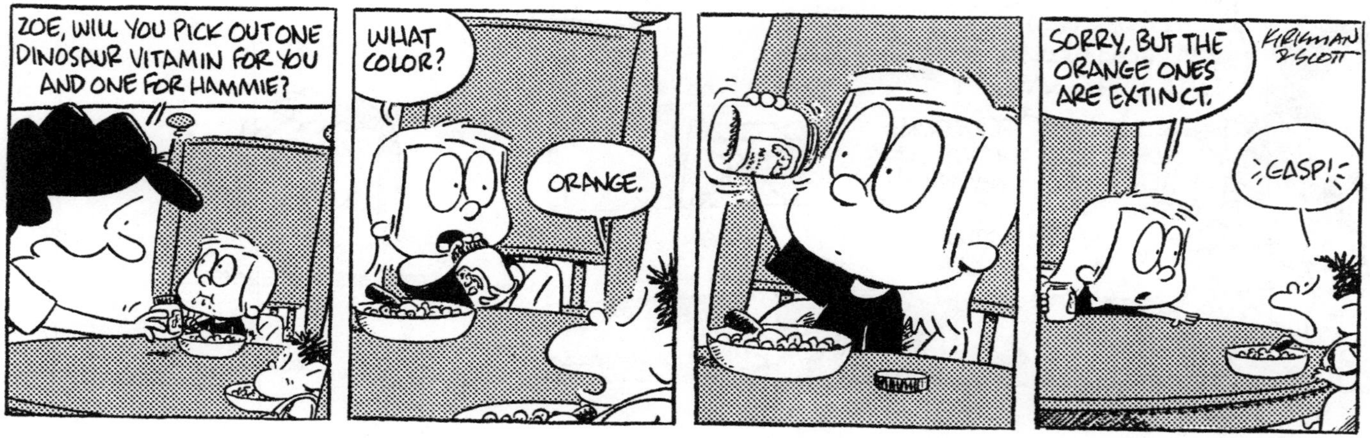
ZOE, WILL YOU PICK OUT ONE DINOSAUR VITAMIN FOR YOU AND ONE FOR HAMMIE?
WHAT COLOR?
ORANGE.
SORRY, BUT THE ORANGE ONES ARE EXTINCT.
KIRKMAN & SCOTT
GASP!

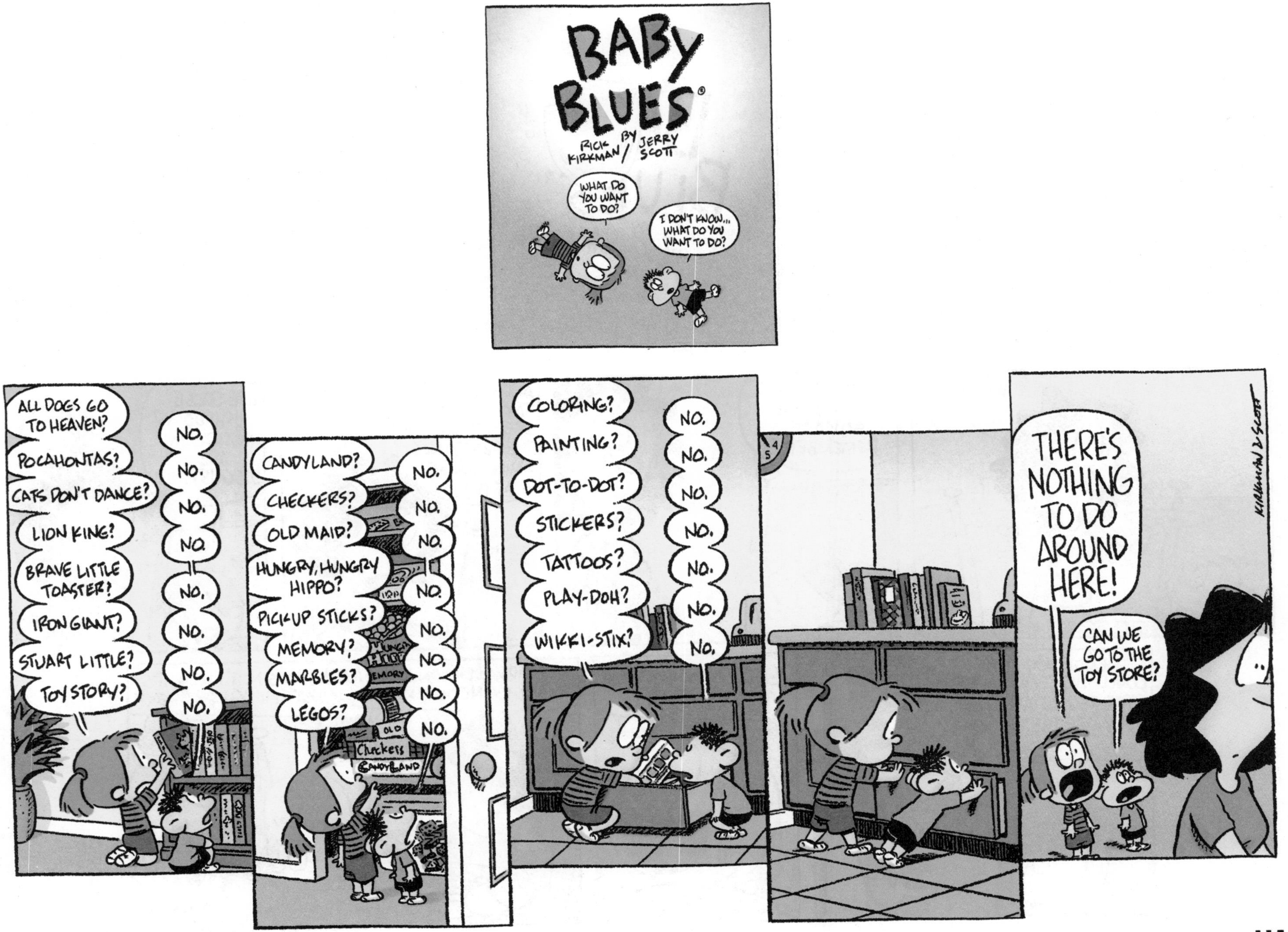
BABY BLUES®
BY RICK KIRKMAN / JERRY SCOTT
WHAT DO YOU WANT TO DO?
I DON'T KNOW... WHAT DO YOU WANT TO DO?
ALL DOGS GO TO HEAVEN?
NO.
POCAHONTAS?
NO.
CATS DON'T DANCE?
NO.
LION KING?
NO.
BRAVE LITTLE TOASTER?
NO.
IRON GIANT?
NO.
STUART LITTLE?
NO.
TOY STORY?
NO.
CANDYLAND?
NO.
CHECKERS?
NO.
OLD MAID?
NO.
HUNGRY, HUNGRY HIPPO?
NO.
PICKUP STICKS?
NO.
MEMORY?
NO.
MARBLES?
NO.
LEGOS?
NO.
COLORING?
NO.
PAINTING?
NO.
DOT-TO-DOT?
NO.
STICKERS?
NO.
TATTOOS?
NO.
PLAY-DOH?
NO.
WIKKI-STIX?
NO.
KIRKMAN & SCOTT
THERE'S NOTHING TO DO AROUND HERE!
CAN WE GO TO THE TOY STORE?

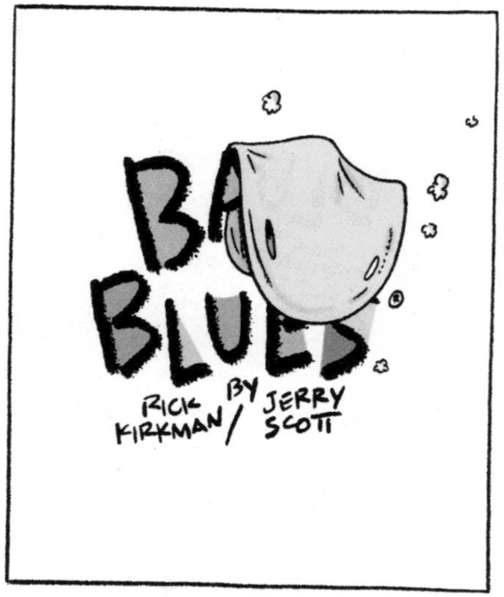
BA
BLUES
RICK KIRKMAN / BY JERRY SCOTT

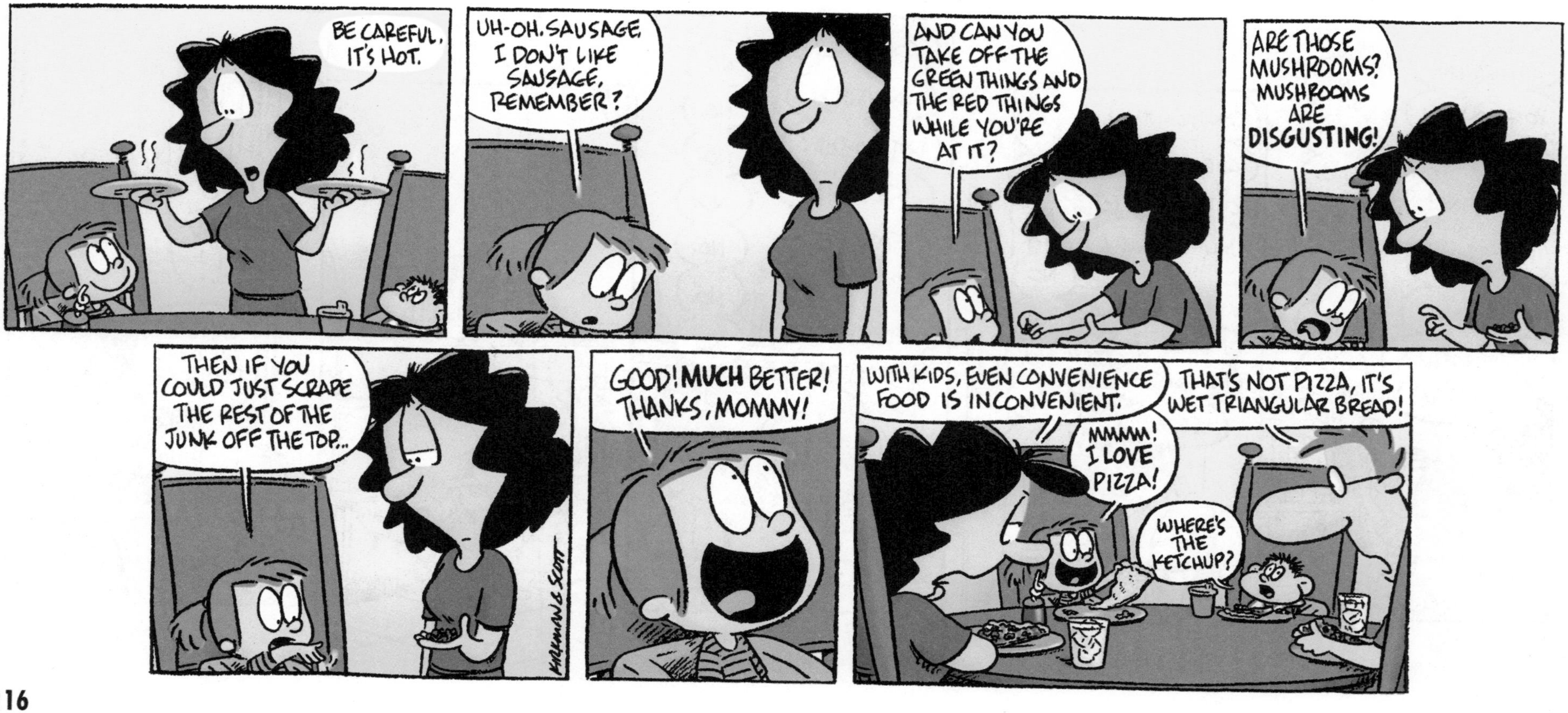
BE CAREFUL, IT'S HOT.
UH-OH, SAUSAGE. I DON'T LIKE SAUSAGE, REMEMBER?
AND CAN YOU TAKE OFF THE GREEN THINGS AND THE RED THINGS WHILE YOU'RE AT IT?
ARE THOSE MUSHROOMS? MUSHROOMS ARE DISGUSTING!
THEN IF YOU COULD JUST SCRAPE THE REST OF THE JUNK OFF THE TOP...
KIRKMAN & SCOTT
GOOD! MUCH BETTER! THANKS, MOMMY!
WITH KIDS, EVEN CONVENIENCE FOOD IS INCONVENIENT.
THAT'S NOT PIZZA, IT'S WET TRIANGULAR BREAD!
MMMM! I LOVE PIZZA!
WHERE'S THE KETCHUP?

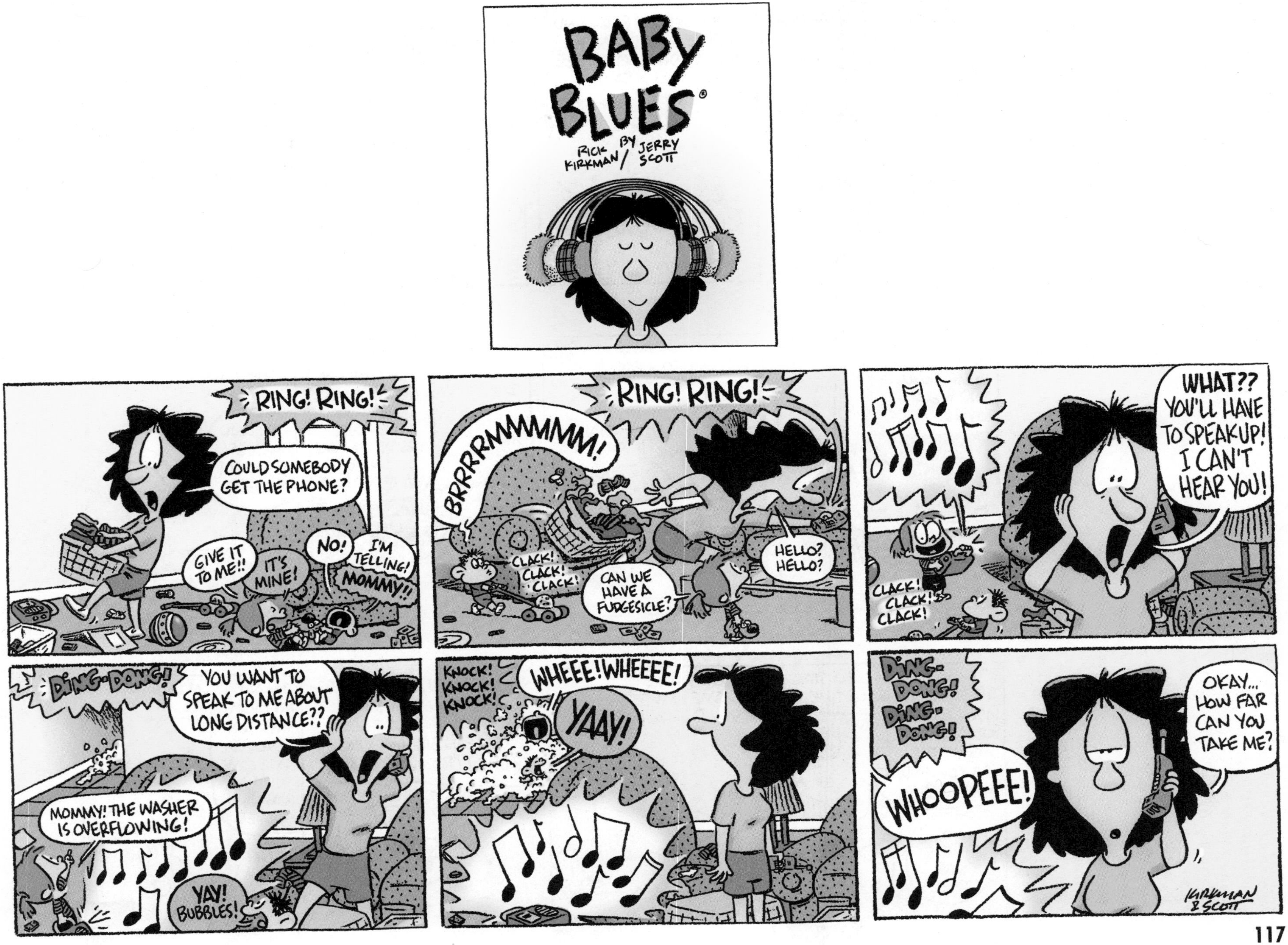
BABY BLUES®
BY RICK KIRKMAN / JERRY SCOTT
RING! RING!
COULD SOMEBODY GET THE PHONE?
GIVE IT TO ME!!
IT'S MINE!
NO!
I'M TELLING!
MOMMY!!
RING! RING!
BRRRRMMMMM!
CLACK! CLACK! CLACK!
CAN WE HAVE A FUDGESICLE?
HELLO? HELLO?
WHAT?? YOU'LL HAVE TO SPEAK UP! I CAN'T HEAR YOU!
CLACK! CLACK! CLACK!
DING-DONG!
YOU WANT TO SPEAK TO ME ABOUT LONG DISTANCE??
MOMMY! THE WASHER IS OVERFLOWING!
YAY! BUBBLES!
KNOCK! KNOCK! KNOCK!
WHEEE! WHEEEE!
YAAY!
DING-DONG! DING-DONG!
OKAY... HOW FAR CAN YOU TAKE ME?
WHOOPEEE!
KIRKMAN & SCOTT

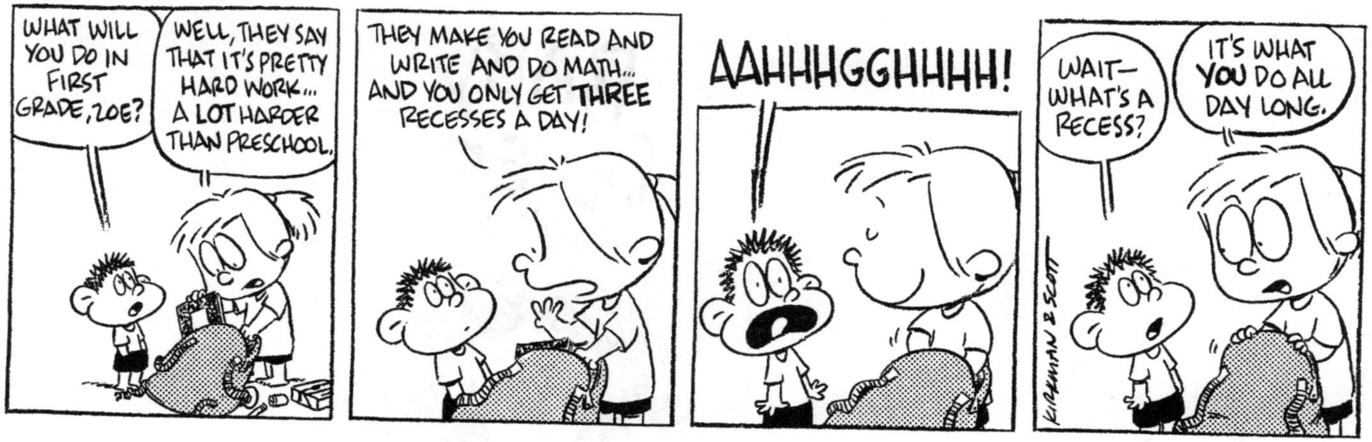
WHAT WILL YOU DO IN FIRST GRADE, ZOE?
WELL, THEY SAY THAT IT'S PRETTY HARD WORK... A LOT HARDER THAN PRESCHOOL.
THEY MAKE YOU READ AND WRITE AND DO MATH... AND YOU ONLY GET THREE RECESSES A DAY!
AAHHHGGHHHH!
WAIT— WHAT'S A RECESS?
IT'S WHAT YOU DO ALL DAY LONG.
KIRKMAN & SCOTT

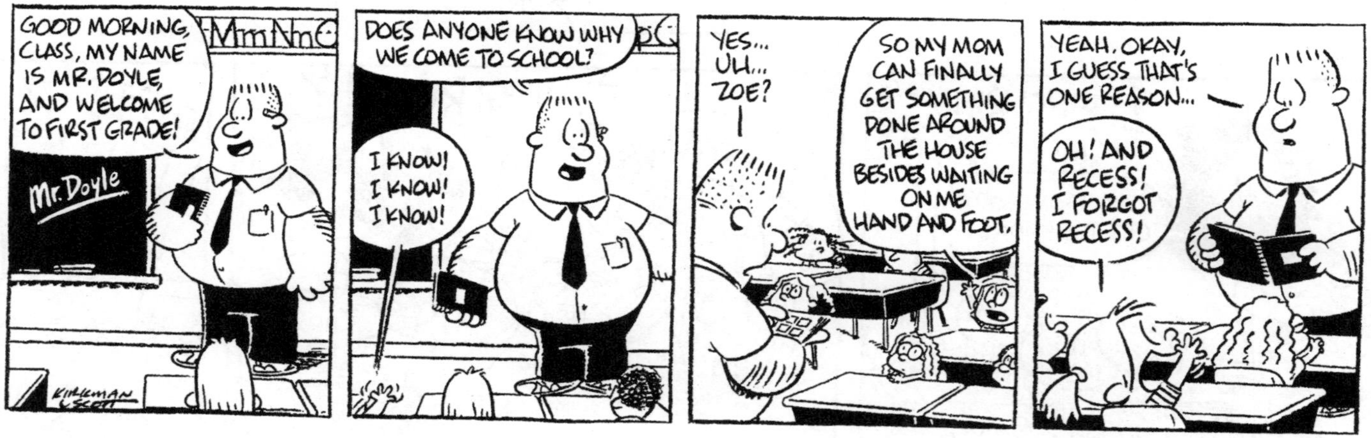
GOOD MORNING, CLASS, MY NAME IS MR. DOYLE, AND WELCOME TO FIRST GRADE!
Mr. Doyle
KIRKMAN & SCOTT
DOES ANYONE KNOW WHY WE COME TO SCHOOL?
I KNOW! I KNOW! I KNOW!
YES... UH... ZOE?
SO MY MOM CAN FINALLY GET SOMETHING DONE AROUND THE HOUSE BESIDES WAITING ON ME HAND AND FOOT.
YEAH. OKAY, I GUESS THAT'S ONE REASON...
OH! AND RECESS! I FORGOT RECESS!

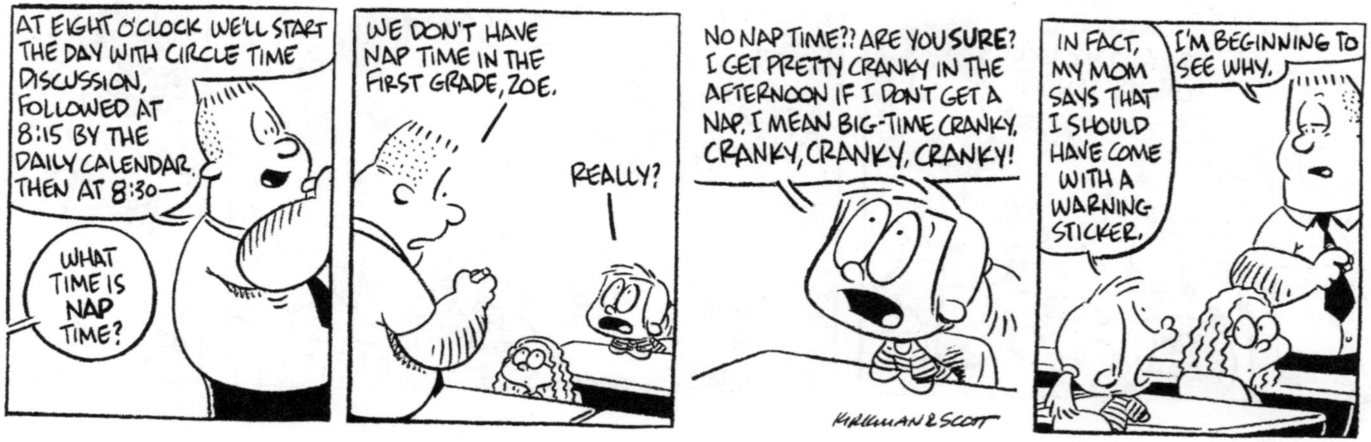
AT EIGHT O'CLOCK WE'LL START THE DAY WITH CIRCLE TIME DISCUSSION, FOLLOWED AT 8:15 BY THE DAILY CALENDAR. THEN AT 8:30—
WHAT TIME IS NAP TIME?
WE DON'T HAVE NAP TIME IN THE FIRST GRADE, ZOE.
REALLY?
NO NAP TIME?? ARE YOU SURE? I GET PRETTY CRANKY IN THE AFTERNOON IF I DON'T GET A NAP. I MEAN BIG-TIME CRANKY. CRANKY, CRANKY, CRANKY!
KIRKMAN & SCOTT
IN FACT, MY MOM SAYS THAT I SHOULD HAVE COME WITH A WARNING STICKER.
I'M BEGINNING TO SEE WHY.

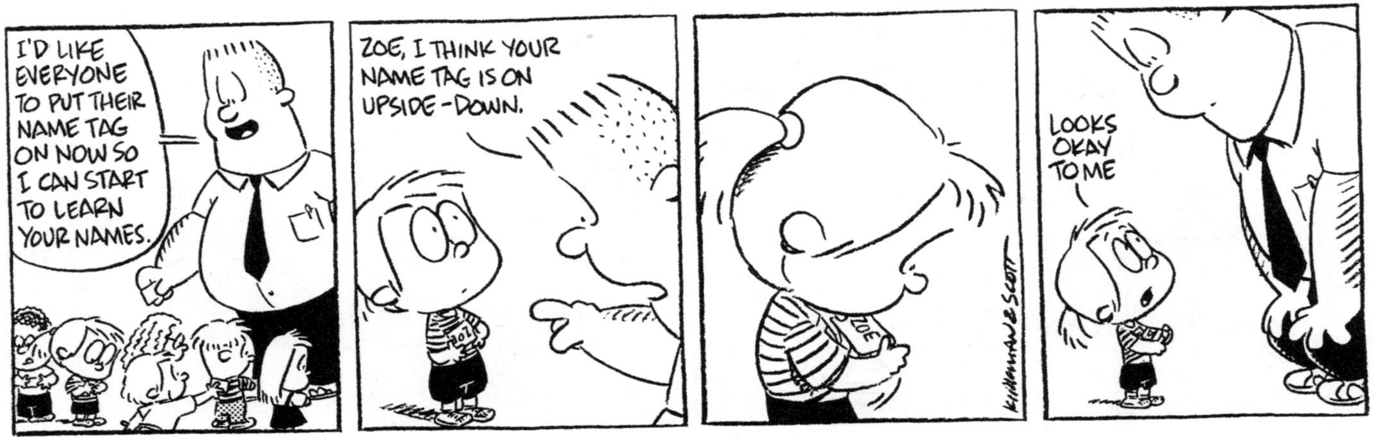
I'D LIKE EVERYONE TO PUT THEIR NAME TAG ON NOW SO I CAN START TO LEARN YOUR NAMES.
ZOE, I THINK YOUR NAME TAG IS ON UPSIDE-DOWN.
KIRKMAN & SCOTT
LOOKS OKAY TO ME

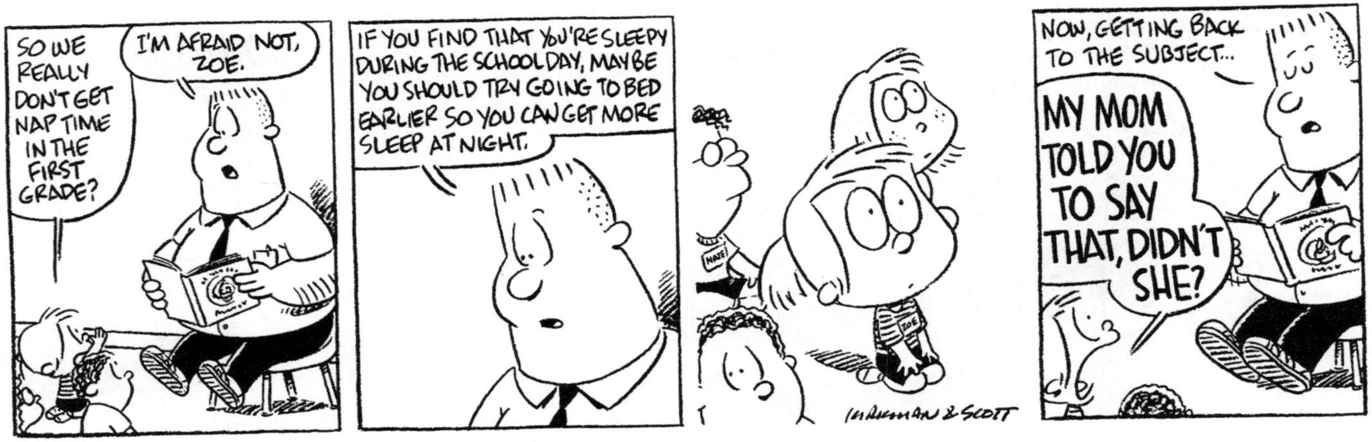
SO WE REALLY DON'T GET NAP TIME IN THE FIRST GRADE?
I'M AFRAID NOT, ZOE.
IF YOU FIND THAT YOU'RE SLEEPY DURING THE SCHOOL DAY, MAYBE YOU SHOULD TRY GOING TO BED EARLIER SO YOU CAN GET MORE SLEEP AT NIGHT.
KIRKMAN & SCOTT
NOW, GETTING BACK TO THE SUBJECT...
MY MOM TOLD YOU TO SAY THAT, DIDN'T SHE?

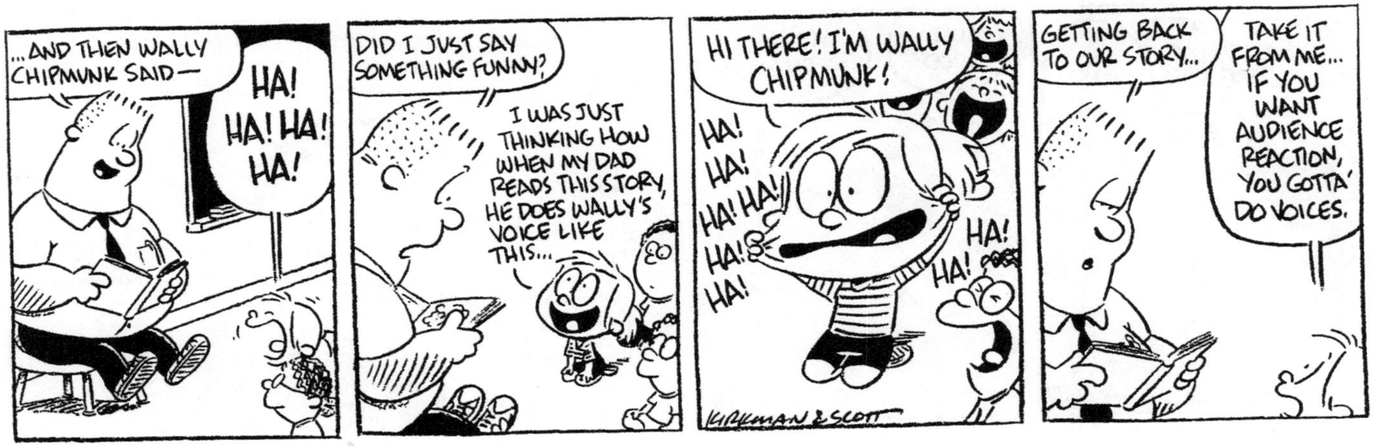
...AND THEN WALLY CHIPMUNK SAID—
HA! HA! HA! HA!
DID I JUST SAY SOMETHING FUNNY?
I WAS JUST THINKING HOW WHEN MY DAD READS THIS STORY, HE DOES WALLY'S VOICE LIKE THIS...
HI THERE! I'M WALLY CHIPMUNK!
HA! HA! HA! HA! HA! HA!
HA! HA!
KIRKMAN & SCOTT
GETTING BACK TO OUR STORY...
TAKE IT FROM ME... IF YOU WANT AUDIENCE REACTION, YOU GOTTA' DO VOICES.

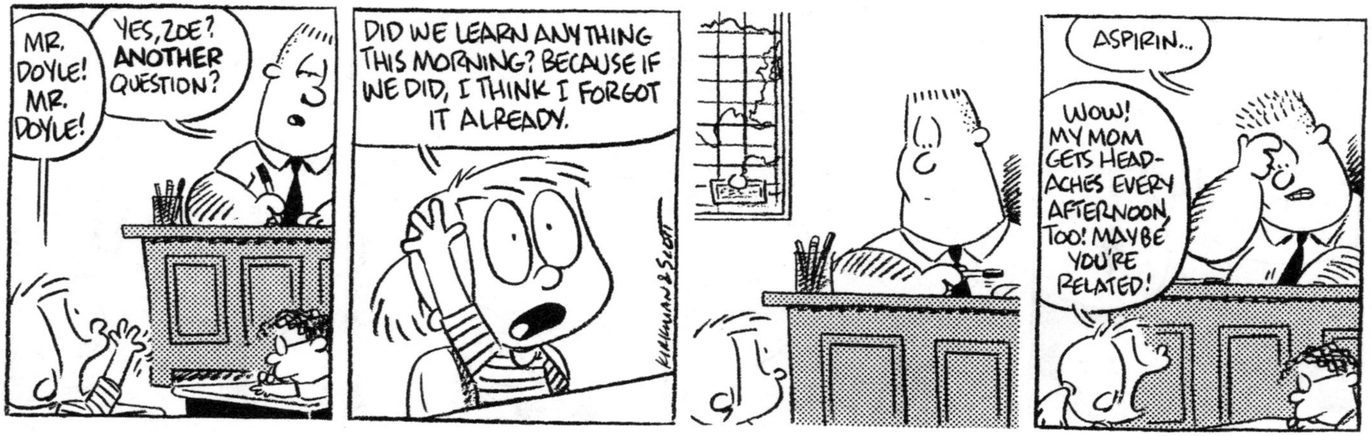
MR. DOYLE! MR. DOYLE!
YES, ZOE? **ANOTHER** QUESTION?
DID WE LEARN ANYTHING THIS MORNING? BECAUSE IF WE DID, I THINK I FORGOT IT ALREADY.
KIRKMAN & SCOTT
ASPIRIN...
WOW! MY MOM GETS HEADACHES EVERY AFTERNOON, TOO! MAYBE YOU'RE RELATED!

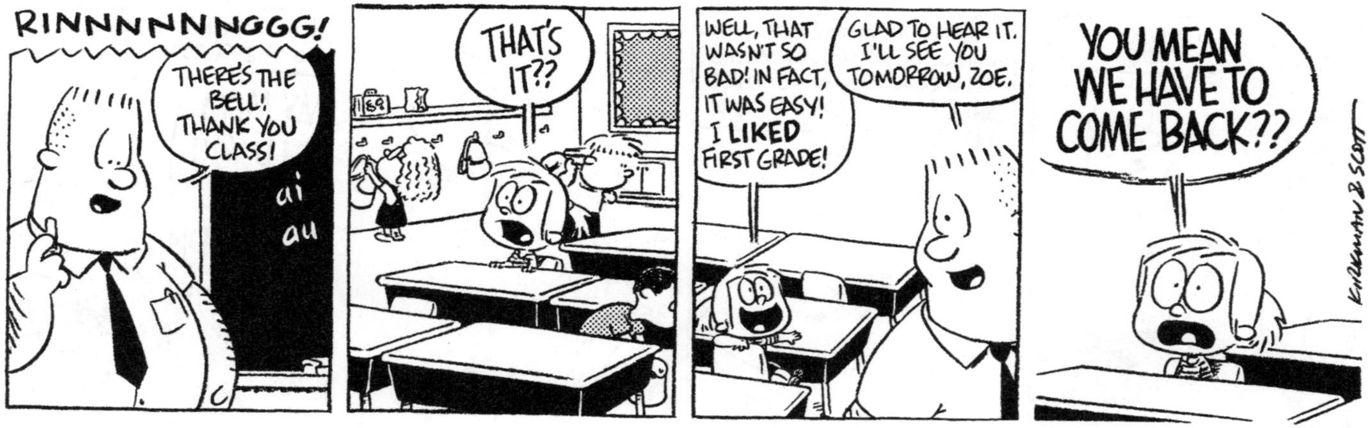
RINNNNNNNGGG!
THERE'S THE BELL! THANK YOU CLASS!
ai
au
THAT'S IT??
WELL, THAT WASN'T SO BAD! IN FACT, IT WAS EASY! I **LIKED** FIRST GRADE!
GLAD TO HEAR IT. I'LL SEE YOU TOMORROW, ZOE.
YOU MEAN WE HAVE TO COME BACK??
KIRKMAN & SCOTT

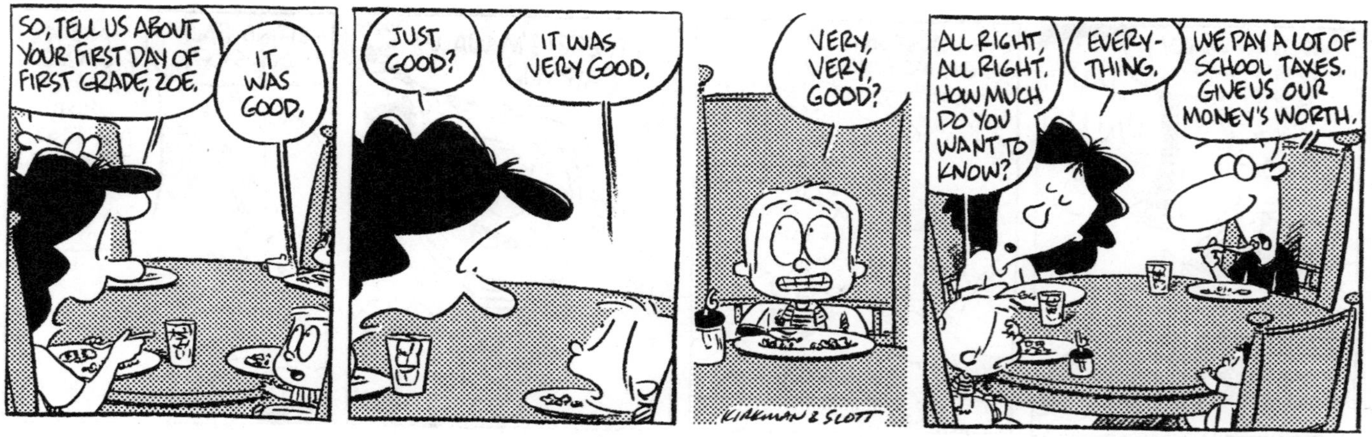
SO, TELL US ABOUT YOUR FIRST DAY OF FIRST GRADE, ZOE.
IT WAS GOOD.
JUST GOOD?
IT WAS VERY GOOD.
VERY, VERY, GOOD?
KIRKMAN & SCOTT
ALL RIGHT, ALL RIGHT. HOW MUCH DO YOU WANT TO KNOW?
EVERYTHING.
WE PAY A LOT OF SCHOOL TAXES. GIVE US OUR MONEY'S WORTH.

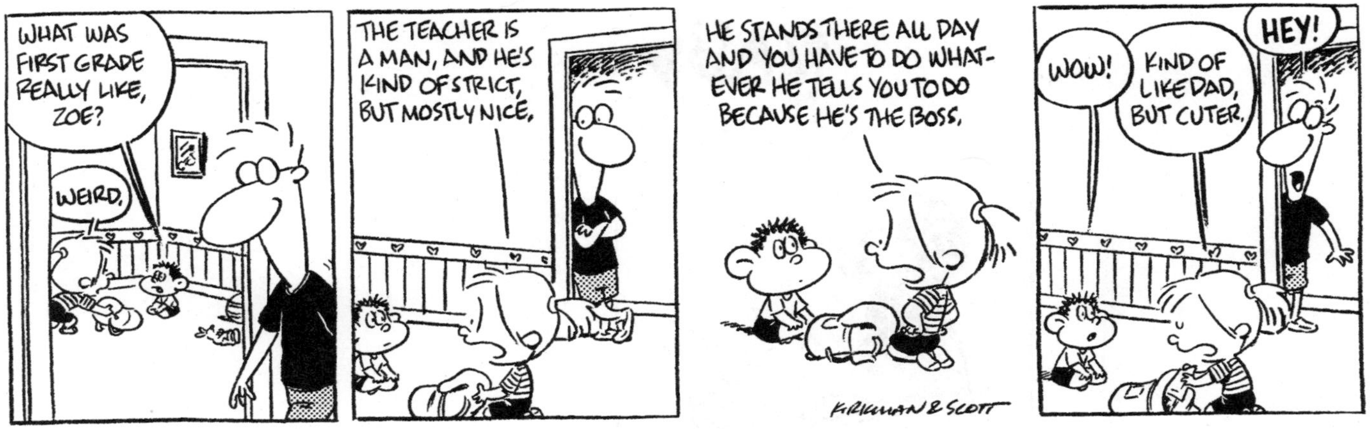
WHAT WAS FIRST GRADE REALLY LIKE, ZOE?
WEIRD.
THE TEACHER IS A MAN, AND HE'S KIND OF STRICT, BUT MOSTLY NICE.
HE STANDS THERE ALL DAY AND YOU HAVE TO DO WHAT-EVER HE TELLS YOU TO DO BECAUSE HE'S THE BOSS.
KIRKMAN & SCOTT
WOW!
KIND OF LIKE DAD, BUT CUTER.
HEY!

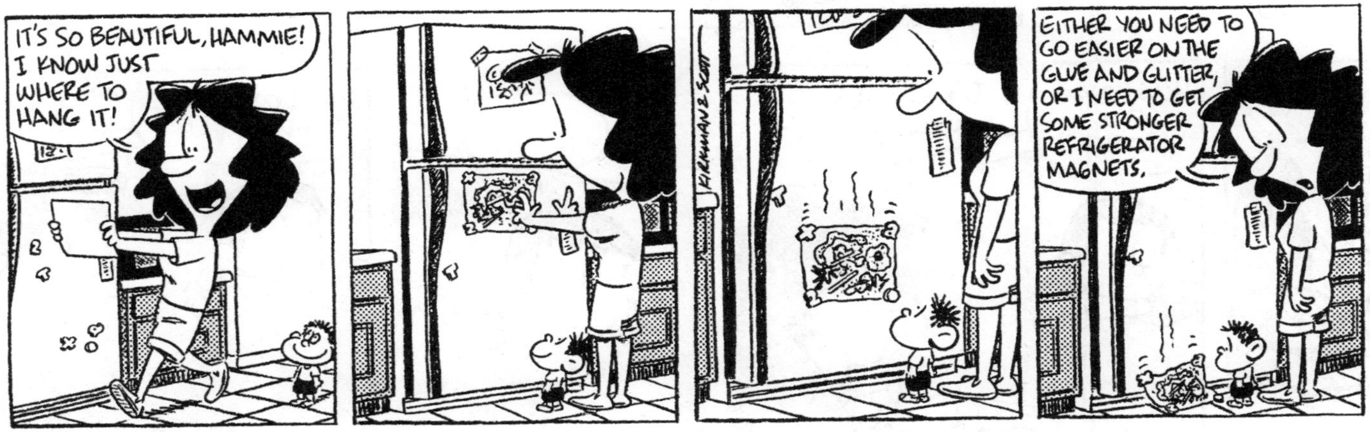
IT'S SO BEAUTIFUL, HAMMIE! I KNOW JUST WHERE TO HANG IT!
KIRKMAN & SCOTT
EITHER YOU NEED TO GO EASIER ON THE GLUE AND GLITTER, OR I NEED TO GET SOME STRONGER REFRIGERATOR MAGNETS.

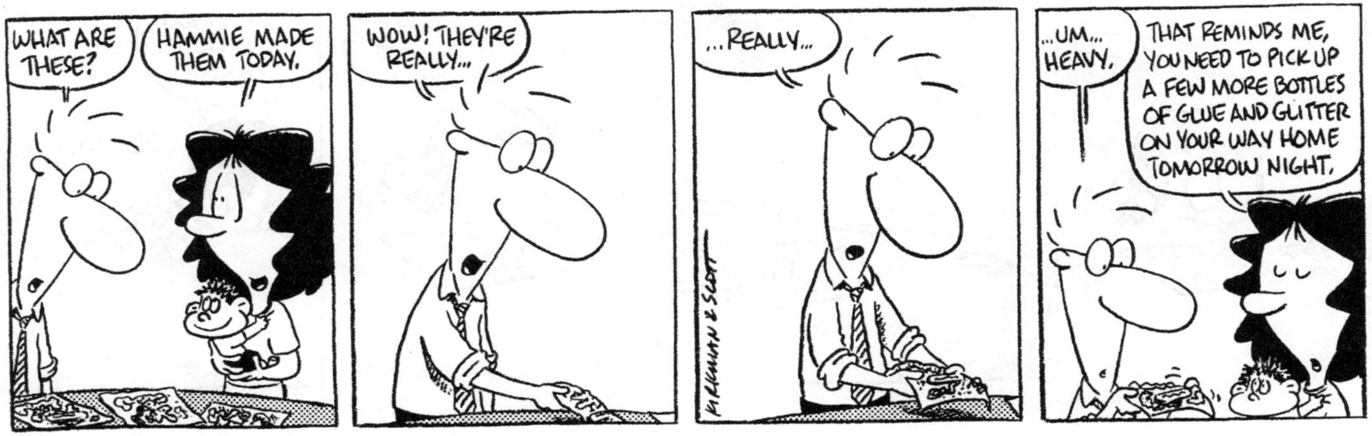
WHAT ARE THESE?
HAMMIE MADE THEM TODAY.
WOW! THEY'RE REALLY...
...REALLY...
KIRKMAN & SCOTT
...UM... HEAVY.
THAT REMINDS ME, YOU NEED TO PICK UP A FEW MORE BOTTLES OF GLUE AND GLITTER ON YOUR WAY HOME TOMORROW NIGHT.

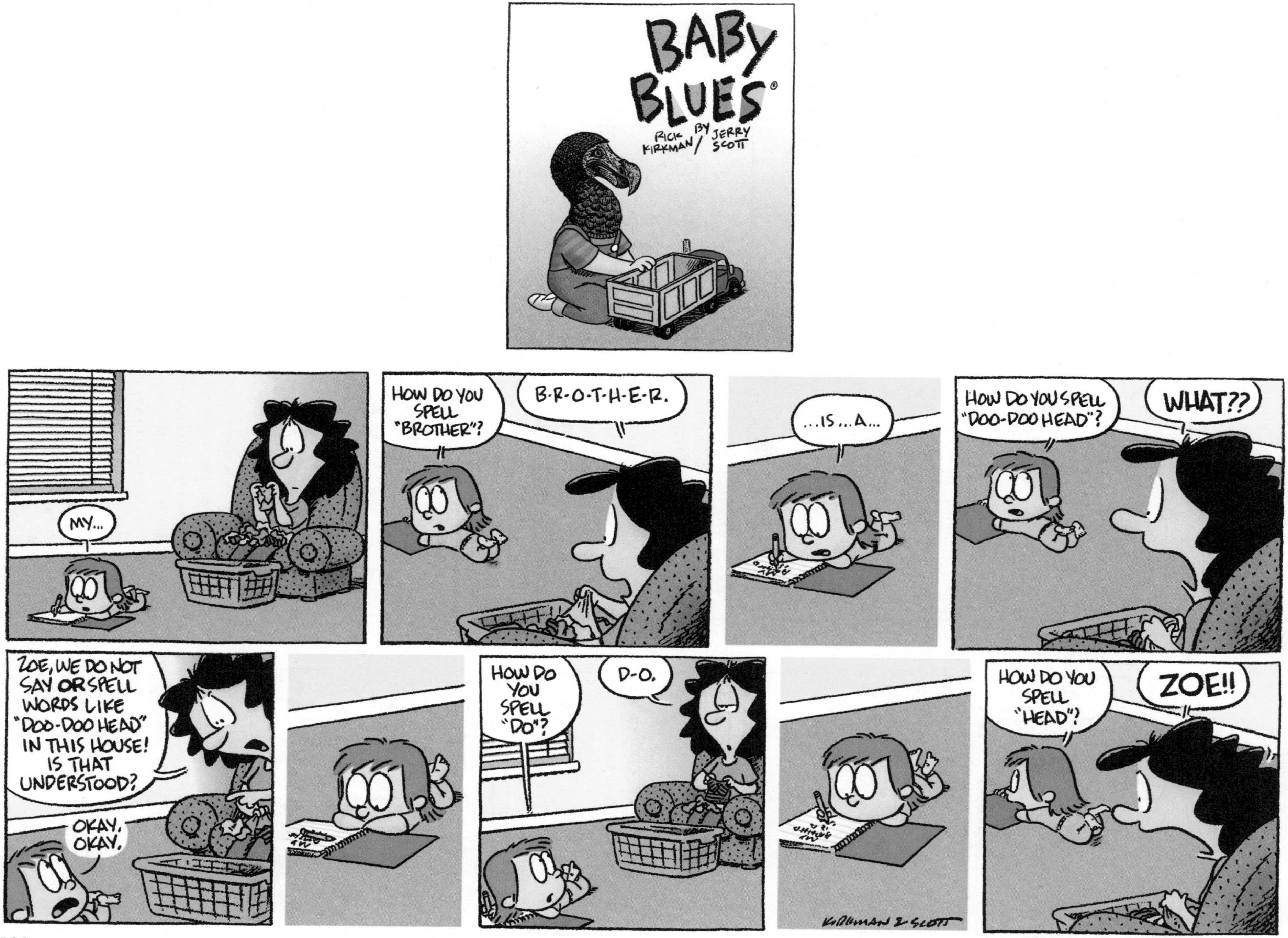
BABY BLUES®
RICK KIRKMAN / BY / JERRY SCOTT
MY...
HOW DO YOU SPELL "BROTHER"?
B-R-O-T-H-E-R.
...IS...A...
HOW DO YOU SPELL "DOO-DOO HEAD"?
WHAT??
ZOE, WE DO NOT SAY OR SPELL WORDS LIKE "DOO-DOO HEAD" IN THIS HOUSE! IS THAT UNDERSTOOD?
OKAY, OKAY.
HOW DO YOU SPELL "DO"?
D-O.
KIRKMAN & SCOTT
HOW DO YOU SPELL "HEAD"?
ZOE!!

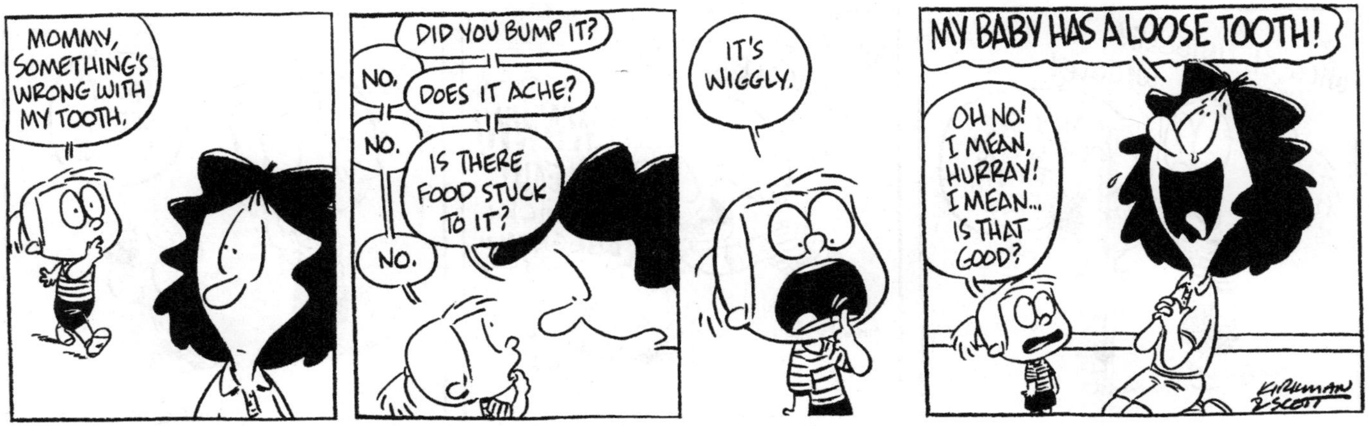
MOMMY, SOMETHING'S WRONG WITH MY TOOTH.
DID YOU BUMP IT?
NO.
DOES IT ACHE?
NO.
IS THERE FOOD STUCK TO IT?
NO.
IT'S WIGGLY.
MY BABY HAS A LOOSE TOOTH!
OH NO! I MEAN, HURRAY! I MEAN... IS THAT GOOD?
KIRKMAN & SCOTT

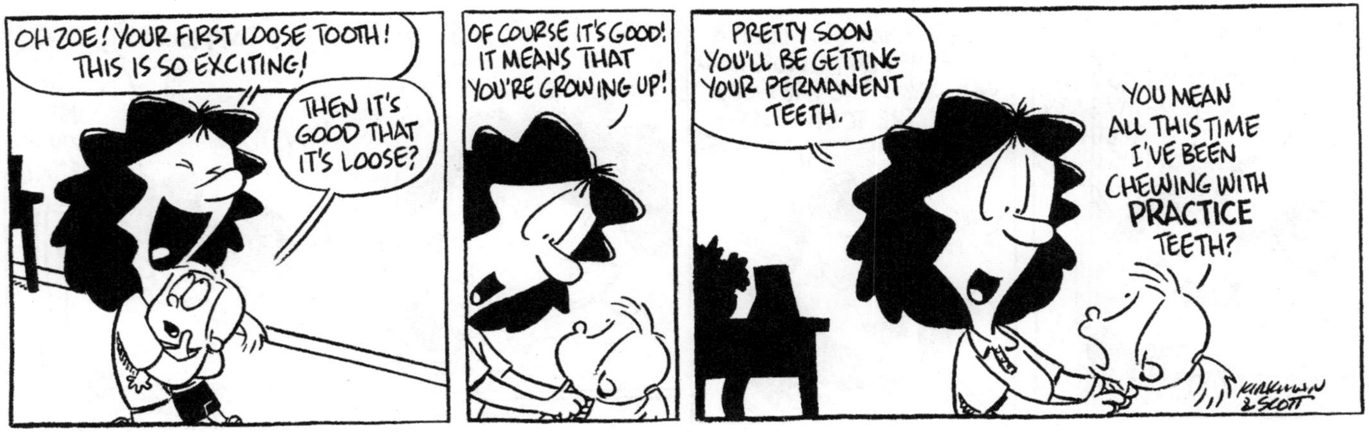
OH ZOE! YOUR FIRST LOOSE TOOTH! THIS IS SO EXCITING!
THEN IT'S GOOD THAT IT'S LOOSE?
OF COURSE IT'S GOOD! IT MEANS THAT YOU'RE GROWING UP!
PRETTY SOON YOU'LL BE GETTING YOUR PERMANENT TEETH.
YOU MEAN ALL THIS TIME I'VE BEEN CHEWING WITH PRACTICE TEETH?
KIRKMAN & SCOTT

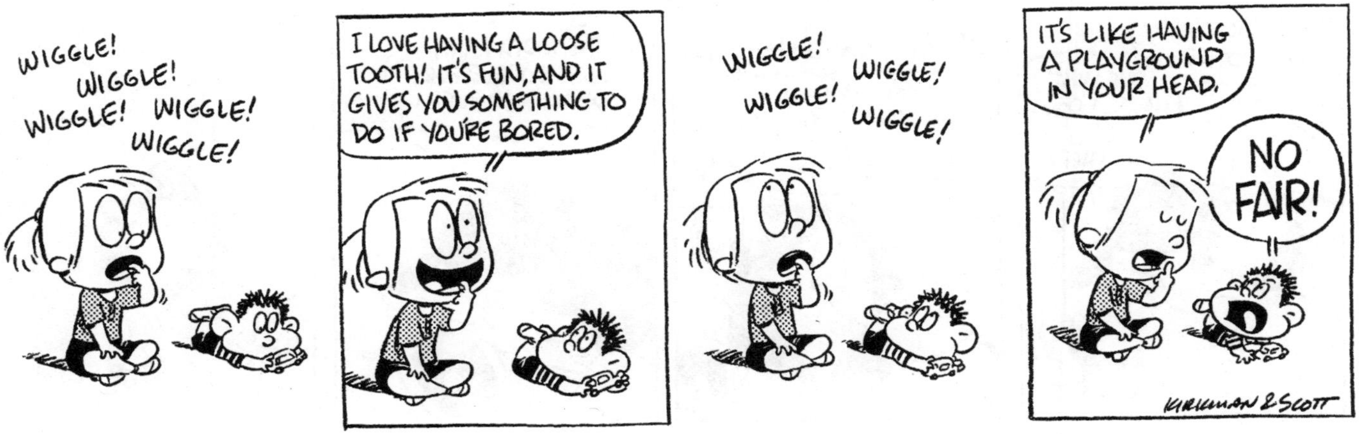
WIGGLE! WIGGLE! WIGGLE! WIGGLE! WIGGLE!
I LOVE HAVING A LOOSE TOOTH! IT'S FUN, AND IT GIVES YOU SOMETHING TO DO IF YOU'RE BORED.
WIGGLE! WIGGLE! WIGGLE! WIGGLE!
IT'S LIKE HAVING A PLAYGROUND IN YOUR HEAD.
NO FAIR!
KIRKMAN & SCOTT

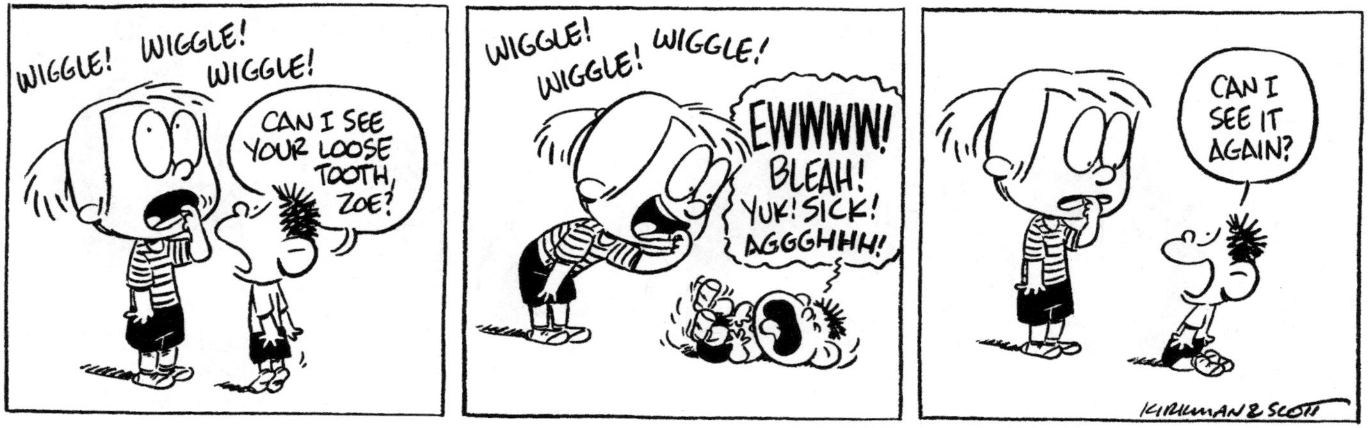
WIGGLE! WIGGLE! WIGGLE!
CAN I SEE YOUR LOOSE TOOTH, ZOE?
WIGGLE! WIGGLE! WIGGLE!
EWWWW! BLEAH! YUK! SICK! AGGGHHH!
CAN I SEE IT AGAIN?
KIRKMAN & SCOTT

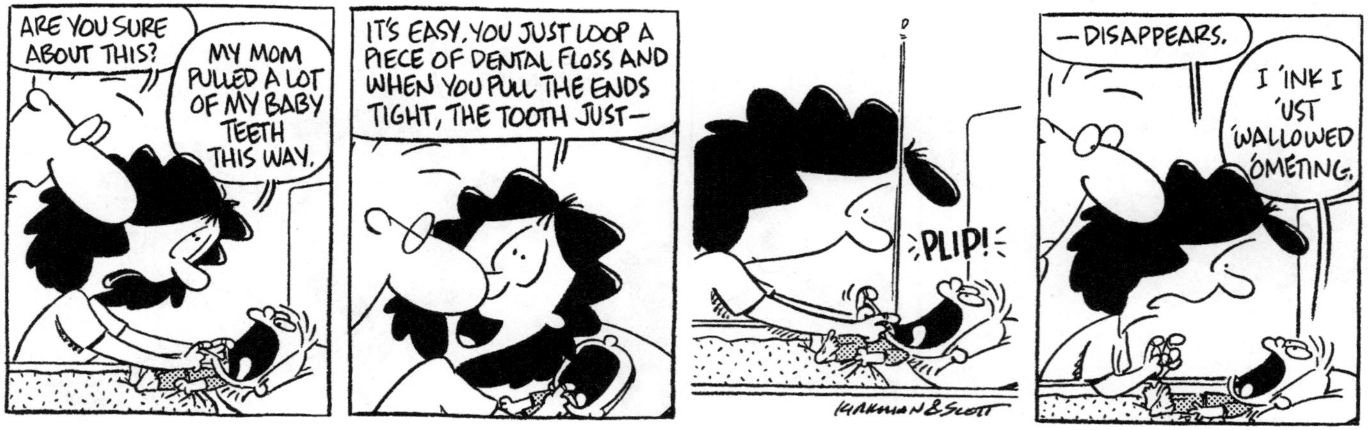
ARE YOU SURE ABOUT THIS?
MY MOM PULLED A LOT OF MY BABY TEETH THIS WAY.
IT'S EASY. YOU JUST LOOP A PIECE OF DENTAL FLOSS AND WHEN YOU PULL THE ENDS TIGHT, THE TOOTH JUST—
PLIP!
KIRKMAN & SCOTT
—DISAPPEARS.
I 'INK I 'UST 'WALLOWED 'OMETING.

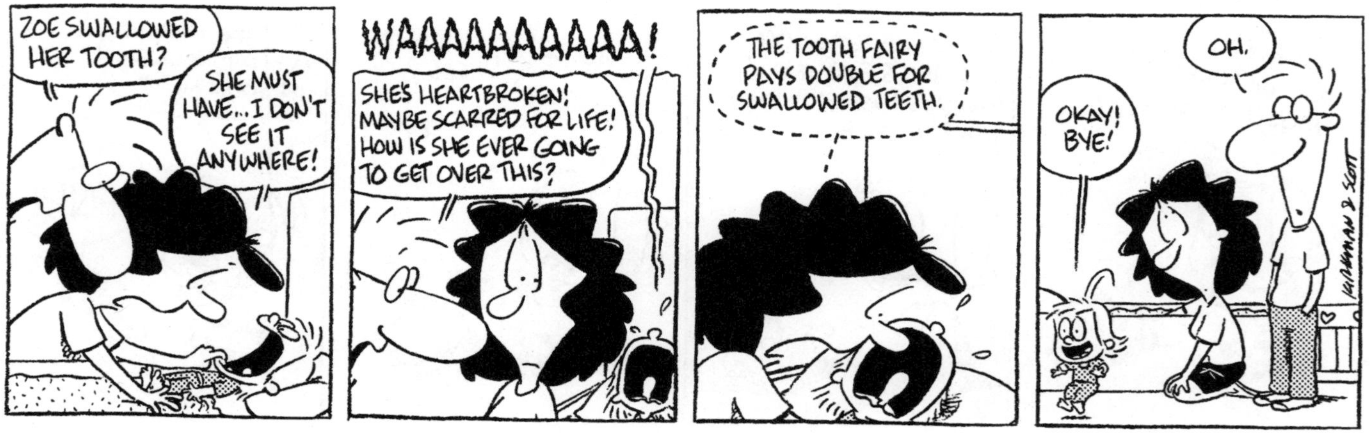
ZOE SWALLOWED HER TOOTH?
SHE MUST HAVE... I DON'T SEE IT ANYWHERE!
WAAAAAAAAAA!
SHE'S HEARTBROKEN! MAYBE SCARRED FOR LIFE! HOW IS SHE EVER GOING TO GET OVER THIS?
THE TOOTH FAIRY PAYS DOUBLE FOR SWALLOWED TEETH.
OH.
OKAY! BYE!
KIRKMAN & SCOTT

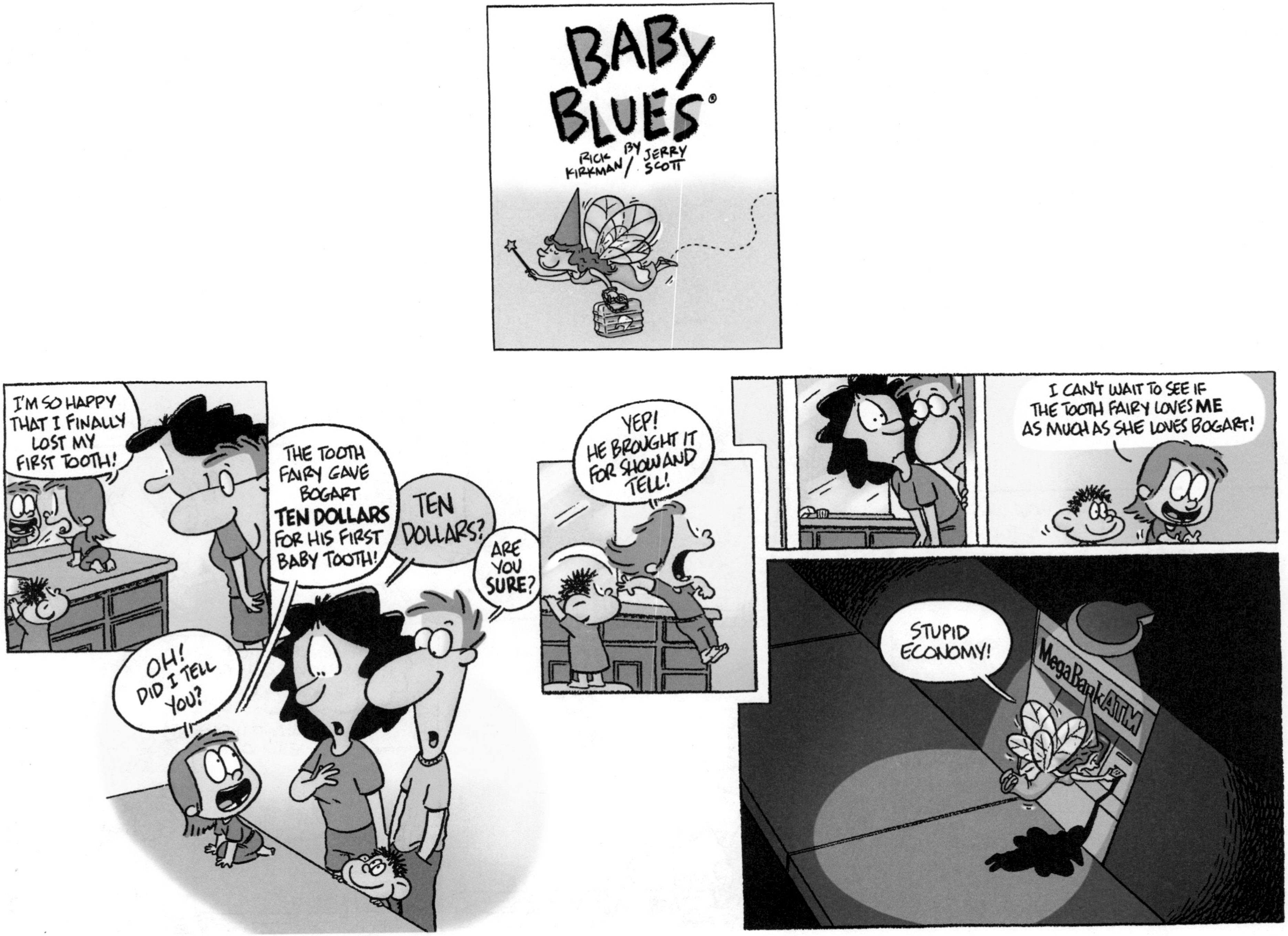
BABY BLUES®
BY RICK KIRKMAN / JERRY SCOTT
I'M SO HAPPY THAT I FINALLY LOST MY FIRST TOOTH!
THE TOOTH FAIRY GAVE BOGART **TEN DOLLARS** FOR HIS FIRST BABY TOOTH!
TEN DOLLARS?
ARE YOU **SURE**?
OH! DID I TELL YOU?
YEP! HE BROUGHT IT FOR SHOW AND TELL!
I CAN'T WAIT TO SEE IF THE TOOTH FAIRY LOVES **ME** AS MUCH AS SHE LOVES BOGART!
STUPID ECONOMY!
MegaBank ATM

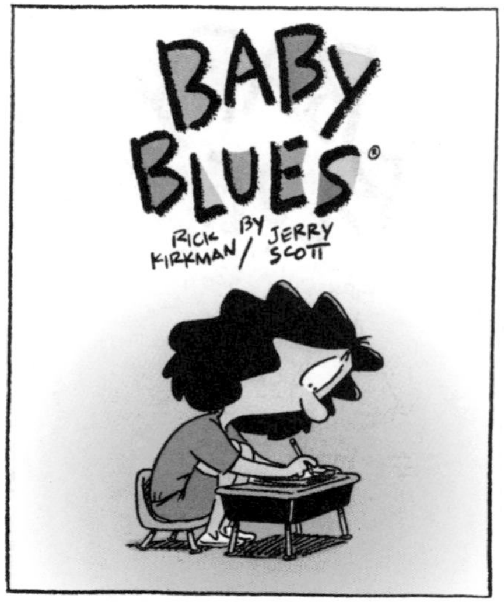
BABY BLUES®
RICK KIRKMAN / BY JERRY SCOTT

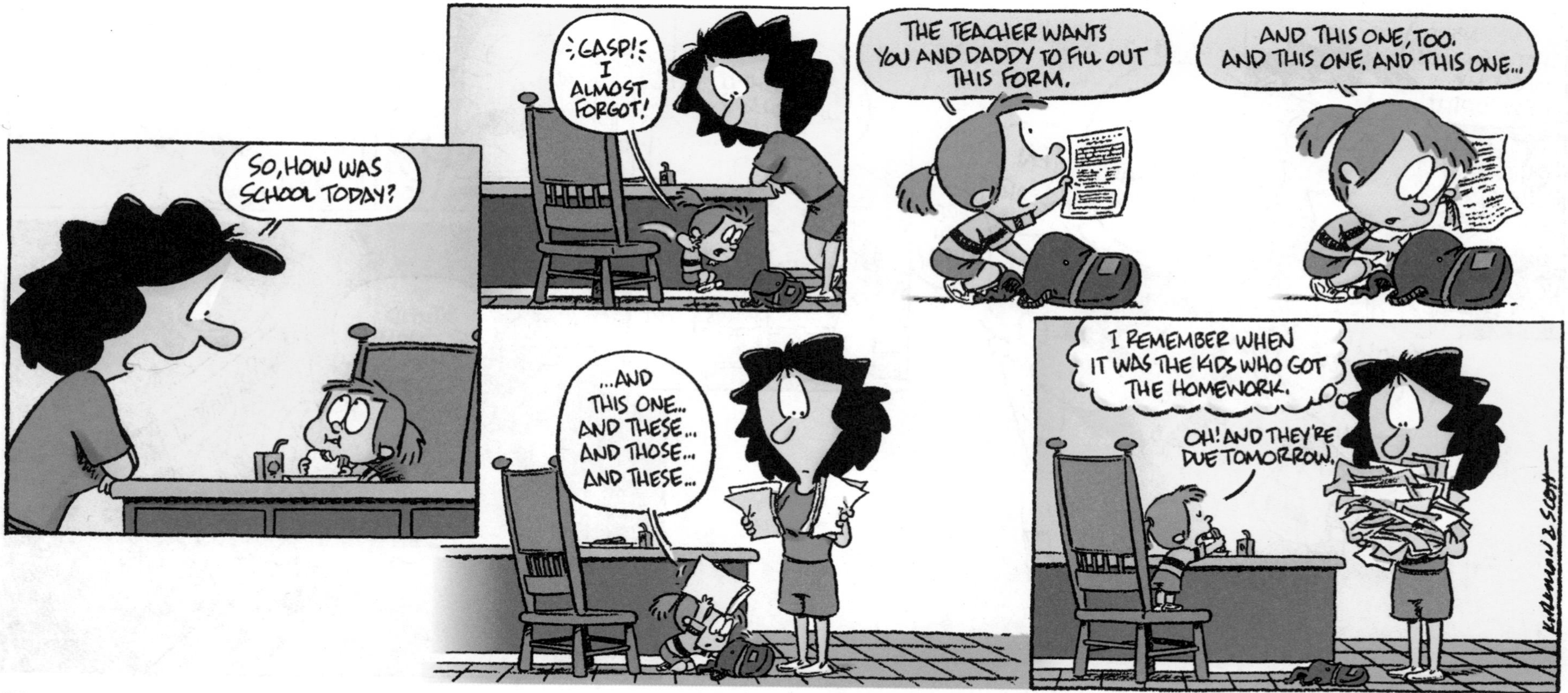
SO, HOW WAS SCHOOL TODAY?
GASP! I ALMOST FORGOT!
THE TEACHER WANTS YOU AND DADDY TO FILL OUT THIS FORM.
AND THIS ONE, TOO. AND THIS ONE. AND THIS ONE...
...AND THIS ONE... AND THESE... AND THOSE... AND THESE...
I REMEMBER WHEN IT WAS THE KIDS WHO GOT THE HOMEWORK.
OH! AND THEY'RE DUE TOMORROW.
KIRKMAN & SCOTT

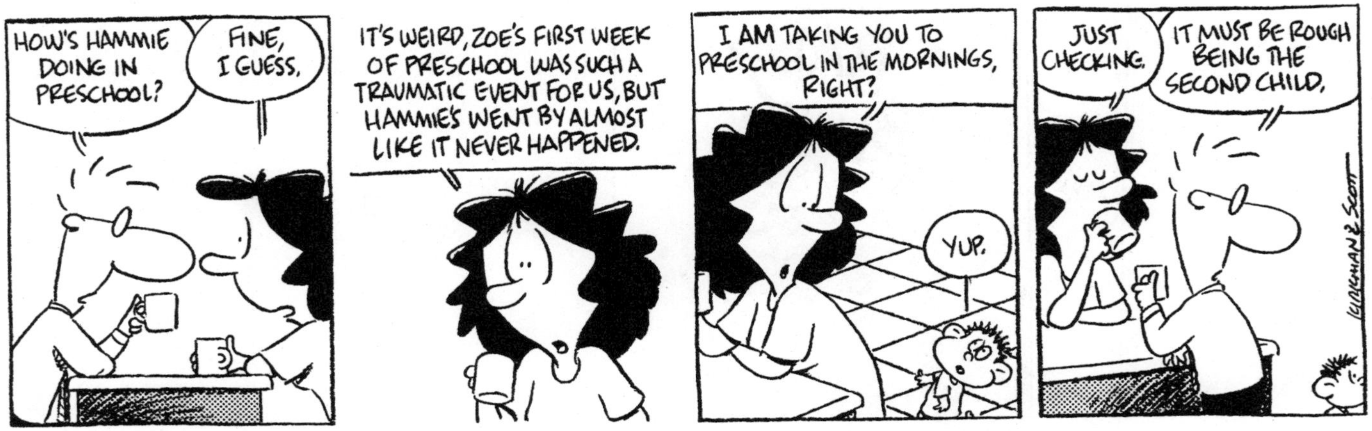
HOW'S HAMMIE DOING IN PRESCHOOL?
FINE, I GUESS.
IT'S WEIRD, ZOE'S FIRST WEEK OF PRESCHOOL WAS SUCH A TRAUMATIC EVENT FOR US, BUT HAMMIE'S WENT BY ALMOST LIKE IT NEVER HAPPENED.
I AM TAKING YOU TO PRESCHOOL IN THE MORNINGS, RIGHT?
YUP.
JUST CHECKING.
IT MUST BE ROUGH BEING THE SECOND CHILD.
KIRKMAN & SCOTT

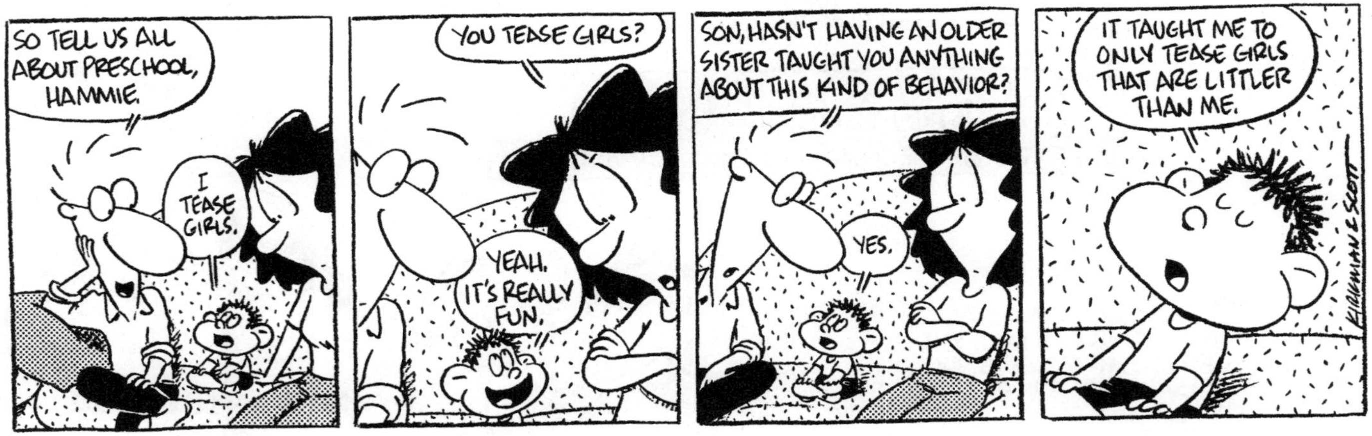
SO TELL US ALL ABOUT PRESCHOOL, HAMMIE.
I TEASE GIRLS.
YOU TEASE GIRLS?
YEAH. IT'S REALLY FUN.
SON, HASN'T HAVING AN OLDER SISTER TAUGHT YOU ANYTHING ABOUT THIS KIND OF BEHAVIOR?
YES.
IT TAUGHT ME TO ONLY TEASE GIRLS THAT ARE LITTLER THAN ME.
KIRKMAN & SCOTT

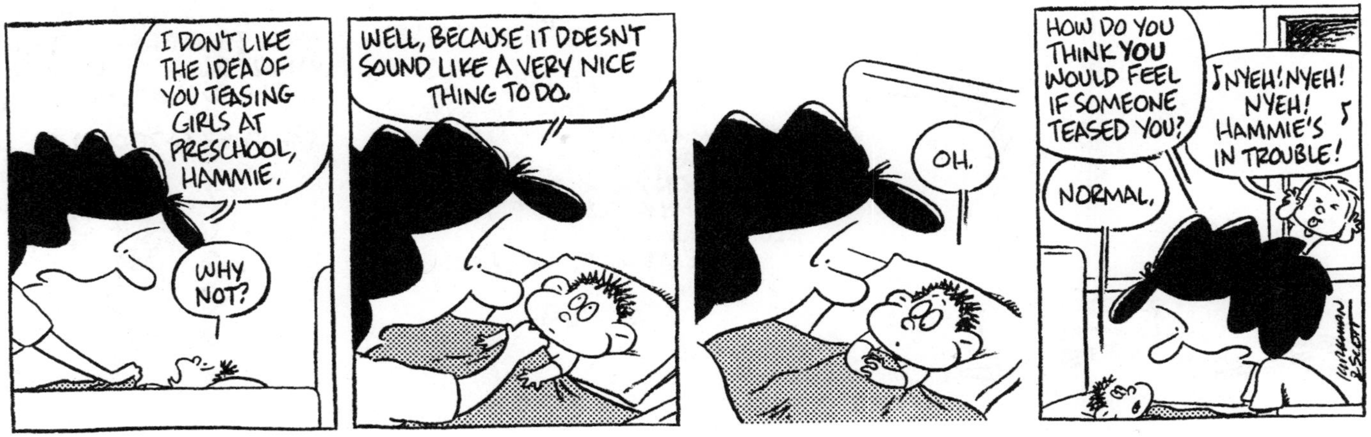
I DON'T LIKE THE IDEA OF YOU TEASING GIRLS AT PRESCHOOL, HAMMIE.
WHY NOT?
WELL, BECAUSE IT DOESN'T SOUND LIKE A VERY NICE THING TO DO.
OH.
HOW DO YOU THINK YOU WOULD FEEL IF SOMEONE TEASED YOU?
NORMAL.
NYEH! NYEH! NYEH! HAMMIE'S IN TROUBLE!

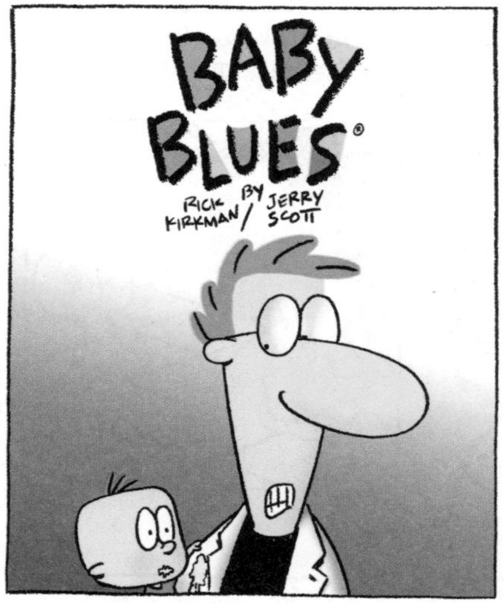
BABY BLUES®
BY RICK KIRKMAN / JERRY SCOTT

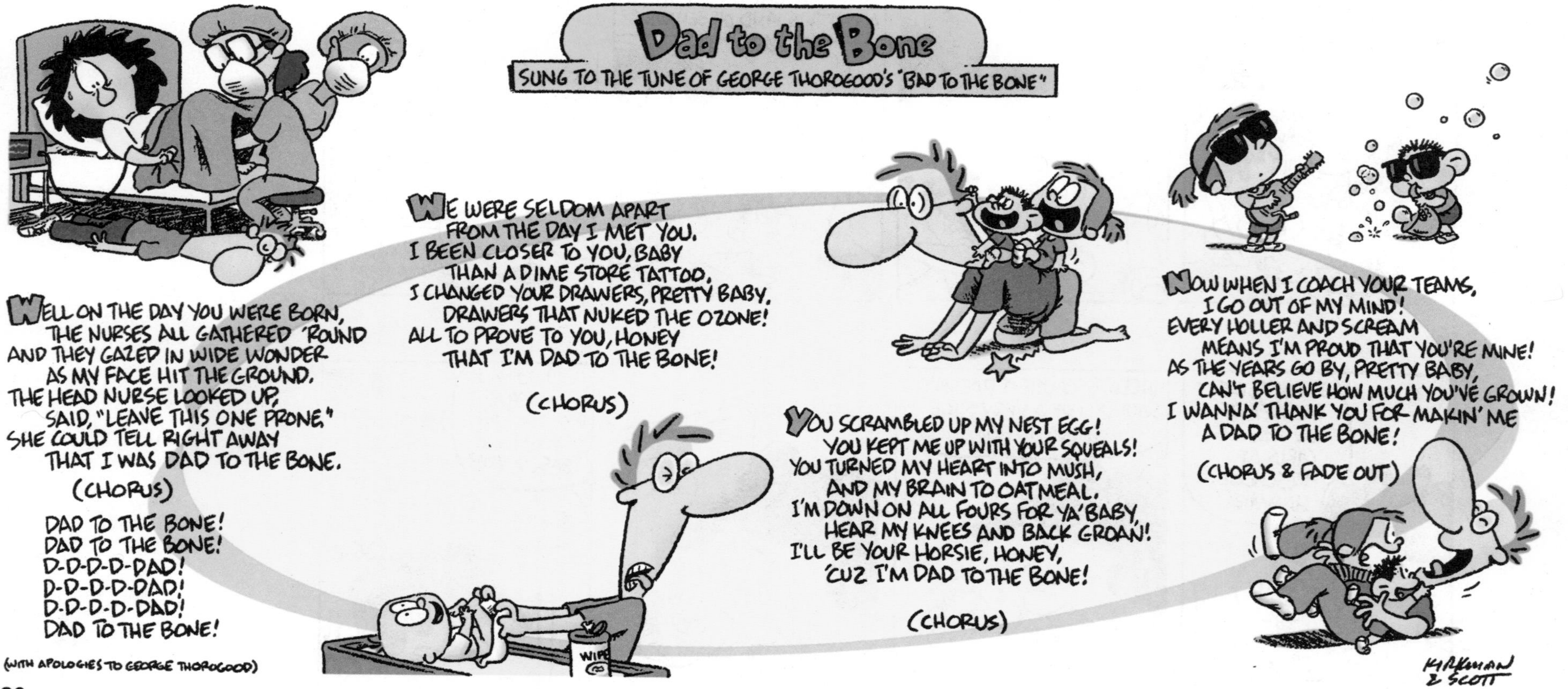
Dad to the Bone
SUNG TO THE TUNE OF GEORGE THOROGOOD'S "BAD TO THE BONE"
WELL ON THE DAY YOU WERE BORN, THE NURSES ALL GATHERED 'ROUND AND THEY GAZED IN WIDE WONDER AS MY FACE HIT THE GROUND. THE HEAD NURSE LOOKED UP, SAID, "LEAVE THIS ONE PRONE." SHE COULD TELL RIGHT AWAY THAT I WAS DAD TO THE BONE.
(CHORUS)
DAD TO THE BONE!
DAD TO THE BONE!
D-D-D-D-DAD!
D-D-D-D-DAD!
D-D-D-D-DAD!
DAD TO THE BONE!
WE WERE SELDOM APART FROM THE DAY I MET YOU. I BEEN CLOSER TO YOU, BABY THAN A DIME STORE TATTOO. I CHANGED YOUR DRAWERS, PRETTY BABY, DRAWERS THAT NUKED THE OZONE! ALL TO PROVE TO YOU, HONEY THAT I'M DAD TO THE BONE!
(CHORUS)
YOU SCRAMBLED UP MY NEST EGG! YOU KEPT ME UP WITH YOUR SQUEALS! YOU TURNED MY HEART INTO MUSH, AND MY BRAIN TO OATMEAL. I'M DOWN ON ALL FOURS FOR YA' BABY, HEAR MY KNEES AND BACK GROAN! I'LL BE YOUR HORSIE, HONEY, 'CUZ I'M DAD TO THE BONE!
(CHORUS)
NOW WHEN I COACH YOUR TEAMS, I GO OUT OF MY MIND! EVERY HOLLER AND SCREAM MEANS I'M PROUD THAT YOU'RE MINE! AS THE YEARS GO BY, PRETTY BABY, CAN'T BELIEVE HOW MUCH YOU'VE GROWN! I WANNA' THANK YOU FOR MAKIN' ME A DAD TO THE BONE!
(CHORUS & FADE OUT)
(WITH APOLOGIES TO GEORGE THOROGOOD)
KIRKMAN & SCOTT

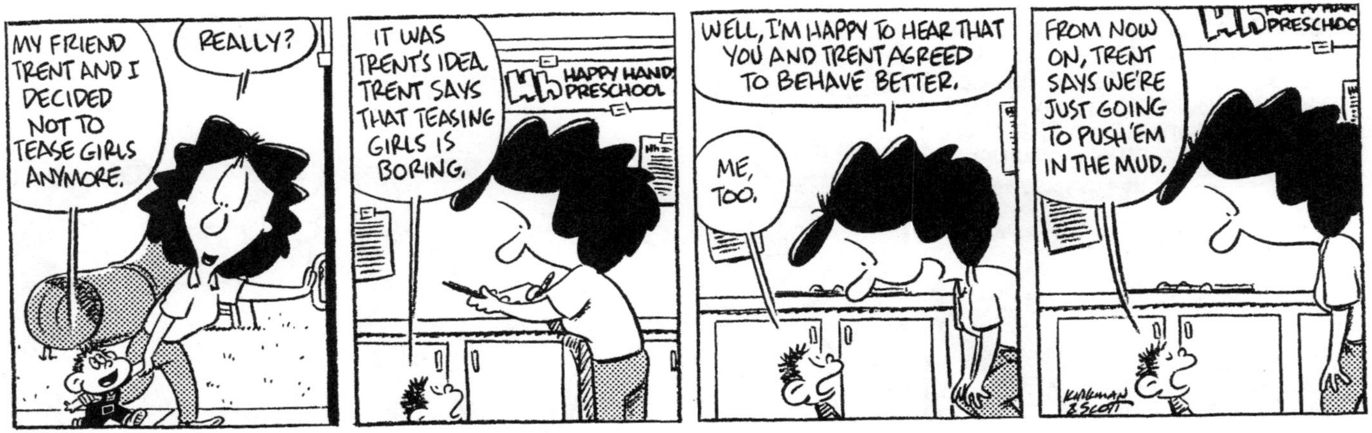
MY FRIEND TRENT AND I DECIDED NOT TO TEASE GIRLS ANYMORE.
REALLY?
IT WAS TRENT'S IDEA. TRENT SAYS THAT TEASING GIRLS IS BORING.
HAPPY HAND PRESCHOOL
WELL, I'M HAPPY TO HEAR THAT YOU AND TRENT AGREED TO BEHAVE BETTER.
ME, TOO.
FROM NOW ON, TRENT SAYS WE'RE JUST GOING TO PUSH 'EM IN THE MUD.
KIRKMAN & SCOTT

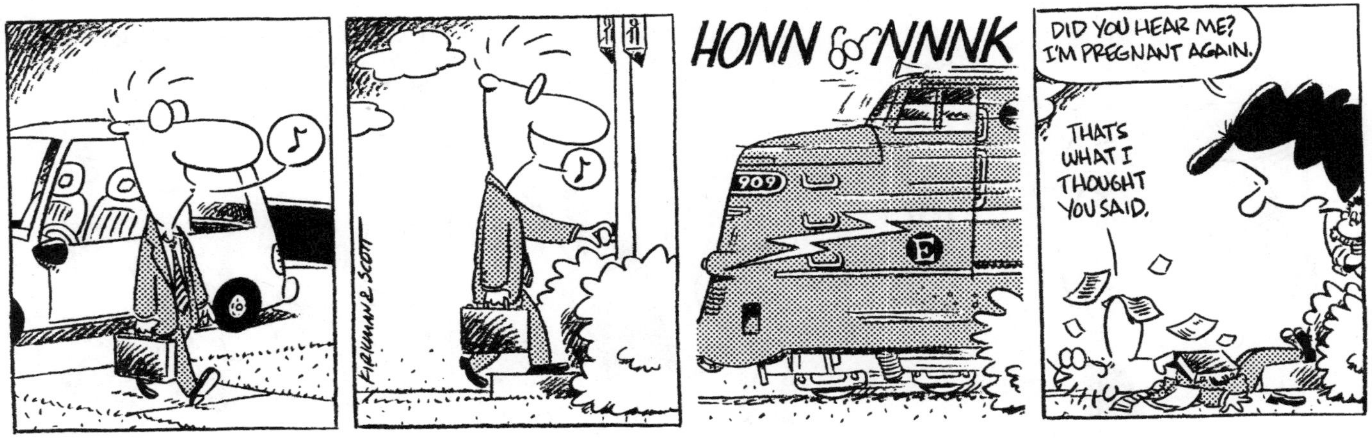
KIRKMAN & SCOTT
HONN NNNK
909
E
DID YOU HEAR ME? I'M PREGNANT AGAIN.
THAT'S WHAT I THOUGHT YOU SAID.

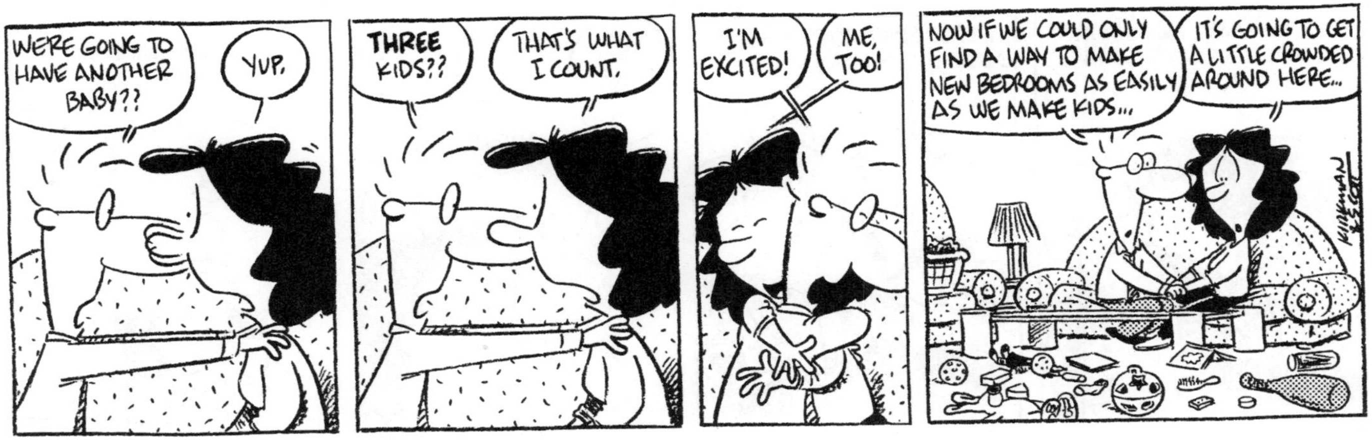
WE'RE GOING TO HAVE ANOTHER BABY??
YUP.
THREE KIDS??
THAT'S WHAT I COUNT.
I'M EXCITED!
ME, TOO!
NOW IF WE COULD ONLY FIND A WAY TO MAKE NEW BEDROOMS AS EASILY AS WE MAKE KIDS...
IT'S GOING TO GET A LITTLE CROWDED AROUND HERE...
KIRKMAN & SCOTT

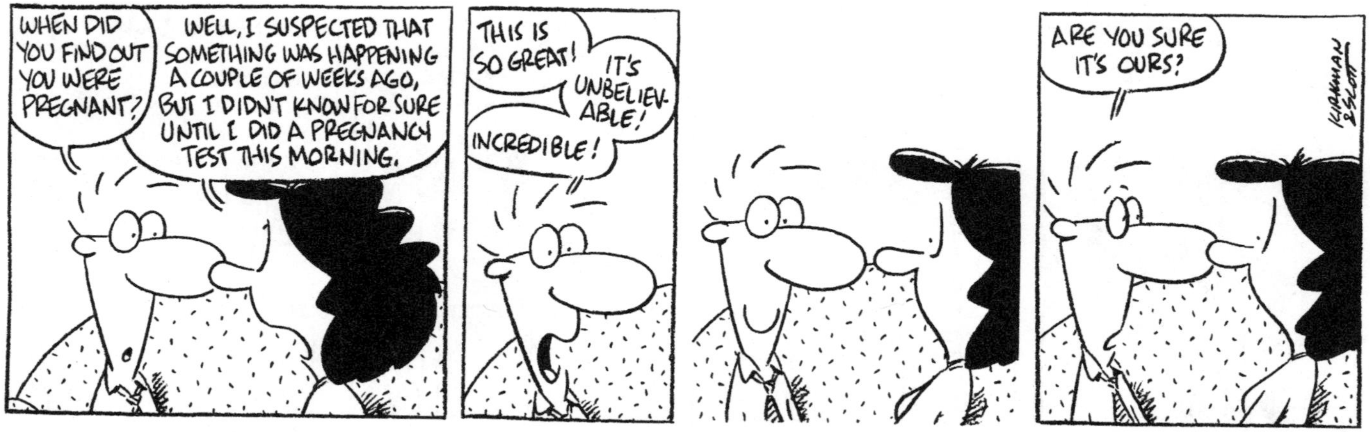
WHEN DID YOU FIND OUT YOU WERE PREGNANT?
WELL, I SUSPECTED THAT SOMETHING WAS HAPPENING A COUPLE OF WEEKS AGO, BUT I DIDN'T KNOW FOR SURE UNTIL I DID A PREGNANCY TEST THIS MORNING.
THIS IS SO GREAT!
IT'S UNBELIEV-ABLE!
INCREDIBLE!
ARE YOU SURE IT'S OURS?
KIRKMAN & SCOTT

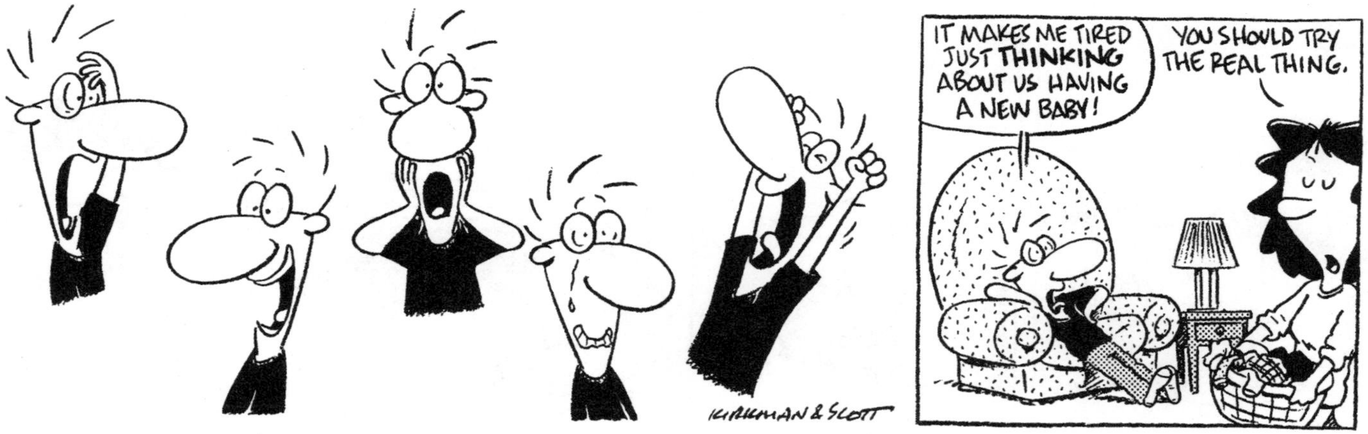
KIRKMAN & SCOTT
IT MAKES ME TIRED JUST **THINKING** ABOUT US HAVING A NEW BABY!
YOU SHOULD TRY THE REAL THING.

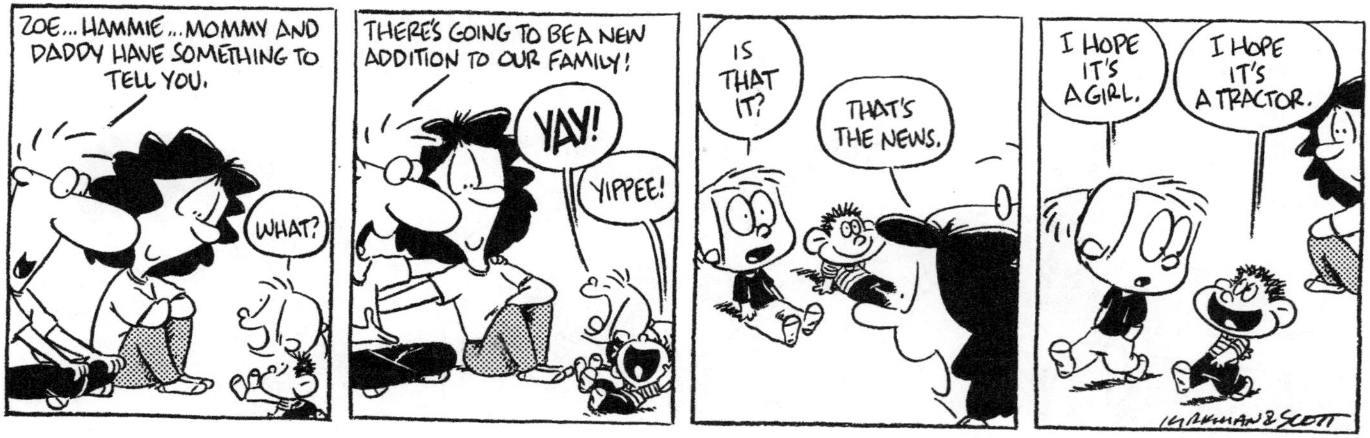
ZOE... HAMMIE... MOMMY AND DADDY HAVE SOMETHING TO TELL YOU.
WHAT?
THERE'S GOING TO BE A NEW ADDITION TO OUR FAMILY!
YAY!
YIPPEE!
IS THAT IT?
THAT'S THE NEWS.
I HOPE IT'S A GIRL.
I HOPE IT'S A TRACTOR.
KIRKMAN & SCOTT

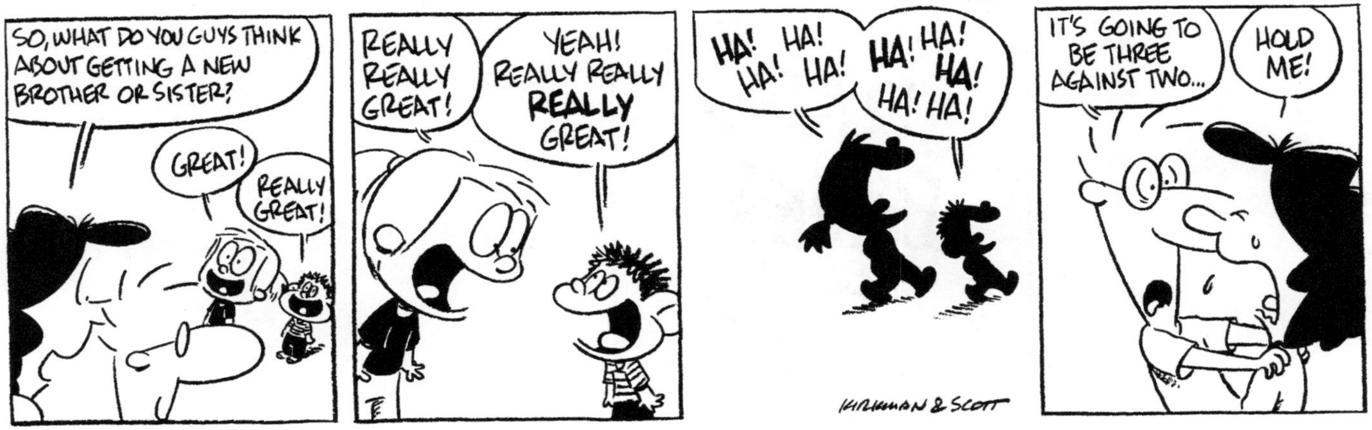
SO, WHAT DO YOU GUYS THINK ABOUT GETTING A NEW BROTHER OR SISTER?
GREAT!
REALLY GREAT!
REALLY REALLY GREAT!
YEAH! REALLY REALLY REALLY GREAT!
HA! HA! HA! HA!
HA! HA! HA! HA! HA!
IT'S GOING TO BE THREE AGAINST TWO...
HOLD ME!
KIRKMAN & SCOTT

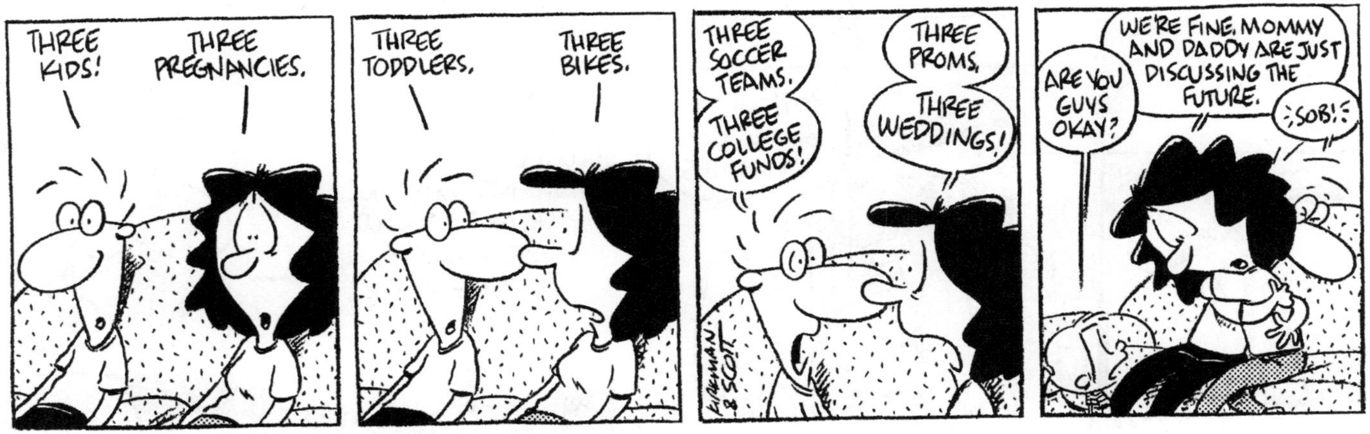
THREE KIDS!
THREE PREGNANCIES.
THREE TODDLERS.
THREE BIKES.
THREE SOCCER TEAMS.
THREE COLLEGE FUNDS!
THREE PROMS.
THREE WEDDINGS!
KIRKMAN & SCOTT
ARE YOU GUYS OKAY?
WE'RE FINE, MOMMY AND DADDY ARE JUST DISCUSSING THE FUTURE.
SOB!

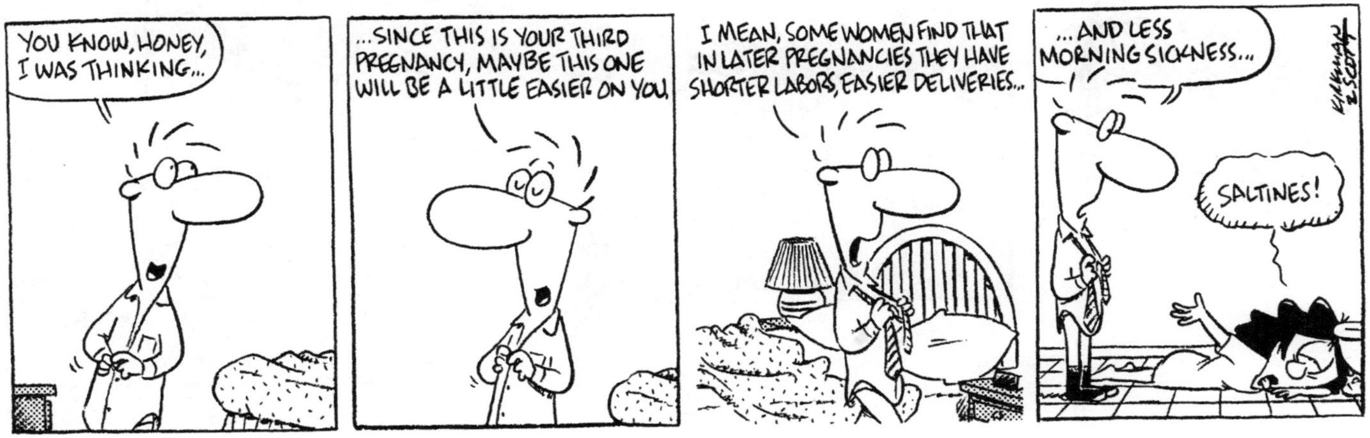
YOU KNOW, HONEY, I WAS THINKING...
...SINCE THIS IS YOUR THIRD PREGNANCY, MAYBE THIS ONE WILL BE A LITTLE EASIER ON YOU.
I MEAN, SOME WOMEN FIND THAT IN LATER PREGNANCIES THEY HAVE SHORTER LABORS, EASIER DELIVERIES...
...AND LESS MORNING SICKNESS...
SALTINES!
KIRKMAN & SCOTT

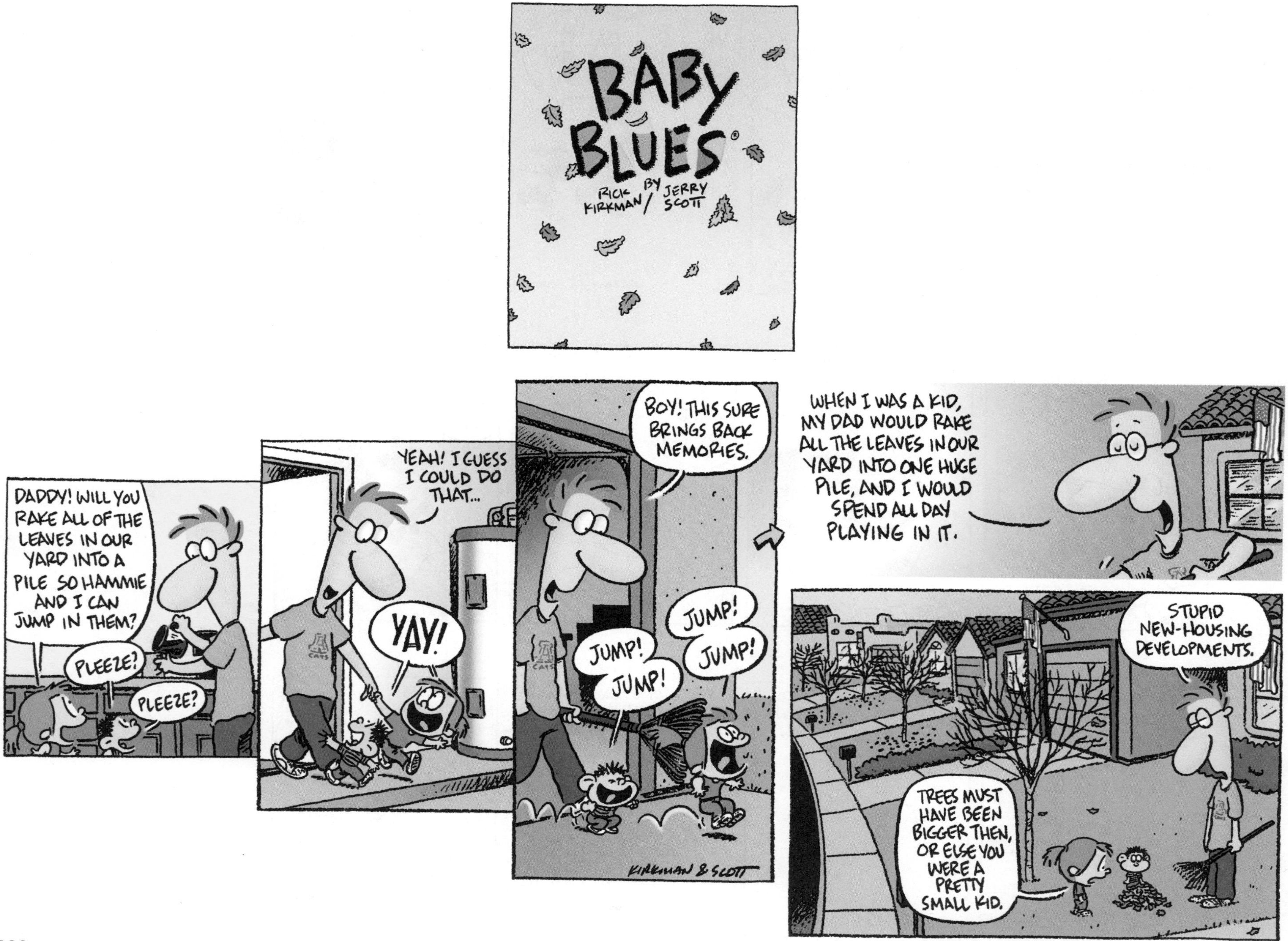
BABY BLUES®
BY RICK KIRKMAN / JERRY SCOTT
DADDY! WILL YOU RAKE ALL OF THE LEAVES IN OUR YARD INTO A PILE SO HAMMIE AND I CAN JUMP IN THEM?
PLEEZE?
PLEEZE?
YEAH! I GUESS I COULD DO THAT...
YAY!
BOY! THIS SURE BRINGS BACK MEMORIES.
JUMP! JUMP!
JUMP! JUMP!
KIRKMAN & SCOTT
WHEN I WAS A KID, MY DAD WOULD RAKE ALL THE LEAVES IN OUR YARD INTO ONE HUGE PILE, AND I WOULD SPEND ALL DAY PLAYING IN IT.
STUPID NEW-HOUSING DEVELOPMENTS.
TREES MUST HAVE BEEN BIGGER THEN, OR ELSE YOU WERE A PRETTY SMALL KID.

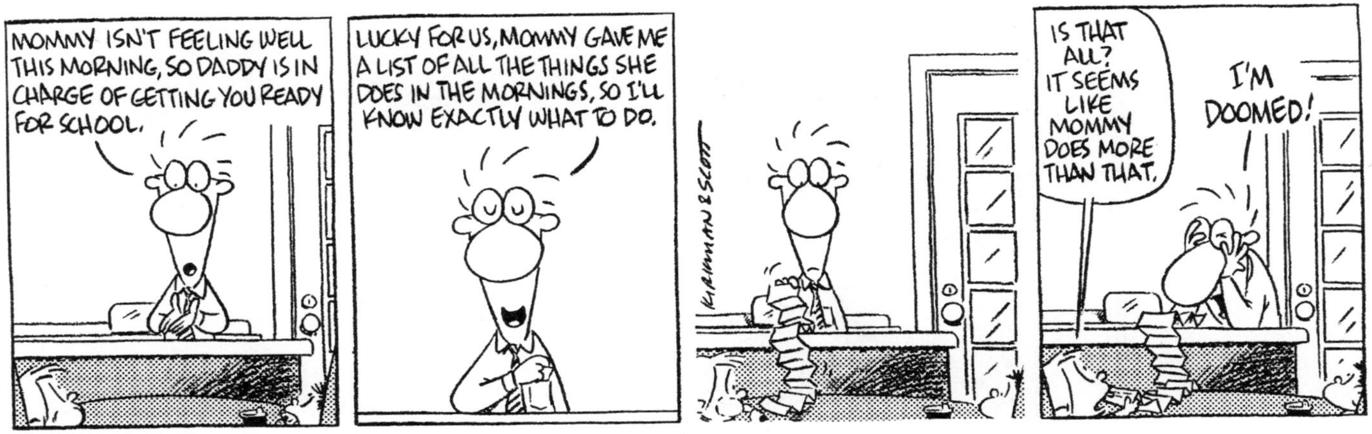
MOMMY ISN'T FEELING WELL THIS MORNING, SO DADDY IS IN CHARGE OF GETTING YOU READY FOR SCHOOL.
LUCKY FOR US, MOMMY GAVE ME A LIST OF ALL THE THINGS SHE DOES IN THE MORNINGS, SO I'LL KNOW EXACTLY WHAT TO DO.
KIRKMAN & SCOTT
IS THAT ALL? IT SEEMS LIKE MOMMY DOES MORE THAN THAT.
I'M DOOMED!

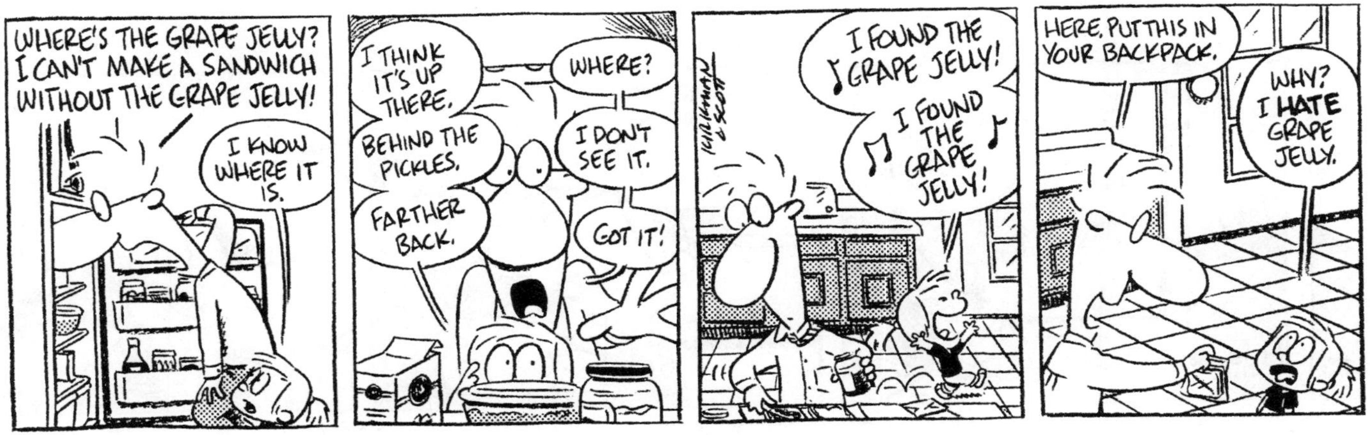
WHERE'S THE GRAPE JELLY? I CAN'T MAKE A SANDWICH WITHOUT THE GRAPE JELLY!
I KNOW WHERE IT IS.
I THINK IT'S UP THERE.
WHERE?
BEHIND THE PICKLES.
I DON'T SEE IT.
FARTHER BACK.
GOT IT!
KIRKMAN & SCOTT
I FOUND THE GRAPE JELLY!
I FOUND THE GRAPE JELLY!
HERE, PUT THIS IN YOUR BACKPACK.
WHY? I HATE GRAPE JELLY.

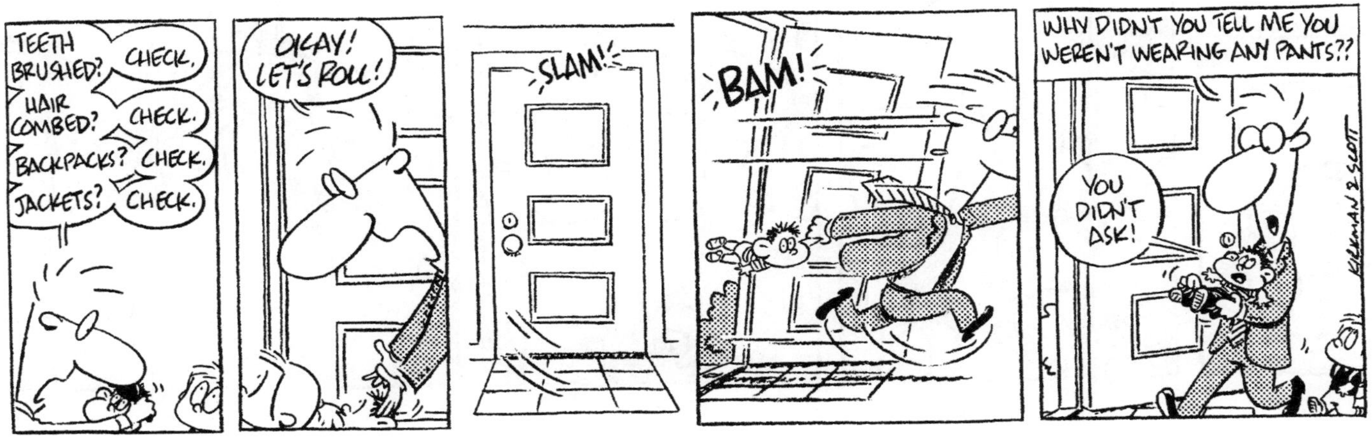
TEETH BRUSHED?
CHECK.
HAIR COMBED?
CHECK.
BACKPACKS?
CHECK.
JACKETS?
CHECK.
OKAY! LET'S ROLL!
SLAM!
BAM!
WHY DIDN'T YOU TELL ME YOU WEREN'T WEARING ANY PANTS??
YOU DIDN'T ASK!
KIRKMAN & SCOTT

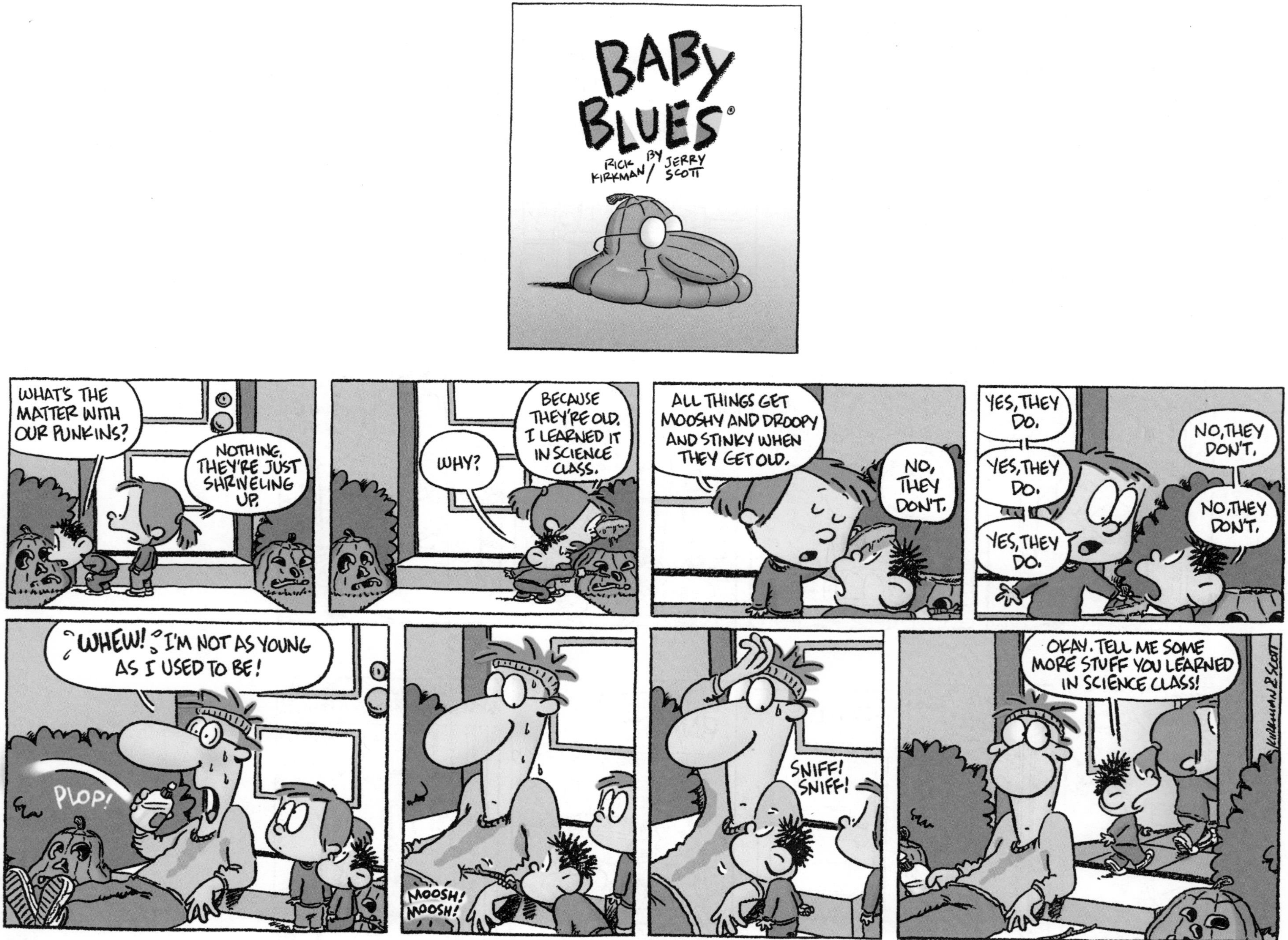
BABY BLUES®
RICK KIRKMAN / BY / JERRY SCOTT
WHAT'S THE MATTER WITH OUR PUNKINS?
NOTHING. THEY'RE JUST SHRIVELING UP.
WHY?
BECAUSE THEY'RE OLD. I LEARNED IT IN SCIENCE CLASS.
ALL THINGS GET MOOSHY AND DROOPY AND STINKY WHEN THEY GET OLD.
NO, THEY DON'T.
YES, THEY DO.
YES, THEY DO.
YES, THEY DO.
NO, THEY DON'T.
NO, THEY DON'T.
WHEW! I'M NOT AS YOUNG AS I USED TO BE!
PLOP!
MOOSH! MOOSH!
SNIFF! SNIFF!
OKAY. TELL ME SOME MORE STUFF YOU LEARNED IN SCIENCE CLASS!
KIRKMAN & SCOTT

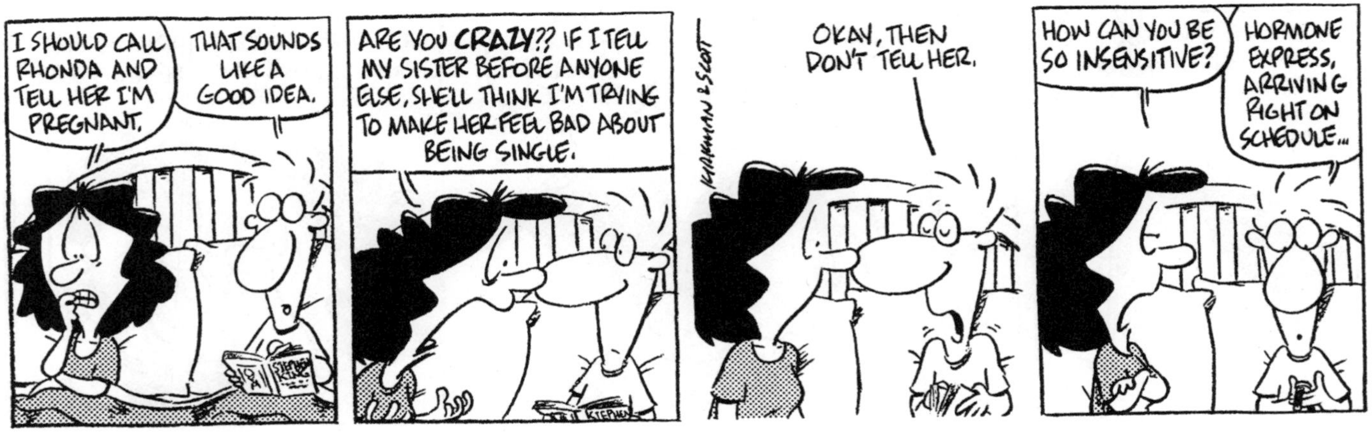
I SHOULD CALL RHONDA AND TELL HER I'M PREGNANT.
THAT SOUNDS LIKE A GOOD IDEA.
ARE YOU CRAZY?? IF I TELL MY SISTER BEFORE ANYONE ELSE, SHE'LL THINK I'M TRYING TO MAKE HER FEEL BAD ABOUT BEING SINGLE.
KIRKMAN & SCOTT
OKAY, THEN DON'T TELL HER.
HOW CAN YOU BE SO INSENSITIVE?
HORMONE EXPRESS, ARRIVING RIGHT ON SCHEDULE...

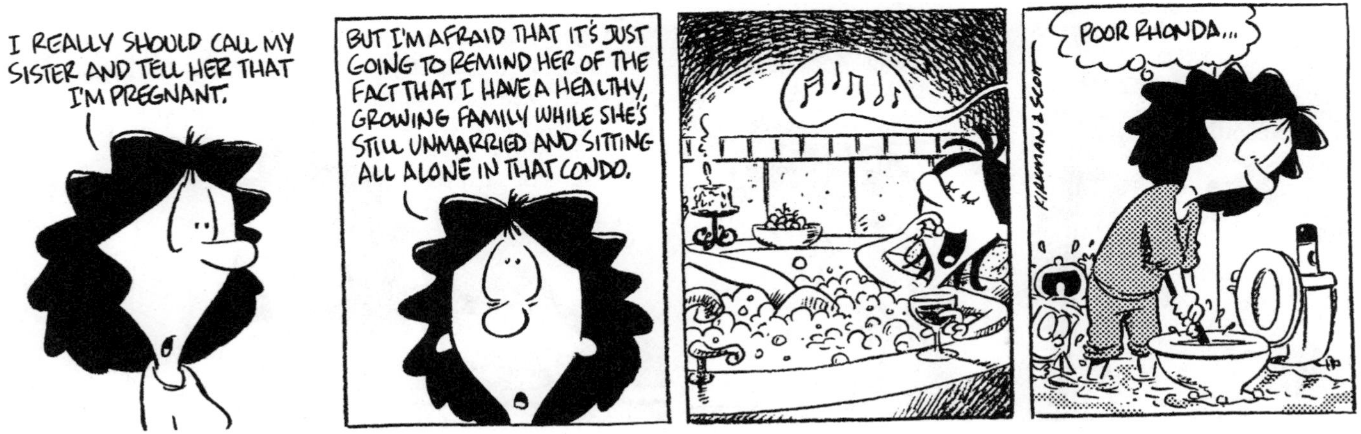
I REALLY SHOULD CALL MY SISTER AND TELL HER THAT I'M PREGNANT.
BUT I'M AFRAID THAT IT'S JUST GOING TO REMIND HER OF THE FACT THAT I HAVE A HEALTHY, GROWING FAMILY WHILE SHE'S STILL UNMARRIED AND SITTING ALL ALONE IN THAT CONDO.
KIRKMAN & SCOTT
POOR RHONDA...

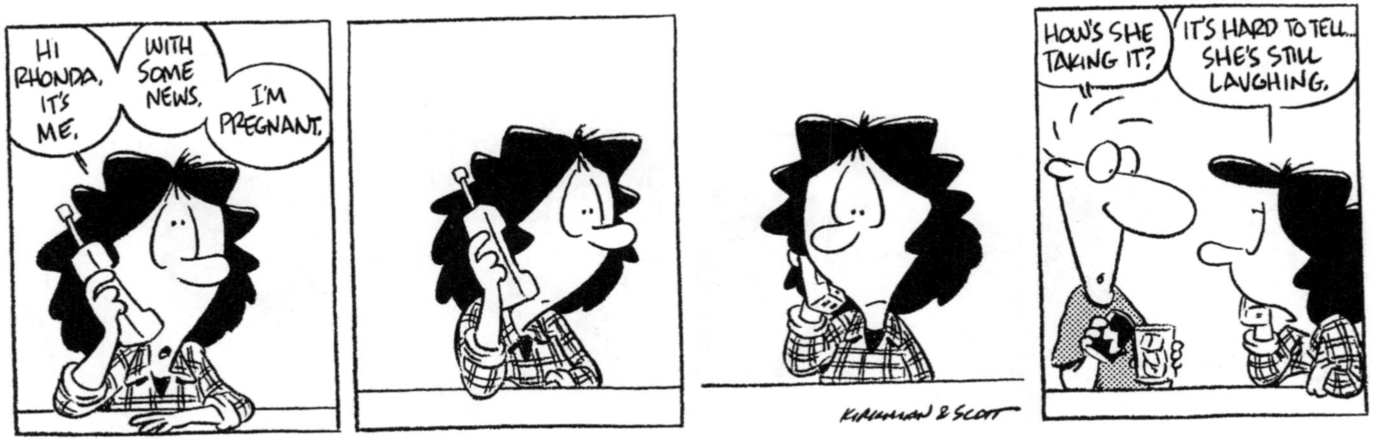
HI RHONDA, IT'S ME.
WITH SOME NEWS.
I'M PREGNANT.
HOW'S SHE TAKING IT?
IT'S HARD TO TELL... SHE'S STILL LAUGHING.
KIRKMAN & SCOTT

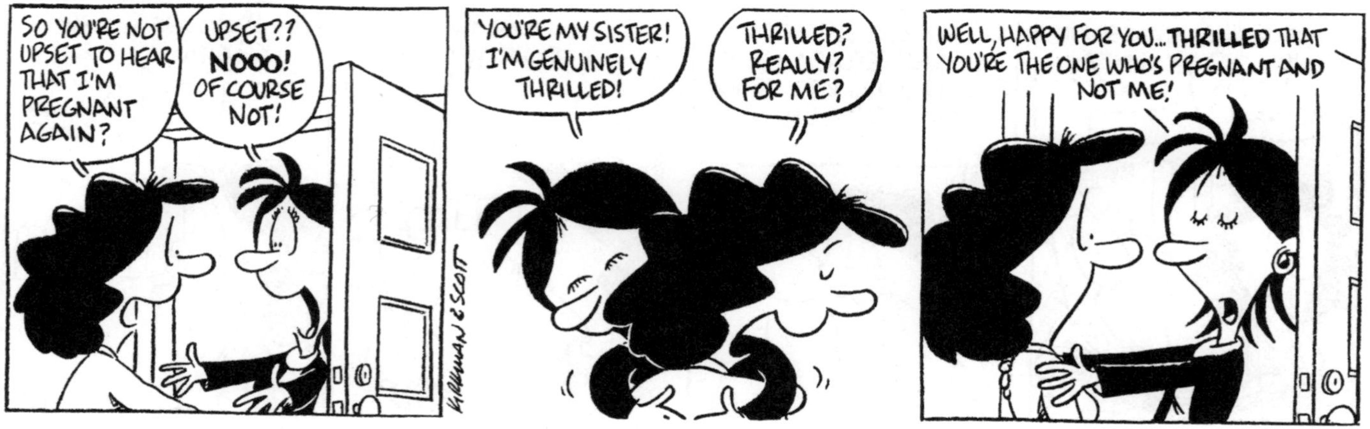
SO YOU'RE NOT UPSET TO HEAR THAT I'M PREGNANT AGAIN?
UPSET?? NOOO! OF COURSE NOT!
KIRKMAN & SCOTT
YOU'RE MY SISTER! I'M GENUINELY THRILLED!
THRILLED? REALLY? FOR ME?
WELL, HAPPY FOR YOU... THRILLED THAT YOU'RE THE ONE WHO'S PREGNANT AND NOT ME!

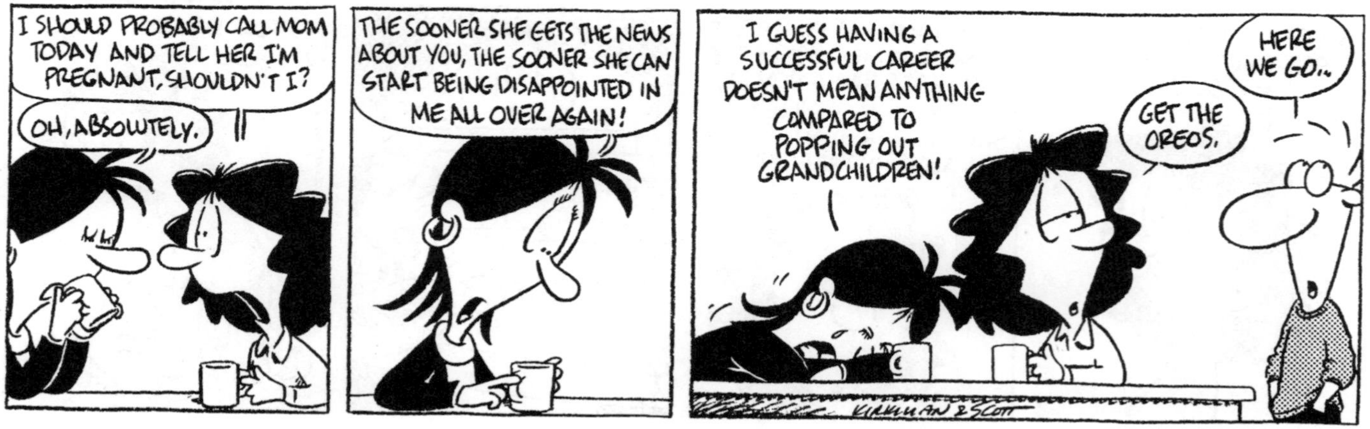
I SHOULD PROBABLY CALL MOM TODAY AND TELL HER I'M PREGNANT, SHOULDN'T I?
OH, ABSOLUTELY.
THE SOONER SHE GETS THE NEWS ABOUT YOU, THE SOONER SHE CAN START BEING DISAPPOINTED IN ME ALL OVER AGAIN!
I GUESS HAVING A SUCCESSFUL CAREER DOESN'T MEAN ANYTHING COMPARED TO POPPING OUT GRANDCHILDREN!
HERE WE GO..
GET THE OREOS.
KIRKMAN & SCOTT

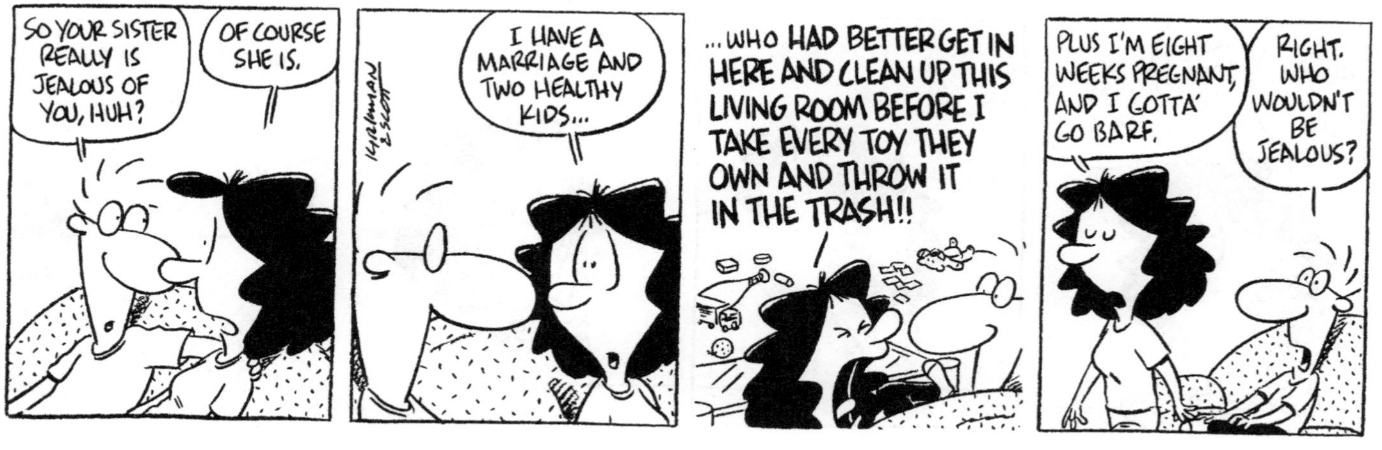
SO YOUR SISTER REALLY IS JEALOUS OF YOU, HUH?
OF COURSE SHE IS.
KIRKMAN & SCOTT
I HAVE A MARRIAGE AND TWO HEALTHY KIDS...
...WHO HAD BETTER GET IN HERE AND CLEAN UP THIS LIVING ROOM BEFORE I TAKE EVERY TOY THEY OWN AND THROW IT IN THE TRASH!!
PLUS I'M EIGHT WEEKS PREGNANT, AND I GOTTA' GO BARF.
RIGHT. WHO WOULDN'T BE JEALOUS?

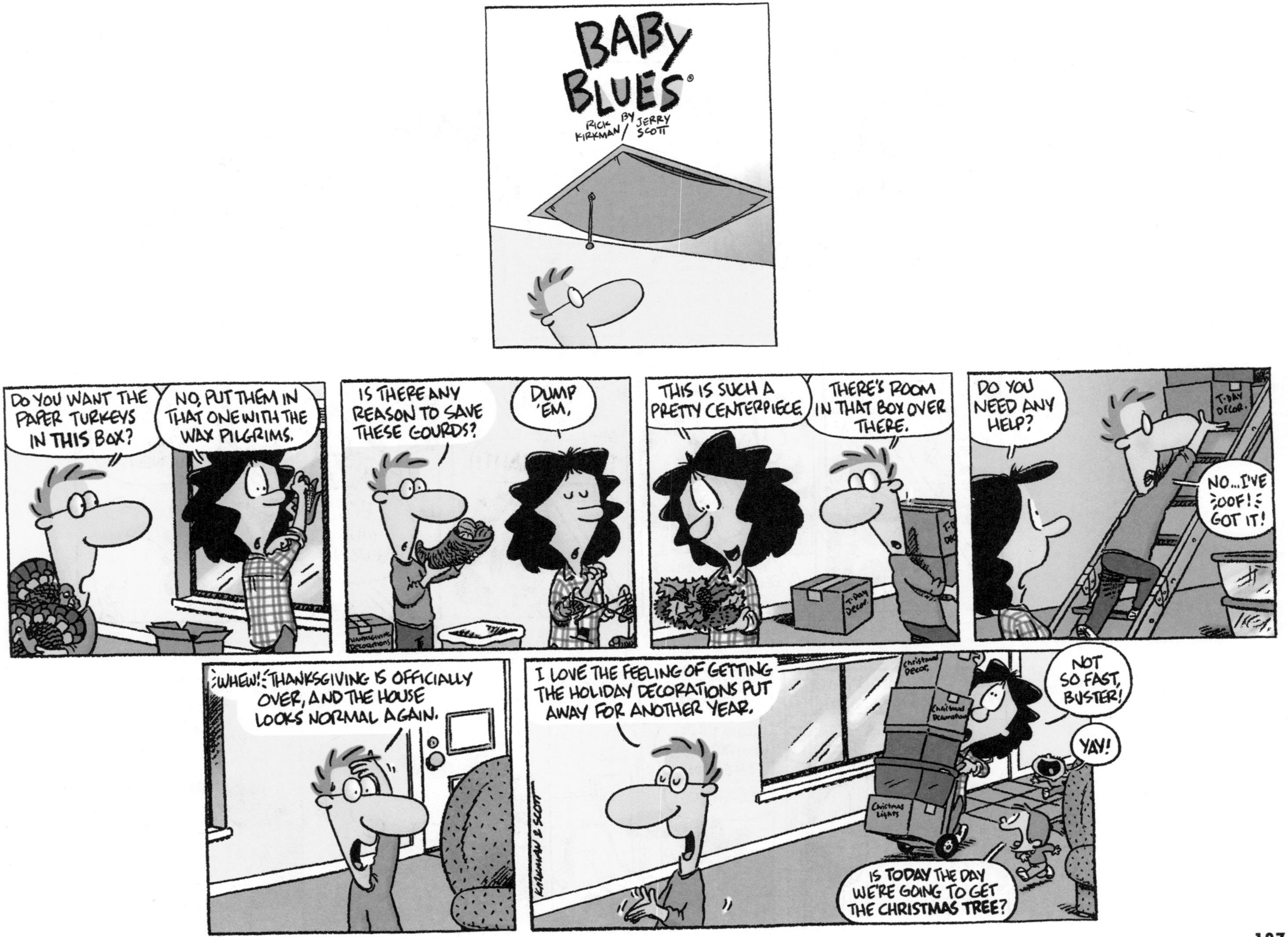
BABY BLUES®
BY RICK KIRKMAN / JERRY SCOTT
DO YOU WANT THE PAPER TURKEYS IN THIS BOX?
NO, PUT THEM IN THAT ONE WITH THE WAX PILGRIMS.
IS THERE ANY REASON TO SAVE THESE GOURDS?
DUMP 'EM.
THIS IS SUCH A PRETTY CENTERPIECE.
THERE'S ROOM IN THAT BOX OVER THERE.
T-DAY DECOR.
DO YOU NEED ANY HELP?
NO... I'VE OOF! GOT IT!
WHEW! THANKSGIVING IS OFFICIALLY OVER, AND THE HOUSE LOOKS NORMAL AGAIN.
KIRKMAN & SCOTT
I LOVE THE FEELING OF GETTING THE HOLIDAY DECORATIONS PUT AWAY FOR ANOTHER YEAR.
NOT SO FAST, BUSTER!
YAY!
IS TODAY THE DAY WE'RE GOING TO GET THE CHRISTMAS TREE?
Christmas Lights

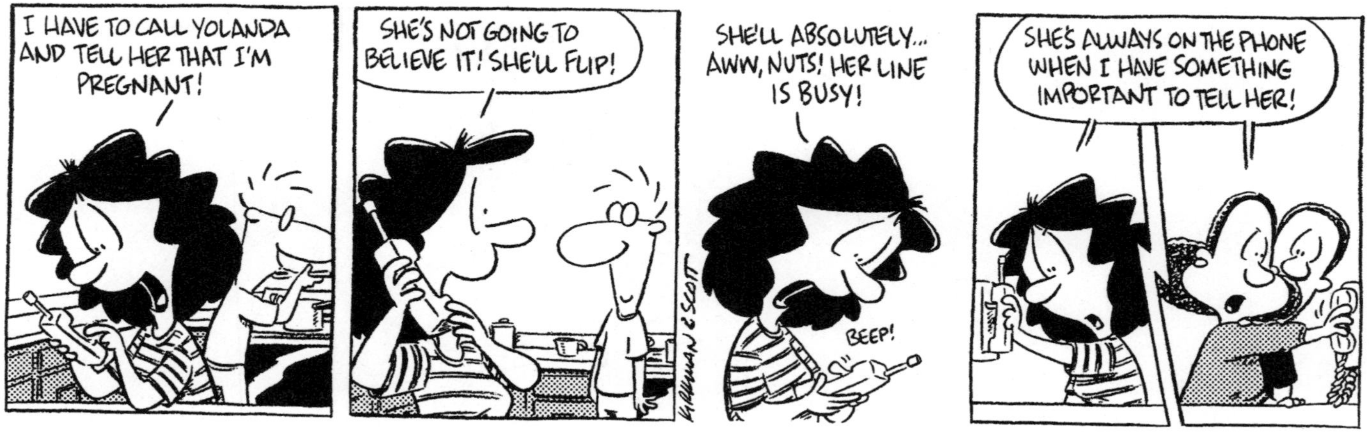
I HAVE TO CALL YOLANDA AND TELL HER THAT I'M PREGNANT!
SHE'S NOT GOING TO BELIEVE IT! SHE'LL FLIP!
KIRKMAN & SCOTT
SHE'LL ABSOLUTELY... AWW, NUTS! HER LINE IS BUSY!
BEEP!
SHE'S ALWAYS ON THE PHONE WHEN I HAVE SOMETHING IMPORTANT TO TELL HER!

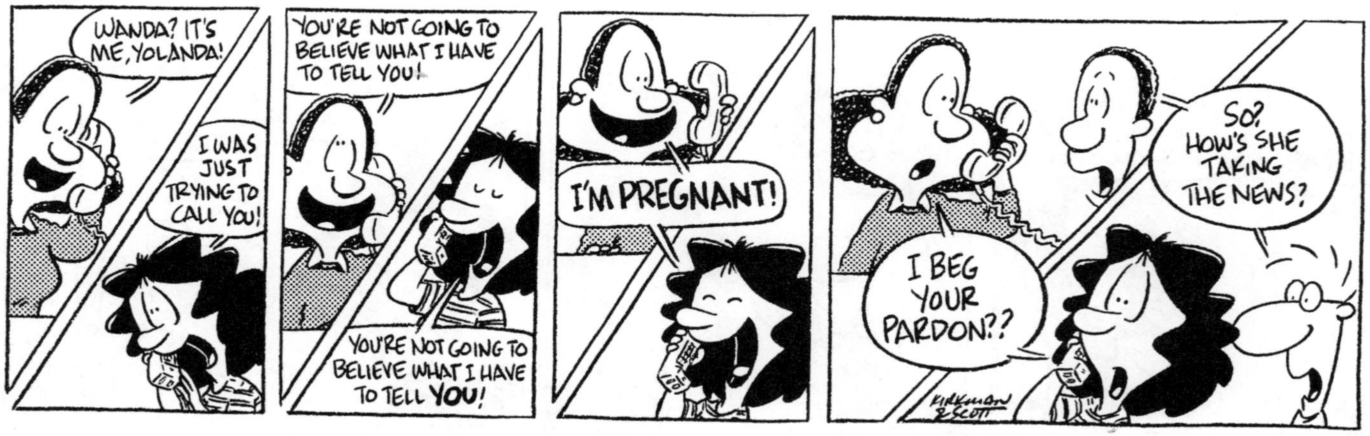
WANDA? IT'S ME, YOLANDA!
I WAS JUST TRYING TO CALL YOU!
YOU'RE NOT GOING TO BELIEVE WHAT I HAVE TO TELL YOU!
YOU'RE NOT GOING TO BELIEVE WHAT I HAVE TO TELL **YOU**!
I'M PREGNANT!
I BEG YOUR PARDON??
SO? HOW'S SHE TAKING THE NEWS?
KIRKMAN & SCOTT

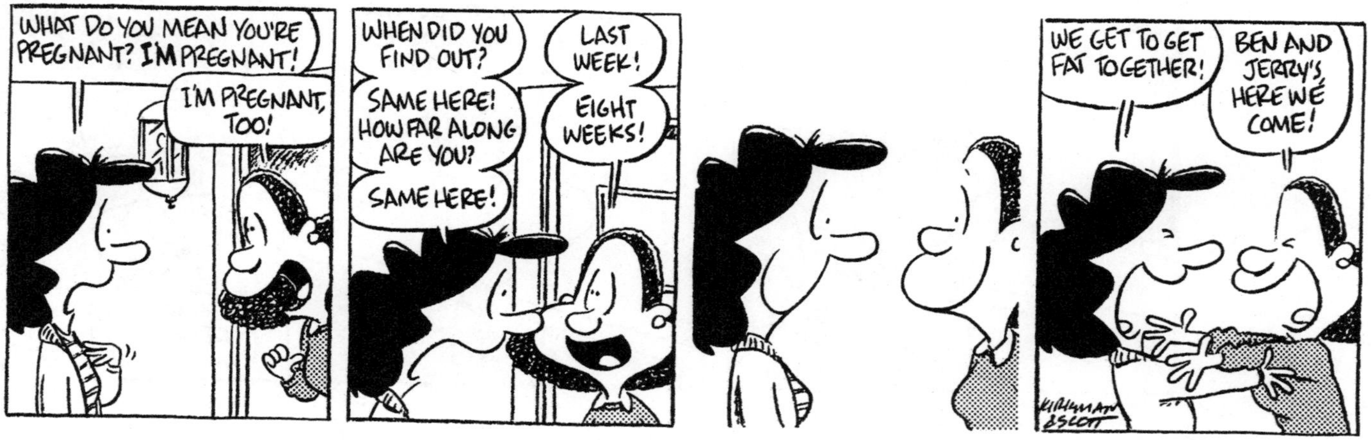
WHAT DO YOU MEAN YOU'RE PREGNANT? **I'M** PREGNANT!
I'M PREGNANT, TOO!
WHEN DID YOU FIND OUT?
LAST WEEK!
SAME HERE! HOW FAR ALONG ARE YOU?
EIGHT WEEKS!
SAME HERE!
WE GET TO GET FAT TOGETHER!
BEN AND JERRY'S, HERE WE COME!
KIRKMAN & SCOTT

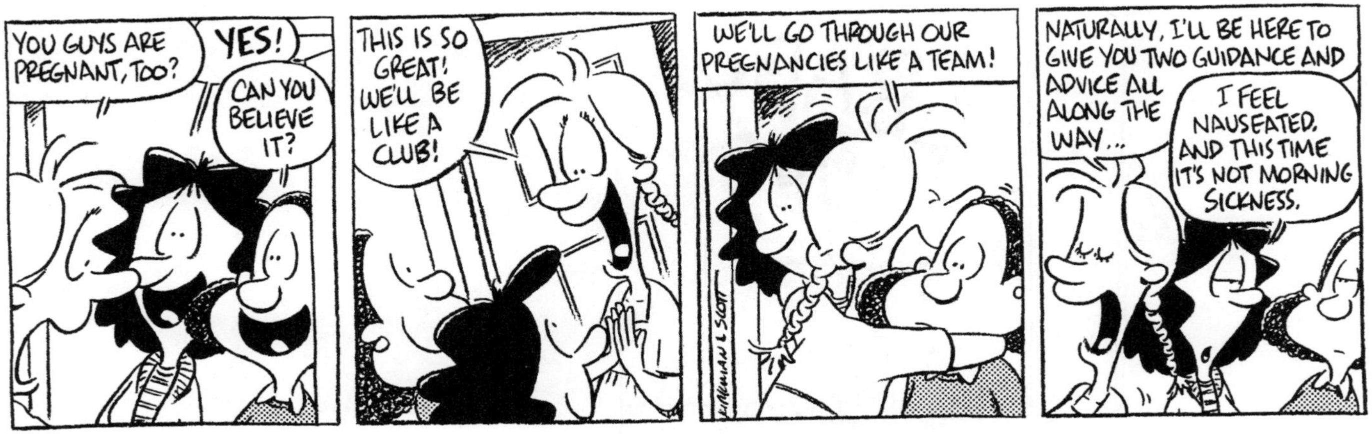
YOU GUYS ARE PREGNANT, TOO?
YES!
CAN YOU BELIEVE IT?
THIS IS SO GREAT! WE'LL BE LIKE A CLUB!
WE'LL GO THROUGH OUR PREGNANCIES LIKE A TEAM!
KIRKMAN & SCOTT
NATURALLY, I'LL BE HERE TO GIVE YOU TWO GUIDANCE AND ADVICE ALL ALONG THE WAY...
I FEEL NAUSEATED, AND THIS TIME IT'S NOT MORNING SICKNESS.

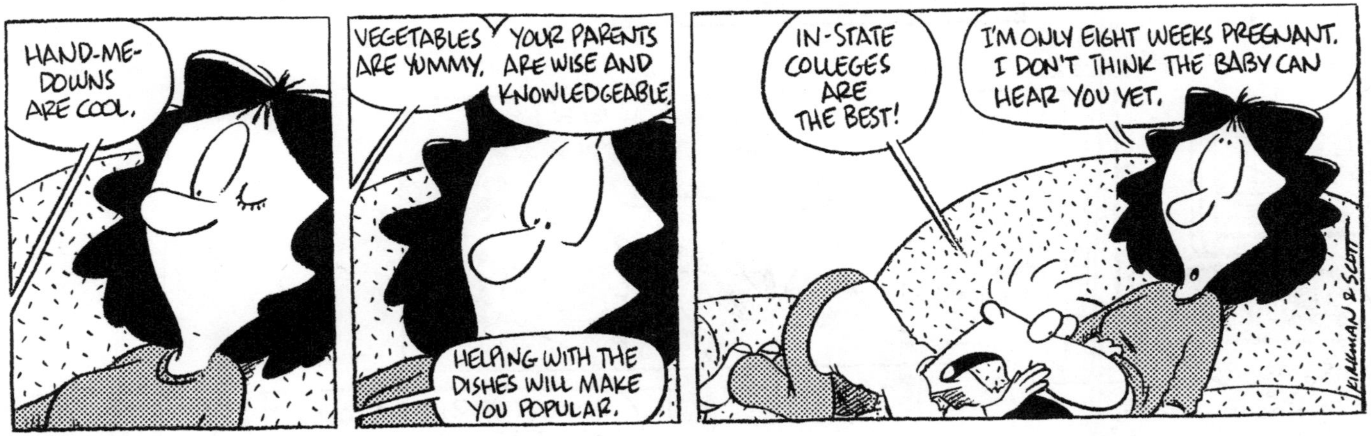
HAND-ME-DOWNS ARE COOL.
VEGETABLES ARE YUMMY.
YOUR PARENTS ARE WISE AND KNOWLEDGEABLE.
HELPING WITH THE DISHES WILL MAKE YOU POPULAR.
IN-STATE COLLEGES ARE THE BEST!
I'M ONLY EIGHT WEEKS PREGNANT. I DON'T THINK THE BABY CAN HEAR YOU YET.
KIRKMAN & SCOTT

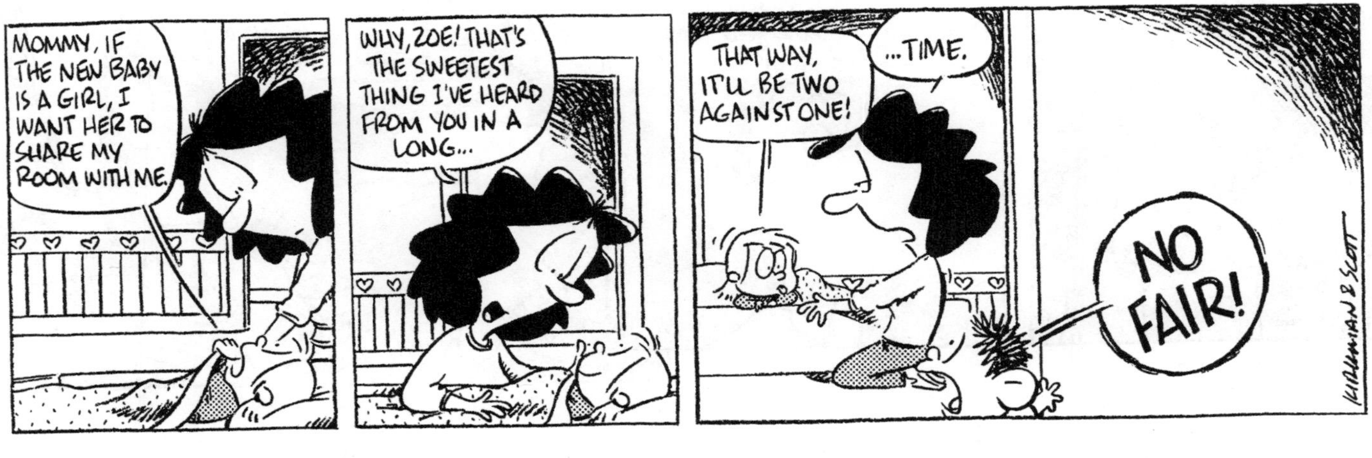
MOMMY, IF THE NEW BABY IS A GIRL, I WANT HER TO SHARE MY ROOM WITH ME.
WHY, ZOE! THAT'S THE SWEETEST THING I'VE HEARD FROM YOU IN A LONG...
THAT WAY, IT'LL BE TWO AGAINST ONE!
...TIME.
NO FAIR!
KIRKMAN & SCOTT

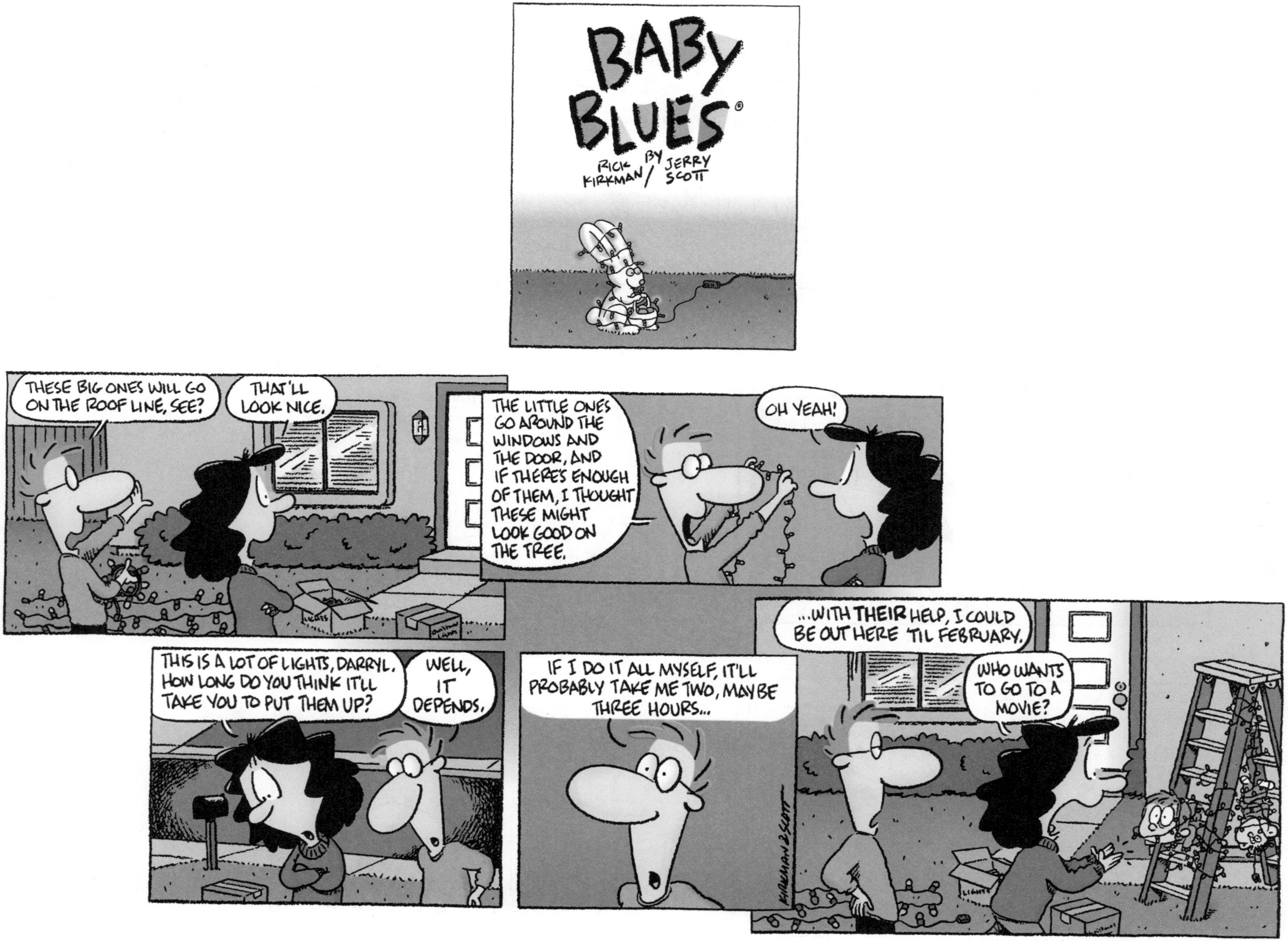
BABY BLUES®
BY RICK KIRKMAN / JERRY SCOTT
THESE BIG ONES WILL GO ON THE ROOF LINE, SEE?
THAT'LL LOOK NICE.
THE LITTLE ONES GO AROUND THE WINDOWS AND THE DOOR, AND IF THERE'S ENOUGH OF THEM, I THOUGHT THESE MIGHT LOOK GOOD ON THE TREE.
OH YEAH!
THIS IS A LOT OF LIGHTS, DARRYL. HOW LONG DO YOU THINK IT'LL TAKE YOU TO PUT THEM UP?
WELL, IT DEPENDS.
IF I DO IT ALL MYSELF, IT'LL PROBABLY TAKE ME TWO, MAYBE THREE HOURS...
...WITH THEIR HELP, I COULD BE OUT HERE 'TIL FEBRUARY.
WHO WANTS TO GO TO A MOVIE?

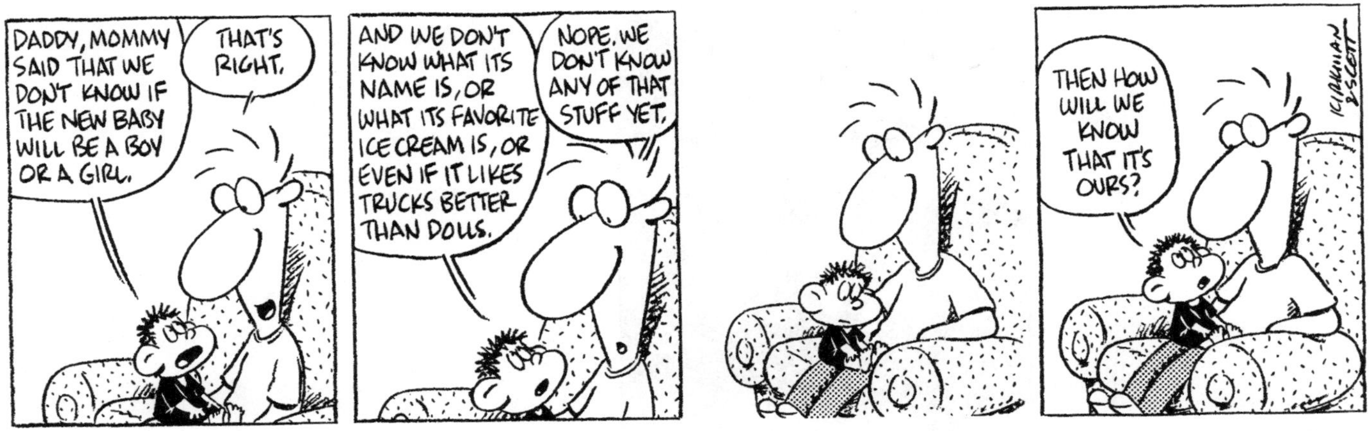
DADDY, MOMMY SAID THAT WE DON'T KNOW IF THE NEW BABY WILL BE A BOY OR A GIRL.
THAT'S RIGHT.
AND WE DON'T KNOW WHAT ITS NAME IS, OR WHAT ITS FAVORITE ICE CREAM IS, OR EVEN IF IT LIKES TRUCKS BETTER THAN DOLLS.
NOPE. WE DON'T KNOW ANY OF THAT STUFF YET.
KIRKMAN & SCOTT
THEN HOW WILL WE KNOW THAT IT'S OURS?

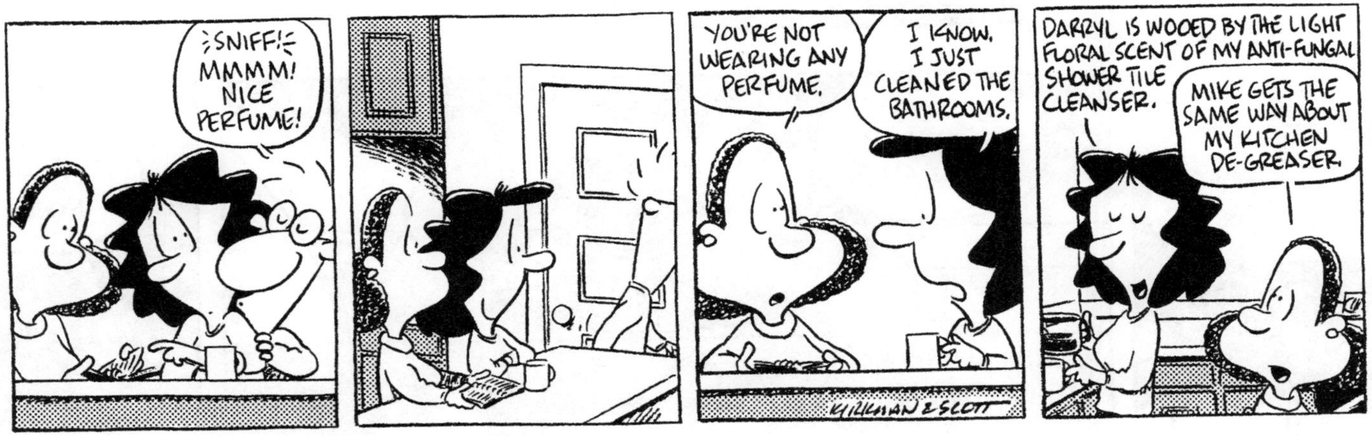
SNIFF!
MMMM! NICE PERFUME!
YOU'RE NOT WEARING ANY PERFUME.
I KNOW. I JUST CLEANED THE BATHROOMS.
KIRKMAN & SCOTT
DARRYL IS WOOED BY THE LIGHT FLORAL SCENT OF MY ANTI-FUNGAL SHOWER TILE CLEANSER.
MIKE GETS THE SAME WAY ABOUT MY KITCHEN DE-GREASER.

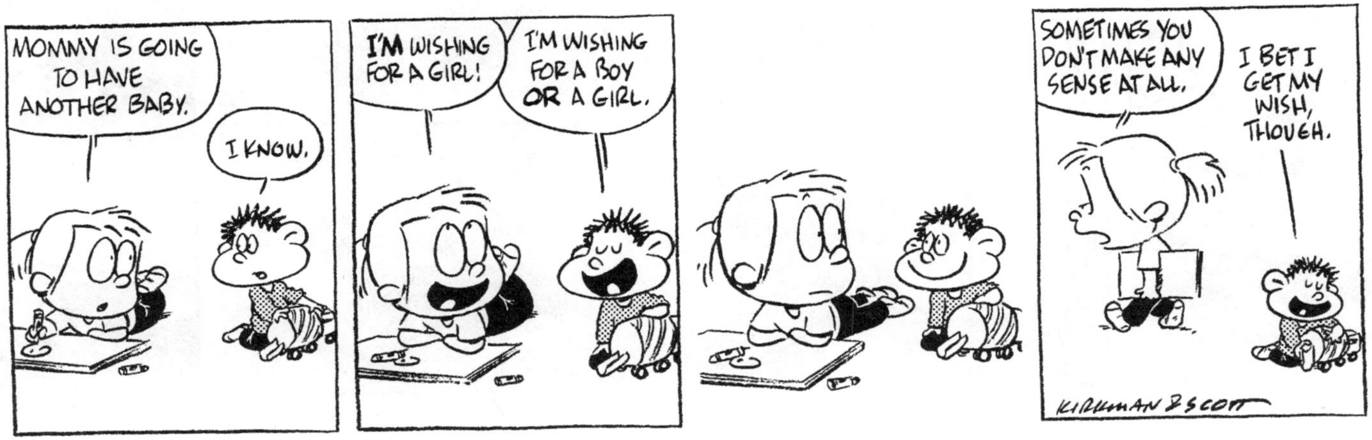
MOMMY IS GOING TO HAVE ANOTHER BABY.
I KNOW.
I'M WISHING FOR A GIRL!
I'M WISHING FOR A BOY OR A GIRL.
SOMETIMES YOU DON'T MAKE ANY SENSE AT ALL.
I BET I GET MY WISH, THOUGH.
KIRKMAN & SCOTT

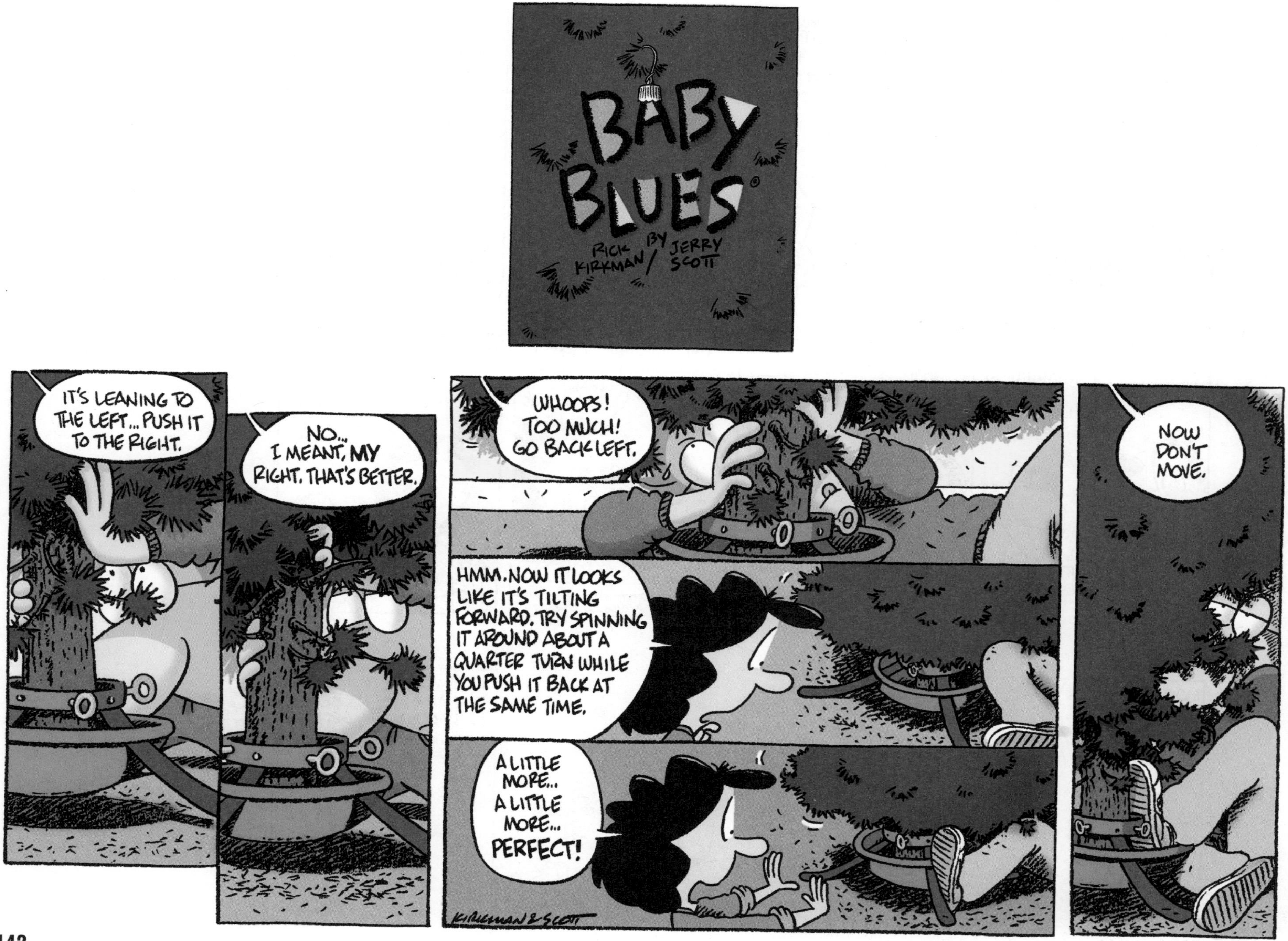
BABY BLUES®
BY RICK KIRKMAN / JERRY SCOTT
IT'S LEANING TO THE LEFT... PUSH IT TO THE RIGHT.
NO... I MEANT, MY RIGHT. THAT'S BETTER.
WHOOPS! TOO MUCH! GO BACK LEFT.
HMM. NOW IT LOOKS LIKE IT'S TILTING FORWARD. TRY SPINNING IT AROUND ABOUT A QUARTER TURN WHILE YOU PUSH IT BACK AT THE SAME TIME.
A LITTLE MORE... A LITTLE MORE... PERFECT!
KIRKMAN & SCOTT
NOW DON'T MOVE.

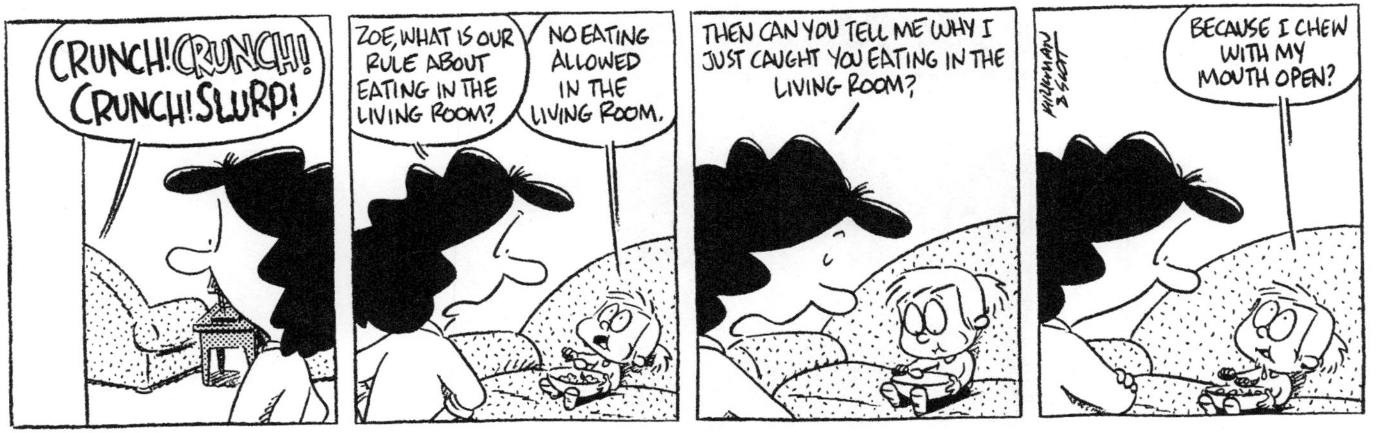
CRUNCH! CRUNCH! CRUNCH! SLURP!
ZOE, WHAT IS OUR RULE ABOUT EATING IN THE LIVING ROOM?
NO EATING ALLOWED IN THE LIVING ROOM.
THEN CAN YOU TELL ME WHY I JUST CAUGHT YOU EATING IN THE LIVING ROOM?
KIRKMAN & SCOTT
BECAUSE I CHEW WITH MY MOUTH OPEN?

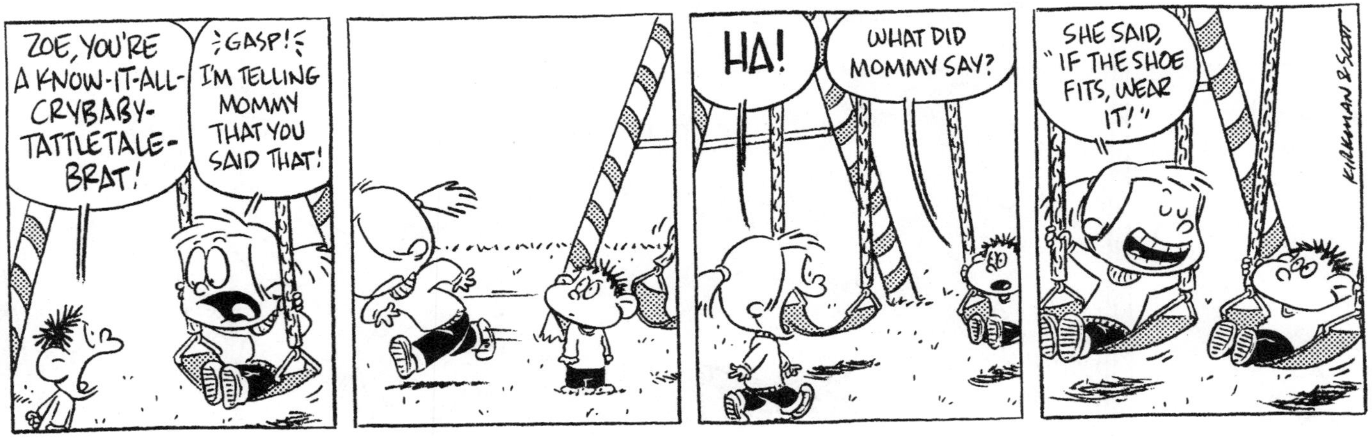
ZOE, YOU'RE A KNOW-IT-ALL-CRYBABY-TATTLETALE-BRAT!
GASP! I'M TELLING MOMMY THAT YOU SAID THAT!
HA!
WHAT DID MOMMY SAY?
SHE SAID, "IF THE SHOE FITS, WEAR IT!"
KIRKMAN & SCOTT

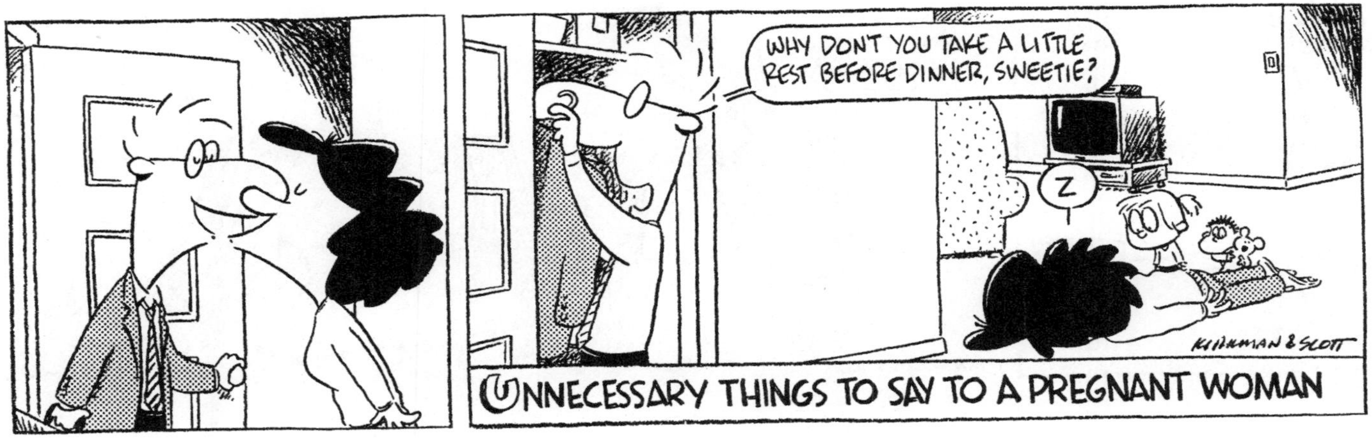
WHY DON'T YOU TAKE A LITTLE REST BEFORE DINNER, SWEETIE?
Z
KIRKMAN & SCOTT
UNNECESSARY THINGS TO SAY TO A PREGNANT WOMAN

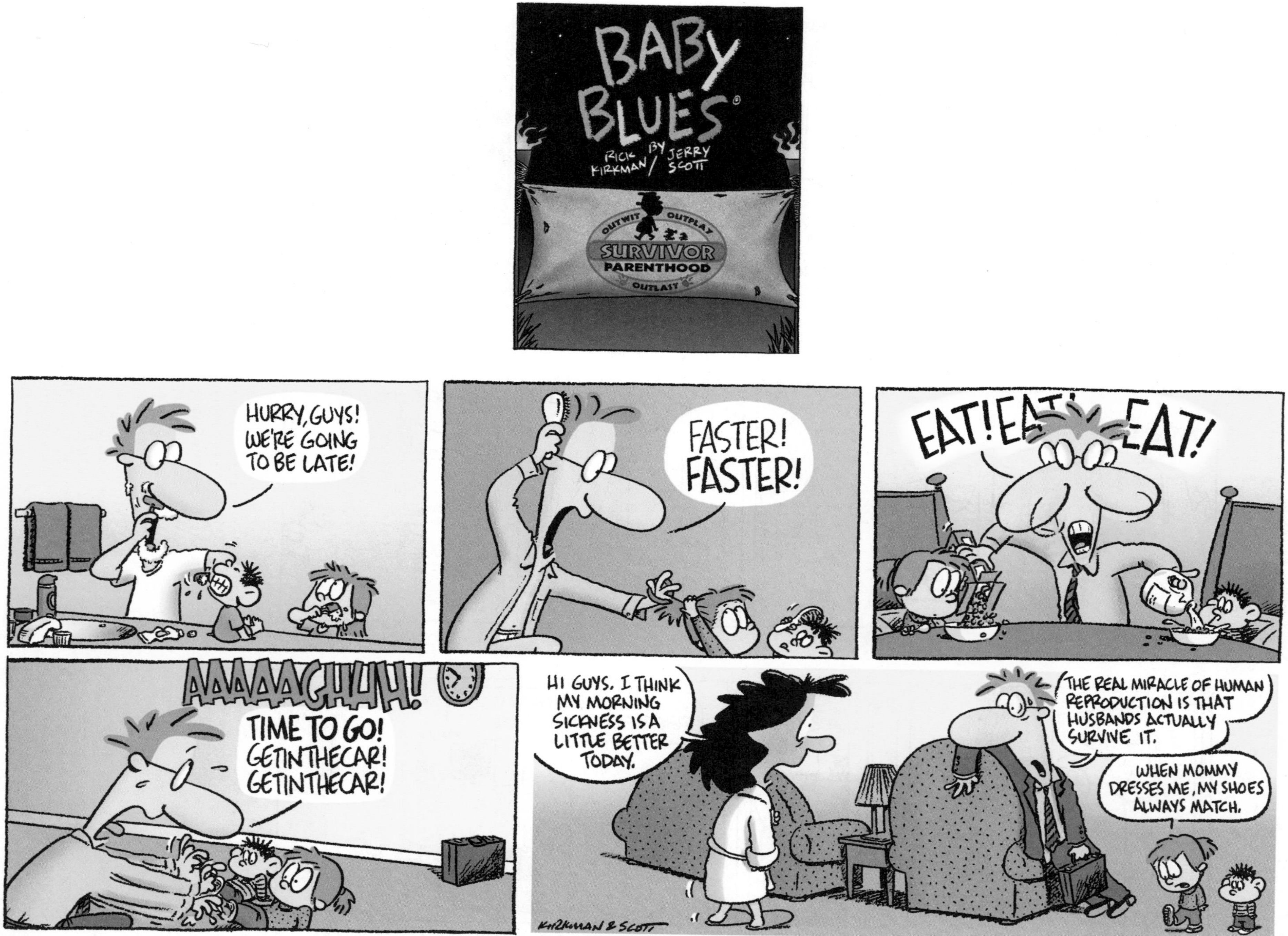
BABY BLUES®
BY RICK KIRKMAN / JERRY SCOTT
OUTWIT OUTPLAY
SURVIVOR
PARENTHOOD
OUTLAST
HURRY, GUYS! WE'RE GOING TO BE LATE!
FASTER! FASTER!
EAT! EAT! EAT!
AAAAAGHHH!
TIME TO GO! GETINTHECAR! GETINTHECAR!
HI GUYS. I THINK MY MORNING SICKNESS IS A LITTLE BETTER TODAY.
THE REAL MIRACLE OF HUMAN REPRODUCTION IS THAT HUSBANDS ACTUALLY SURVIVE IT.
WHEN MOMMY DRESSES ME, MY SHOES ALWAYS MATCH.
KIRKMAN & SCOTT

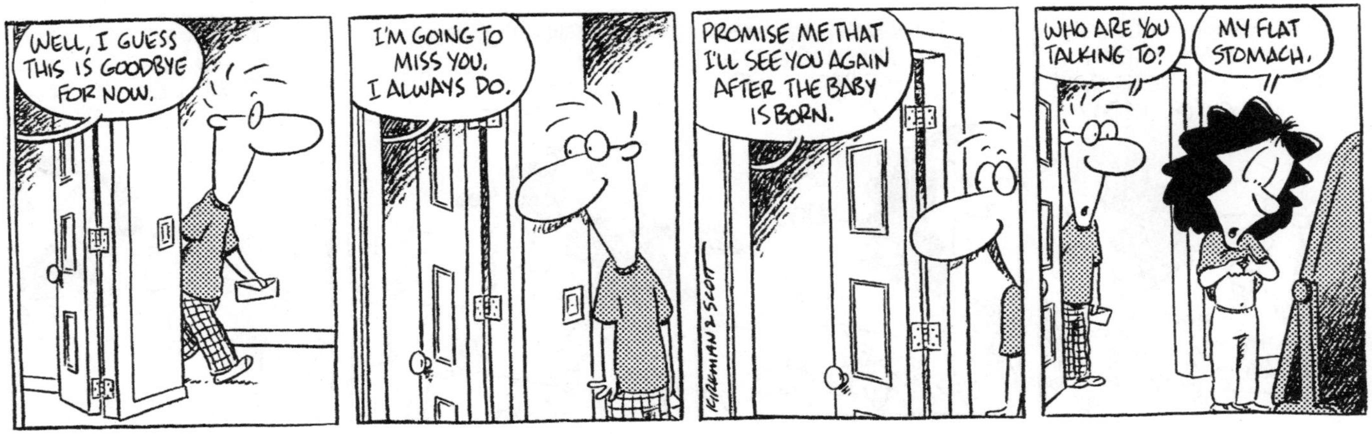
WELL, I GUESS THIS IS GOODBYE FOR NOW.
I'M GOING TO MISS YOU. I ALWAYS DO.
PROMISE ME THAT I'LL SEE YOU AGAIN AFTER THE BABY IS BORN.
KIRKMAN & SCOTT
WHO ARE YOU TALKING TO?
MY FLAT STOMACH.

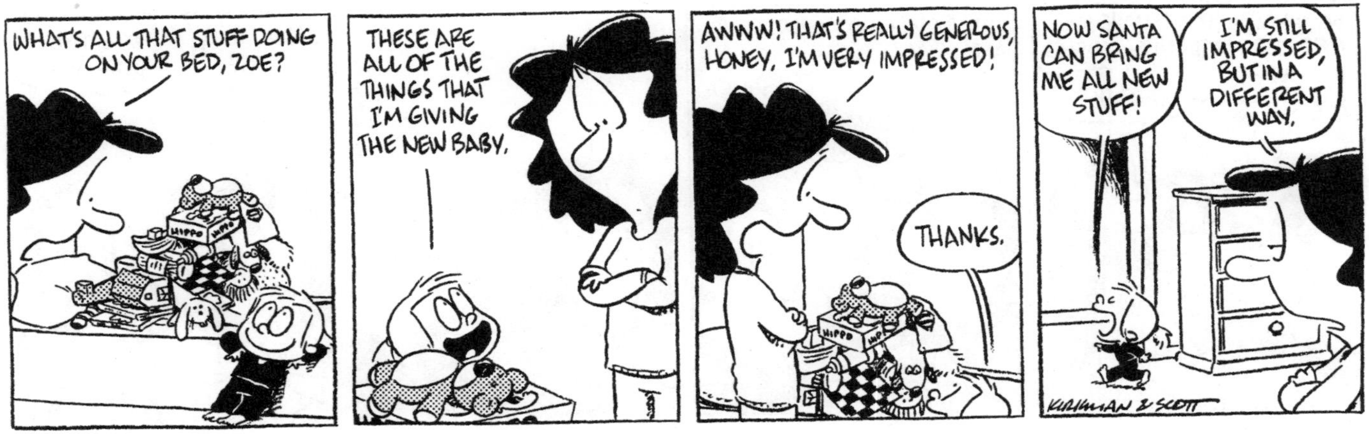
WHAT'S ALL THAT STUFF DOING ON YOUR BED, ZOE?
THESE ARE ALL OF THE THINGS THAT I'M GIVING THE NEW BABY.
AWWW! THAT'S REALLY GENEROUS, HONEY. I'M VERY IMPRESSED!
THANKS.
NOW SANTA CAN BRING ME ALL NEW STUFF!
I'M STILL IMPRESSED, BUT IN A DIFFERENT WAY.
KIRKMAN & SCOTT

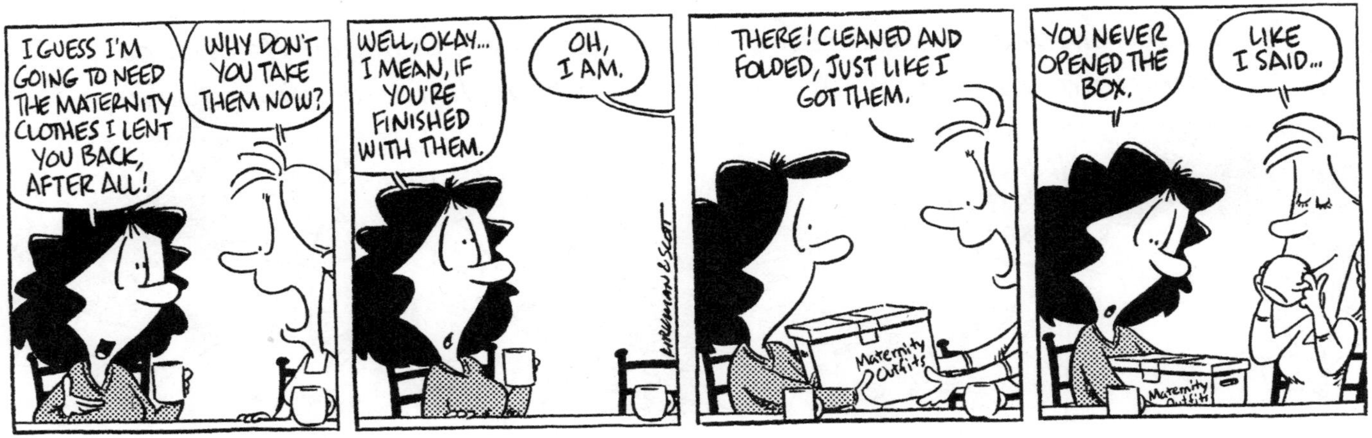
I GUESS I'M GOING TO NEED THE MATERNITY CLOTHES I LENT YOU BACK, AFTER ALL!
WHY DON'T YOU TAKE THEM NOW?
WELL, OKAY... I MEAN, IF YOU'RE FINISHED WITH THEM.
OH, I AM.
KIRKMAN & SCOTT
THERE! CLEANED AND FOLDED, JUST LIKE I GOT THEM.
Maternity Outfits
YOU NEVER OPENED THE BOX.
LIKE I SAID...

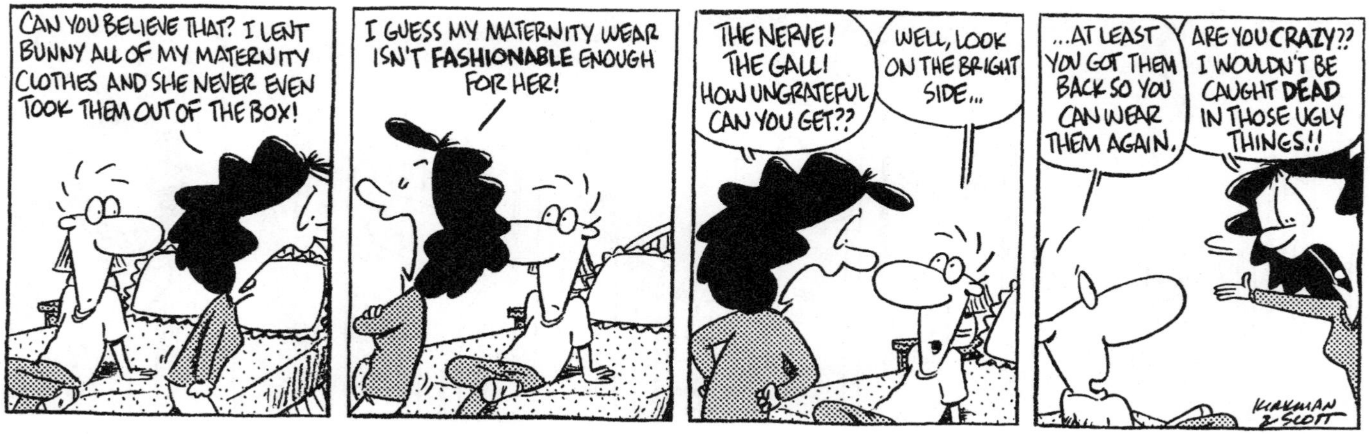
CAN YOU BELIEVE THAT? I LENT BUNNY ALL OF MY MATERNITY CLOTHES AND SHE NEVER EVEN TOOK THEM OUT OF THE BOX!
I GUESS MY MATERNITY WEAR ISN'T FASHIONABLE ENOUGH FOR HER!
THE NERVE! THE GALL! HOW UNGRATEFUL CAN YOU GET??
WELL, LOOK ON THE BRIGHT SIDE...
...AT LEAST YOU GOT THEM BACK SO YOU CAN WEAR THEM AGAIN.
ARE YOU CRAZY?? I WOULDN'T BE CAUGHT DEAD IN THOSE UGLY THINGS!!
KIRKMAN & SCOTT

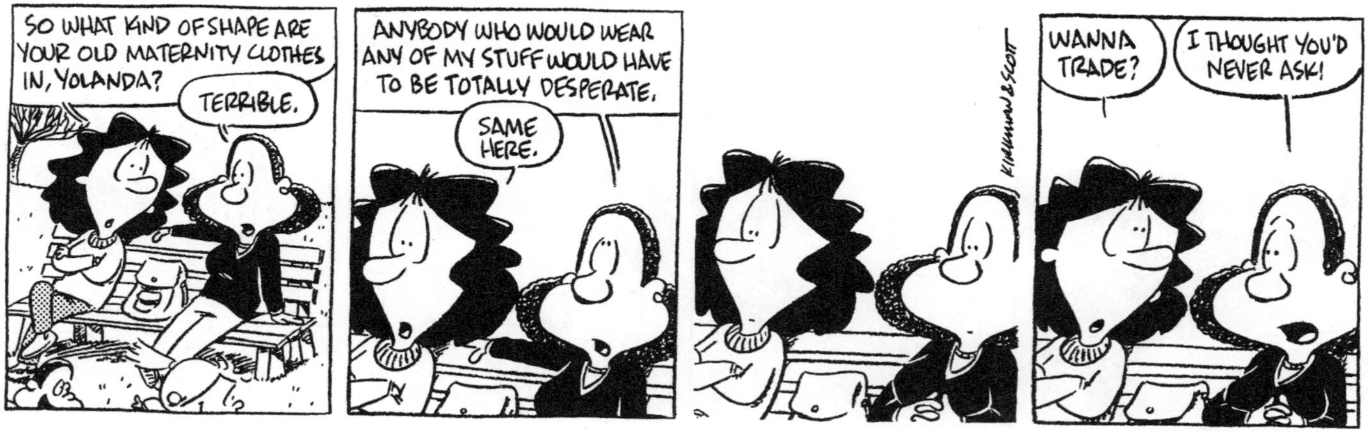
SO WHAT KIND OF SHAPE ARE YOUR OLD MATERNITY CLOTHES IN, YOLANDA?
TERRIBLE.
ANYBODY WHO WOULD WEAR ANY OF MY STUFF WOULD HAVE TO BE TOTALLY DESPERATE.
SAME HERE.
KIRKMAN & SCOTT
WANNA TRADE?
I THOUGHT YOU'D NEVER ASK!

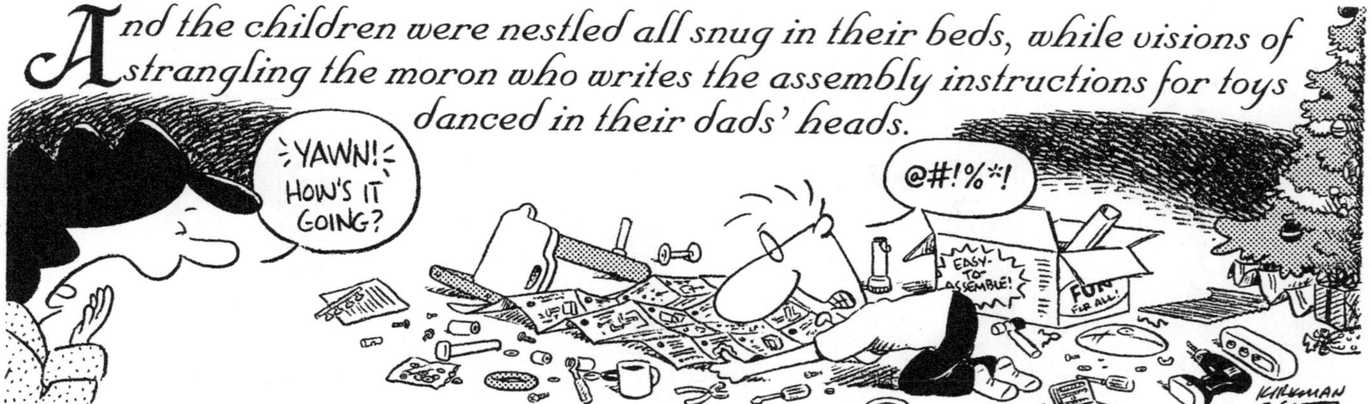
And the children were nestled all snug in their beds, while visions of strangling the moron who writes the assembly instructions for toys danced in their dads' heads.
YAWN! HOW'S IT GOING?
@#!%*!
EASY-TO-ASSEMBLE!
FUN FOR ALL!
KIRKMAN & SCOTT

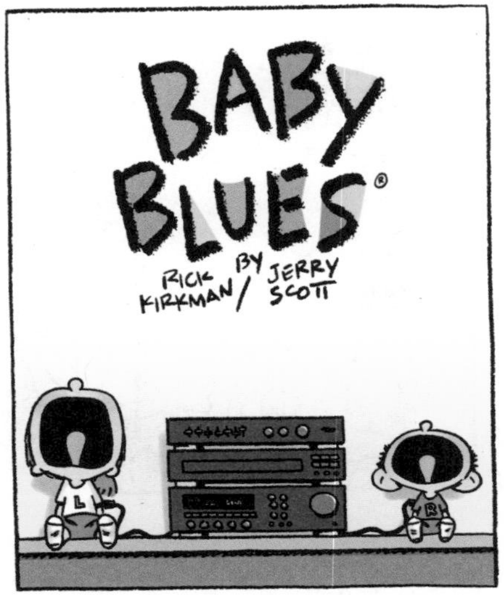
BABY BLUES®
BY RICK KIRKMAN / JERRY SCOTT

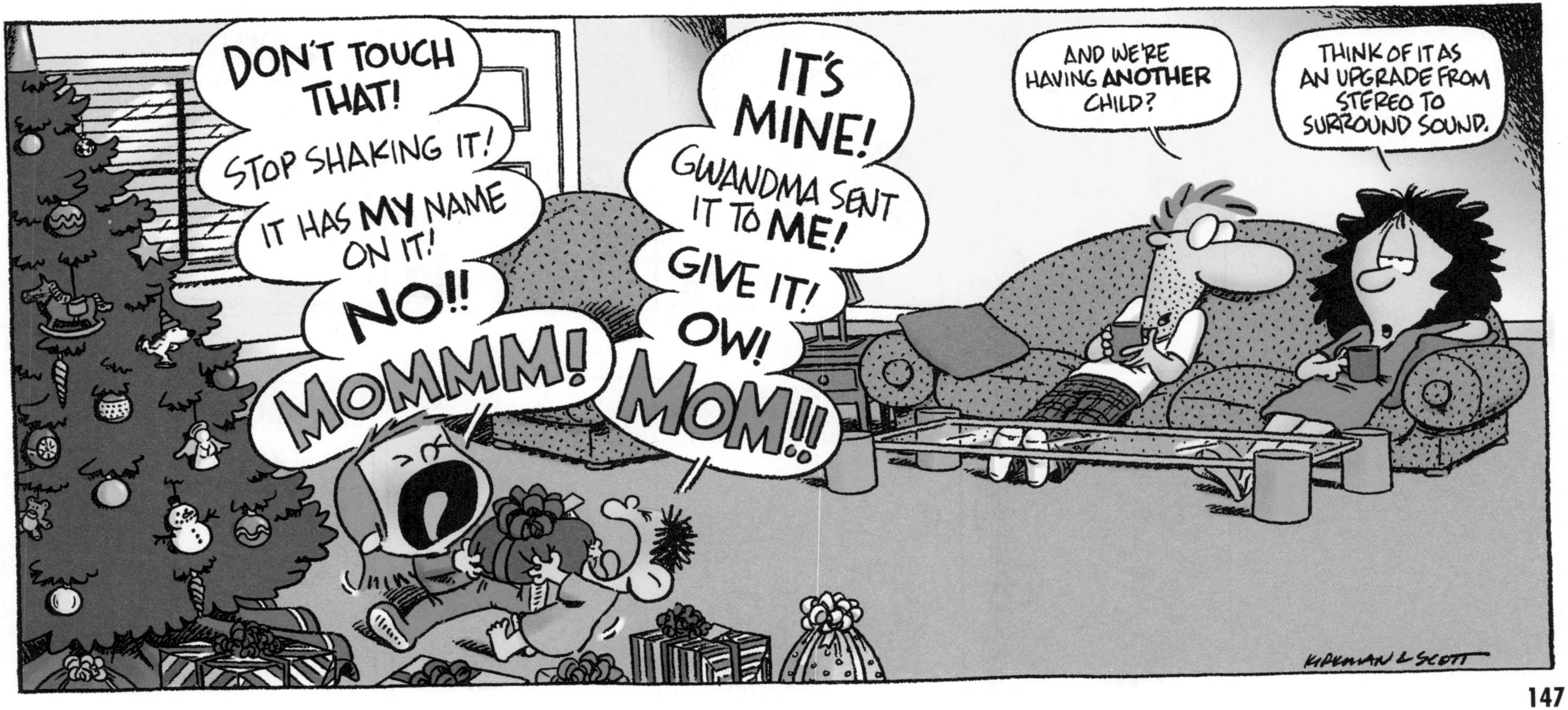
DON'T TOUCH THAT!
IT'S MINE!
STOP SHAKING IT!
GWANDMA SENT IT TO **ME**!
IT HAS **MY** NAME ON IT!
GIVE IT!
NO!!
OW!
MOMMM!
MOM!!
AND WE'RE HAVING **ANOTHER** CHILD?
THINK OF IT AS AN UPGRADE FROM STEREO TO SURROUND SOUND.
KIRKMAN & SCOTT

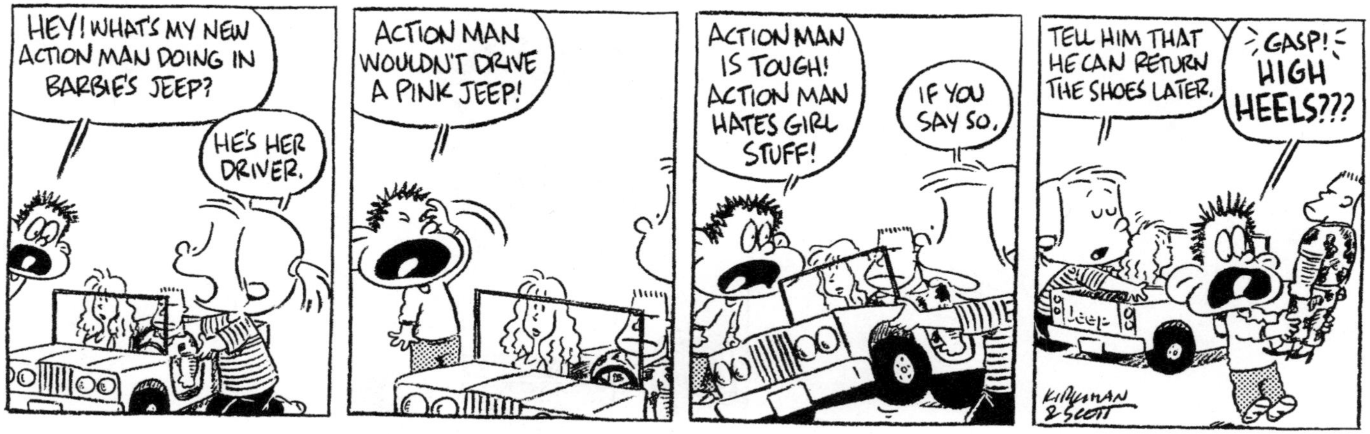
HEY! WHAT'S MY NEW ACTION MAN DOING IN BARBIE'S JEEP?
HE'S HER DRIVER.
ACTION MAN WOULDN'T DRIVE A PINK JEEP!
ACTION MAN IS TOUGH! ACTION MAN HATES GIRL STUFF!
IF YOU SAY SO.
TELL HIM THAT HE CAN RETURN THE SHOES LATER.
GASP! HIGH HEELS???
Jeep
KIRKMAN & SCOTT

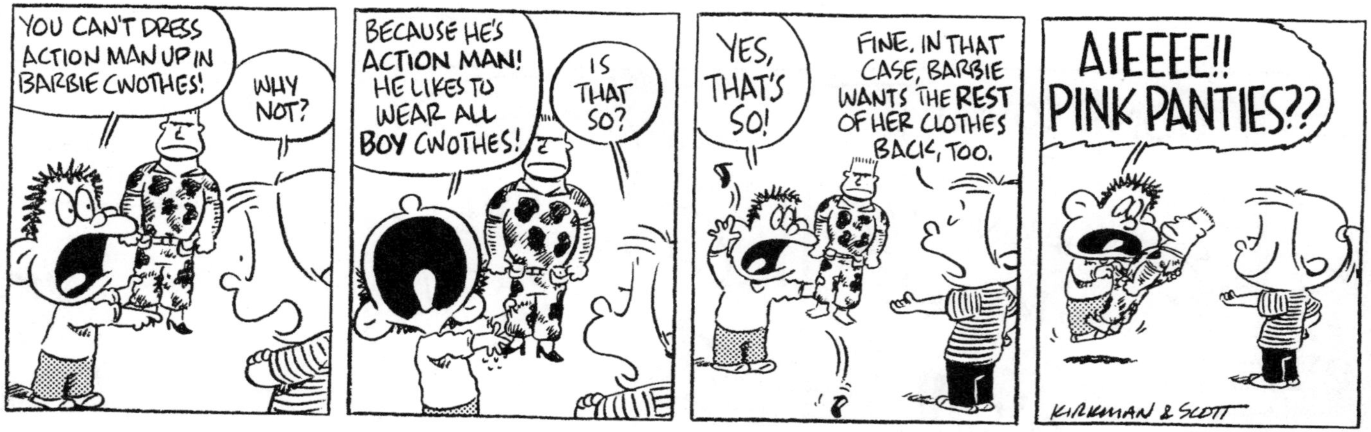
YOU CAN'T DRESS ACTION MAN UP IN BARBIE CWOTHES!
WHY NOT?
BECAUSE HE'S ACTION MAN! HE LIKES TO WEAR ALL BOY CWOTHES!
IS THAT SO?
YES, THAT'S SO!
FINE. IN THAT CASE, BARBIE WANTS THE REST OF HER CLOTHES BACK, TOO.
AIEEEE!! PINK PANTIES??
KIRKMAN & SCOTT

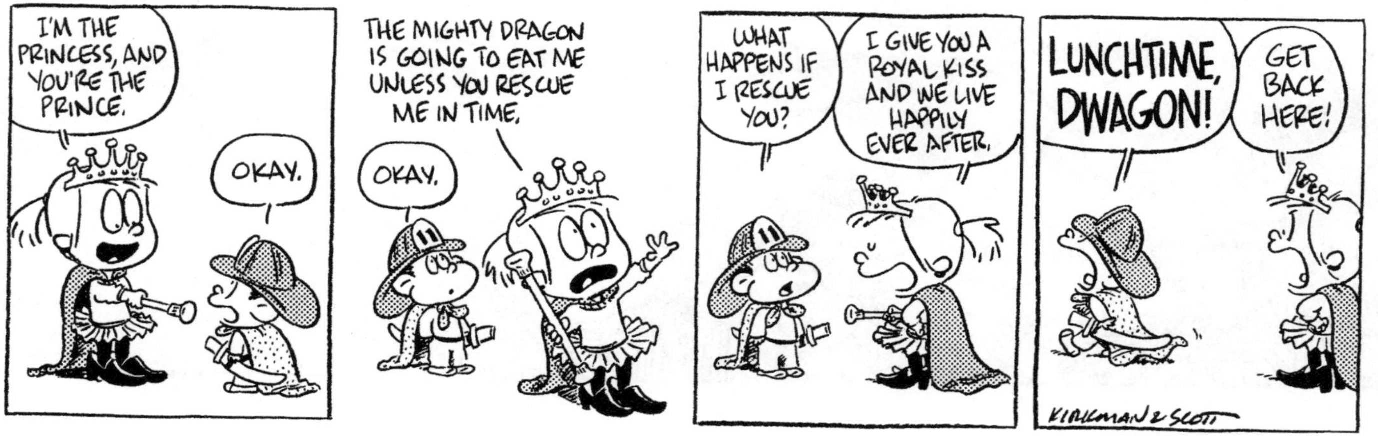
I'M THE PRINCESS, AND YOU'RE THE PRINCE.
OKAY.
THE MIGHTY DRAGON IS GOING TO EAT ME UNLESS YOU RESCUE ME IN TIME.
OKAY.
WHAT HAPPENS IF I RESCUE YOU?
I GIVE YOU A ROYAL KISS AND WE LIVE HAPPILY EVER AFTER.
LUNCHTIME, DWAGON!
GET BACK HERE!
KIRKMAN & SCOTT

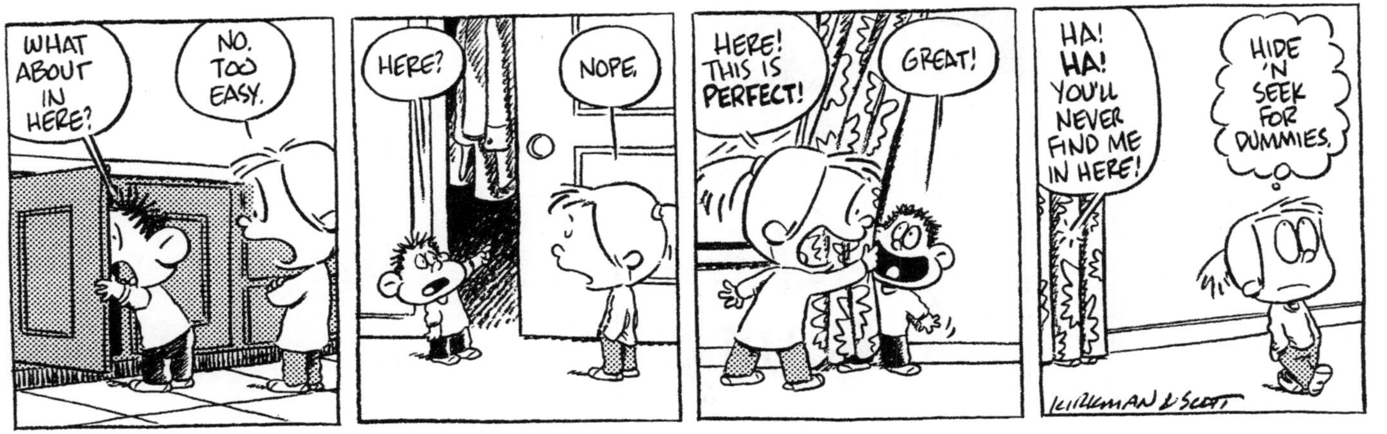
WHAT ABOUT IN HERE?
NO. TOO EASY.
HERE?
NOPE.
HERE! THIS IS **PERFECT!**
GREAT!
HA! **HA!** YOU'LL NEVER FIND ME IN HERE!
HIDE 'N SEEK FOR DUMMIES.
KIRKMAN & SCOTT

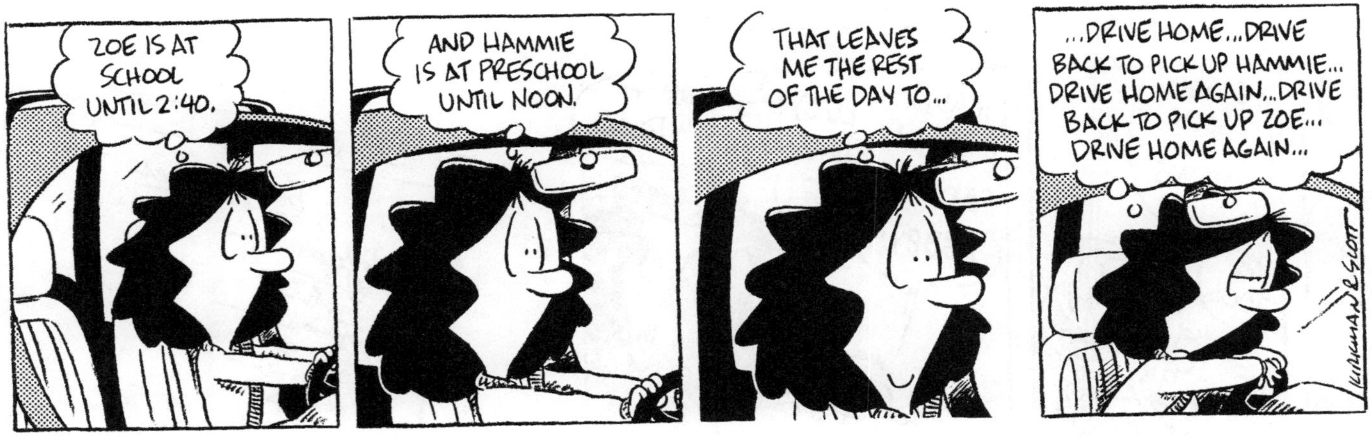
ZOE IS AT SCHOOL UNTIL 2:40.
AND HAMMIE IS AT PRESCHOOL UNTIL NOON.
THAT LEAVES ME THE REST OF THE DAY TO...
...DRIVE HOME...DRIVE BACK TO PICK UP HAMMIE... DRIVE HOME AGAIN...DRIVE BACK TO PICK UP ZOE... DRIVE HOME AGAIN...
KIRKMAN & SCOTT

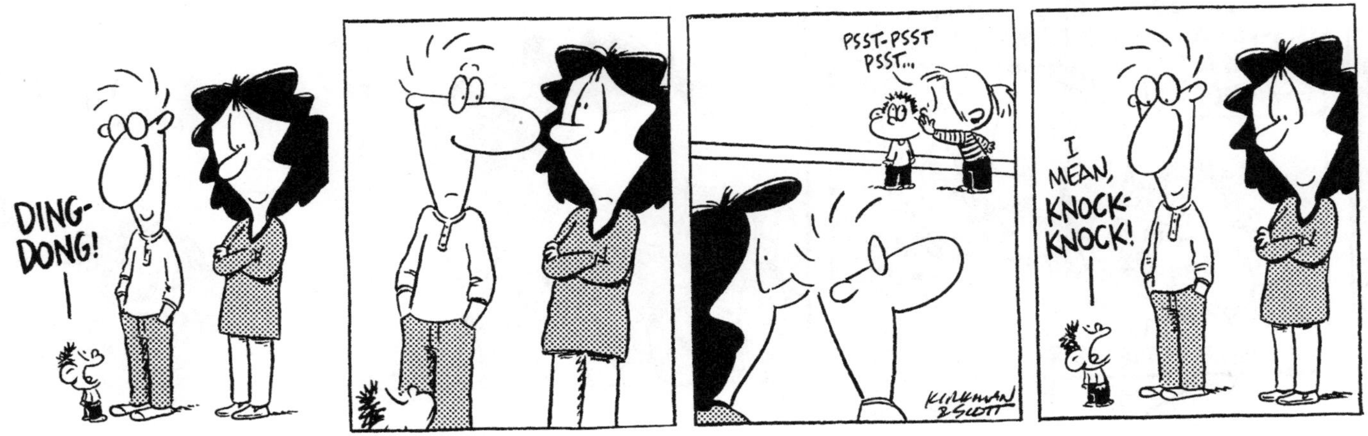
DING-DONG!
PSST-PSST PSST...
KIRKMAN & SCOTT
I MEAN, KNOCK-KNOCK!

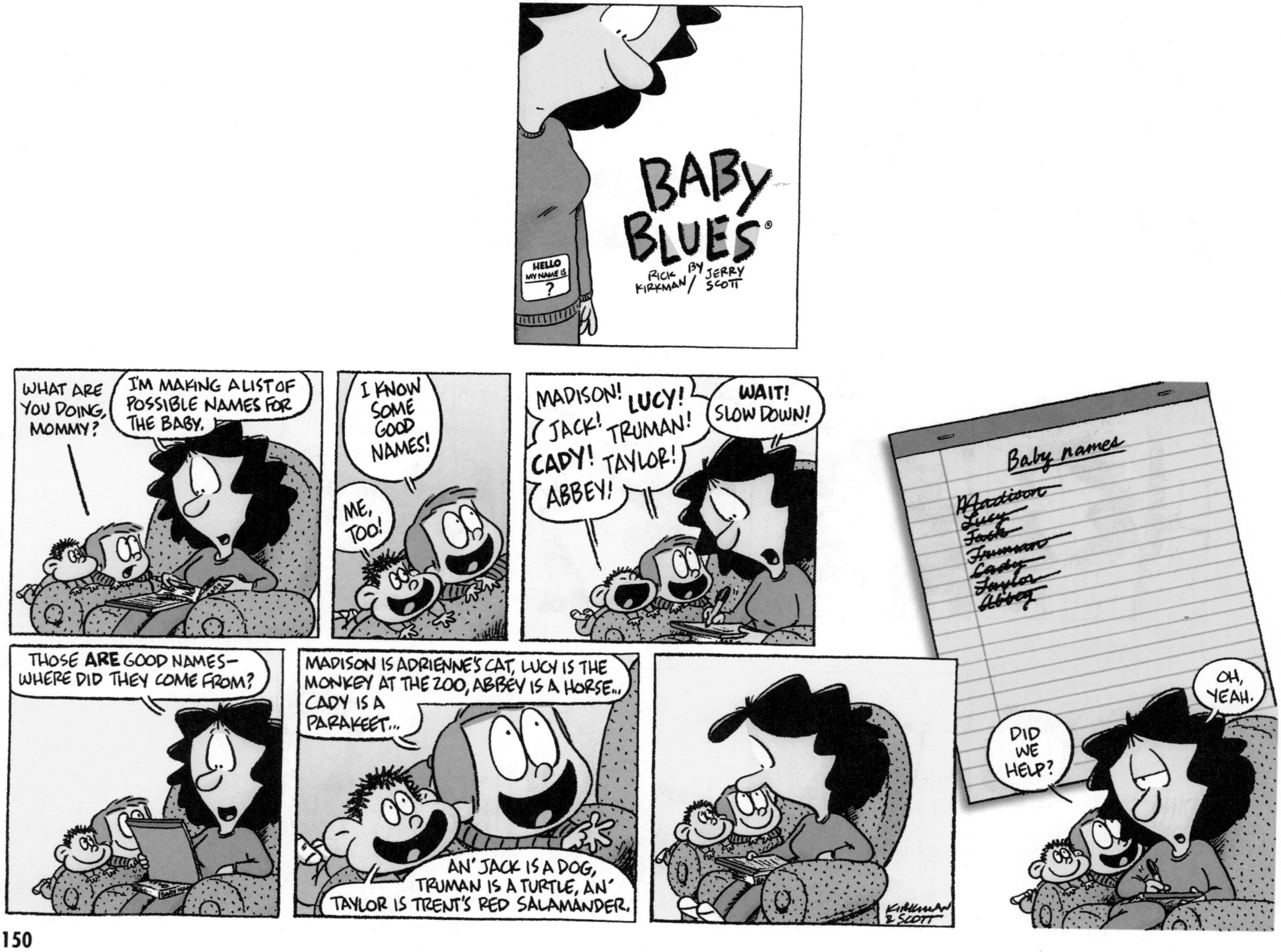
BABY BLUES®
BY RICK KIRKMAN / JERRY SCOTT
HELLO MY NAME IS ?
WHAT ARE YOU DOING, MOMMY?
I'M MAKING A LIST OF POSSIBLE NAMES FOR THE BABY.
I KNOW SOME GOOD NAMES!
ME, TOO!
MADISON! JACK! CADY! ABBEY!
LUCY! TRUMAN! TAYLOR!
WAIT! SLOW DOWN!
Baby names
Madison
Lucy
Jack
Truman
Cady
Taylor
Abbey
THOSE ARE GOOD NAMES— WHERE DID THEY COME FROM?
MADISON IS ADRIENNE'S CAT, LUCY IS THE MONKEY AT THE ZOO, ABBEY IS A HORSE... CADY IS A PARAKEET...
AN' JACK IS A DOG, TRUMAN IS A TURTLE, AN' TAYLOR IS TRENT'S RED SALAMANDER.
DID WE HELP?
OH, YEAH.

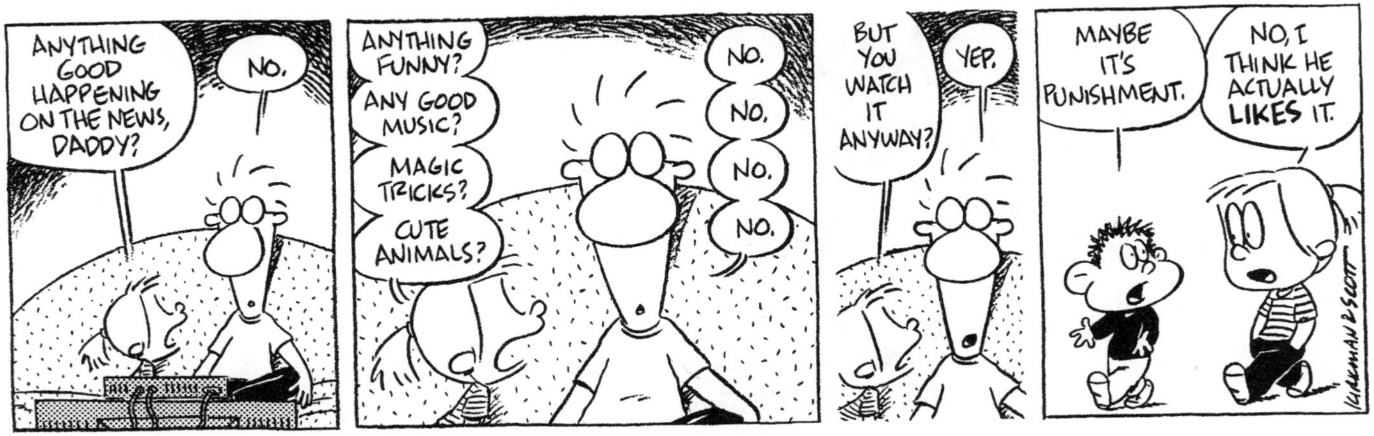
ANYTHING GOOD HAPPENING ON THE NEWS, DADDY?
NO.
ANYTHING FUNNY?
NO.
ANY GOOD MUSIC?
NO.
MAGIC TRICKS?
NO.
CUTE ANIMALS?
NO.
BUT YOU WATCH IT ANYWAY?
YEP.
MAYBE IT'S PUNISHMENT.
NO, I THINK HE ACTUALLY **LIKES** IT.
KIRKMAN & SCOTT

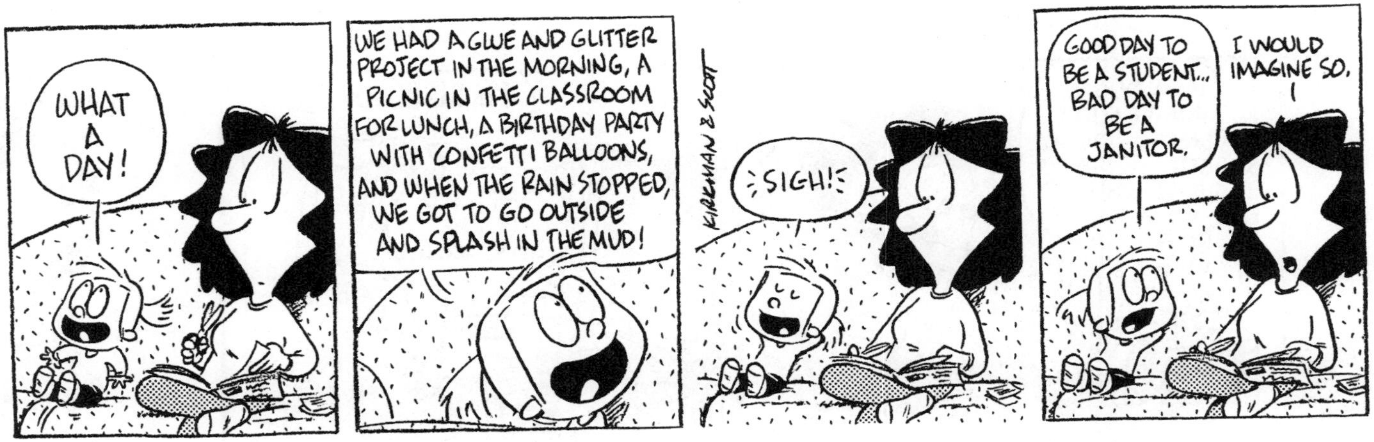
WHAT A DAY!
WE HAD A GLUE AND GLITTER PROJECT IN THE MORNING, A PICNIC IN THE CLASSROOM FOR LUNCH, A BIRTHDAY PARTY WITH CONFETTI BALLOONS, AND WHEN THE RAIN STOPPED, WE GOT TO GO OUTSIDE AND SPLASH IN THE MUD!
KIRKMAN & SCOTT
SIGH!
GOOD DAY TO BE A STUDENT... BAD DAY TO BE A JANITOR.
I WOULD IMAGINE SO.

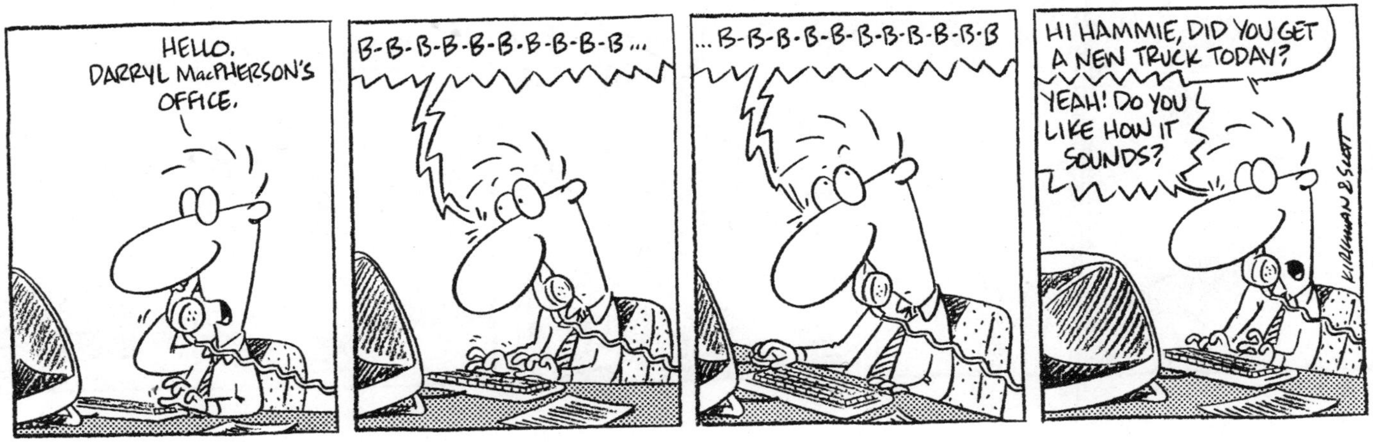
HELLO. DARRYL MacPHERSON'S OFFICE.
B-B-B-B-B-B-B-B-B-B-B...
...B-B-B-B-B-B-B-B-B-B-B
HI HAMMIE, DID YOU GET A NEW TRUCK TODAY?
YEAH! DO YOU LIKE HOW IT SOUNDS?
KIRKMAN & SCOTT

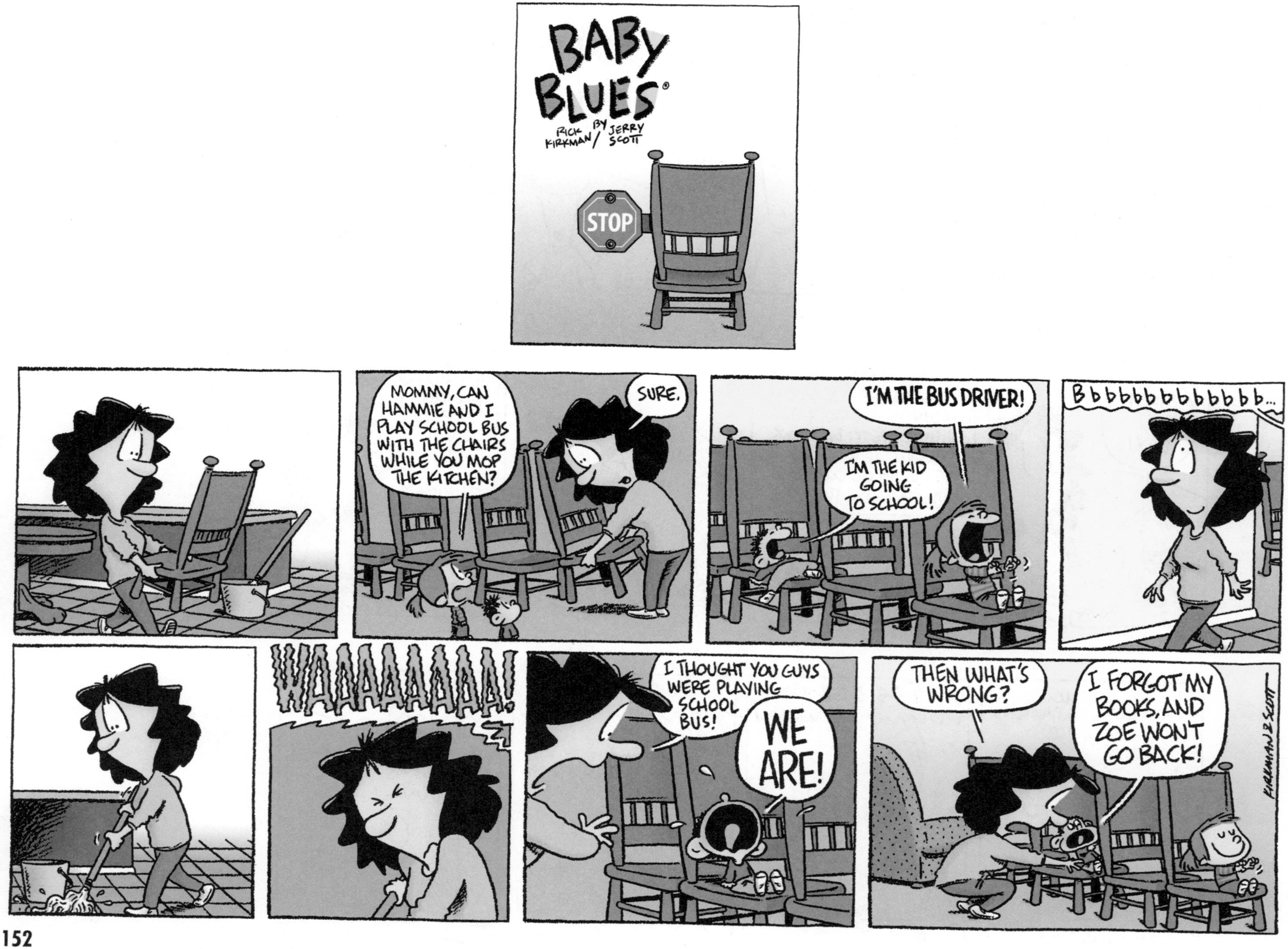
BABY BLUES®
BY RICK KIRKMAN / JERRY SCOTT
STOP
MOMMY, CAN HAMMIE AND I PLAY SCHOOL BUS WITH THE CHAIRS WHILE YOU MOP THE KITCHEN?
SURE.
I'M THE BUS DRIVER!
I'M THE KID GOING TO SCHOOL!
Bbbbbbbbbbbbbb...
WAAAAAAAA!
I THOUGHT YOU GUYS WERE PLAYING SCHOOL BUS!
WE ARE!
THEN WHAT'S WRONG?
I FORGOT MY BOOKS, AND ZOE WON'T GO BACK!
KIRKMAN & SCOTT

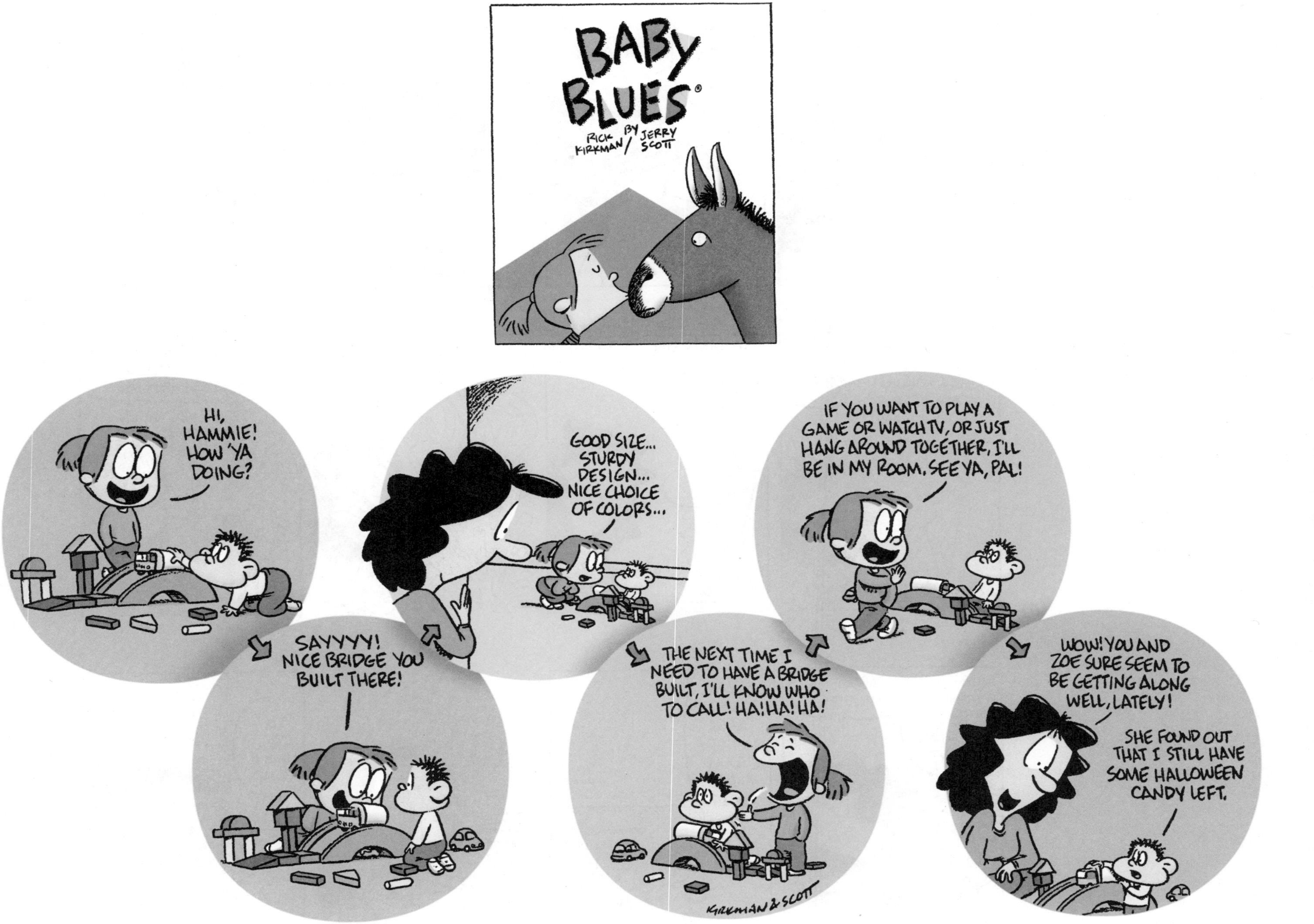
BABY BLUES®
RICK KIRKMAN / BY JERRY SCOTT
HI, HAMMIE! HOW 'YA DOING?
SAYYYY! NICE BRIDGE YOU BUILT THERE!
GOOD SIZE... STURDY DESIGN... NICE CHOICE OF COLORS...
THE NEXT TIME I NEED TO HAVE A BRIDGE BUILT, I'LL KNOW WHO TO CALL! HA! HA! HA!
IF YOU WANT TO PLAY A GAME OR WATCH TV, OR JUST HANG AROUND TOGETHER, I'LL BE IN MY ROOM. SEE YA, PAL!
WOW! YOU AND ZOE SURE SEEM TO BE GETTING ALONG WELL, LATELY!
SHE FOUND OUT THAT I STILL HAVE SOME HALLOWEEN CANDY LEFT.
KIRKMAN & SCOTT

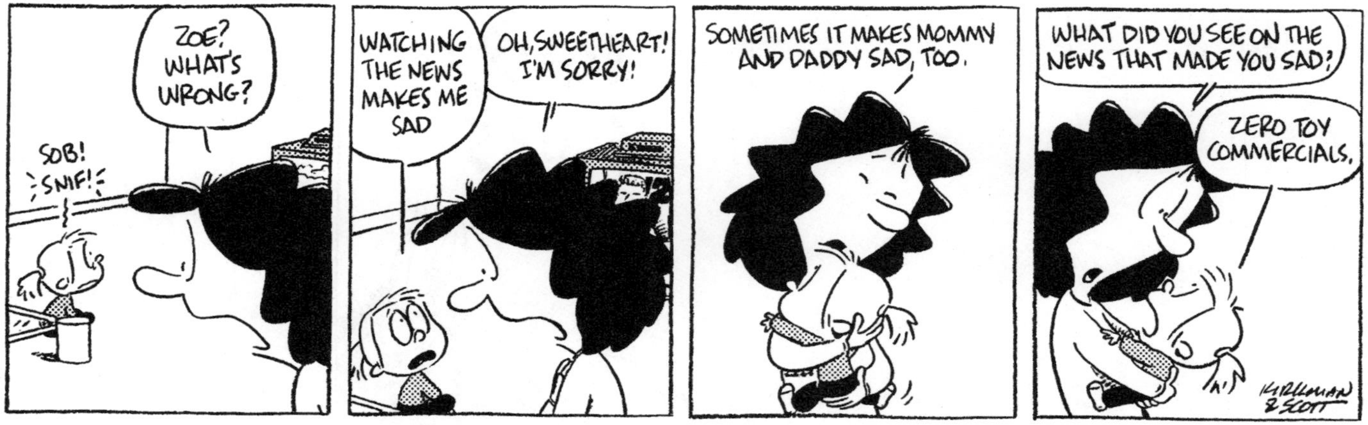
SOB! SNIF!
ZOE? WHAT'S WRONG?
WATCHING THE NEWS MAKES ME SAD
OH, SWEETHEART! I'M SORRY!
SOMETIMES IT MAKES MOMMY AND DADDY SAD, TOO.
WHAT DID YOU SEE ON THE NEWS THAT MADE YOU SAD?
ZERO TOY COMMERCIALS.
KIRKMAN & SCOTT

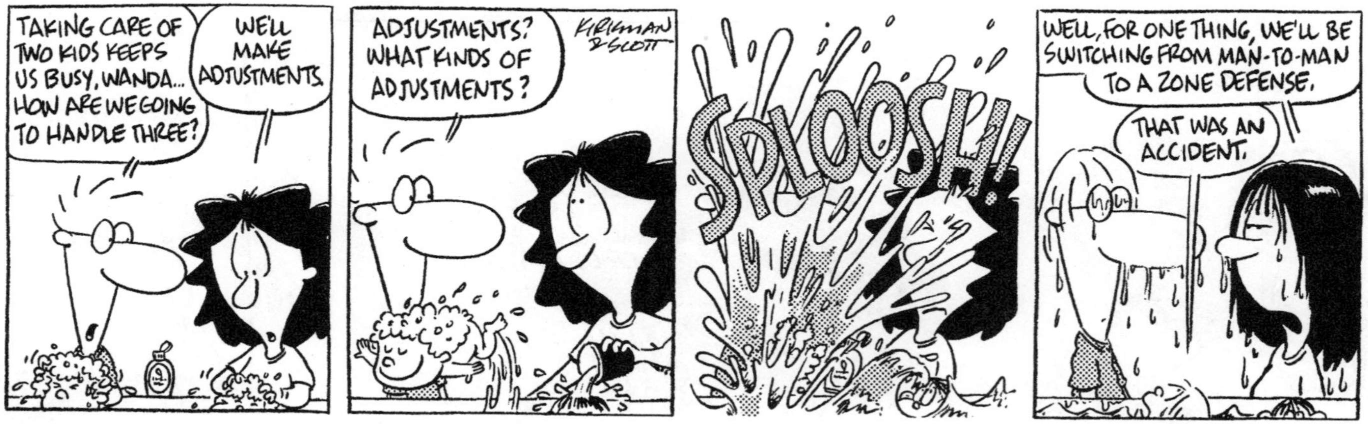
TAKING CARE OF TWO KIDS KEEPS US BUSY, WANDA... HOW ARE WE GOING TO HANDLE THREE?
WE'LL MAKE ADJUSTMENTS.
ADJUSTMENTS? WHAT KINDS OF ADJUSTMENTS?
KIRKMAN & SCOTT
SPLOOSH!!
WELL, FOR ONE THING, WE'LL BE SWITCHING FROM MAN-TO-MAN TO A ZONE DEFENSE.
THAT WAS AN ACCIDENT.

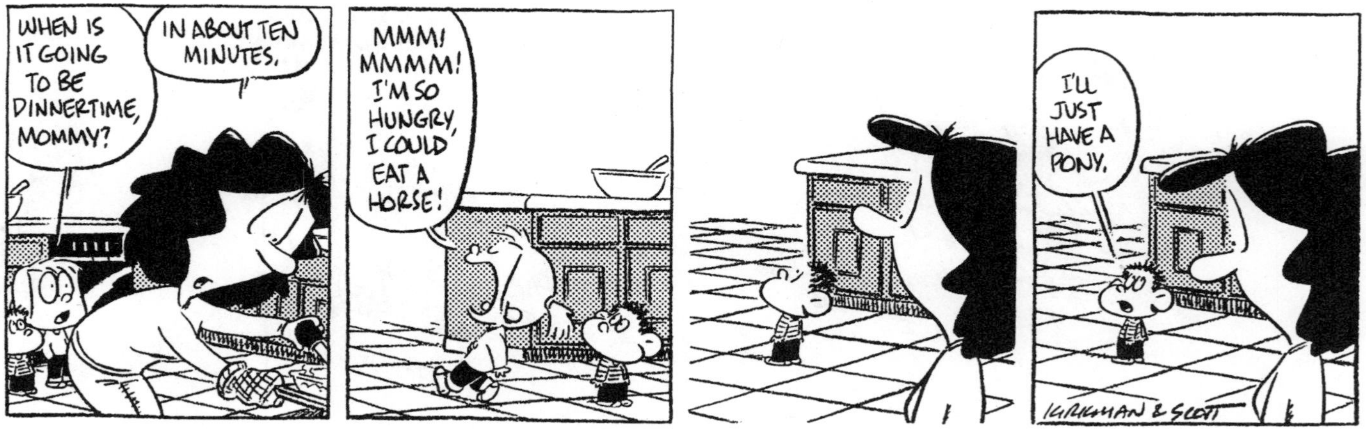
WHEN IS IT GOING TO BE DINNERTIME, MOMMY?
IN ABOUT TEN MINUTES.
MMM! MMMM! I'M SO HUNGRY, I COULD EAT A HORSE!
I'LL JUST HAVE A PONY.
KIRKMAN & SCOTT

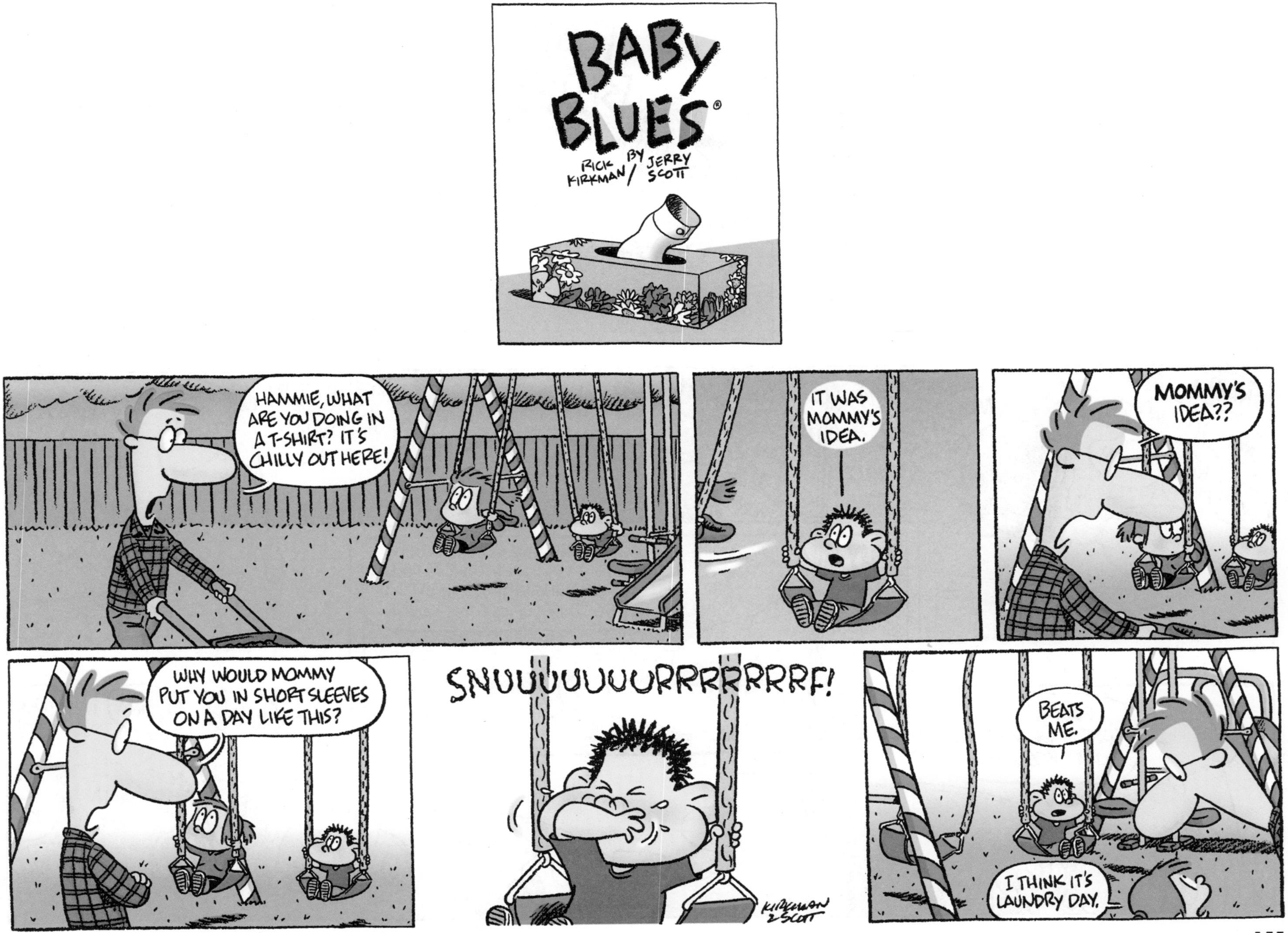
BABY BLUES®
BY RICK KIRKMAN / JERRY SCOTT
HAMMIE, WHAT ARE YOU DOING IN A T-SHIRT? IT'S CHILLY OUT HERE!
IT WAS MOMMY'S IDEA.
MOMMY'S IDEA??
WHY WOULD MOMMY PUT YOU IN SHORT SLEEVES ON A DAY LIKE THIS?
SNUUUUUUURRRRRRRF!
KIRKMAN & SCOTT
BEATS ME.
I THINK IT'S LAUNDRY DAY.

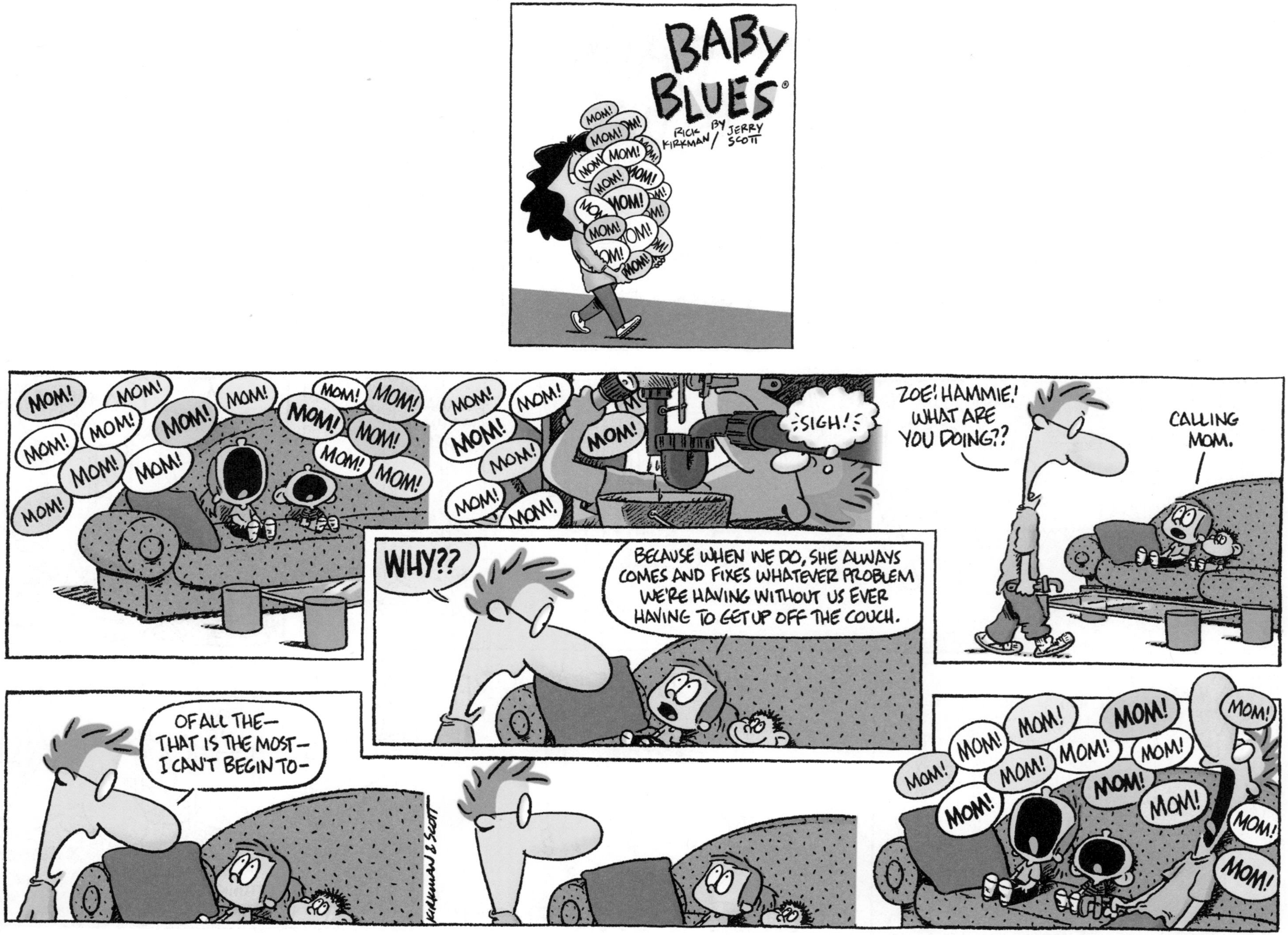
BABY BLUES®
BY RICK KIRKMAN / JERRY SCOTT
MOM!
MOM!
MOM!
SIGH!
ZOE! HAMMIE! WHAT ARE YOU DOING??
CALLING MOM.
WHY??
BECAUSE WHEN WE DO, SHE ALWAYS COMES AND FIXES WHATEVER PROBLEM WE'RE HAVING WITHOUT US EVER HAVING TO GET UP OFF THE COUCH.
OF ALL THE— THAT IS THE MOST— I CAN'T BEGIN TO—
KIRKMAN & SCOTT
MOM!

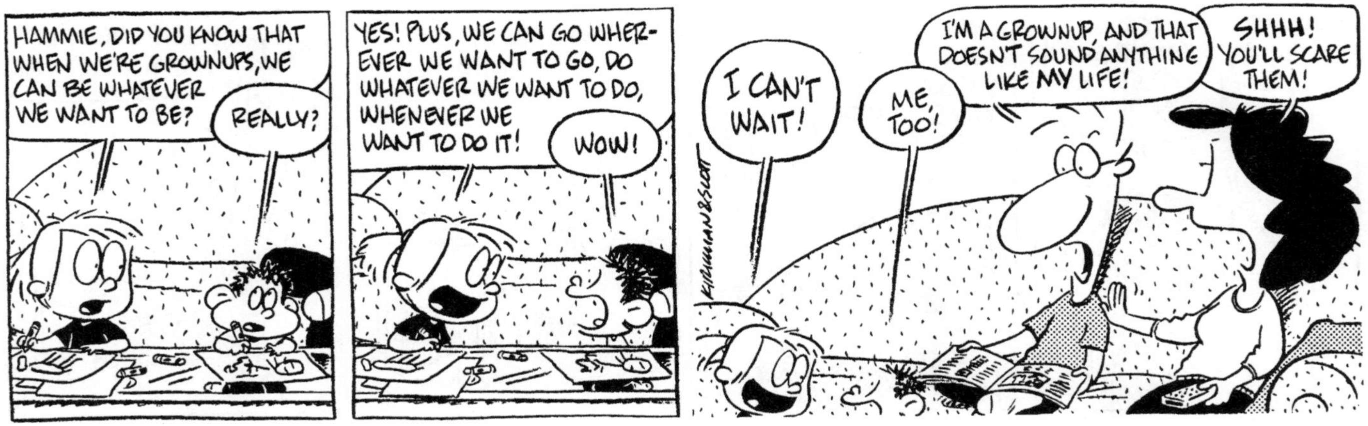
HAMMIE, DID YOU KNOW THAT WHEN WE'RE GROWNUPS, WE CAN BE WHATEVER WE WANT TO BE?
REALLY?
YES! PLUS, WE CAN GO WHEREVER WE WANT TO GO, DO WHATEVER WE WANT TO DO, WHENEVER WE WANT TO DO IT!
WOW!
I CAN'T WAIT!
ME, TOO!
I'M A GROWNUP, AND THAT DOESN'T SOUND ANYTHING LIKE MY LIFE!
SHHH! YOU'LL SCARE THEM!
KIRKMAN & SCOTT

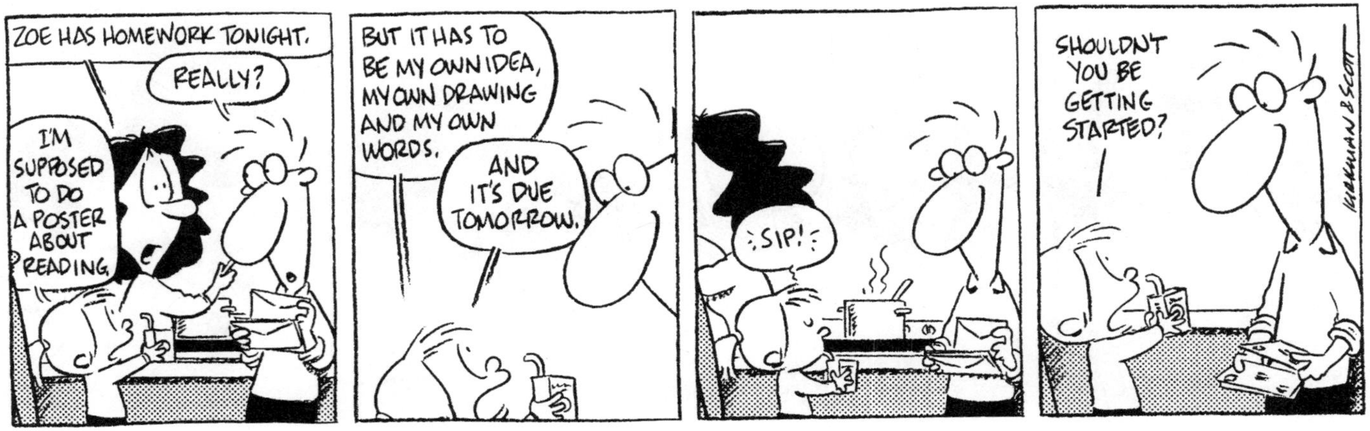
ZOE HAS HOMEWORK TONIGHT.
REALLY?
I'M SUPPOSED TO DO A POSTER ABOUT READING.
BUT IT HAS TO BE MY OWN IDEA, MY OWN DRAWING AND MY OWN WORDS.
AND IT'S DUE TOMORROW.
SIP!
SHOULDN'T YOU BE GETTING STARTED?
KIRKMAN & SCOTT

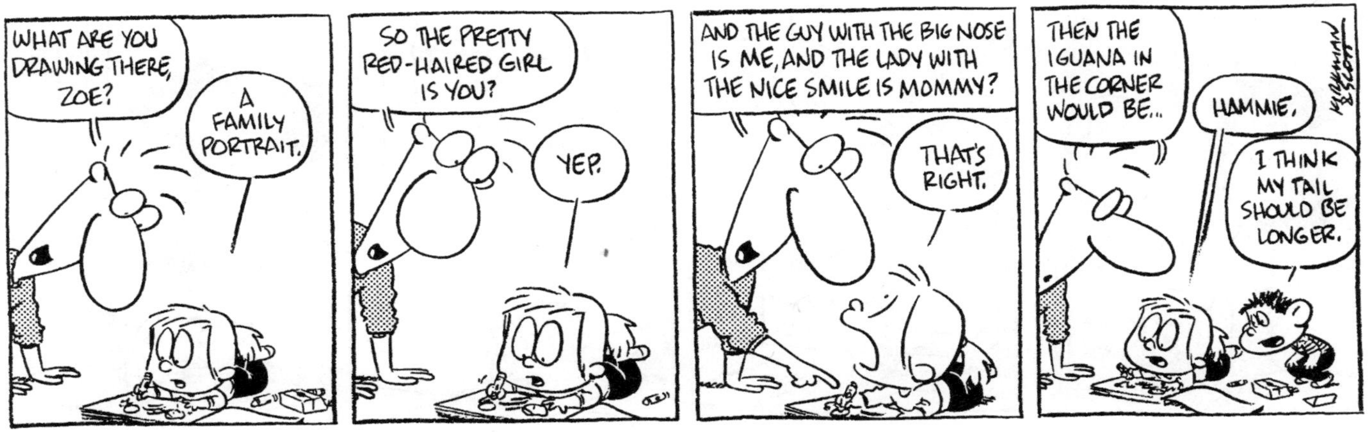
WHAT ARE YOU DRAWING THERE, ZOE?
A FAMILY PORTRAIT.
SO THE PRETTY RED-HAIRED GIRL IS YOU?
YEP.
AND THE GUY WITH THE BIG NOSE IS ME, AND THE LADY WITH THE NICE SMILE IS MOMMY?
THAT'S RIGHT.
THEN THE IGUANA IN THE CORNER WOULD BE...
HAMMIE.
I THINK MY TAIL SHOULD BE LONGER.
KIRKMAN & SCOTT

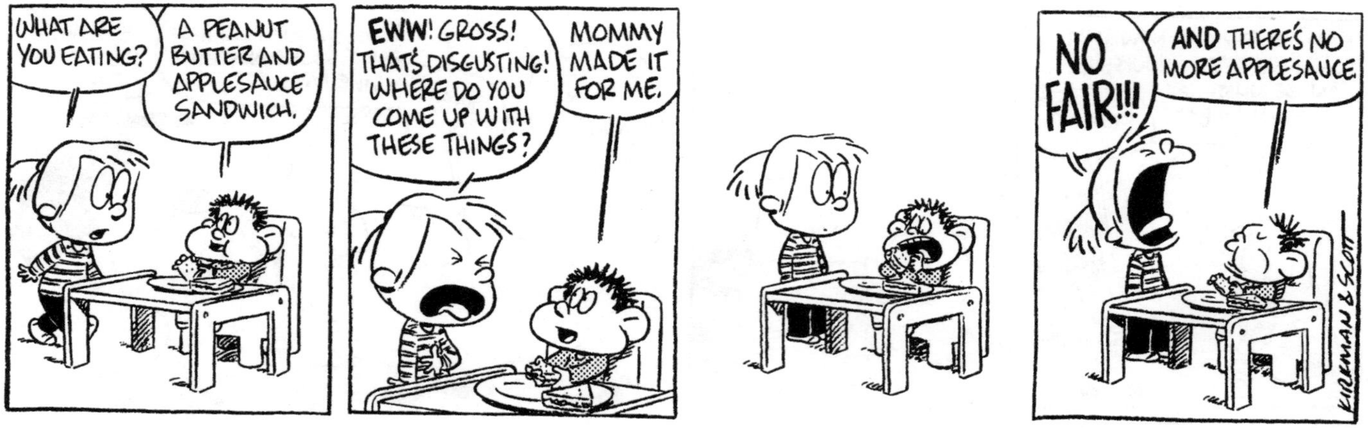
WHAT ARE YOU EATING?
A PEANUT BUTTER AND APPLESAUCE SANDWICH.
EWW! GROSS! THAT'S DISGUSTING! WHERE DO YOU COME UP WITH THESE THINGS?
MOMMY MADE IT FOR ME.
NO FAIR!!!
AND THERE'S NO MORE APPLESAUCE.
KIRKMAN & SCOTT

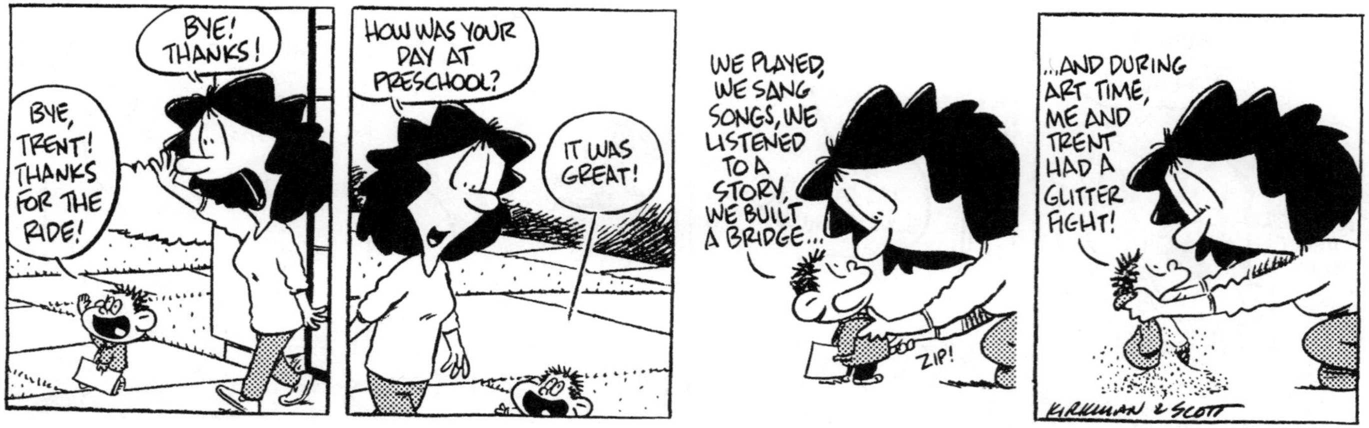
BYE! THANKS!
BYE, TRENT! THANKS FOR THE RIDE!
HOW WAS YOUR DAY AT PRESCHOOL?
IT WAS GREAT!
WE PLAYED, WE SANG SONGS, WE LISTENED TO A STORY, WE BUILT A BRIDGE...
ZIP!
...AND DURING ART TIME, ME AND TRENT HAD A GLITTER FIGHT!
KIRKMAN & SCOTT

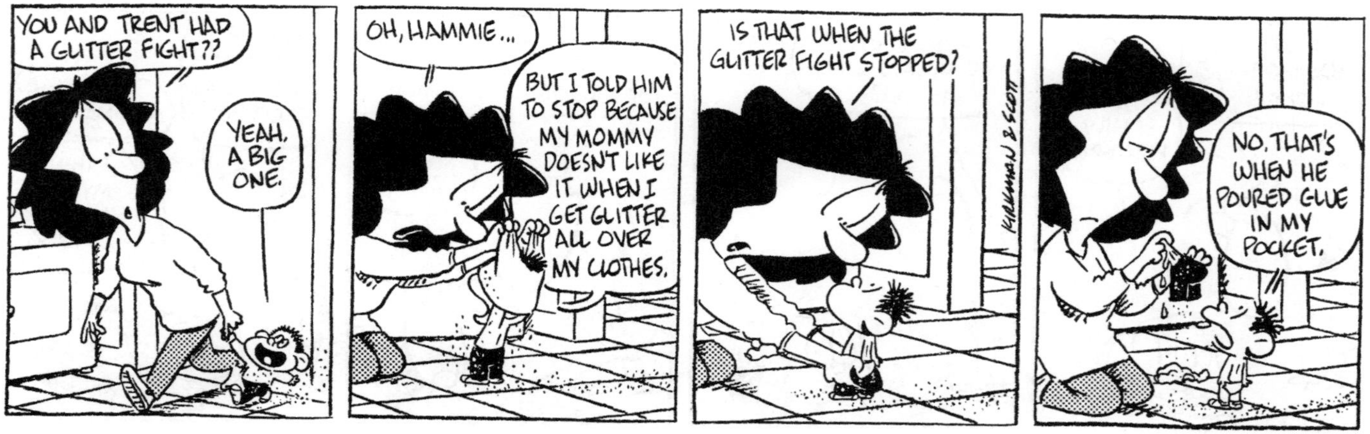
YOU AND TRENT HAD A GLITTER FIGHT??
YEAH, A BIG ONE.
OH, HAMMIE...
BUT I TOLD HIM TO STOP BECAUSE MY MOMMY DOESN'T LIKE IT WHEN I GET GLITTER ALL OVER MY CLOTHES.
IS THAT WHEN THE GLITTER FIGHT STOPPED?
KIRKMAN & SCOTT
NO, THAT'S WHEN HE POURED GLUE IN MY POCKET.

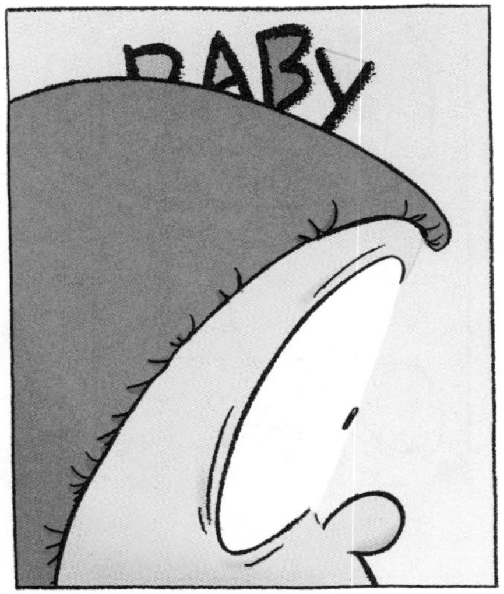
BABY

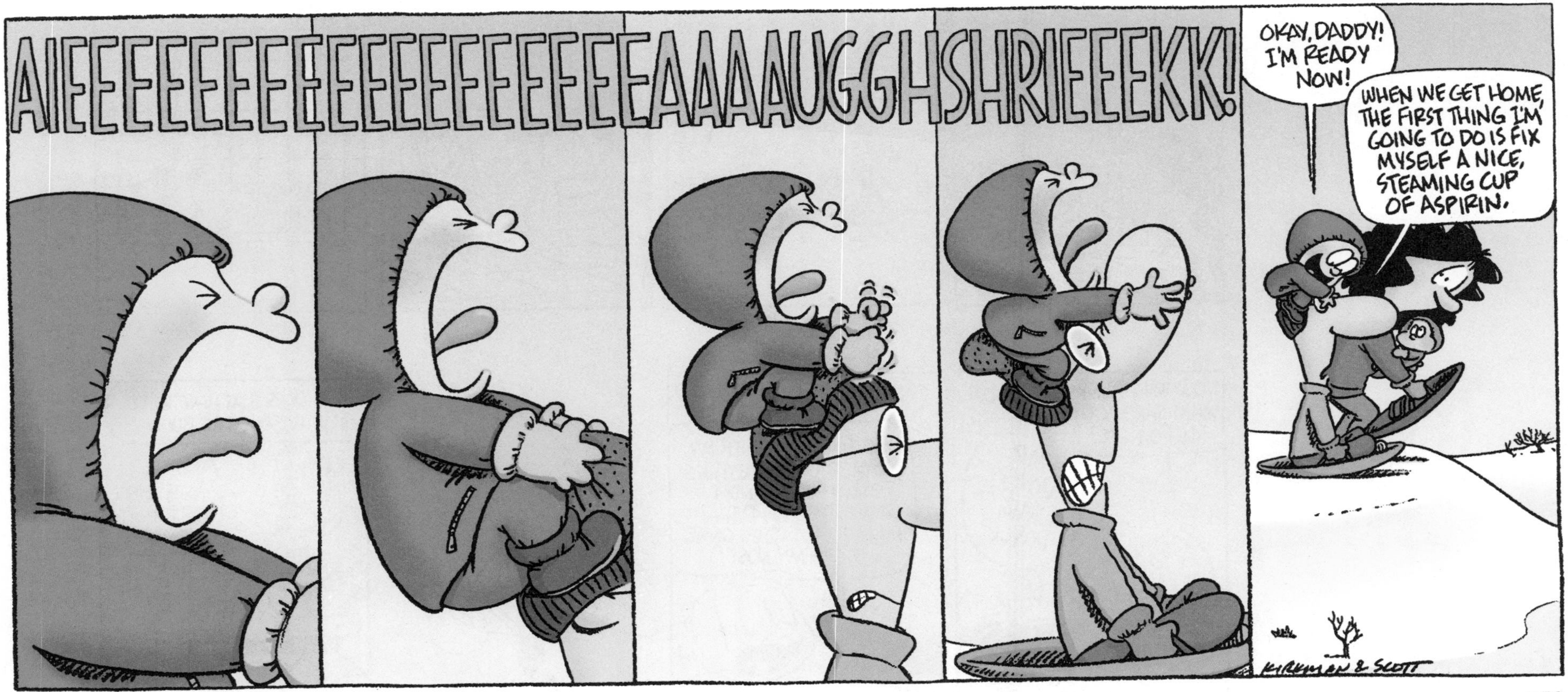
AIEEEEEEEEEEEEEEEEEEEEEAAAAUGGHSHRIEEEKK!
OKAY, DADDY! I'M READY NOW!
WHEN WE GET HOME, THE FIRST THING I'M GOING TO DO IS FIX MYSELF A NICE, STEAMING CUP OF ASPIRIN.
KIRKMAN & SCOTT

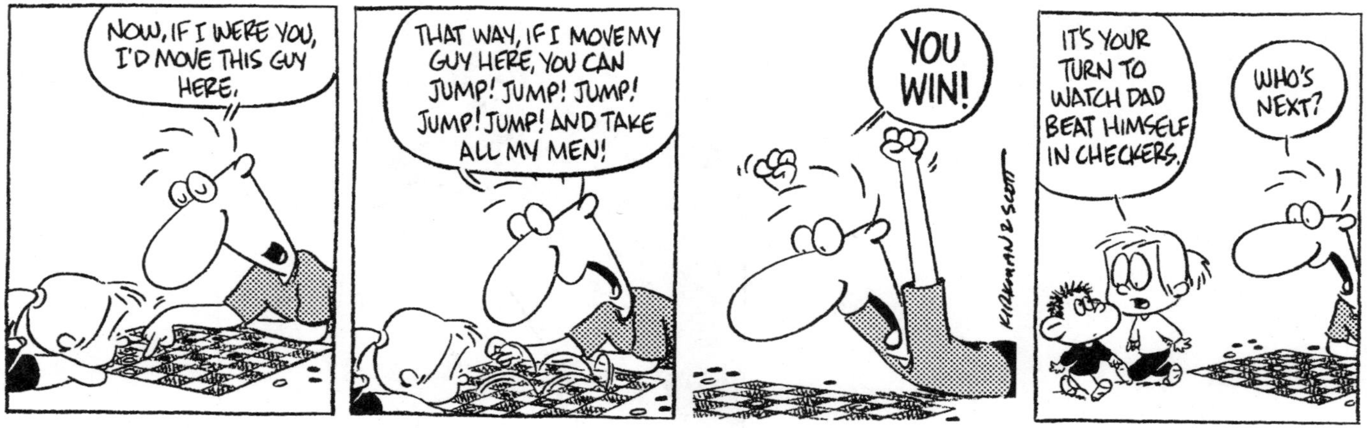
NOW, IF I WERE YOU, I'D MOVE THIS GUY HERE.
THAT WAY, IF I MOVE MY GUY HERE, YOU CAN JUMP! JUMP! JUMP! JUMP! JUMP! AND TAKE ALL MY MEN!
YOU WIN!
KIRKMAN & SCOTT
IT'S YOUR TURN TO WATCH DAD BEAT HIMSELF IN CHECKERS.
WHO'S NEXT?

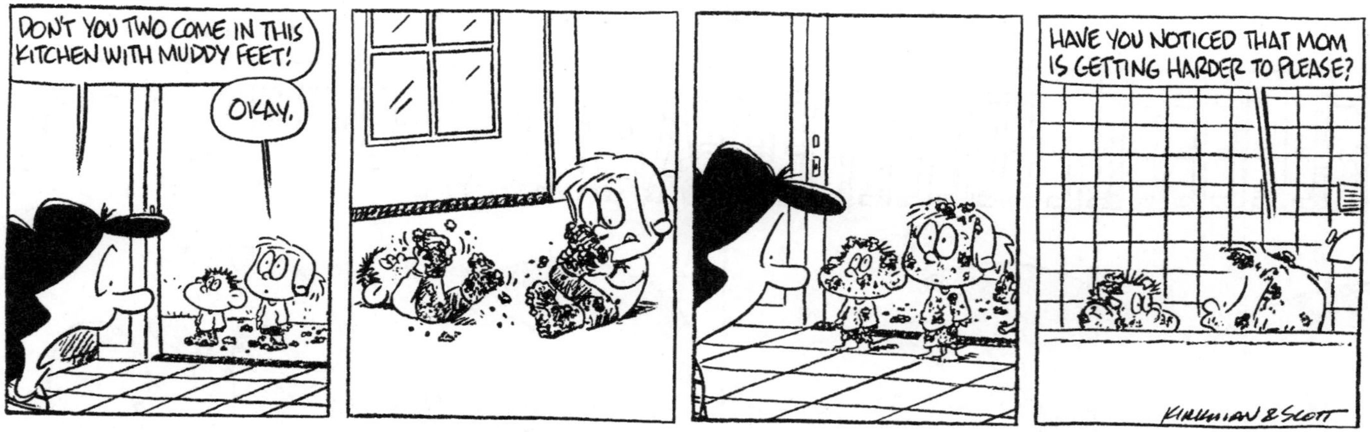
DON'T YOU TWO COME IN THIS KITCHEN WITH MUDDY FEET!
OKAY.
HAVE YOU NOTICED THAT MOM IS GETTING HARDER TO PLEASE?
KIRKMAN & SCOTT

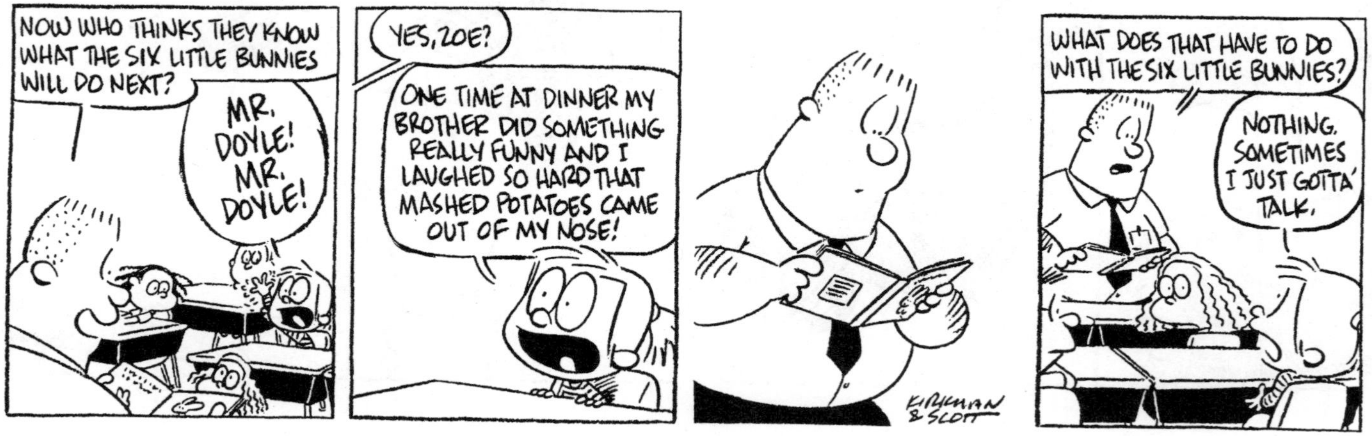
NOW WHO THINKS THEY KNOW WHAT THE SIX LITTLE BUNNIES WILL DO NEXT?
MR. DOYLE! MR. DOYLE!
YES, ZOE?
ONE TIME AT DINNER MY BROTHER DID SOMETHING REALLY FUNNY AND I LAUGHED SO HARD THAT MASHED POTATOES CAME OUT OF MY NOSE!
KIRKMAN & SCOTT
WHAT DOES THAT HAVE TO DO WITH THE SIX LITTLE BUNNIES?
NOTHING. SOMETIMES I JUST GOTTA' TALK.

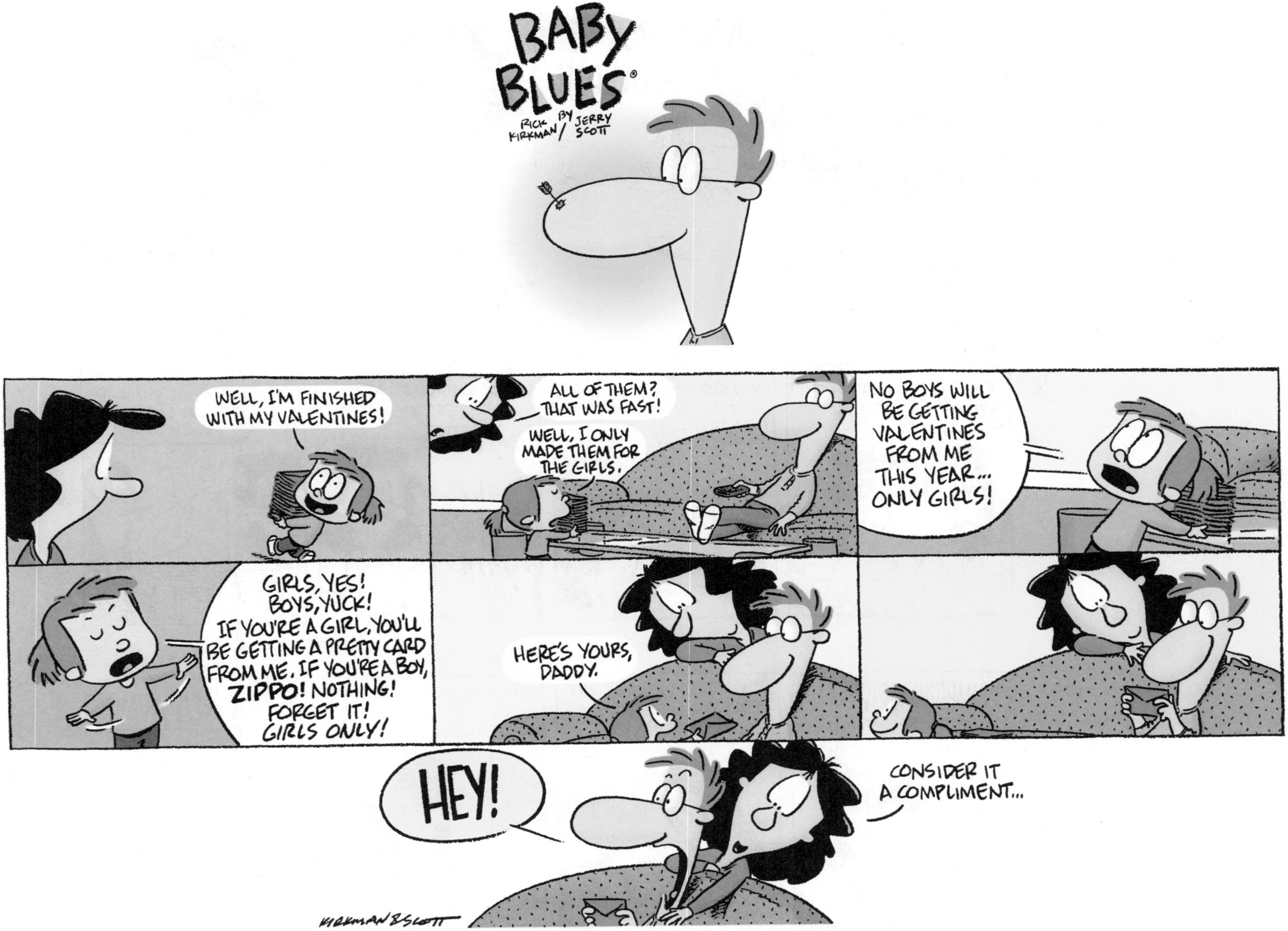
BABY BLUES®
BY RICK KIRKMAN / JERRY SCOTT
WELL, I'M FINISHED WITH MY VALENTINES!
ALL OF THEM? THAT WAS FAST!
WELL, I ONLY MADE THEM FOR THE GIRLS.
NO BOYS WILL BE GETTING VALENTINES FROM ME THIS YEAR... ONLY GIRLS!
GIRLS, YES! BOYS, YUCK! IF YOU'RE A GIRL, YOU'LL BE GETTING A PRETTY CARD FROM ME. IF YOU'RE A BOY, ZIPPO! NOTHING! FORGET IT! GIRLS ONLY!
HERE'S YOURS, DADDY.
HEY!
CONSIDER IT A COMPLIMENT...
KIRKMAN & SCOTT

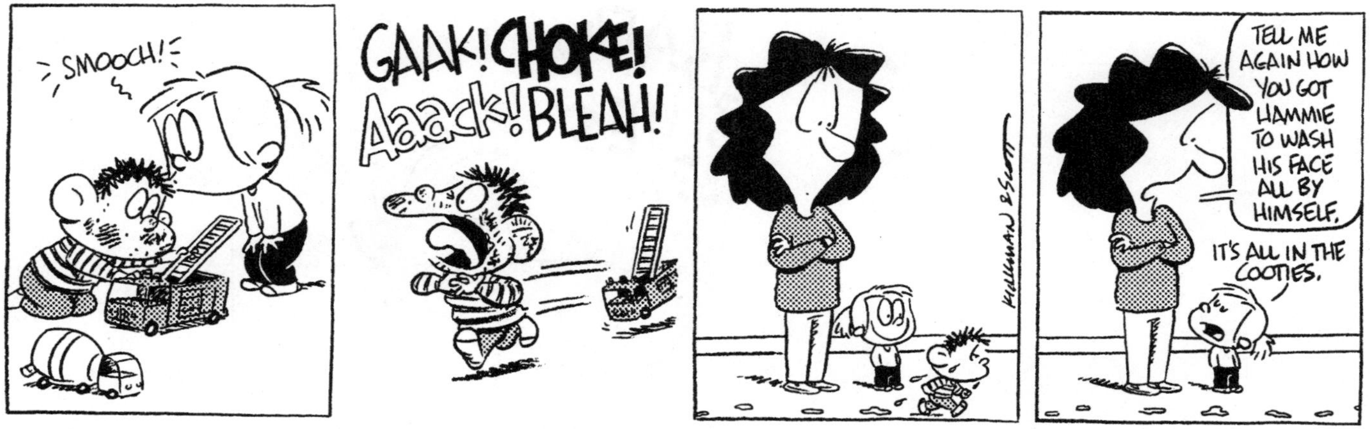
SMOOCH!
GAAK! CHOKE! Aaack! BLEAH!
KIRKMAN & SCOTT
TELL ME AGAIN HOW YOU GOT HAMMIE TO WASH HIS FACE ALL BY HIMSELF.
IT'S ALL IN THE COOTIES.

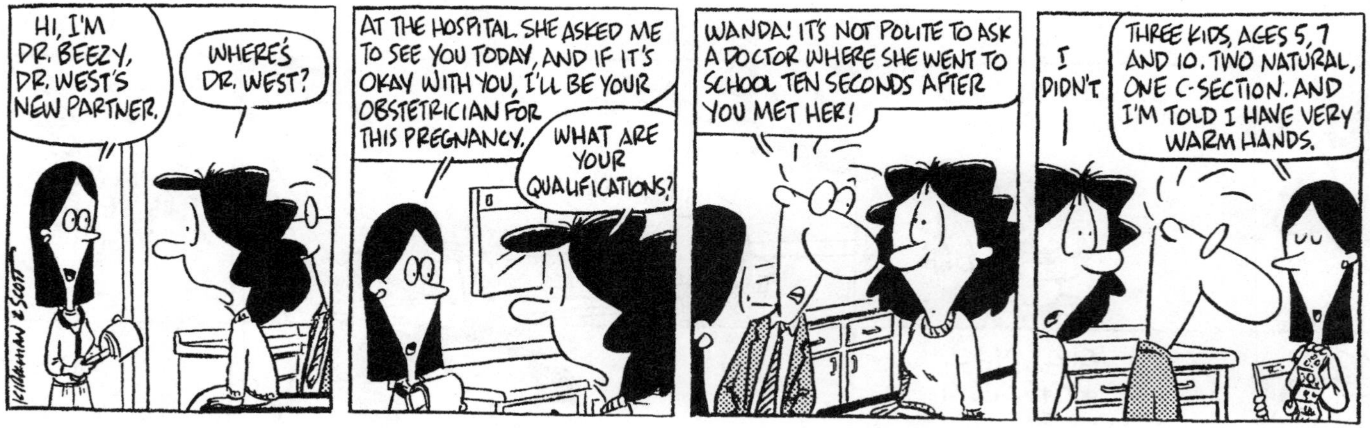
HI, I'M DR. BEEZY, DR. WEST'S NEW PARTNER.
WHERE'S DR. WEST?
KIRKMAN & SCOTT
AT THE HOSPITAL. SHE ASKED ME TO SEE YOU TODAY, AND IF IT'S OKAY WITH YOU, I'LL BE YOUR OBSTETRICIAN FOR THIS PREGNANCY.
WHAT ARE YOUR QUALIFICATIONS?
WANDA! IT'S NOT POLITE TO ASK A DOCTOR WHERE SHE WENT TO SCHOOL TEN SECONDS AFTER YOU MET HER!
I DIDN'T
THREE KIDS, AGES 5, 7 AND 10. TWO NATURAL, ONE C-SECTION. AND I'M TOLD I HAVE VERY WARM HANDS.

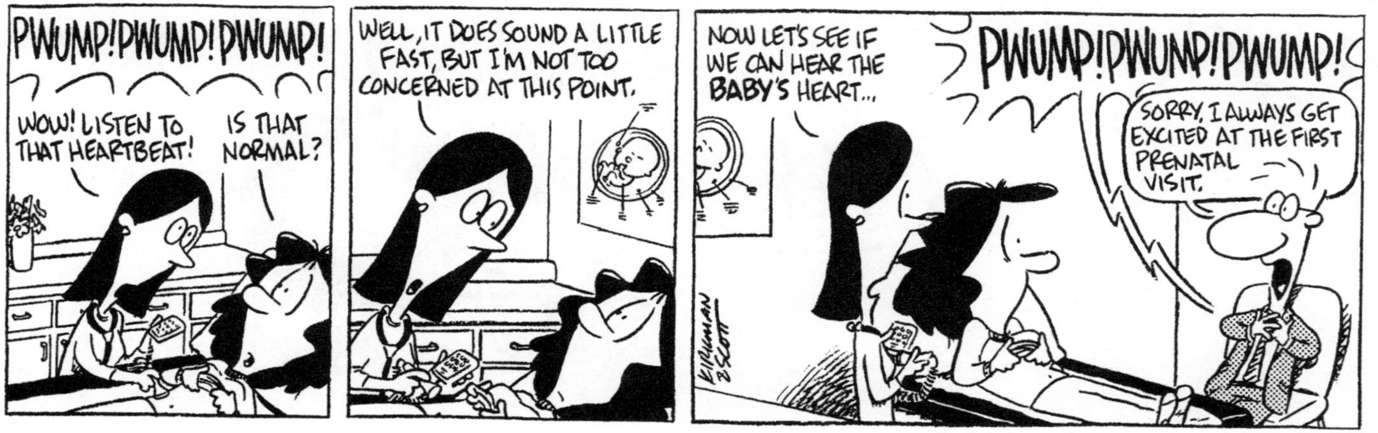
PWUMP! PWUMP! PWUMP!
WOW! LISTEN TO THAT HEARTBEAT!
IS THAT NORMAL?
WELL, IT DOES SOUND A LITTLE FAST, BUT I'M NOT TOO CONCERNED AT THIS POINT.
NOW LET'S SEE IF WE CAN HEAR THE BABY'S HEART...
PWUMP! PWUMP! PWUMP!
KIRKMAN & SCOTT
SORRY, I ALWAYS GET EXCITED AT THE FIRST PRENATAL VISIT.

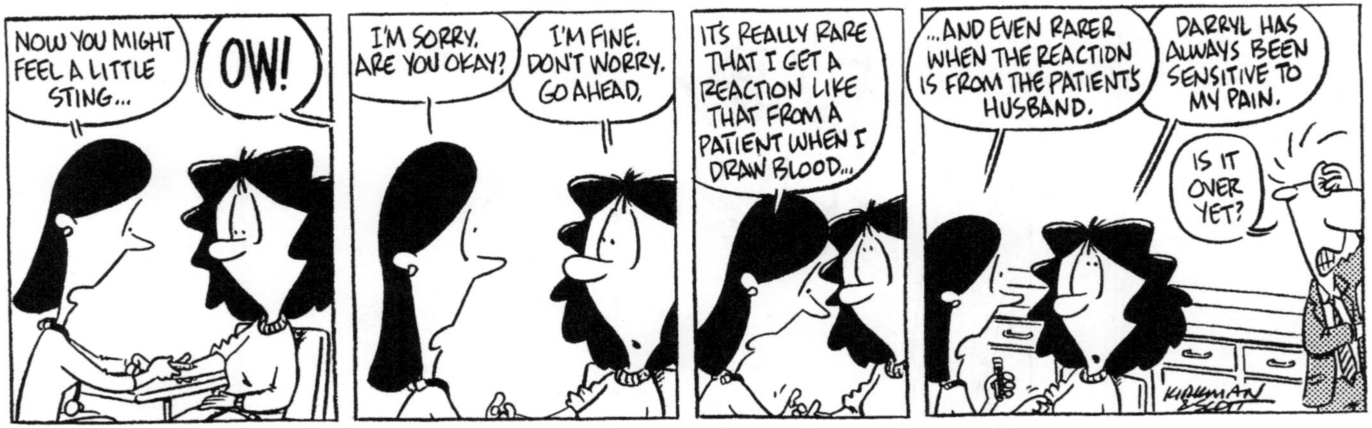
NOW YOU MIGHT FEEL A LITTLE STING...
OW!
I'M SORRY. ARE YOU OKAY?
I'M FINE. DON'T WORRY. GO AHEAD.
IT'S REALLY RARE THAT I GET A REACTION LIKE THAT FROM A PATIENT WHEN I DRAW BLOOD...
...AND EVEN RARER WHEN THE REACTION IS FROM THE PATIENT'S HUSBAND.
DARRYL HAS ALWAYS BEEN SENSITIVE TO MY PAIN.
IS IT OVER YET?
KIRKMAN & SCOTT

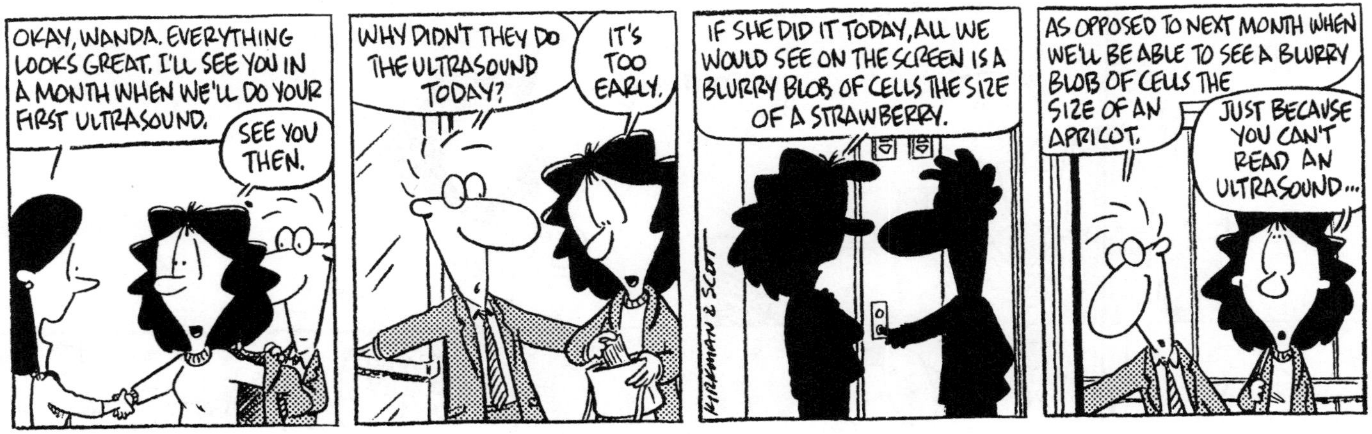
OKAY, WANDA. EVERYTHING LOOKS GREAT. I'LL SEE YOU IN A MONTH WHEN WE'LL DO YOUR FIRST ULTRASOUND.
SEE YOU THEN.
WHY DIDN'T THEY DO THE ULTRASOUND TODAY?
IT'S TOO EARLY.
IF SHE DID IT TODAY, ALL WE WOULD SEE ON THE SCREEN IS A BLURRY BLOB OF CELLS THE SIZE OF A STRAWBERRY.
KIRKMAN & SCOTT
AS OPPOSED TO NEXT MONTH WHEN WE'LL BE ABLE TO SEE A BLURRY BLOB OF CELLS THE SIZE OF AN APRICOT.
JUST BECAUSE YOU CAN'T READ AN ULTRASOUND...

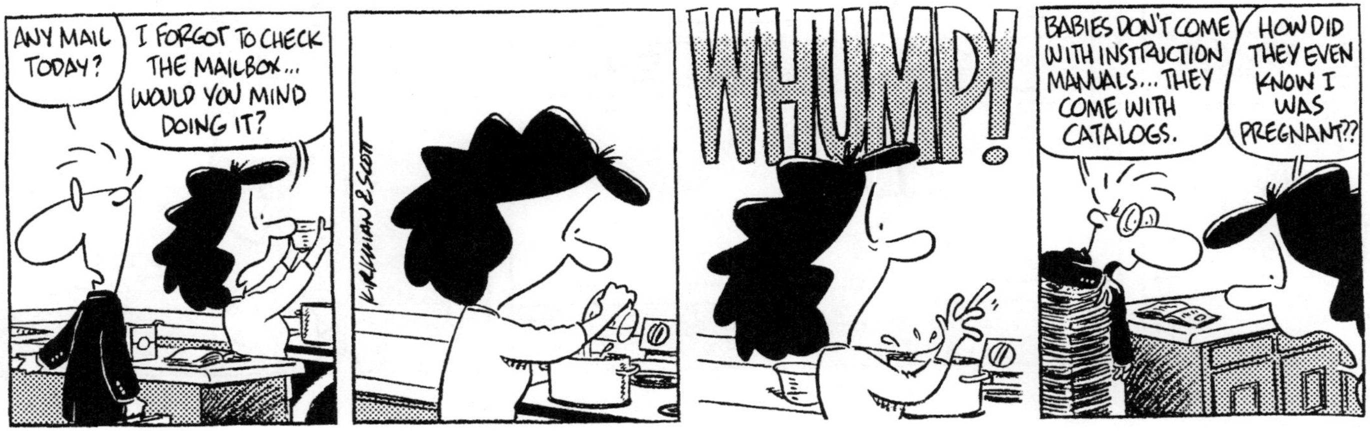
ANY MAIL TODAY?
I FORGOT TO CHECK THE MAILBOX... WOULD YOU MIND DOING IT?
KIRKMAN & SCOTT
WHUMP!
BABIES DON'T COME WITH INSTRUCTION MANUALS... THEY COME WITH CATALOGS.
HOW DID THEY EVEN KNOW I WAS PREGNANT??

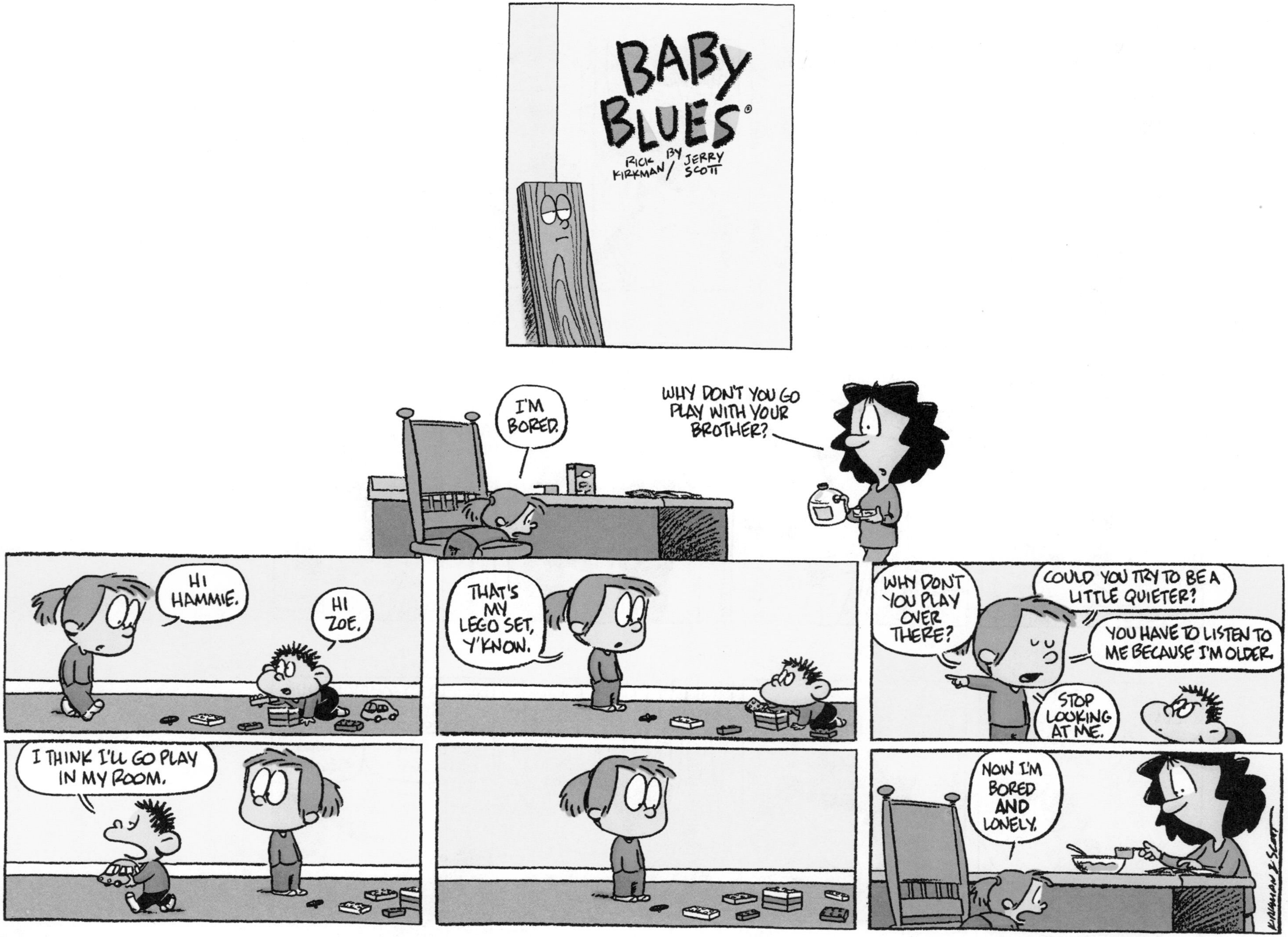
BABY BLUES®
BY RICK KIRKMAN / JERRY SCOTT
I'M BORED.
WHY DON'T YOU GO PLAY WITH YOUR BROTHER?
HI HAMMIE.
HI ZOE.
THAT'S MY LEGO SET, Y'KNOW.
WHY DON'T YOU PLAY OVER THERE?
COULD YOU TRY TO BE A LITTLE QUIETER?
YOU HAVE TO LISTEN TO ME BECAUSE I'M OLDER.
STOP LOOKING AT ME.
I THINK I'LL GO PLAY IN MY ROOM.
NOW I'M BORED AND LONELY.

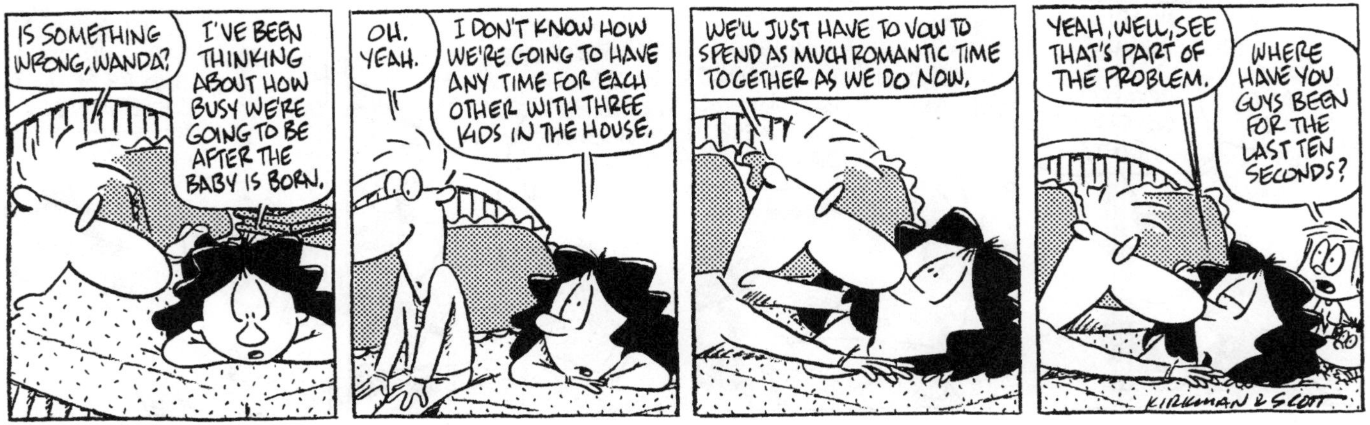
IS SOMETHING WRONG, WANDA?
I'VE BEEN THINKING ABOUT HOW BUSY WE'RE GOING TO BE AFTER THE BABY IS BORN.
OH. YEAH.
I DON'T KNOW HOW WE'RE GOING TO HAVE ANY TIME FOR EACH OTHER WITH THREE KIDS IN THE HOUSE.
WE'LL JUST HAVE TO VOW TO SPEND AS MUCH ROMANTIC TIME TOGETHER AS WE DO NOW.
YEAH, WELL, SEE THAT'S PART OF THE PROBLEM.
WHERE HAVE YOU GUYS BEEN FOR THE LAST TEN SECONDS?
KIRKMAN & SCOTT

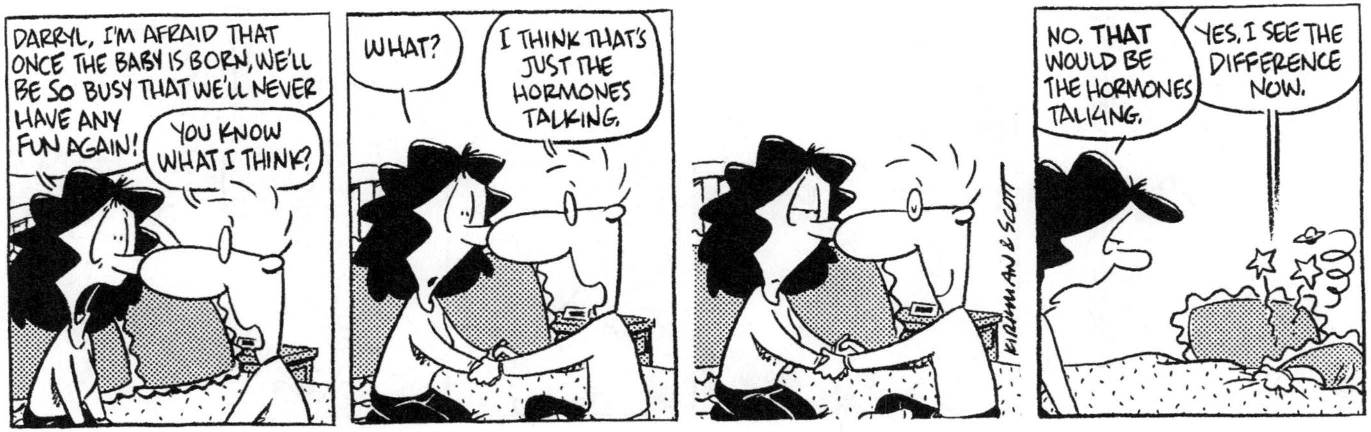
DARRYL, I'M AFRAID THAT ONCE THE BABY IS BORN, WE'LL BE SO BUSY THAT WE'LL NEVER HAVE ANY FUN AGAIN!
YOU KNOW WHAT I THINK?
WHAT?
I THINK THAT'S JUST THE HORMONES TALKING.
KIRKMAN & SCOTT
NO. **THAT** WOULD BE THE HORMONES TALKING.
YES. I SEE THE DIFFERENCE NOW.

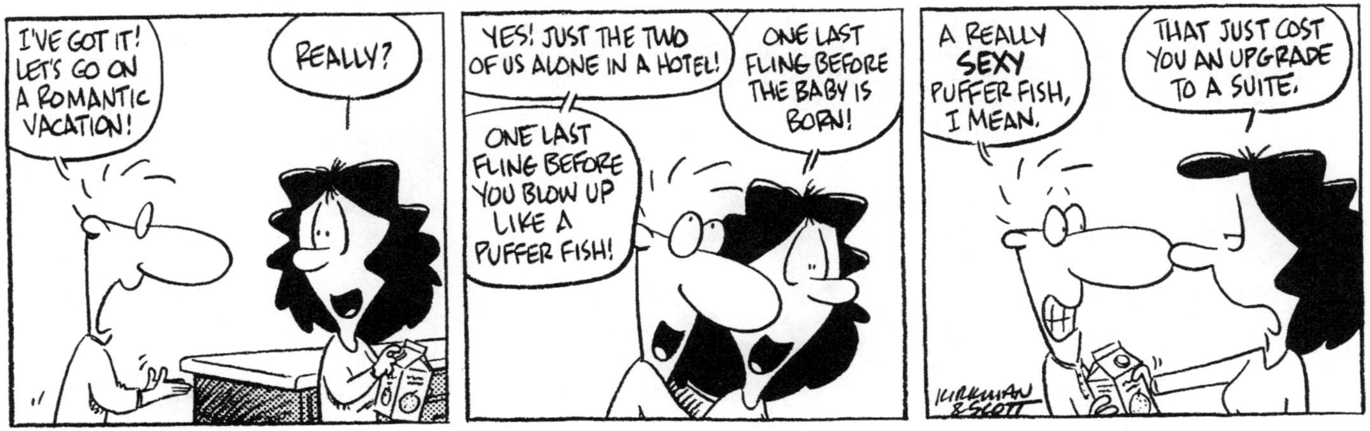
I'VE GOT IT! LET'S GO ON A ROMANTIC VACATION!
REALLY?
YES! JUST THE TWO OF US ALONE IN A HOTEL!
ONE LAST FLING BEFORE THE BABY IS BORN!
ONE LAST FLING BEFORE YOU BLOW UP LIKE A PUFFER FISH!
A REALLY **SEXY** PUFFER FISH, I MEAN.
THAT JUST COST YOU AN UPGRADE TO A SUITE.
KIRKMAN & SCOTT

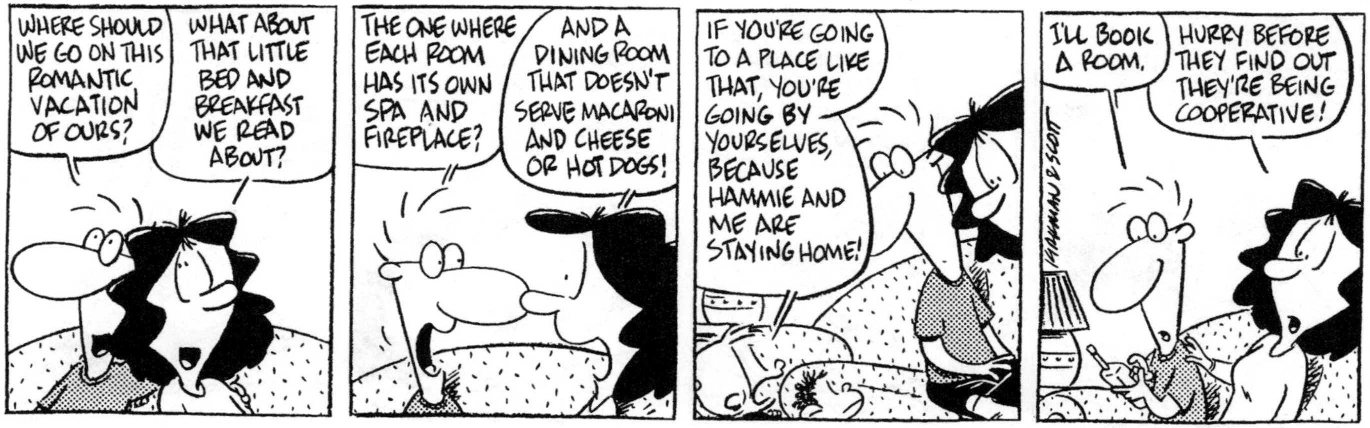
WHERE SHOULD WE GO ON THIS ROMANTIC VACATION OF OURS?
WHAT ABOUT THAT LITTLE BED AND BREAKFAST WE READ ABOUT?
THE ONE WHERE EACH ROOM HAS ITS OWN SPA AND FIREPLACE?
AND A DINING ROOM THAT DOESN'T SERVE MACARONI AND CHEESE OR HOT DOGS!
IF YOU'RE GOING TO A PLACE LIKE THAT, YOU'RE GOING BY YOURSELVES, BECAUSE HAMMIE AND ME ARE STAYING HOME!
I'LL BOOK A ROOM.
HURRY BEFORE THEY FIND OUT THEY'RE BEING COOPERATIVE!
KIRKMAN & SCOTT

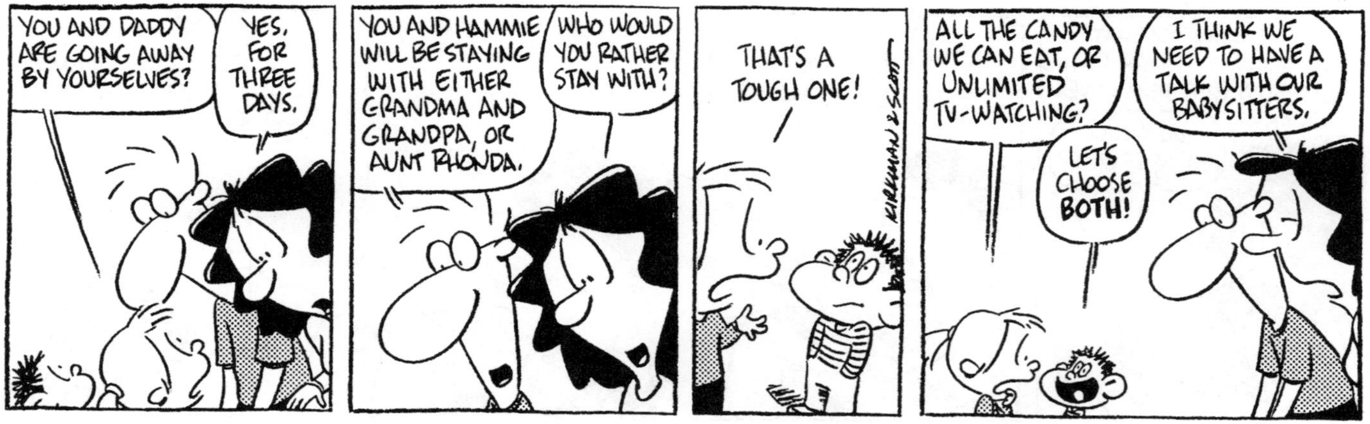
YOU AND DADDY ARE GOING AWAY BY YOURSELVES?
YES, FOR THREE DAYS.
YOU AND HAMMIE WILL BE STAYING WITH EITHER GRANDMA AND GRANDPA, OR AUNT RHONDA.
WHO WOULD YOU RATHER STAY WITH?
THAT'S A TOUGH ONE!
KIRKMAN & SCOTT
ALL THE CANDY WE CAN EAT, OR UNLIMITED TV-WATCHING?
LET'S CHOOSE **BOTH**!
I THINK WE NEED TO HAVE A TALK WITH OUR BABYSITTERS.

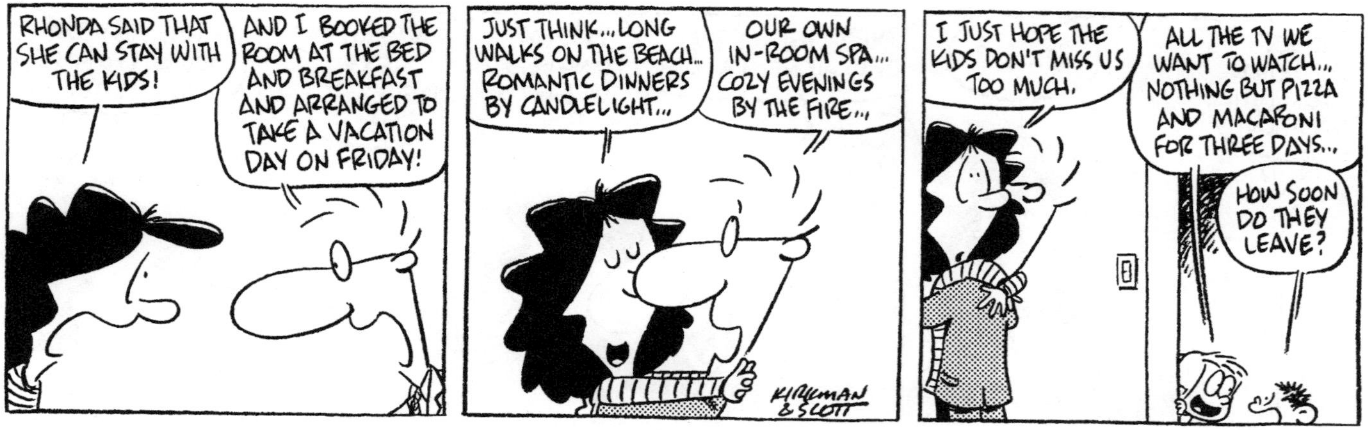
RHONDA SAID THAT SHE CAN STAY WITH THE KIDS!
AND I BOOKED THE ROOM AT THE BED AND BREAKFAST AND ARRANGED TO TAKE A VACATION DAY ON FRIDAY!
JUST THINK... LONG WALKS ON THE BEACH... ROMANTIC DINNERS BY CANDLELIGHT...
OUR OWN IN-ROOM SPA... COZY EVENINGS BY THE FIRE...
KIRKMAN & SCOTT
I JUST HOPE THE KIDS DON'T MISS US TOO MUCH.
ALL THE TV WE WANT TO WATCH... NOTHING BUT PIZZA AND MACARONI FOR THREE DAYS...
HOW SOON DO THEY LEAVE?

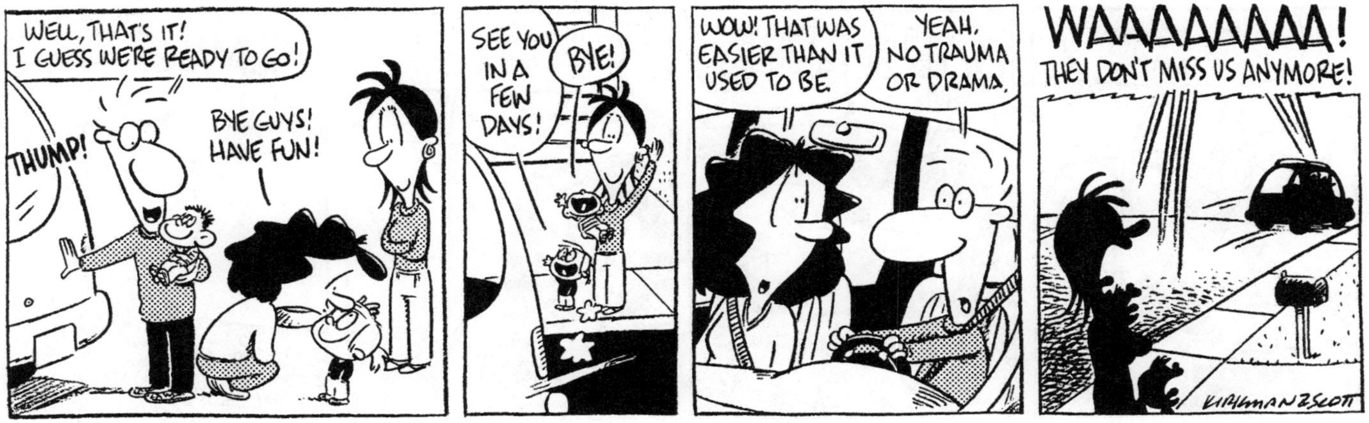
WELL, THAT'S IT! I GUESS WE'RE READY TO GO!
THUMP!
BYE GUYS! HAVE FUN!
SEE YOU IN A FEW DAYS!
BYE!
WOW! THAT WAS EASIER THAN IT USED TO BE.
YEAH, NO TRAUMA OR DRAMA.
WAAAAAAAA!
THEY DON'T MISS US ANYMORE!
KIRKMAN & SCOTT

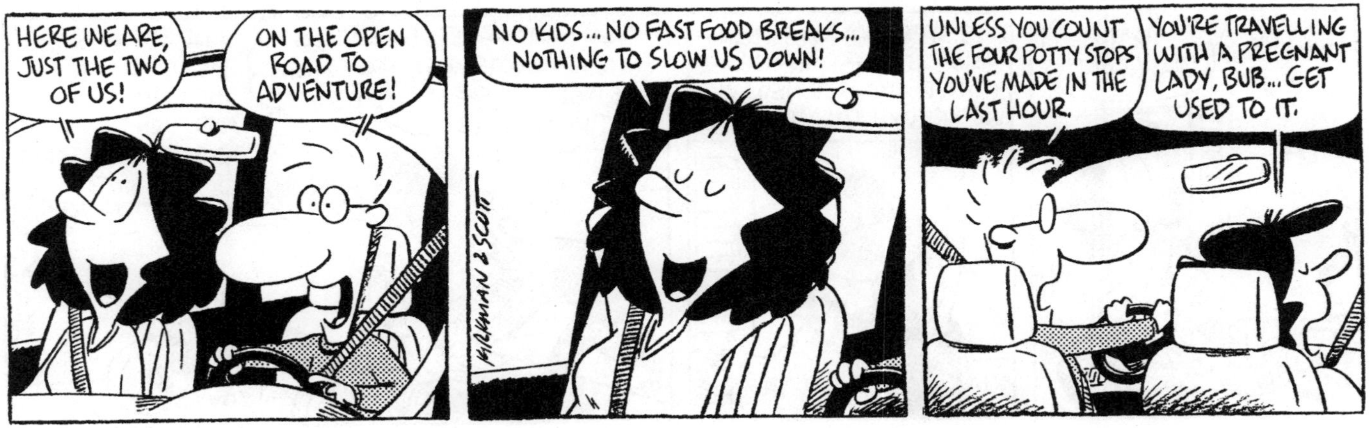
HERE WE ARE, JUST THE TWO OF US!
ON THE OPEN ROAD TO ADVENTURE!
KIRKMAN & SCOTT
NO KIDS... NO FAST FOOD BREAKS... NOTHING TO SLOW US DOWN!
UNLESS YOU COUNT THE FOUR POTTY STOPS YOU'VE MADE IN THE LAST HOUR.
YOU'RE TRAVELLING WITH A PREGNANT LADY, BUB... GET USED TO IT.

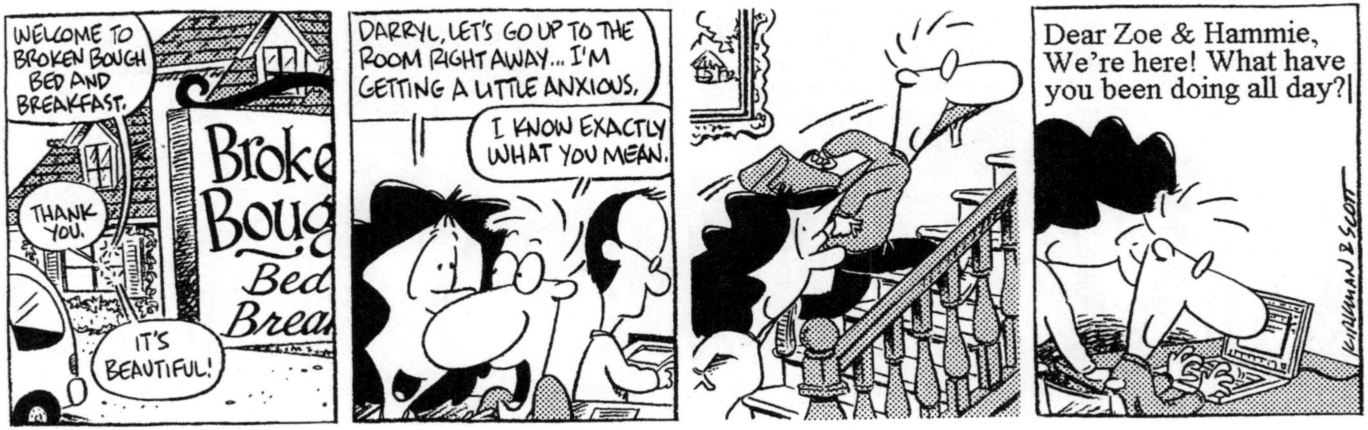
WELCOME TO BROKEN BOUGH BED AND BREAKFAST.
THANK YOU.
IT'S BEAUTIFUL!
DARRYL, LET'S GO UP TO THE ROOM RIGHT AWAY... I'M GETTING A LITTLE ANXIOUS.
I KNOW EXACTLY WHAT YOU MEAN.
KIRKMAN & SCOTT
Dear Zoe & Hammie,
We're here! What have you been doing all day?

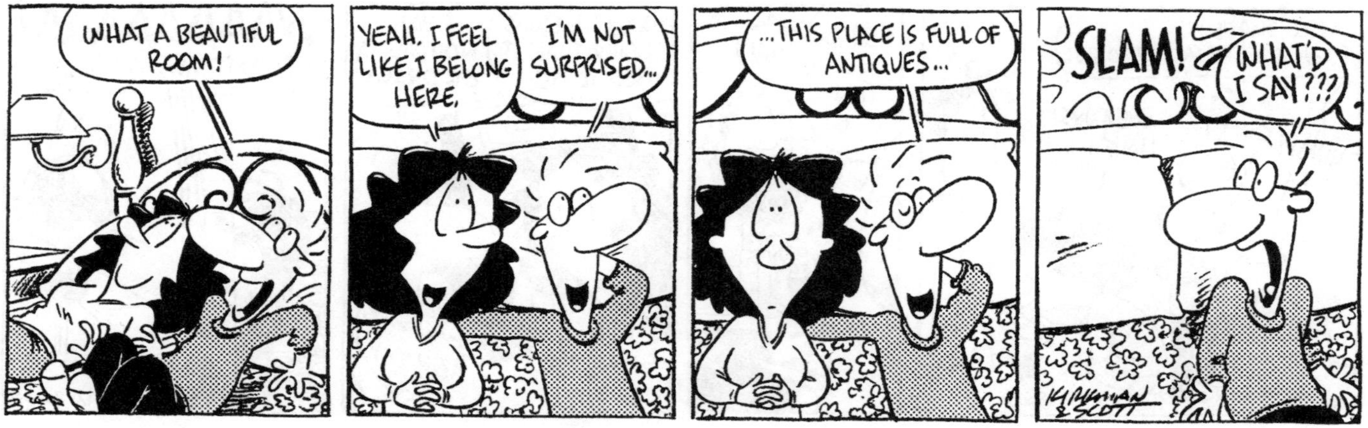
WHAT A BEAUTIFUL ROOM!
YEAH. I FEEL LIKE I BELONG HERE.
I'M NOT SURPRISED...
...THIS PLACE IS FULL OF ANTIQUES...
SLAM!
WHAT'D I SAY???
KIRKMAN & SCOTT

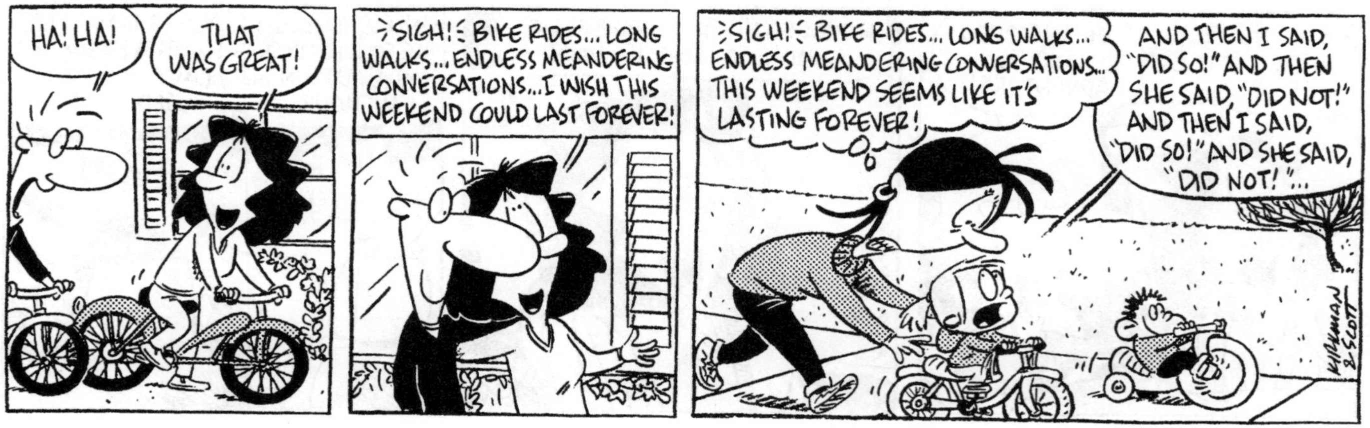
HA! HA!
THAT WAS GREAT!
SIGH! BIKE RIDES... LONG WALKS... ENDLESS MEANDERING CONVERSATIONS... I WISH THIS WEEKEND COULD LAST FOREVER!
SIGH! BIKE RIDES... LONG WALKS... ENDLESS MEANDERING CONVERSATIONS... THIS WEEKEND SEEMS LIKE IT'S LASTING FOREVER!
AND THEN I SAID, "DID SO!" AND THEN SHE SAID, "DID NOT!" AND THEN I SAID, "DID SO!" AND SHE SAID, "DID NOT!"...
KIRKMAN & SCOTT

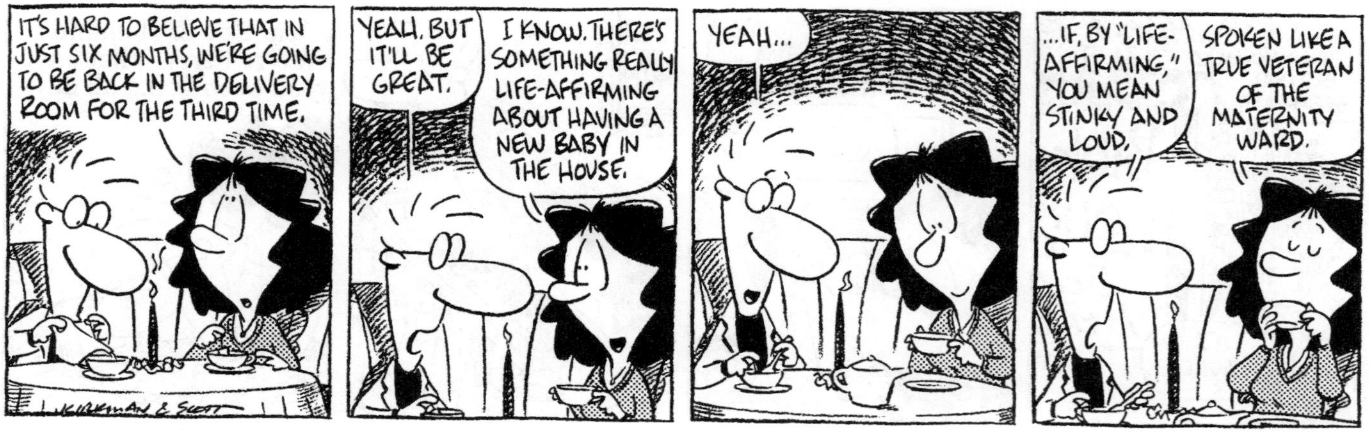
IT'S HARD TO BELIEVE THAT IN JUST SIX MONTHS, WE'RE GOING TO BE BACK IN THE DELIVERY ROOM FOR THE THIRD TIME.
YEAH. BUT IT'LL BE GREAT.
I KNOW. THERE'S SOMETHING REALLY LIFE-AFFIRMING ABOUT HAVING A NEW BABY IN THE HOUSE.
YEAH...
...IF, BY "LIFE-AFFIRMING," YOU MEAN STINKY AND LOUD.
SPOKEN LIKE A TRUE VETERAN OF THE MATERNITY WARD.
KIRKMAN & SCOTT

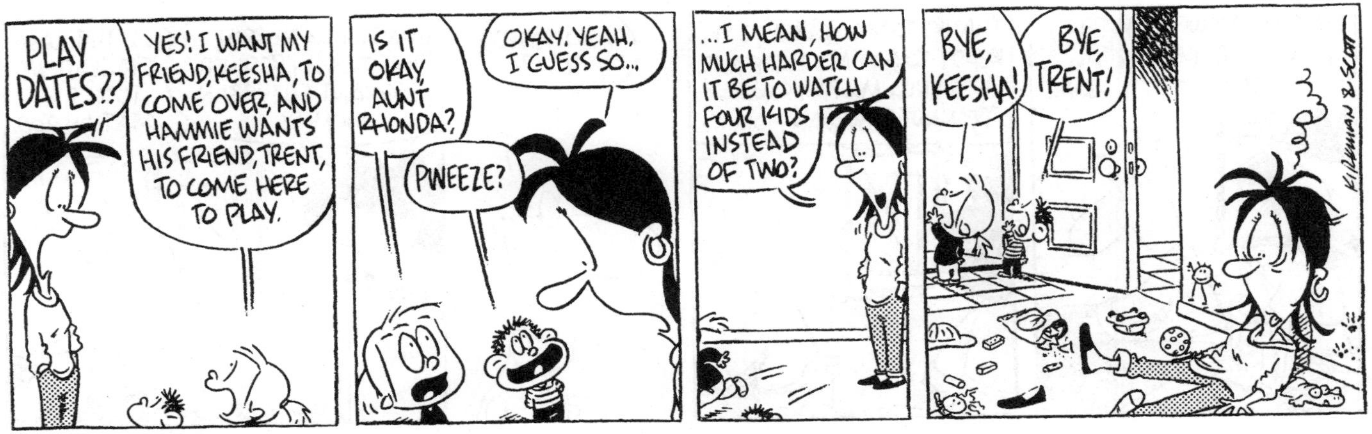
PLAY DATES??
YES! I WANT MY FRIEND, KEESHA, TO COME OVER, AND HAMMIE WANTS HIS FRIEND, TRENT, TO COME HERE TO PLAY.
IS IT OKAY, AUNT RHONDA?
PWEEZE?
OKAY, YEAH. I GUESS SO...
...I MEAN, HOW MUCH HARDER CAN IT BE TO WATCH FOUR KIDS INSTEAD OF TWO?
BYE, KEESHA!
BYE, TRENT!
KIRKMAN & SCOTT

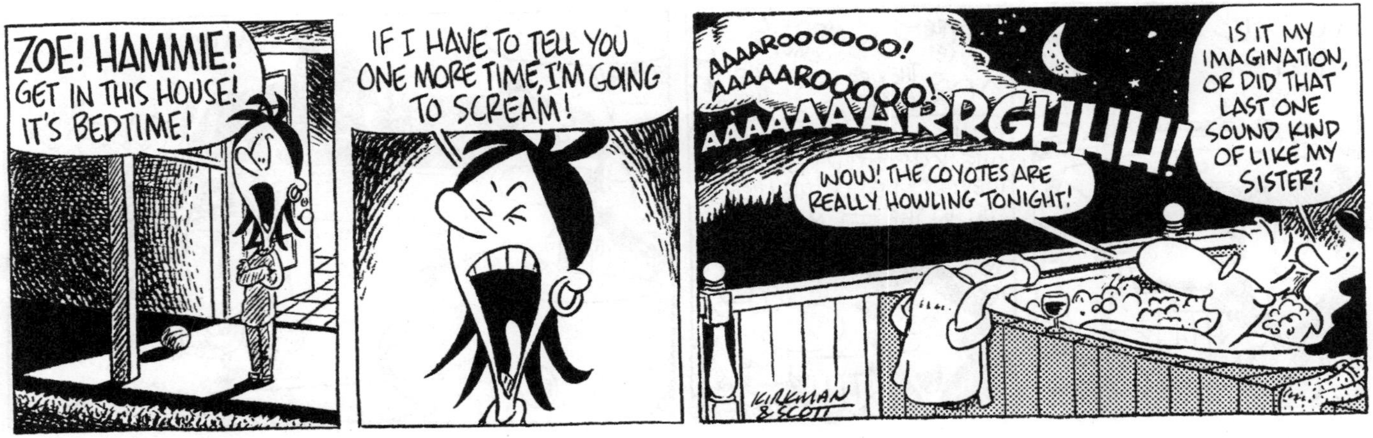
ZOE! HAMMIE! GET IN THIS HOUSE! IT'S BEDTIME!
IF I HAVE TO TELL YOU ONE MORE TIME, I'M GOING TO SCREAM!
AAAAROOOOOOO!
AAAAAROOOOOO!
AAAAAAAARRGHHH!
WOW! THE COYOTES ARE REALLY HOWLING TONIGHT!
IS IT MY IMAGINATION, OR DID THAT LAST ONE SOUND KIND OF LIKE MY SISTER?
KIRKMAN & SCOTT

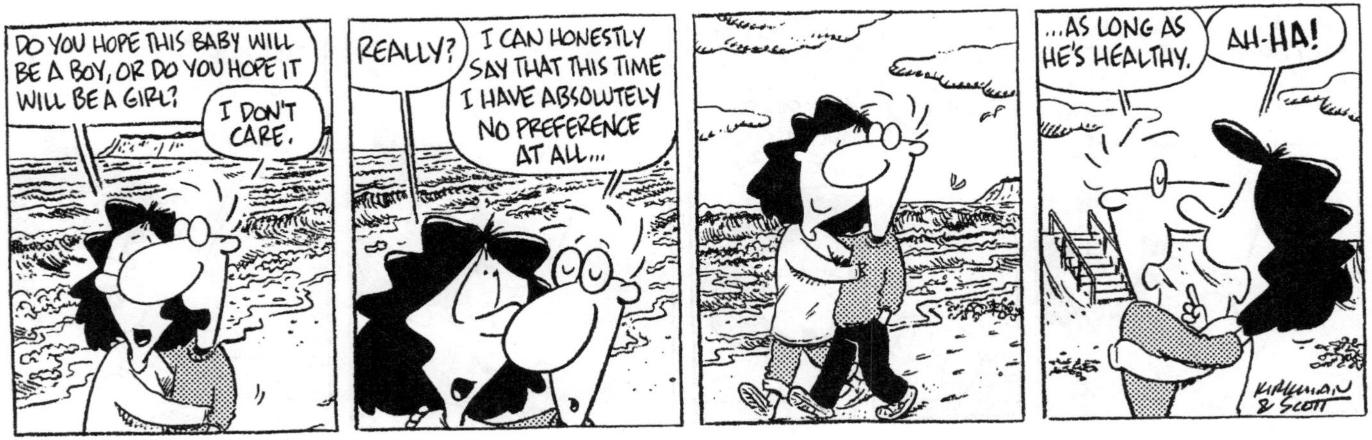
DO YOU HOPE THIS BABY WILL BE A BOY, OR DO YOU HOPE IT WILL BE A GIRL?
I DON'T CARE.
REALLY?
I CAN HONESTLY SAY THAT THIS TIME I HAVE ABSOLUTELY NO PREFERENCE AT ALL...
...AS LONG AS HE'S HEALTHY.
AH-HA!
KIRKMAN & SCOTT

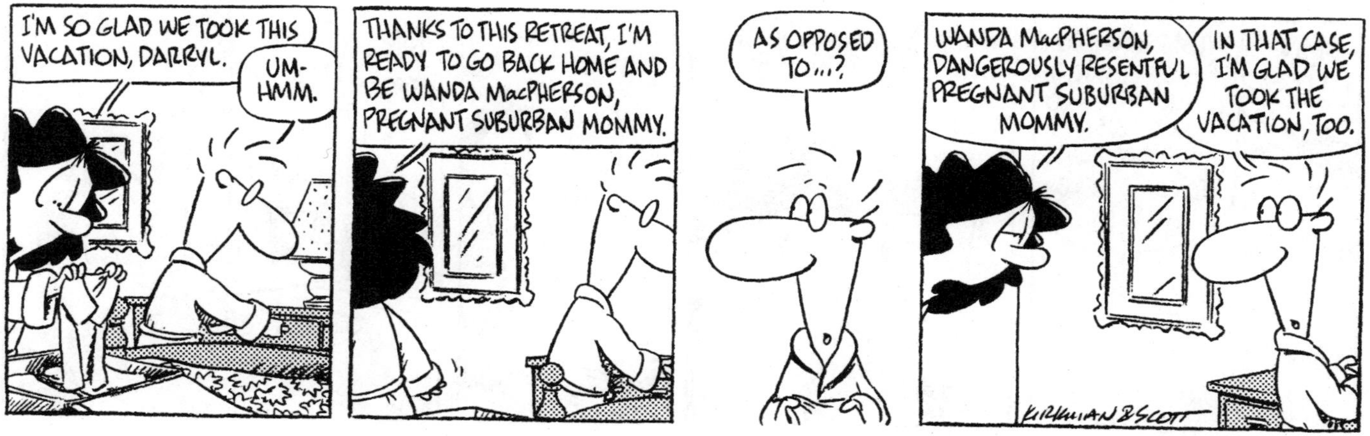
I'M SO GLAD WE TOOK THIS VACATION, DARRYL.
UM-HMM.
THANKS TO THIS RETREAT, I'M READY TO GO BACK HOME AND BE WANDA MacPHERSON, PREGNANT SUBURBAN MOMMY.
AS OPPOSED TO...?
WANDA MacPHERSON, DANGEROUSLY RESENTFUL PREGNANT SUBURBAN MOMMY.
IN THAT CASE, I'M GLAD WE TOOK THE VACATION, TOO.
KIRKMAN & SCOTT

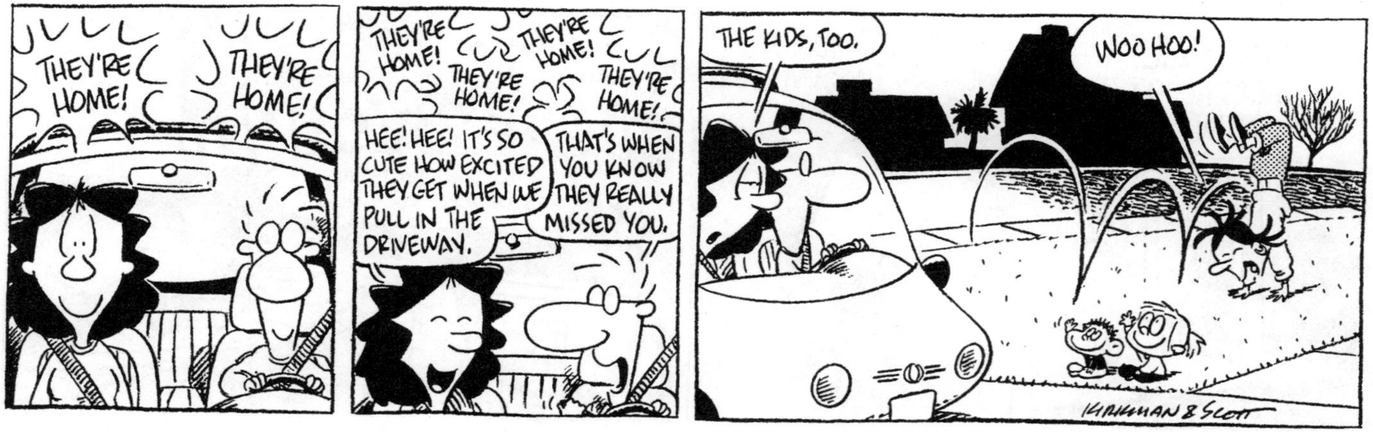
THEY'RE HOME!
THEY'RE HOME!
THEY'RE HOME!
THEY'RE HOME!
THEY'RE HOME!
THEY'RE HOME!
HEE! HEE! IT'S SO CUTE HOW EXCITED THEY GET WHEN WE PULL IN THE DRIVEWAY.
THAT'S WHEN YOU KNOW THEY REALLY MISSED YOU.
THE KIDS, TOO.
WOO HOO!
KIRKMAN & SCOTT

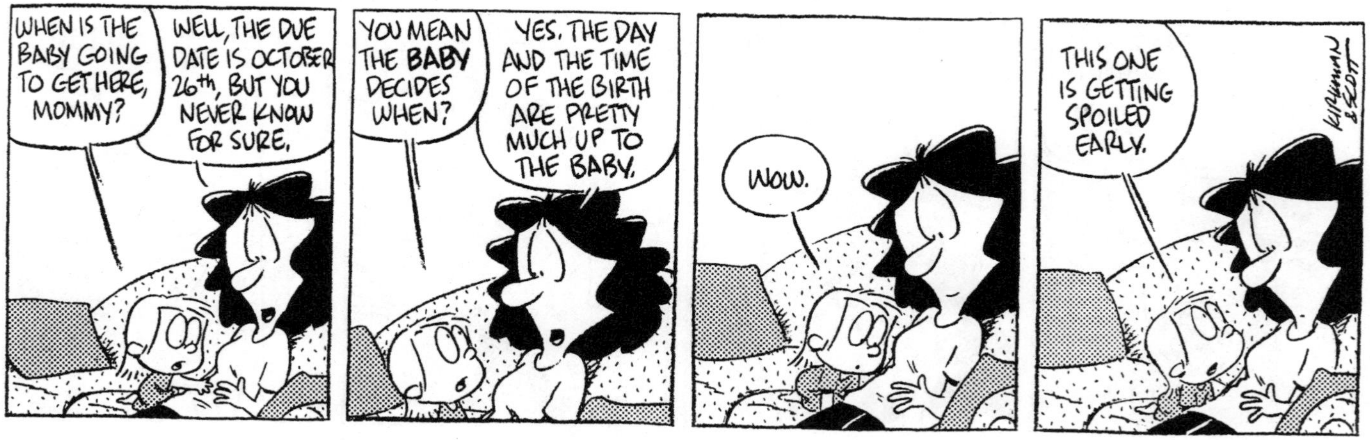
WHEN IS THE BABY GOING TO GET HERE, MOMMY?
WELL, THE DUE DATE IS OCTOBER 26th, BUT YOU NEVER KNOW FOR SURE.
YOU MEAN THE **BABY** DECIDES WHEN?
YES. THE DAY AND THE TIME OF THE BIRTH ARE PRETTY MUCH UP TO THE BABY.
WOW.
THIS ONE IS GETTING SPOILED EARLY.
KIRKMAN & SCOTT

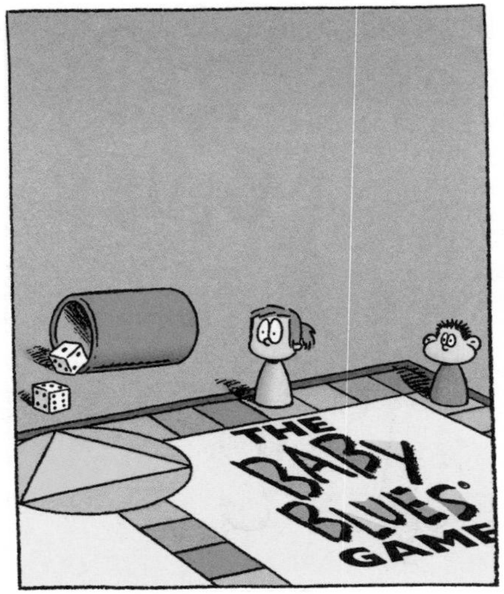
THE
BABY
BLUES
GAME

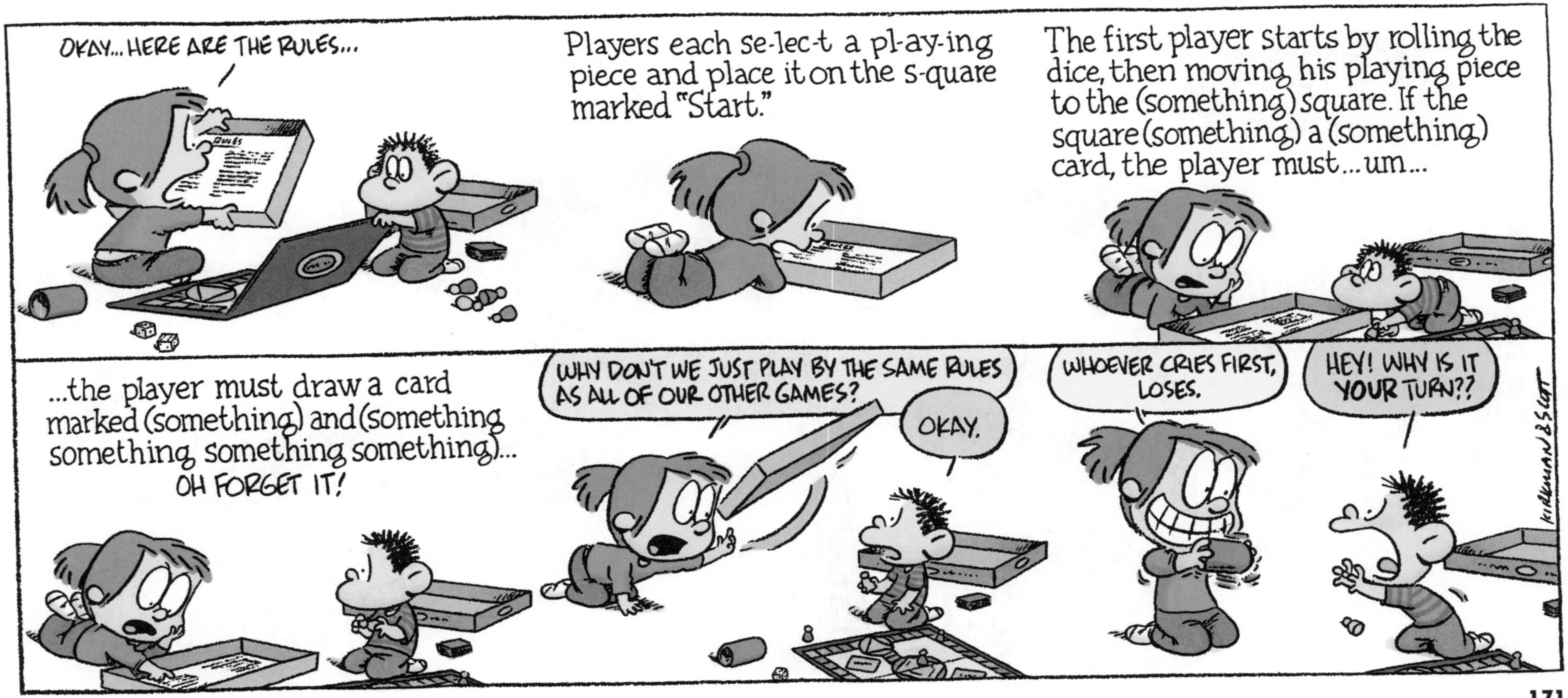
OKAY... HERE ARE THE RULES...
RULES
Players each se-lec-t a pl-ay-ing piece and place it on the s-quare marked "Start."
The first player starts by rolling the dice, then moving his playing piece to the (something) square. If the square (something) a (something) card, the player must... um...
...the player must draw a card marked (something) and (something something, something something)... OH FORGET IT!
WHY DON'T WE JUST PLAY BY THE SAME RULES AS ALL OF OUR OTHER GAMES?
OKAY.
WHOEVER CRIES FIRST, LOSES.
HEY! WHY IS IT YOUR TURN??
KIRKMAN & SCOTT

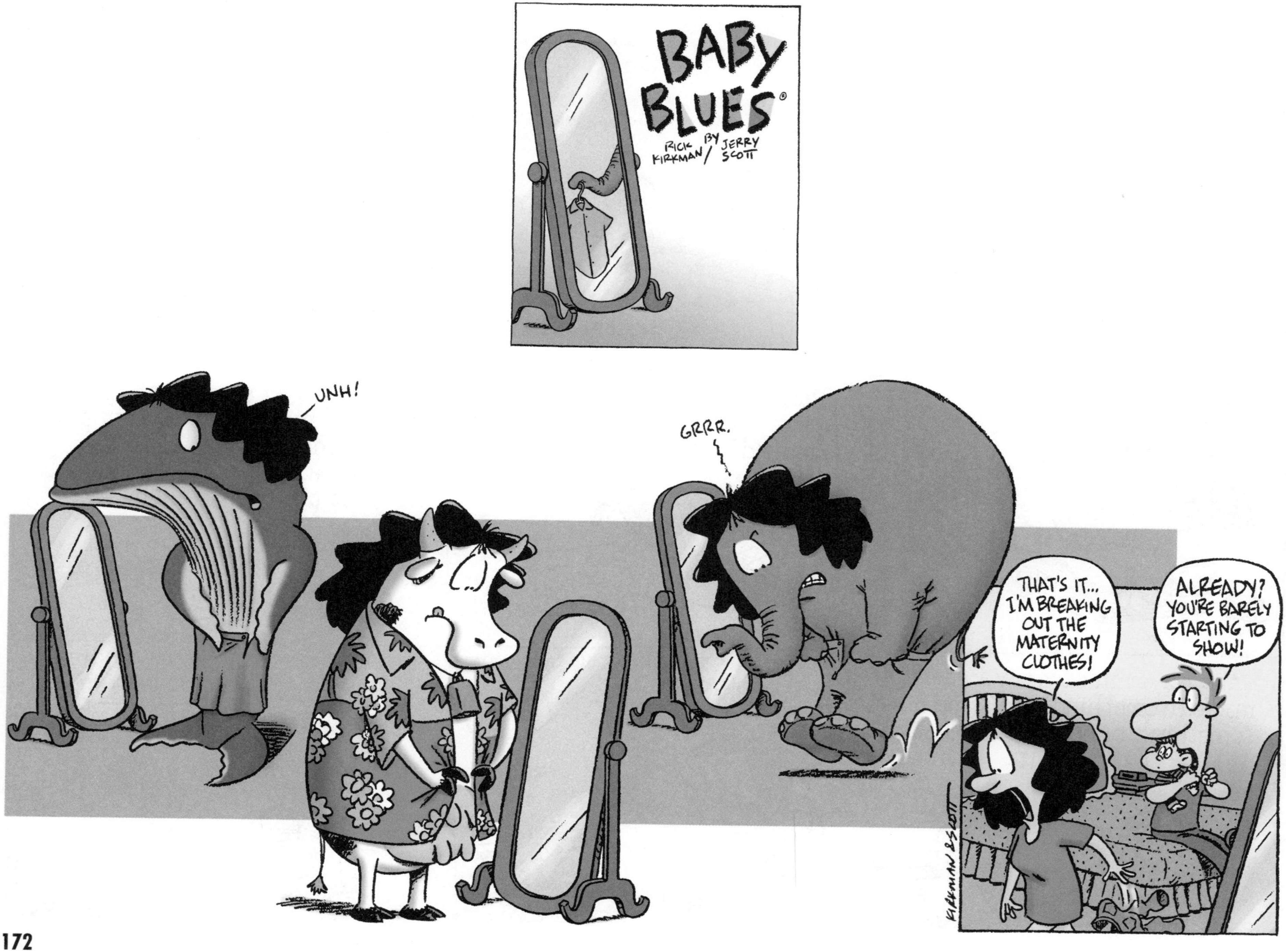
BABY BLUES®
RICK KIRKMAN / BY JERRY SCOTT
UNH!
GRRR.
THAT'S IT... I'M BREAKING OUT THE MATERNITY CLOTHES!
ALREADY? YOU'RE BARELY STARTING TO SHOW!
KIRKMAN & SCOTT

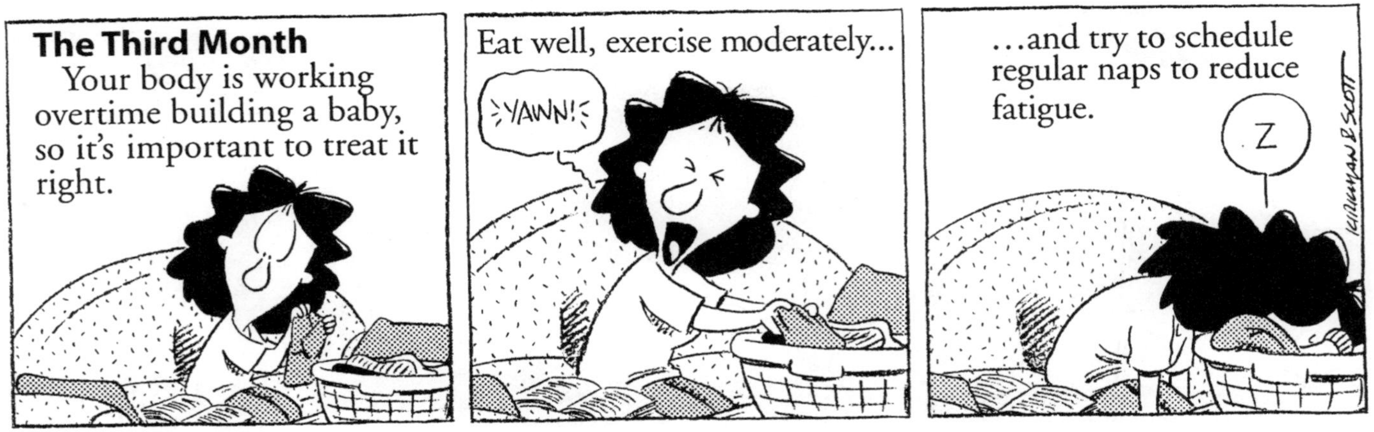
The Third Month
Your body is working overtime building a baby, so it's important to treat it right.
Eat well, exercise moderately...
YAWN!
...and try to schedule regular naps to reduce fatigue.
Z

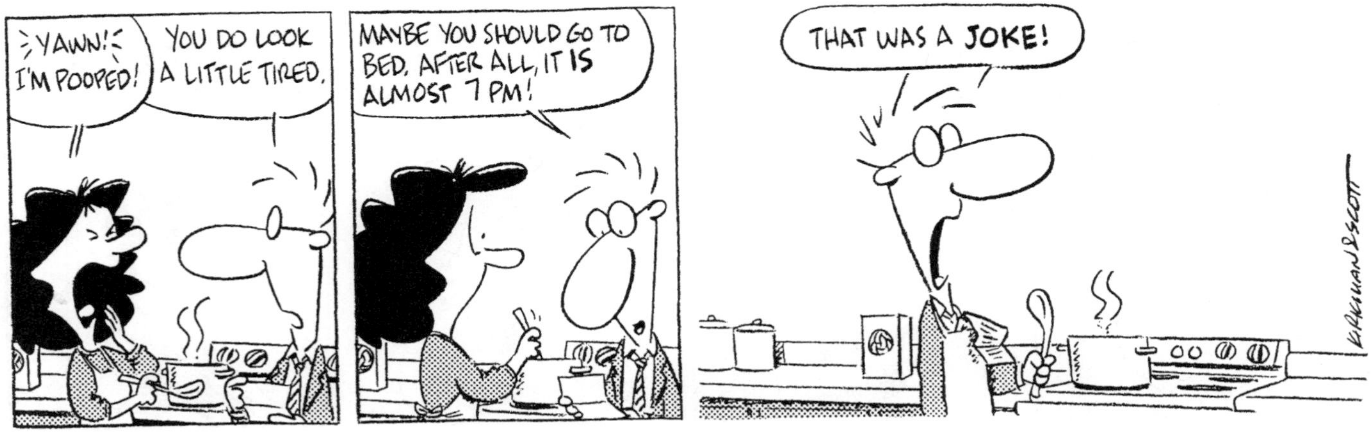
YAWN! I'M POOPED!
YOU DO LOOK A LITTLE TIRED.
MAYBE YOU SHOULD GO TO BED. AFTER ALL, IT IS ALMOST 7 PM!
THAT WAS A JOKE!

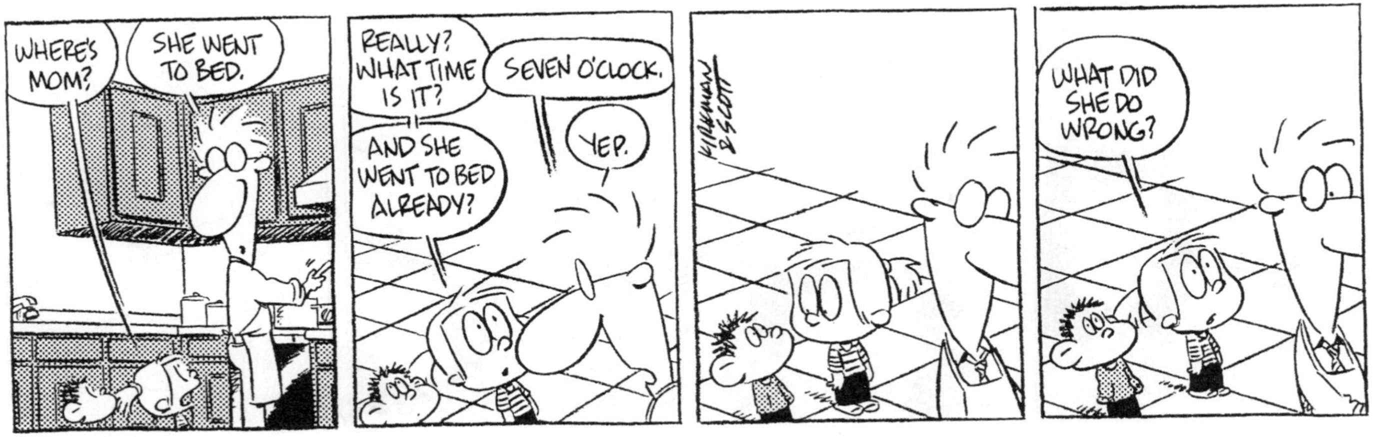
WHERE'S MOM?
SHE WENT TO BED.
REALLY? WHAT TIME IS IT?
SEVEN O'CLOCK.
AND SHE WENT TO BED ALREADY?
YEP.
WHAT DID SHE DO WRONG?

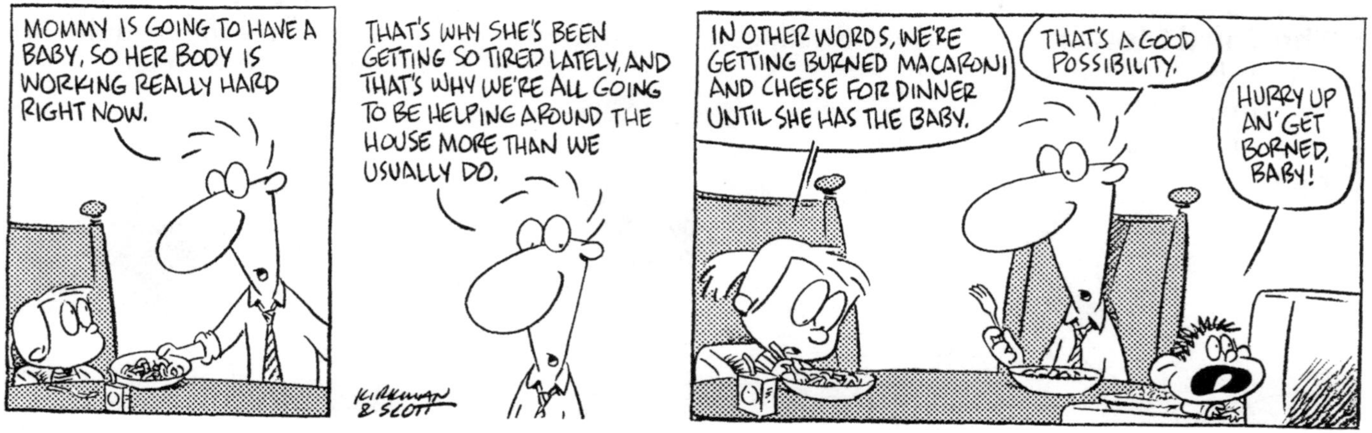
MOMMY IS GOING TO HAVE A BABY, SO HER BODY IS WORKING REALLY HARD RIGHT NOW.
THAT'S WHY SHE'S BEEN GETTING SO TIRED LATELY, AND THAT'S WHY WE'RE ALL GOING TO BE HELPING AROUND THE HOUSE MORE THAN WE USUALLY DO.
KIRKMAN & SCOTT
IN OTHER WORDS, WE'RE GETTING BURNED MACARONI AND CHEESE FOR DINNER UNTIL SHE HAS THE BABY.
THAT'S A GOOD POSSIBILITY.
HURRY UP AN' GET BORNED, BABY!

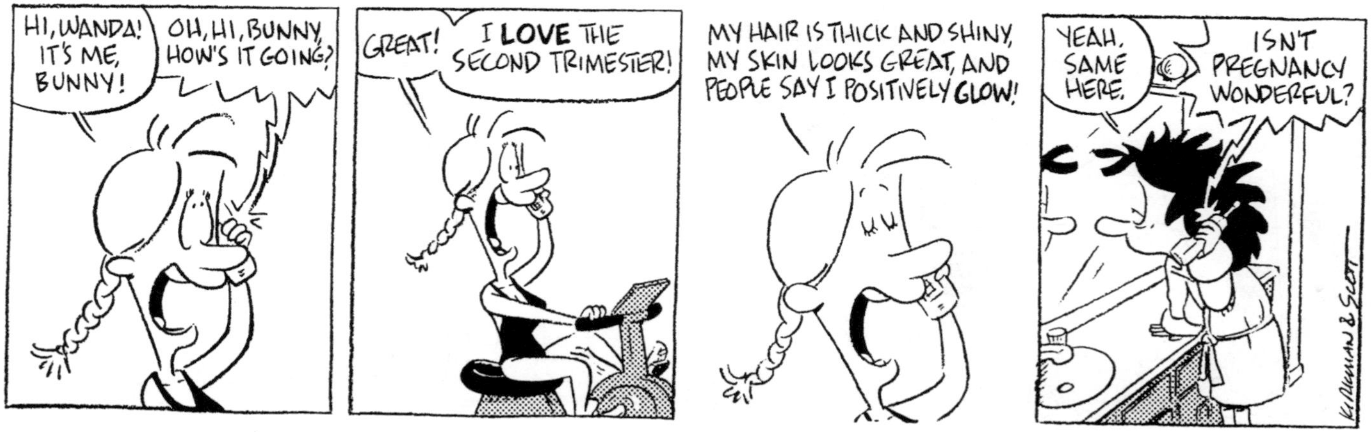
HI, WANDA! IT'S ME, BUNNY!
OH, HI, BUNNY, HOW'S IT GOING?
GREAT!
I LOVE THE SECOND TRIMESTER!
MY HAIR IS THICK AND SHINY, MY SKIN LOOKS GREAT, AND PEOPLE SAY I POSITIVELY GLOW!
YEAH, SAME HERE.
ISN'T PREGNANCY WONDERFUL?
KIRKMAN & SCOTT

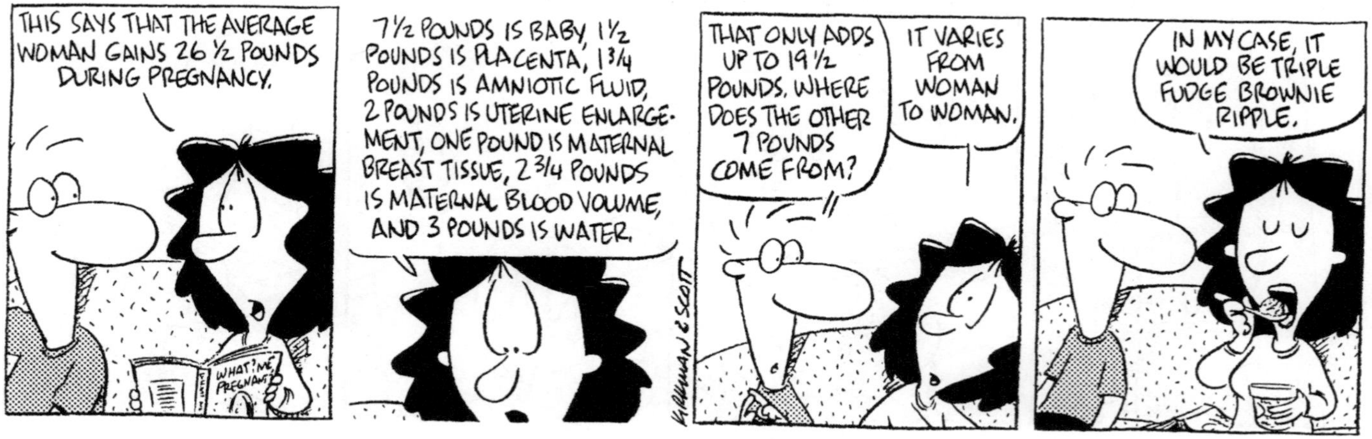
THIS SAYS THAT THE AVERAGE WOMAN GAINS 26 ½ POUNDS DURING PREGNANCY.
WHAT? ME, PREGNANT?
7½ POUNDS IS BABY, 1½ POUNDS IS PLACENTA, 1¾ POUNDS IS AMNIOTIC FLUID, 2 POUNDS IS UTERINE ENLARGEMENT, ONE POUND IS MATERNAL BREAST TISSUE, 2¾ POUNDS IS MATERNAL BLOOD VOLUME, AND 3 POUNDS IS WATER.
KIRKMAN & SCOTT
THAT ONLY ADDS UP TO 19 ½ POUNDS. WHERE DOES THE OTHER 7 POUNDS COME FROM?
IT VARIES FROM WOMAN TO WOMAN.
IN MY CASE, IT WOULD BE TRIPLE FUDGE BROWNIE RIPPLE.

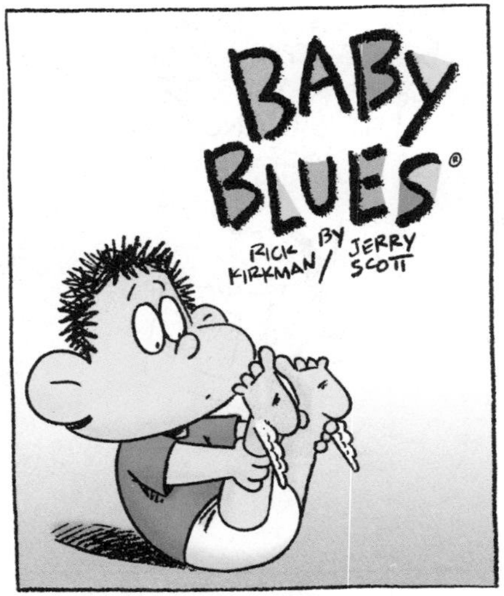
BABY BLUES®
BY RICK KIRKMAN / JERRY SCOTT

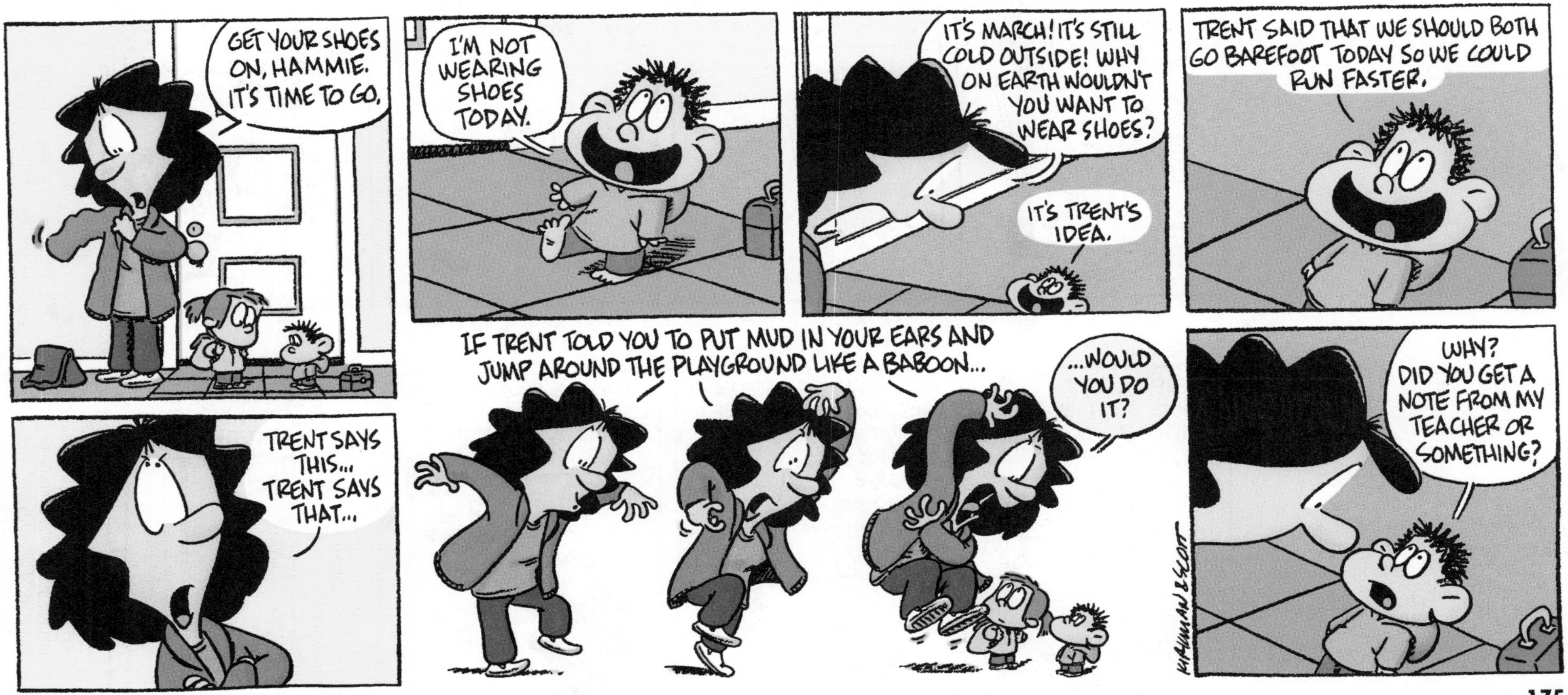
GET YOUR SHOES ON, HAMMIE. IT'S TIME TO GO.
I'M NOT WEARING SHOES TODAY.
IT'S MARCH! IT'S STILL COLD OUTSIDE! WHY ON EARTH WOULDN'T YOU WANT TO WEAR SHOES?
IT'S TRENT'S IDEA.
TRENT SAID THAT WE SHOULD BOTH GO BAREFOOT TODAY SO WE COULD RUN FASTER.
TRENT SAYS THIS... TRENT SAYS THAT...
IF TRENT TOLD YOU TO PUT MUD IN YOUR EARS AND JUMP AROUND THE PLAYGROUND LIKE A BABOON...
...WOULD YOU DO IT?
KIRKMAN & SCOTT
WHY? DID YOU GET A NOTE FROM MY TEACHER OR SOMETHING?

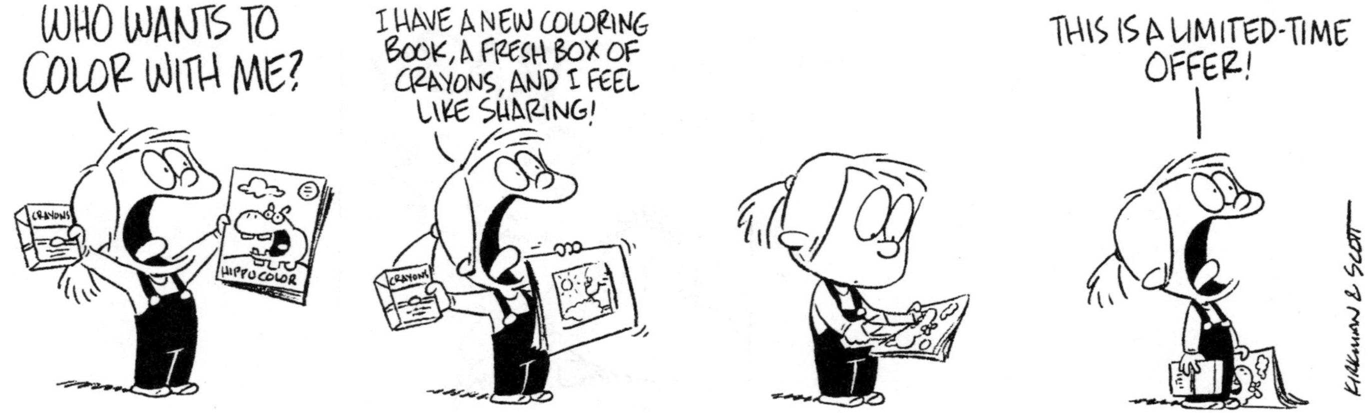
WHO WANTS TO COLOR WITH ME?
CRAYONS
HIPPO COLOR
I HAVE A NEW COLORING BOOK, A FRESH BOX OF CRAYONS, AND I FEEL LIKE SHARING!
CRAYONS
THIS IS A LIMITED-TIME OFFER!
KIRKMAN & SCOTT

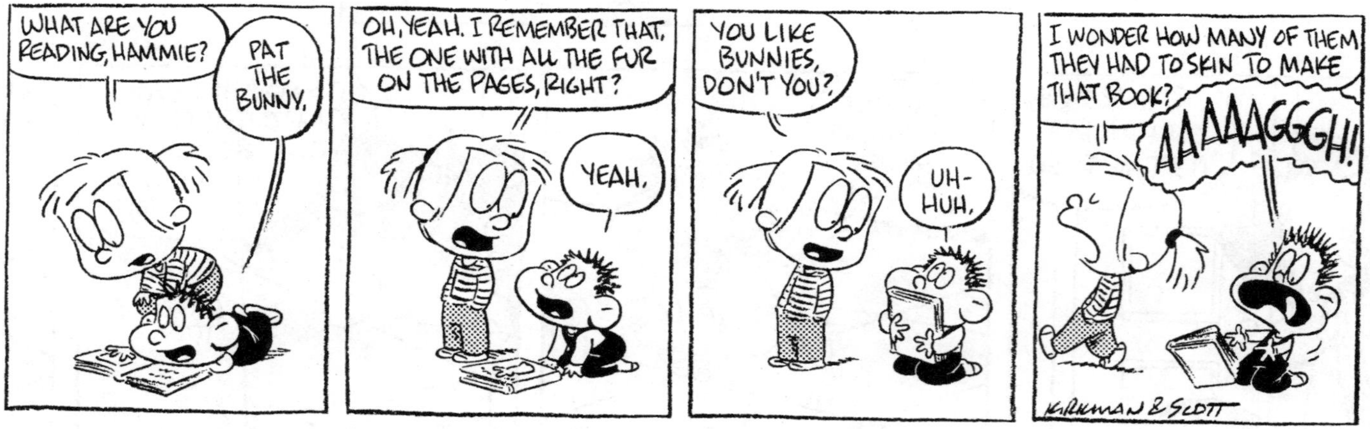
WHAT ARE YOU READING, HAMMIE?
PAT THE BUNNY.
OH, YEAH. I REMEMBER THAT. THE ONE WITH ALL THE FUR ON THE PAGES, RIGHT?
YEAH.
YOU LIKE BUNNIES, DON'T YOU?
UH-HUH.
I WONDER HOW MANY OF THEM THEY HAD TO SKIN TO MAKE THAT BOOK?
AAAAAGGGH!
KIRKMAN & SCOTT

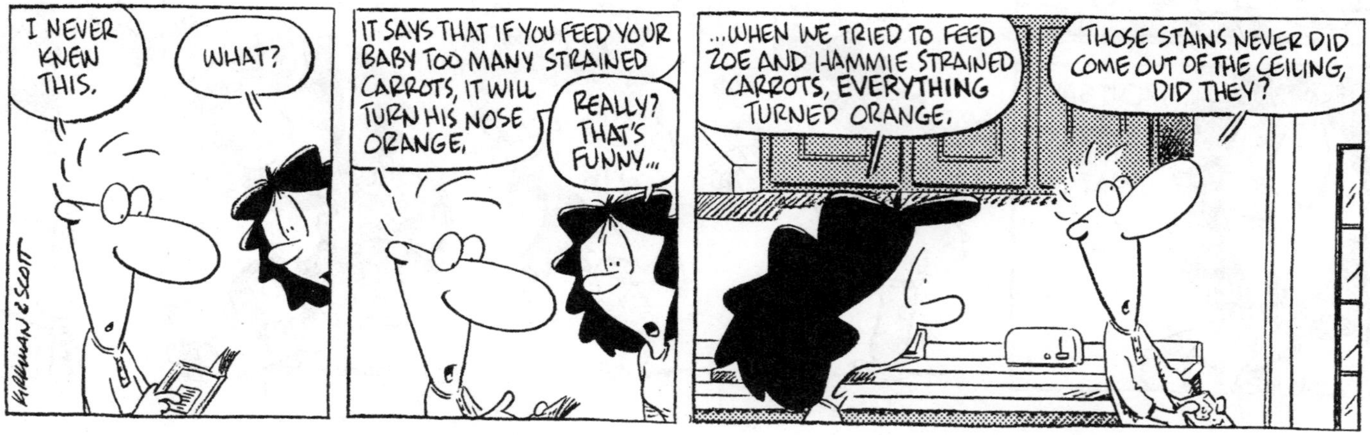
I NEVER KNEW THIS.
WHAT?
KIRKMAN & SCOTT
IT SAYS THAT IF YOU FEED YOUR BABY TOO MANY STRAINED CARROTS, IT WILL TURN HIS NOSE ORANGE.
REALLY? THAT'S FUNNY...
...WHEN WE TRIED TO FEED ZOE AND HAMMIE STRAINED CARROTS, EVERYTHING TURNED ORANGE.
THOSE STAINS NEVER DID COME OUT OF THE CEILING, DID THEY?

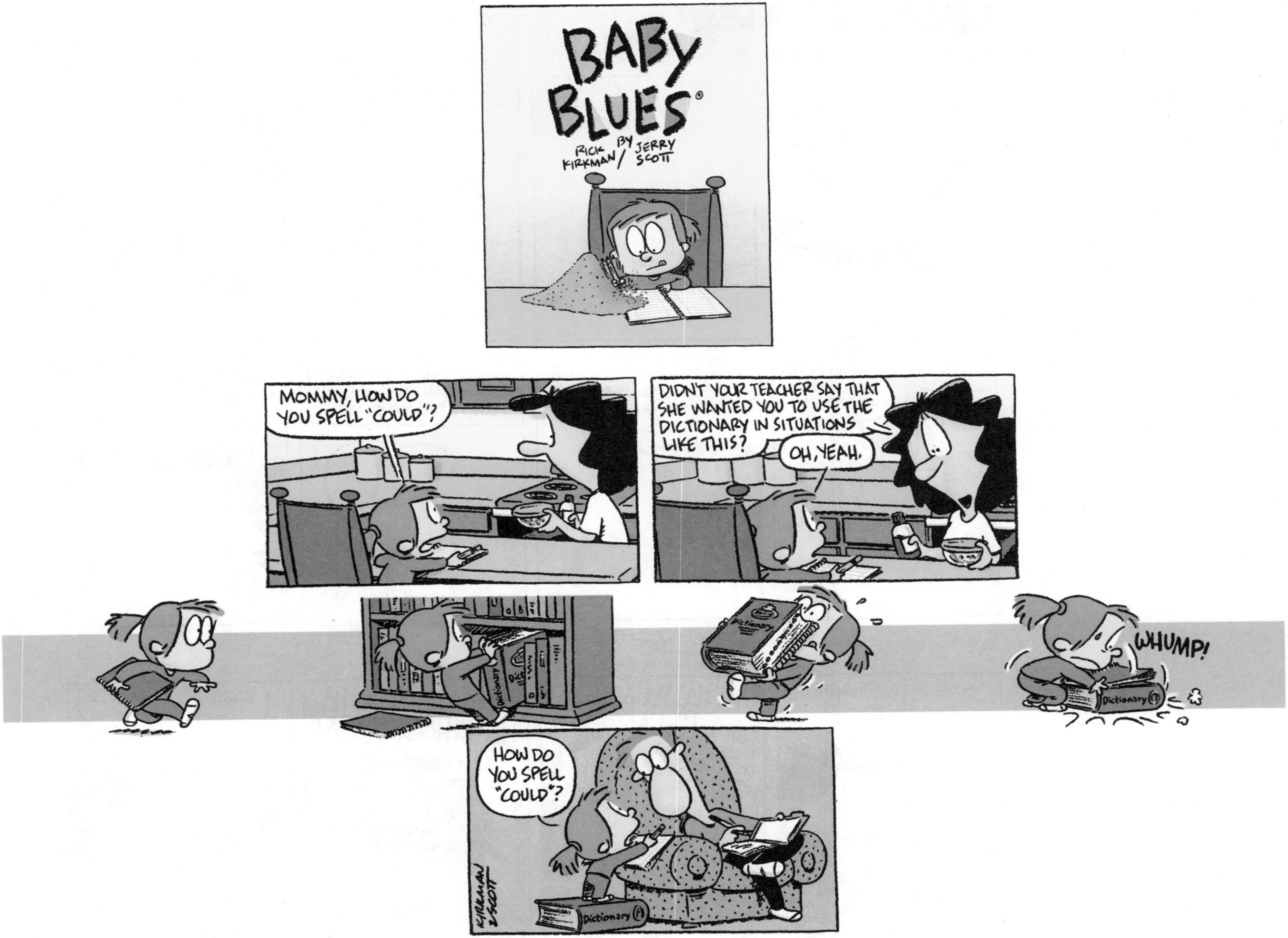
BABY BLUES®
RICK KIRKMAN / BY JERRY SCOTT
MOMMY, HOW DO YOU SPELL "COULD"?
DIDN'T YOUR TEACHER SAY THAT SHE WANTED YOU TO USE THE DICTIONARY IN SITUATIONS LIKE THIS?
OH, YEAH.
Dictionary
WHUMP!
Dictionary
HOW DO YOU SPELL "COULD"?
Dictionary
KIRKMAN & SCOTT

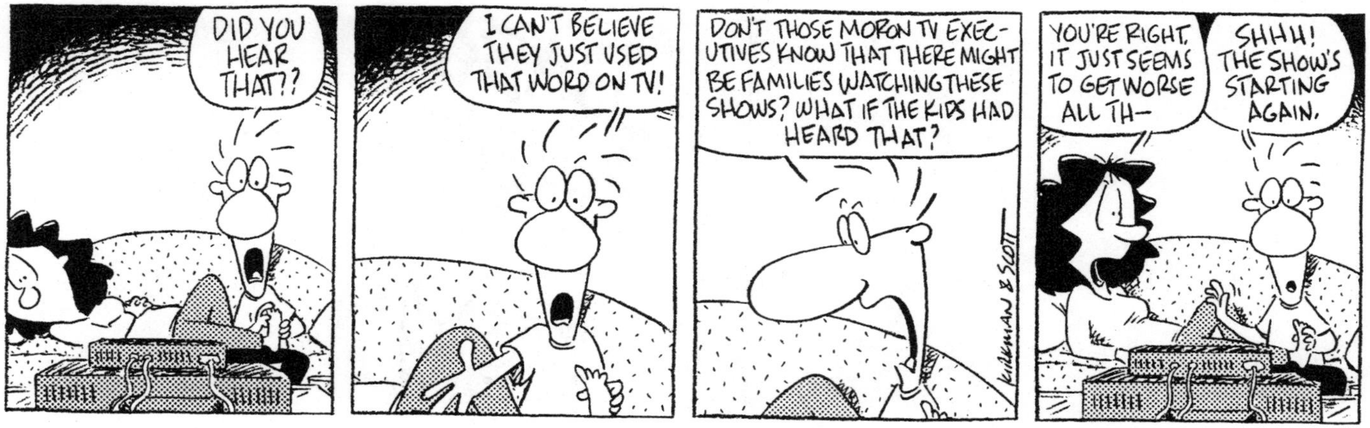
DID YOU HEAR THAT??
I CAN'T BELIEVE THEY JUST USED THAT WORD ON TV!
DON'T THOSE MORON TV EXECUTIVES KNOW THAT THERE MIGHT BE FAMILIES WATCHING THESE SHOWS? WHAT IF THE KIDS HAD HEARD THAT?
KIRKMAN & SCOTT
YOU'RE RIGHT. IT JUST SEEMS TO GET WORSE ALL TH—
SHHH! THE SHOW'S STARTING AGAIN.

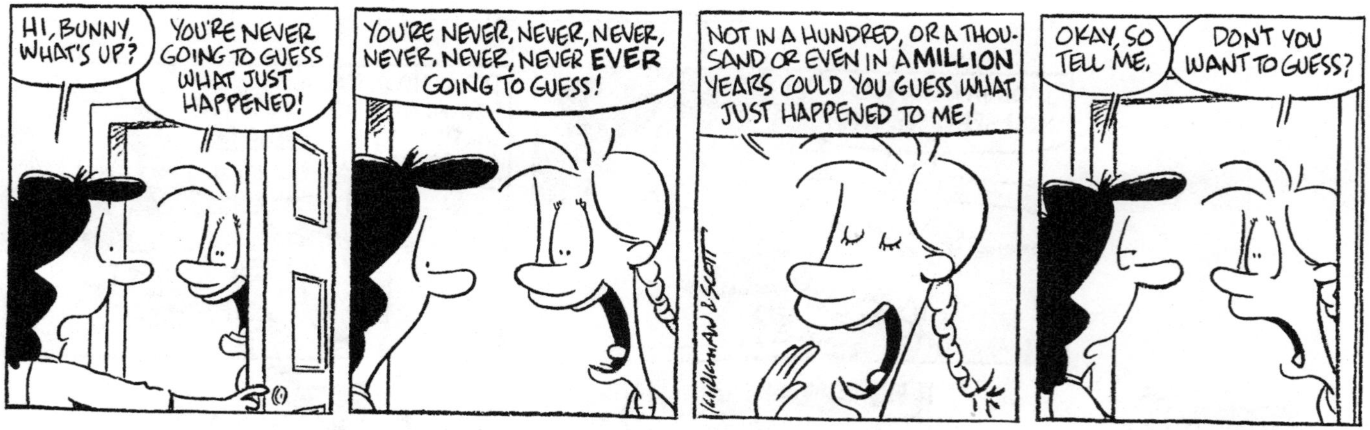
HI, BUNNY. WHAT'S UP?
YOU'RE NEVER GOING TO GUESS WHAT JUST HAPPENED!
YOU'RE NEVER, NEVER, NEVER, NEVER, NEVER, NEVER **EVER** GOING TO GUESS!
KIRKMAN & SCOTT
NOT IN A HUNDRED, OR A THOUSAND OR EVEN IN A **MILLION** YEARS COULD YOU GUESS WHAT JUST HAPPENED TO ME!
OKAY, SO TELL ME.
DON'T YOU WANT TO GUESS?

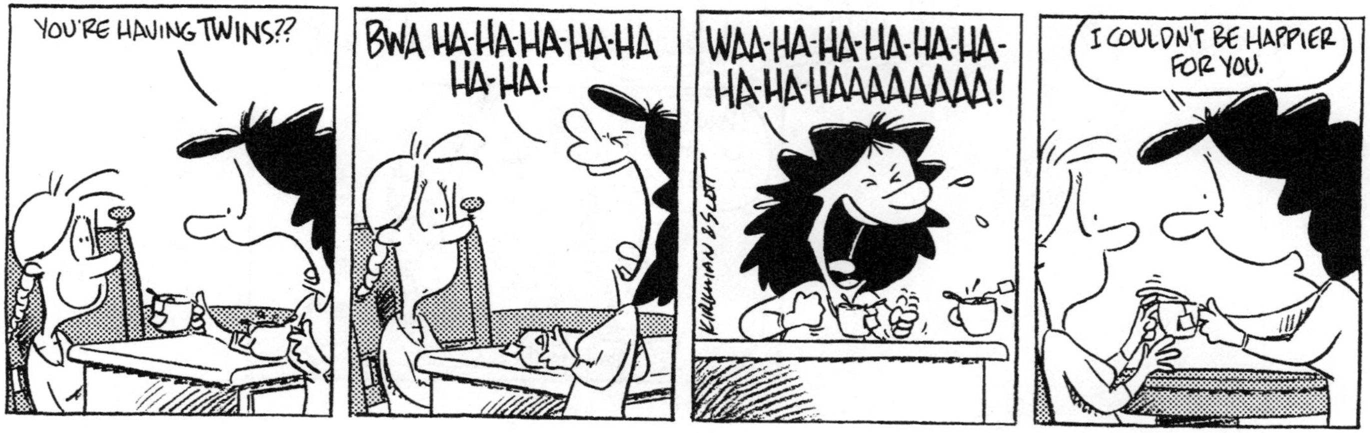
YOU'RE HAVING **TWINS**??
BWA HA-HA-HA-HA-HA HA-HA!
WAA-HA-HA-HA-HA-HA-HA-HA-HAAAAAAAA!
KIRKMAN & SCOTT
I COULDN'T BE HAPPIER FOR YOU.

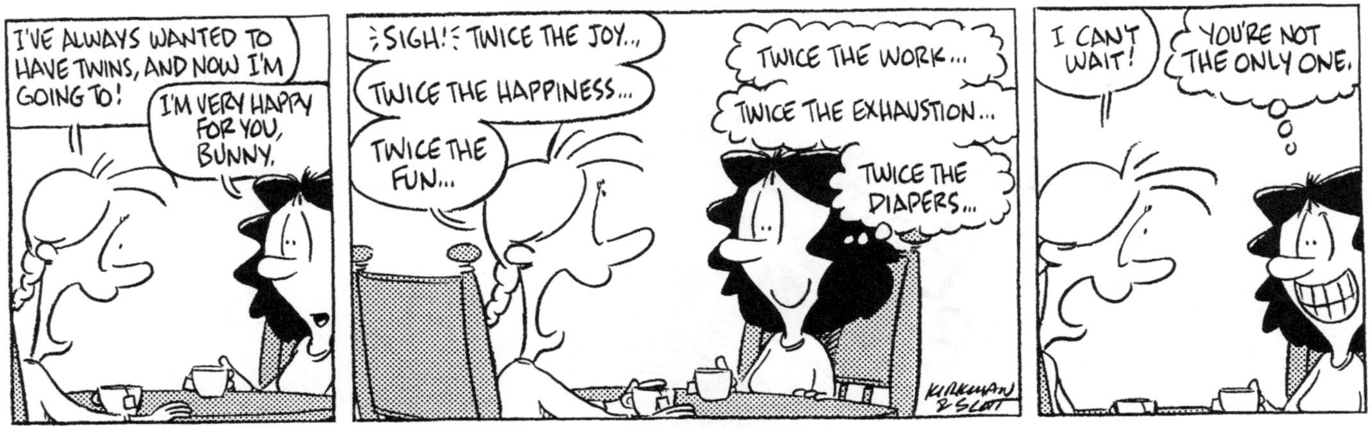
I'VE ALWAYS WANTED TO HAVE TWINS, AND NOW I'M GOING TO!
I'M VERY HAPPY FOR YOU, BUNNY.
SIGH! TWICE THE JOY...
TWICE THE HAPPINESS...
TWICE THE FUN...
TWICE THE WORK...
TWICE THE EXHAUSTION...
TWICE THE DIAPERS...
KIRKMAN & SCOTT
I CAN'T WAIT!
YOU'RE NOT THE ONLY ONE.

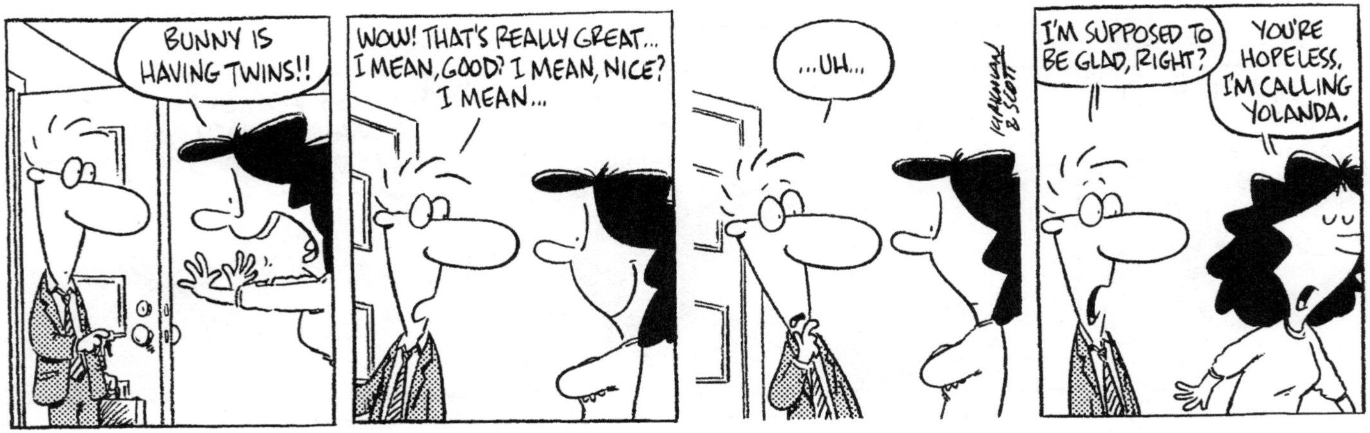
BUNNY IS HAVING TWINS!!
WOW! THAT'S REALLY GREAT... I MEAN, GOOD? I MEAN, NICE? I MEAN...
...UH...
KIRKMAN & SCOTT
I'M SUPPOSED TO BE GLAD, RIGHT?
YOU'RE HOPELESS. I'M CALLING YOLANDA.

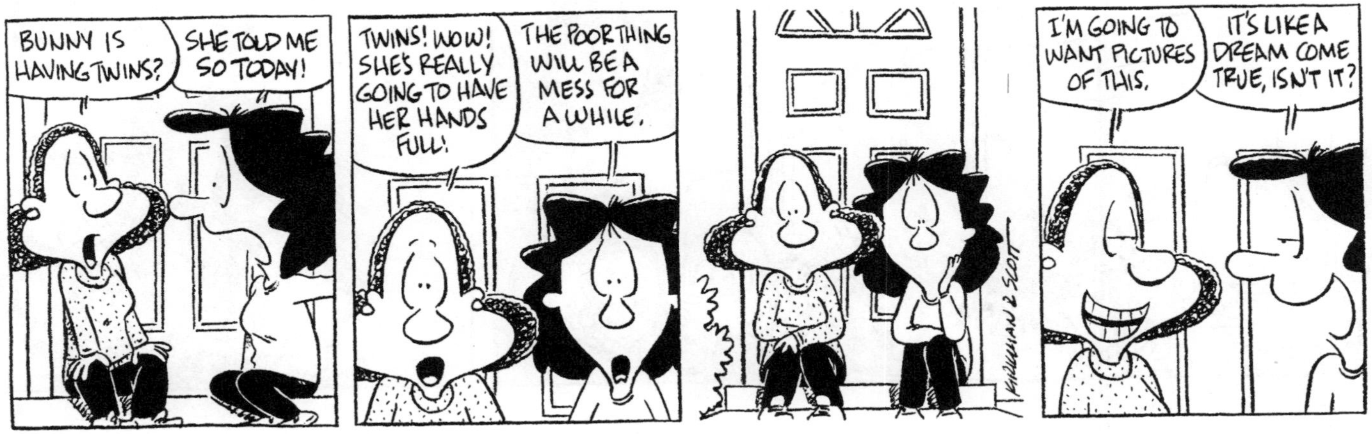
BUNNY IS HAVING TWINS?
SHE TOLD ME SO TODAY!
TWINS! WOW! SHE'S REALLY GOING TO HAVE HER HANDS FULL!
THE POOR THING WILL BE A MESS FOR A WHILE.
KIRKMAN & SCOTT
I'M GOING TO WANT PICTURES OF THIS.
IT'S LIKE A DREAM COME TRUE, ISN'T IT?

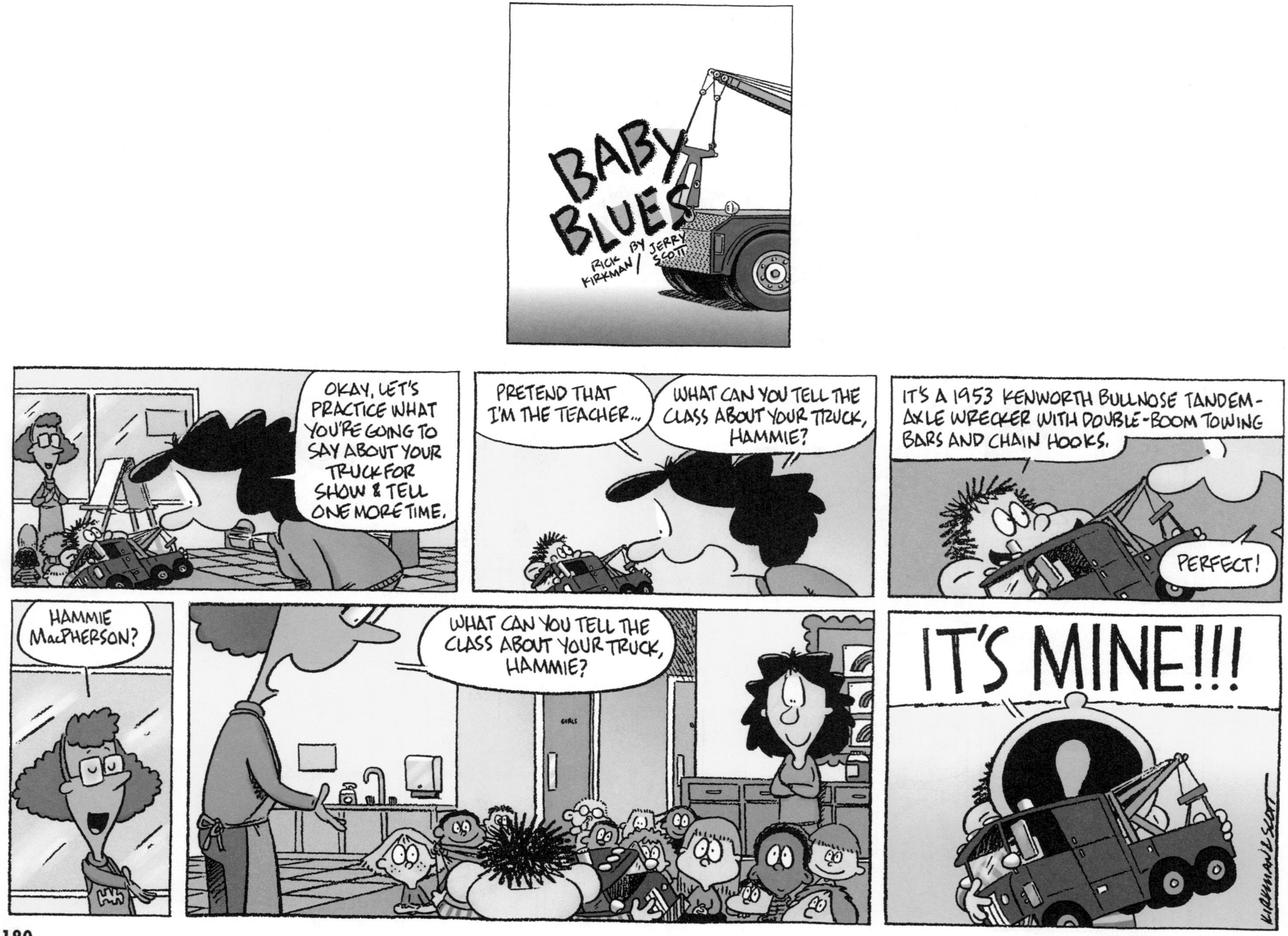
BABY BLUES
BY RICK KIRKMAN / JERRY SCOTT
OKAY, LET'S PRACTICE WHAT YOU'RE GOING TO SAY ABOUT YOUR TRUCK FOR SHOW & TELL ONE MORE TIME.
PRETEND THAT I'M THE TEACHER...
WHAT CAN YOU TELL THE CLASS ABOUT YOUR TRUCK, HAMMIE?
IT'S A 1953 KENWORTH BULLNOSE TANDEM-AXLE WRECKER WITH DOUBLE-BOOM TOWING BARS AND CHAIN HOOKS.
PERFECT!
HAMMIE MacPHERSON?
WHAT CAN YOU TELL THE CLASS ABOUT YOUR TRUCK, HAMMIE?
IT'S MINE!!!

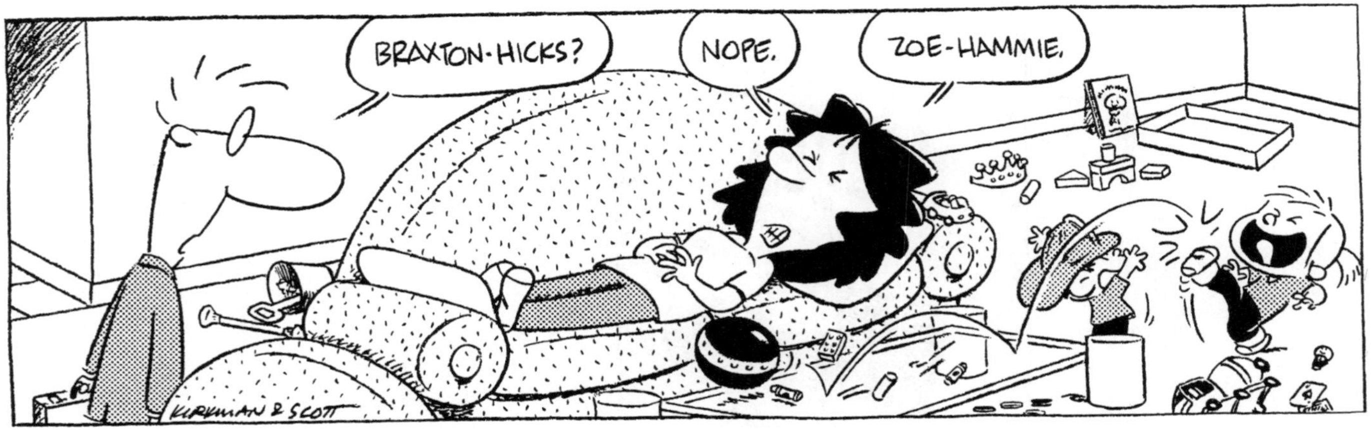
BRAXTON-HICKS?
NOPE.
ZOE-HAMMIE.
KIRKMAN & SCOTT

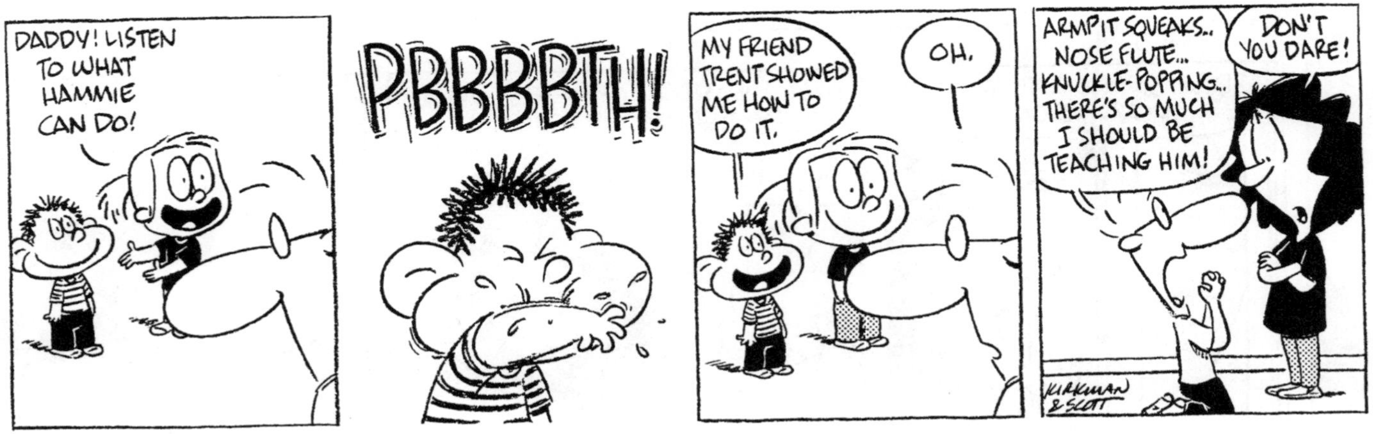
DADDY! LISTEN TO WHAT HAMMIE CAN DO!
PBBBBTH!
MY FRIEND TRENT SHOWED ME HOW TO DO IT.
OH.
ARMPIT SQUEAKS.. NOSE FLUTE... KNUCKLE-POPPING.. THERE'S SO MUCH I SHOULD BE TEACHING HIM!
DON'T YOU DARE!
KIRKMAN & SCOTT

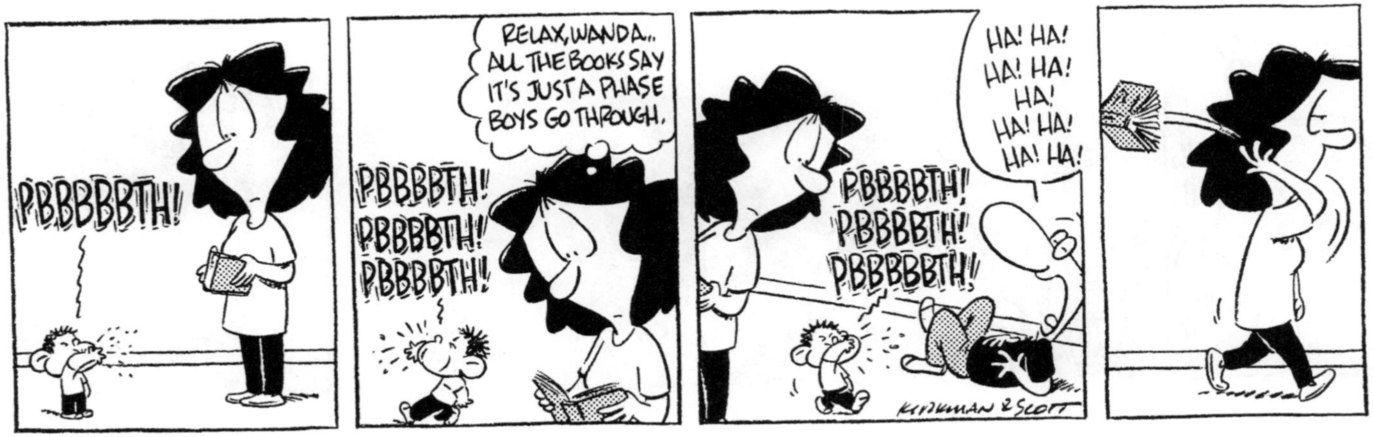
PBBBBBTH!
RELAX, WANDA.. ALL THE BOOKS SAY IT'S JUST A PHASE BOYS GO THROUGH.
PBBBBTH! PBBBBTH! PBBBBTH!
HA! HA! HA! HA! HA! HA! HA! HA! HA!
PBBBBTH! PBBBBTH! PBBBBBTH!
KIRKMAN & SCOTT

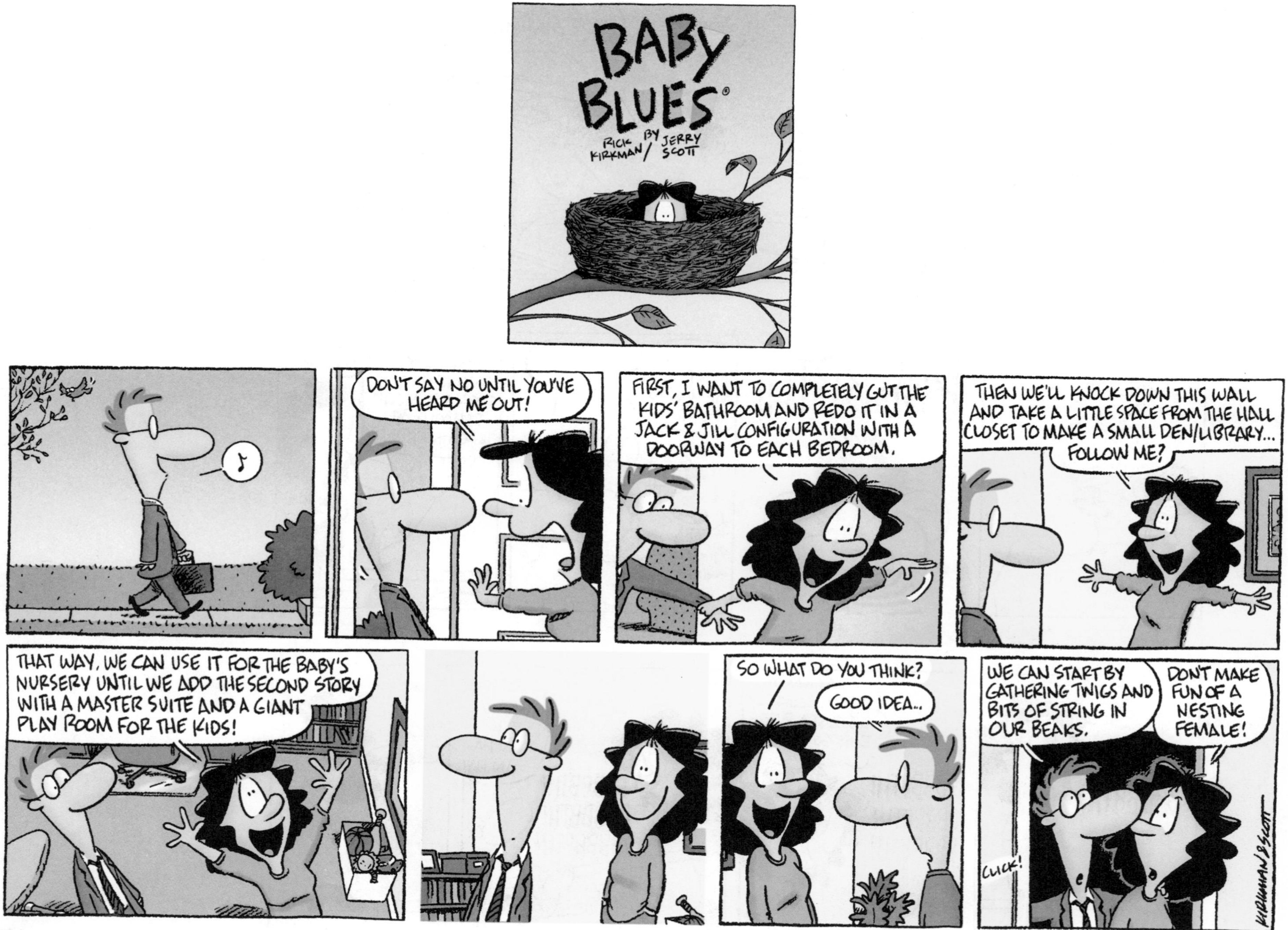
BABY BLUES®
BY RICK KIRKMAN / JERRY SCOTT
DON'T SAY NO UNTIL YOU'VE HEARD ME OUT!
FIRST, I WANT TO COMPLETELY GUT THE KIDS' BATHROOM AND REDO IT IN A JACK & JILL CONFIGURATION WITH A DOORWAY TO EACH BEDROOM.
THEN WE'LL KNOCK DOWN THIS WALL AND TAKE A LITTLE SPACE FROM THE HALL CLOSET TO MAKE A SMALL DEN/LIBRARY...
FOLLOW ME?
THAT WAY, WE CAN USE IT FOR THE BABY'S NURSERY UNTIL WE ADD THE SECOND STORY WITH A MASTER SUITE AND A GIANT PLAY ROOM FOR THE KIDS!
SO WHAT DO YOU THINK?
GOOD IDEA...
WE CAN START BY GATHERING TWIGS AND BITS OF STRING IN OUR BEAKS.
DON'T MAKE FUN OF A NESTING FEMALE!
CLICK!
KIRKMAN & SCOTT

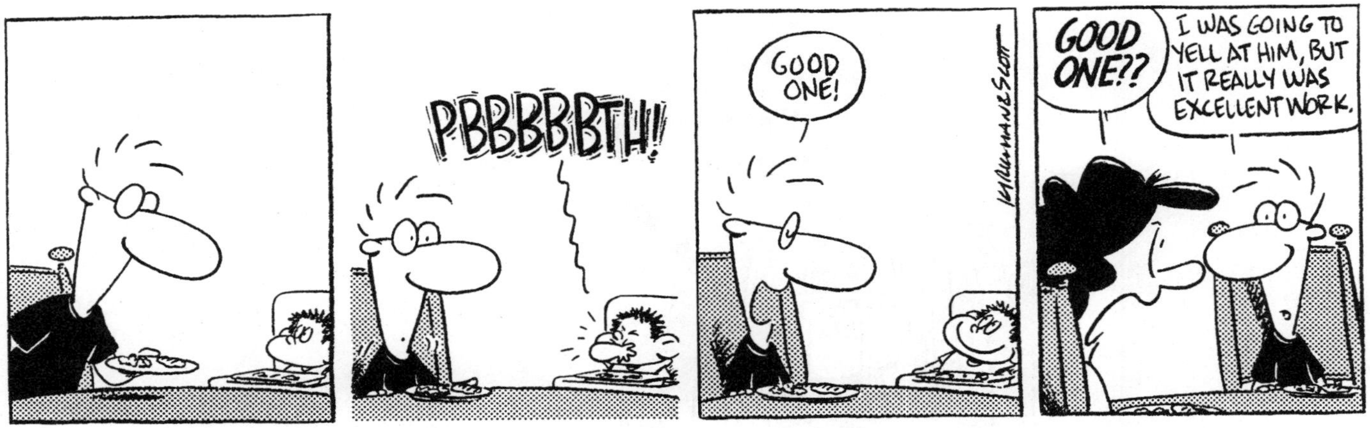
PBBBBBTH!
GOOD ONE!
KIRKMAN & SCOTT
GOOD ONE??
I WAS GOING TO YELL AT HIM, BUT IT REALLY WAS EXCELLENT WORK.

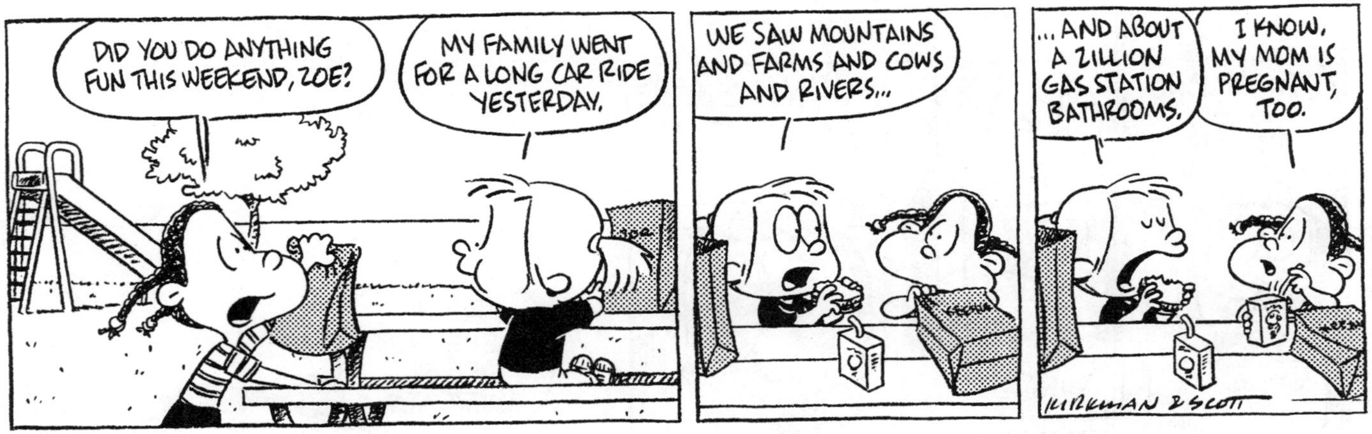
DID YOU DO ANYTHING FUN THIS WEEKEND, ZOE?
MY FAMILY WENT FOR A LONG CAR RIDE YESTERDAY.
WE SAW MOUNTAINS AND FARMS AND COWS AND RIVERS...
...AND ABOUT A ZILLION GAS STATION BATHROOMS.
I KNOW. MY MOM IS PREGNANT, TOO.
KIRKMAN & SCOTT

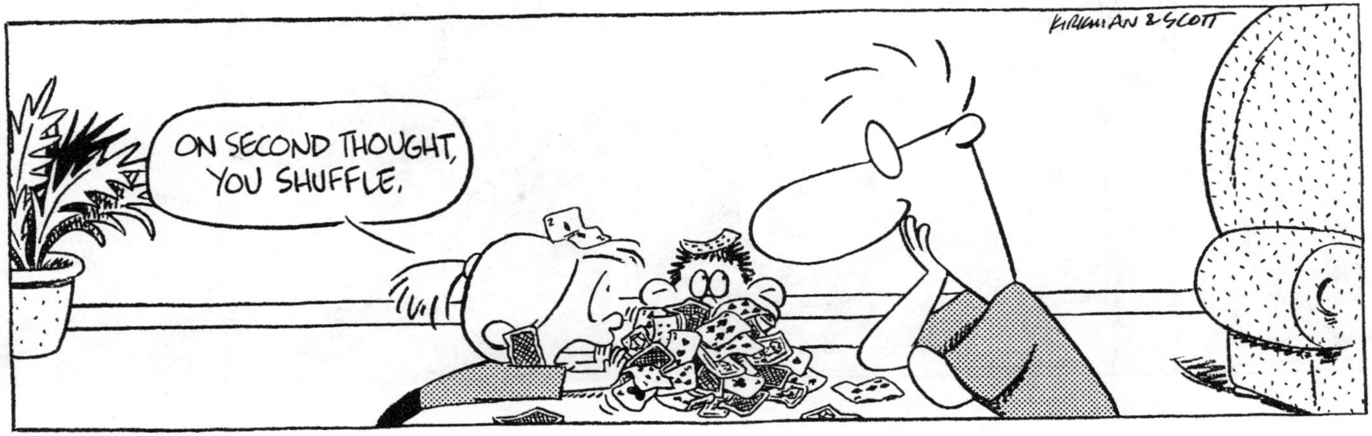
KIRKMAN & SCOTT
ON SECOND THOUGHT, YOU SHUFFLE.

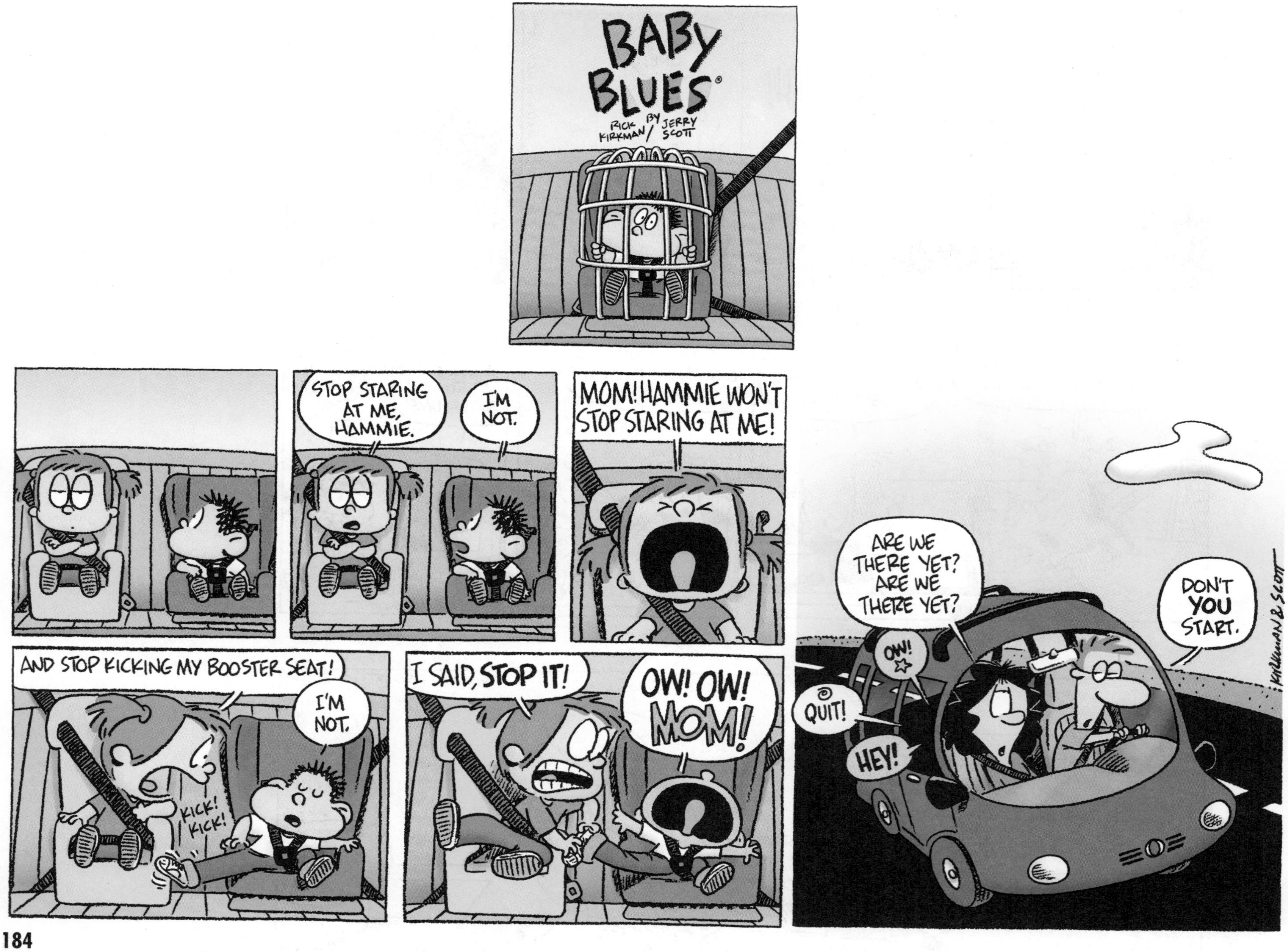
BABY BLUES®
BY RICK KIRKMAN / JERRY SCOTT
STOP STARING AT ME, HAMMIE.
I'M NOT.
MOM! HAMMIE WON'T STOP STARING AT ME!
AND STOP KICKING MY BOOSTER SEAT!
I'M NOT.
KICK! KICK!
I SAID, STOP IT!
OW! OW! MOM!
ARE WE THERE YET? ARE WE THERE YET?
OW!
QUIT!
HEY!
DON'T YOU START.
KIRKMAN & SCOTT

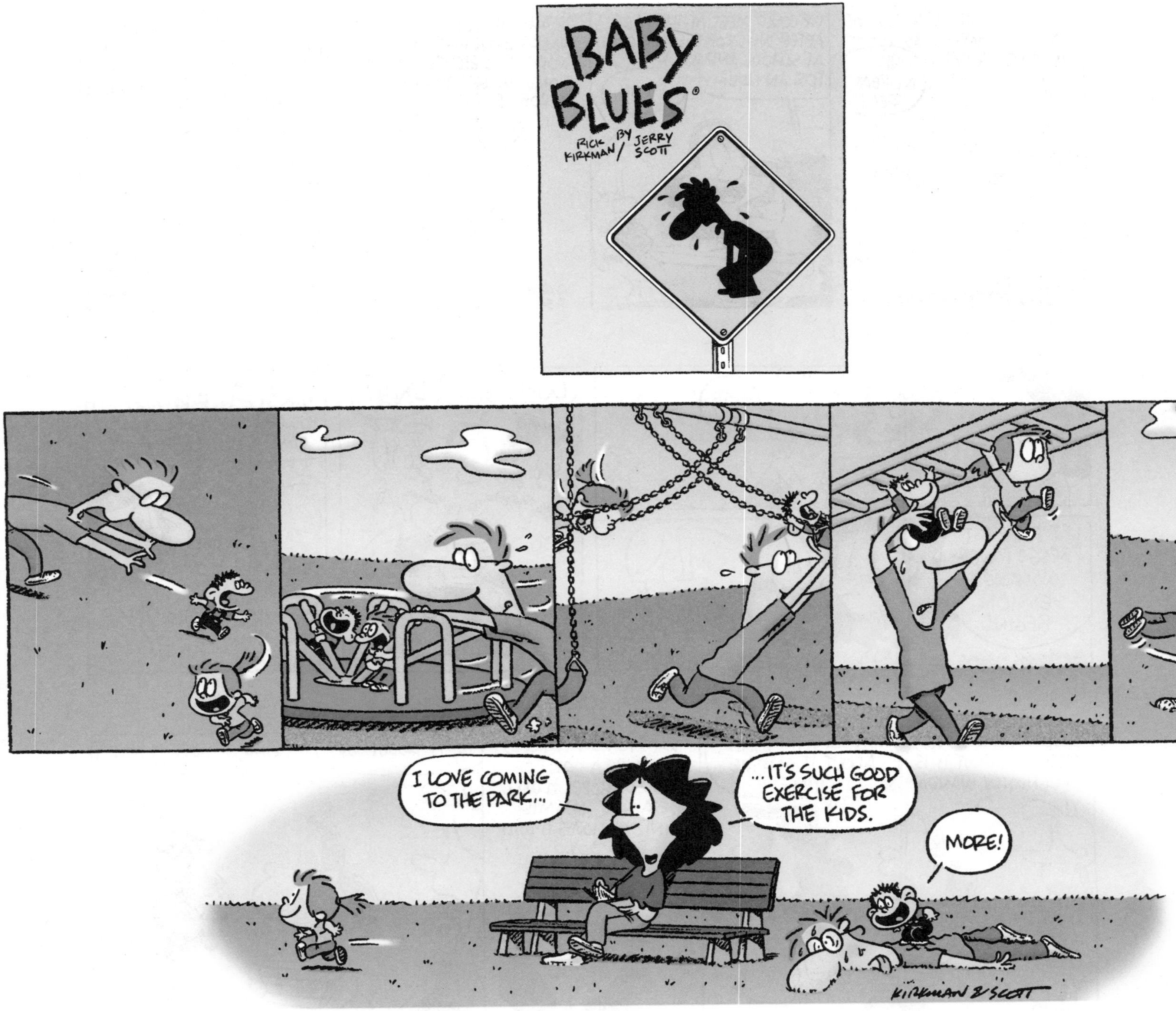
BABY BLUES®
BY RICK KIRKMAN / JERRY SCOTT
I LOVE COMING TO THE PARK...
...IT'S SUCH GOOD EXERCISE FOR THE KIDS.
MORE!
KIRKMAN & SCOTT

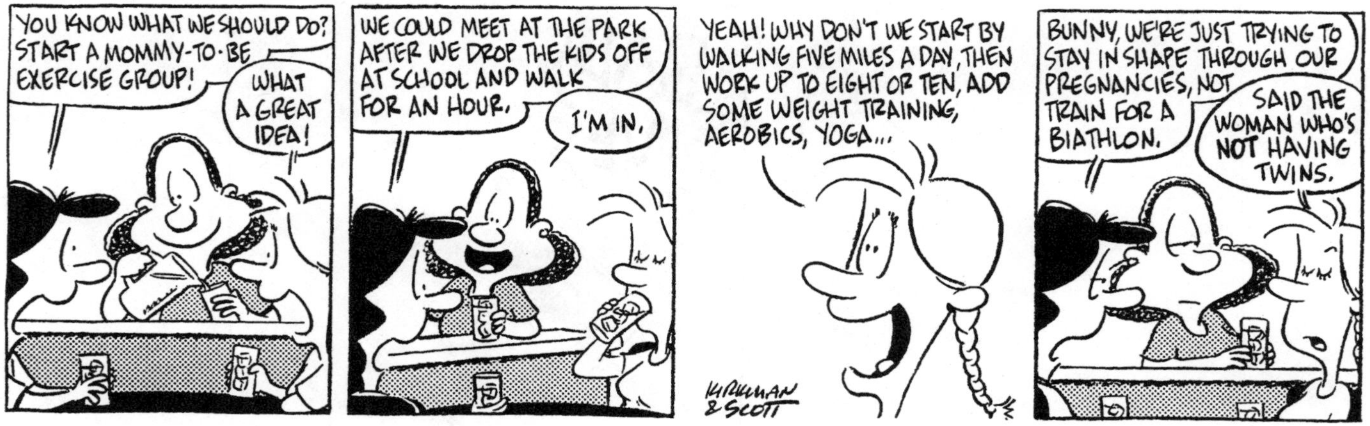
YOU KNOW WHAT WE SHOULD DO? START A MOMMY-TO-BE EXERCISE GROUP!
WHAT A GREAT IDEA!
WE COULD MEET AT THE PARK AFTER WE DROP THE KIDS OFF AT SCHOOL AND WALK FOR AN HOUR.
I'M IN.
YEAH! WHY DON'T WE START BY WALKING FIVE MILES A DAY, THEN WORK UP TO EIGHT OR TEN, ADD SOME WEIGHT TRAINING, AEROBICS, YOGA...
KIRKMAN & SCOTT
BUNNY, WE'RE JUST TRYING TO STAY IN SHAPE THROUGH OUR PREGNANCIES, NOT TRAIN FOR A BIATHLON.
SAID THE WOMAN WHO'S NOT HAVING TWINS.

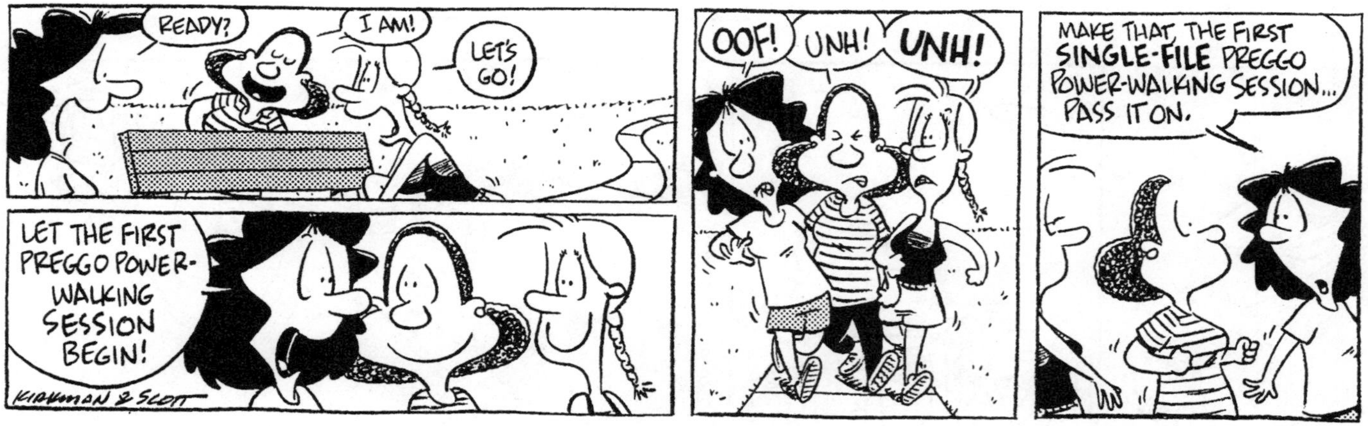
READY?
I AM!
LET'S GO!
LET THE FIRST PREGGO POWER-WALKING SESSION BEGIN!
KIRKMAN & SCOTT
OOF!
UNH!
UNH!
MAKE THAT, THE FIRST SINGLE-FILE PREGGO POWER-WALKING SESSION... PASS IT ON.

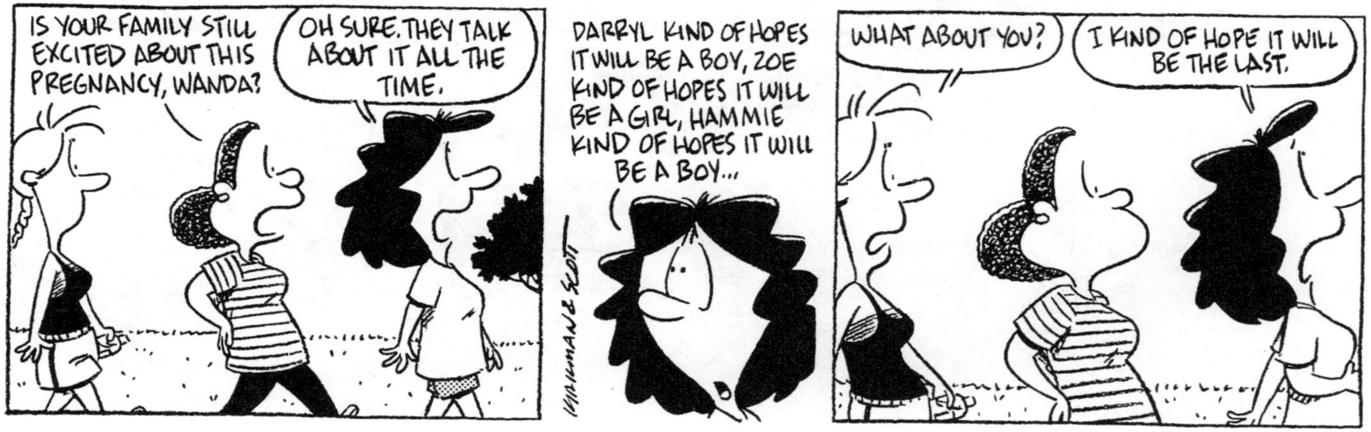
IS YOUR FAMILY STILL EXCITED ABOUT THIS PREGNANCY, WANDA?
OH SURE. THEY TALK ABOUT IT ALL THE TIME.
KIRKMAN & SCOTT
DARRYL KIND OF HOPES IT WILL BE A BOY, ZOE KIND OF HOPES IT WILL BE A GIRL, HAMMIE KIND OF HOPES IT WILL BE A BOY...
WHAT ABOUT YOU?
I KIND OF HOPE IT WILL BE THE LAST.

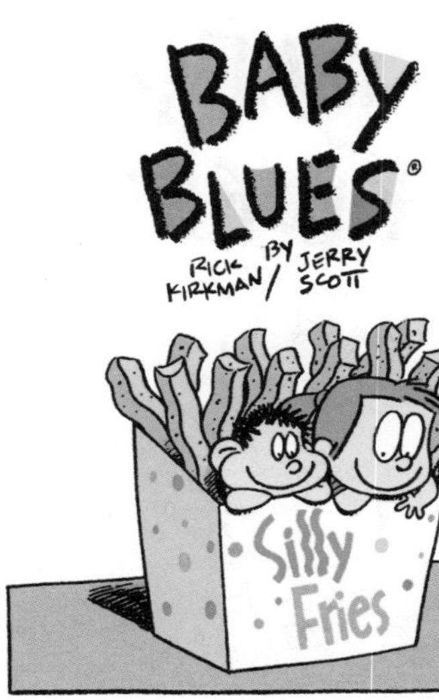
BABY BLUES®
BY RICK KIRKMAN / JERRY SCOTT
Silly Fries

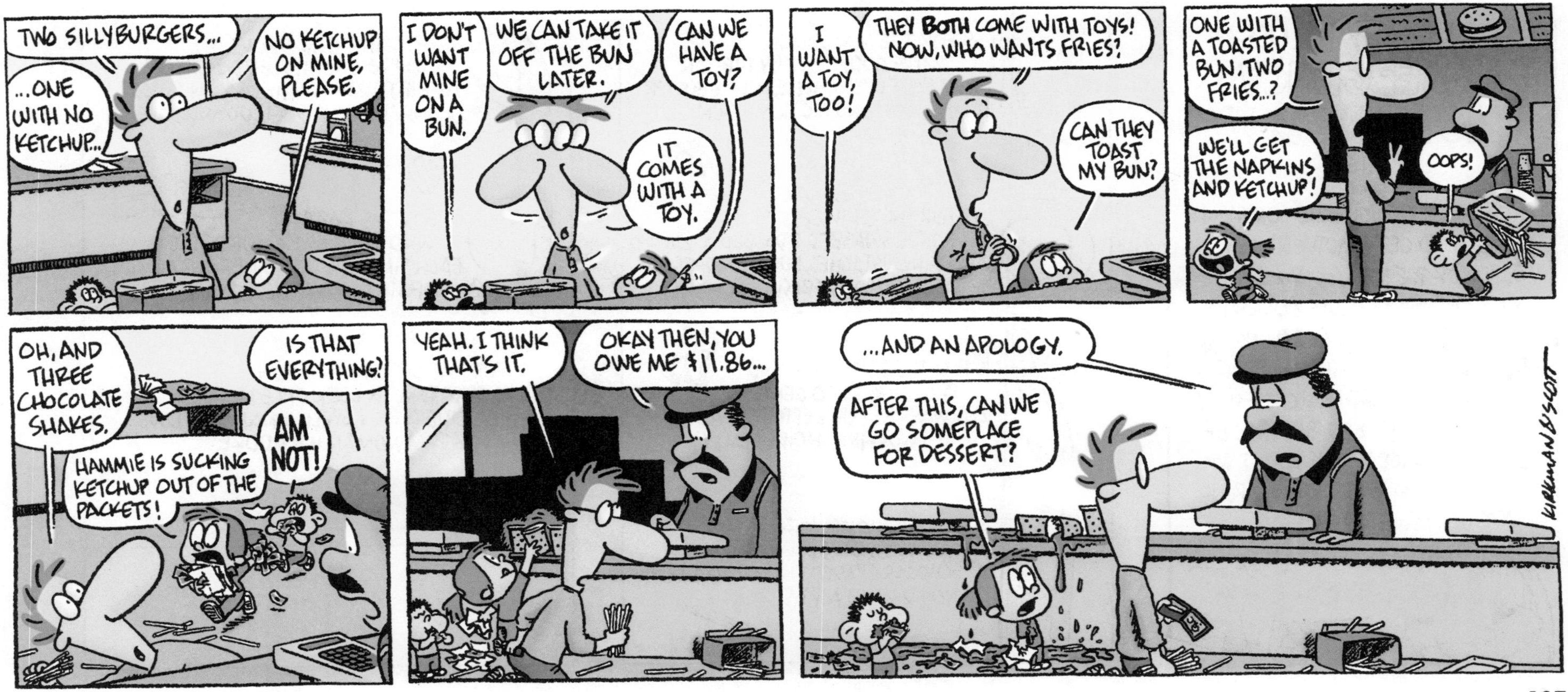
TWO SILLYBURGERS...
...ONE WITH NO KETCHUP...
NO KETCHUP ON MINE, PLEASE.
I DON'T WANT MINE ON A BUN.
WE CAN TAKE IT OFF THE BUN LATER.
CAN WE HAVE A TOY?
IT COMES WITH A TOY.
I WANT A TOY, TOO!
THEY BOTH COME WITH TOYS! NOW, WHO WANTS FRIES?
CAN THEY TOAST MY BUN?
ONE WITH A TOASTED BUN. TWO FRIES...?
WE'LL GET THE NAPKINS AND KETCHUP!
OOPS!
OH, AND THREE CHOCOLATE SHAKES.
IS THAT EVERYTHING?
HAMMIE IS SUCKING KETCHUP OUT OF THE PACKETS!
AM NOT!
YEAH. I THINK THAT'S IT.
OKAY THEN, YOU OWE ME $11.86...
...AND AN APOLOGY.
AFTER THIS, CAN WE GO SOMEPLACE FOR DESSERT?
KIRKMAN & SCOTT

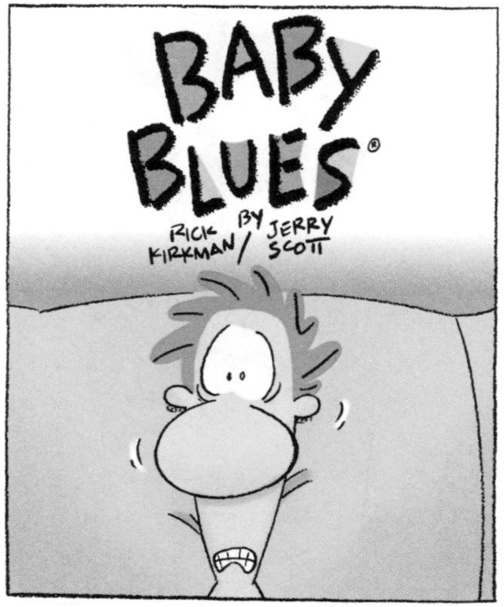
BABY BLUES®
BY RICK KIRKMAN / JERRY SCOTT

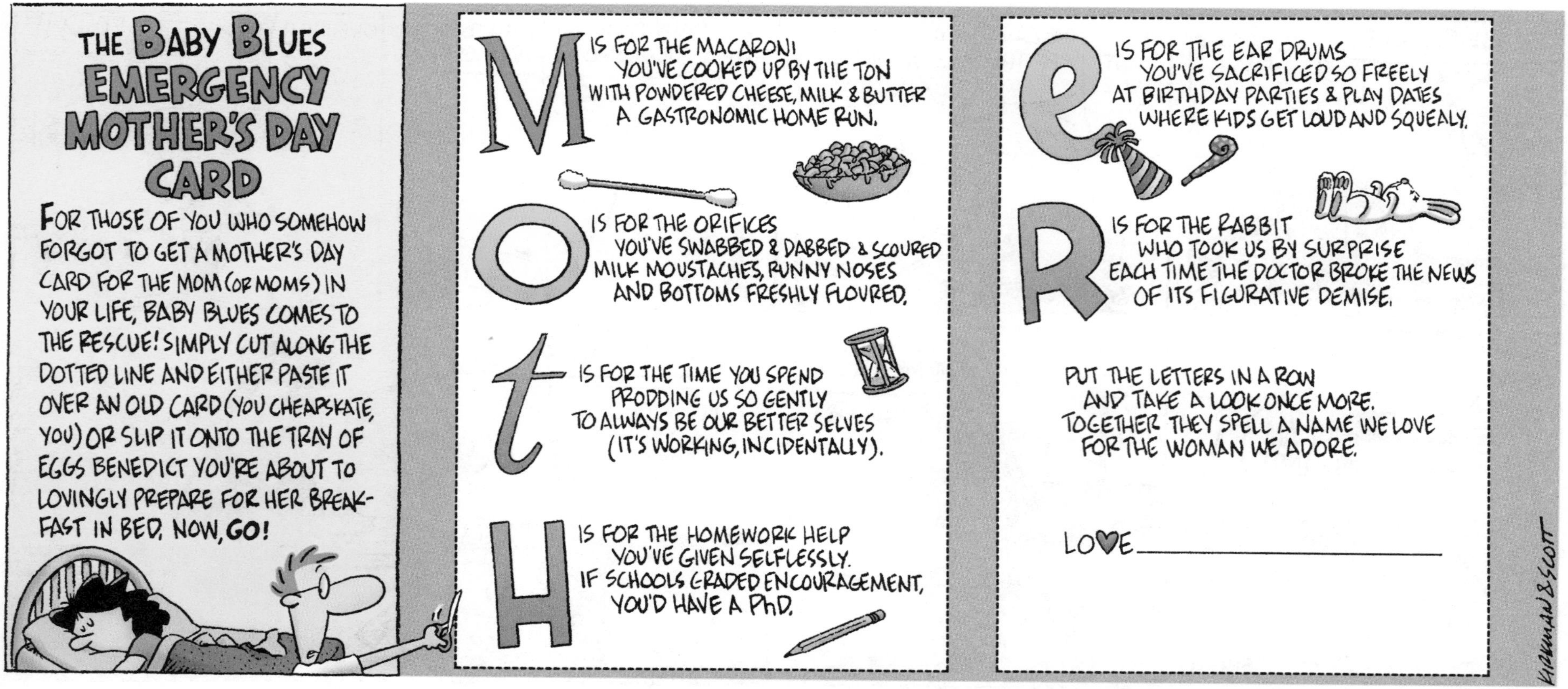
THE BABY BLUES EMERGENCY MOTHER'S DAY CARD
FOR THOSE OF YOU WHO SOMEHOW FORGOT TO GET A MOTHER'S DAY CARD FOR THE MOM (OR MOMS) IN YOUR LIFE, BABY BLUES COMES TO THE RESCUE! SIMPLY CUT ALONG THE DOTTED LINE AND EITHER PASTE IT OVER AN OLD CARD (YOU CHEAPSKATE, YOU) OR SLIP IT ONTO THE TRAY OF EGGS BENEDICT YOU'RE ABOUT TO LOVINGLY PREPARE FOR HER BREAKFAST IN BED. NOW, GO!
M IS FOR THE MACARONI YOU'VE COOKED UP BY THE TON WITH POWDERED CHEESE, MILK & BUTTER A GASTRONOMIC HOME RUN.
O IS FOR THE ORIFICES YOU'VE SWABBED & DABBED & SCOURED MILK MOUSTACHES, RUNNY NOSES AND BOTTOMS FRESHLY FLOURED.
t IS FOR THE TIME YOU SPEND PRODDING US SO GENTLY TO ALWAYS BE OUR BETTER SELVES (IT'S WORKING, INCIDENTALLY).
H IS FOR THE HOMEWORK HELP YOU'VE GIVEN SELFLESSLY. IF SCHOOLS GRADED ENCOURAGEMENT, YOU'D HAVE A PhD.
e IS FOR THE EAR DRUMS YOU'VE SACRIFICED SO FREELY AT BIRTHDAY PARTIES & PLAY DATES WHERE KIDS GET LOUD AND SQUEALY.
R IS FOR THE RABBIT WHO TOOK US BY SURPRISE EACH TIME THE DOCTOR BROKE THE NEWS OF ITS FIGURATIVE DEMISE.
PUT THE LETTERS IN A ROW AND TAKE A LOOK ONCE MORE. TOGETHER THEY SPELL A NAME WE LOVE FOR THE WOMAN WE ADORE.
LOVE ____________
KIRKMAN & SCOTT

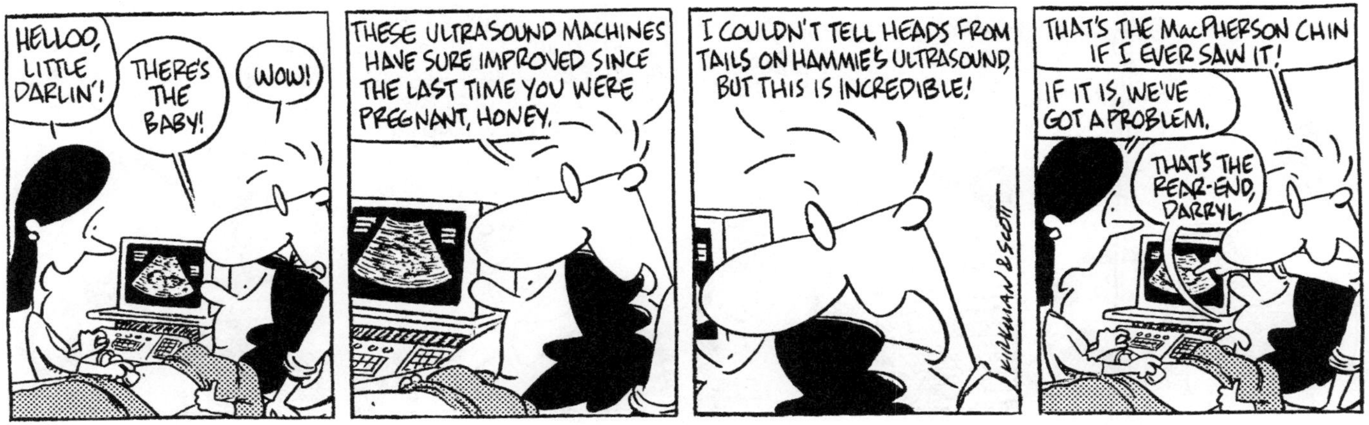
HELLOO, LITTLE DARLIN'!
THERE'S THE BABY!
WOW!
THESE ULTRASOUND MACHINES HAVE SURE IMPROVED SINCE THE LAST TIME YOU WERE PREGNANT, HONEY.
I COULDN'T TELL HEADS FROM TAILS ON HAMMIE'S ULTRASOUND, BUT THIS IS INCREDIBLE!
KIRKMAN & SCOTT
THAT'S THE MacPHERSON CHIN IF I EVER SAW IT!
IF IT IS, WE'VE GOT A PROBLEM.
THAT'S THE REAR-END, DARRYL.

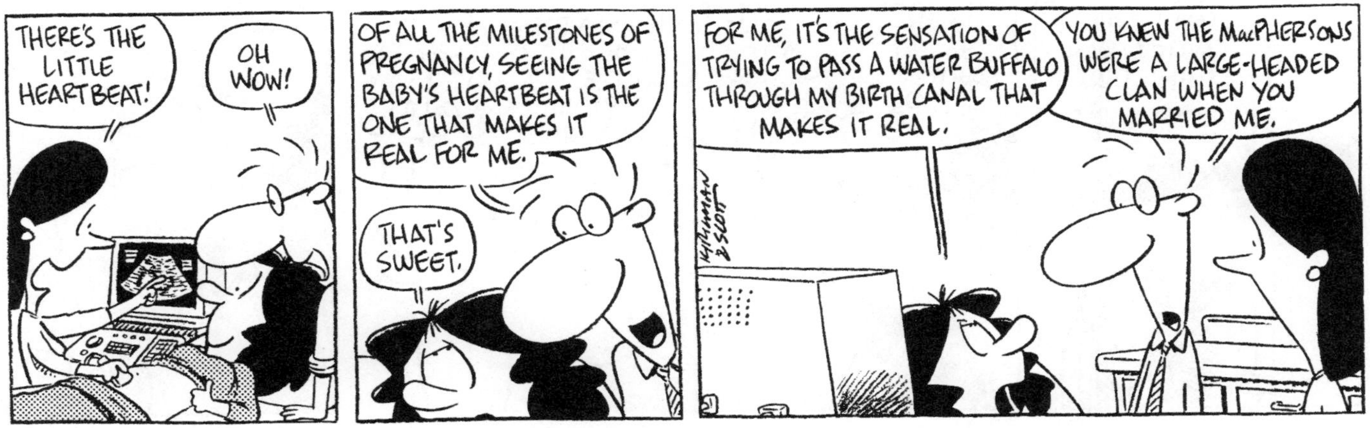
THERE'S THE LITTLE HEARTBEAT!
OH WOW!
OF ALL THE MILESTONES OF PREGNANCY, SEEING THE BABY'S HEARTBEAT IS THE ONE THAT MAKES IT REAL FOR ME.
THAT'S SWEET.
KIRKMAN & SCOTT
FOR ME, IT'S THE SENSATION OF TRYING TO PASS A WATER BUFFALO THROUGH MY BIRTH CANAL THAT MAKES IT REAL.
YOU KNEW THE MacPHERSONS WERE A LARGE-HEADED CLAN WHEN YOU MARRIED ME.

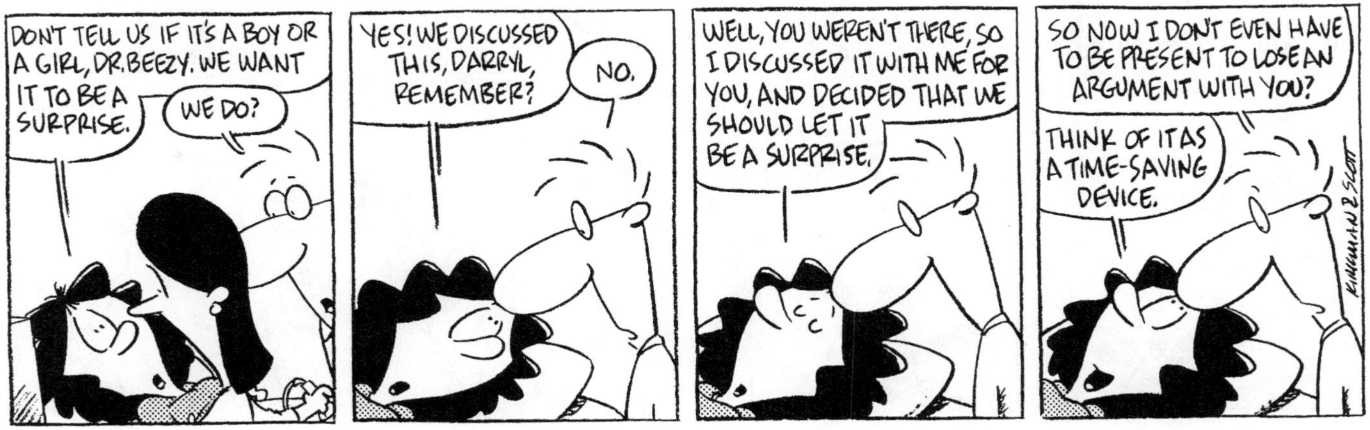
DON'T TELL US IF IT'S A BOY OR A GIRL, DR. BEEZY. WE WANT IT TO BE A SURPRISE.
WE DO?
YES! WE DISCUSSED THIS, DARRYL, REMEMBER?
NO.
WELL, YOU WEREN'T THERE, SO I DISCUSSED IT WITH ME FOR YOU, AND DECIDED THAT WE SHOULD LET IT BE A SURPRISE.
SO NOW I DON'T EVEN HAVE TO BE PRESENT TO LOSE AN ARGUMENT WITH YOU?
THINK OF IT AS A TIME-SAVING DEVICE.
KIRKMAN & SCOTT

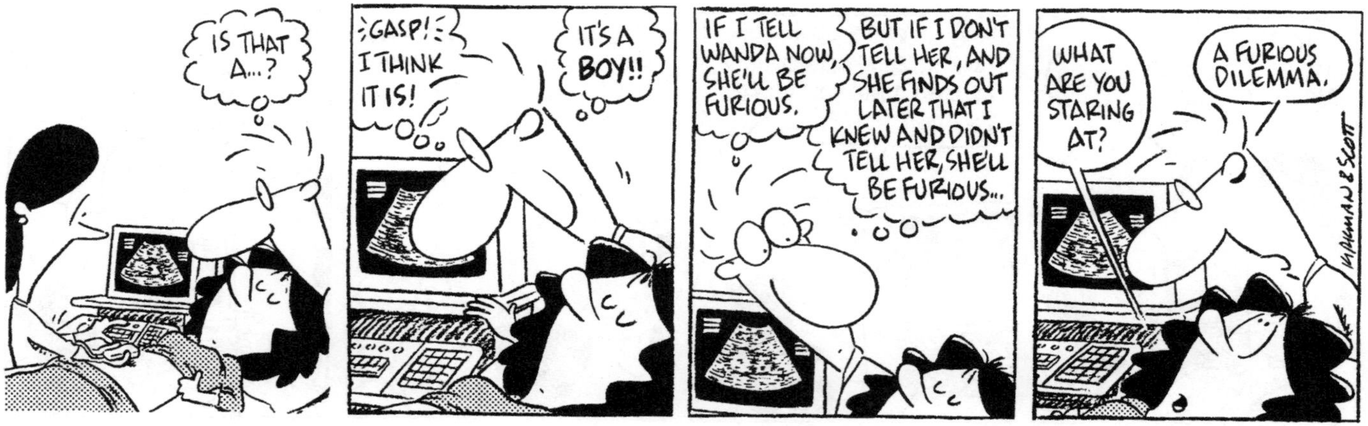
IS THAT A...?
GASP! I THINK IT IS!
IT'S A BOY!!
IF I TELL WANDA NOW, SHE'LL BE FURIOUS.
BUT IF I DON'T TELL HER, AND SHE FINDS OUT LATER THAT I KNEW AND DIDN'T TELL HER, SHE'LL BE FURIOUS...
WHAT ARE YOU STARING AT?
A FURIOUS DILEMMA.
KIRKMAN & SCOTT

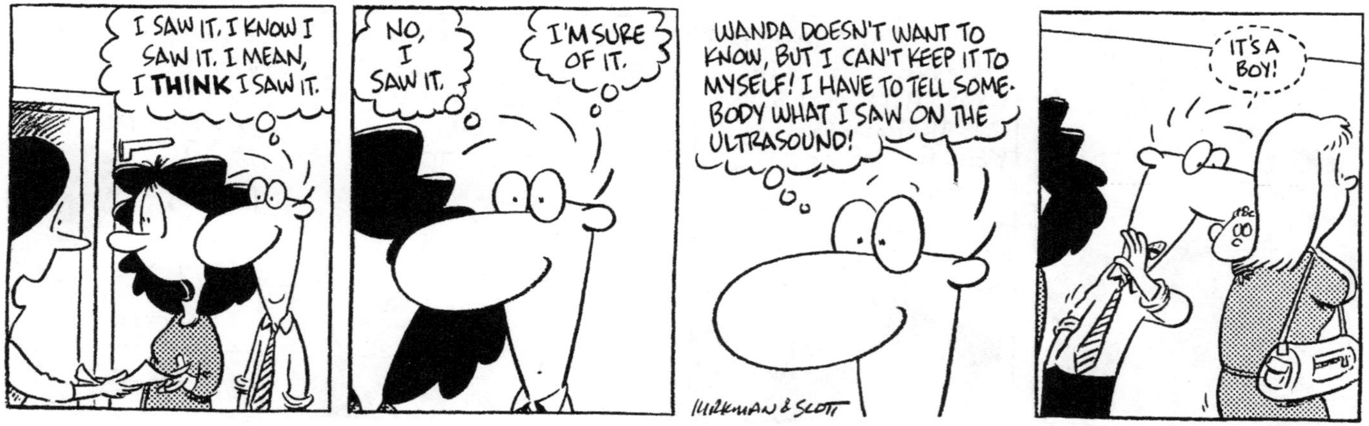
I SAW IT. I KNOW I SAW IT. I MEAN, I THINK I SAW IT.
NO, I SAW IT.
I'M SURE OF IT.
WANDA DOESN'T WANT TO KNOW, BUT I CAN'T KEEP IT TO MYSELF! I HAVE TO TELL SOMEBODY WHAT I SAW ON THE ULTRASOUND!
KIRKMAN & SCOTT
IT'S A BOY!

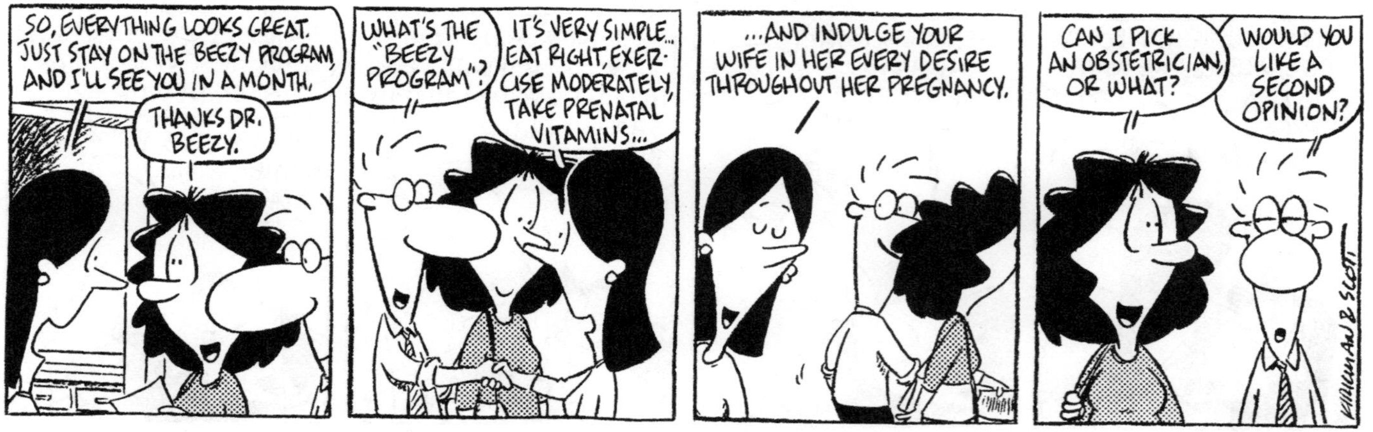
SO, EVERYTHING LOOKS GREAT. JUST STAY ON THE BEEZY PROGRAM AND I'LL SEE YOU IN A MONTH.
THANKS DR. BEEZY.
WHAT'S THE "BEEZY PROGRAM"?
IT'S VERY SIMPLE... EAT RIGHT, EXERCISE MODERATELY, TAKE PRENATAL VITAMINS...
...AND INDULGE YOUR WIFE IN HER EVERY DESIRE THROUGHOUT HER PREGNANCY.
CAN I PICK AN OBSTETRICIAN, OR WHAT?
WOULD YOU LIKE A SECOND OPINION?
KIRKMAN & SCOTT

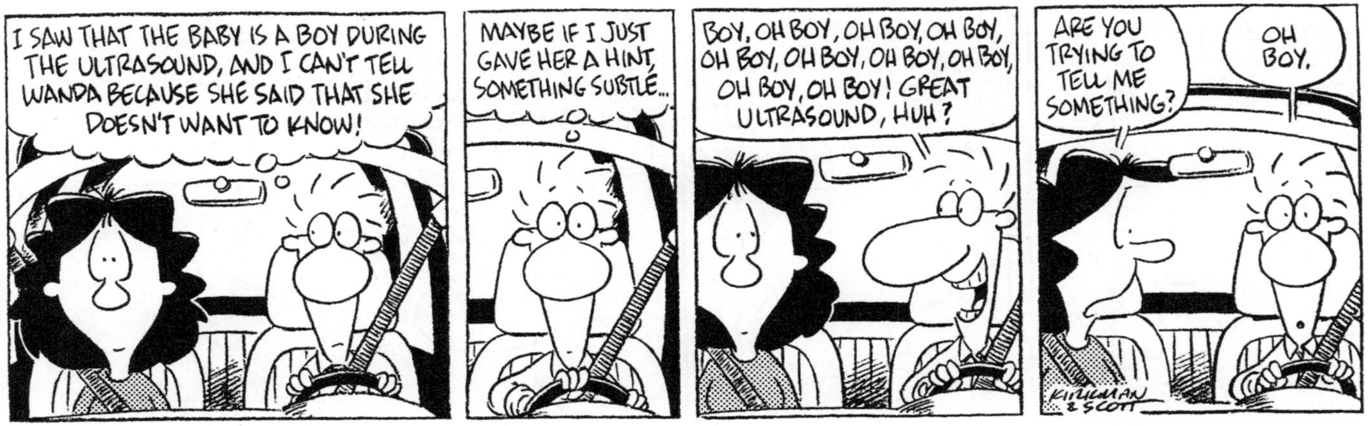
I SAW THAT THE BABY IS A BOY DURING THE ULTRASOUND, AND I CAN'T TELL WANDA BECAUSE SHE SAID THAT SHE DOESN'T WANT TO KNOW!
MAYBE IF I JUST GAVE HER A HINT, SOMETHING SUBTLE...
BOY, OH BOY, OH BOY, OH BOY, OH BOY, OH BOY, OH BOY, OH BOY, OH BOY, OH BOY! GREAT ULTRASOUND, HUH?
ARE YOU TRYING TO TELL ME SOMETHING?
OH BOY.
KIRKMAN & SCOTT

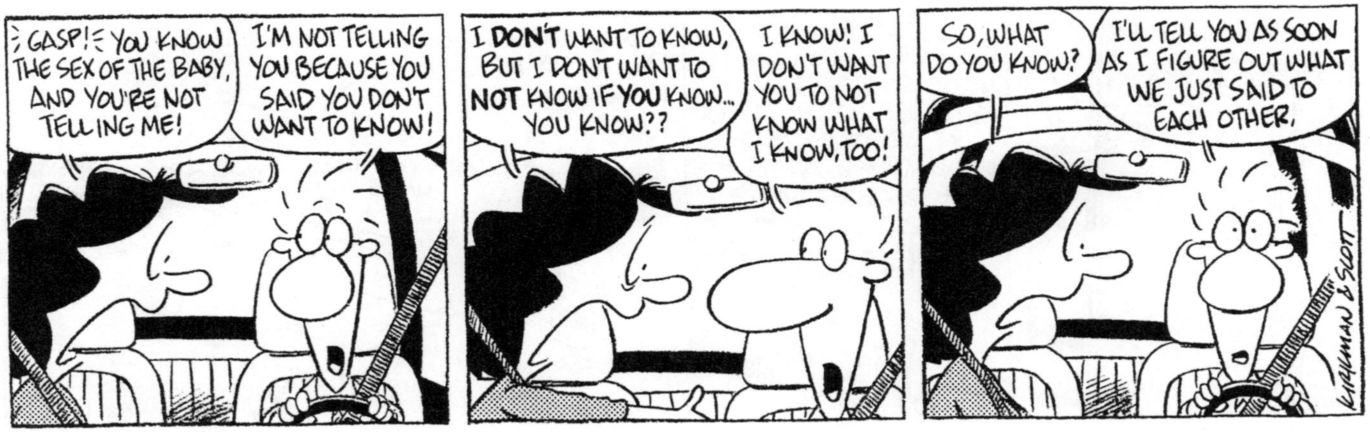
GASP! YOU KNOW THE SEX OF THE BABY, AND YOU'RE NOT TELLING ME!
I'M NOT TELLING YOU BECAUSE YOU SAID YOU DON'T WANT TO KNOW!
I **DON'T** WANT TO KNOW, BUT I DON'T WANT TO **NOT** KNOW IF **YOU** KNOW... YOU KNOW??
I KNOW! I DON'T WANT YOU TO NOT KNOW WHAT I KNOW, TOO!
SO, WHAT DO YOU KNOW?
I'LL TELL YOU AS SOON AS I FIGURE OUT WHAT WE JUST SAID TO EACH OTHER.
KIRKMAN & SCOTT

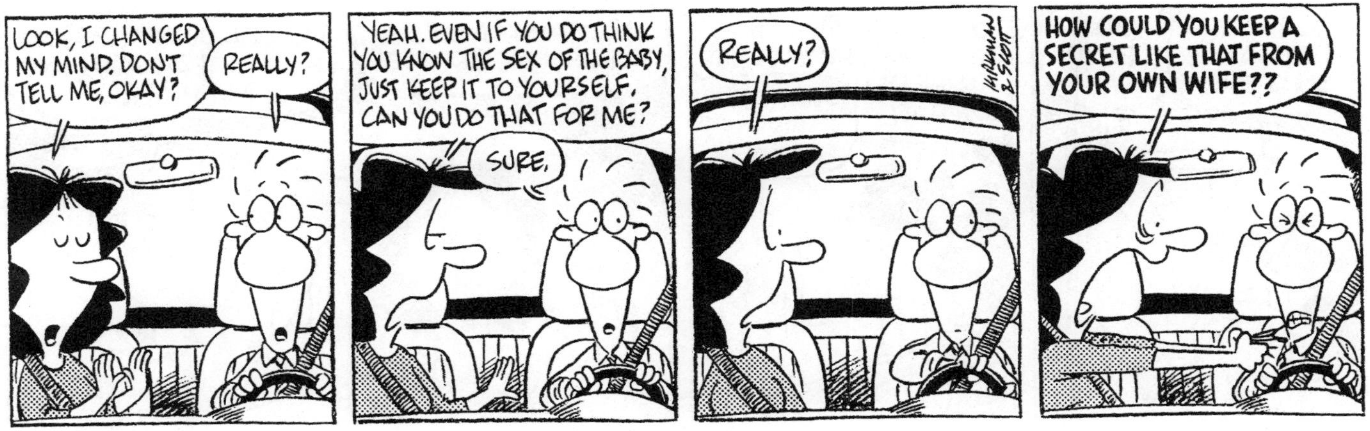
LOOK, I CHANGED MY MIND. DON'T TELL ME, OKAY?
REALLY?
YEAH. EVEN IF YOU DO THINK YOU KNOW THE SEX OF THE BABY, JUST KEEP IT TO YOURSELF. CAN YOU DO THAT FOR ME?
SURE.
REALLY?
KIRKMAN & SCOTT
HOW COULD YOU KEEP A SECRET LIKE THAT FROM YOUR OWN WIFE??

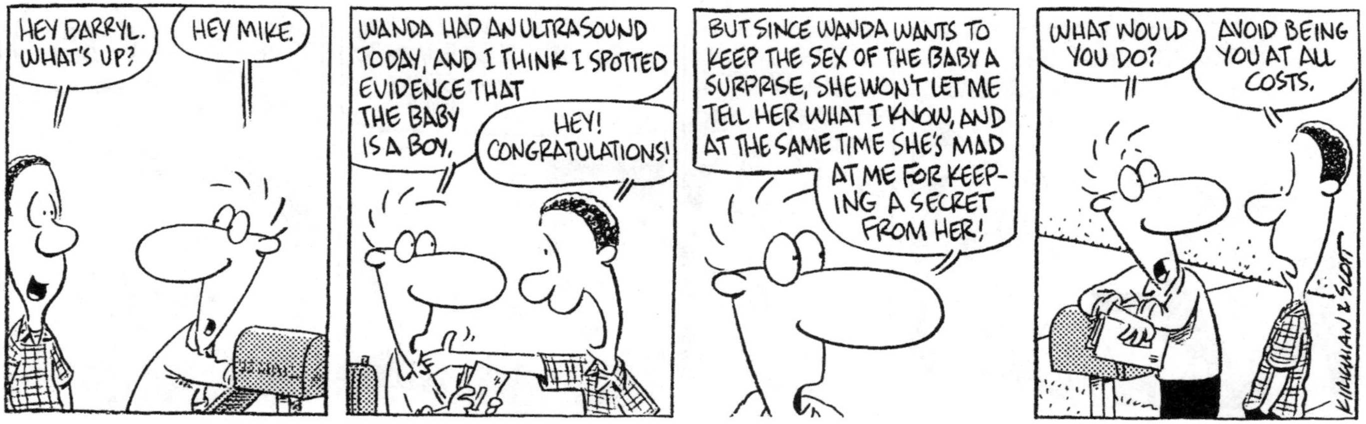
HEY DARRYL. WHAT'S UP?
HEY MIKE.
WANDA HAD AN ULTRASOUND TODAY, AND I THINK I SPOTTED EVIDENCE THAT THE BABY IS A BOY.
HEY! CONGRATULATIONS!
BUT SINCE WANDA WANTS TO KEEP THE SEX OF THE BABY A SURPRISE, SHE WON'T LET ME TELL HER WHAT I KNOW, AND AT THE SAME TIME SHE'S MAD AT ME FOR KEEPING A SECRET FROM HER!
WHAT WOULD YOU DO?
AVOID BEING YOU AT ALL COSTS.
KIRKMAN & SCOTT

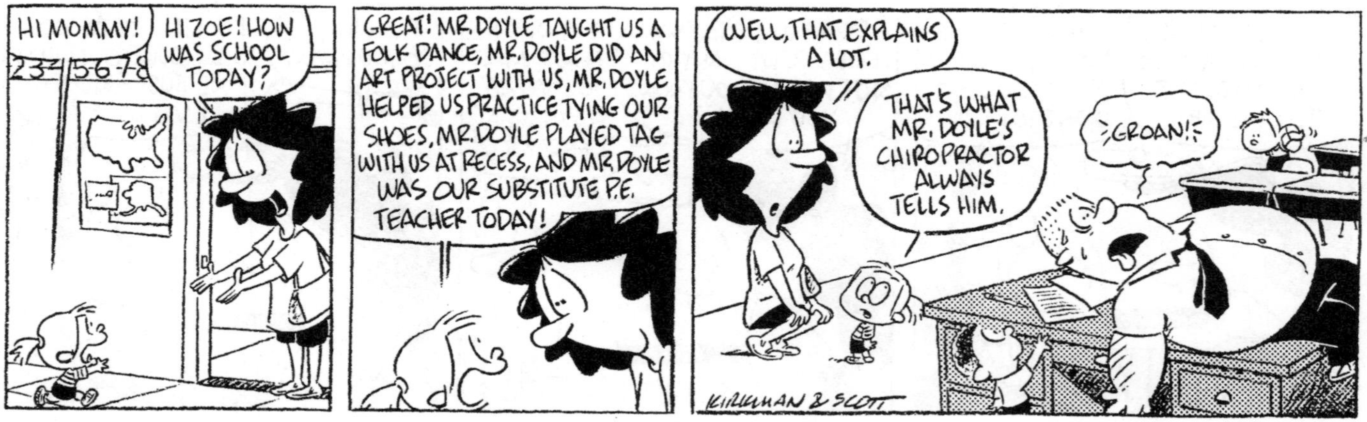
HI MOMMY!
HI ZOE! HOW WAS SCHOOL TODAY?
GREAT! MR. DOYLE TAUGHT US A FOLK DANCE, MR. DOYLE DID AN ART PROJECT WITH US, MR. DOYLE HELPED US PRACTICE TYING OUR SHOES, MR. DOYLE PLAYED TAG WITH US AT RECESS, AND MR. DOYLE WAS OUR SUBSTITUTE P.E. TEACHER TODAY!
WELL, THAT EXPLAINS A LOT.
THAT'S WHAT MR. DOYLE'S CHIROPRACTOR ALWAYS TELLS HIM.
GROAN!
KIRKMAN & SCOTT

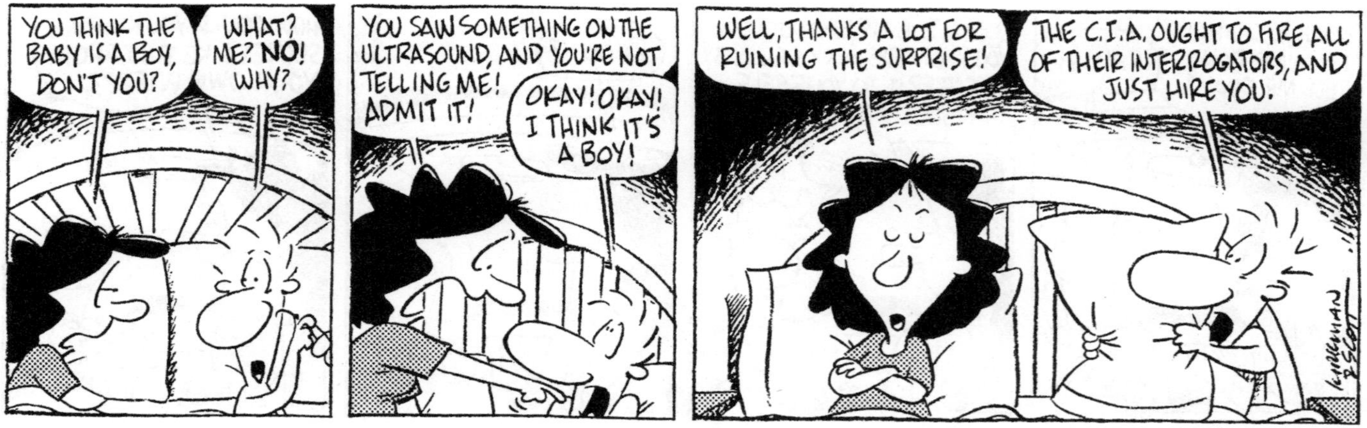
YOU THINK THE BABY IS A BOY, DON'T YOU?
WHAT? ME? NO! WHY?
YOU SAW SOMETHING ON THE ULTRASOUND, AND YOU'RE NOT TELLING ME! ADMIT IT!
OKAY! OKAY! I THINK IT'S A BOY!
WELL, THANKS A LOT FOR RUINING THE SURPRISE!
THE C.I.A. OUGHT TO FIRE ALL OF THEIR INTERROGATORS, AND JUST HIRE YOU.
KIRKMAN & SCOTT

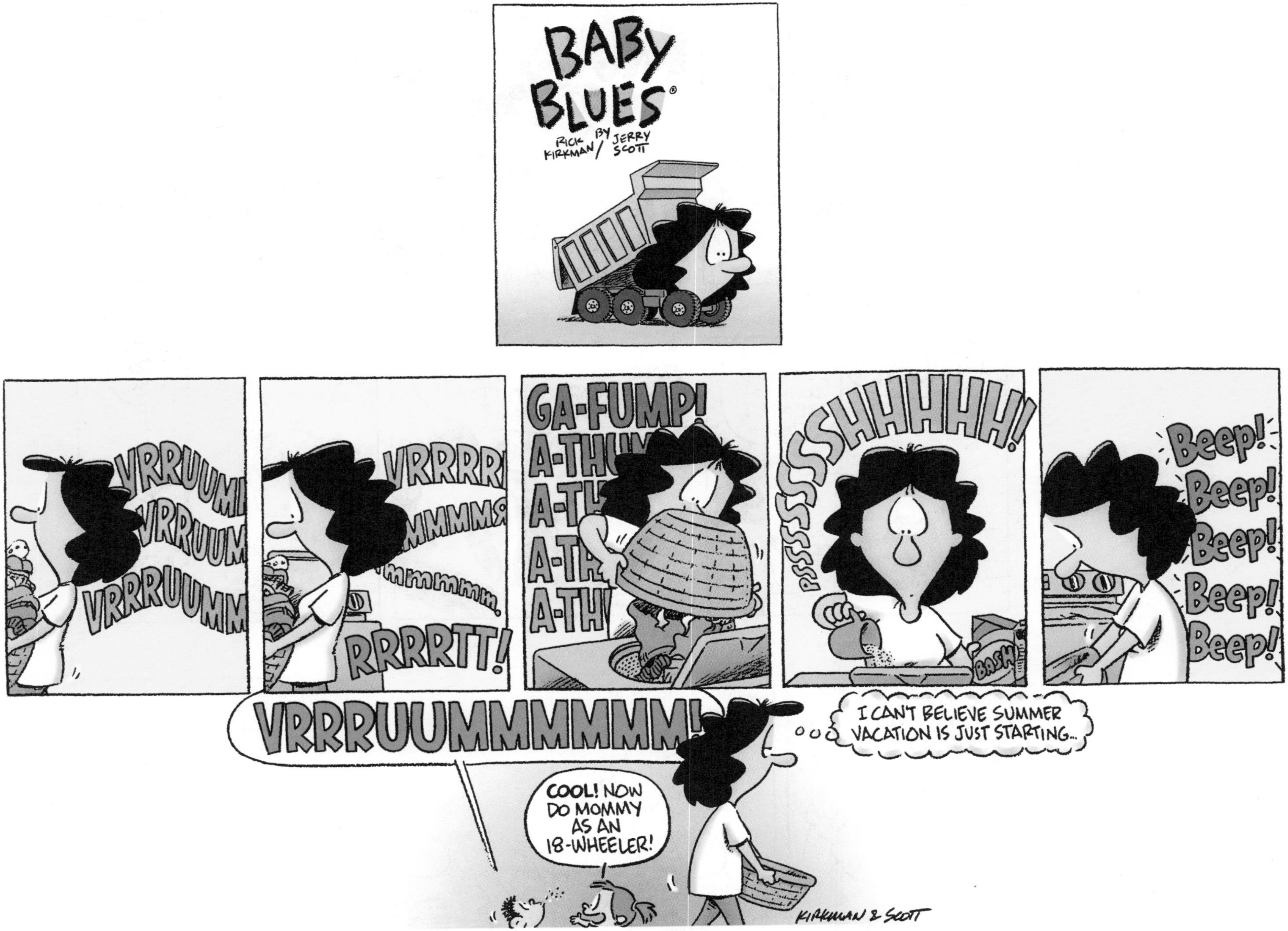
BABY BLUES®
BY RICK KIRKMAN / JERRY SCOTT
VRRUUM! VRRUUM VRRRUUMM
VRRRRR MMMMR mmmmmm. RRRRTT!
GA-FUMP! A-TH A-TH A-TH A-TH
PSSSSSSSHHHHHH!
BASH
Beep! Beep! Beep! Beep! Beep!
VRRRUUMMMMMM!
I CAN'T BELIEVE SUMMER VACATION IS JUST STARTING...
COOL! NOW DO MOMMY AS AN 18-WHEELER!
KIRKMAN & SCOTT

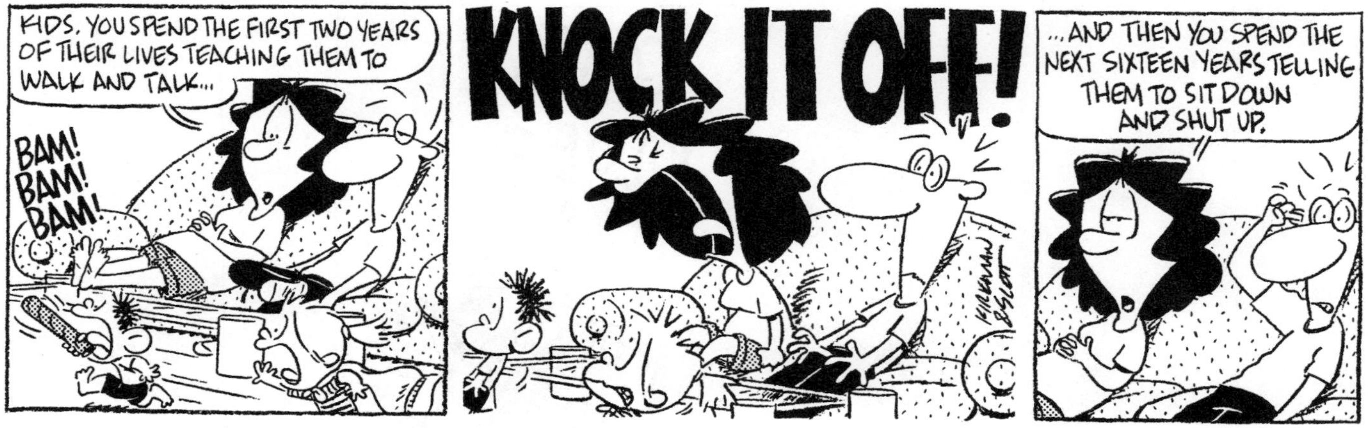
KIDS. YOU SPEND THE FIRST TWO YEARS OF THEIR LIVES TEACHING THEM TO WALK AND TALK...
BAM! BAM! BAM!
KNOCK IT OFF!
KIRKMAN & SCOTT
...AND THEN YOU SPEND THE NEXT SIXTEEN YEARS TELLING THEM TO SIT DOWN AND SHUT UP.

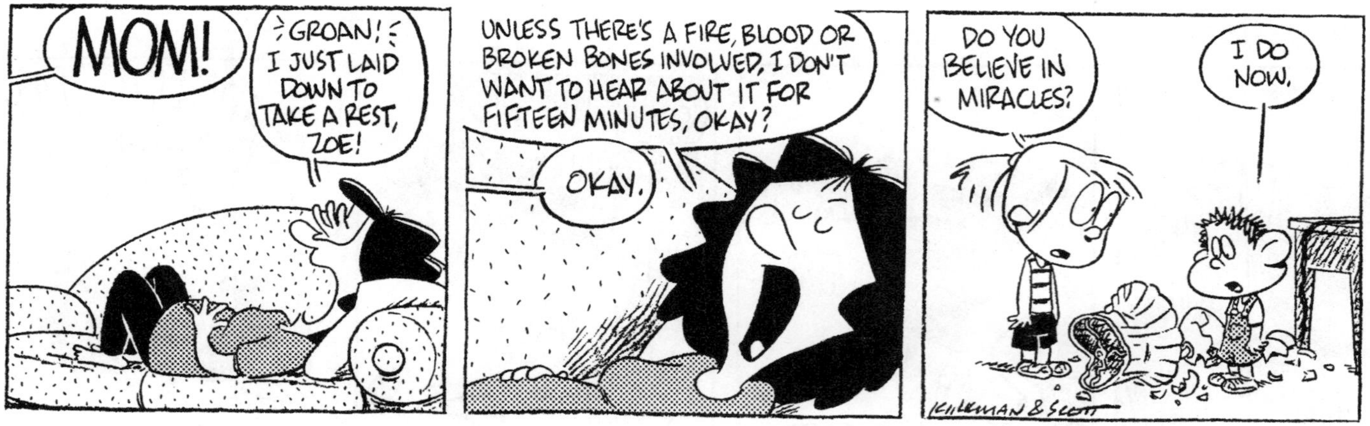
MOM!
GROAN! I JUST LAID DOWN TO TAKE A REST, ZOE!
UNLESS THERE'S A FIRE, BLOOD OR BROKEN BONES INVOLVED, I DON'T WANT TO HEAR ABOUT IT FOR FIFTEEN MINUTES, OKAY?
OKAY.
DO YOU BELIEVE IN MIRACLES?
I DO NOW.
KIRKMAN & SCOTT

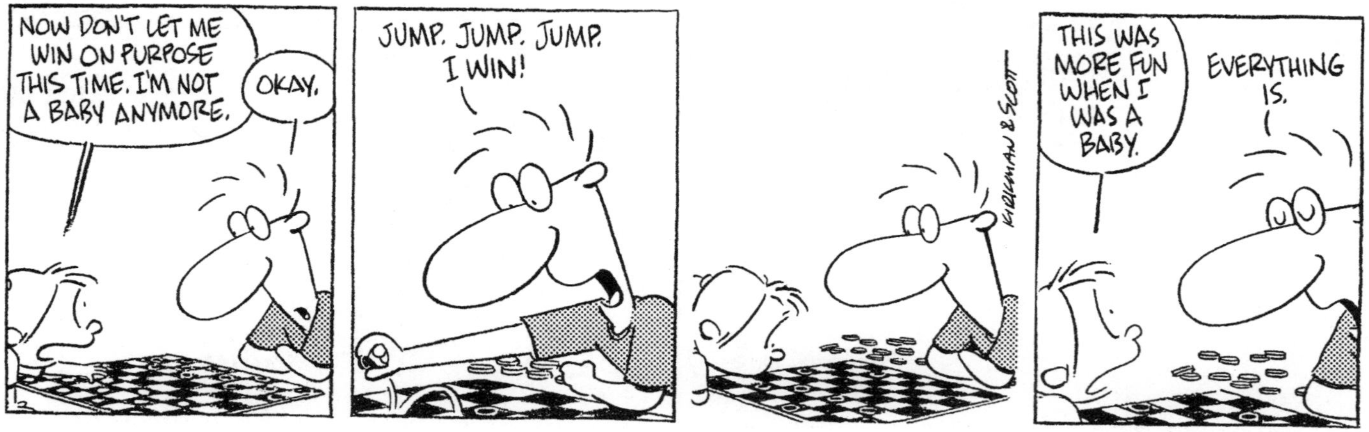
NOW DON'T LET ME WIN ON PURPOSE THIS TIME. I'M NOT A BABY ANYMORE.
OKAY.
JUMP. JUMP. JUMP. I WIN!
KIRKMAN & SCOTT
THIS WAS MORE FUN WHEN I WAS A BABY.
EVERYTHING IS.

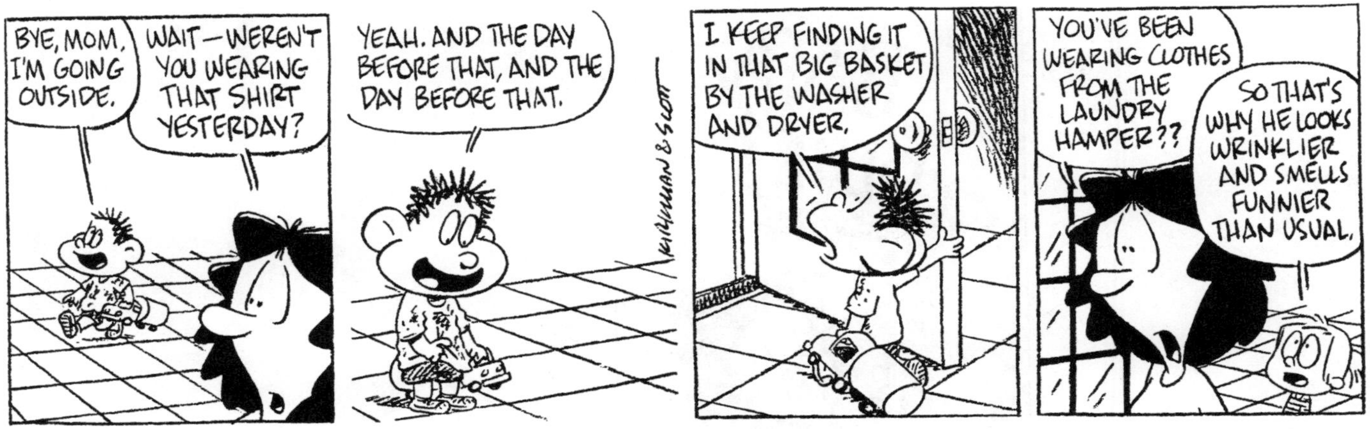
BYE, MOM, I'M GOING OUTSIDE.
WAIT—WEREN'T YOU WEARING THAT SHIRT YESTERDAY?
YEAH. AND THE DAY BEFORE THAT, AND THE DAY BEFORE THAT.
KIRKMAN & SCOTT
I KEEP FINDING IT IN THAT BIG BASKET BY THE WASHER AND DRYER.
YOU'VE BEEN WEARING CLOTHES FROM THE LAUNDRY HAMPER??
SO THAT'S WHY HE LOOKS WRINKLIER AND SMELLS FUNNIER THAN USUAL.

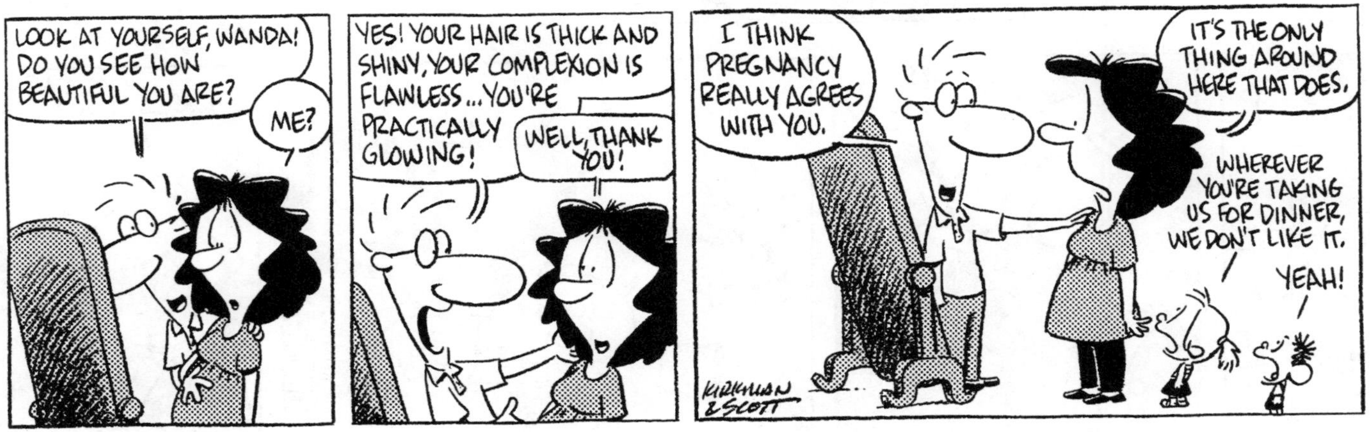
LOOK AT YOURSELF, WANDA! DO YOU SEE HOW BEAUTIFUL YOU ARE?
ME?
YES! YOUR HAIR IS THICK AND SHINY, YOUR COMPLEXION IS FLAWLESS... YOU'RE PRACTICALLY GLOWING!
WELL, THANK YOU!
I THINK PREGNANCY REALLY AGREES WITH YOU.
IT'S THE ONLY THING AROUND HERE THAT DOES.
WHEREVER YOU'RE TAKING US FOR DINNER, WE DON'T LIKE IT.
YEAH!
KIRKMAN & SCOTT

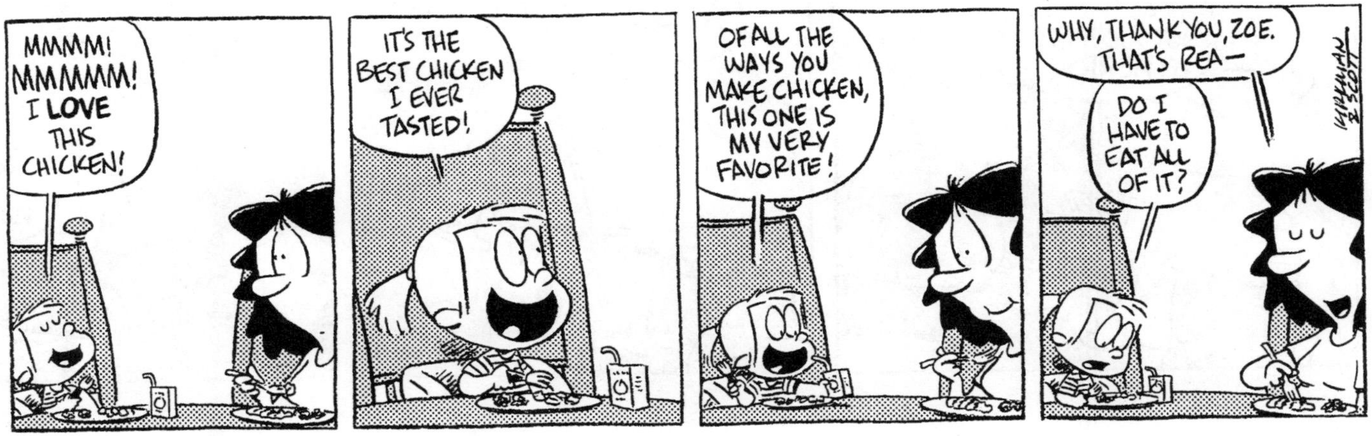
MMMM! MMMMM! I **LOVE** THIS CHICKEN!
IT'S THE BEST CHICKEN I EVER TASTED!
OF ALL THE WAYS YOU MAKE CHICKEN, THIS ONE IS MY VERY FAVORITE!
WHY, THANK YOU, ZOE. THAT'S REA—
DO I HAVE TO EAT ALL OF IT?
KIRKMAN & SCOTT

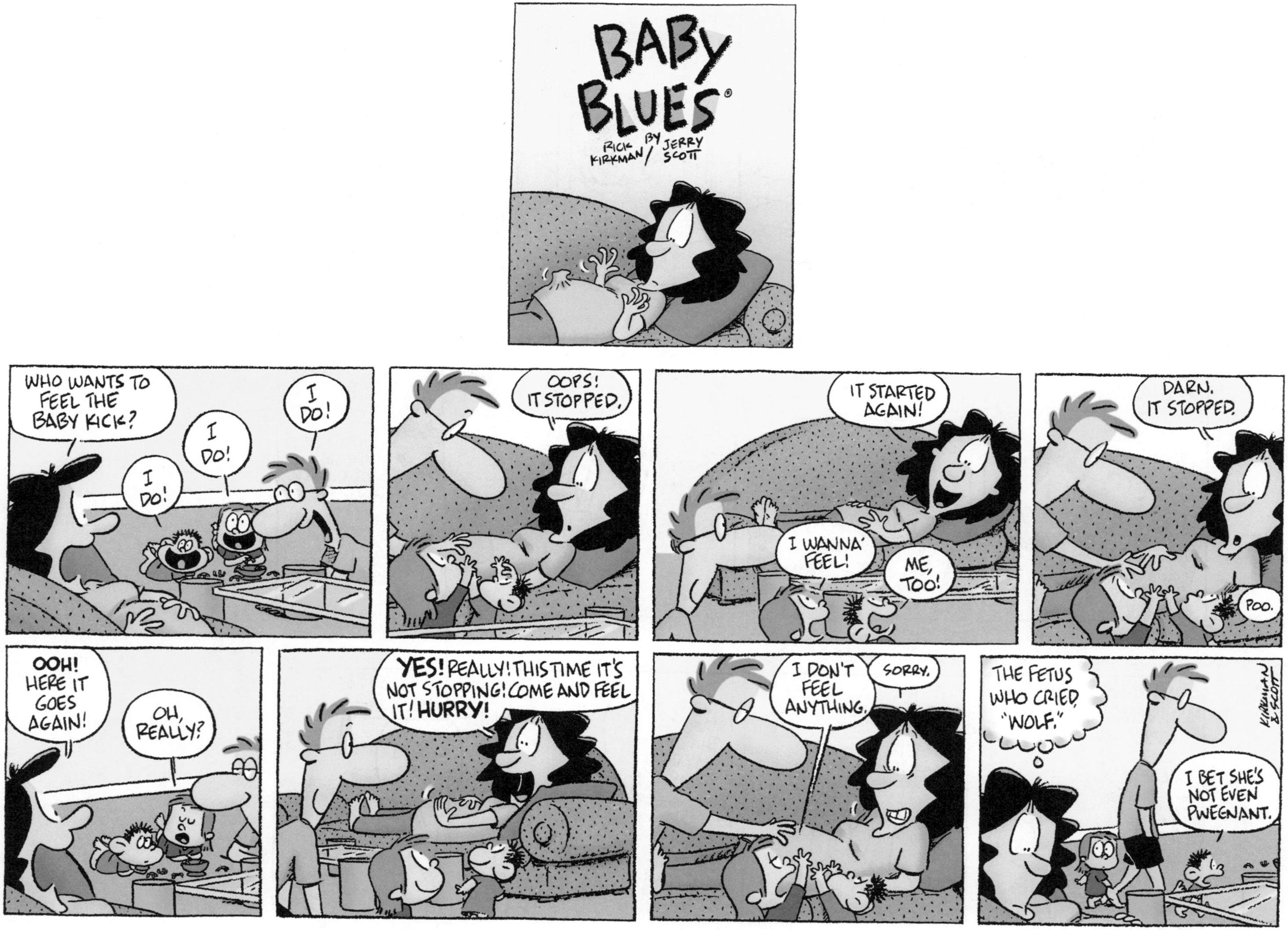
BABY BLUES®
RICK KIRKMAN / BY JERRY SCOTT
WHO WANTS TO FEEL THE BABY KICK?
I DO!
I DO!
I DO!
OOPS! IT STOPPED.
IT STARTED AGAIN!
I WANNA' FEEL!
ME, TOO!
DARN. IT STOPPED.
POO.
OOH! HERE IT GOES AGAIN!
OH, REALLY?
YES! REALLY! THIS TIME IT'S NOT STOPPING! COME AND FEEL IT! HURRY!
I DON'T FEEL ANYTHING.
SORRY.
THE FETUS WHO CRIED "WOLF."
I BET SHE'S NOT EVEN PWEGNANT.
KIRKMAN & SCOTT

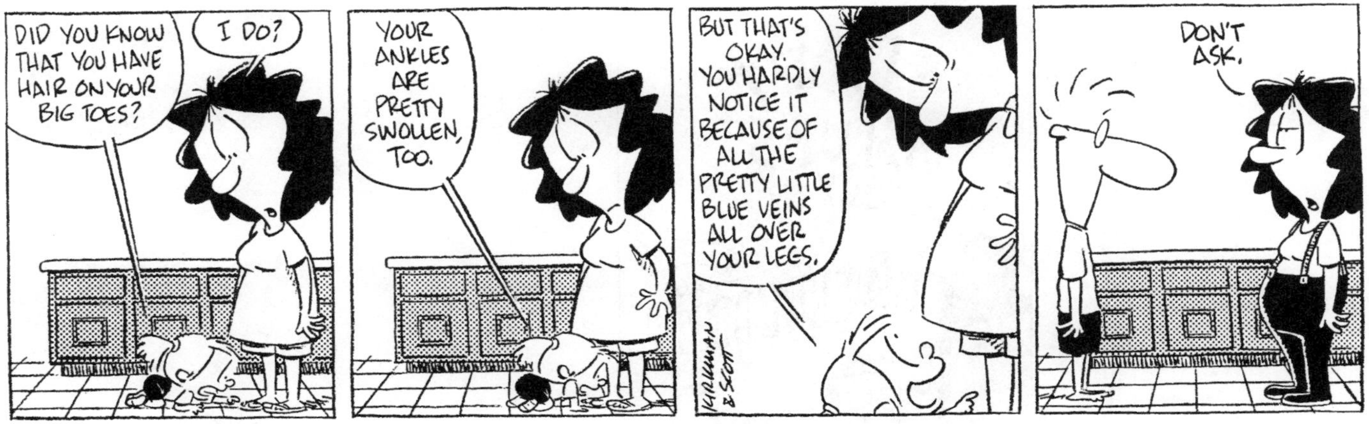
DID YOU KNOW THAT YOU HAVE HAIR ON YOUR BIG TOES?
I DO?
YOUR ANKLES ARE PRETTY SWOLLEN, TOO.
BUT THAT'S OKAY. YOU HARDLY NOTICE IT BECAUSE OF ALL THE PRETTY LITTLE BLUE VEINS ALL OVER YOUR LEGS.
DON'T ASK.

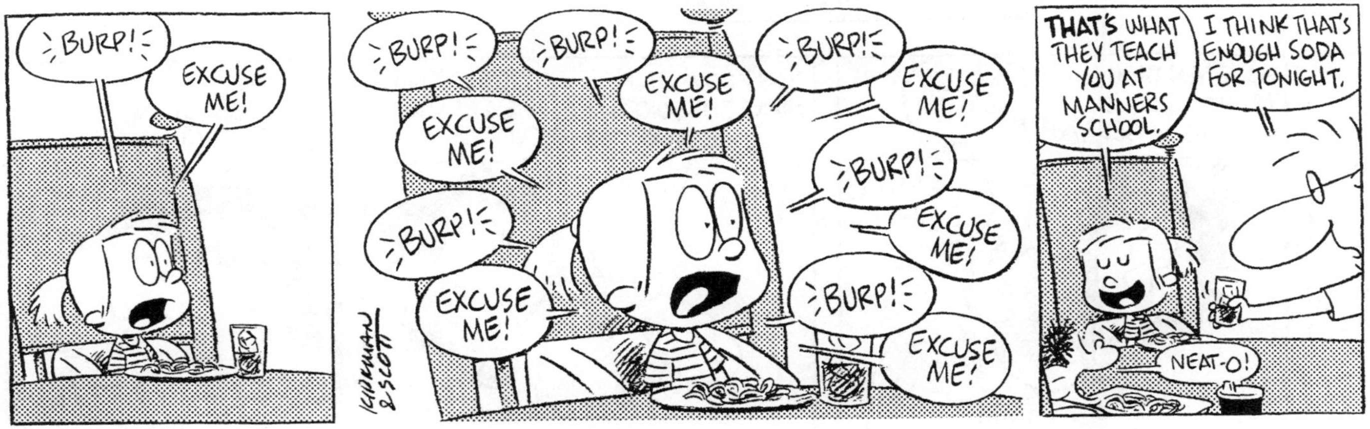
BURP!
EXCUSE ME!
BURP!
BURP!
EXCUSE ME!
EXCUSE ME!
BURP!
EXCUSE ME!
BURP!
BURP!
EXCUSE ME!
EXCUSE ME!
BURP!
EXCUSE ME!
THAT'S WHAT THEY TEACH YOU AT MANNERS SCHOOL.
I THINK THAT'S ENOUGH SODA FOR TONIGHT.
NEAT-O!

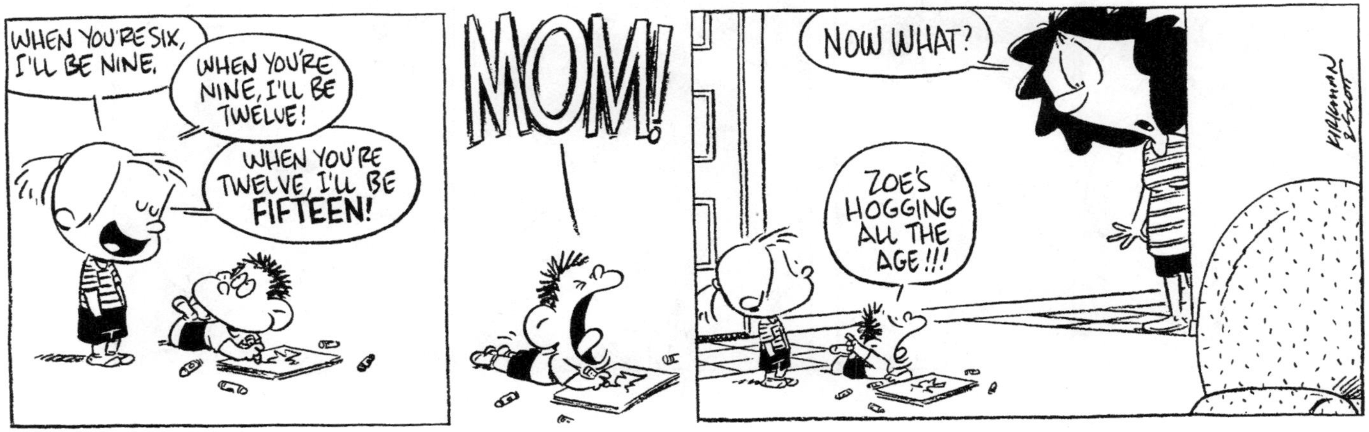
WHEN YOU'RE SIX, I'LL BE NINE.
WHEN YOU'RE NINE, I'LL BE TWELVE!
WHEN YOU'RE TWELVE, I'LL BE **FIFTEEN!**
MOM!
NOW WHAT?
ZOE'S HOGGING ALL THE AGE!!!

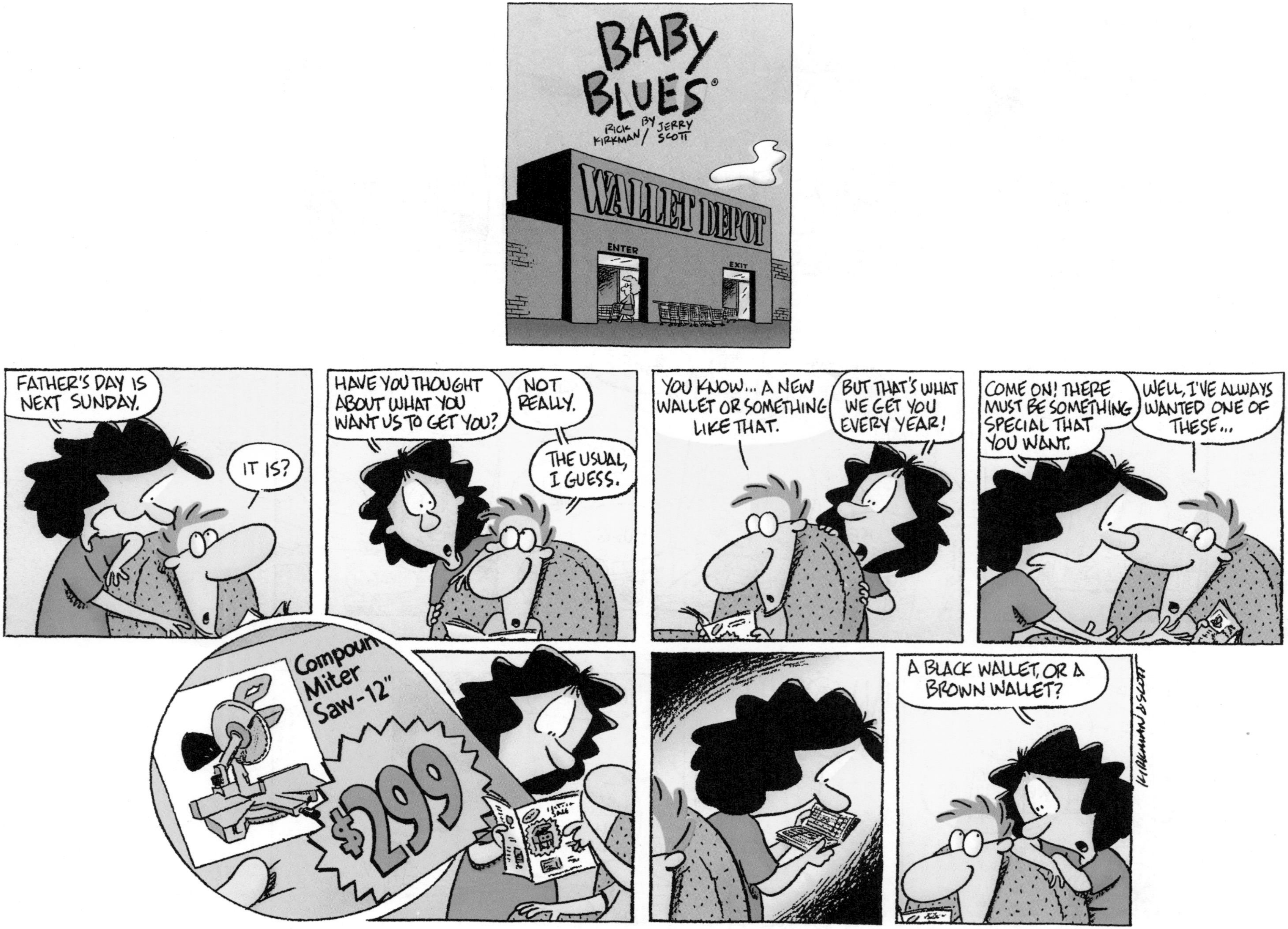
BABY BLUES®
BY RICK KIRKMAN / JERRY SCOTT
WALLET DEPOT
ENTER
EXIT
FATHER'S DAY IS NEXT SUNDAY.
IT IS?
HAVE YOU THOUGHT ABOUT WHAT YOU WANT US TO GET YOU?
NOT REALLY.
THE USUAL, I GUESS.
YOU KNOW... A NEW WALLET OR SOMETHING LIKE THAT.
BUT THAT'S WHAT WE GET YOU EVERY YEAR!
COME ON! THERE MUST BE SOMETHING SPECIAL THAT YOU WANT.
WELL, I'VE ALWAYS WANTED ONE OF THESE...
Compoun Miter Saw-12"
$299
A BLACK WALLET, OR A BROWN WALLET?
KIRKMAN & SCOTT

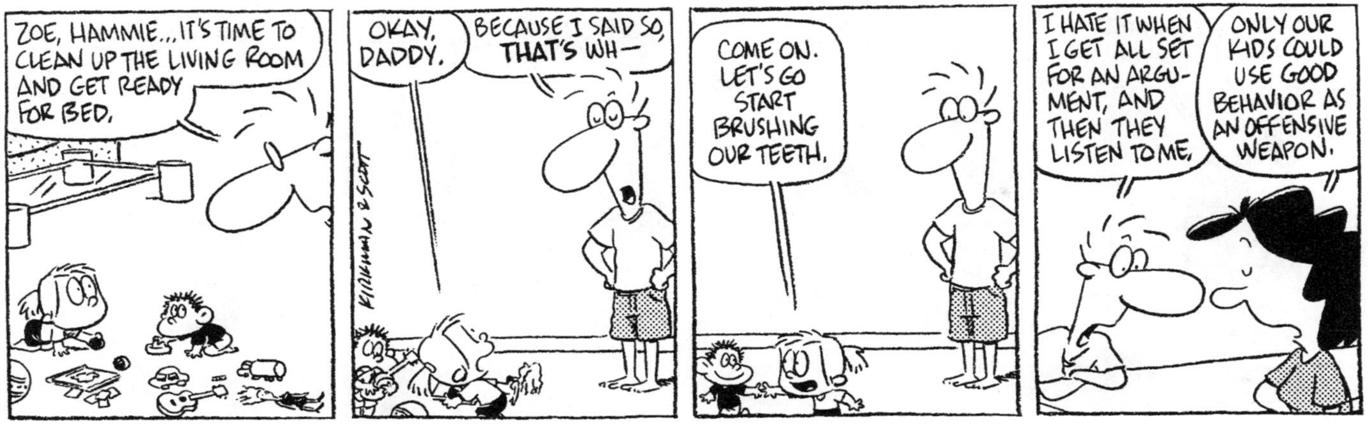
ZOE, HAMMIE... IT'S TIME TO CLEAN UP THE LIVING ROOM AND GET READY FOR BED.
OKAY, DADDY.
BECAUSE I SAID SO, THAT'S WH—
COME ON. LET'S GO START BRUSHING OUR TEETH.
I HATE IT WHEN I GET ALL SET FOR AN ARGUMENT, AND THEN THEY LISTEN TO ME.
ONLY OUR KIDS COULD USE GOOD BEHAVIOR AS AN OFFENSIVE WEAPON.
KIRKMAN & SCOTT

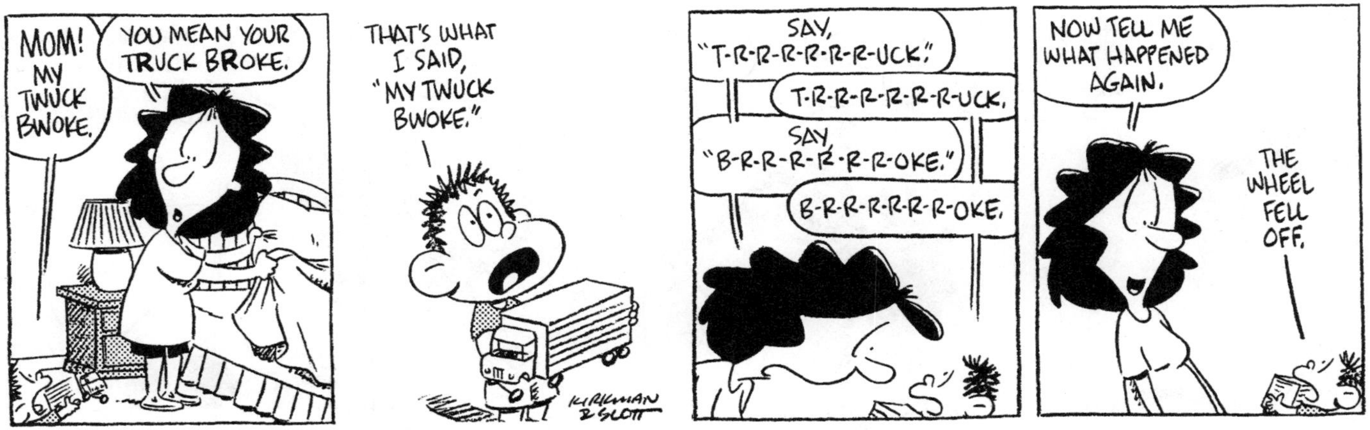
MOM! MY TWUCK BWOKE.
YOU MEAN YOUR TRUCK BROKE.
THAT'S WHAT I SAID, "MY TWUCK BWOKE."
KIRKMAN & SCOTT
SAY, "T-R-R-R-R-R-R-UCK."
T-R-R-R-R-R-R-UCK.
SAY, "B-R-R-R-R-R-R-OKE."
B-R-R-R-R-R-R-OKE.
NOW TELL ME WHAT HAPPENED AGAIN.
THE WHEEL FELL OFF.

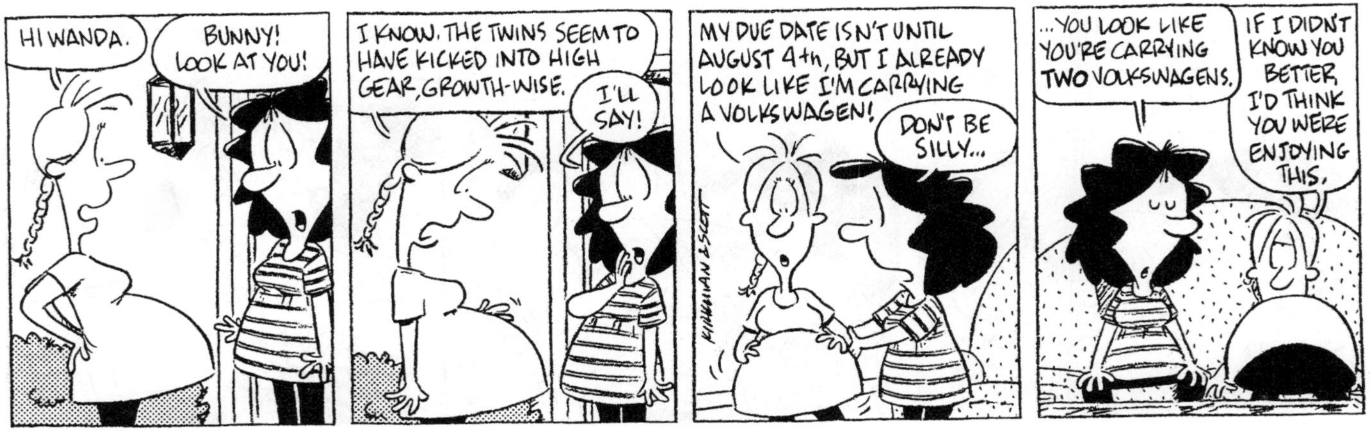
HI WANDA.
BUNNY! LOOK AT YOU!
I KNOW. THE TWINS SEEM TO HAVE KICKED INTO HIGH GEAR, GROWTH-WISE.
I'LL SAY!
MY DUE DATE ISN'T UNTIL AUGUST 4th, BUT I ALREADY LOOK LIKE I'M CARRYING A VOLKSWAGEN!
DON'T BE SILLY...
...YOU LOOK LIKE YOU'RE CARRYING TWO VOLKSWAGENS.
IF I DIDN'T KNOW YOU BETTER, I'D THINK YOU WERE ENJOYING THIS.
KIRKMAN & SCOTT

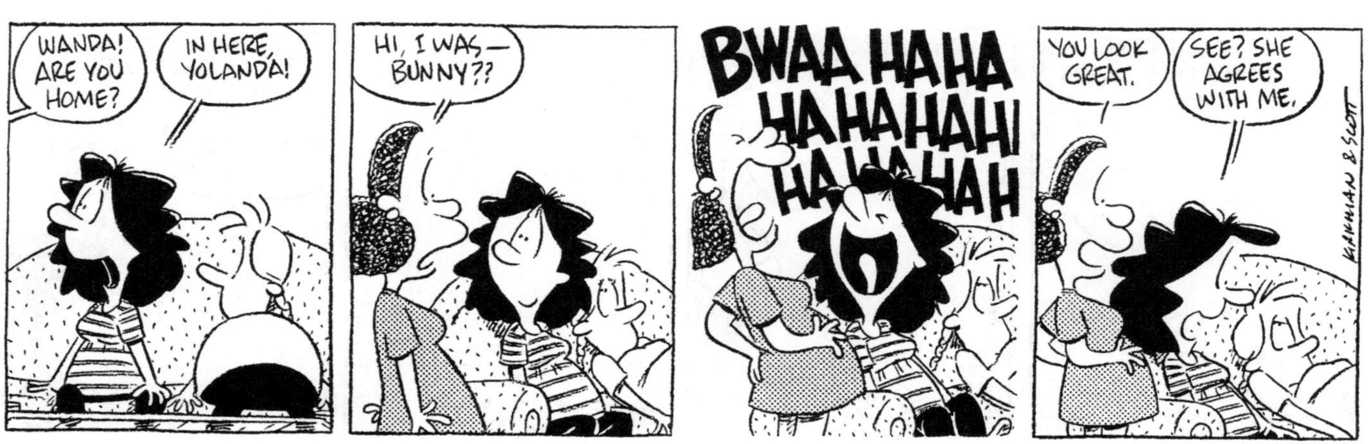
WANDA! ARE YOU HOME?
IN HERE, YOLANDA!
HI, I WAS— BUNNY??
BWAA HA HA HA HA HA HI HA HA HA H
YOU LOOK GREAT.
SEE? SHE AGREES WITH ME.
KIRKMAN & SCOTT

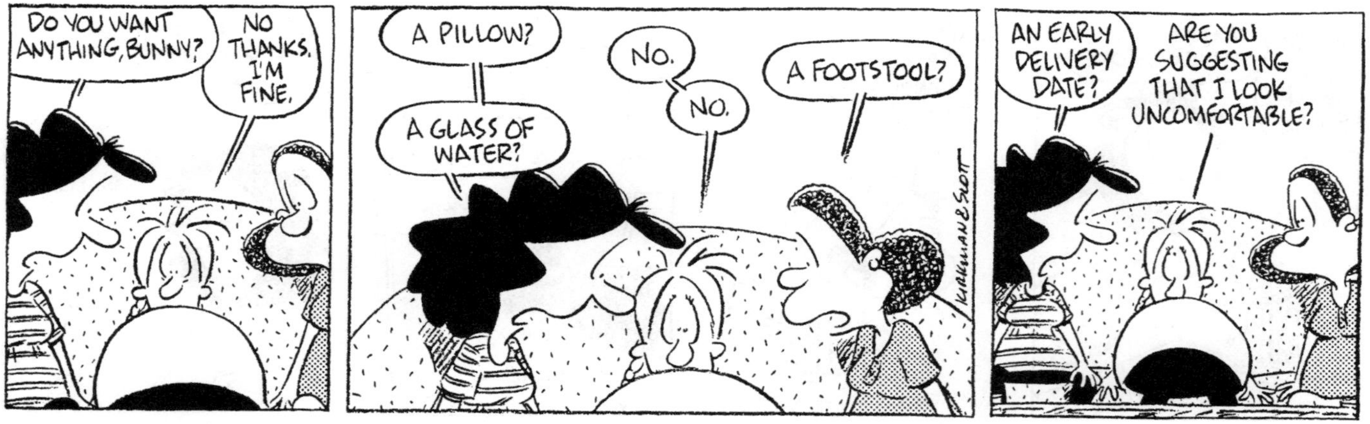
DO YOU WANT ANYTHING, BUNNY?
NO THANKS. I'M FINE.
A PILLOW?
A GLASS OF WATER?
NO.
NO.
A FOOTSTOOL?
KIRKMAN & SCOTT
AN EARLY DELIVERY DATE?
ARE YOU SUGGESTING THAT I LOOK UNCOMFORTABLE?

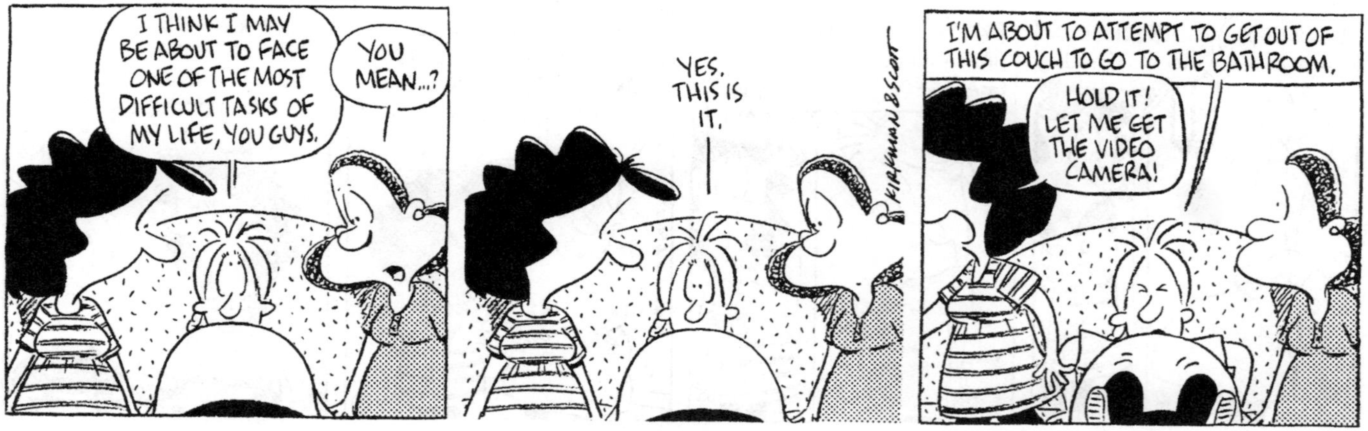
I THINK I MAY BE ABOUT TO FACE ONE OF THE MOST DIFFICULT TASKS OF MY LIFE, YOU GUYS.
YOU MEAN...?
YES. THIS IS IT.
KIRKMAN & SCOTT
I'M ABOUT TO ATTEMPT TO GET OUT OF THIS COUCH TO GO TO THE BATHROOM.
HOLD IT! LET ME GET THE VIDEO CAMERA!

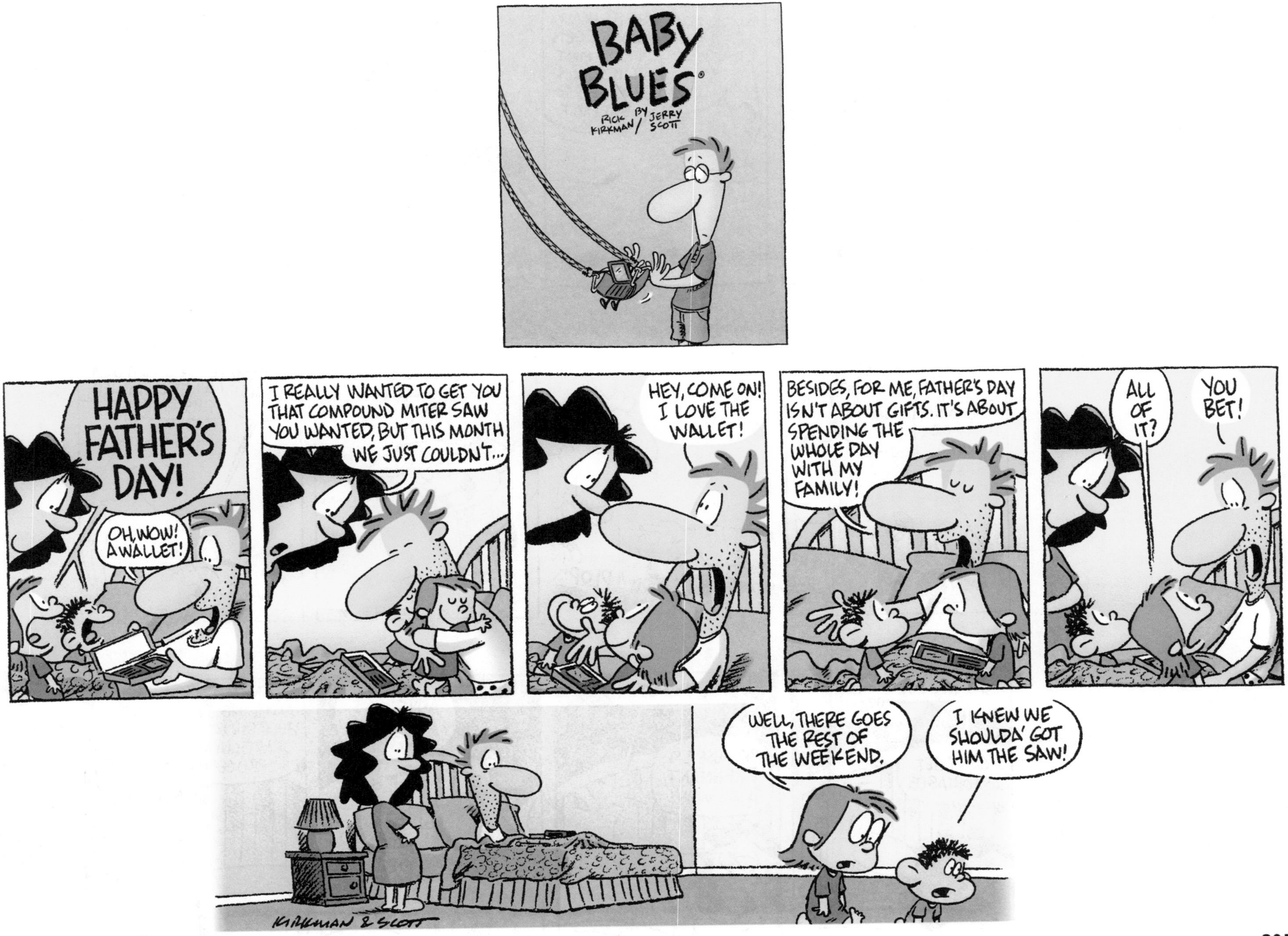
BABY BLUES®
RICK KIRKMAN / BY / JERRY SCOTT
HAPPY FATHER'S DAY!
OH, WOW! A WALLET!
I REALLY WANTED TO GET YOU THAT COMPOUND MITER SAW YOU WANTED, BUT THIS MONTH WE JUST COULDN'T...
HEY, COME ON! I LOVE THE WALLET!
BESIDES, FOR ME, FATHER'S DAY ISN'T ABOUT GIFTS. IT'S ABOUT SPENDING THE WHOLE DAY WITH MY FAMILY!
ALL OF IT?
YOU BET!
WELL, THERE GOES THE REST OF THE WEEKEND.
I KNEW WE SHOULDA' GOT HIM THE SAW!
KIRKMAN & SCOTT

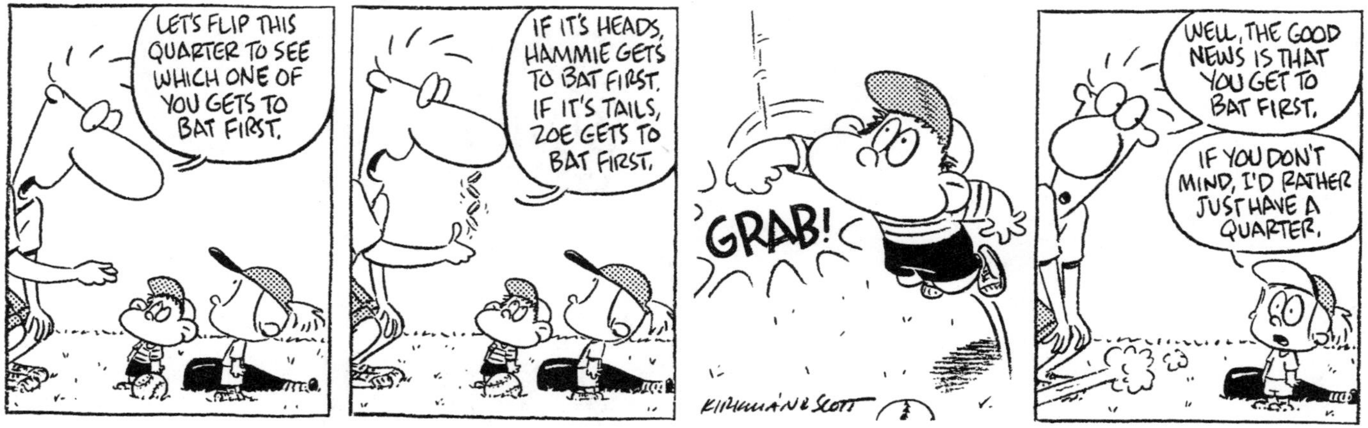
LET'S FLIP THIS QUARTER TO SEE WHICH ONE OF YOU GETS TO BAT FIRST.
IF IT'S HEADS, HAMMIE GETS TO BAT FIRST. IF IT'S TAILS, ZOE GETS TO BAT FIRST.
GRAB!
WELL, THE GOOD NEWS IS THAT YOU GET TO BAT FIRST.
IF YOU DON'T MIND, I'D RATHER JUST HAVE A QUARTER.
KIRKMAN & SCOTT

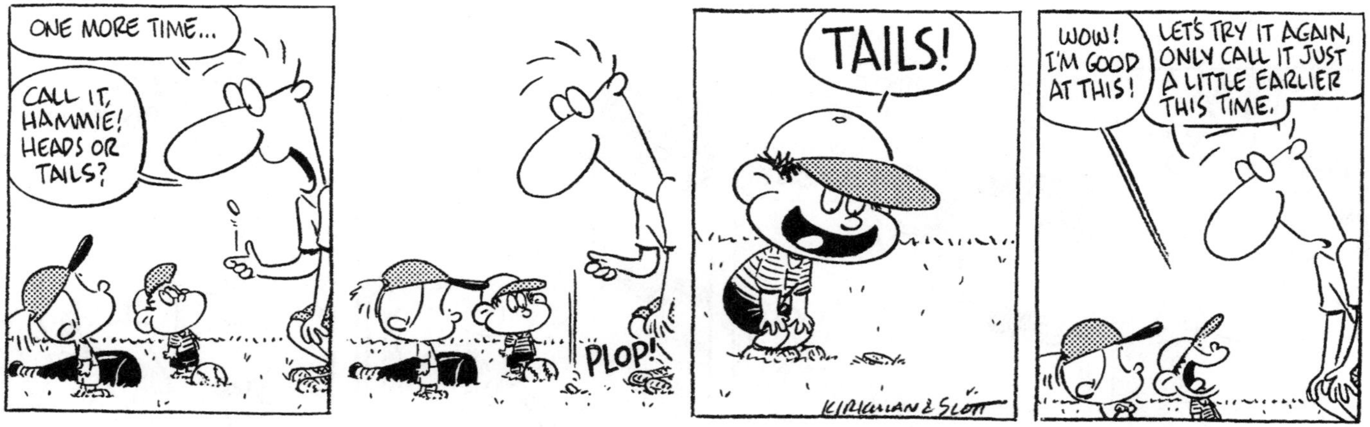
ONE MORE TIME...
CALL IT, HAMMIE! HEADS OR TAILS?
PLOP!
TAILS!
KIRKMAN & SCOTT
WOW! I'M GOOD AT THIS!
LET'S TRY IT AGAIN, ONLY CALL IT JUST A LITTLE EARLIER THIS TIME.

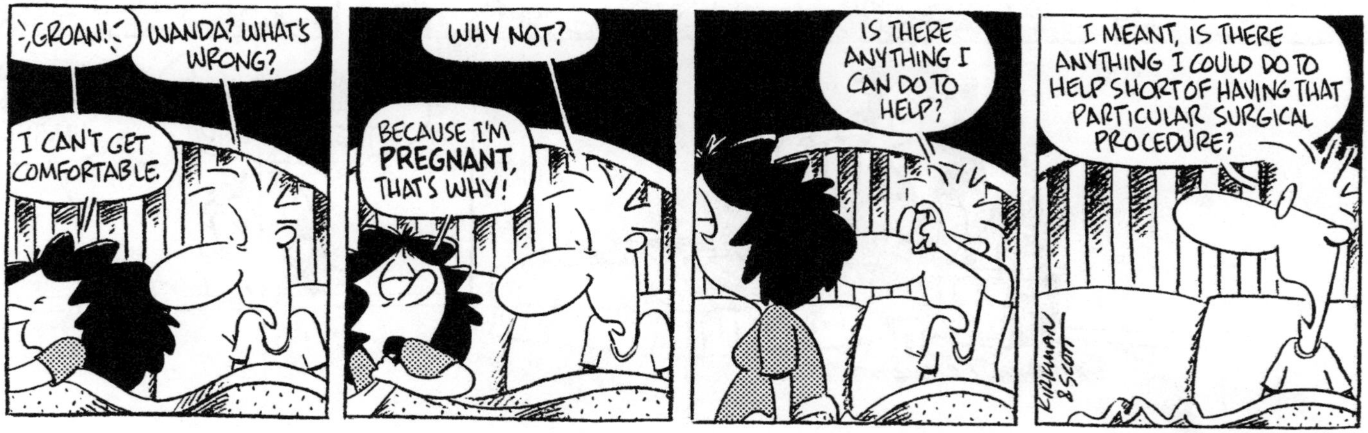
GROAN!
WANDA? WHAT'S WRONG?
I CAN'T GET COMFORTABLE.
WHY NOT?
BECAUSE I'M PREGNANT, THAT'S WHY!
IS THERE ANYTHING I CAN DO TO HELP?
I MEANT, IS THERE ANYTHING I COULD DO TO HELP SHORT OF HAVING THAT PARTICULAR SURGICAL PROCEDURE?
KIRKMAN & SCOTT

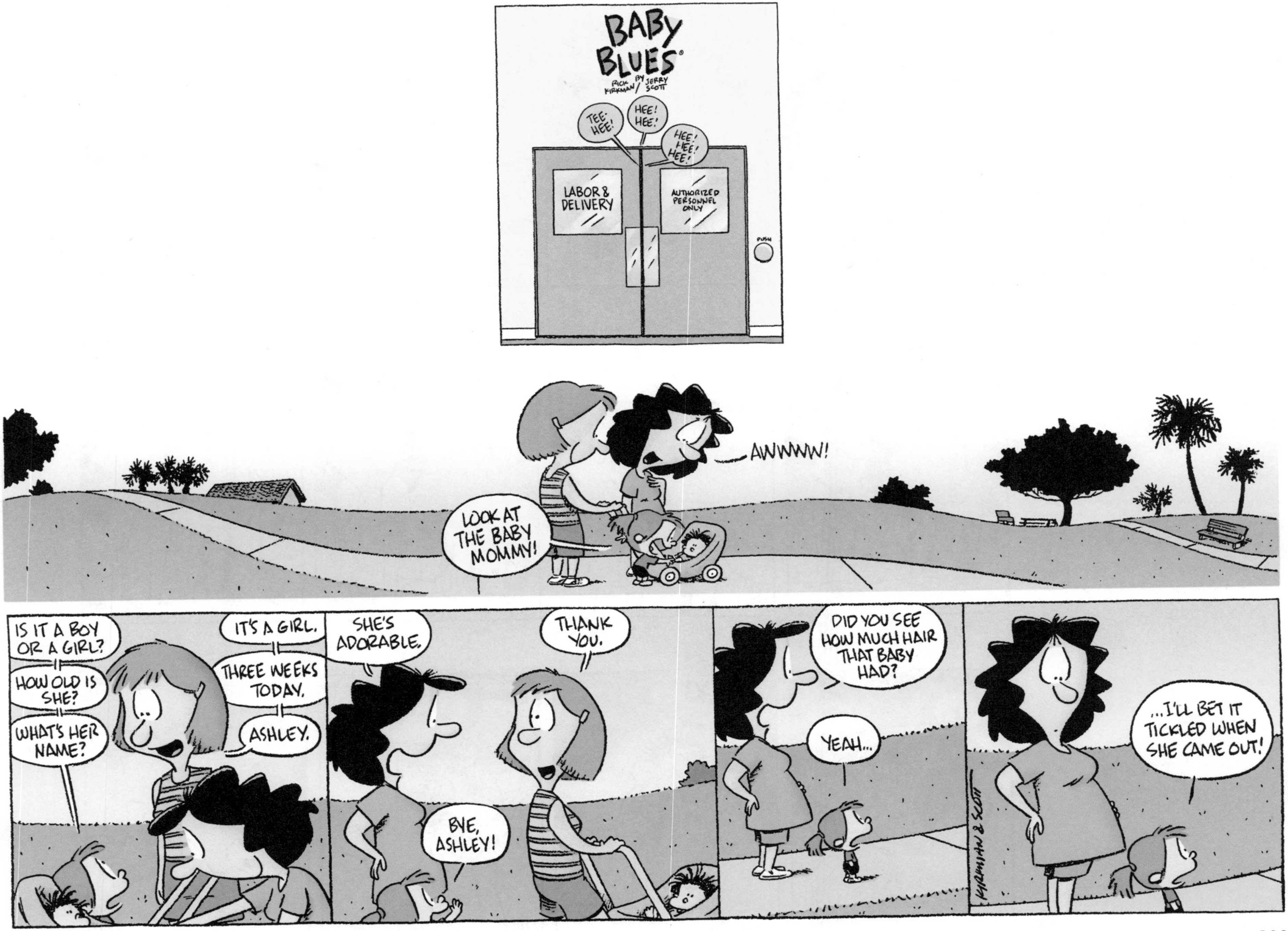
BABY BLUES®
BY RICK KIRKMAN / JERRY SCOTT
TEE-HEE!
HEE! HEE!
HEE! HEE! HEE!
LABOR & DELIVERY
AUTHORIZED PERSONNEL ONLY
PUSH
LOOK AT THE BABY MOMMY!
AWWWW!
IS IT A BOY OR A GIRL?
IT'S A GIRL.
HOW OLD IS SHE?
THREE WEEKS TODAY.
WHAT'S HER NAME?
ASHLEY.
SHE'S ADORABLE.
THANK YOU.
BYE, ASHLEY!
DID YOU SEE HOW MUCH HAIR THAT BABY HAD?
YEAH...
...I'LL BET IT TICKLED WHEN SHE CAME OUT!

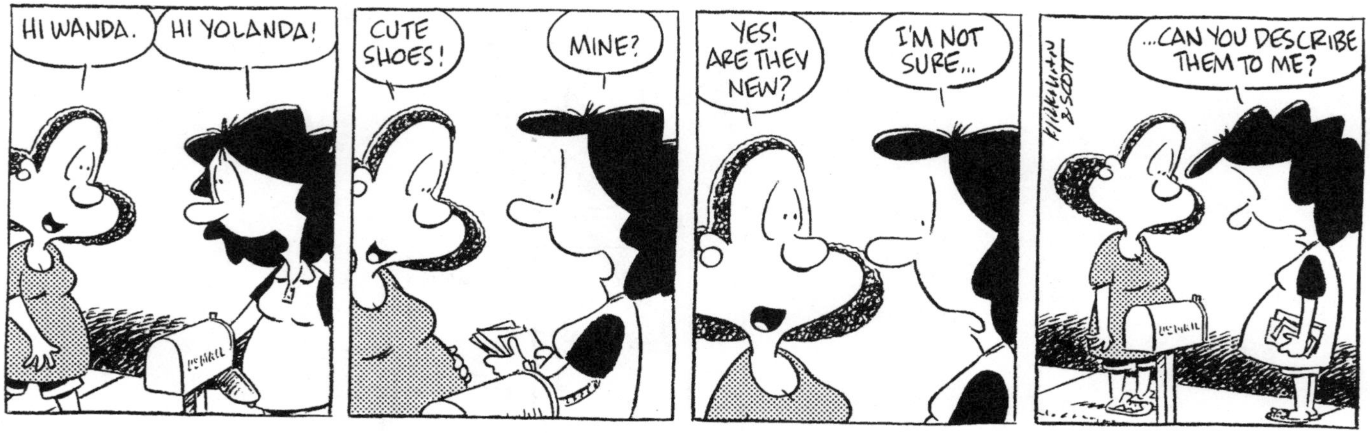
HI WANDA.
HI YOLANDA!
CUTE SHOES!
MINE?
YES! ARE THEY NEW?
I'M NOT SURE...
...CAN YOU DESCRIBE THEM TO ME?

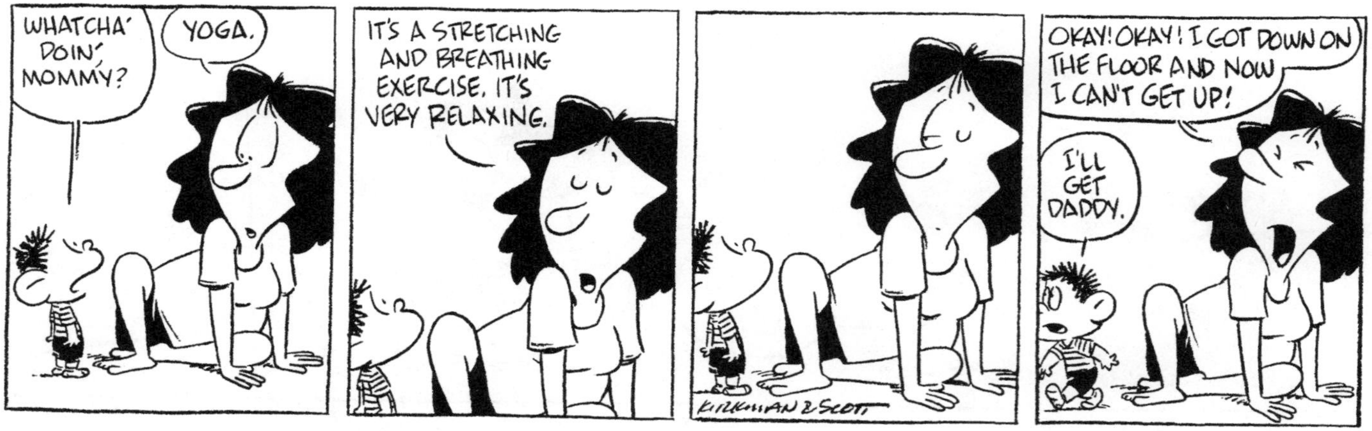
WHATCHA' DOIN' MOMMY?
YOGA.
IT'S A STRETCHING AND BREATHING EXERCISE. IT'S VERY RELAXING.
KIRKMAN & SCOTT
OKAY! OKAY! I GOT DOWN ON THE FLOOR AND NOW I CAN'T GET UP!
I'LL GET DADDY.

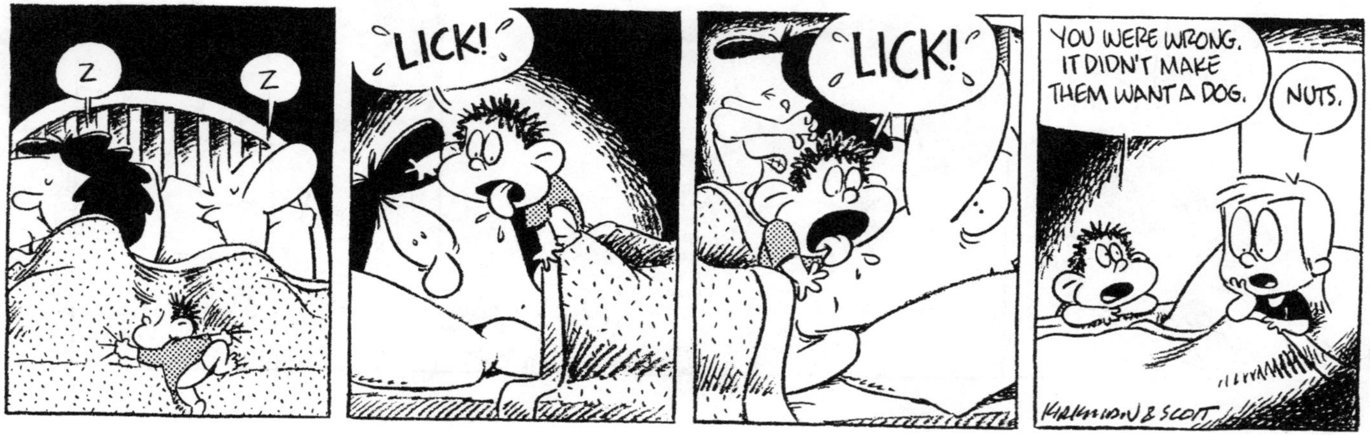
Z
Z
LICK!
LICK!
YOU WERE WRONG. IT DIDN'T MAKE THEM WANT A DOG.
NUTS.
KIRKMAN & SCOTT

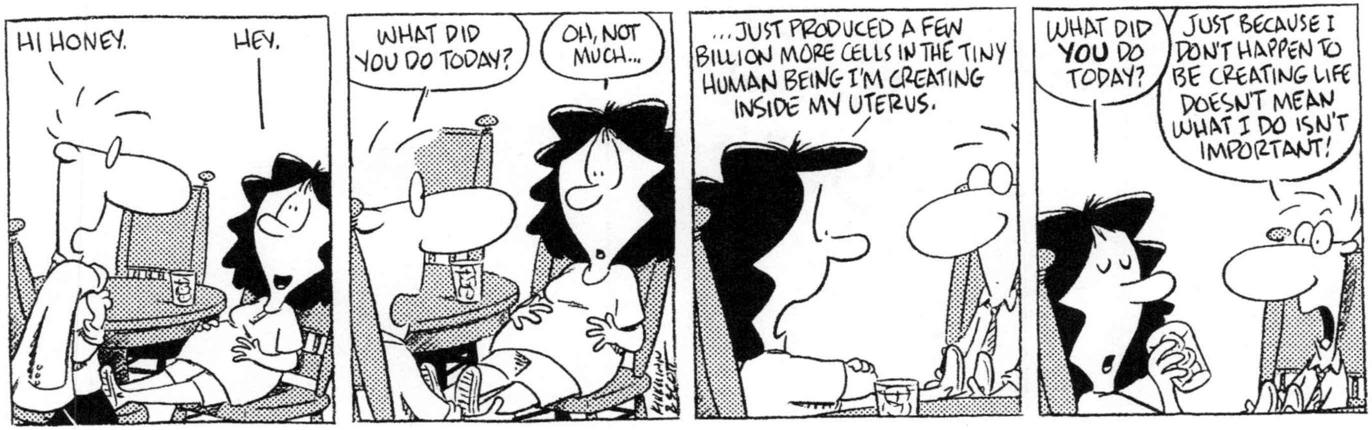
HI HONEY.
HEY.
WHAT DID YOU DO TODAY?
OH, NOT MUCH...
...JUST PRODUCED A FEW BILLION MORE CELLS IN THE TINY HUMAN BEING I'M CREATING INSIDE MY UTERUS.
WHAT DID **YOU** DO TODAY?
JUST BECAUSE I DON'T HAPPEN TO BE CREATING LIFE DOESN'T MEAN WHAT I DO ISN'T IMPORTANT!

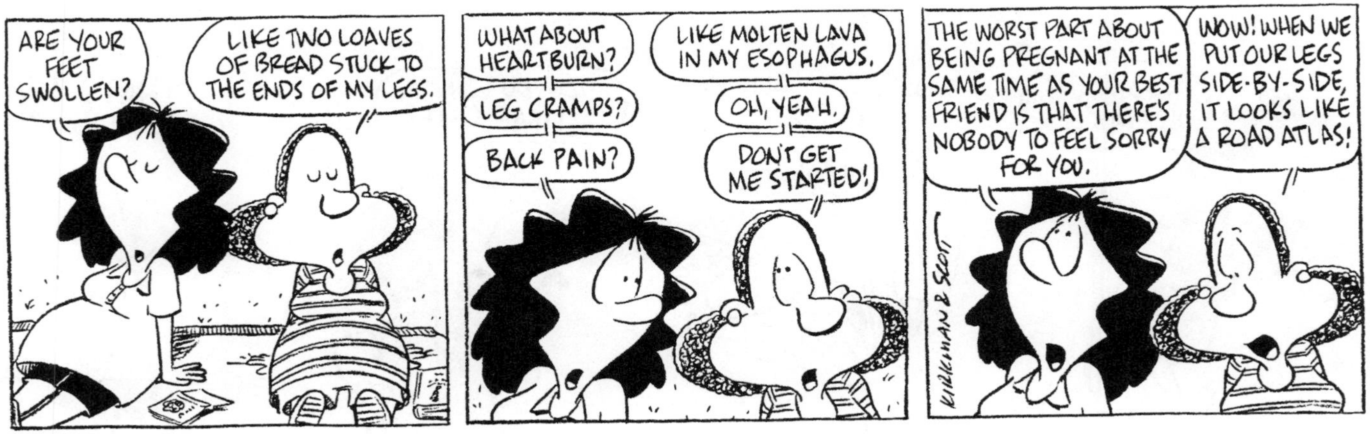
ARE YOUR FEET SWOLLEN?
LIKE TWO LOAVES OF BREAD STUCK TO THE ENDS OF MY LEGS.
WHAT ABOUT HEARTBURN?
LIKE MOLTEN LAVA IN MY ESOPHAGUS.
LEG CRAMPS?
OH, YEAH.
BACK PAIN?
DON'T GET ME STARTED!
THE WORST PART ABOUT BEING PREGNANT AT THE SAME TIME AS YOUR BEST FRIEND IS THAT THERE'S NOBODY TO FEEL SORRY FOR YOU.
WOW! WHEN WE PUT OUR LEGS SIDE-BY-SIDE, IT LOOKS LIKE A ROAD ATLAS!

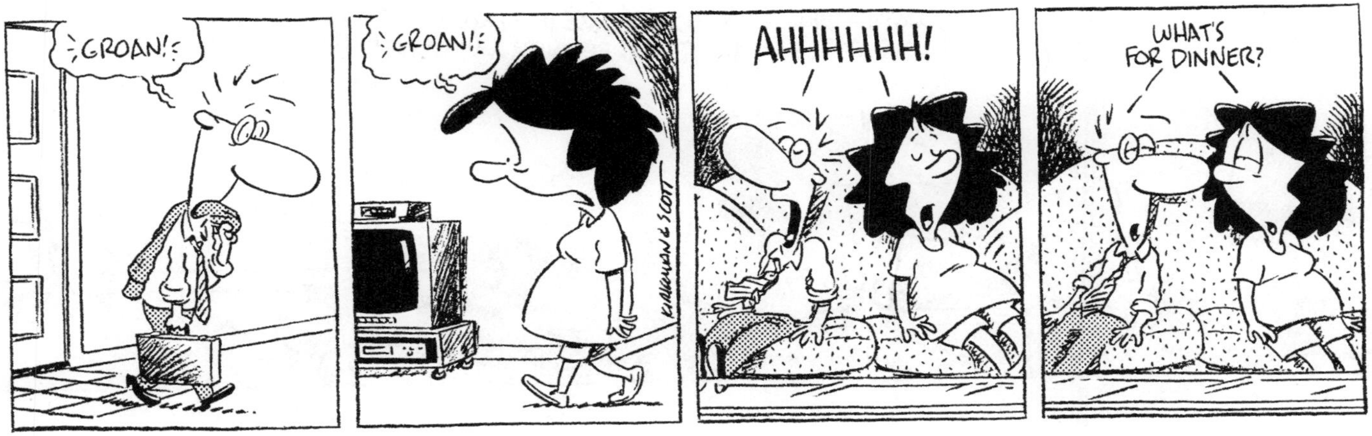
GROAN!
GROAN!
AHHHHHH!
WHAT'S FOR DINNER?

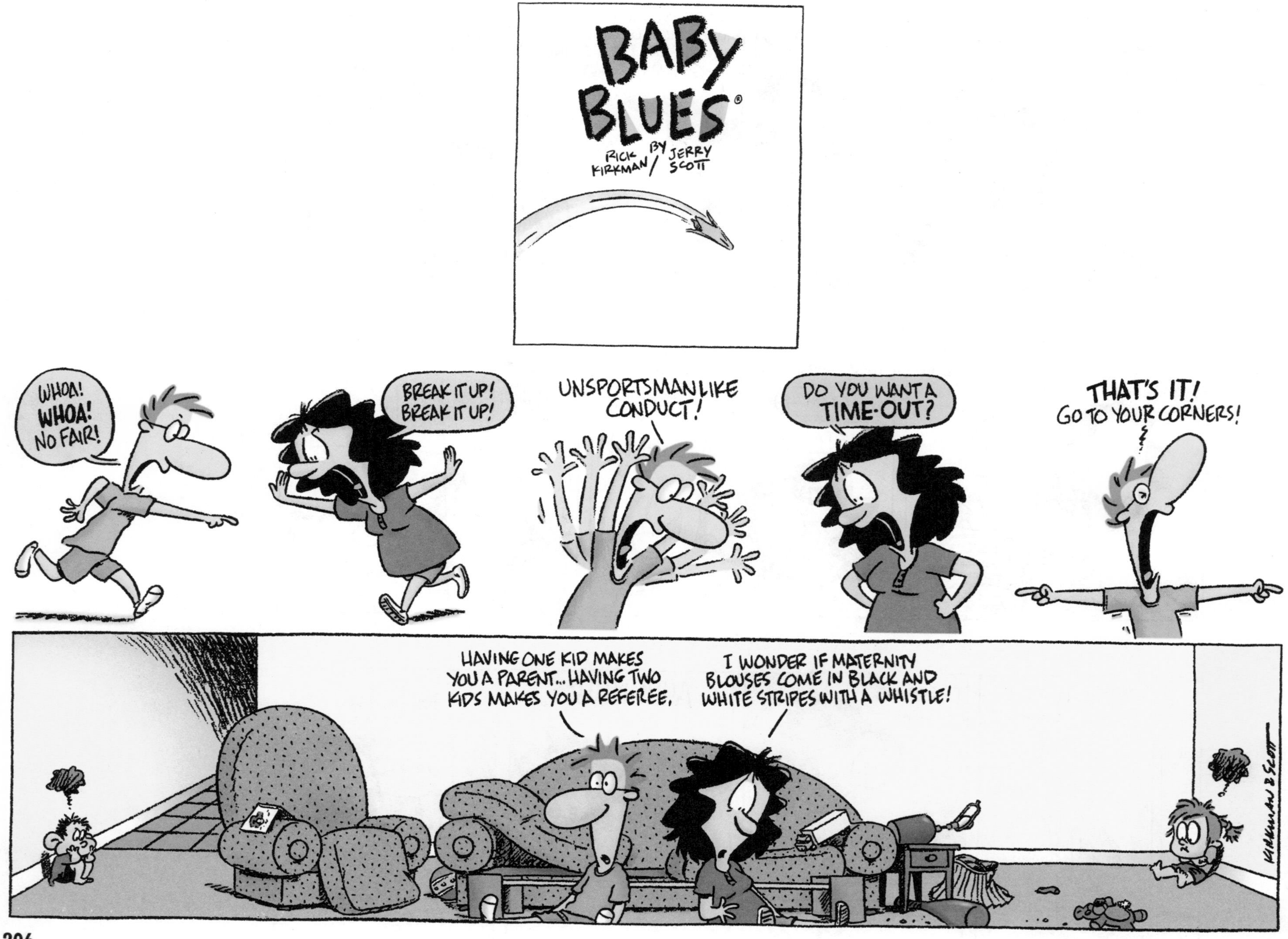
BABY BLUES®
BY RICK KIRKMAN / JERRY SCOTT
WHOA! WHOA! NO FAIR!
BREAK IT UP! BREAK IT UP!
UNSPORTSMANLIKE CONDUCT!
DO YOU WANT A TIME-OUT?
THAT'S IT! GO TO YOUR CORNERS!
HAVING ONE KID MAKES YOU A PARENT... HAVING TWO KIDS MAKES YOU A REFEREE.
I WONDER IF MATERNITY BLOUSES COME IN BLACK AND WHITE STRIPES WITH A WHISTLE!
KIRKMAN & SCOTT

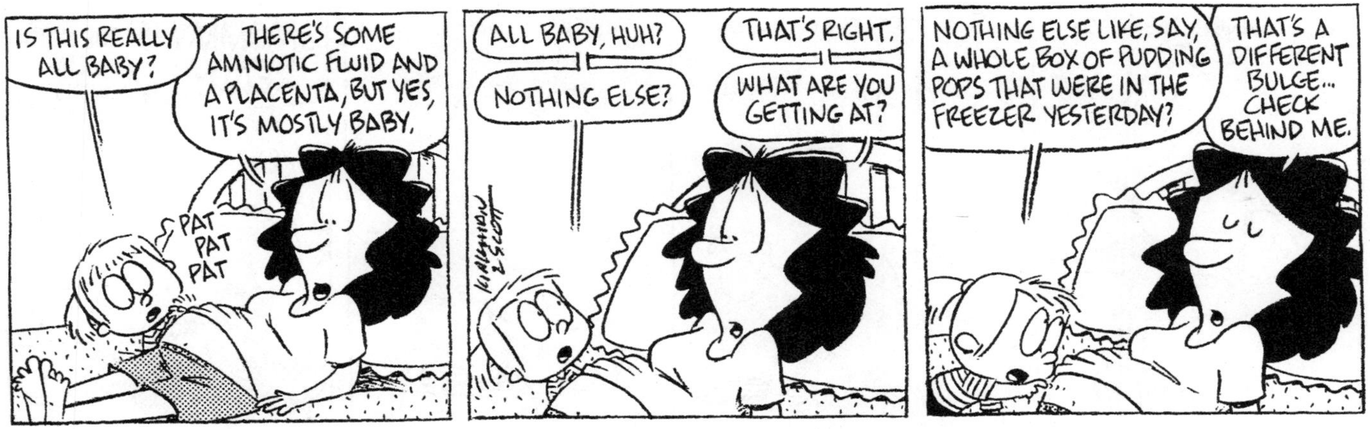
IS THIS REALLY ALL BABY?
THERE'S SOME AMNIOTIC FLUID AND A PLACENTA, BUT YES, IT'S MOSTLY BABY.
PAT PAT PAT
ALL BABY, HUH?
THAT'S RIGHT.
NOTHING ELSE?
WHAT ARE YOU GETTING AT?
NOTHING ELSE LIKE, SAY, A WHOLE BOX OF PUDDING POPS THAT WERE IN THE FREEZER YESTERDAY?
THAT'S A DIFFERENT BULGE... CHECK BEHIND ME.

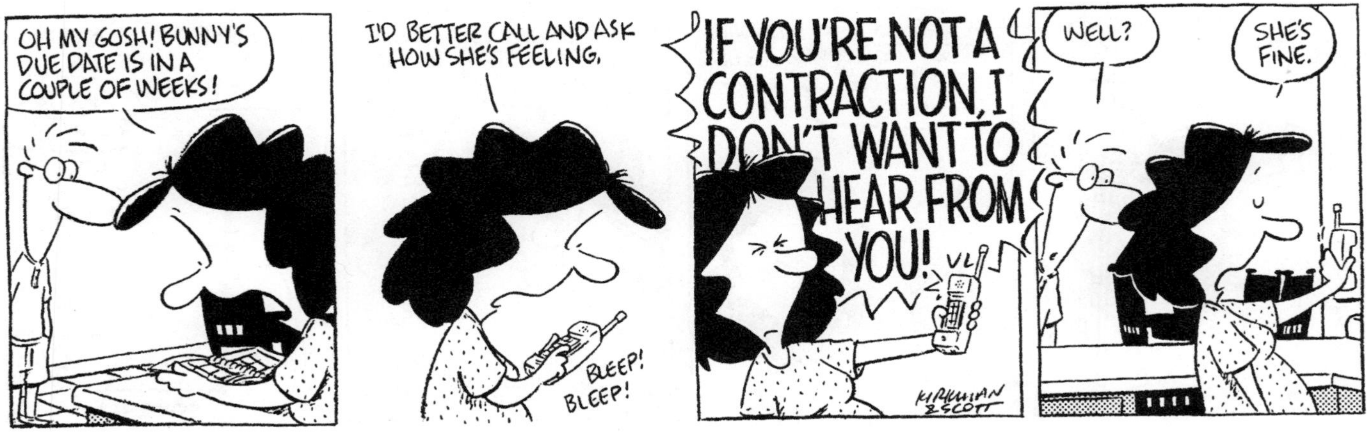
OH MY GOSH! BUNNY'S DUE DATE IS IN A COUPLE OF WEEKS!
I'D BETTER CALL AND ASK HOW SHE'S FEELING.
BLEEP! BLEEP!
IF YOU'RE NOT A CONTRACTION, I DON'T WANT TO HEAR FROM YOU!
WELL?
SHE'S FINE.

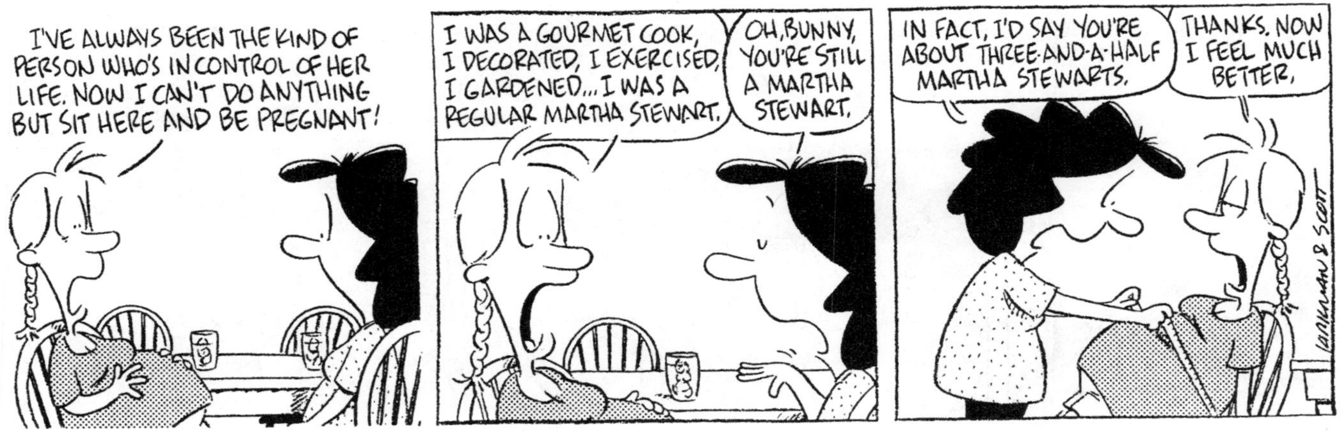
I'VE ALWAYS BEEN THE KIND OF PERSON WHO'S IN CONTROL OF HER LIFE. NOW I CAN'T DO ANYTHING BUT SIT HERE AND BE PREGNANT!
I WAS A GOURMET COOK, I DECORATED, I EXERCISED, I GARDENED... I WAS A REGULAR MARTHA STEWART.
OH, BUNNY, YOU'RE STILL A MARTHA STEWART.
IN FACT, I'D SAY YOU'RE ABOUT THREE-AND-A-HALF MARTHA STEWARTS.
THANKS. NOW I FEEL MUCH BETTER.

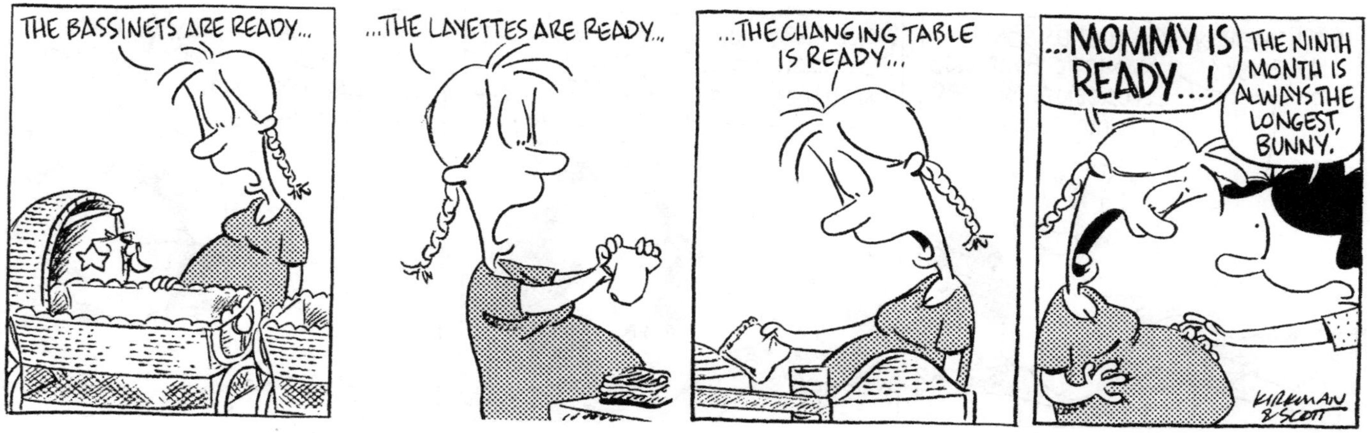
THE BASSINETS ARE READY...
...THE LAYETTES ARE READY...
...THE CHANGING TABLE IS READY...
...MOMMY IS READY...!
THE NINTH MONTH IS ALWAYS THE LONGEST, BUNNY.
KIRKMAN & SCOTT

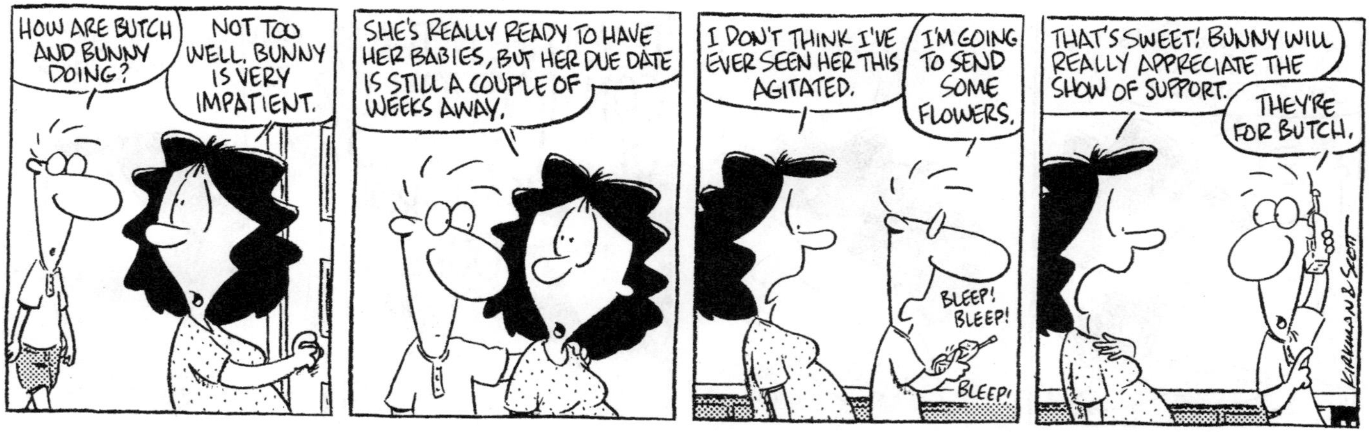
HOW ARE BUTCH AND BUNNY DOING?
NOT TOO WELL. BUNNY IS VERY IMPATIENT.
SHE'S REALLY READY TO HAVE HER BABIES, BUT HER DUE DATE IS STILL A COUPLE OF WEEKS AWAY.
I DON'T THINK I'VE EVER SEEN HER THIS AGITATED.
I'M GOING TO SEND SOME FLOWERS.
BLEEP! BLEEP!
BLEEP!
THAT'S SWEET! BUNNY WILL REALLY APPRECIATE THE SHOW OF SUPPORT.
THEY'RE FOR BUTCH.
KIRKMAN & SCOTT

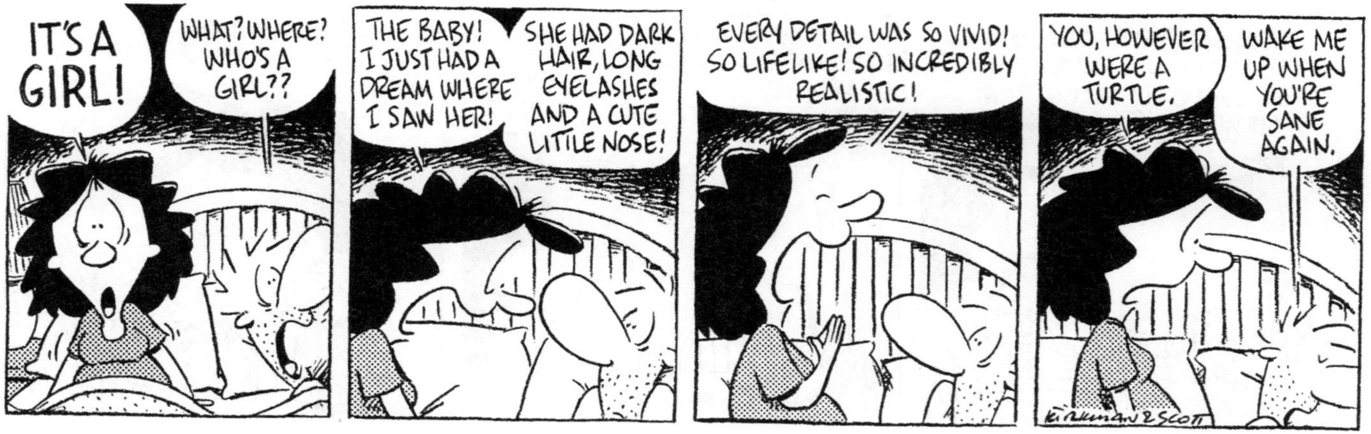
IT'S A GIRL!
WHAT? WHERE? WHO'S A GIRL??
THE BABY! I JUST HAD A DREAM WHERE I SAW HER!
SHE HAD DARK HAIR, LONG EYELASHES AND A CUTE LITTLE NOSE!
EVERY DETAIL WAS SO VIVID! SO LIFELIKE! SO INCREDIBLY REALISTIC!
YOU, HOWEVER WERE A TURTLE.
WAKE ME UP WHEN YOU'RE SANE AGAIN.
KIRKMAN & SCOTT

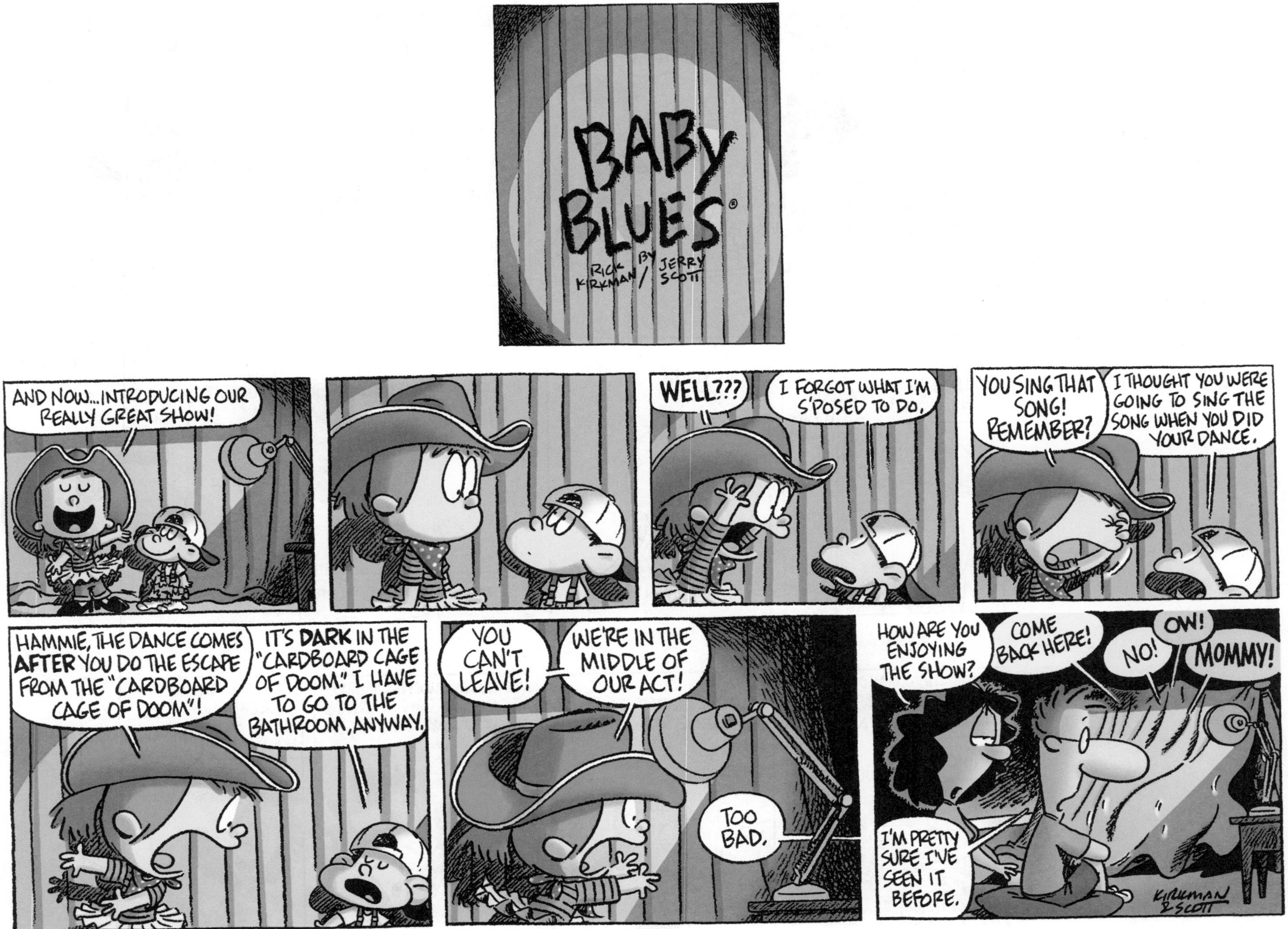
BABY BLUES®
BY RICK KIRKMAN / JERRY SCOTT
AND NOW...INTRODUCING OUR REALLY GREAT SHOW!
WELL???
I FORGOT WHAT I'M S'POSED TO DO.
YOU SING THAT SONG! REMEMBER?
I THOUGHT YOU WERE GOING TO SING THE SONG WHEN YOU DID YOUR DANCE.
HAMMIE, THE DANCE COMES AFTER YOU DO THE ESCAPE FROM THE "CARDBOARD CAGE OF DOOM"!
IT'S DARK IN THE "CARDBOARD CAGE OF DOOM." I HAVE TO GO TO THE BATHROOM, ANYWAY.
YOU CAN'T LEAVE!
WE'RE IN THE MIDDLE OF OUR ACT!
TOO BAD.
HOW ARE YOU ENJOYING THE SHOW?
COME BACK HERE!
NO!
OW!
MOMMY!
I'M PRETTY SURE I'VE SEEN IT BEFORE.
KIRKMAN & SCOTT

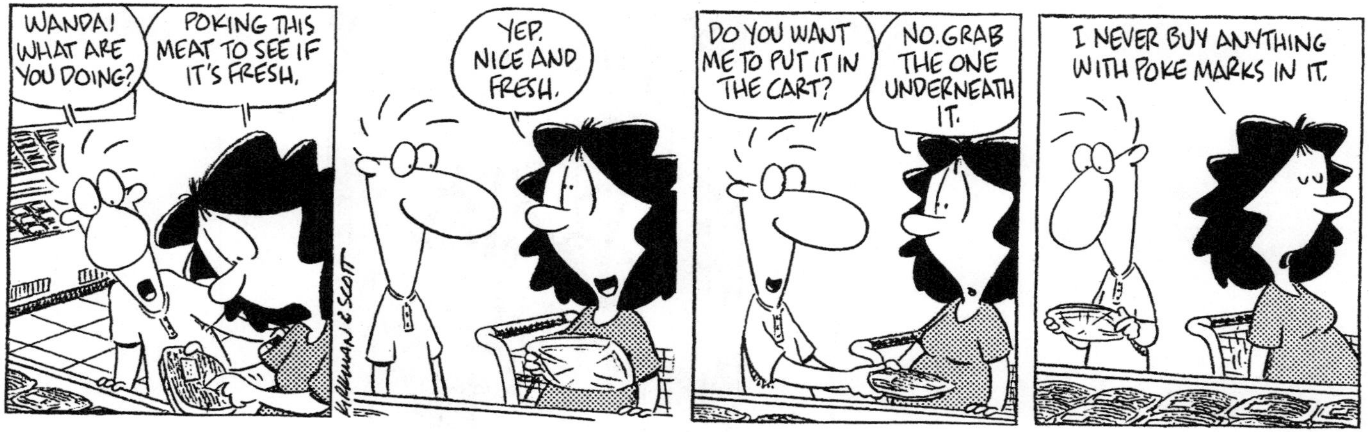
WANDA! WHAT ARE YOU DOING?
POKING THIS MEAT TO SEE IF IT'S FRESH.
YEP. NICE AND FRESH.
DO YOU WANT ME TO PUT IT IN THE CART?
NO. GRAB THE ONE UNDERNEATH IT.
I NEVER BUY ANYTHING WITH POKE MARKS IN IT.

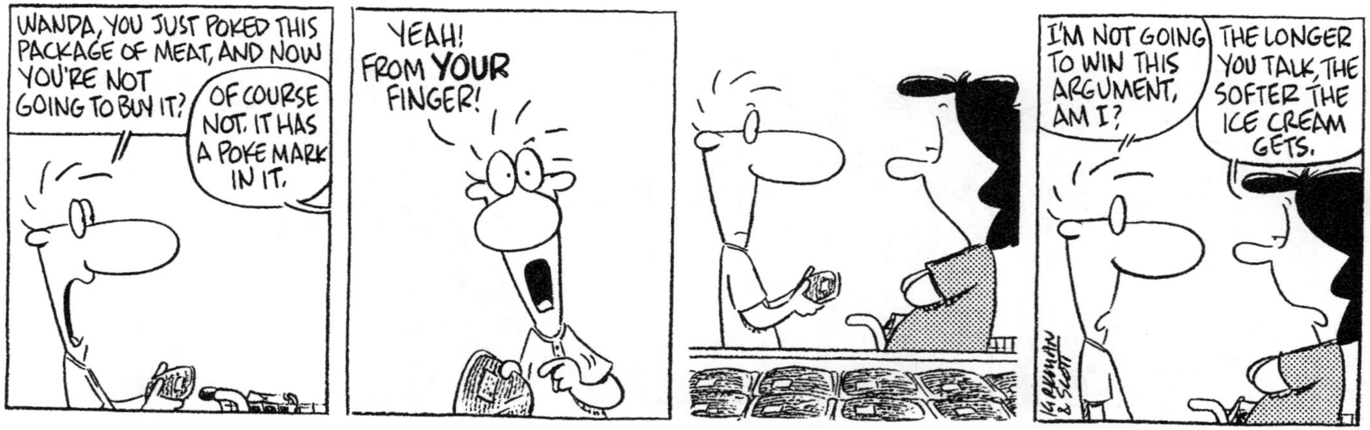
WANDA, YOU JUST POKED THIS PACKAGE OF MEAT, AND NOW YOU'RE NOT GOING TO BUY IT?
OF COURSE NOT. IT HAS A POKE MARK IN IT.
YEAH! FROM **YOUR** FINGER!
I'M NOT GOING TO WIN THIS ARGUMENT, AM I?
THE LONGER YOU TALK, THE SOFTER THE ICE CREAM GETS.

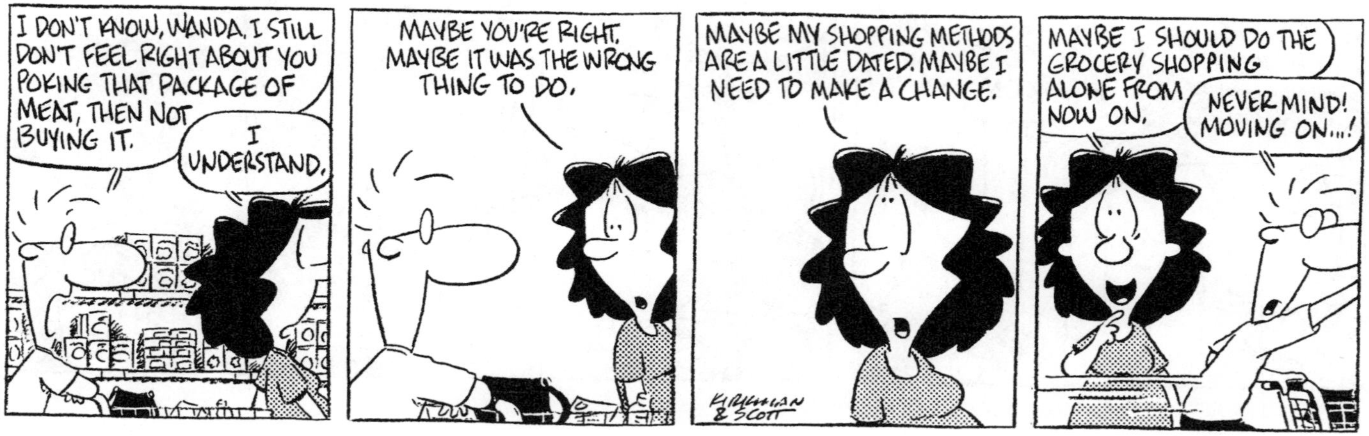
I DON'T KNOW, WANDA. I STILL DON'T FEEL RIGHT ABOUT YOU POKING THAT PACKAGE OF MEAT, THEN NOT BUYING IT.
I UNDERSTAND.
MAYBE YOU'RE RIGHT. MAYBE IT WAS THE WRONG THING TO DO.
MAYBE MY SHOPPING METHODS ARE A LITTLE DATED. MAYBE I NEED TO MAKE A CHANGE.
MAYBE I SHOULD DO THE GROCERY SHOPPING ALONE FROM NOW ON.
NEVER MIND! MOVING ON...!

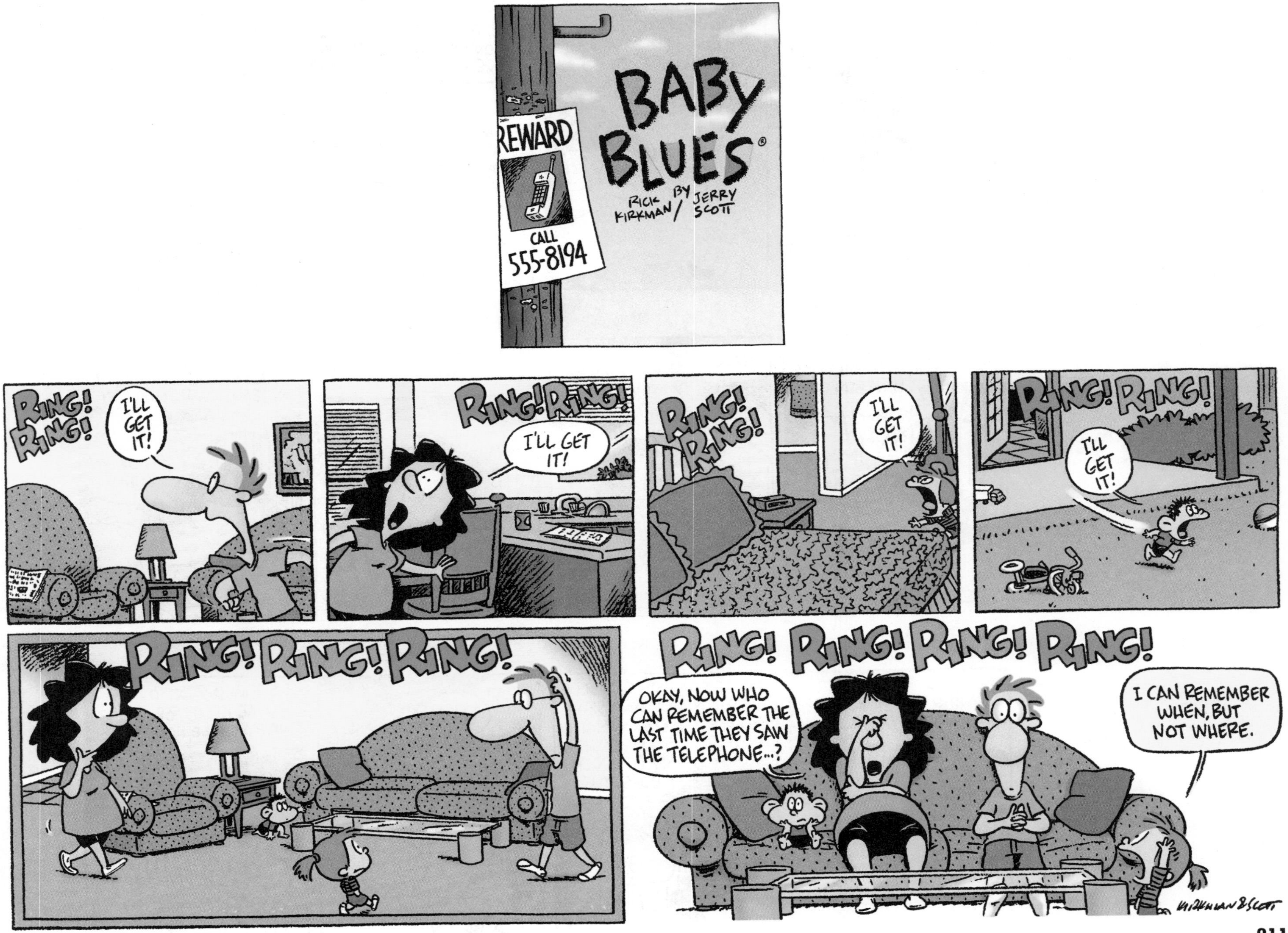
REWARD
CALL
555-8194
BABY BLUES®
BY RICK KIRKMAN / JERRY SCOTT
RING! RING!
I'LL GET IT!
RING! RING!
I'LL GET IT!
RING! RING!
I'LL GET IT!
RING! RING!
I'LL GET IT!
RING! RING! RING!
RING! RING! RING! RING!
OKAY, NOW WHO CAN REMEMBER THE LAST TIME THEY SAW THE TELEPHONE...?
I CAN REMEMBER WHEN, BUT NOT WHERE.
KIRKMAN & SCOTT

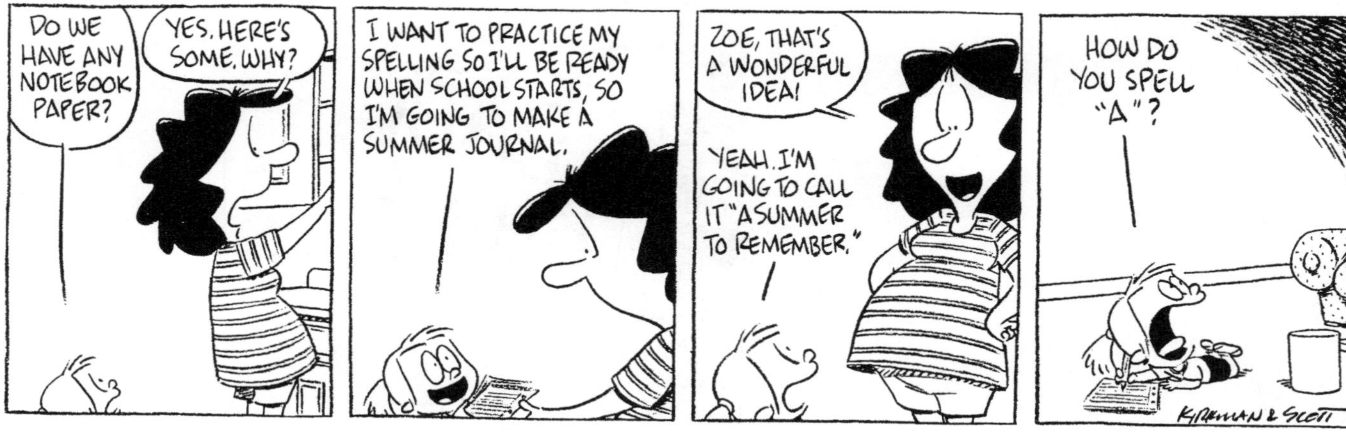
DO WE HAVE ANY NOTEBOOK PAPER?
YES. HERE'S SOME. WHY?
I WANT TO PRACTICE MY SPELLING SO I'LL BE READY WHEN SCHOOL STARTS, SO I'M GOING TO MAKE A SUMMER JOURNAL.
ZOE, THAT'S A WONDERFUL IDEA!
YEAH. I'M GOING TO CALL IT "A SUMMER TO REMEMBER."
HOW DO YOU SPELL "A"?
KIRKMAN & SCOTT

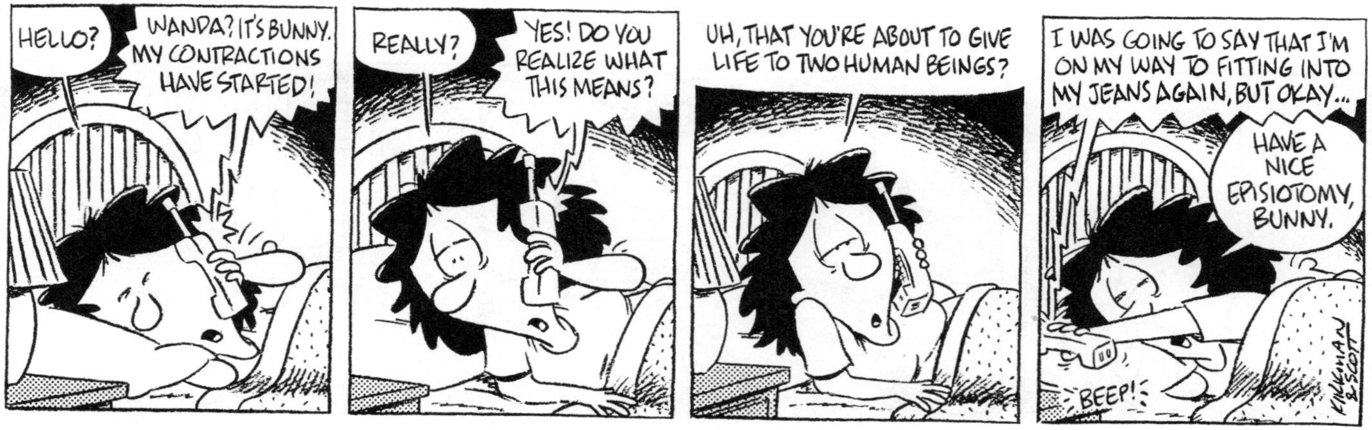
HELLO?
WANDA? IT'S BUNNY. MY CONTRACTIONS HAVE STARTED!
REALLY?
YES! DO YOU REALIZE WHAT THIS MEANS?
UH, THAT YOU'RE ABOUT TO GIVE LIFE TO TWO HUMAN BEINGS?
I WAS GOING TO SAY THAT I'M ON MY WAY TO FITTING INTO MY JEANS AGAIN, BUT OKAY...
HAVE A NICE EPISIOTOMY, BUNNY.
BEEP!
KIRKMAN & SCOTT

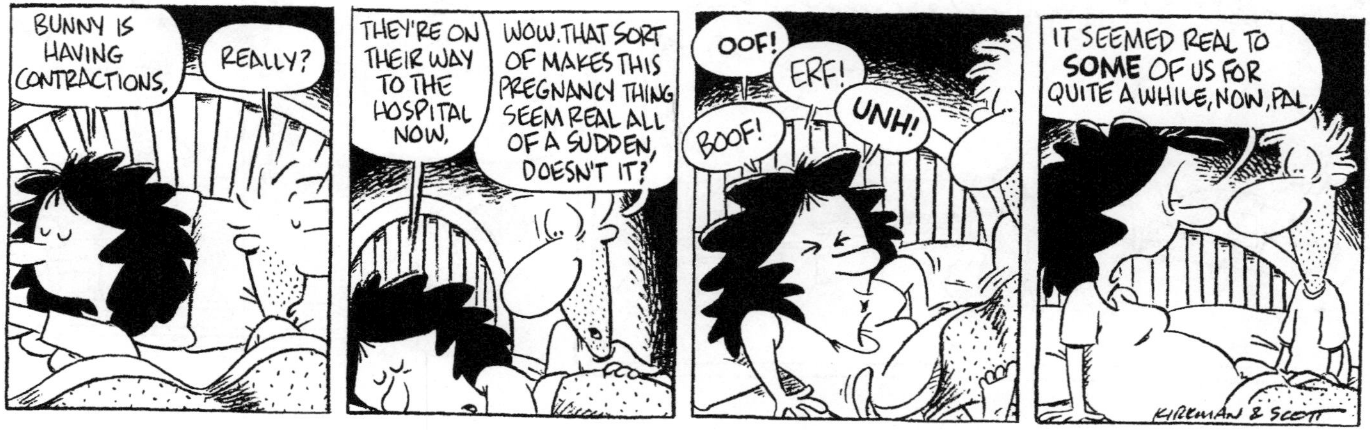
BUNNY IS HAVING CONTRACTIONS.
REALLY?
THEY'RE ON THEIR WAY TO THE HOSPITAL NOW.
WOW. THAT SORT OF MAKES THIS PREGNANCY THING SEEM REAL ALL OF A SUDDEN, DOESN'T IT?
OOF!
ERF!
BOOF!
UNH!
IT SEEMED REAL TO SOME OF US FOR QUITE A WHILE, NOW, PAL.
KIRKMAN & SCOTT

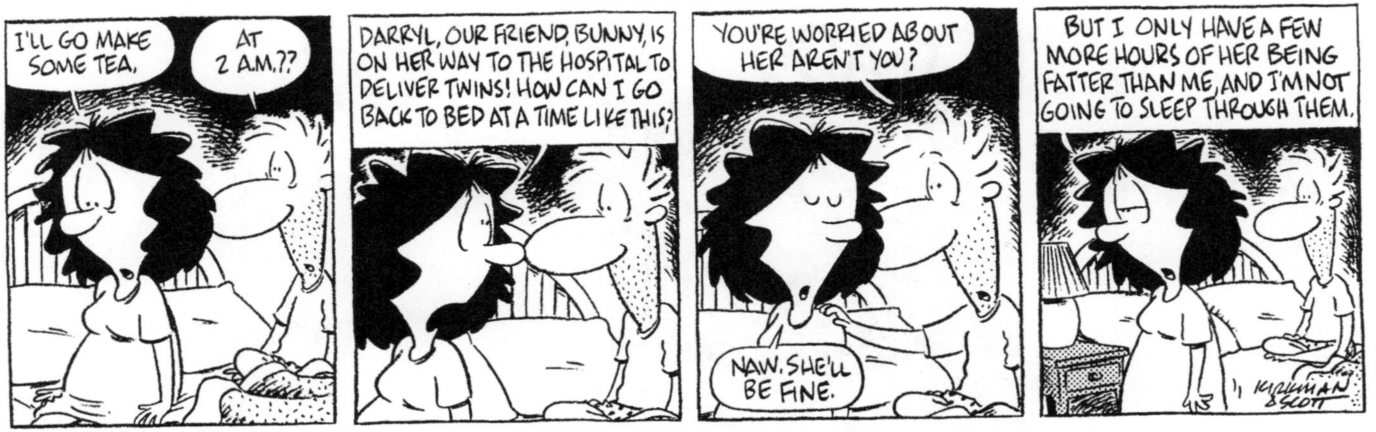
I'LL GO MAKE SOME TEA.
AT 2 A.M.??
DARRYL, OUR FRIEND, BUNNY, IS ON HER WAY TO THE HOSPITAL TO DELIVER TWINS! HOW CAN I GO BACK TO BED AT A TIME LIKE THIS?
YOU'RE WORRIED ABOUT HER AREN'T YOU?
NAW. SHE'LL BE FINE.
BUT I ONLY HAVE A FEW MORE HOURS OF HER BEING FATTER THAN ME, AND I'M NOT GOING TO SLEEP THROUGH THEM.
KIRKMAN & SCOTT

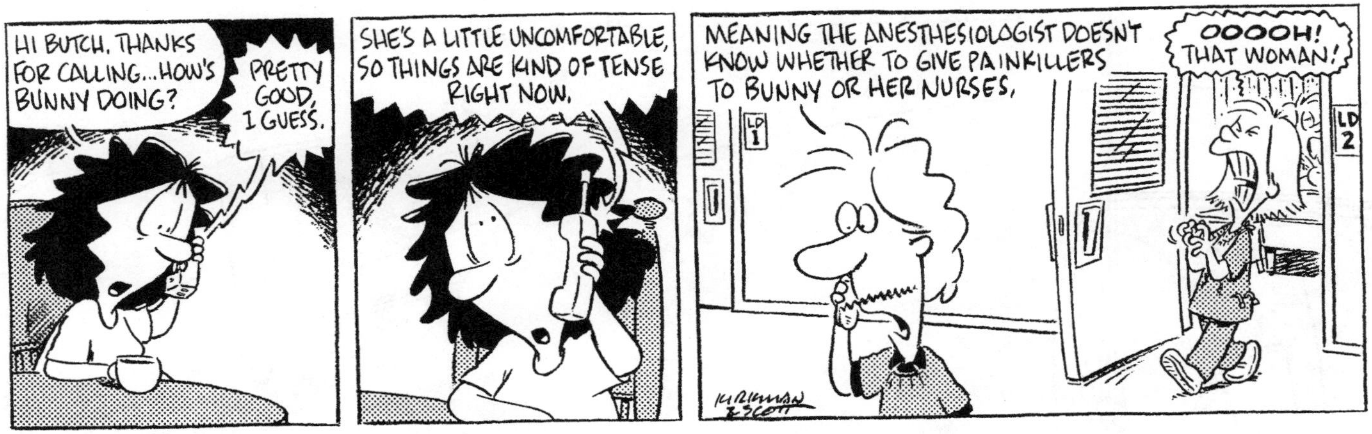
HI BUTCH. THANKS FOR CALLING... HOW'S BUNNY DOING?
PRETTY GOOD, I GUESS.
SHE'S A LITTLE UNCOMFORTABLE, SO THINGS ARE KIND OF TENSE RIGHT NOW.
MEANING THE ANESTHESIOLOGIST DOESN'T KNOW WHETHER TO GIVE PAINKILLERS TO BUNNY OR HER NURSES.
OOOOH! THAT WOMAN!
LD 1
LD 2
KIRKMAN & SCOTT

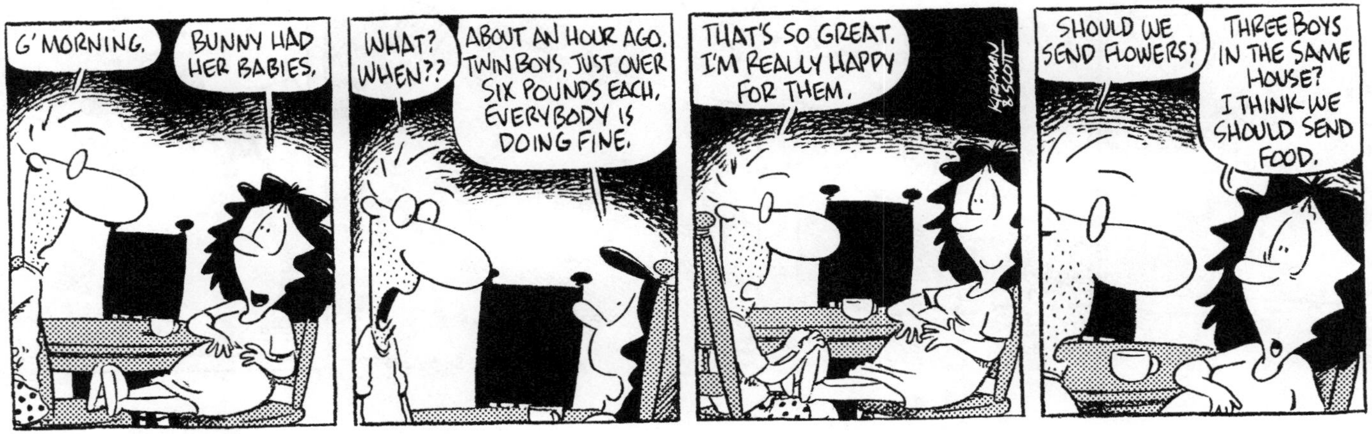
G'MORNING.
BUNNY HAD HER BABIES.
WHAT? WHEN??
ABOUT AN HOUR AGO. TWIN BOYS, JUST OVER SIX POUNDS EACH. EVERYBODY IS DOING FINE.
THAT'S SO GREAT. I'M REALLY HAPPY FOR THEM.
KIRKMAN & SCOTT
SHOULD WE SEND FLOWERS?
THREE BOYS IN THE SAME HOUSE? I THINK WE SHOULD SEND FOOD.

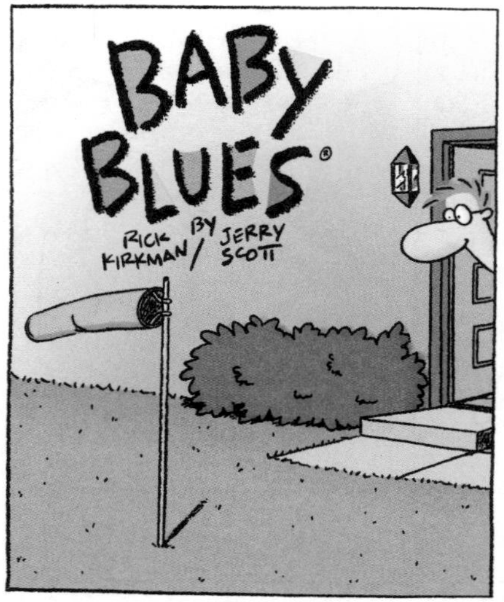
BABY BLUES®
BY RICK KIRKMAN / JERRY SCOTT

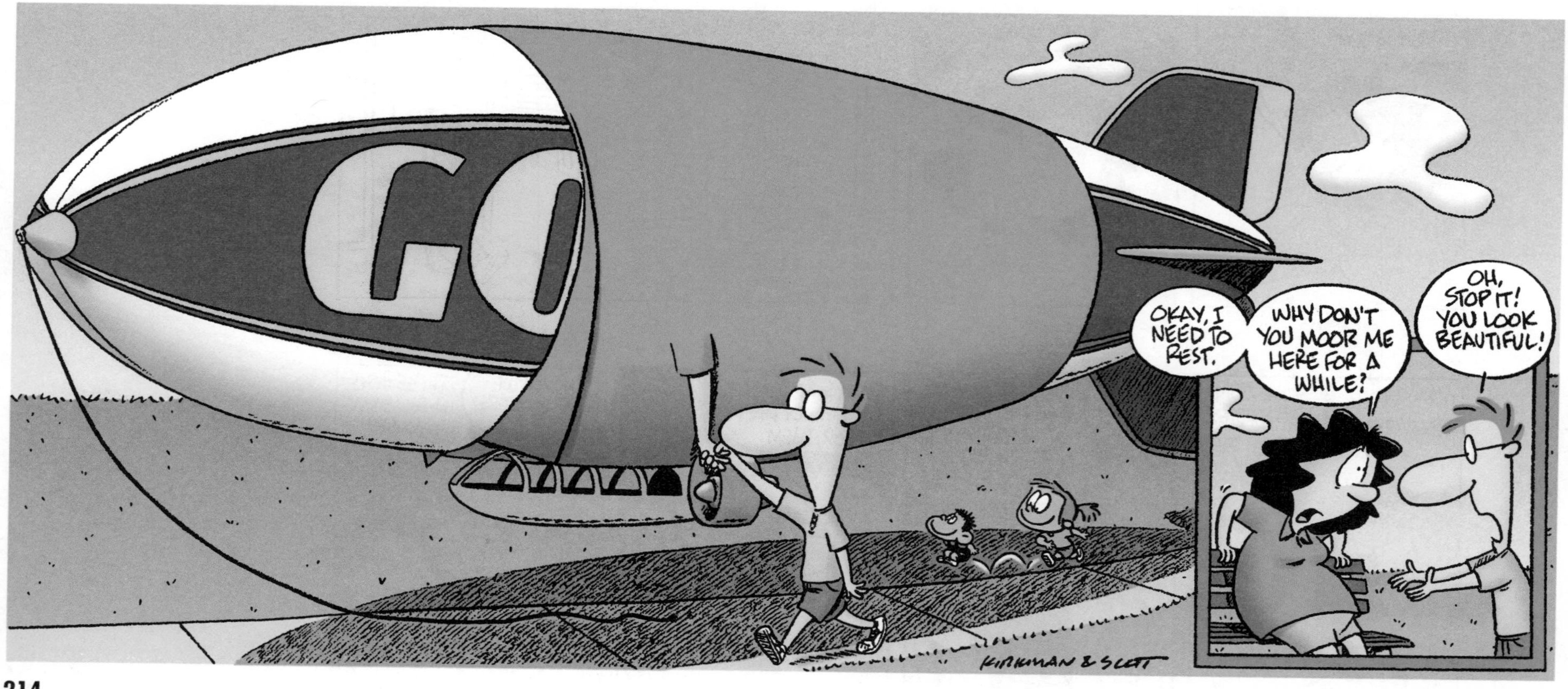
GO
OKAY, I NEED TO REST.
WHY DON'T YOU MOOR ME HERE FOR A WHILE?
OH, STOP IT! YOU LOOK BEAUTIFUL!
KIRKMAN & SCOTT

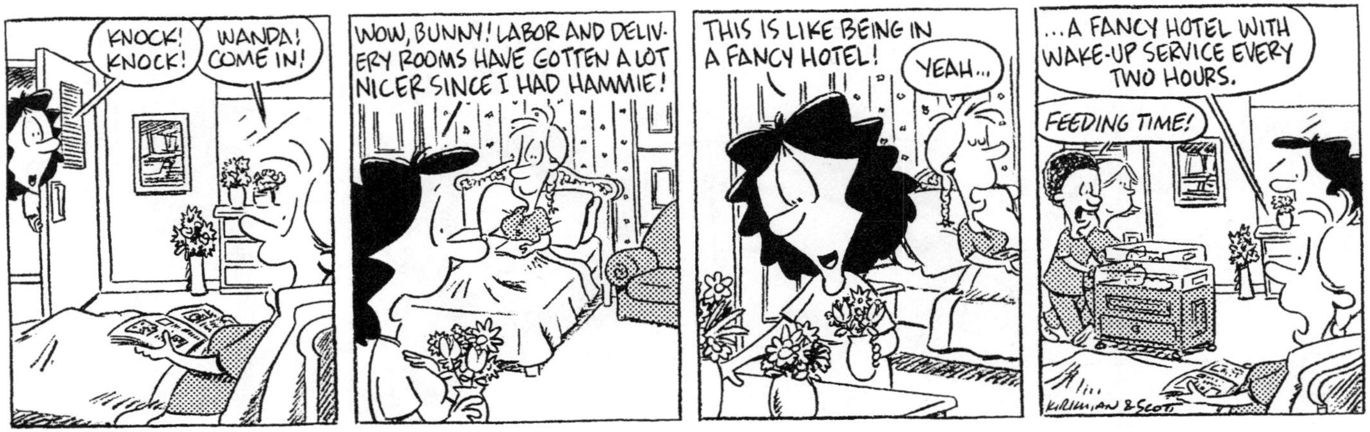
KNOCK! KNOCK!
WANDA! COME IN!
WOW, BUNNY! LABOR AND DELIVERY ROOMS HAVE GOTTEN A LOT NICER SINCE I HAD HAMMIE!
THIS IS LIKE BEING IN A FANCY HOTEL!
YEAH...
...A FANCY HOTEL WITH WAKE-UP SERVICE EVERY TWO HOURS.
FEEDING TIME!
KIRKMAN & SCOTT

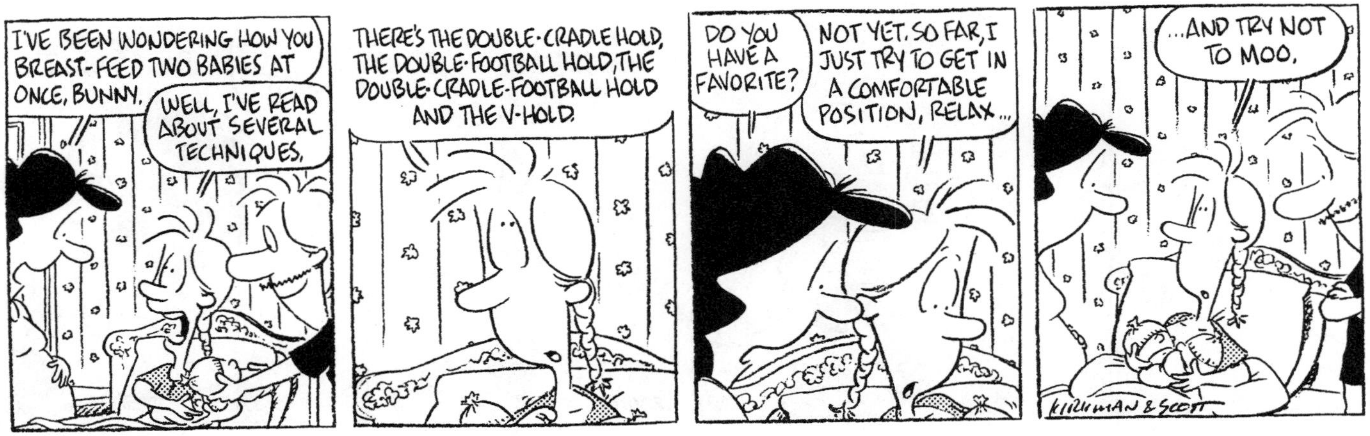
I'VE BEEN WONDERING HOW YOU BREAST-FEED TWO BABIES AT ONCE, BUNNY.
WELL, I'VE READ ABOUT SEVERAL TECHNIQUES.
THERE'S THE DOUBLE-CRADLE HOLD, THE DOUBLE-FOOTBALL HOLD, THE DOUBLE-CRADLE-FOOTBALL HOLD AND THE V-HOLD.
DO YOU HAVE A FAVORITE?
NOT YET. SO FAR, I JUST TRY TO GET IN A COMFORTABLE POSITION, RELAX...
...AND TRY NOT TO MOO.
KIRKMAN & SCOTT

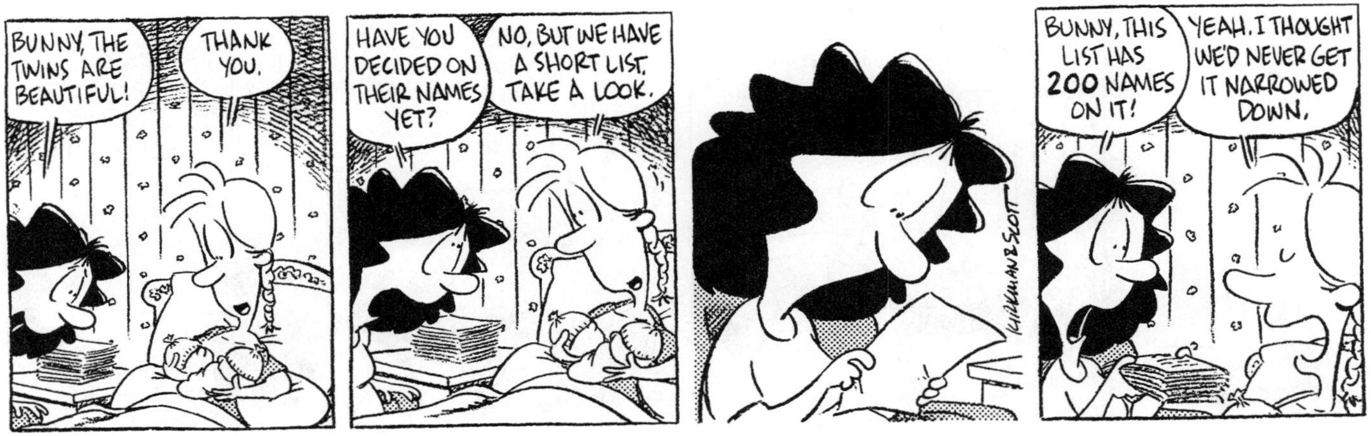
BUNNY, THE TWINS ARE BEAUTIFUL!
THANK YOU.
HAVE YOU DECIDED ON THEIR NAMES YET?
NO, BUT WE HAVE A SHORT LIST. TAKE A LOOK.
KIRKMAN & SCOTT
BUNNY, THIS LIST HAS 200 NAMES ON IT!
YEAH. I THOUGHT WE'D NEVER GET IT NARROWED DOWN.

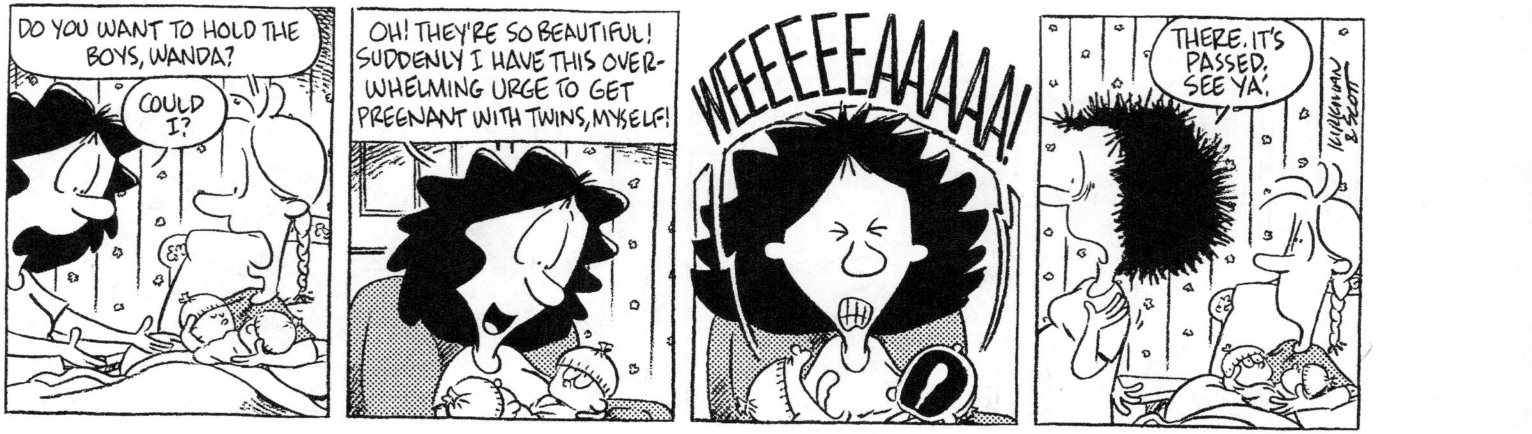
DO YOU WANT TO HOLD THE BOYS, WANDA?
COULD I?
OH! THEY'RE SO BEAUTIFUL! SUDDENLY I HAVE THIS OVER-WHELMING URGE TO GET PREGNANT WITH TWINS, MYSELF!
WEEEEEEAAAAA!
THERE. IT'S PASSED. SEE YA.
KIRKMAN & SCOTT

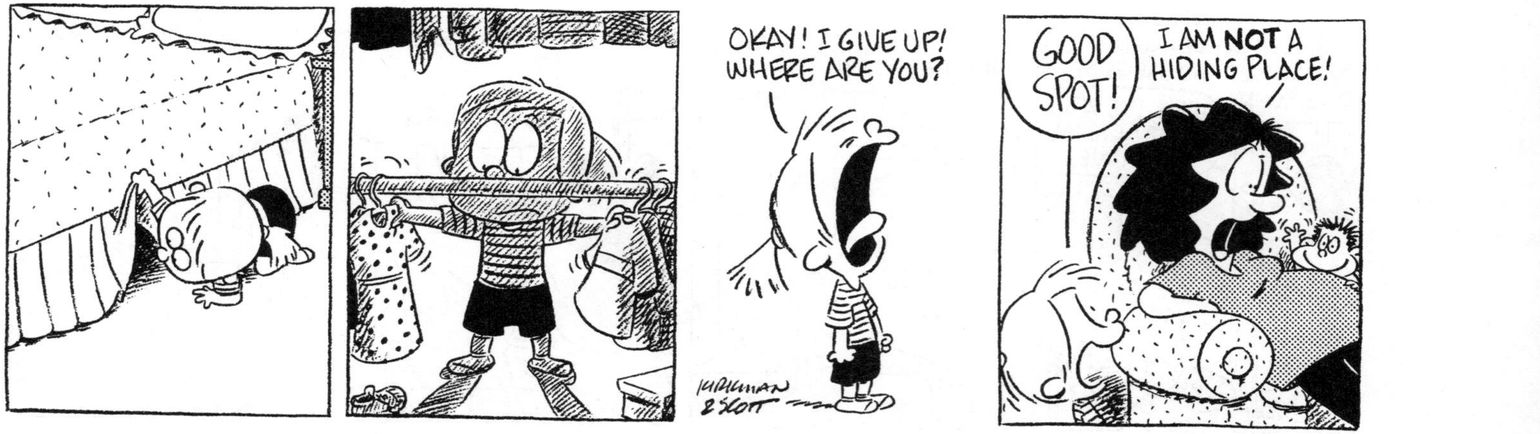
OKAY! I GIVE UP! WHERE ARE YOU?
KIRKMAN & SCOTT
GOOD SPOT!
I AM **NOT** A HIDING PLACE!

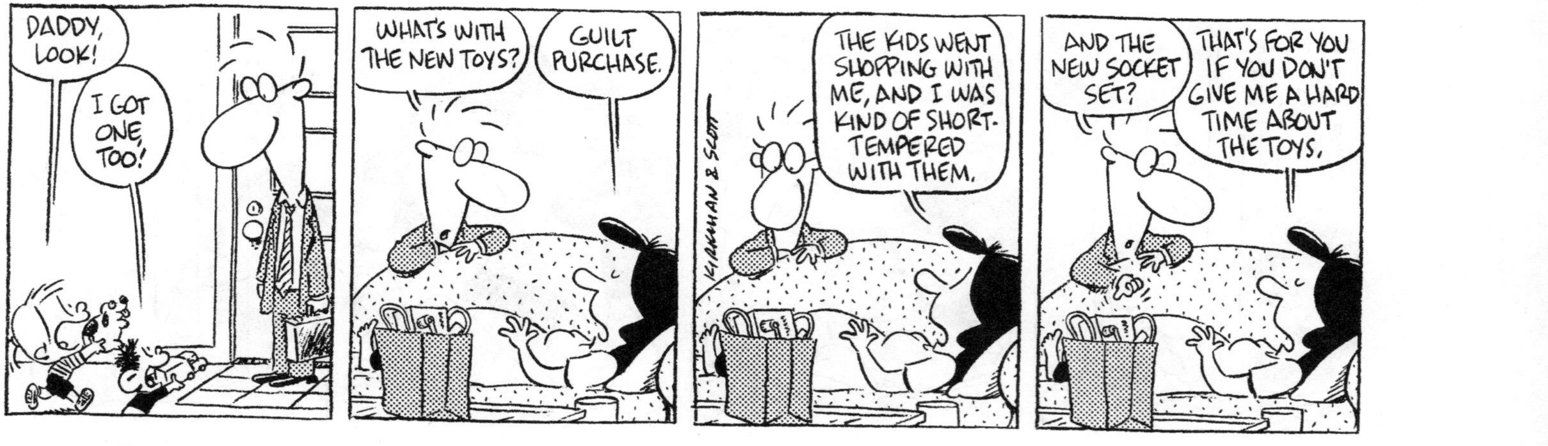
DADDY, LOOK!
I GOT ONE, TOO!
WHAT'S WITH THE NEW TOYS?
GUILT PURCHASE.
KIRKMAN & SCOTT
THE KIDS WENT SHOPPING WITH ME, AND I WAS KIND OF SHORT-TEMPERED WITH THEM.
AND THE NEW SOCKET SET?
THAT'S FOR YOU IF YOU DON'T GIVE ME A HARD TIME ABOUT THE TOYS.

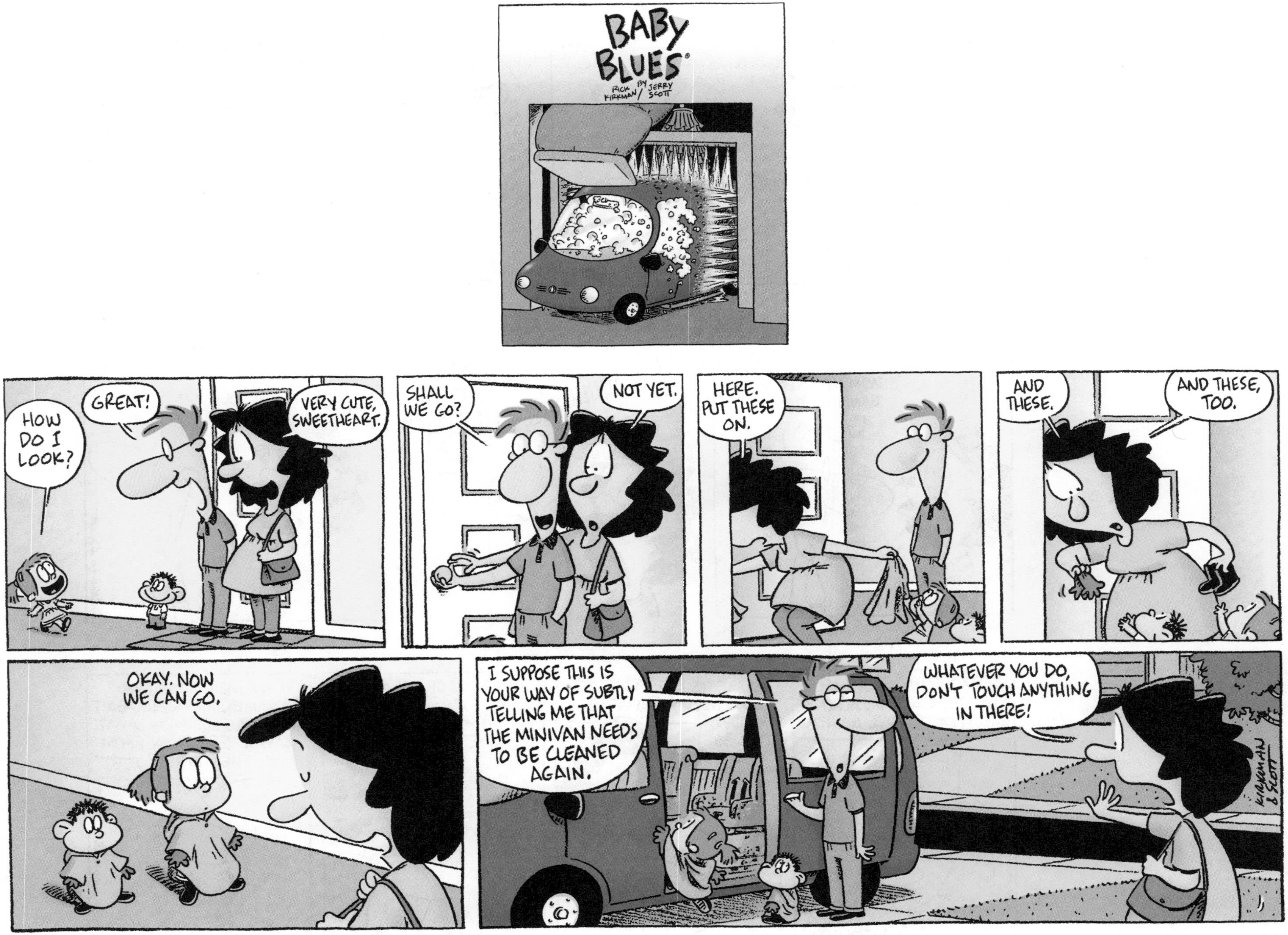
BABY BLUES®
BY RICK KIRKMAN / JERRY SCOTT
HOW DO I LOOK?
GREAT!
VERY CUTE, SWEETHEART.
SHALL WE GO?
NOT YET.
HERE. PUT THESE ON.
AND THESE.
AND THESE, TOO.
OKAY. NOW WE CAN GO.
I SUPPOSE THIS IS YOUR WAY OF SUBTLY TELLING ME THAT THE MINIVAN NEEDS TO BE CLEANED AGAIN.
WHATEVER YOU DO, DON'T TOUCH ANYTHING IN THERE!
KIRKMAN & SCOTT

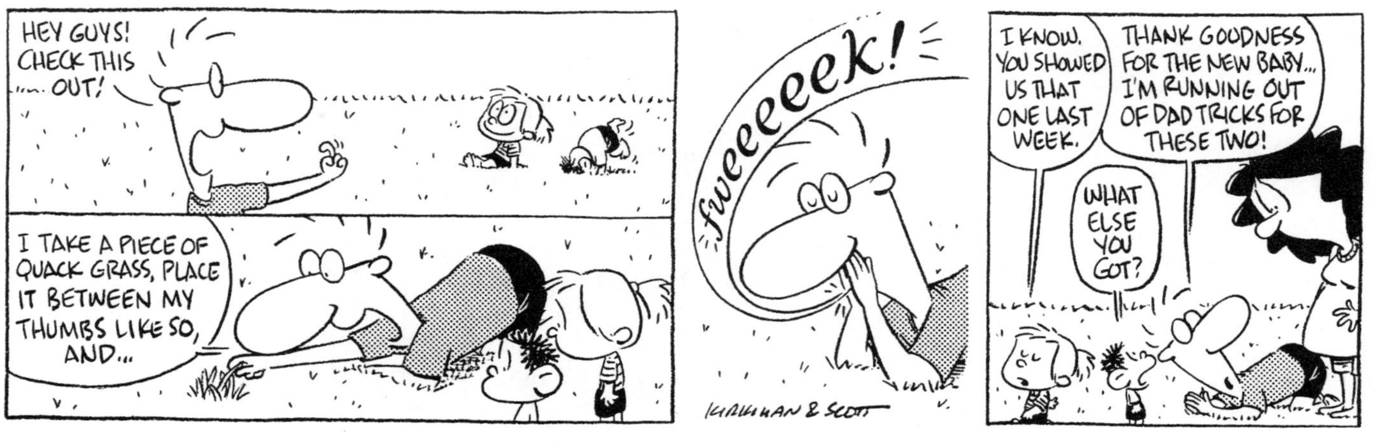
HEY GUYS! CHECK THIS OUT!
I TAKE A PIECE OF QUACK GRASS, PLACE IT BETWEEN MY THUMBS LIKE SO, AND...
fweeeeek!
I KNOW. YOU SHOWED US THAT ONE LAST WEEK.
WHAT ELSE YOU GOT?
THANK GOODNESS FOR THE NEW BABY... I'M RUNNING OUT OF DAD TRICKS FOR THESE TWO!
KIRKMAN & SCOTT

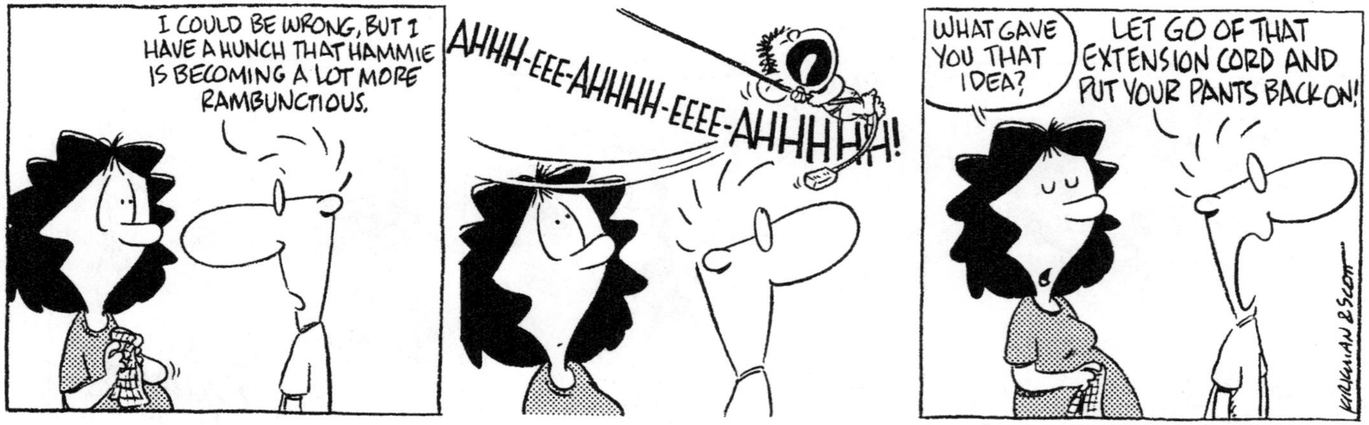
I COULD BE WRONG, BUT I HAVE A HUNCH THAT HAMMIE IS BECOMING A LOT MORE RAMBUNCTIOUS.
AHHH-EEE-AHHHH-EEEE-AHHHHH!
WHAT GAVE YOU THAT IDEA?
LET GO OF THAT EXTENSION CORD AND PUT YOUR PANTS BACK ON!
KIRKMAN & SCOTT

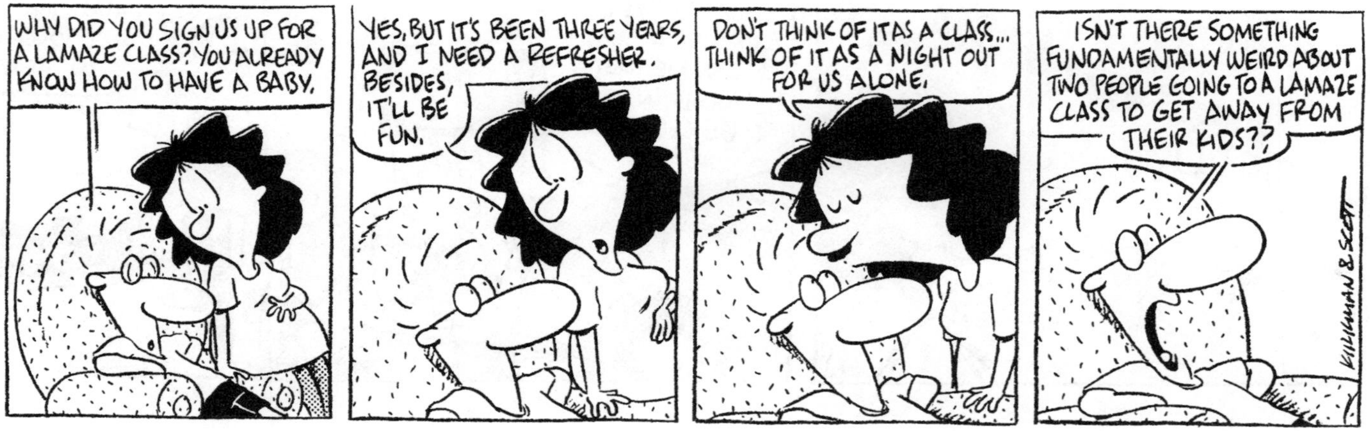
WHY DID YOU SIGN US UP FOR A LAMAZE CLASS? YOU ALREADY KNOW HOW TO HAVE A BABY.
YES, BUT IT'S BEEN THREE YEARS, AND I NEED A REFRESHER.
BESIDES, IT'LL BE FUN.
DON'T THINK OF IT AS A CLASS... THINK OF IT AS A NIGHT OUT FOR US ALONE.
ISN'T THERE SOMETHING FUNDAMENTALLY WEIRD ABOUT TWO PEOPLE GOING TO A LAMAZE CLASS TO GET AWAY FROM THEIR KIDS??
KIRKMAN & SCOTT

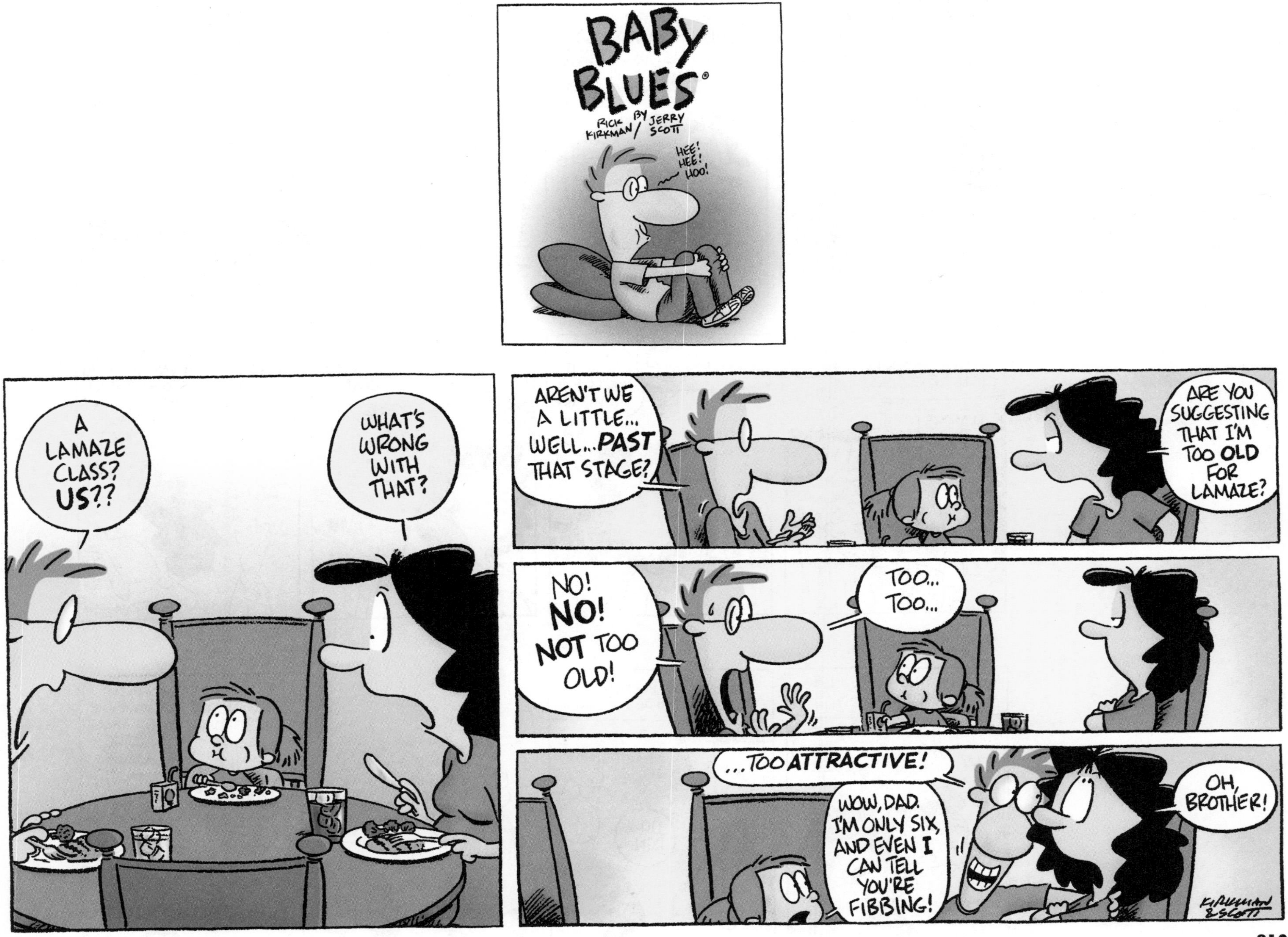
BABY BLUES®
BY RICK KIRKMAN / JERRY SCOTT
HEE! HEE! HOO!
A LAMAZE CLASS? US??
WHAT'S WRONG WITH THAT?
AREN'T WE A LITTLE... WELL...PAST THAT STAGE?
ARE YOU SUGGESTING THAT I'M TOO OLD FOR LAMAZE?
NO! NO! NOT TOO OLD!
TOO... TOO...
...TOO ATTRACTIVE!
OH, BROTHER!
WOW, DAD. I'M ONLY SIX, AND EVEN I CAN TELL YOU'RE FIBBING!
KIRKMAN & SCOTT

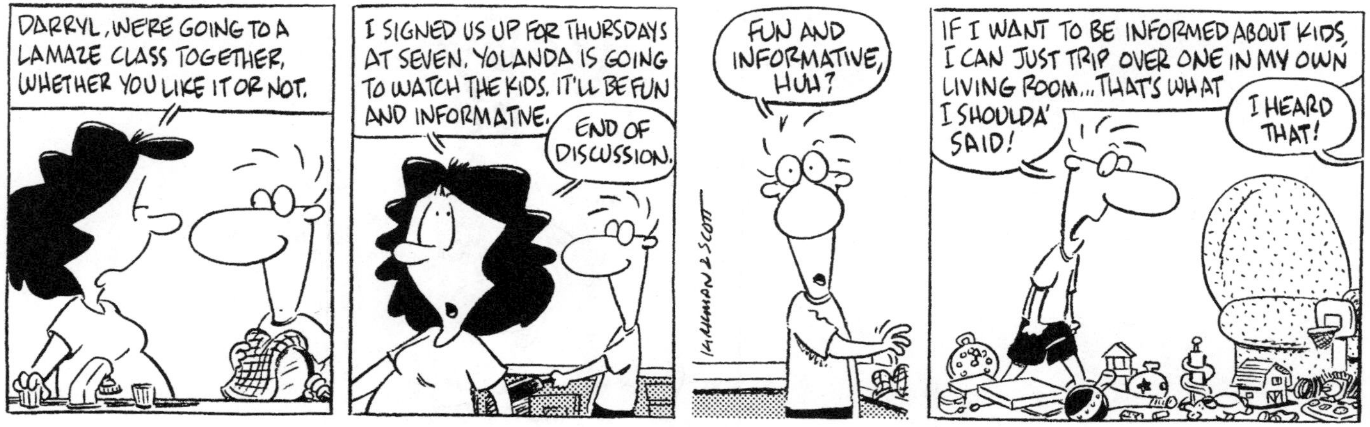
DARRYL, WE'RE GOING TO A LAMAZE CLASS TOGETHER, WHETHER YOU LIKE IT OR NOT.
I SIGNED US UP FOR THURSDAYS AT SEVEN. YOLANDA IS GOING TO WATCH THE KIDS. IT'LL BE FUN AND INFORMATIVE.
END OF DISCUSSION.
KIRKMAN & SCOTT
FUN AND INFORMATIVE, HUH?
IF I WANT TO BE INFORMED ABOUT KIDS, I CAN JUST TRIP OVER ONE IN MY OWN LIVING ROOM... THAT'S WHAT I SHOULDA' SAID!
I HEARD THAT!

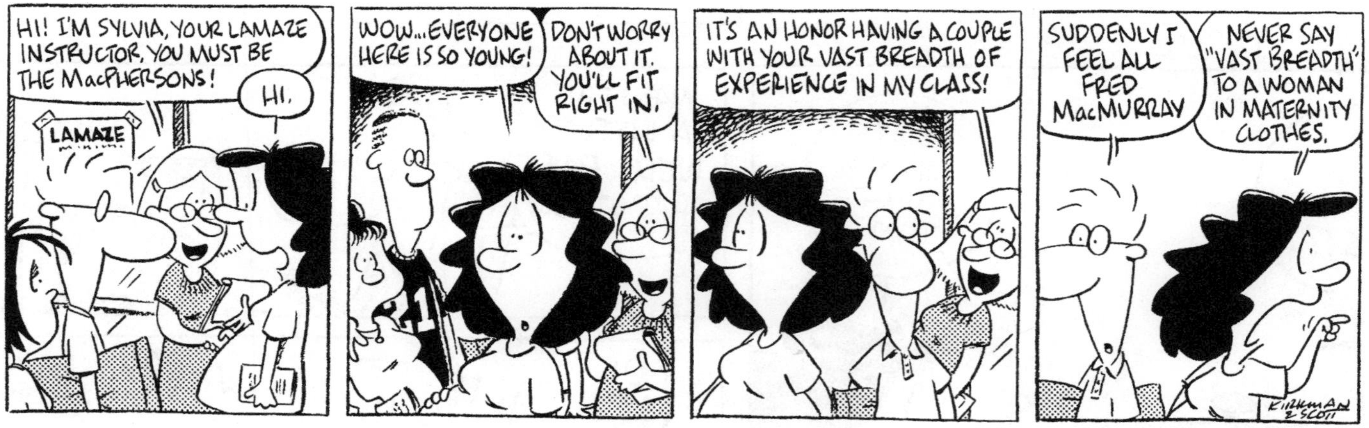
HI! I'M SYLVIA, YOUR LAMAZE INSTRUCTOR. YOU MUST BE THE MacPHERSONS!
HI.
LAMAZE
WOW... EVERYONE HERE IS SO YOUNG!
DON'T WORRY ABOUT IT. YOU'LL FIT RIGHT IN.
IT'S AN HONOR HAVING A COUPLE WITH YOUR VAST BREADTH OF EXPERIENCE IN MY CLASS!
SUDDENLY I FEEL ALL FRED MacMURRAY
NEVER SAY "VAST BREADTH" TO A WOMAN IN MATERNITY CLOTHES.
KIRKMAN & SCOTT

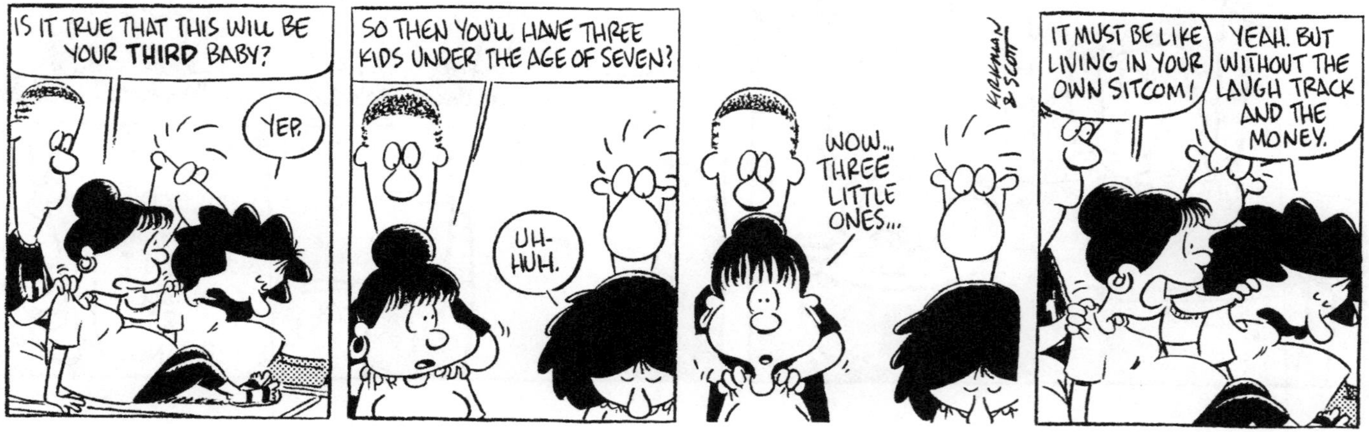
IS IT TRUE THAT THIS WILL BE YOUR THIRD BABY?
YEP.
SO THEN YOU'LL HAVE THREE KIDS UNDER THE AGE OF SEVEN?
UH-HUH.
WOW... THREE LITTLE ONES...
KIRKMAN & SCOTT
IT MUST BE LIKE LIVING IN YOUR OWN SITCOM!
YEAH. BUT WITHOUT THE LAUGH TRACK AND THE MONEY.

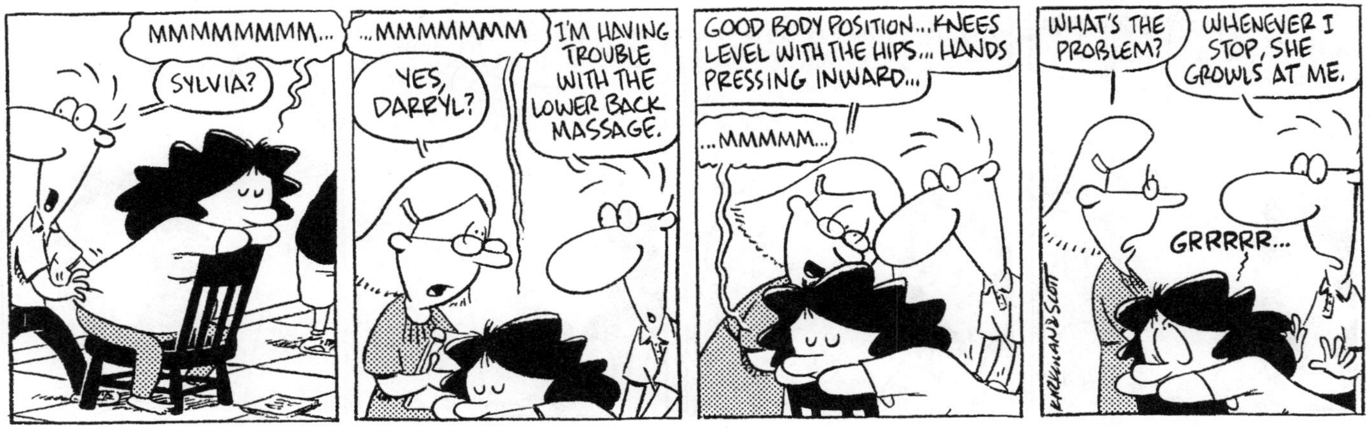
MMMMMMMM...
SYLVIA?
...MMMMMMM
YES, DARRYL?
I'M HAVING TROUBLE WITH THE LOWER BACK MASSAGE.
GOOD BODY POSITION... KNEES LEVEL WITH THE HIPS... HANDS PRESSING INWARD...
...MMMMM...
WHAT'S THE PROBLEM?
WHENEVER I STOP, SHE GROWLS AT ME.
GRRRRR...

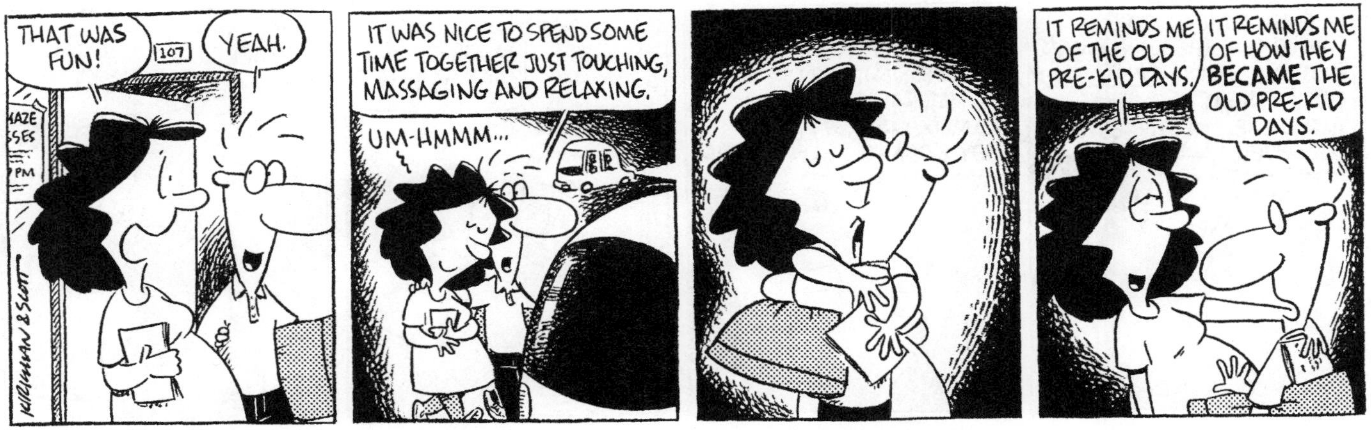
THAT WAS FUN!
107
YEAH.
IT WAS NICE TO SPEND SOME TIME TOGETHER JUST TOUCHING, MASSAGING AND RELAXING.
UM-HMMM...
IT REMINDS ME OF THE OLD PRE-KID DAYS.
IT REMINDS ME OF HOW THEY BECAME THE OLD PRE-KID DAYS.

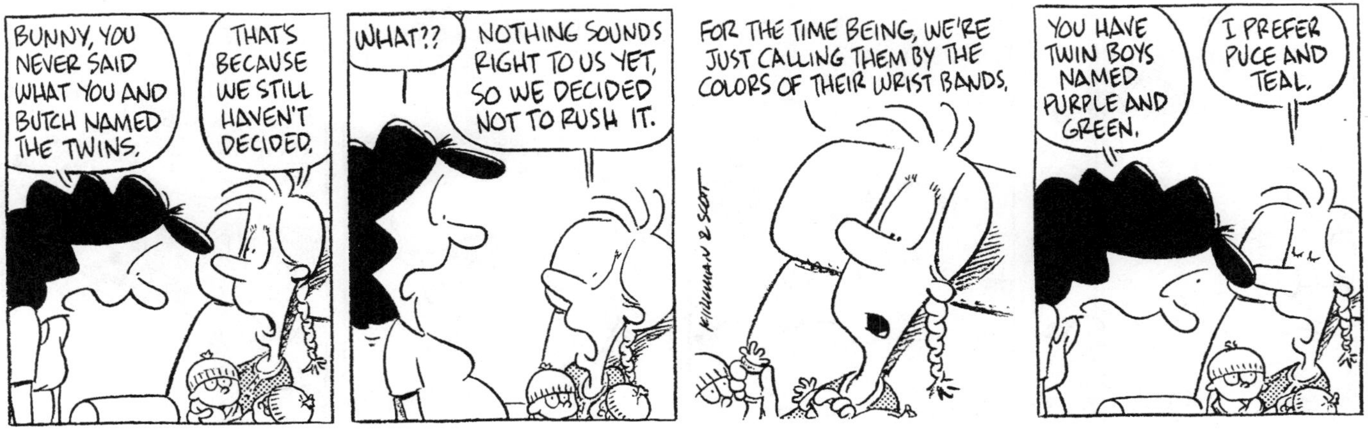
BUNNY, YOU NEVER SAID WHAT YOU AND BUTCH NAMED THE TWINS.
THAT'S BECAUSE WE STILL HAVEN'T DECIDED.
WHAT??
NOTHING SOUNDS RIGHT TO US YET, SO WE DECIDED NOT TO RUSH IT.
FOR THE TIME BEING, WE'RE JUST CALLING THEM BY THE COLORS OF THEIR WRIST BANDS.
YOU HAVE TWIN BOYS NAMED PURPLE AND GREEN.
I PREFER PUCE AND TEAL.

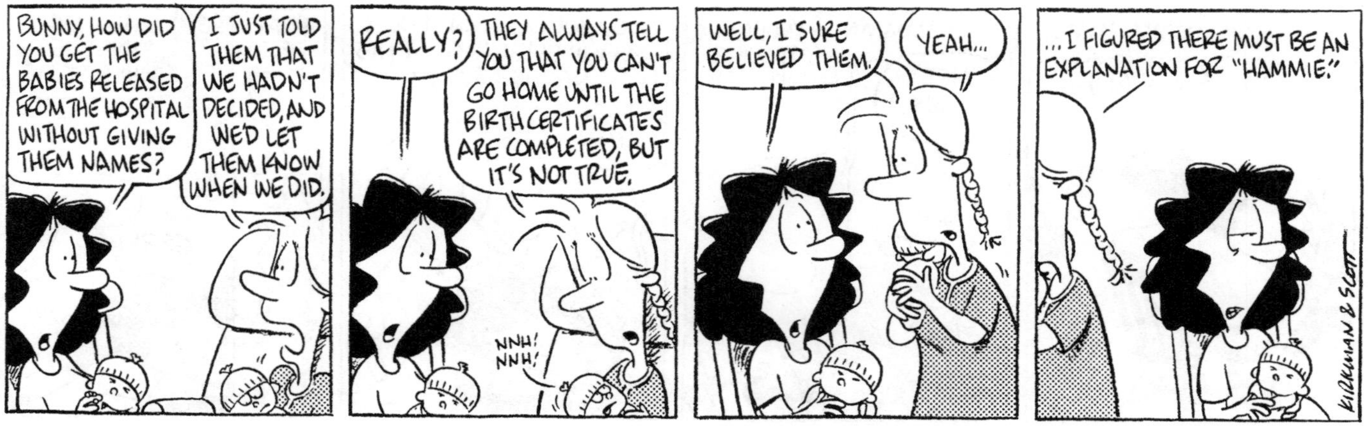
BUNNY, HOW DID YOU GET THE BABIES RELEASED FROM THE HOSPITAL WITHOUT GIVING THEM NAMES?
I JUST TOLD THEM THAT WE HADN'T DECIDED, AND WE'D LET THEM KNOW WHEN WE DID.
REALLY?
THEY ALWAYS TELL YOU THAT YOU CAN'T GO HOME UNTIL THE BIRTH CERTIFICATES ARE COMPLETED, BUT IT'S NOT TRUE.
NNH! NNH!
WELL, I SURE BELIEVED THEM.
YEAH...
...I FIGURED THERE MUST BE AN EXPLANATION FOR "HAMMIE."
KIRKMAN & SCOTT

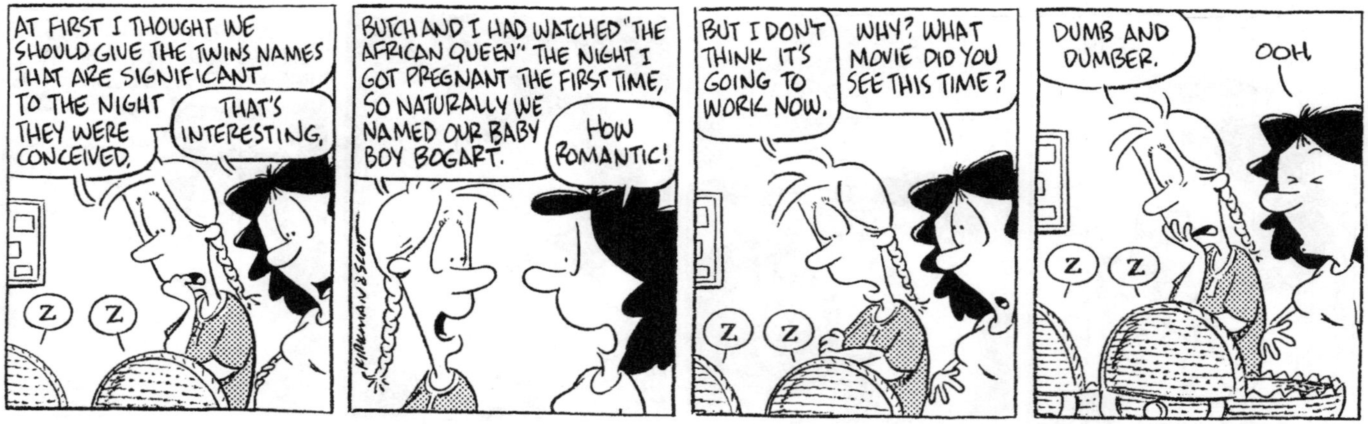
AT FIRST I THOUGHT WE SHOULD GIVE THE TWINS NAMES THAT ARE SIGNIFICANT TO THE NIGHT THEY WERE CONCEIVED.
THAT'S INTERESTING.
Z
Z
BUTCH AND I HAD WATCHED "THE AFRICAN QUEEN" THE NIGHT I GOT PREGNANT THE FIRST TIME, SO NATURALLY WE NAMED OUR BABY BOY BOGART.
HOW ROMANTIC!
KIRKMAN & SCOTT
BUT I DON'T THINK IT'S GOING TO WORK NOW.
WHY? WHAT MOVIE DID YOU SEE THIS TIME?
Z
Z
DUMB AND DUMBER.
OOH.
Z
Z

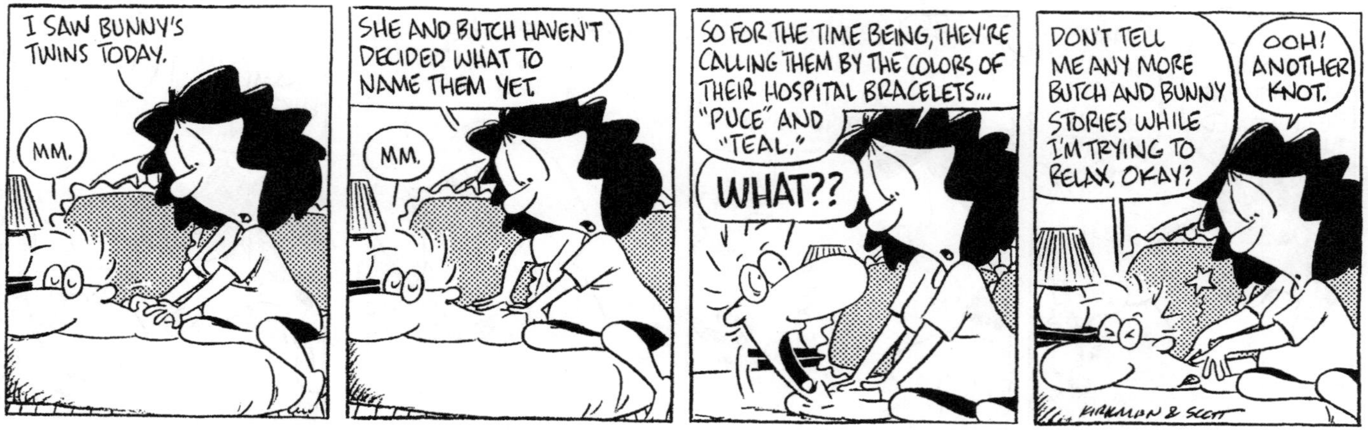
I SAW BUNNY'S TWINS TODAY.
MM.
SHE AND BUTCH HAVEN'T DECIDED WHAT TO NAME THEM YET.
MM.
SO FOR THE TIME BEING, THEY'RE CALLING THEM BY THE COLORS OF THEIR HOSPITAL BRACELETS... "PUCE" AND "TEAL."
WHAT??
DON'T TELL ME ANY MORE BUTCH AND BUNNY STORIES WHILE I'M TRYING TO RELAX, OKAY?
OOH! ANOTHER KNOT.
KIRKMAN & SCOTT

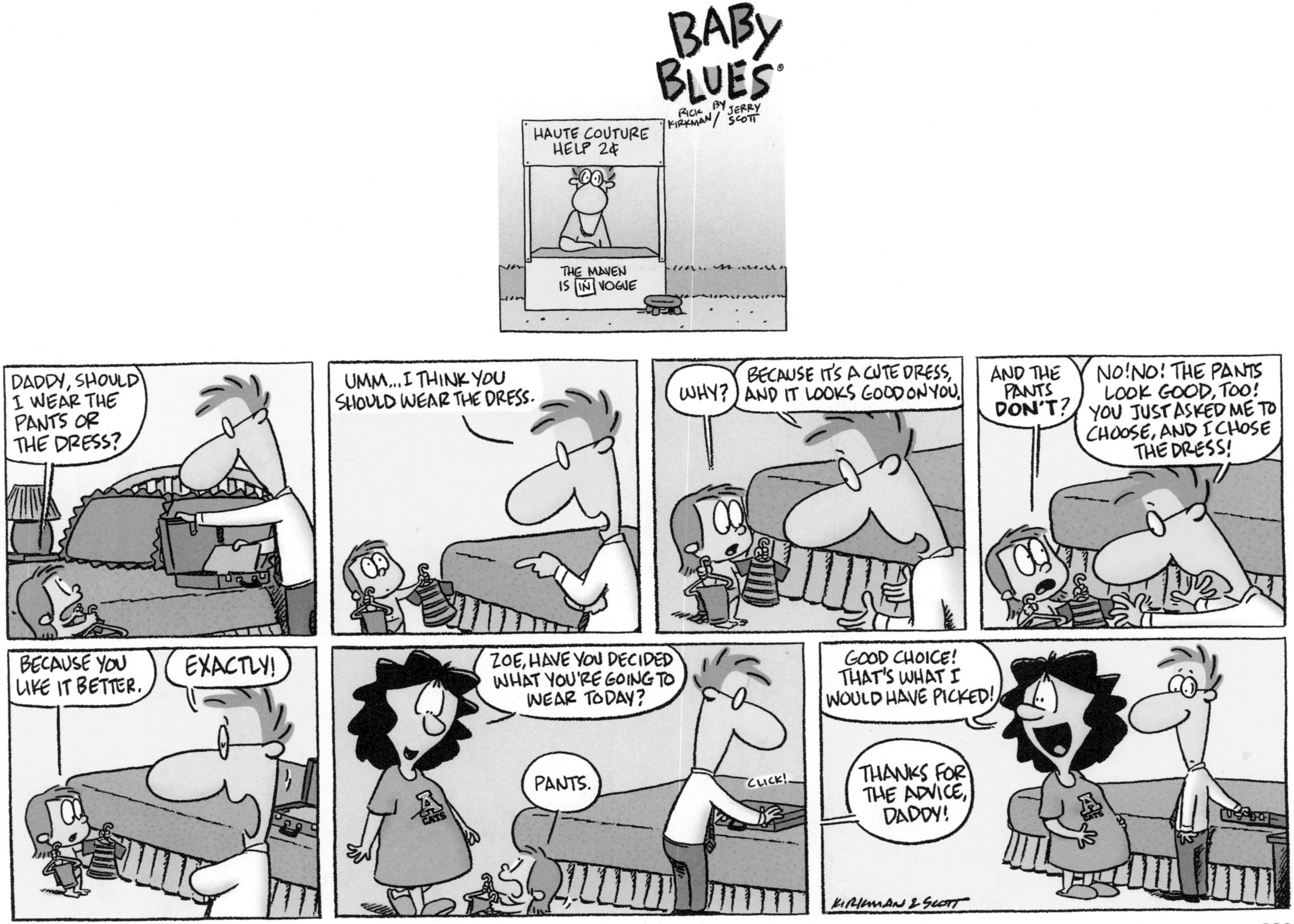
BABY BLUES®
BY RICK KIRKMAN / JERRY SCOTT
HAUTE COUTURE HELP 2¢
THE MAVEN IS IN VOGUE
DADDY, SHOULD I WEAR THE PANTS OR THE DRESS?
UMM... I THINK YOU SHOULD WEAR THE DRESS.
WHY?
BECAUSE IT'S A CUTE DRESS, AND IT LOOKS GOOD ON YOU.
AND THE PANTS DON'T?
NO! NO! THE PANTS LOOK GOOD, TOO! YOU JUST ASKED ME TO CHOOSE, AND I CHOSE THE DRESS!
BECAUSE YOU LIKE IT BETTER.
EXACTLY!
ZOE, HAVE YOU DECIDED WHAT YOU'RE GOING TO WEAR TODAY?
PANTS.
CLICK!
GOOD CHOICE! THAT'S WHAT I WOULD HAVE PICKED!
THANKS FOR THE ADVICE, DADDY!
KIRKMAN & SCOTT

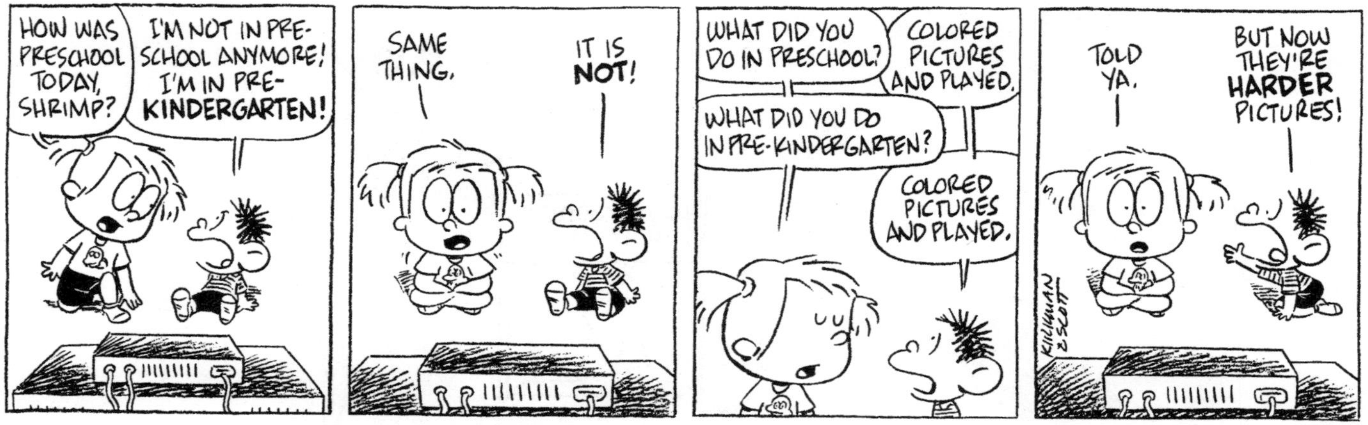
HOW WAS PRESCHOOL TODAY, SHRIMP?
I'M NOT IN PRESCHOOL ANYMORE! I'M IN PRE-KINDERGARTEN!
SAME THING.
IT IS NOT!
WHAT DID YOU DO IN PRESCHOOL?
COLORED PICTURES AND PLAYED.
WHAT DID YOU DO IN PRE-KINDERGARTEN?
COLORED PICTURES AND PLAYED.
TOLD YA.
BUT NOW THEY'RE HARDER PICTURES!

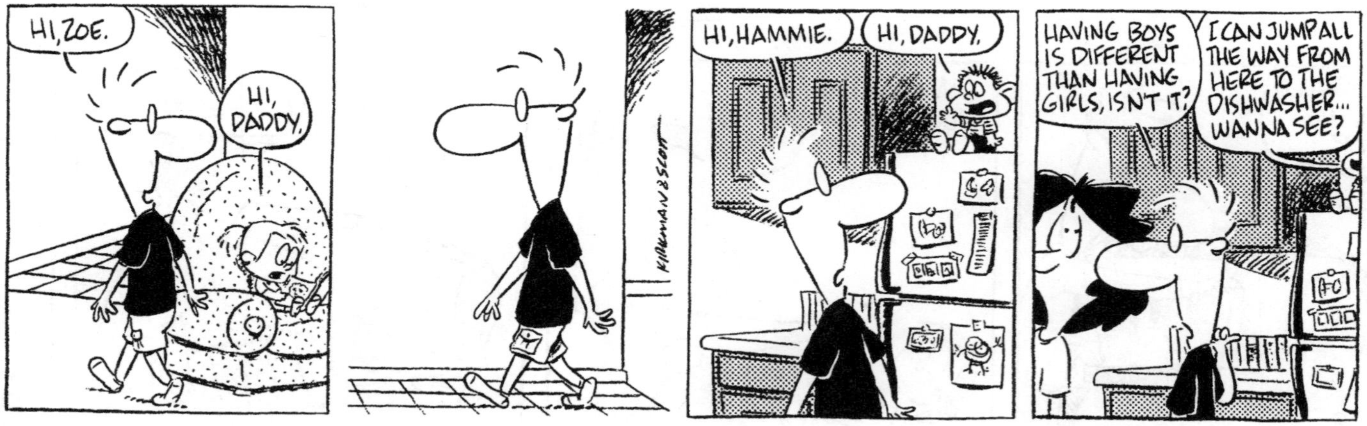
HI, ZOE.
HI, DADDY.
HI, HAMMIE.
HI, DADDY.
HAVING BOYS IS DIFFERENT THAN HAVING GIRLS, ISN'T IT?
I CAN JUMP ALL THE WAY FROM HERE TO THE DISHWASHER... WANNA SEE?

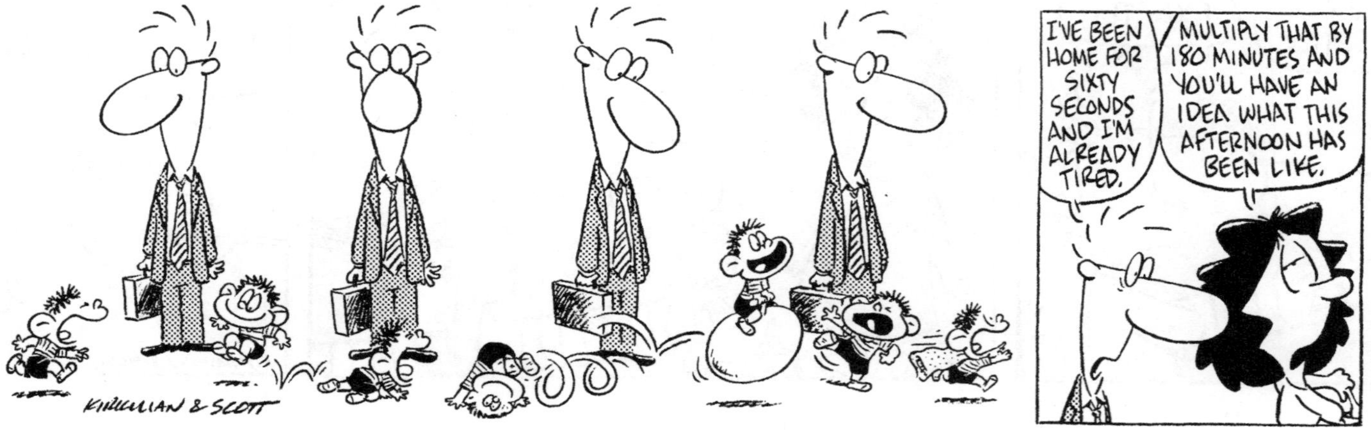
KIRKMAN & SCOTT
I'VE BEEN HOME FOR SIXTY SECONDS AND I'M ALREADY TIRED.
MULTIPLY THAT BY 180 MINUTES AND YOU'LL HAVE AN IDEA WHAT THIS AFTERNOON HAS BEEN LIKE.

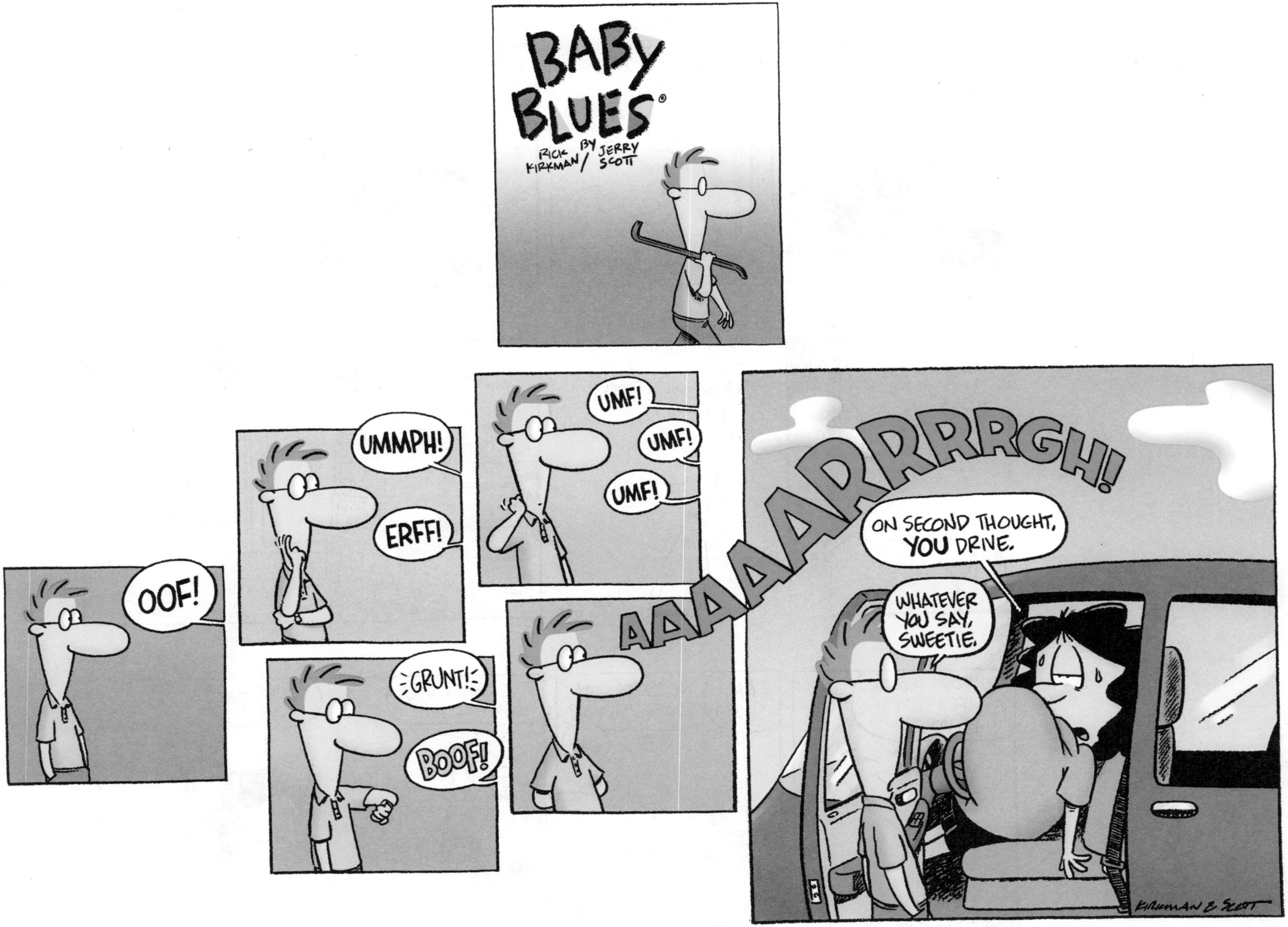
BABY BLUES®
BY RICK KIRKMAN / JERRY SCOTT
OOF!
UMMPH!
ERFF!
GRUNT!
BOOF!
UMF!
UMF!
UMF!
AAAAAARRRRRGH!
ON SECOND THOUGHT, YOU DRIVE.
WHATEVER YOU SAY, SWEETIE.
KIRKMAN & SCOTT

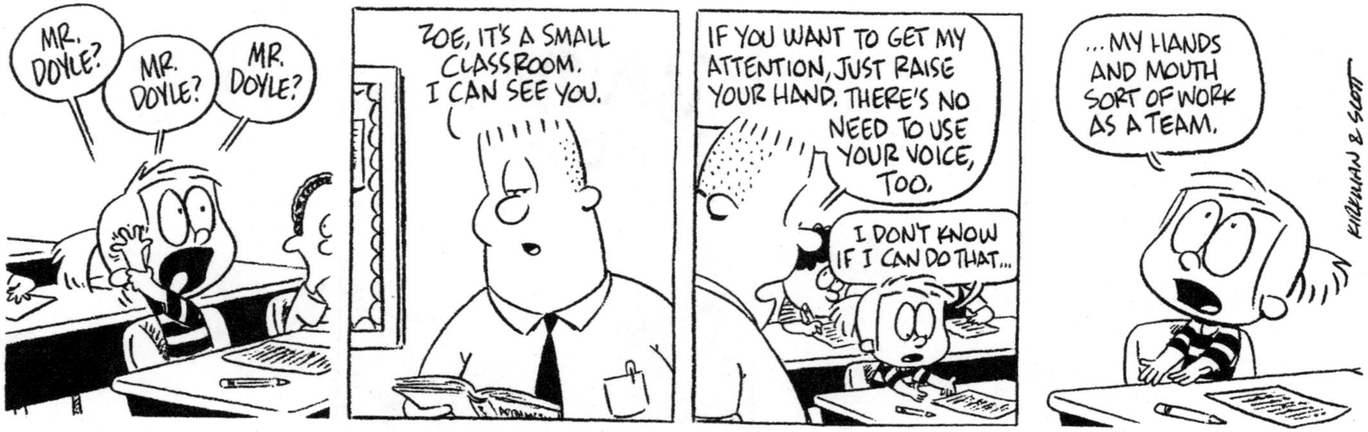
MR. DOYLE?
MR. DOYLE?
MR. DOYLE?
ZOE, IT'S A SMALL CLASSROOM. I CAN SEE YOU.
IF YOU WANT TO GET MY ATTENTION, JUST RAISE YOUR HAND. THERE'S NO NEED TO USE YOUR VOICE, TOO.
I DON'T KNOW IF I CAN DO THAT...
...MY HANDS AND MOUTH SORT OF WORK AS A TEAM.
KIRKMAN & SCOTT

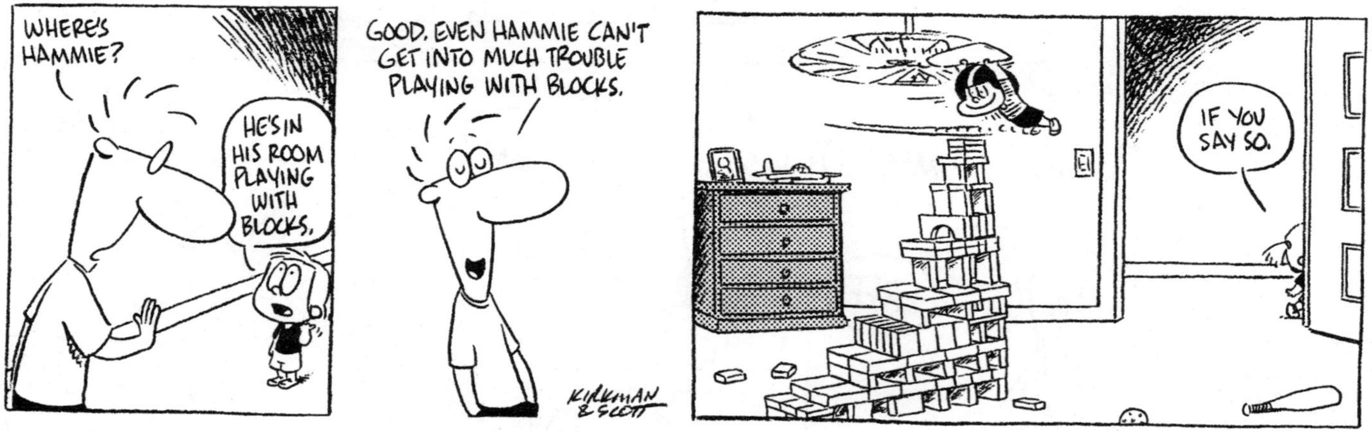
WHERE'S HAMMIE?
HE'S IN HIS ROOM PLAYING WITH BLOCKS.
GOOD. EVEN HAMMIE CAN'T GET INTO MUCH TROUBLE PLAYING WITH BLOCKS.
KIRKMAN & SCOTT
IF YOU SAY SO.

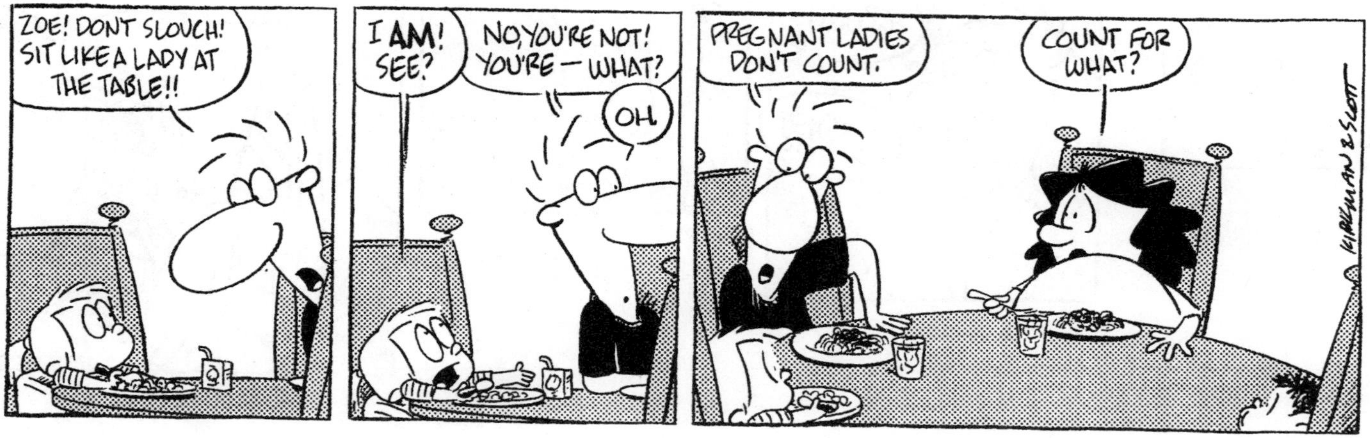
ZOE! DON'T SLOUCH! SIT LIKE A LADY AT THE TABLE!!
I AM! SEE?
NO, YOU'RE NOT! YOU'RE — WHAT?
OH.
PREGNANT LADIES DON'T COUNT.
COUNT FOR WHAT?
KIRKMAN & SCOTT

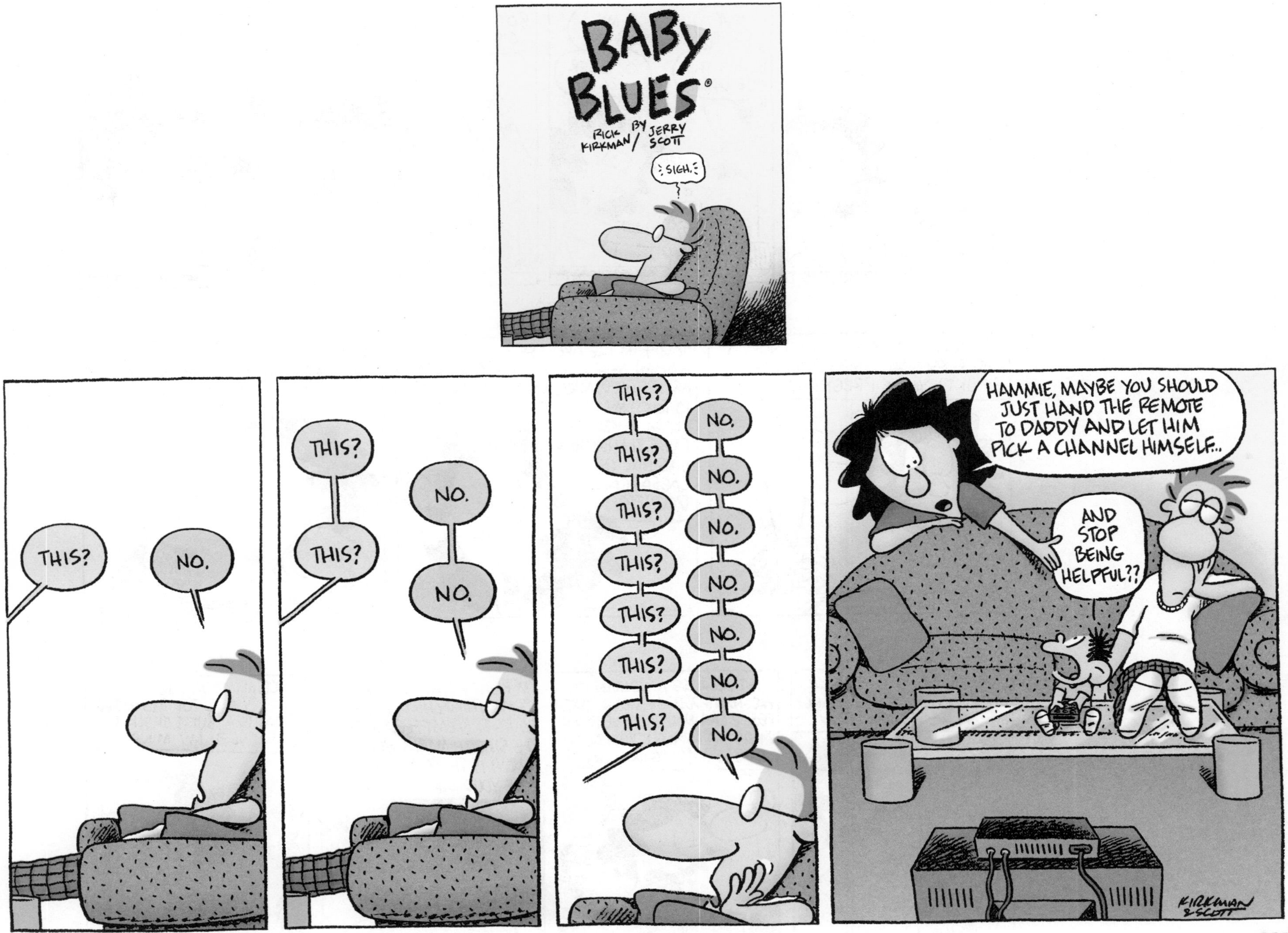
BABY BLUES®
BY RICK KIRKMAN / JERRY SCOTT
SIGH.
THIS?
NO.
THIS?
THIS?
NO.
NO.
THIS?
THIS?
THIS?
THIS?
THIS?
THIS?
THIS?
NO.
NO.
NO.
NO.
NO.
NO.
NO.
HAMMIE, MAYBE YOU SHOULD JUST HAND THE REMOTE TO DADDY AND LET HIM PICK A CHANNEL HIMSELF...
AND STOP BEING HELPFUL??
KIRKMAN & SCOTT

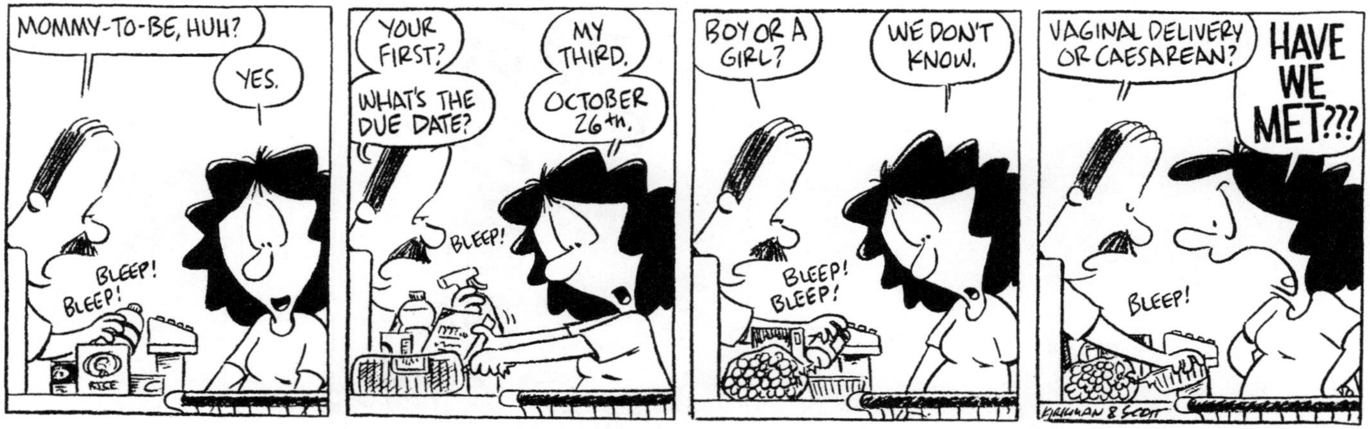
MOMMY-TO-BE, HUH?
YES.
BLEEP! BLEEP!
YOUR FIRST?
WHAT'S THE DUE DATE?
MY THIRD.
OCTOBER 26th.
BLEEP!
BOY OR A GIRL?
WE DON'T KNOW.
BLEEP! BLEEP!
VAGINAL DELIVERY OR CAESAREAN?
HAVE WE MET???
BLEEP!
KIRKMAN & SCOTT

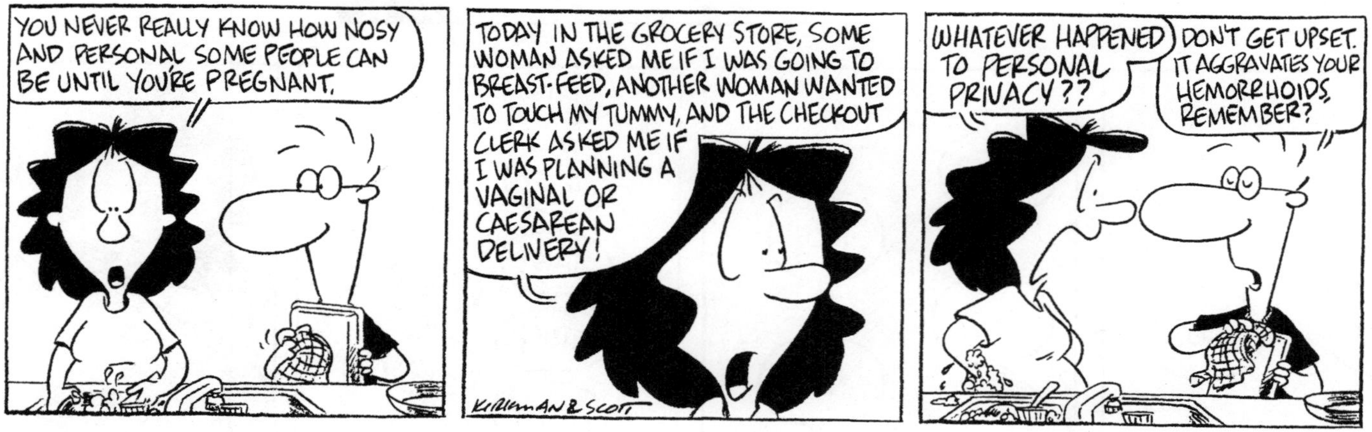
YOU NEVER REALLY KNOW HOW NOSY AND PERSONAL SOME PEOPLE CAN BE UNTIL YOU'RE PREGNANT.
TODAY IN THE GROCERY STORE, SOME WOMAN ASKED ME IF I WAS GOING TO BREAST-FEED, ANOTHER WOMAN WANTED TO TOUCH MY TUMMY, AND THE CHECKOUT CLERK ASKED ME IF I WAS PLANNING A VAGINAL OR CAESAREAN DELIVERY!
KIRKMAN & SCOTT
WHATEVER HAPPENED TO PERSONAL PRIVACY??
DON'T GET UPSET. IT AGGRAVATES YOUR HEMORRHOIDS, REMEMBER?

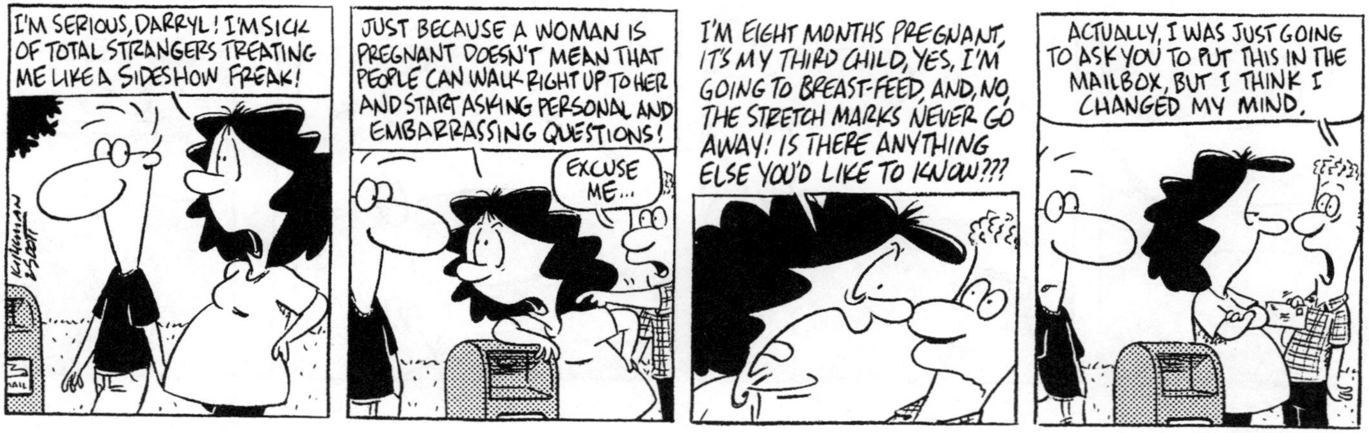
I'M SERIOUS, DARRYL! I'M SICK OF TOTAL STRANGERS TREATING ME LIKE A SIDESHOW FREAK!
KIRKMAN & SCOTT
JUST BECAUSE A WOMAN IS PREGNANT DOESN'T MEAN THAT PEOPLE CAN WALK RIGHT UP TO HER AND START ASKING PERSONAL AND EMBARRASSING QUESTIONS!
EXCUSE ME...
I'M EIGHT MONTHS PREGNANT, IT'S MY THIRD CHILD, YES, I'M GOING TO BREAST-FEED, AND, NO, THE STRETCH MARKS NEVER GO AWAY! IS THERE ANYTHING ELSE YOU'D LIKE TO KNOW???
ACTUALLY, I WAS JUST GOING TO ASK YOU TO PUT THIS IN THE MAILBOX, BUT I THINK I CHANGED MY MIND.

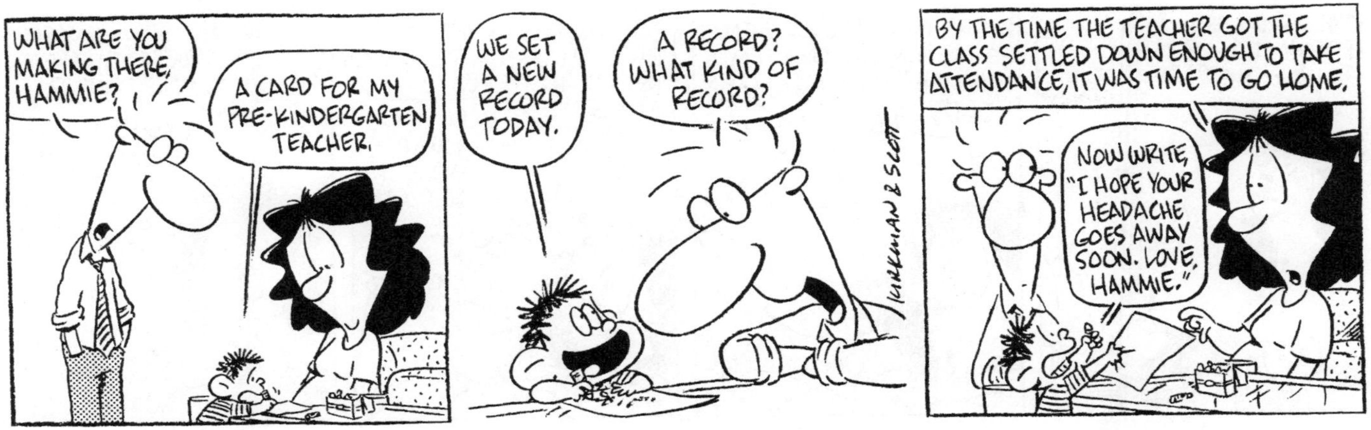
WHAT ARE YOU MAKING THERE, HAMMIE?
A CARD FOR MY PRE-KINDERGARTEN TEACHER.
WE SET A NEW RECORD TODAY.
A RECORD? WHAT KIND OF RECORD?
BY THE TIME THE TEACHER GOT THE CLASS SETTLED DOWN ENOUGH TO TAKE ATTENDANCE, IT WAS TIME TO GO HOME.
NOW WRITE, "I HOPE YOUR HEADACHE GOES AWAY SOON. LOVE, HAMMIE."
KIRKMAN & SCOTT

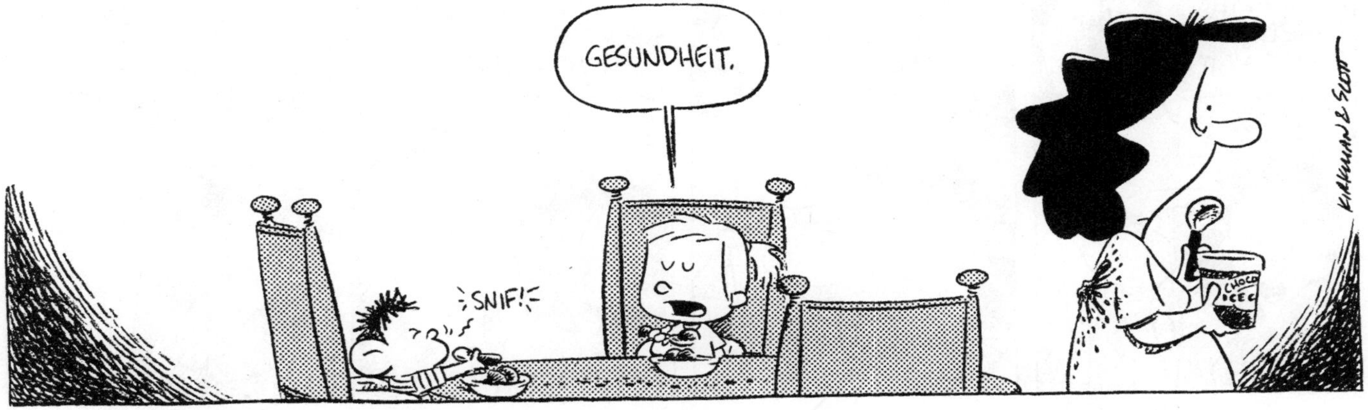
GESUNDHEIT.
SNIF!
KIRKMAN & SCOTT

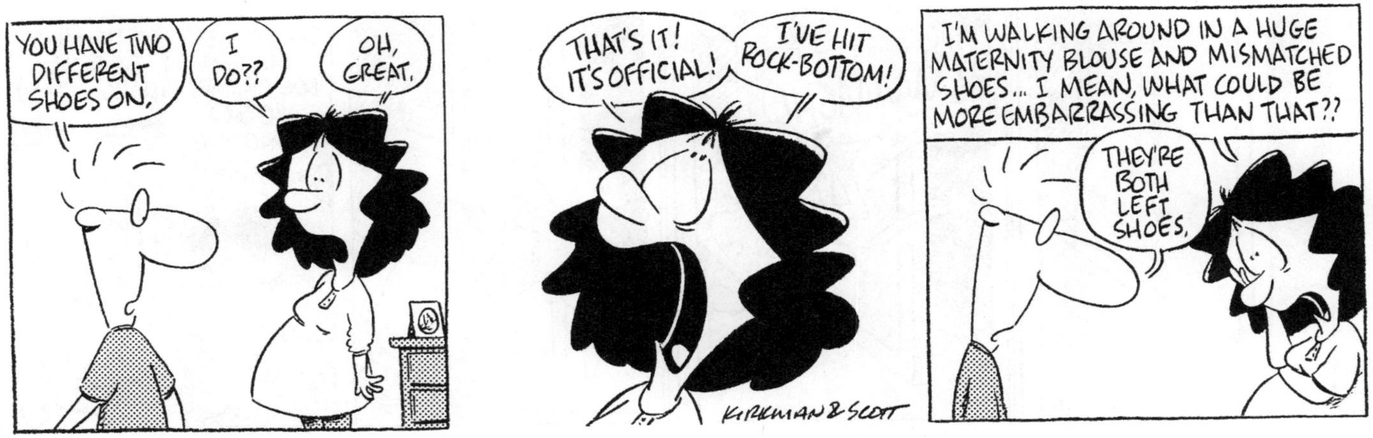
YOU HAVE TWO DIFFERENT SHOES ON.
I DO??
OH, GREAT.
THAT'S IT! IT'S OFFICIAL!
I'VE HIT ROCK-BOTTOM!
I'M WALKING AROUND IN A HUGE MATERNITY BLOUSE AND MISMATCHED SHOES... I MEAN, WHAT COULD BE MORE EMBARRASSING THAN THAT??
THEY'RE BOTH LEFT SHOES.
KIRKMAN & SCOTT

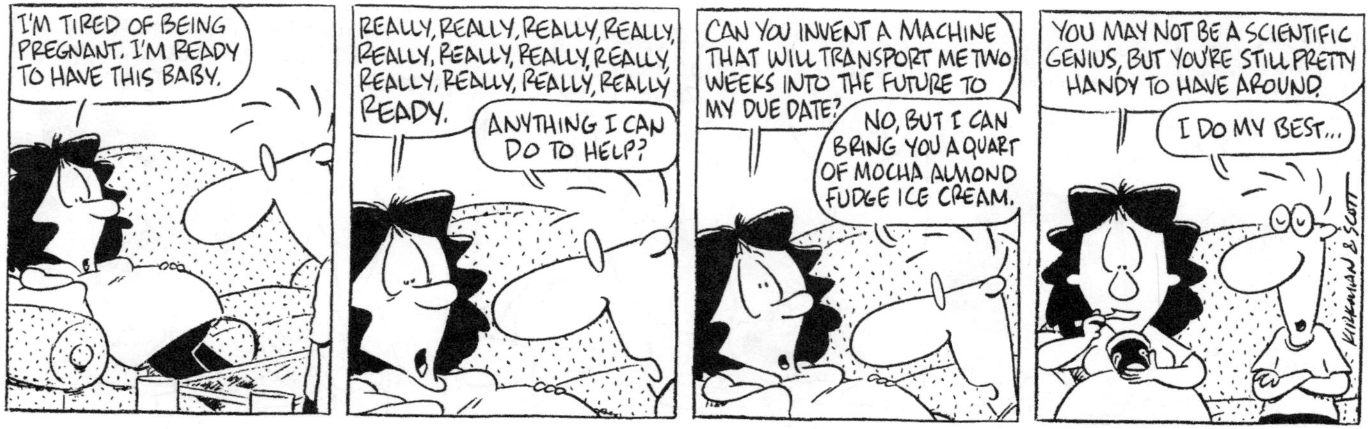
I'M TIRED OF BEING PREGNANT. I'M READY TO HAVE THIS BABY.
REALLY, REALLY, REALLY, REALLY, REALLY, REALLY, REALLY, REALLY, REALLY, REALLY, REALLY, REALLY READY.
ANYTHING I CAN DO TO HELP?
CAN YOU INVENT A MACHINE THAT WILL TRANSPORT ME TWO WEEKS INTO THE FUTURE TO MY DUE DATE?
NO, BUT I CAN BRING YOU A QUART OF MOCHA ALMOND FUDGE ICE CREAM.
YOU MAY NOT BE A SCIENTIFIC GENIUS, BUT YOU'RE STILL PRETTY HANDY TO HAVE AROUND.
I DO MY BEST...
KIRKMAN & SCOTT

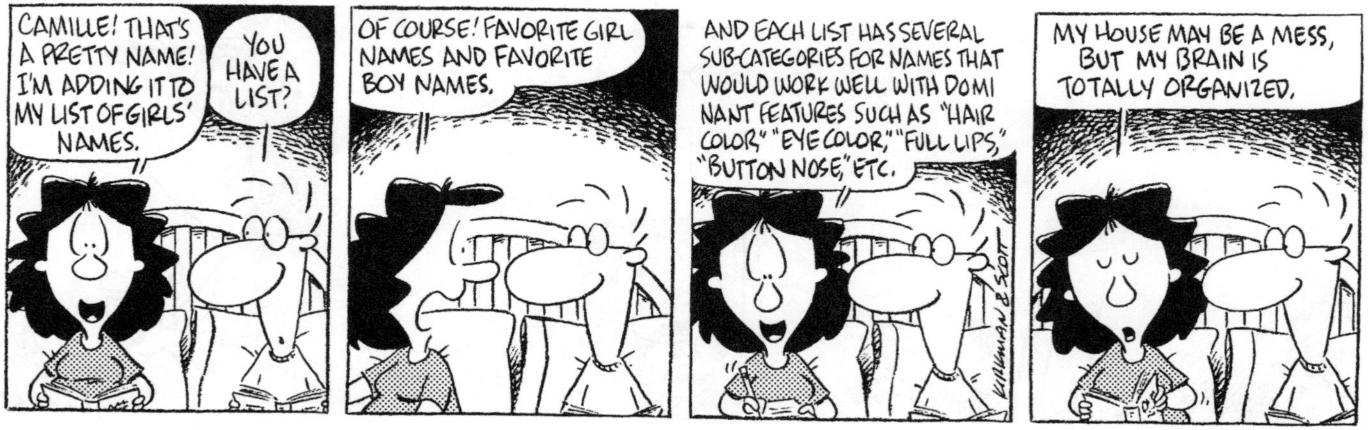
CAMILLE! THAT'S A PRETTY NAME! I'M ADDING IT TO MY LIST OF GIRLS' NAMES.
YOU HAVE A LIST?
OF COURSE! FAVORITE GIRL NAMES AND FAVORITE BOY NAMES.
AND EACH LIST HAS SEVERAL SUB-CATEGORIES FOR NAMES THAT WOULD WORK WELL WITH DOMINANT FEATURES SUCH AS "HAIR COLOR," "EYE COLOR," "FULL LIPS," "BUTTON NOSE," ETC.
KIRKMAN & SCOTT
MY HOUSE MAY BE A MESS, BUT MY BRAIN IS TOTALLY ORGANIZED.

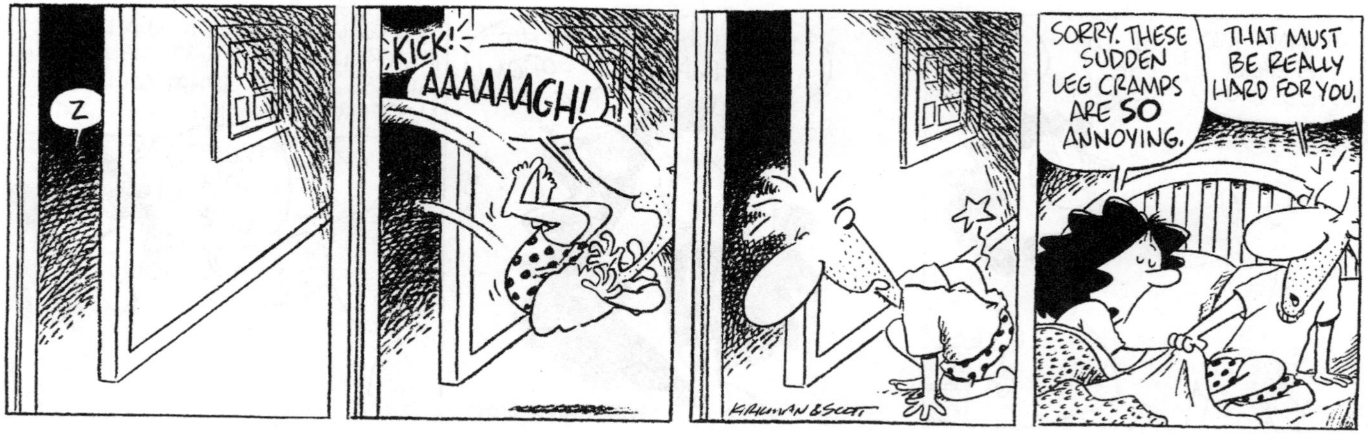
Z
KICK!
AAAAAAGH!
KIRKMAN & SCOTT
SORRY. THESE SUDDEN LEG CRAMPS ARE SO ANNOYING.
THAT MUST BE REALLY HARD FOR YOU.

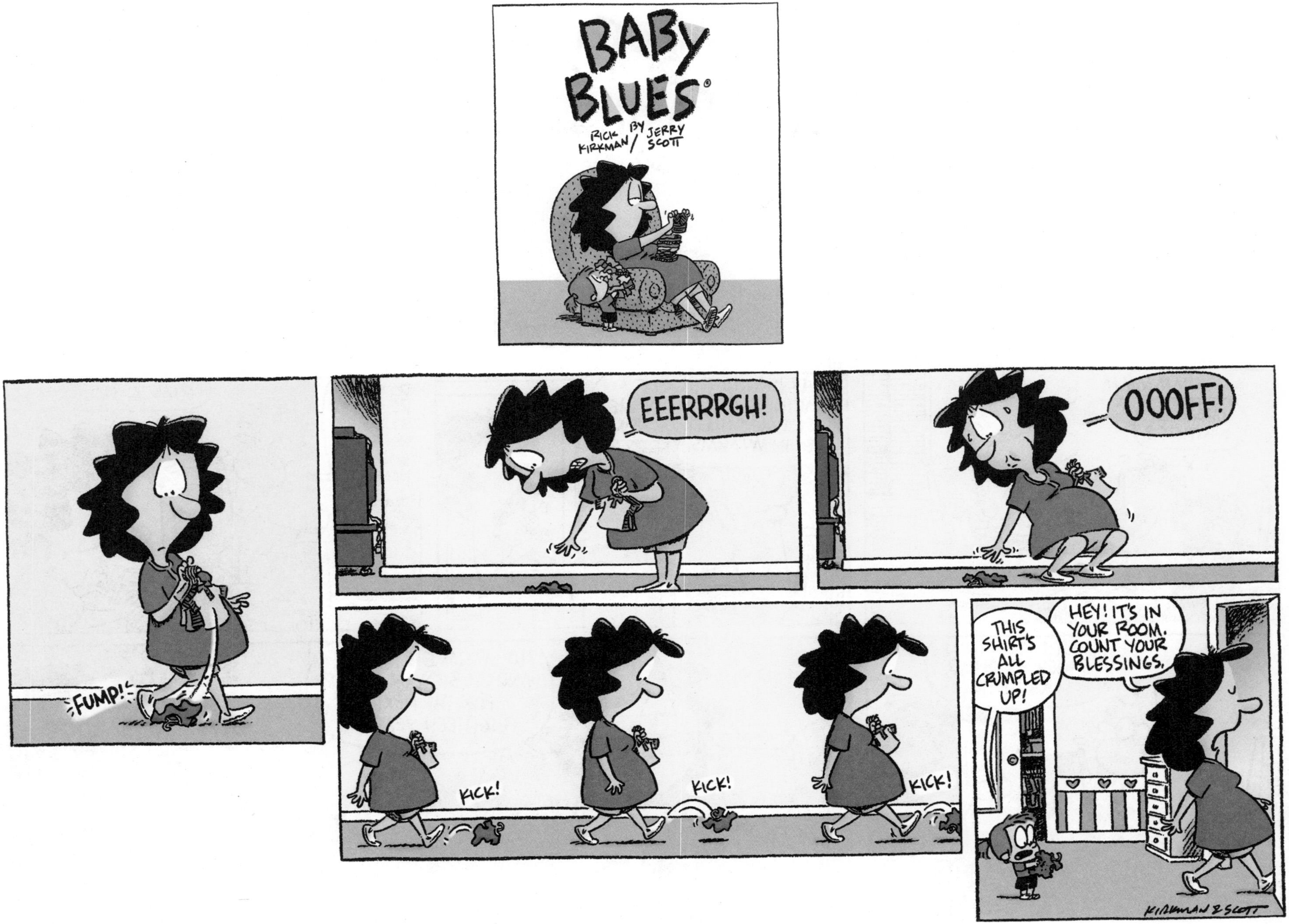
BABY BLUES®
BY RICK KIRKMAN / JERRY SCOTT
FUMP!
EEERRRGH!
OOOFF!
KICK!
KICK!
KICK!
THIS SHIRT'S ALL CRUMPLED UP!
HEY! IT'S IN YOUR ROOM. COUNT YOUR BLESSINGS.
KIRKMAN & SCOTT

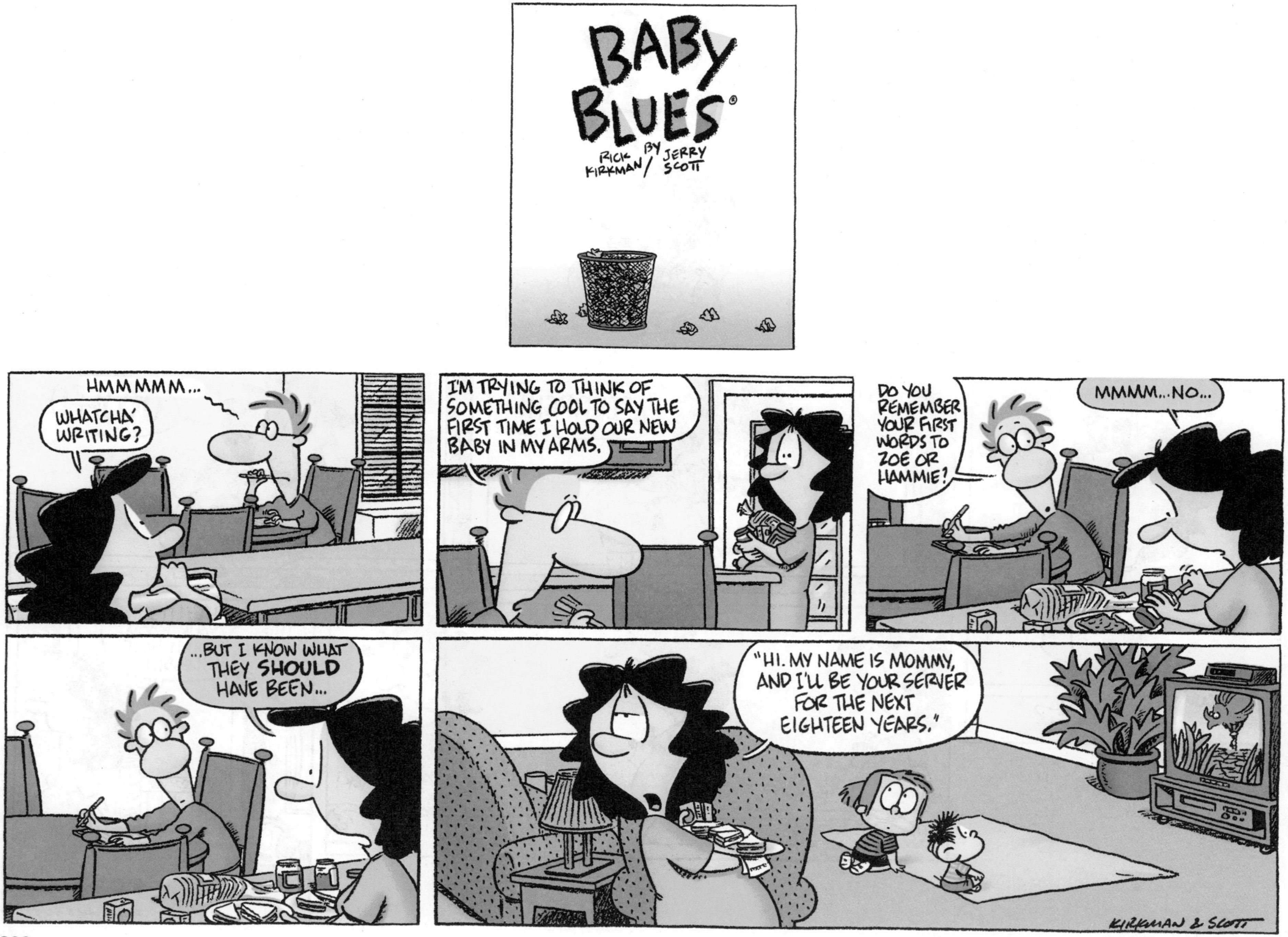
BABY BLUES®
BY RICK KIRKMAN / JERRY SCOTT
HMMMMM...
WHATCHA' WRITING?
I'M TRYING TO THINK OF SOMETHING COOL TO SAY THE FIRST TIME I HOLD OUR NEW BABY IN MY ARMS.
DO YOU REMEMBER YOUR FIRST WORDS TO ZOE OR HAMMIE?
MMMM...NO...
...BUT I KNOW WHAT THEY **SHOULD** HAVE BEEN...
"HI. MY NAME IS MOMMY, AND I'LL BE YOUR SERVER FOR THE NEXT EIGHTEEN YEARS."
KIRKMAN & SCOTT

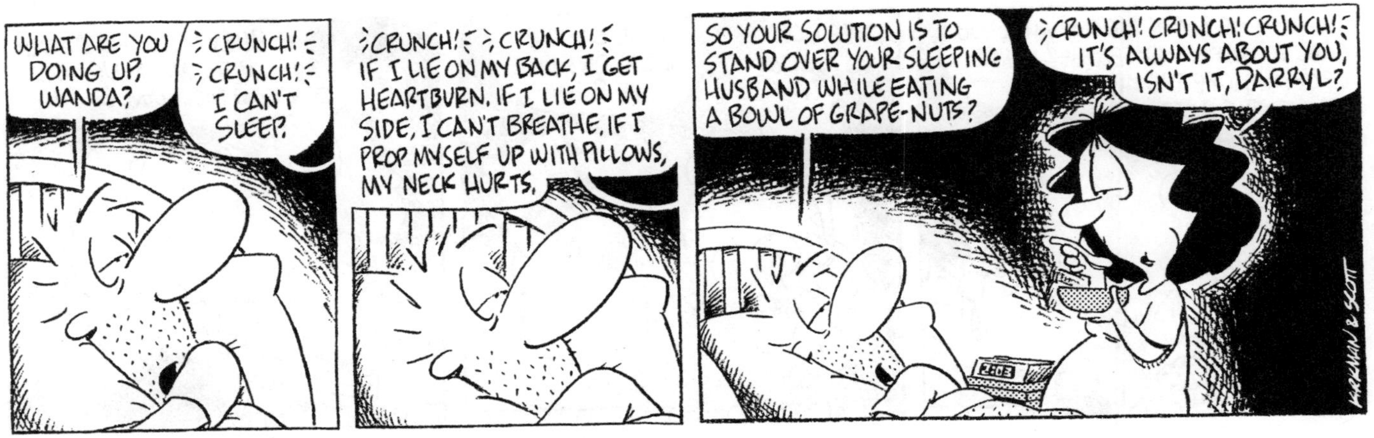
WHAT ARE YOU DOING UP, WANDA?
CRUNCH! CRUNCH! I CAN'T SLEEP.
CRUNCH! CRUNCH! IF I LIE ON MY BACK, I GET HEARTBURN. IF I LIE ON MY SIDE, I CAN'T BREATHE. IF I PROP MYSELF UP WITH PILLOWS, MY NECK HURTS.
SO YOUR SOLUTION IS TO STAND OVER YOUR SLEEPING HUSBAND WHILE EATING A BOWL OF GRAPE-NUTS?
CRUNCH! CRUNCH! CRUNCH! IT'S ALWAYS ABOUT YOU, ISN'T IT, DARRYL?
KIRKMAN & SCOTT

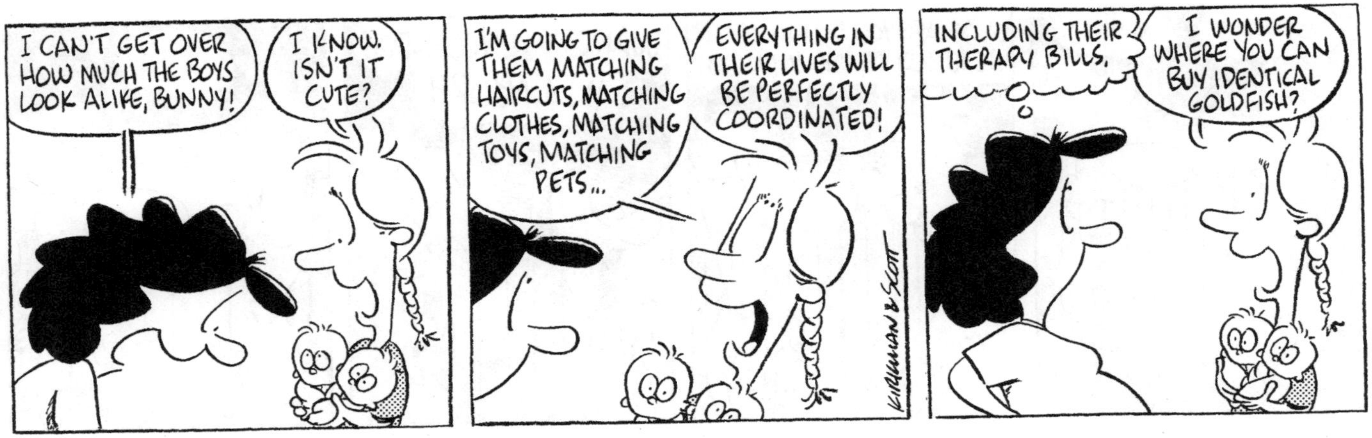
I CAN'T GET OVER HOW MUCH THE BOYS LOOK ALIKE, BUNNY!
I KNOW. ISN'T IT CUTE?
I'M GOING TO GIVE THEM MATCHING HAIRCUTS, MATCHING CLOTHES, MATCHING TOYS, MATCHING PETS...
EVERYTHING IN THEIR LIVES WILL BE PERFECTLY COORDINATED!
KIRKMAN & SCOTT
INCLUDING THEIR THERAPY BILLS.
I WONDER WHERE YOU CAN BUY IDENTICAL GOLDFISH?

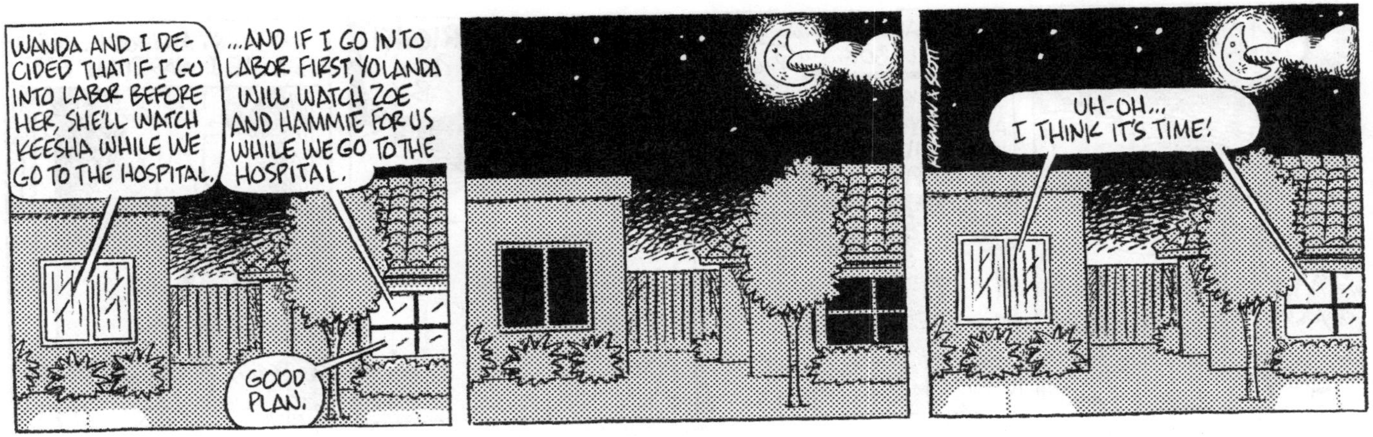
WANDA AND I DECIDED THAT IF I GO INTO LABOR BEFORE HER, SHE'LL WATCH KEESHA WHILE WE GO TO THE HOSPITAL.
...AND IF I GO INTO LABOR FIRST, YOLANDA WILL WATCH ZOE AND HAMMIE FOR US WHILE WE GO TO THE HOSPITAL.
GOOD PLAN.
KIRKMAN & SCOTT
UH-OH... I THINK IT'S TIME!

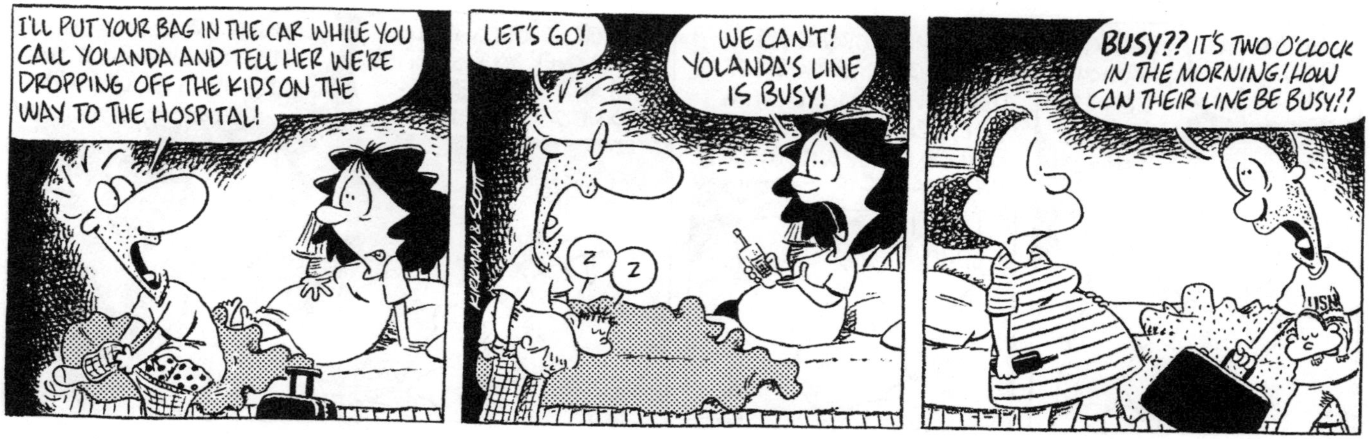
I'LL PUT YOUR BAG IN THE CAR WHILE YOU CALL YOLANDA AND TELL HER WE'RE DROPPING OFF THE KIDS ON THE WAY TO THE HOSPITAL!
KIRKMAN & SCOTT
LET'S GO!
WE CAN'T! YOLANDA'S LINE IS BUSY!
Z Z
BUSY?? IT'S TWO O'CLOCK IN THE MORNING! HOW CAN THEIR LINE BE BUSY??
USN

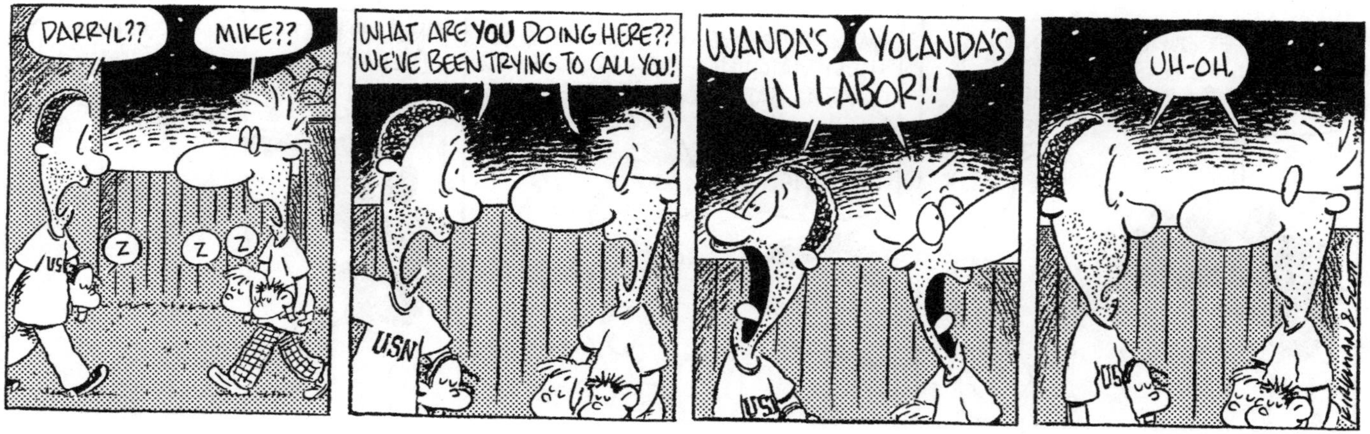
DARRYL??
MIKE??
Z
Z Z
WHAT ARE YOU DOING HERE?? WE'VE BEEN TRYING TO CALL YOU!
USN
WANDA'S
YOLANDA'S
IN LABOR!!
UH-OH
KIRKMAN & SCOTT

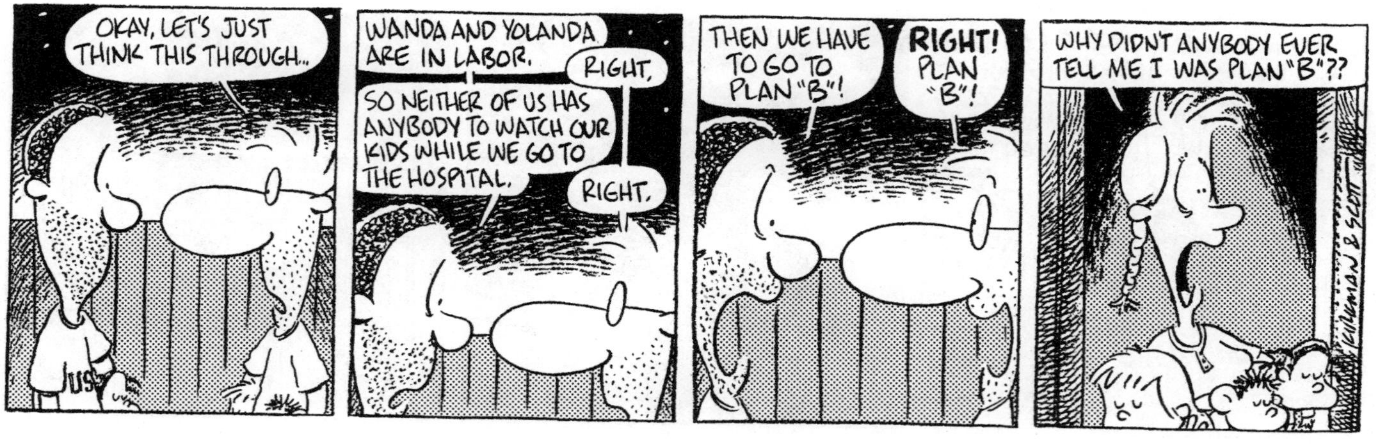
OKAY, LET'S JUST THINK THIS THROUGH...
WANDA AND YOLANDA ARE IN LABOR.
RIGHT.
SO NEITHER OF US HAS ANYBODY TO WATCH OUR KIDS WHILE WE GO TO THE HOSPITAL.
RIGHT.
THEN WE HAVE TO GO TO PLAN "B"!
RIGHT! PLAN "B"!
WHY DIDN'T ANYBODY EVER TELL ME I WAS PLAN "B"??
KIRKMAN & SCOTT

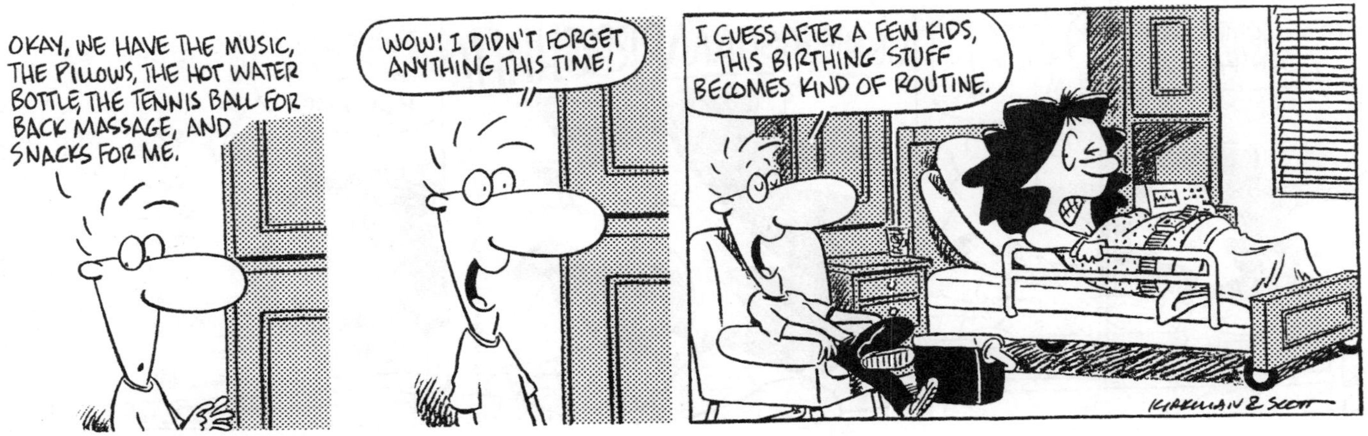
OKAY, WE HAVE THE MUSIC, THE PILLOWS, THE HOT WATER BOTTLE, THE TENNIS BALL FOR BACK MASSAGE, AND SNACKS FOR ME.
WOW! I DIDN'T FORGET ANYTHING THIS TIME!
I GUESS AFTER A FEW KIDS, THIS BIRTHING STUFF BECOMES KIND OF ROUTINE.
KIRKMAN & SCOTT

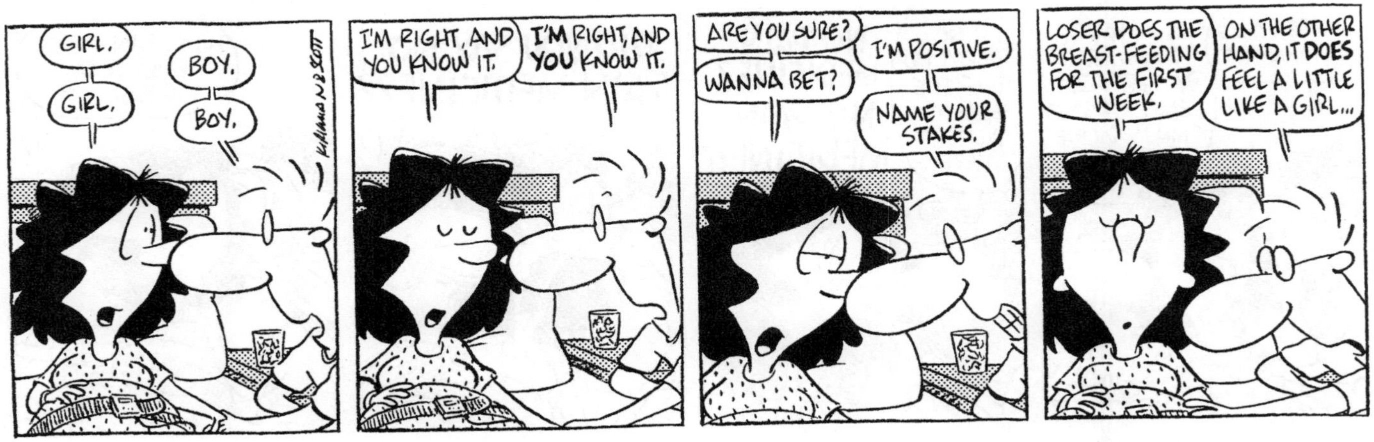
GIRL.
GIRL.
BOY.
BOY.
KIRKMAN & SCOTT
I'M RIGHT, AND YOU KNOW IT.
I'M RIGHT, AND YOU KNOW IT.
ARE YOU SURE?
I'M POSITIVE.
WANNA BET?
NAME YOUR STAKES.
LOSER DOES THE BREAST-FEEDING FOR THE FIRST WEEK.
ON THE OTHER HAND, IT DOES FEEL A LITTLE LIKE A GIRL...

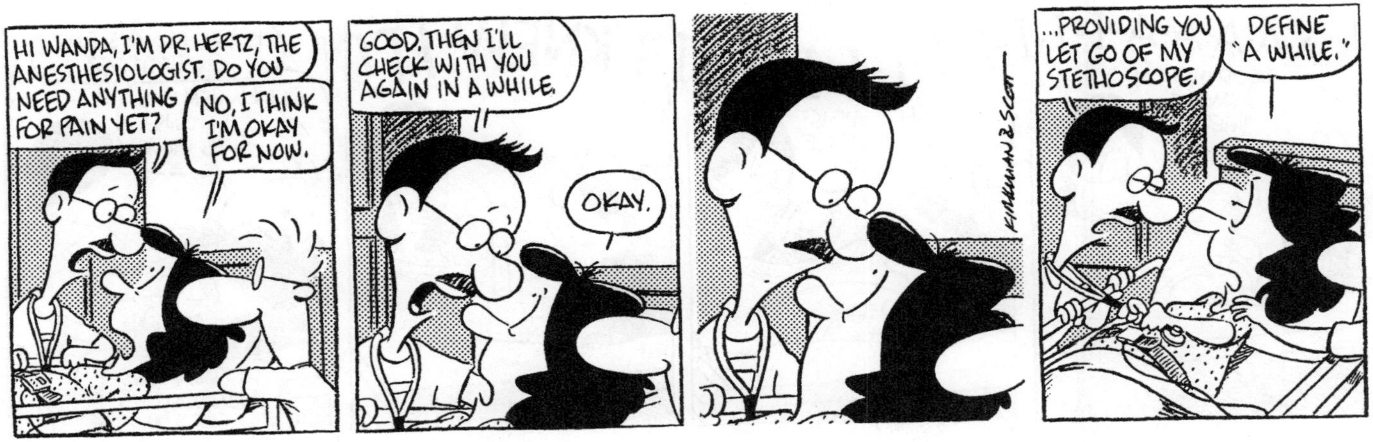
HI WANDA, I'M DR. HERTZ, THE ANESTHESIOLOGIST. DO YOU NEED ANYTHING FOR PAIN YET?
NO, I THINK I'M OKAY FOR NOW.
GOOD, THEN I'LL CHECK WITH YOU AGAIN IN A WHILE.
OKAY.
KIRKMAN & SCOTT
...PROVIDING YOU LET GO OF MY STETHOSCOPE.
DEFINE "A WHILE."

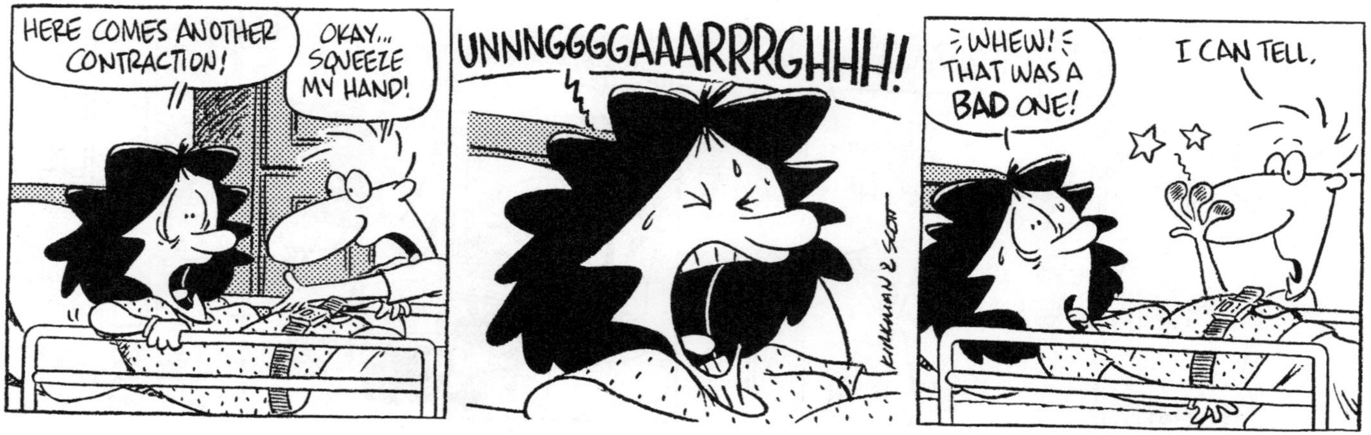
HERE COMES ANOTHER CONTRACTION!
OKAY... SQUEEZE MY HAND!
UNNNGGGGAAARRRGHHH!
WHEW! THAT WAS A BAD ONE!
I CAN TELL.

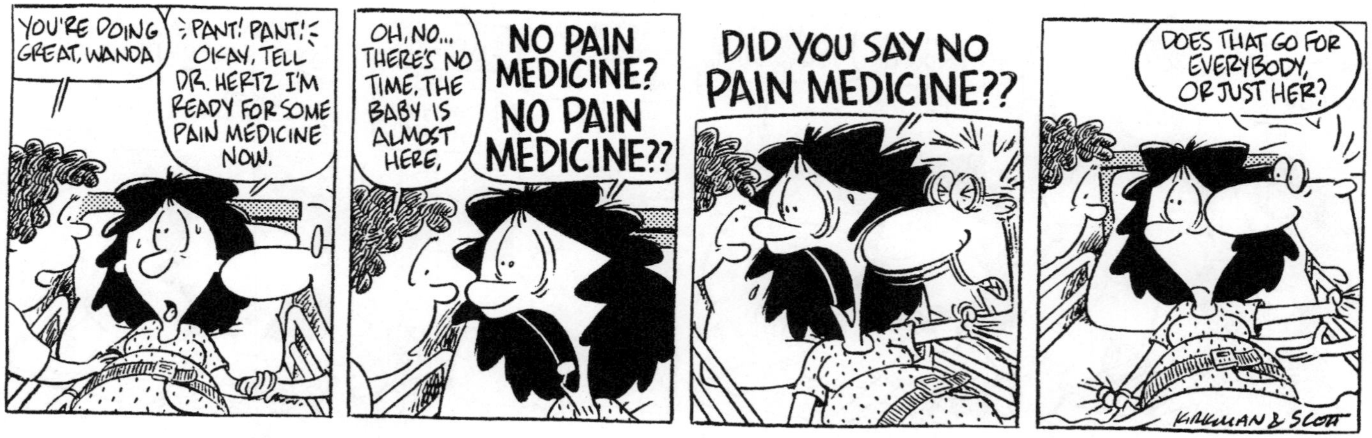
YOU'RE DOING GREAT, WANDA
PANT! PANT! OKAY, TELL DR. HERTZ I'M READY FOR SOME PAIN MEDICINE NOW.
OH, NO... THERE'S NO TIME. THE BABY IS ALMOST HERE.
NO PAIN MEDICINE? NO PAIN MEDICINE??
DID YOU SAY NO PAIN MEDICINE??
DOES THAT GO FOR EVERYBODY, OR JUST HER?
KIRKMAN & SCOTT

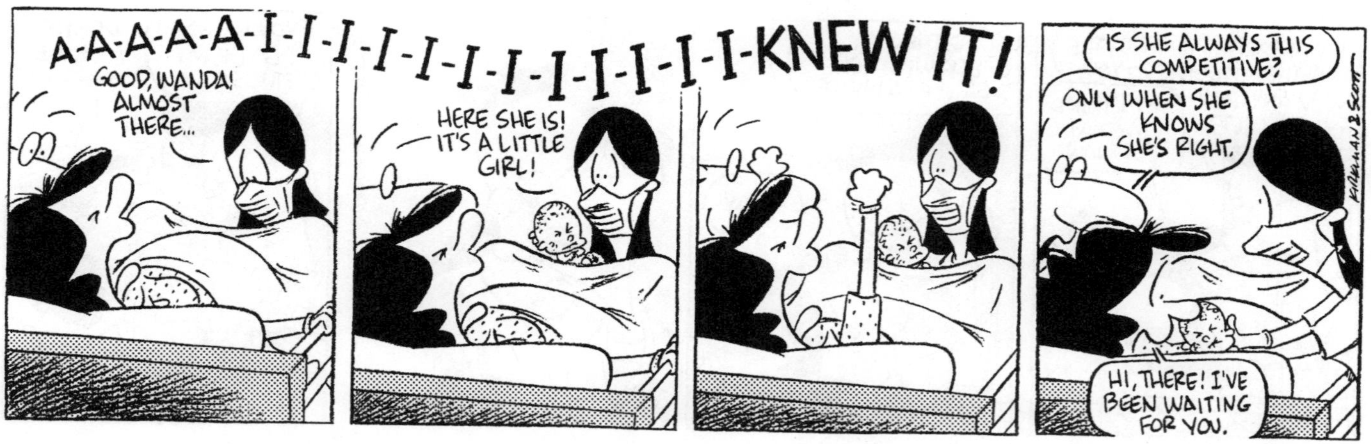
A-A-A-A-A-I-I-I-I-I-I-I-I-I-I-I-I-I-I-KNEW IT!
GOOD, WANDA! ALMOST THERE...
HERE SHE IS! IT'S A LITTLE GIRL!
IS SHE ALWAYS THIS COMPETITIVE?
ONLY WHEN SHE KNOWS SHE'S RIGHT.
HI, THERE! I'VE BEEN WAITING FOR YOU.

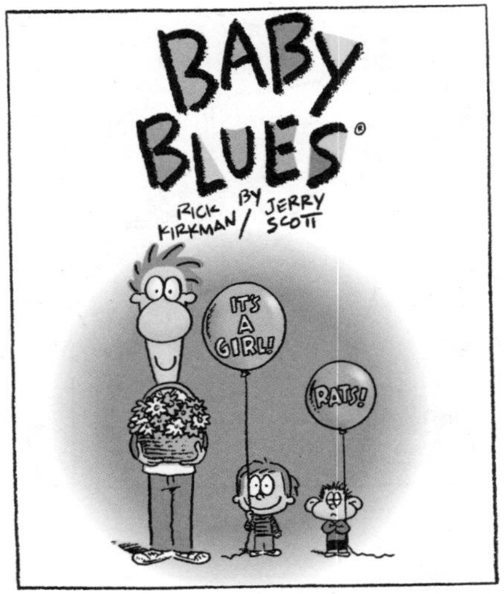
BABY BLUES®
BY RICK KIRKMAN / JERRY SCOTT
IT'S A GIRL!
RATS!

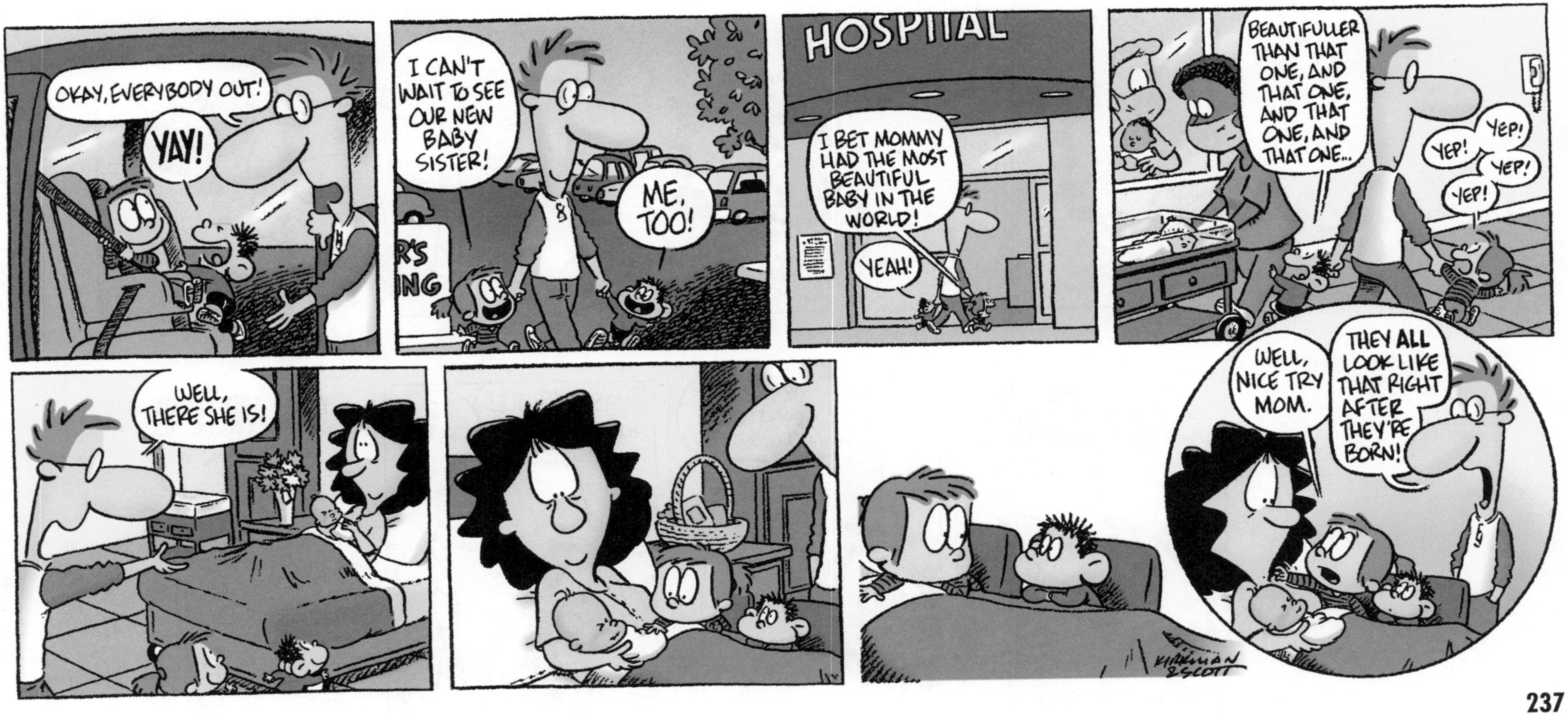
OKAY, EVERYBODY OUT!
YAY!
I CAN'T WAIT TO SEE OUR NEW BABY SISTER!
ME, TOO!
HOSPITAL
I BET MOMMY HAD THE MOST BEAUTIFUL BABY IN THE WORLD!
YEAH!
BEAUTIFULLER THAN THAT ONE, AND THAT ONE, AND THAT ONE, AND THAT ONE...
YEP!
YEP!
YEP!
YEP!
WELL, THERE SHE IS!
WELL, NICE TRY MOM.
THEY ALL LOOK LIKE THAT RIGHT AFTER THEY'RE BORN!
KIRKMAN & SCOTT

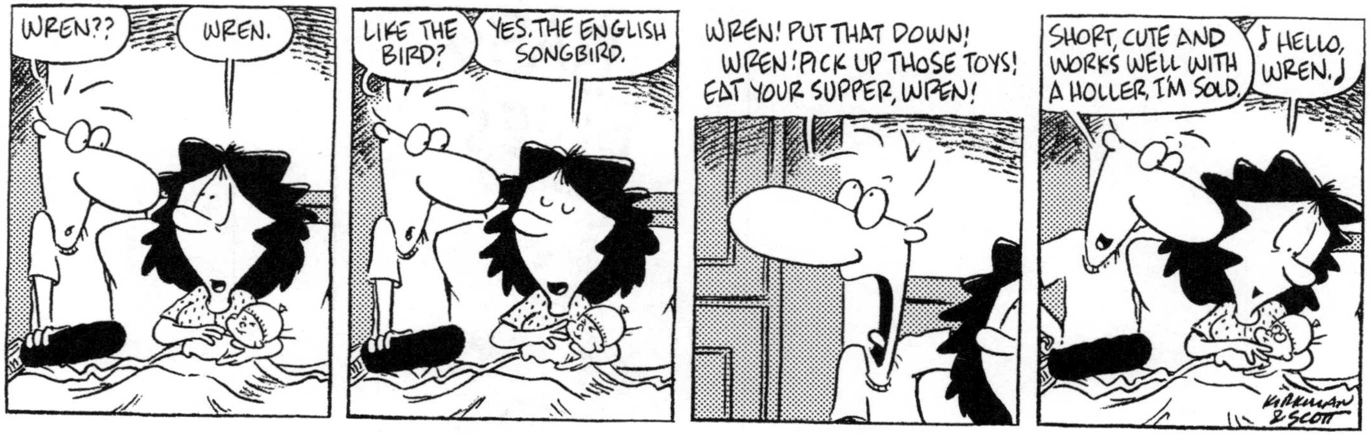
WREN??
WREN.
LIKE THE BIRD?
YES. THE ENGLISH SONGBIRD.
WREN! PUT THAT DOWN! WREN! PICK UP THOSE TOYS! EAT YOUR SUPPER, WREN!
SHORT, CUTE AND WORKS WELL WITH A HOLLER. I'M SOLD.
♪ HELLO, WREN. ♪
KIRKMAN & SCOTT

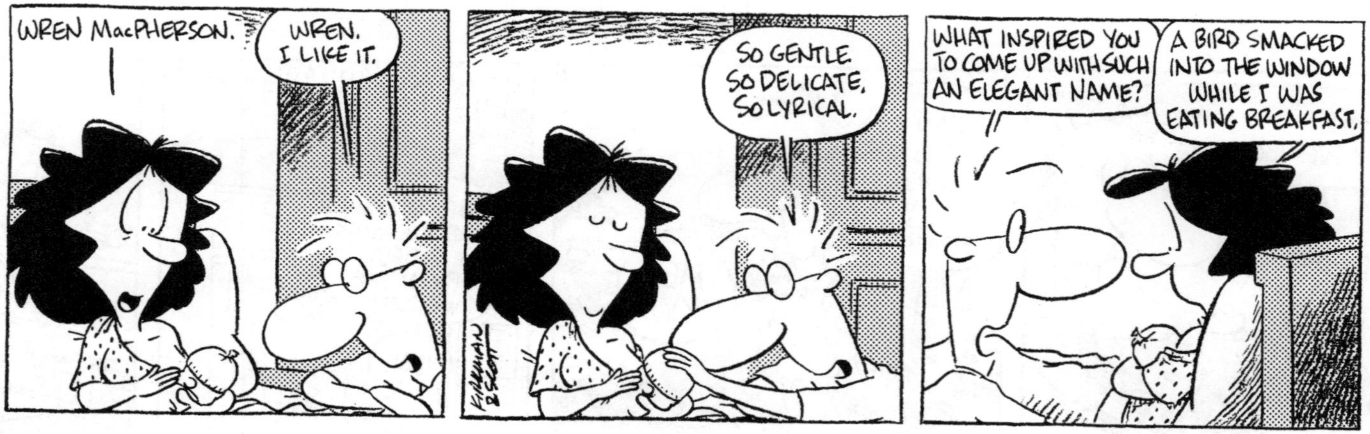
WREN MacPHERSON.
WREN. I LIKE IT.
KIRKMAN & SCOTT
SO GENTLE. SO DELICATE. SO LYRICAL.
WHAT INSPIRED YOU TO COME UP WITH SUCH AN ELEGANT NAME?
A BIRD SMACKED INTO THE WINDOW WHILE I WAS EATING BREAKFAST.

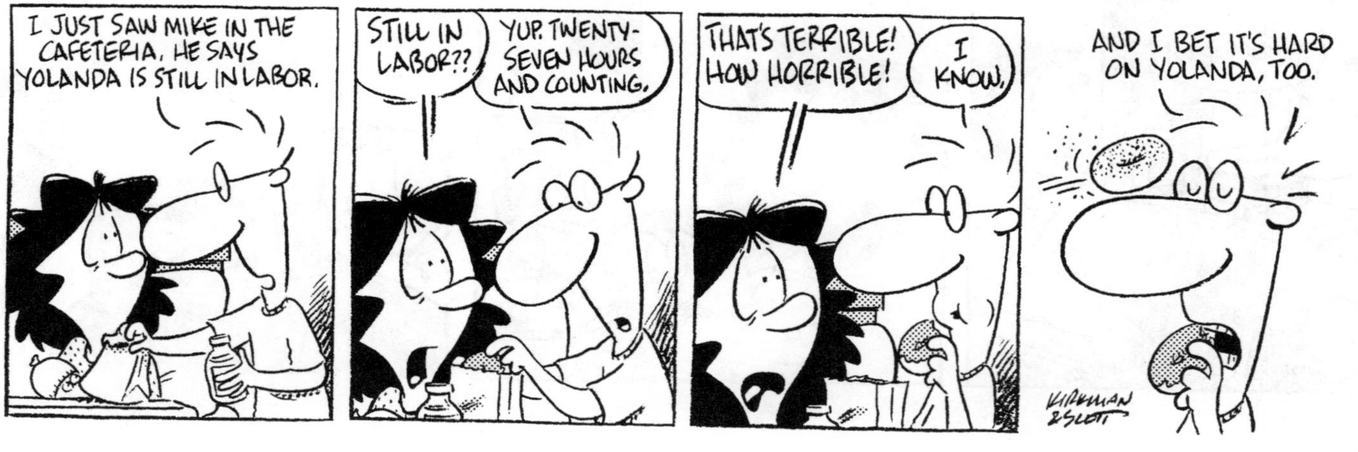
I JUST SAW MIKE IN THE CAFETERIA. HE SAYS YOLANDA IS STILL IN LABOR.
STILL IN LABOR??
YUP. TWENTY-SEVEN HOURS AND COUNTING.
THAT'S TERRIBLE! HOW HORRIBLE!
I KNOW.
AND I BET IT'S HARD ON YOLANDA, TOO.
KIRKMAN & SCOTT

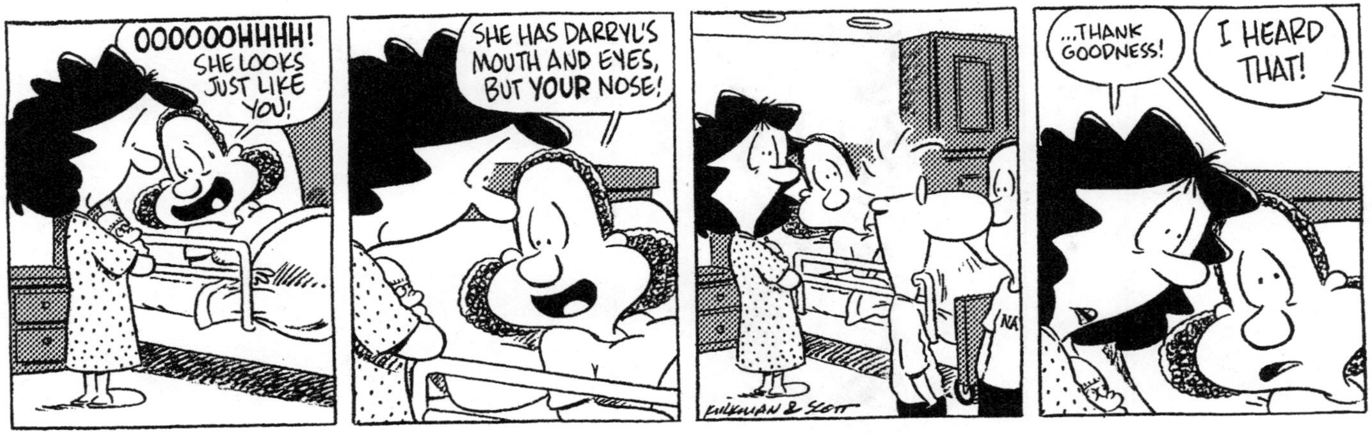
OOOOOOHHHH! SHE LOOKS JUST LIKE YOU!
SHE HAS DARRYL'S MOUTH AND EYES, BUT YOUR NOSE!
KIRKMAN & SCOTT
...THANK GOODNESS!
I HEARD THAT!

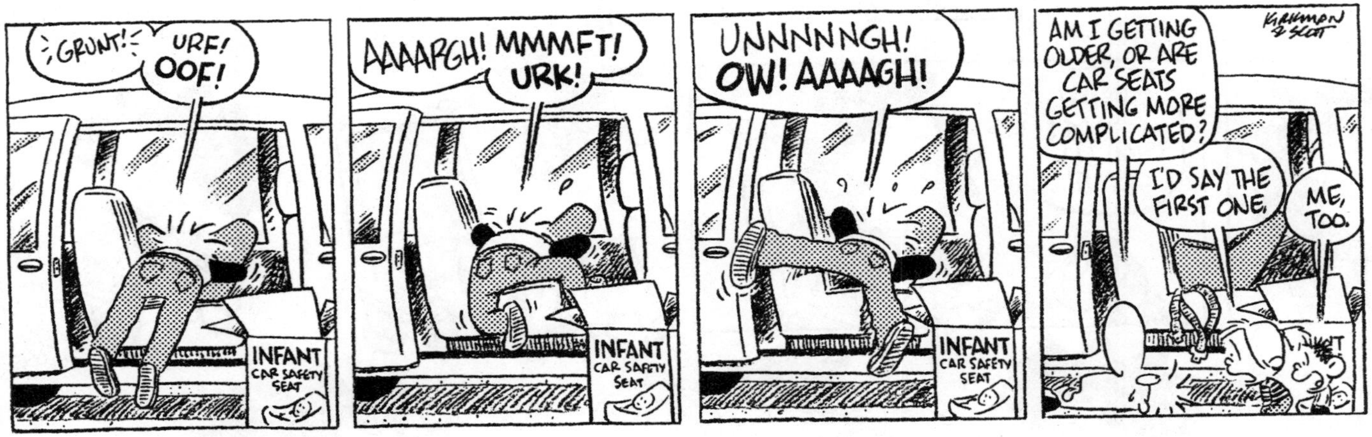
GRUNT!
URF! OOF!
INFANT CAR SAFETY SEAT
AAAARGH! MMMFT! URK!
INFANT CAR SAFETY SEAT
UNNNNNGH! OW! AAAAGH!
INFANT CAR SAFETY SEAT
KIRKMAN & SCOTT
AM I GETTING OLDER, OR ARE CAR SEATS GETTING MORE COMPLICATED?
I'D SAY THE FIRST ONE.
ME, TOO.

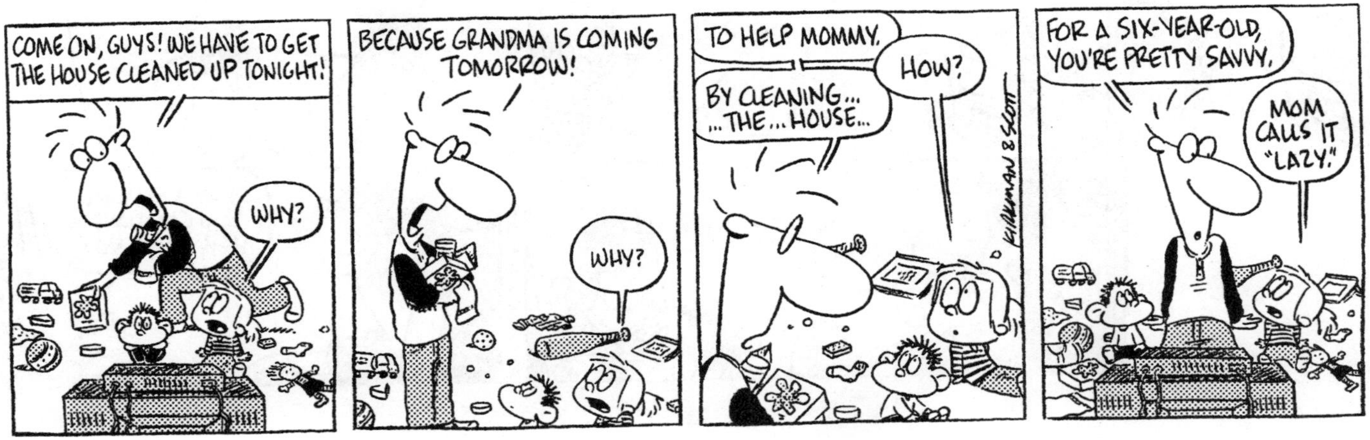
COME ON, GUYS! WE HAVE TO GET THE HOUSE CLEANED UP TONIGHT!
WHY?
BECAUSE GRANDMA IS COMING TOMORROW!
WHY?
TO HELP MOMMY.
HOW?
BY CLEANING... ...THE... HOUSE...
KIRKMAN & SCOTT
FOR A SIX-YEAR-OLD, YOU'RE PRETTY SAVVY.
MOM CALLS IT "LAZY."

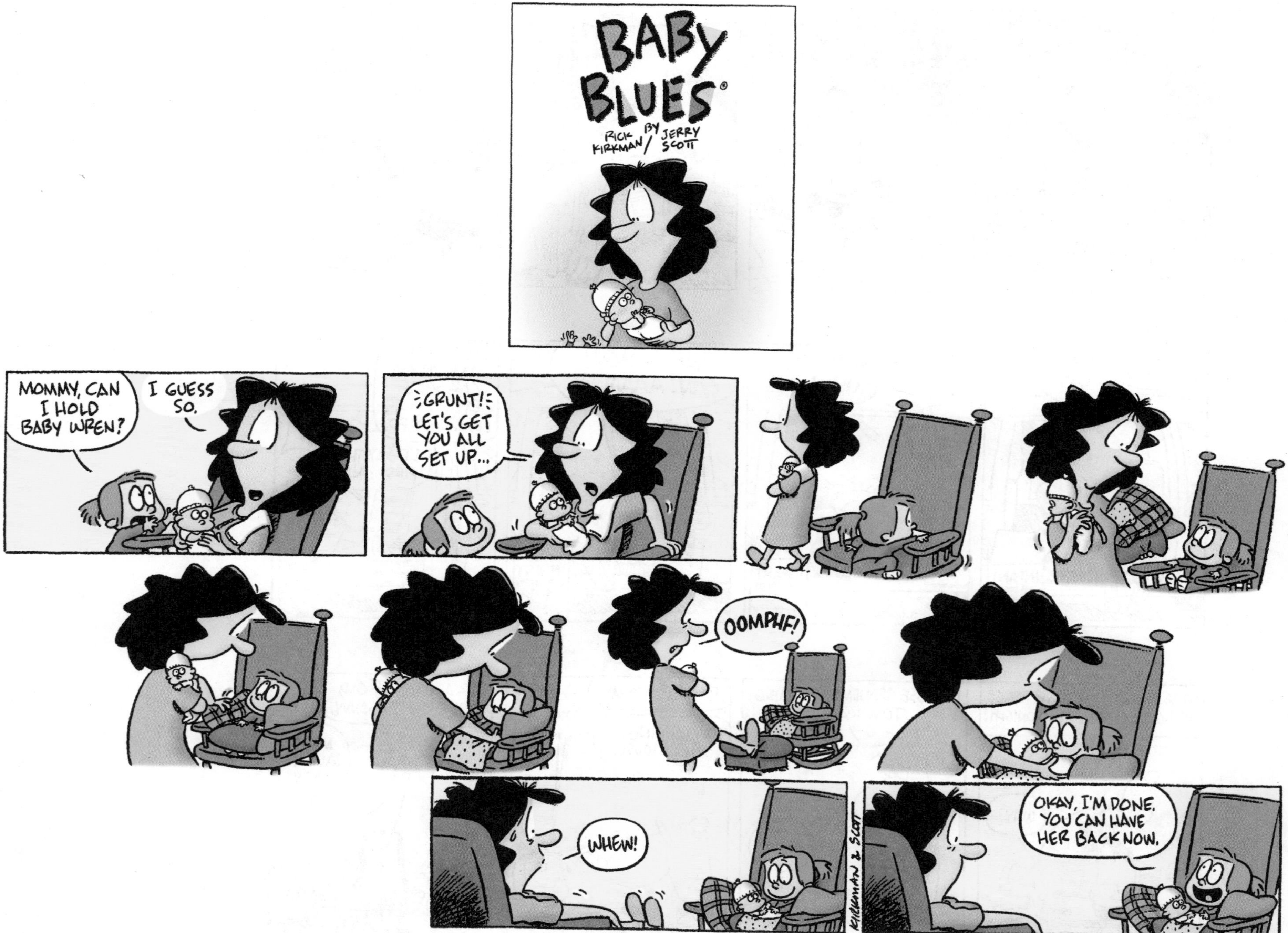
BABY BLUES®
BY RICK KIRKMAN / JERRY SCOTT
MOMMY, CAN I HOLD BABY WREN?
I GUESS SO.
GRUNT!
LET'S GET YOU ALL SET UP...
OOMPHF!
WHEW!
KIRKMAN & SCOTT
OKAY, I'M DONE. YOU CAN HAVE HER BACK NOW.

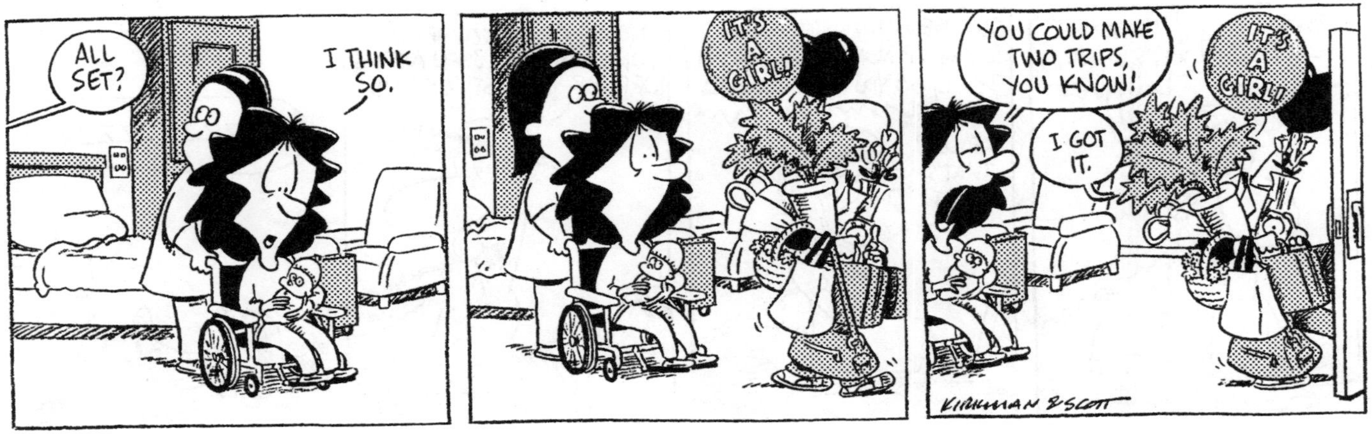
ALL SET?
I THINK SO.
IT'S A GIRL!
YOU COULD MAKE TWO TRIPS, YOU KNOW!
I GOT IT.
IT'S A GIRL!
KIRKMAN & SCOTT

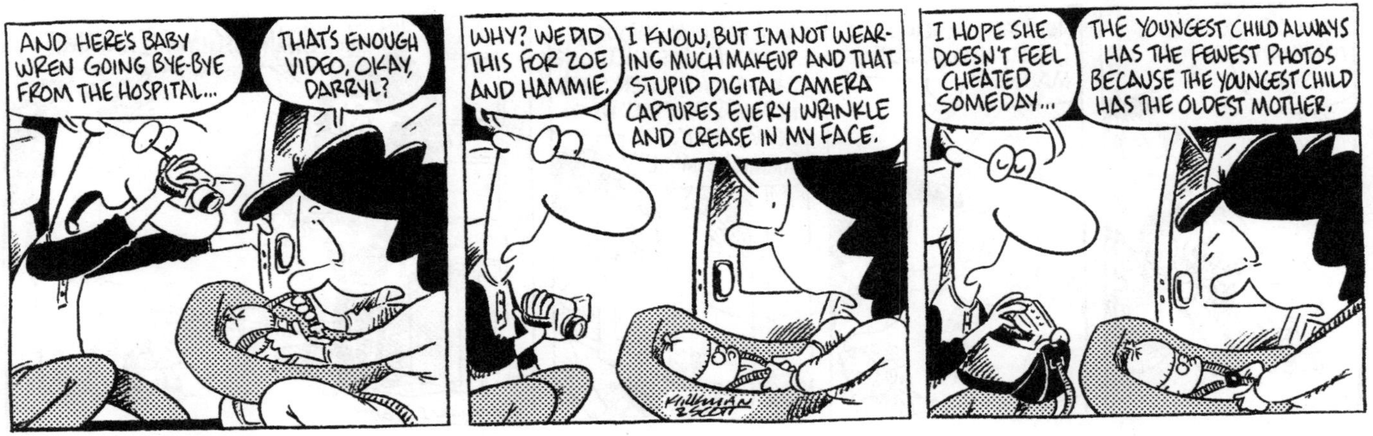
AND HERE'S BABY WREN GOING BYE-BYE FROM THE HOSPITAL...
THAT'S ENOUGH VIDEO, OKAY, DARRYL?
WHY? WE DID THIS FOR ZOE AND HAMMIE.
I KNOW, BUT I'M NOT WEARING MUCH MAKEUP AND THAT STUPID DIGITAL CAMERA CAPTURES EVERY WRINKLE AND CREASE IN MY FACE.
KIRKMAN & SCOTT
I HOPE SHE DOESN'T FEEL CHEATED SOMEDAY...
THE YOUNGEST CHILD ALWAYS HAS THE FEWEST PHOTOS BECAUSE THE YOUNGEST CHILD HAS THE OLDEST MOTHER.

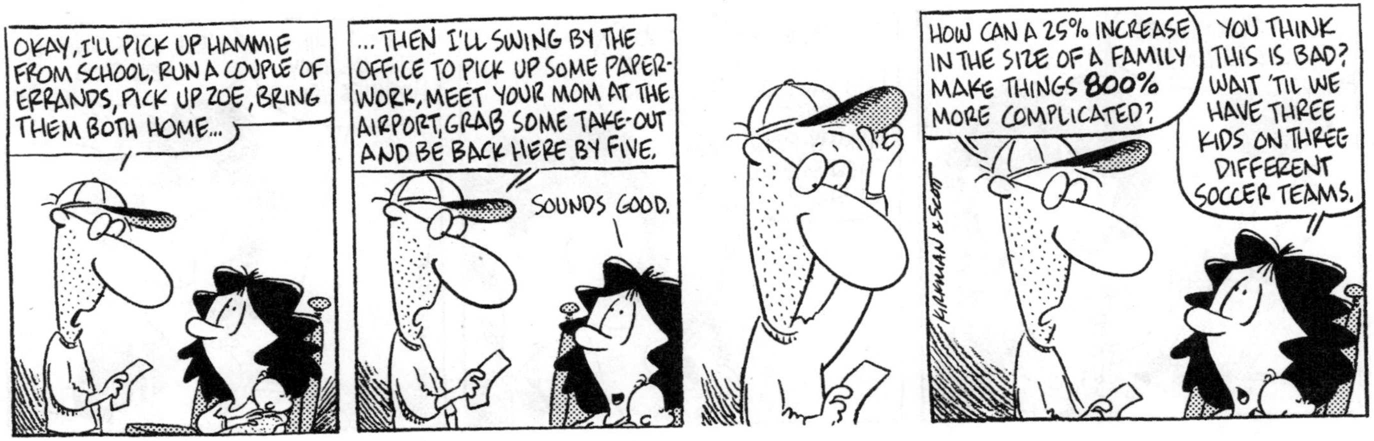
OKAY, I'LL PICK UP HAMMIE FROM SCHOOL, RUN A COUPLE OF ERRANDS, PICK UP ZOE, BRING THEM BOTH HOME...
...THEN I'LL SWING BY THE OFFICE TO PICK UP SOME PAPERWORK, MEET YOUR MOM AT THE AIRPORT, GRAB SOME TAKE-OUT AND BE BACK HERE BY FIVE.
SOUNDS GOOD.
KIRKMAN & SCOTT
HOW CAN A 25% INCREASE IN THE SIZE OF A FAMILY MAKE THINGS 800% MORE COMPLICATED?
YOU THINK THIS IS BAD? WAIT 'TIL WE HAVE THREE KIDS ON THREE DIFFERENT SOCCER TEAMS.

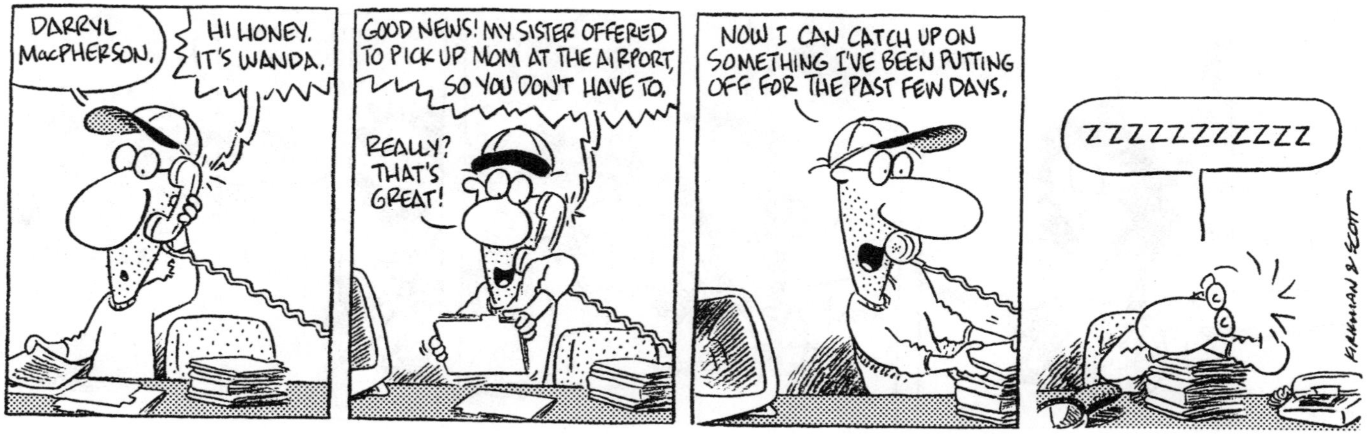
DARRYL MacPHERSON.
HI HONEY. IT'S WANDA.
GOOD NEWS! MY SISTER OFFERED TO PICK UP MOM AT THE AIRPORT, SO YOU DON'T HAVE TO.
REALLY? THAT'S GREAT!
NOW I CAN CATCH UP ON SOMETHING I'VE BEEN PUTTING OFF FOR THE PAST FEW DAYS.
ZZZZZZZZZZZ
KIRKMAN & SCOTT

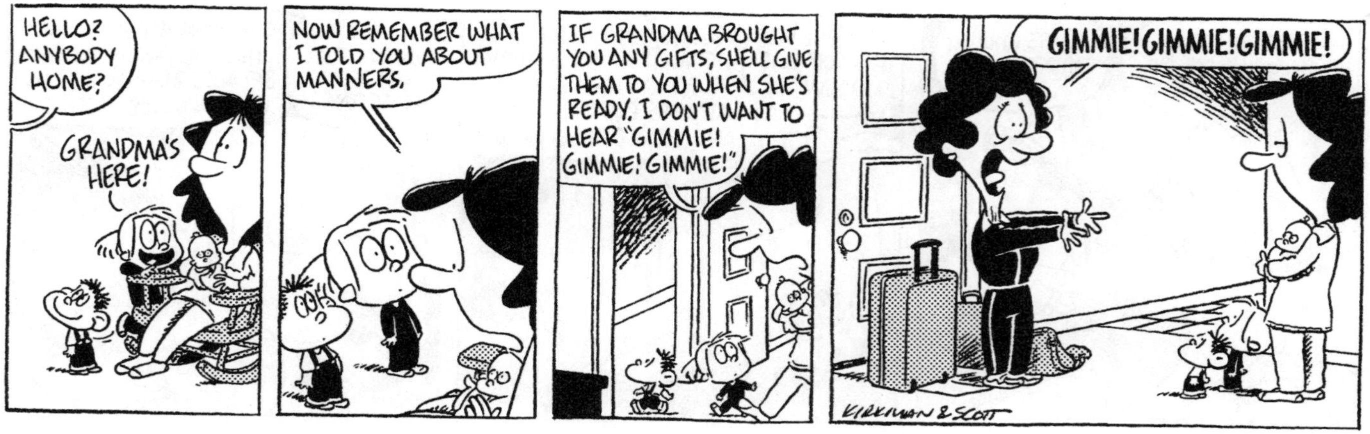
HELLO? ANYBODY HOME?
GRANDMA'S HERE!
NOW REMEMBER WHAT I TOLD YOU ABOUT MANNERS.
IF GRANDMA BROUGHT YOU ANY GIFTS, SHE'LL GIVE THEM TO YOU WHEN SHE'S READY. I DON'T WANT TO HEAR "GIMMIE! GIMMIE! GIMMIE!"
GIMMIE! GIMMIE! GIMMIE!
KIRKMAN & SCOTT

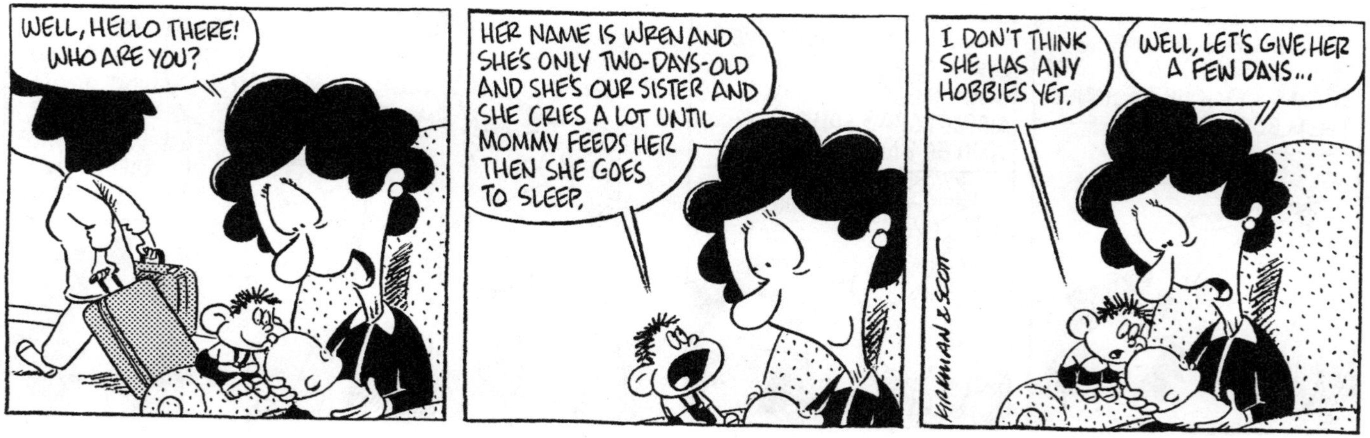
WELL, HELLO THERE! WHO ARE YOU?
HER NAME IS WREN AND SHE'S ONLY TWO-DAYS-OLD AND SHE'S OUR SISTER AND SHE CRIES A LOT UNTIL MOMMY FEEDS HER THEN SHE GOES TO SLEEP.
KIRKMAN & SCOTT
I DON'T THINK SHE HAS ANY HOBBIES YET.
WELL, LET'S GIVE HER A FEW DAYS...

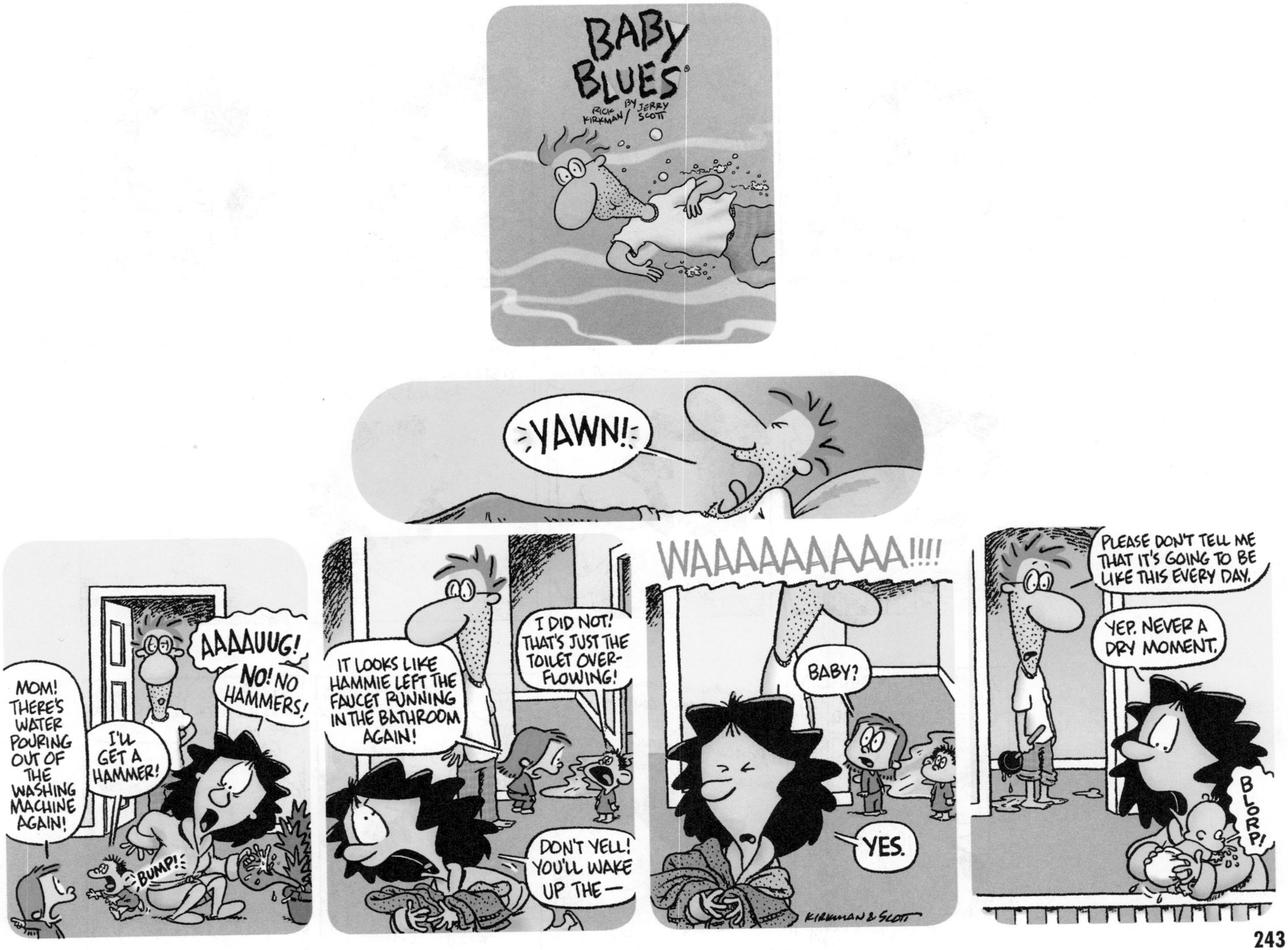
BABY BLUES®
BY RICK KIRKMAN / JERRY SCOTT
YAWN!
MOM! THERE'S WATER POURING OUT OF THE WASHING MACHINE AGAIN!
I'LL GET A HAMMER!
AAAAUUG!
NO! NO HAMMERS!
BUMP!
IT LOOKS LIKE HAMMIE LEFT THE FAUCET RUNNING IN THE BATHROOM AGAIN!
I DID NOT! THAT'S JUST THE TOILET OVER-FLOWING!
DON'T YELL! YOU'LL WAKE UP THE—
WAAAAAAAAAA!!!!
BABY?
YES.
KIRKMAN & SCOTT
PLEASE DON'T TELL ME THAT IT'S GOING TO BE LIKE THIS EVERY DAY.
YEP. NEVER A DRY MOMENT.
BLORP!

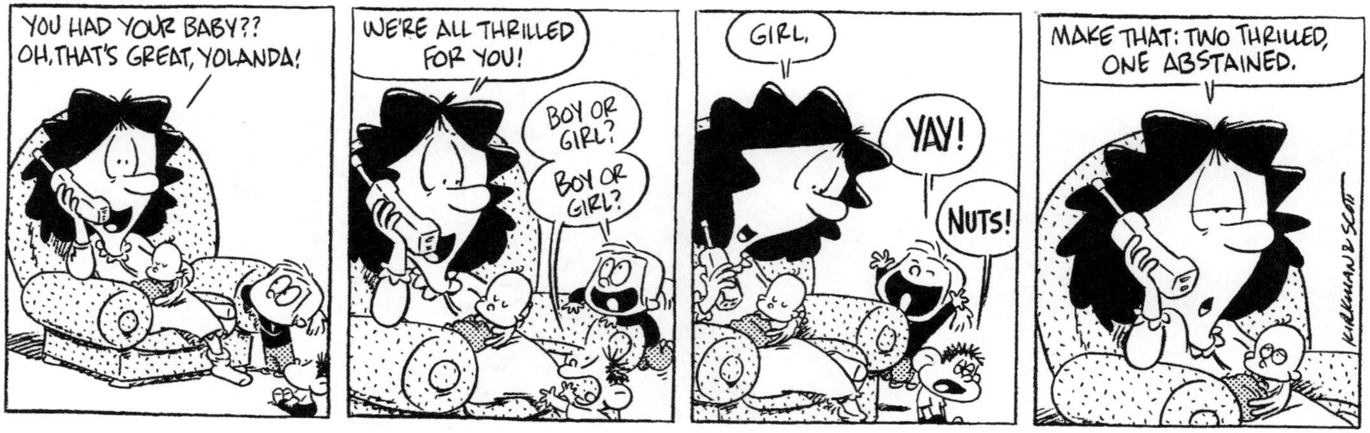
YOU HAD YOUR BABY?? OH, THAT'S GREAT, YOLANDA!
WE'RE ALL THRILLED FOR YOU!
BOY OR GIRL?
BOY OR GIRL?
GIRL.
YAY!
NUTS!
MAKE THAT: TWO THRILLED, ONE ABSTAINED.
KIRKMAN & SCOTT

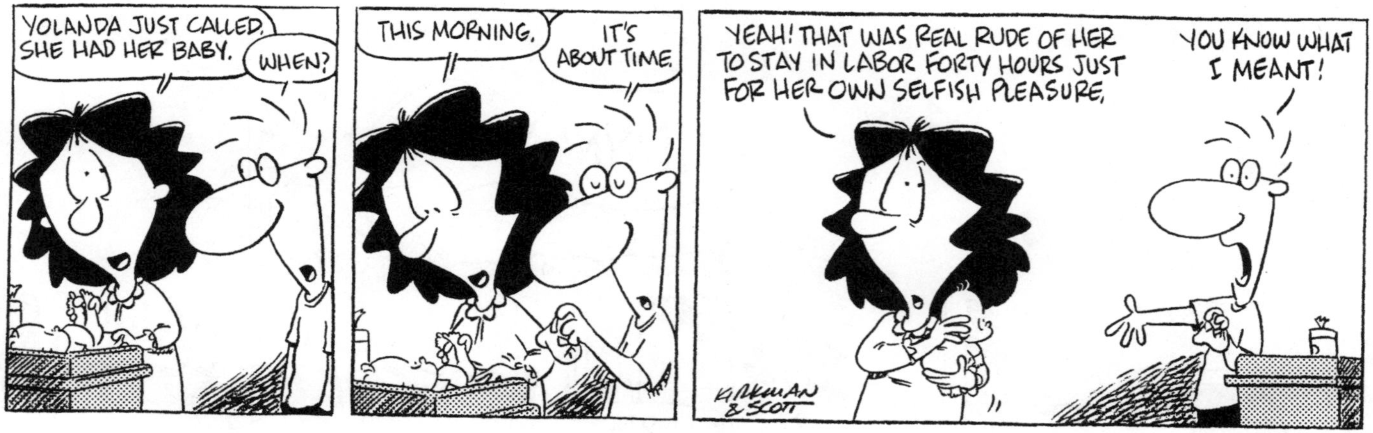
YOLANDA JUST CALLED. SHE HAD HER BABY.
WHEN?
THIS MORNING.
IT'S ABOUT TIME.
YEAH! THAT WAS REAL RUDE OF HER TO STAY IN LABOR FORTY HOURS JUST FOR HER OWN SELFISH PLEASURE.
YOU KNOW WHAT I MEANT!
KIRKMAN & SCOTT

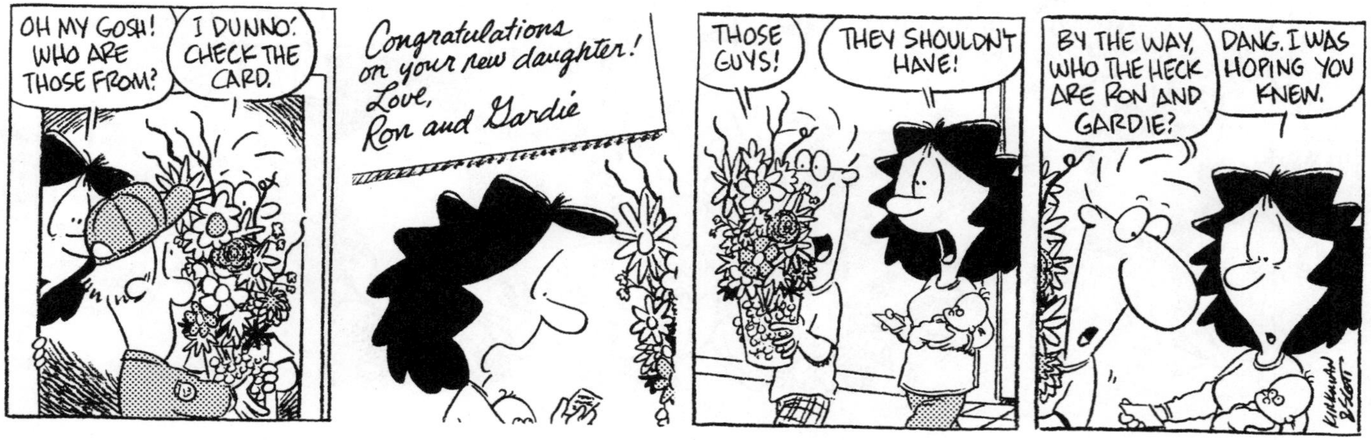
OH MY GOSH! WHO ARE THOSE FROM?
I DUNNO. CHECK THE CARD.
Congratulations on your new daughter! Love, Ron and Gardie
THOSE GUYS!
THEY SHOULDN'T HAVE!
BY THE WAY, WHO THE HECK ARE RON AND GARDIE?
DANG. I WAS HOPING YOU KNEW.
KIRKMAN & SCOTT

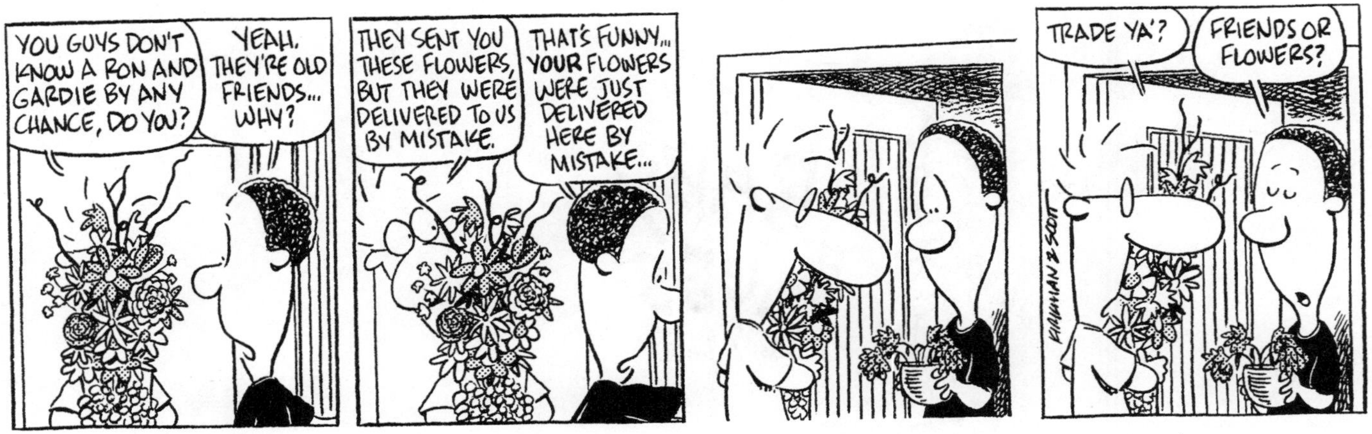
YOU GUYS DON'T KNOW A RON AND GARDIE BY ANY CHANCE, DO YOU?
YEAH. THEY'RE OLD FRIENDS... WHY?
THEY SENT YOU THESE FLOWERS, BUT THEY WERE DELIVERED TO US BY MISTAKE.
THAT'S FUNNY... **YOUR** FLOWERS WERE JUST DELIVERED HERE BY MISTAKE...
TRADE YA'?
FRIENDS OR FLOWERS?
KIRKMAN & SCOTT

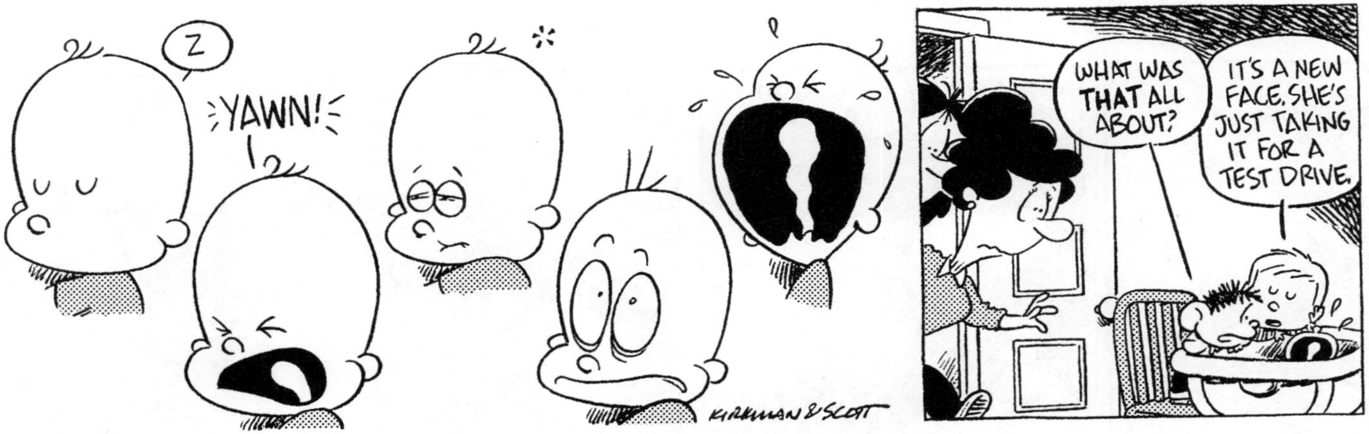
Z
YAWN!
WHAT WAS **THAT** ALL ABOUT?
IT'S A NEW FACE. SHE'S JUST TAKING IT FOR A TEST DRIVE.
KIRKMAN & SCOTT

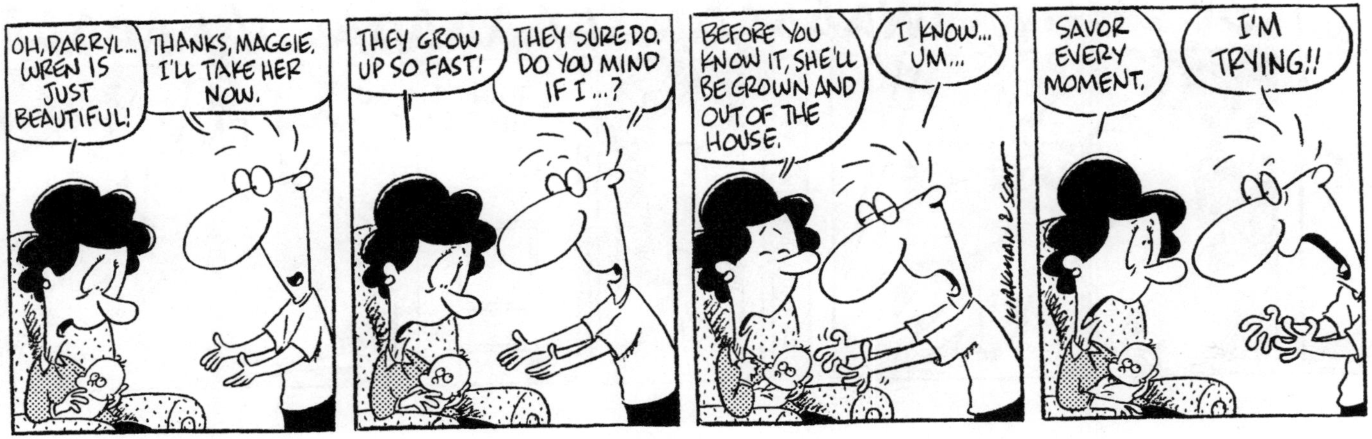
OH, DARRYL... WREN IS JUST BEAUTIFUL!
THANKS, MAGGIE. I'LL TAKE HER NOW.
THEY GROW UP SO FAST!
THEY SURE DO. DO YOU MIND IF I ...?
BEFORE YOU KNOW IT, SHE'LL BE GROWN AND OUT OF THE HOUSE.
I KNOW... UM...
SAVOR EVERY MOMENT.
I'M TRYING!!
KIRKMAN & SCOTT

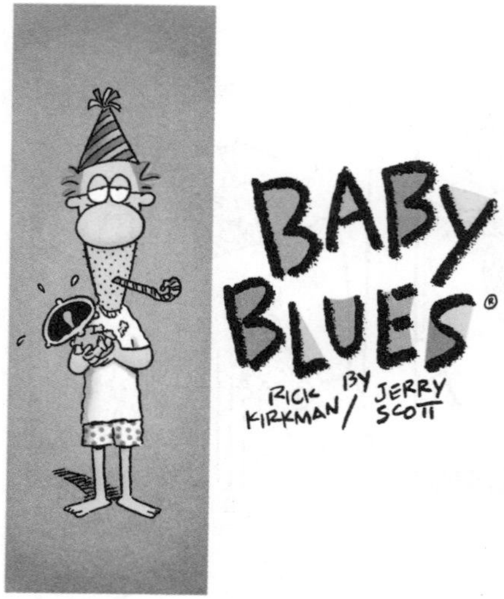
BABY BLUES®
BY RICK KIRKMAN / JERRY SCOTT

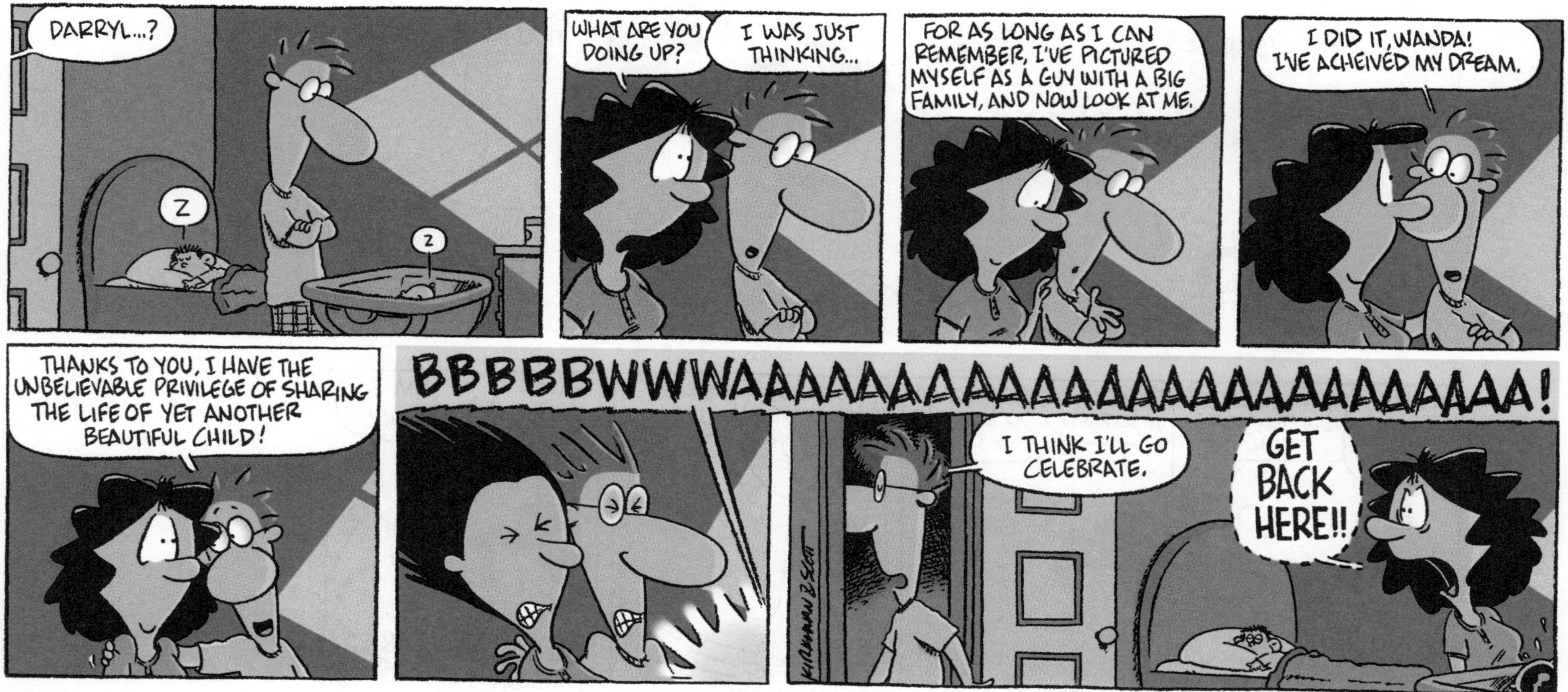
DARRYL...?
Z
Z
WHAT ARE YOU DOING UP?
I WAS JUST THINKING...
FOR AS LONG AS I CAN REMEMBER, I'VE PICTURED MYSELF AS A GUY WITH A BIG FAMILY, AND NOW LOOK AT ME.
I DID IT, WANDA! I'VE ACHEIVED MY DREAM.
THANKS TO YOU, I HAVE THE UNBELIEVABLE PRIVILEGE OF SHARING THE LIFE OF YET ANOTHER BEAUTIFUL CHILD!
BBBBBWWWAAAAAAAAAAAAAAAAAAAAAA!
I THINK I'LL GO CELEBRATE.
GET BACK HERE!!

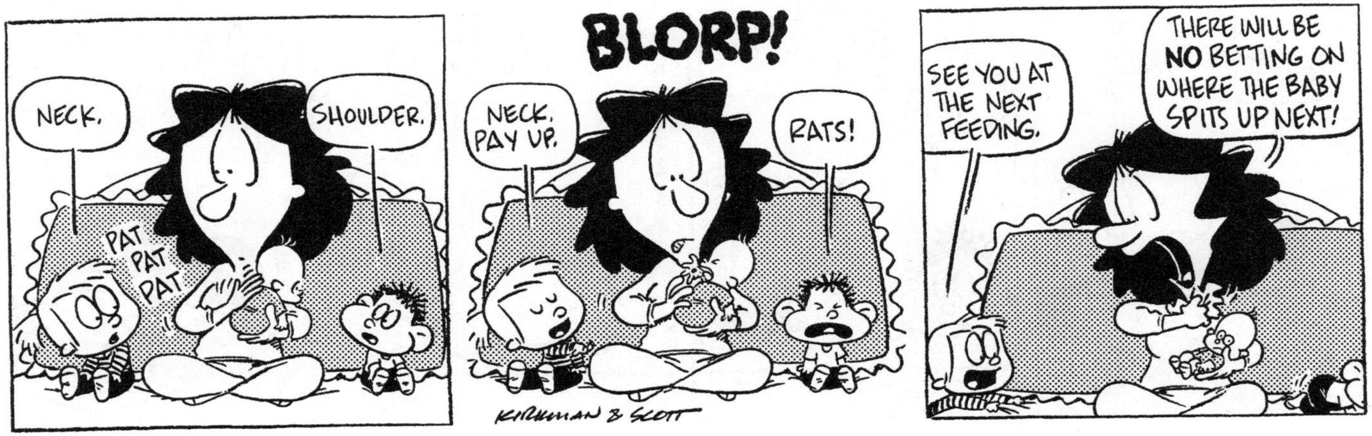
NECK.
SHOULDER.
PAT PAT PAT
BLORP!
NECK. PAY UP.
RATS!
SEE YOU AT THE NEXT FEEDING.
THERE WILL BE **NO** BETTING ON WHERE THE BABY SPITS UP NEXT!
KIRKMAN & SCOTT

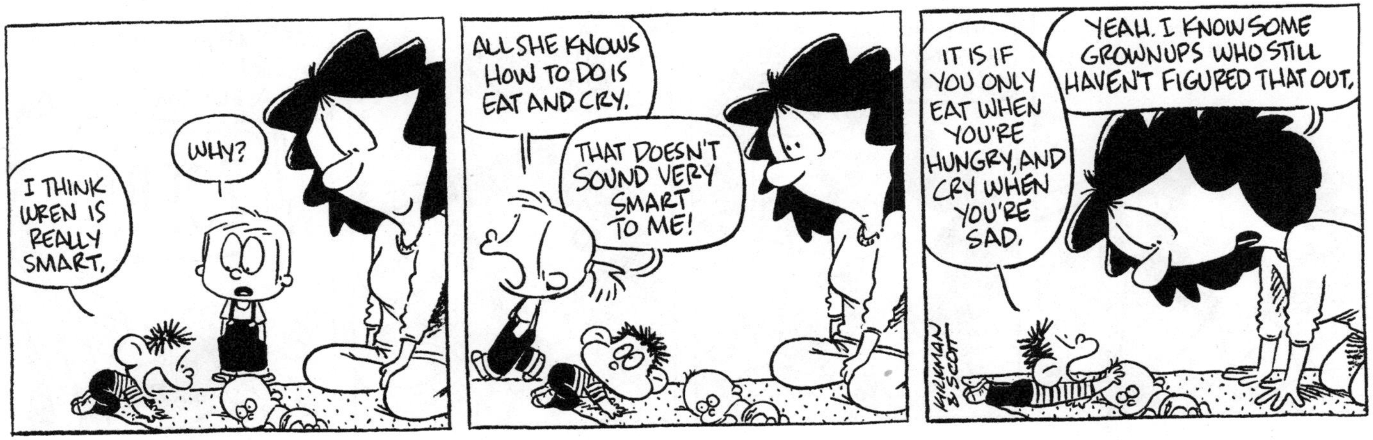
I THINK WREN IS REALLY SMART.
WHY?
ALL SHE KNOWS HOW TO DO IS EAT AND CRY.
THAT DOESN'T SOUND VERY SMART TO ME!
IT IS IF YOU ONLY EAT WHEN YOU'RE HUNGRY, AND CRY WHEN YOU'RE SAD.
YEAH. I KNOW SOME GROWNUPS WHO STILL HAVEN'T FIGURED THAT OUT.
KIRKMAN & SCOTT

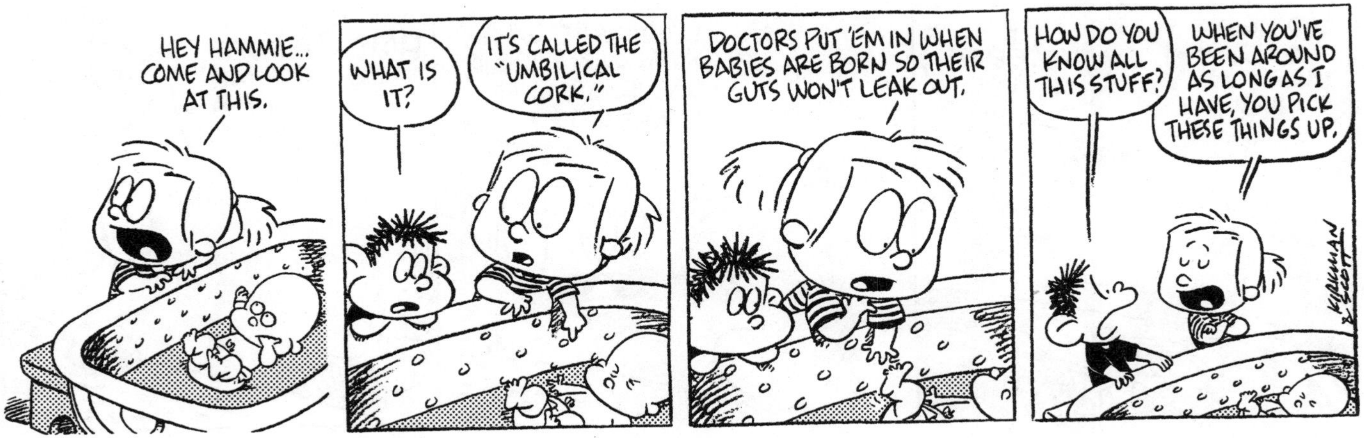
HEY HAMMIE... COME AND LOOK AT THIS.
WHAT IS IT?
IT'S CALLED THE "UMBILICAL CORK."
DOCTORS PUT 'EM IN WHEN BABIES ARE BORN SO THEIR GUTS WON'T LEAK OUT.
HOW DO YOU KNOW ALL THIS STUFF?
WHEN YOU'VE BEEN AROUND AS LONG AS I HAVE, YOU PICK THESE THINGS UP.
KIRKMAN & SCOTT

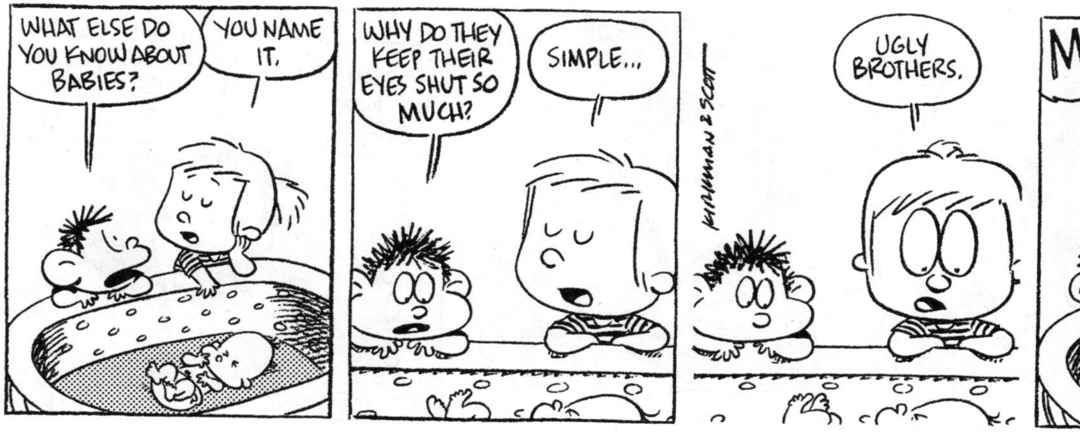
WHAT ELSE DO YOU KNOW ABOUT BABIES?
YOU NAME IT.
WHY DO THEY KEEP THEIR EYES SHUT SO MUCH?
SIMPLE...
KIRKMAN & SCOTT
UGLY BROTHERS.
MO-O-MM!
SURE... BLAME THE EXPERT.

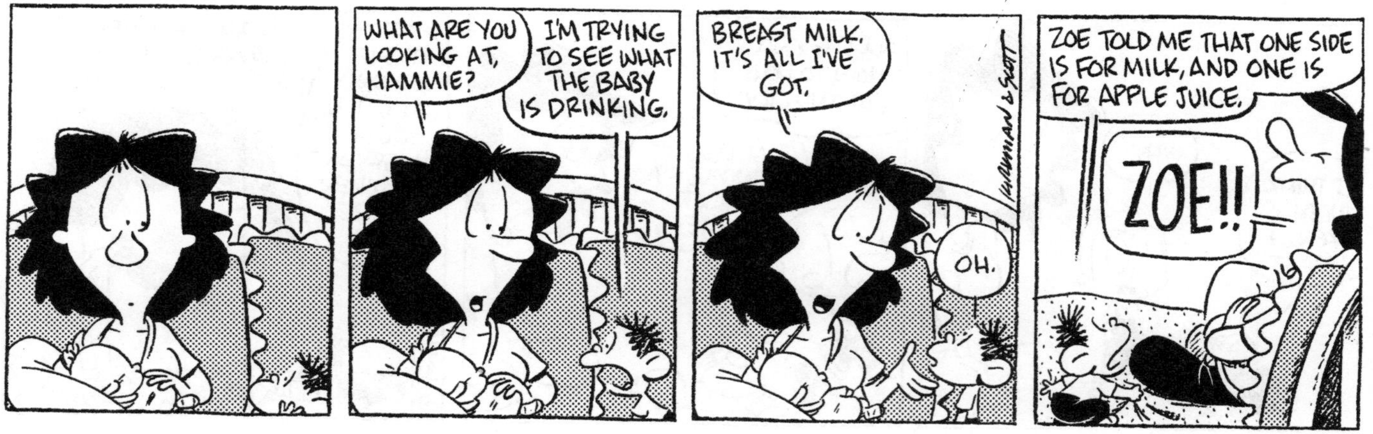
WHAT ARE YOU LOOKING AT, HAMMIE?
I'M TRYING TO SEE WHAT THE BABY IS DRINKING.
BREAST MILK. IT'S ALL I'VE GOT.
OH.
KIRKMAN & SCOTT
ZOE TOLD ME THAT ONE SIDE IS FOR MILK, AND ONE IS FOR APPLE JUICE.
ZOE!!

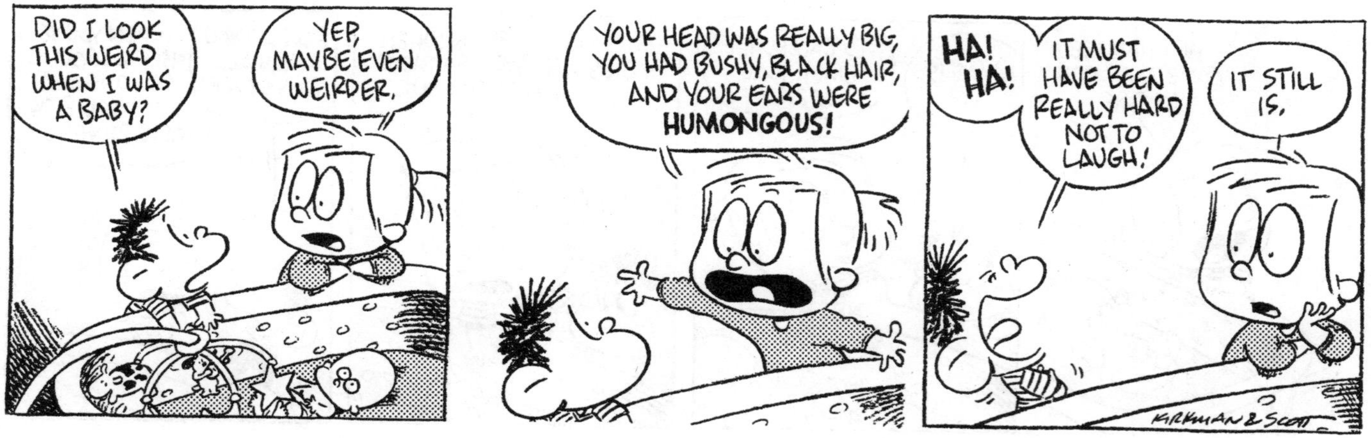
DID I LOOK THIS WEIRD WHEN I WAS A BABY?
YEP, MAYBE EVEN WEIRDER.
YOUR HEAD WAS REALLY BIG, YOU HAD BUSHY, BLACK HAIR, AND YOUR EARS WERE **HUMONGOUS!**
HA! HA!
IT MUST HAVE BEEN REALLY HARD NOT TO LAUGH!
IT STILL IS.
KIRKMAN & SCOTT

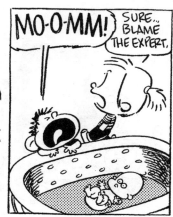

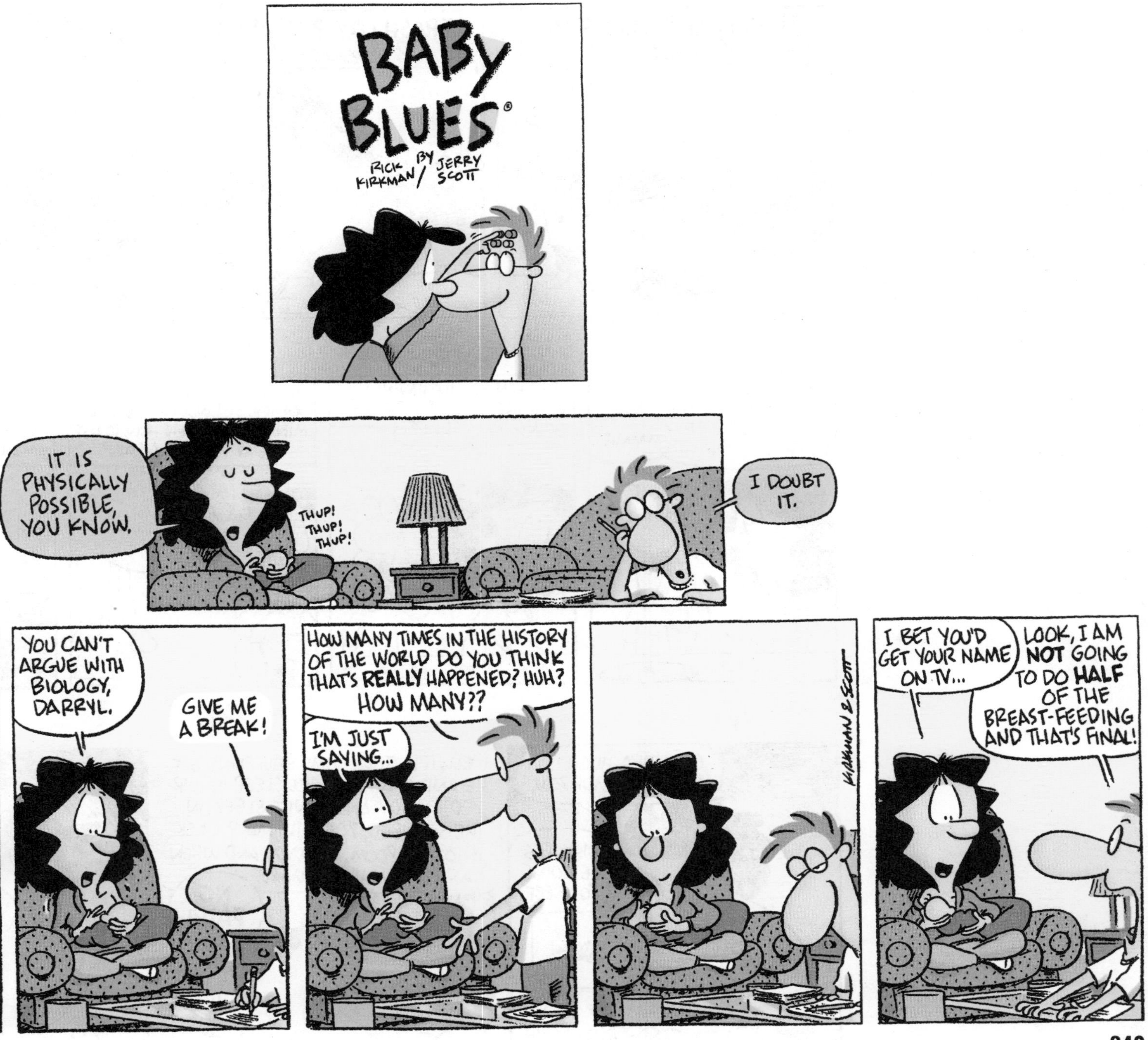
BABY BLUES®
BY RICK KIRKMAN / JERRY SCOTT
IT IS PHYSICALLY POSSIBLE, YOU KNOW.
THUP! THUP! THUP!
I DOUBT IT.
NO, REALLY! I SAW IT ON THE LEARNING CHANNEL.
OH, WELL, THEN...!
YOU CAN'T ARGUE WITH BIOLOGY, DARRYL.
GIVE ME A BREAK!
HOW MANY TIMES IN THE HISTORY OF THE WORLD DO YOU THINK THAT'S REALLY HAPPENED? HUH? HOW MANY??
I'M JUST SAYING...
KIRKMAN & SCOTT
I BET YOU'D GET YOUR NAME ON TV...
LOOK, I AM NOT GOING TO DO HALF OF THE BREAST-FEEDING AND THAT'S FINAL!

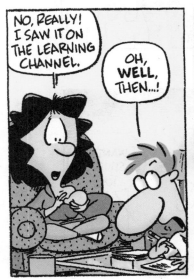

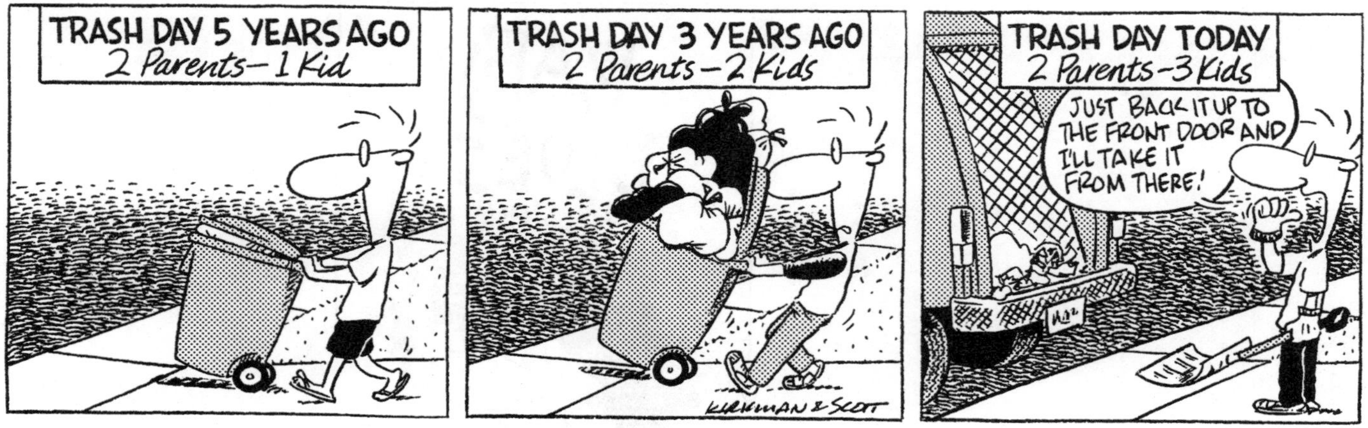
TRASH DAY 5 YEARS AGO
2 Parents – 1 Kid
TRASH DAY 3 YEARS AGO
2 Parents – 2 Kids
KIRKMAN & SCOTT
TRASH DAY TODAY
2 Parents – 3 Kids
JUST BACK IT UP TO THE FRONT DOOR AND I'LL TAKE IT FROM THERE!

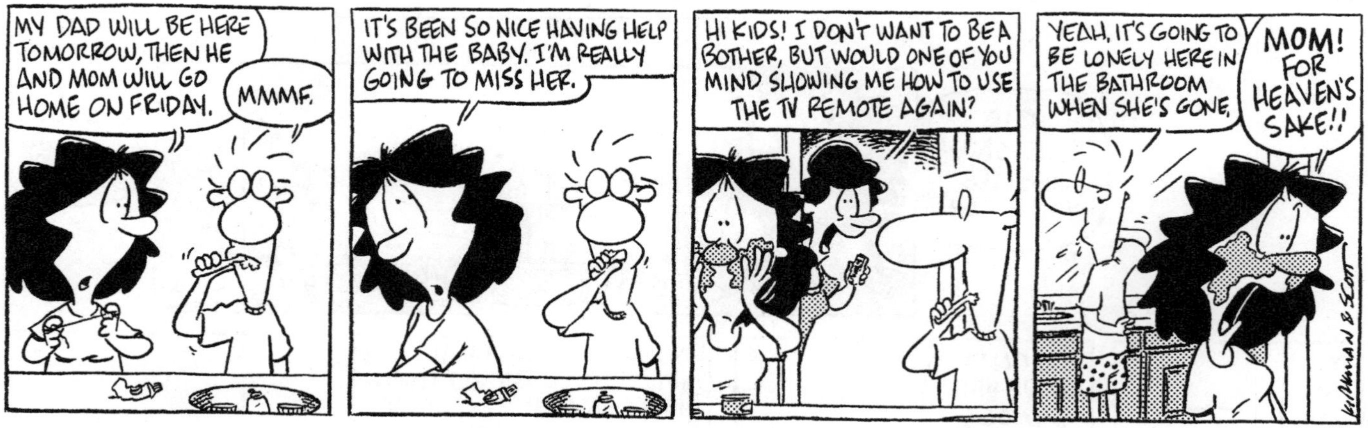
MY DAD WILL BE HERE TOMORROW, THEN HE AND MOM WILL GO HOME ON FRIDAY.
MMMF.
IT'S BEEN SO NICE HAVING HELP WITH THE BABY. I'M REALLY GOING TO MISS HER.
HI KIDS! I DON'T WANT TO BE A BOTHER, BUT WOULD ONE OF YOU MIND SHOWING ME HOW TO USE THE TV REMOTE AGAIN?
YEAH, IT'S GOING TO BE LONELY HERE IN THE BATHROOM WHEN SHE'S GONE.
MOM! FOR HEAVEN'S SAKE!!
KIRKMAN & SCOTT

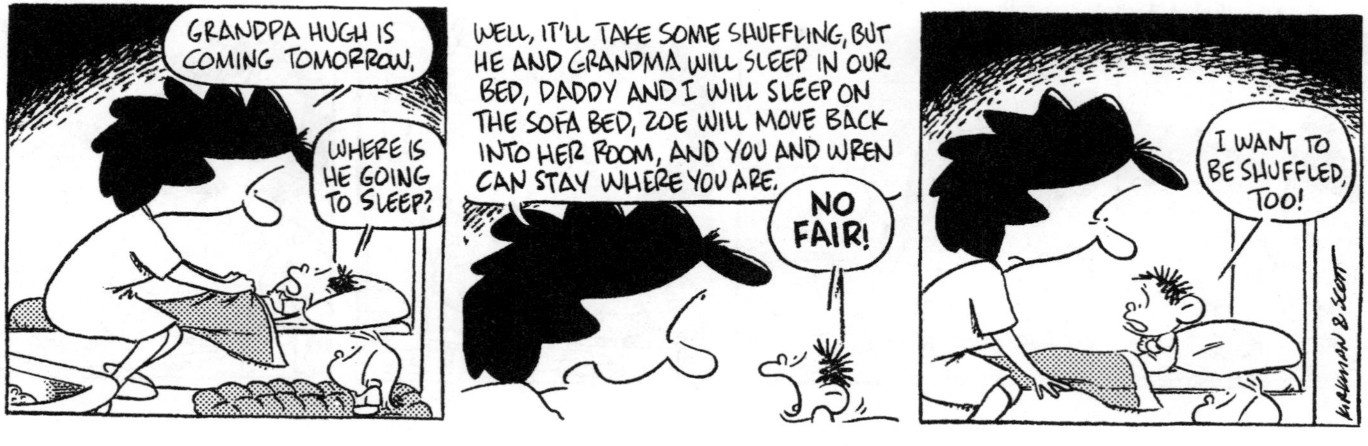
GRANDPA HUGH IS COMING TOMORROW.
WHERE IS HE GOING TO SLEEP?
WELL, IT'LL TAKE SOME SHUFFLING, BUT HE AND GRANDMA WILL SLEEP IN OUR BED, DADDY AND I WILL SLEEP ON THE SOFA BED, ZOE WILL MOVE BACK INTO HER ROOM, AND YOU AND WREN CAN STAY WHERE YOU ARE.
NO FAIR!
I WANT TO BE SHUFFLED, TOO!
KIRKMAN & SCOTT

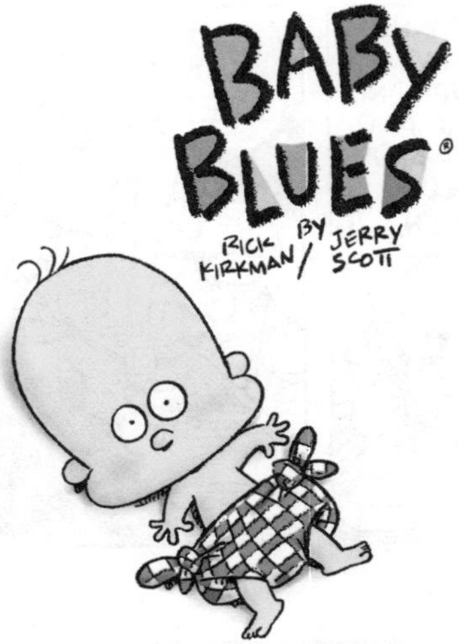
BABY BLUES®
RICK KIRKMAN / BY / JERRY SCOTT

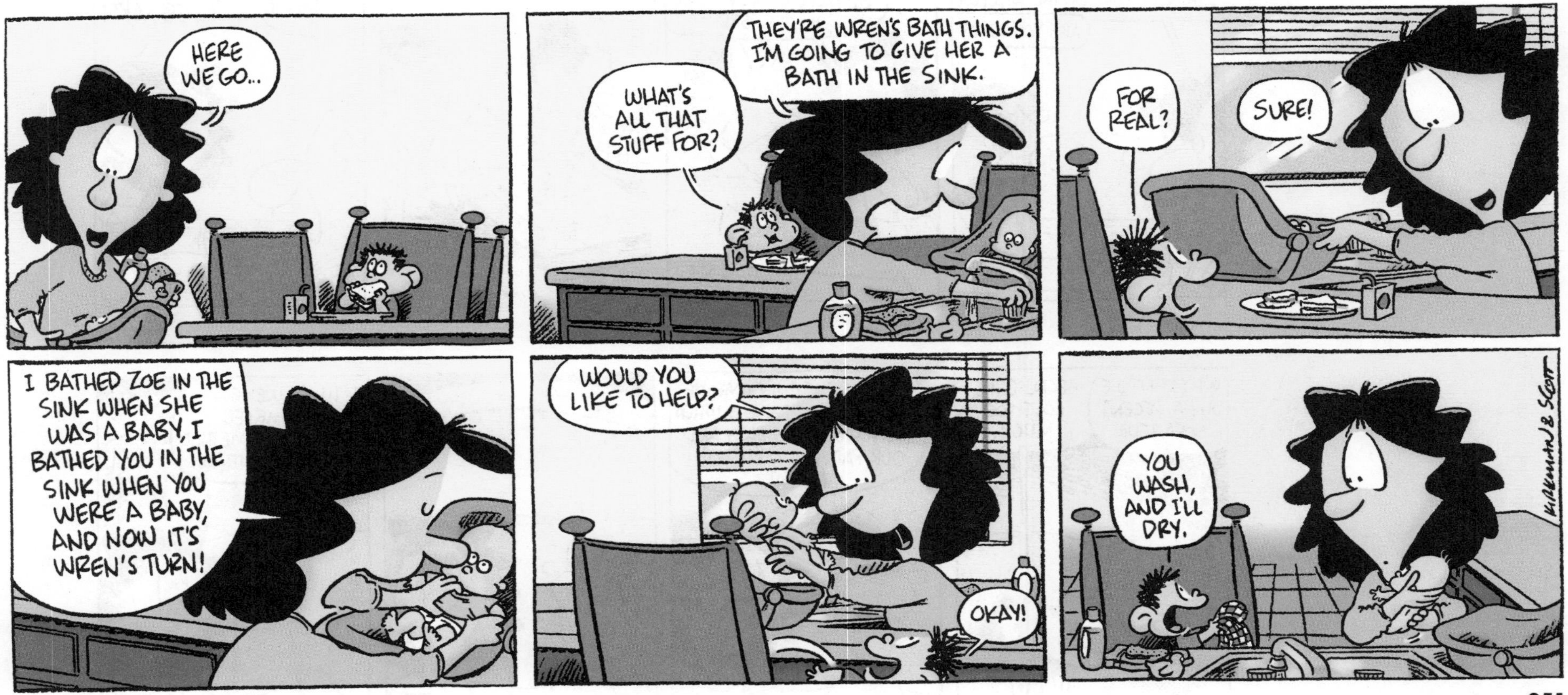
HERE WE GO...
WHAT'S ALL THAT STUFF FOR?
THEY'RE WREN'S BATH THINGS. I'M GOING TO GIVE HER A BATH IN THE SINK.
FOR REAL?
SURE!
I BATHED ZOE IN THE SINK WHEN SHE WAS A BABY, I BATHED YOU IN THE SINK WHEN YOU WERE A BABY, AND NOW IT'S WREN'S TURN!
WOULD YOU LIKE TO HELP?
OKAY!
YOU WASH, AND I'LL DRY.
KIRKMAN & SCOTT

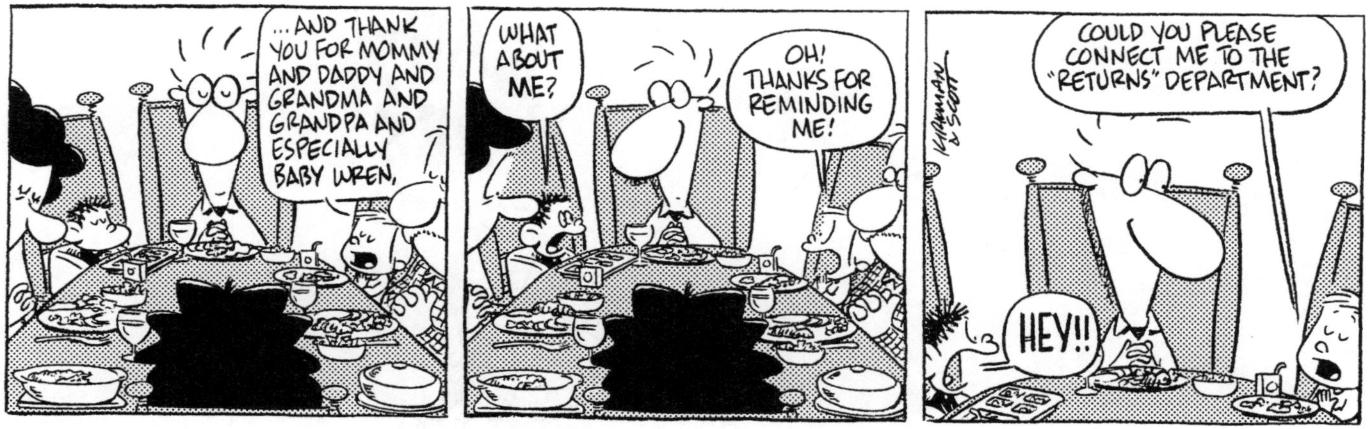

...AND THANK YOU FOR MOMMY AND DADDY AND GRANDMA AND GRANDPA AND ESPECIALLY BABY WREN,
WHAT ABOUT ME?
OH! THANKS FOR REMINDING ME!
COULD YOU PLEASE CONNECT ME TO THE "RETURNS" DEPARTMENT?
HEY!!

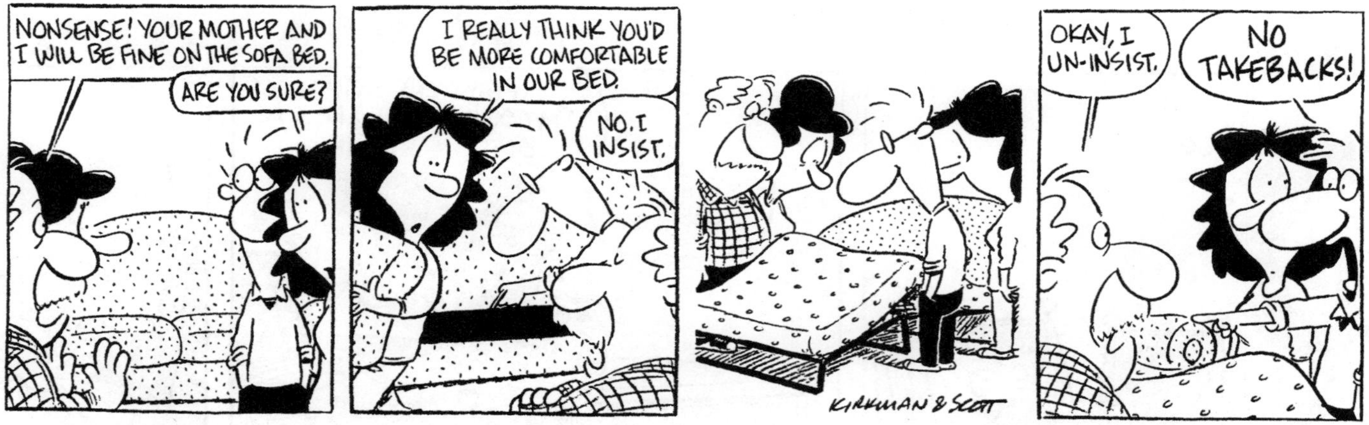

NONSENSE! YOUR MOTHER AND I WILL BE FINE ON THE SOFA BED.
ARE YOU SURE?
I REALLY THINK YOU'D BE MORE COMFORTABLE IN OUR BED.
NO. I INSIST.
KIRKMAN & SCOTT
OKAY, I UN-INSIST.
NO TAKEBACKS!

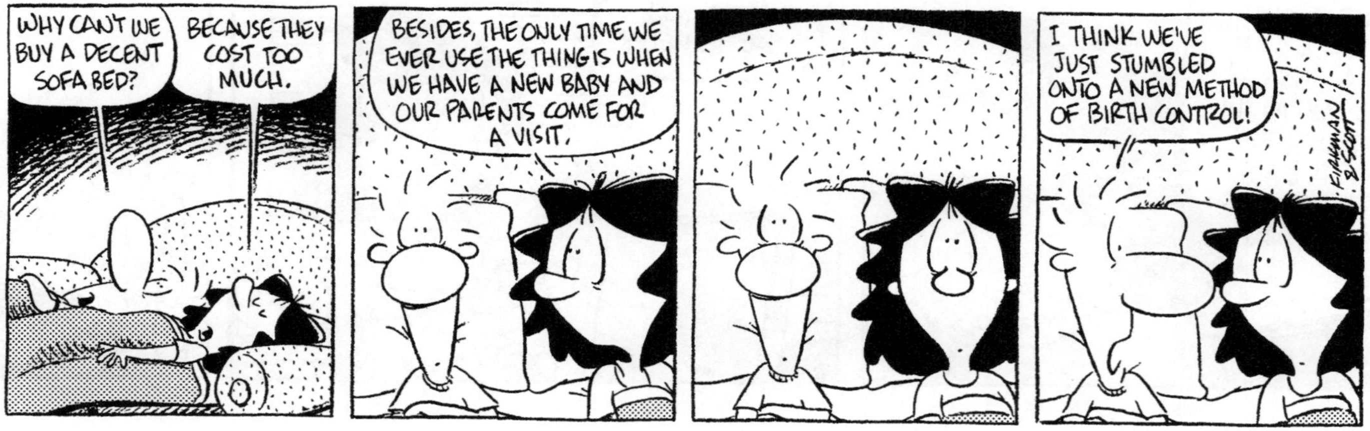

WHY CAN'T WE BUY A DECENT SOFA BED?
BECAUSE THEY COST TOO MUCH.
BESIDES, THE ONLY TIME WE EVER USE THE THING IS WHEN WE HAVE A NEW BABY AND OUR PARENTS COME FOR A VISIT.
I THINK WE'VE JUST STUMBLED ONTO A NEW METHOD OF BIRTH CONTROL!

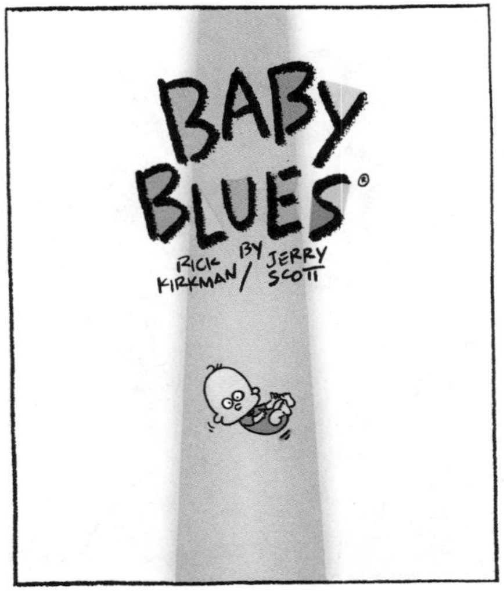
BABY BLUES®
RICK KIRKMAN / BY JERRY SCOTT

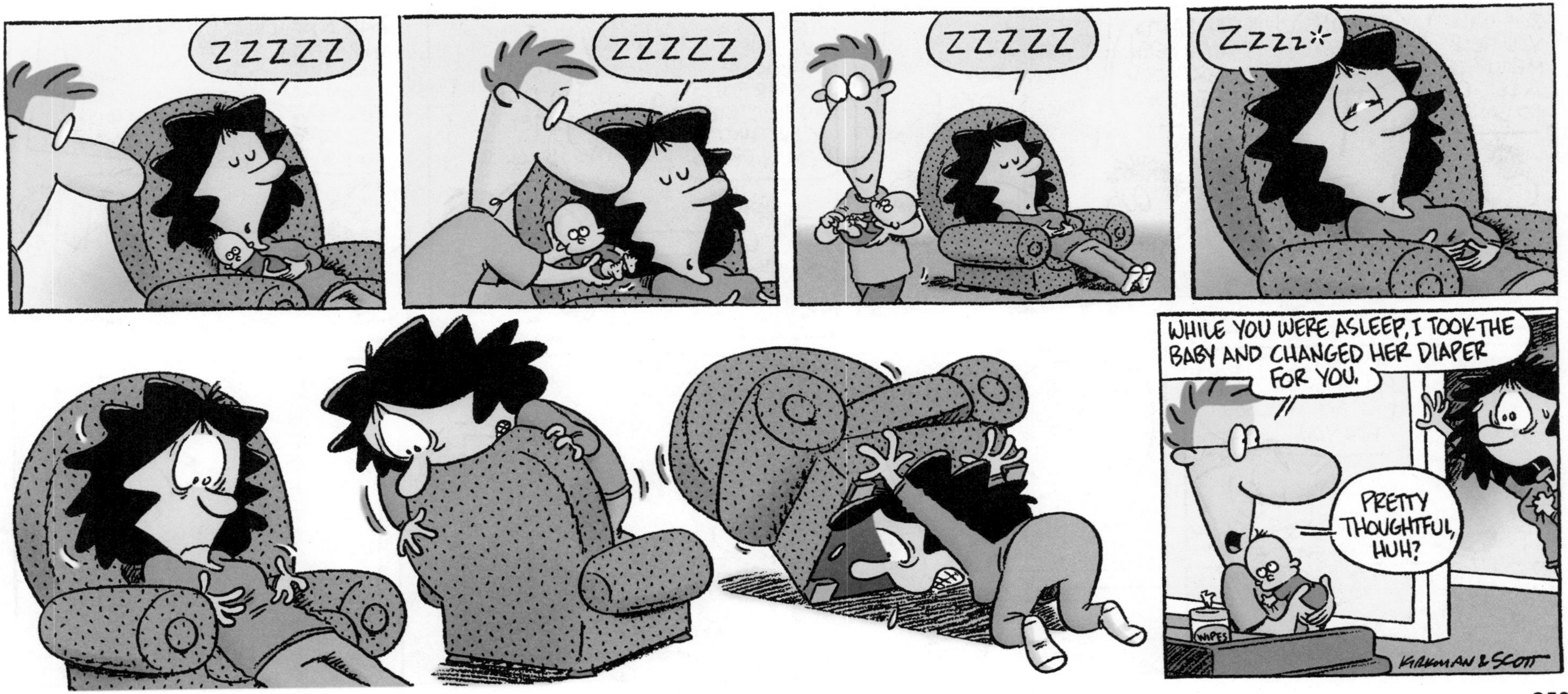
ZZZZZ
ZZZZZ
ZZZZZ
Zzzz
WHILE YOU WERE ASLEEP, I TOOK THE BABY AND CHANGED HER DIAPER FOR YOU.
PRETTY THOUGHTFUL, HUH?
WIPES
KIRKMAN & SCOTT

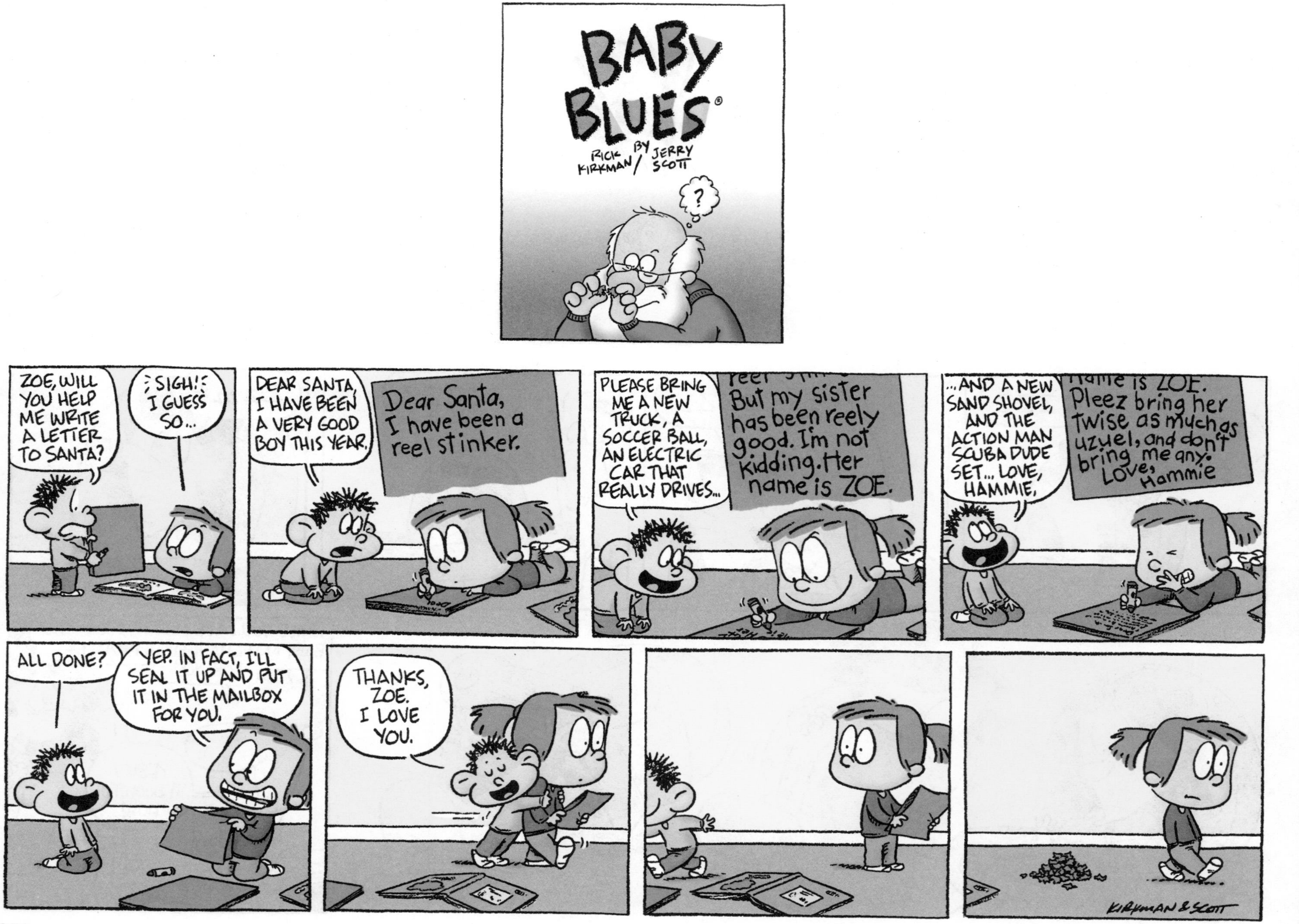
BABY BLUES®
BY RICK KIRKMAN / JERRY SCOTT
?
ZOE, WILL YOU HELP ME WRITE A LETTER TO SANTA?
SIGH! I GUESS SO...
DEAR SANTA, I HAVE BEEN A VERY GOOD BOY THIS YEAR.
Dear Santa, I have been a reel stinker.
PLEASE BRING ME A NEW TRUCK, A SOCCER BALL, AN ELECTRIC CAR THAT REALLY DRIVES...
But my sister has been reely good. I'm not kidding. Her name is ZOE.
...AND A NEW SAND SHOVEL, AND THE ACTION MAN SCUBA DUDE SET... LOVE, HAMMIE.
Pleez bring her twise as much as uzuel, and don't bring me any. Love, Hammie
ALL DONE?
YEP. IN FACT, I'LL SEAL IT UP AND PUT IT IN THE MAILBOX FOR YOU.
THANKS, ZOE. I LOVE YOU.
KIRKMAN & SCOTT

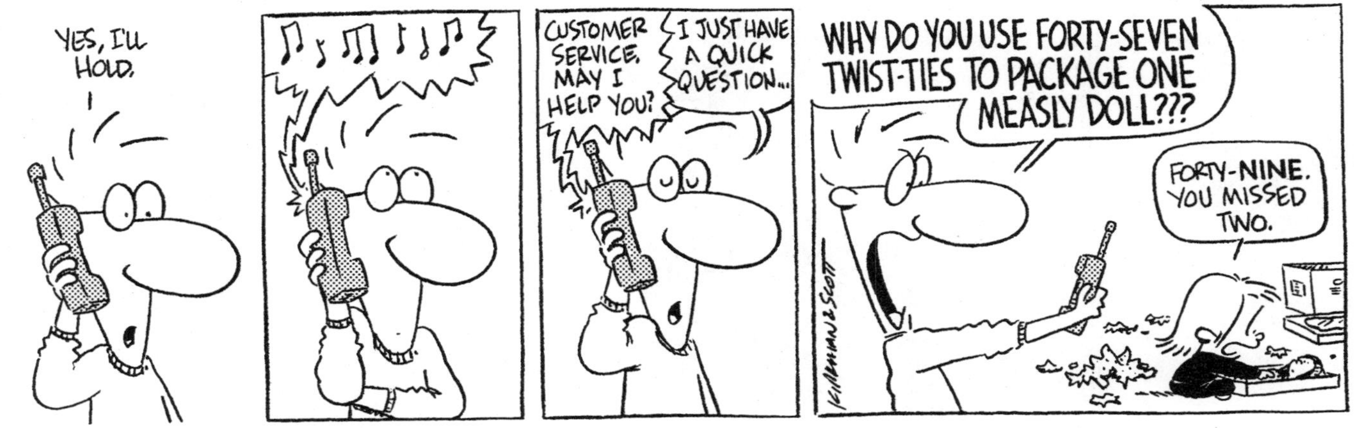
YES, I'LL HOLD.
CUSTOMER SERVICE. MAY I HELP YOU?
I JUST HAVE A QUICK QUESTION...
WHY DO YOU USE FORTY-SEVEN TWIST-TIES TO PACKAGE ONE MEASLY DOLL???
FORTY-NINE. YOU MISSED TWO.

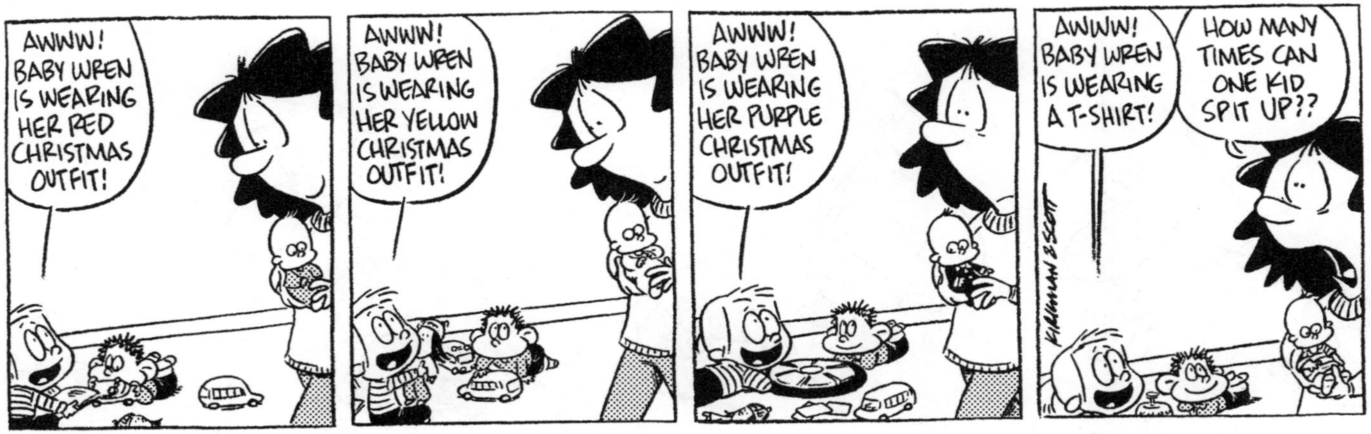
AWWW! BABY WREN IS WEARING HER RED CHRISTMAS OUTFIT!
AWWW! BABY WREN IS WEARING HER YELLOW CHRISTMAS OUTFIT!
AWWW! BABY WREN IS WEARING HER PURPLE CHRISTMAS OUTFIT!
AWWW! BABY WREN IS WEARING A T-SHIRT!
HOW MANY TIMES CAN ONE KID SPIT UP??

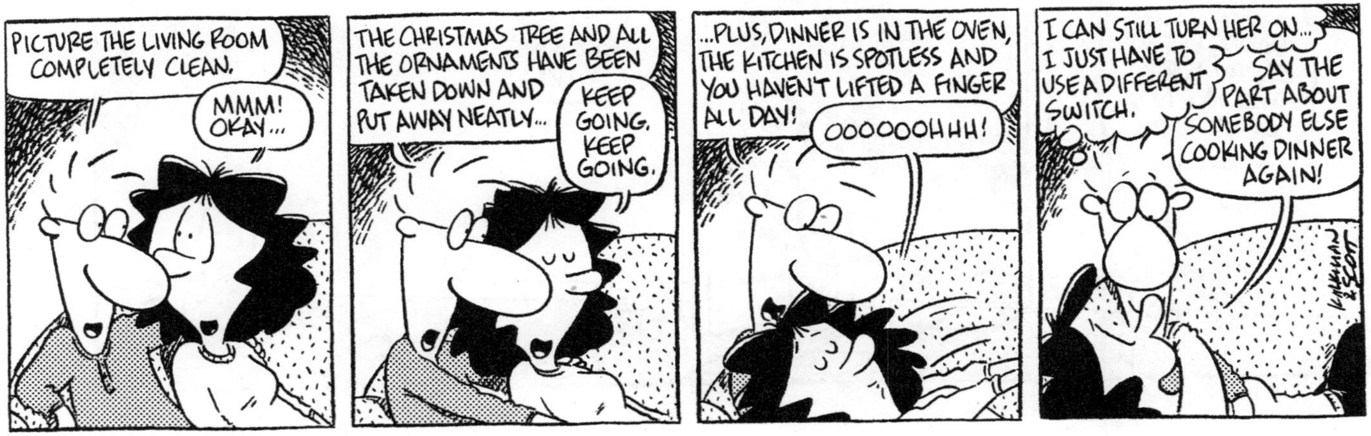
PICTURE THE LIVING ROOM COMPLETELY CLEAN.
MMM! OKAY...
THE CHRISTMAS TREE AND ALL THE ORNAMENTS HAVE BEEN TAKEN DOWN AND PUT AWAY NEATLY...
KEEP GOING. KEEP GOING.
...PLUS, DINNER IS IN THE OVEN, THE KITCHEN IS SPOTLESS AND YOU HAVEN'T LIFTED A FINGER ALL DAY!
OOOOOOHHH!
I CAN STILL TURN HER ON... I JUST HAVE TO USE A DIFFERENT SWITCH.
SAY THE PART ABOUT SOMEBODY ELSE COOKING DINNER AGAIN!

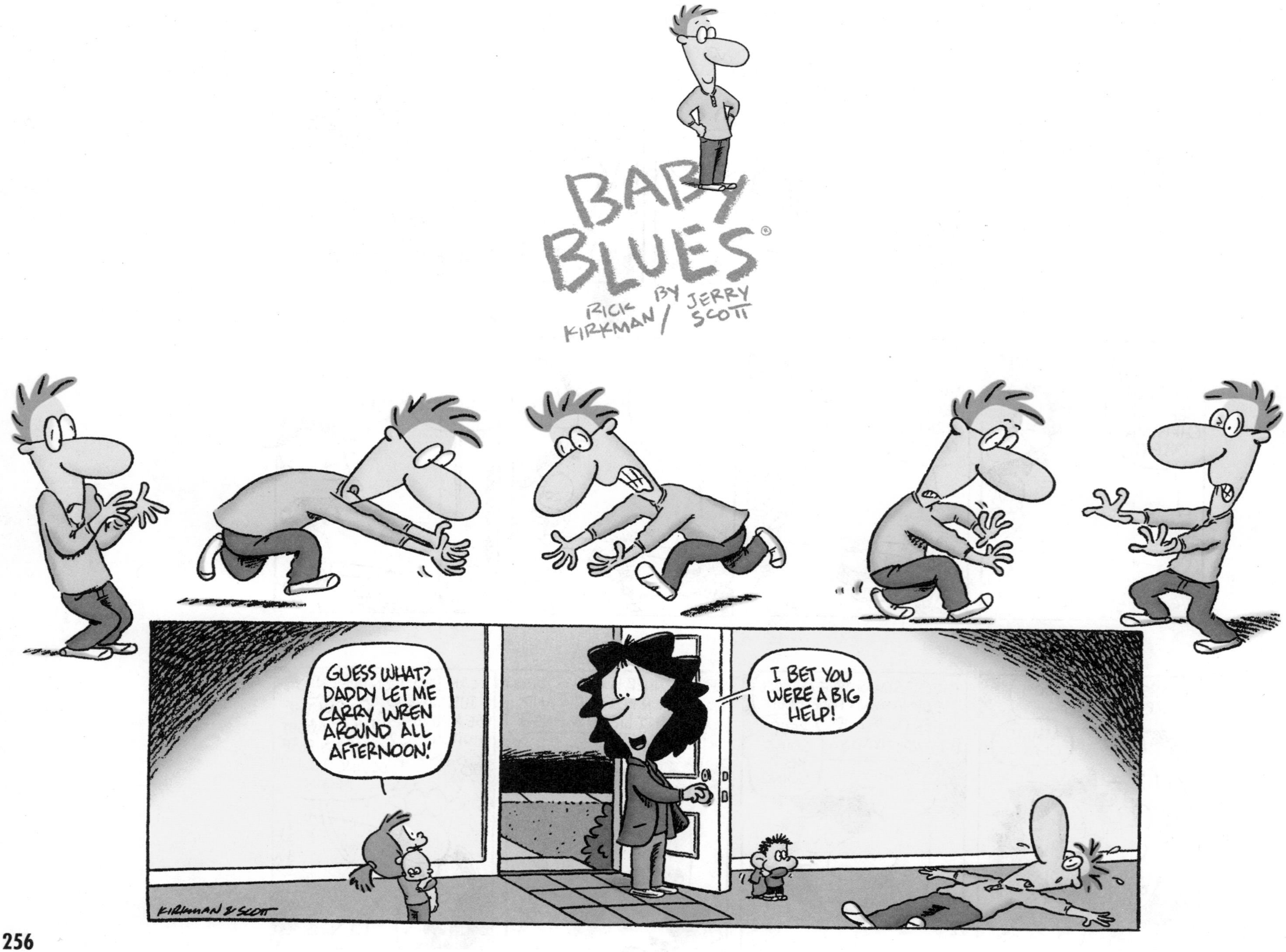
BABY BLUES®
BY RICK KIRKMAN / JERRY SCOTT
GUESS WHAT? DADDY LET ME CARRY WREN AROUND ALL AFTERNOON!
I BET YOU WERE A BIG HELP!
KIRKMAN & SCOTT